FROMMER'S

SOUTH AMERICA

ON $35 A DAY

ARNOLD AND HARRIET GREENBERG

□

1989–1990

Published by Prentice Hall Trade Division
A Division of Simon & Schuster Inc.
Gulf + Western Building
One Gulf + Western Plaza
New York, NY 10023

ISBN 0-13-823709-3
ISSN 0277-7827

Manufactured in the United States of America

*Although every effort was made to ensure the accuracy
of price information appearing in this book,
it should be kept in mind that prices
can and do fluctuate in the course of time.*

CONTENTS

MAPS

READ THIS FIRST

□ □ □

This 13th edition of *South America on $35 a Day* has been freshly updated and revised. It contains new information about Ecuador's fascinating Indian markets, a renewed emphasis on Chile's wonderful museums, and a reworking of the chapter on Panama. Places have been revisited and reappraised, with scores of new finds replacing fading and unacceptable ones. It is an easier task to find high-quality budget hotels and restaurants in South America now than it was 24 years ago when we wrote the first edition of this guide. This is because the influx of tourists has created a demand for new establishments and many new places have opened. The quality of the places listed in this guide has also risen dramatically, while fortunately prices in South America have not climbed as sharply as they have in other parts of the world. Even the continent's elegant five-star stops are far less expensive than comparable hotels in New York and London. It is startling to find these fine hotels priced at the level of three-star European stops. What all this means is that South America is the perfect destination for the budget traveler and now is the perfect time to visit.

We have tried to list prices carefully and accurately, but this, always a difficult task, has become more difficult than ever. Inflation is rampant in South America and many currencies fluctuate wildly against the dollar. In some cases the prices in local currency have been adjusted to stay on par with the dollar, but in other cases, such as in Venezuela and Colombia, that has not happened. Prices are actually lower today than they were two years ago. A situation such as this cannot continue for long and it's just a matter of time till the prices are adjusted. We therefore cannot guarantee that the prices listed here will be those that you encounter when you take your trip.

As an example, the bolívar of Caracas fell from 14 to the dollar in 1985 to 39 to the dollar in late 1988. A cab ride from the airport that just a few years ago would have cost a staggering $30 is now a very manageable $8. When you budget your trip, check the existing rates and keep abreast of changes that have occurred. Add 10% to the prices listed here when you travel in 1990. If things turn out to be less expensive, you can splurge on purchases or even bring some money back home with you.

We are pleased with the countless letters we receive suggesting new places to stay and new adventures to take. It tells us that more people are visiting South America than ever before. We want to encourage you to write. Your suggestions make an impact on this book.

In previous years most tourists to South America were first-time visitors who had made several excursions to Europe and to many other parts of the world as well. However, on recent trips to update this edition, we met scores of travelers throughout the continent who were making second and even third trips to South America. Traveling with previous editions of this guide, they were as impressed (as we are) with the wide variety of experiences a trip to South America offers, and with the distinct traditions of each country. If you accept South America on its terms, not on your own preconceived ones, you will enjoy your trip immensely.

A FEW OBSERVATIONS: Political stability, always the bugaboo of travel to South America, has shown tremendous growth. There are democratically elected, energetic presidents throughout the continent. Our southern neighbors have begun to receive some favorable press coverage, or at least balanced press coverage. For years it was common to read about Latin America's problems and instability and extremely rare to read about its artists, writers, sports figures, and film stars. North Americans are becoming more aware of Latin America's cultural heritage, and this has resulted in a surge of traveler interest. We'd like to say "We told you so," but we'll be content to sit back and read the happy letters from vacationers who've "done the continent."

Latin American imports are finding their way into American homes and many shops now stock woven ponchos and Panamanian molas. Argentinian leather goods and Brazil's gemstones are the rage everywhere.

The Inca ruins of Peru and Bolivia are finally being discovered (there's even a Marriott in Cuzco) and Machú Picchú is no longer thought to be a rare tropical disease.

Brazil in particular is experiencing an incredible tourist boom—understandable considering how remarkable its beaches are and how unforgettable Rio is!

Finally, tour operators are jumping on the bandwagon and there are charter flights to Rio and excellent package tours to other countries as well. Do your homework and you should be able to take advantage of this trend.

With each trip, we are struck by the tangible economic and social changes that have taken place in much of South America. There is a growing middle class that is a vital part of each country. There is a definite upscale feeling in Argentina and Brazil. Under the leadership of dynamic businessmen (such as Hans Stern of Rio, who operates over 100 jewelry shops internationally) and new leadership in many of the countries, the continent is pushing vigorously ahead. Today there are shops in most of the continent's capital cities that would be at home in New York or Paris, yet they reflect a uniquely South American ambience.

Through the years we have seen South America grow. We have seen it change. But there is something about it, the singular, intangible nature of the experience, that always remains the same. Come and share it with us!

Arnold and Harriet Greenberg

To Susan Brushaber
Our sincerest thanks for your assistance
in the preparation of this edition
of this guide.
Muchas gracias

To Mike and Doug
Congratulations on your graduations
With love
Mom and Dad

INFLATION ALERT: We don't have to tell you that inflation has hit South America as it has everywhere else. In researching this book we have made every effort to obtain up-to-the-minute prices, but even the most conscientious researcher cannot keep up with the current pace of inflation. As we go to press, we believe we have obtained the most reliable data possible. Nonetheless, in the lifetime of this edition—particularly its second year (1990)—the wise traveler will add 15% to 20% to the prices quoted throughout these pages.

A DISCLAIMER: Although every effort was made to ensure the accuracy of the prices and travel information appearing in this book, it should be kept in mind that prices do fluctuate in the course of time, and that information does change under the impact of the varied and volatile factors that affect the travel industry. Readers should also note that the establishments described under Readers' Selections or Suggestions have not in many cases been inspected by the authors and that the opinions expressed there are those of the individual reader(s) only. They do not in any way represent the opinions of the publisher or authors of this guide.

CHAPTER I

SOUTH AMERICA ON $35 A DAY

□ □ □

1. THE REASON WHY

2. GETTING THERE

3. USEFUL INFORMATION

**4. THE DOLLARWISE TRAVEL CLUB—HOW
TO SAVE MONEY ON ALL YOUR TRAVELS**

The southern half of the Americas—thought by some North Americans to be a semiprimitive continent one step away from revolution—is actually one of the world's great travel oases. It offers sights and attractions, adventures and experiences that cause the offerings of many other areas to seem pale and insignificant.

Think, for instance, of what you can do and see in a 21- to 30-day trip to South America.

□ You can begin by sunning and swimming in the blue waters of Rio's Guanabara Bay, off the shores of luxurious—and free—Copacabana Beach, where the swimmers beside you might be the millionaire owner of a cocoa plantation and a sultry nightclub dancer.

□ Then on to Buenos Aires, where you will dine on a superb three-quarter-inch-thick steak, after enjoying a Teatro Colón performance of *Aïda,* more polished than at La Scala.

□ If you ski, you'll want to test the challenging slopes of Portillo, not far from Santiago, the former scene of the World Alpine Ski championships.

□ Visit Rapa Nui (Easter Island) and climb into the center of a volcano to inspect the mute monoliths that stand, lie, and have fallen there.

□ Next you'll explore a jungle village only hours by bus from La Paz, a mountain city where the temperatures are 40° cooler than the community below.

□ Explore Ecuador's Galápagos Islands and come away with your own theory of evolution.

□ Then a dramatic visit underground into a church set in a salt mine outside Bogotá.

□ A must, too, is a cruise through the Panama Canal, which to this day remains an incredible engineering achievement.

□ And finally, a climactic journey to the blood-stirring world of the Inca high in the Peruvian Andes, where life is as it was five centuries ago, and where you will see an incredible marvel—Machú Picchú, the legendary "Lost City of the Incas."

Now, that is some holiday by any standard!

To add excitement you can come to Rio in February and immerse yourself in the most frenzied carnival atmosphere you will ever hope to see. Or anytime of the year in any South American city, you can shout yourself into laryngitis at one of the innumerable *"futbol"* (soccer) matches that draw up to 200,000 partisan fans.

Still more?

Then add the hypnotic beauty of these cities:

Quito—where it is spring-like all year round, despite its equatorial location, and from which you can make a one-day excursion to a jungle settlement and stare transfixed at half-naked Indians with torsos brilliantly painted to ward off evil spirits.

Lima—where the conquistadores in 1535 spawned a sea-level Spanish colonial city (after razing the gold-rich Inca mountain cities), and where today the suburbs are stylish and sophisticated.

Santiago—where the air is so sharp and clean you can almost taste it, and where the residents are as warm and generous as in Copenhagen.

La Paz—where the Indians still marvel at the mighty iron birds that roar in and out of this 2½-mile-high city (highest capital in the world), and where the open-air stalls make European flea markets seem tame indeed.

Caracas—where from Mount Ávila you can have a stunning view of the city, and, when it is running, take a cable-car ride down 7,000 feet to the Caribbean beaches below.

Margarita—where the blue sky and sandy beaches rival any other Caribbean isle at half the price.

Cartagena—a walled colonial city surrounded by blue water and sandy beaches.

Iguaçu Falls—the world's mightiest waterfall, located on the frontier between Argentina and Brazil.

For shoppers, good buys are everywhere—in alligator, lizard, suede, alpaca, silver, gemstones, hand-woven wool rugs, and intricately designed woodcarvings—at prices that are far lower than in the U.S.

Little wonder that we think South America is a sadly overlooked travel paradise that inevitably—some veteran travel experts tell us within five years—will begin to rival Europe as the number-one destination for U.S. and Canadian travelers. Let's look into the misconceptions that have kept many North Americans from going there earlier:

1. THE REASON WHY

South America, as we've said, virtually overflows with the kind of magic that usually draws travelers in droves. The continent is exotic, cosmopolitan, history-rich, scenically stunning, and lower priced than Europe. And yes, you jaded budget travelers who never thought you'd see the day—the budget hotels come equipped with private baths.

Yet somehow the southerly portion of the Western Hemisphere is shunned by the bulk of North American tourists as if it were a desert stop called Dullsville.

U.S. travelers at the drop of a tourist brochure skip off to Western Europe,

Scandinavia, Hawaii, Japan, the Caribbean, the Near East, and even to Eastern Europe. There are even 21-day Rotary charters to Beijing.

But South America is virtually ignored. To learn how completely, consider these statistics: over seven million U.S. travelers went abroad in 1987—with about two million of us winding up in Europe. South America drew to its cities, beaches, mountains, and plains only about 800,000 U.S. travelers—an absurdly low percentage of the total. While current levels are considerably higher, still the figures are inexplicably low, particularly when you remember that all of Western Europe, including Scandinavia, could fit comfortably into Brazil.

"I WOULDN'T DREAM OF GOING THERE . . .": Something is wrong somewhere when a continent with such sophisticated and alive cities as Rio and Buenos Aires fails to attract worldly U.S. travelers.

To find out why, we made a thoroughly nonscientific survey of everyone we know who has traveled abroad in recent years. The misconceptions we discovered were astonishing.

"If, before your last trip abroad," we asked them, "someone had suggested you visit South America, what would you have answered?"

Many of those polled said they would have expressed surprise if the question had even been put to them. "Why, we've never considered South America!" was a common first response.

Then the explanation came fast as to why they probably would have replied "Not a chance" to the query. In general there were three broad objections, and we have decided to list them, coupled with our own reactions.

Objection No. 1: "The governments are unstable and it might be dangerous—especially for U.S. citizens."

Of course there have been coups in South America in which governments were toppled overnight. But not nearly as many as you might believe. And even fewer have involved the firing of a single shot. The impression of constant unrest was, we suggest, fostered in large part by our press, which seemed to focus solely on Latin America's problems and crises. This is not to suggest that these countries do not have problems. They do! However, those problems do not interfere with a vacationer's visit. You rarely saw an article about Rio, one of the world's great cities, except at Carnival time. Virtually nothing was written about the great beaches, skiing, and sights of the area.

Never in our South American travels have we encountered any personal hostility, nor have we observed any unpleasantness directed at any U.S. citizen. What anti-U.S. sentiment we have noticed has been expressed in slogans chalked on fences or in newspaper editorials critical of specific U.S. policies. We were in Rio when (then Vice-President) George Bush visited. He was a guest at one of the hotels. He was often cheered by Cariocas who recognized him and he was booed by others. Sound familiar?

On the contrary, private U.S. citizens are welcomed in Latin America. In city after city, the residents we've met have questioned us closely about U.S. customs, sports, and national politics—never with belligerence but rather to learn. Most have relatives living here or have lived here themselves for short periods of time. Most would love to return.

As illustrations of pro-U.S. sentiment you will see photos of the late President Kennedy all over many cities—in hotels, restaurants, and public buildings. Numerous schools are named after him. President Reagan was also well liked here.

Recently, a young Peruvian couple we met while waiting for a restaurant table in Lima invited us to their home later that evening. There we were introduced to several of their friends, and we could not have felt more at ease if this had taken place in Chicago. Nor was this an isolated instance of friendship. We have been corresponding regularly with a young Colombian businessman we met in Bogotá.

Rio and Buenos Aires are so cosmopolitan that North Americans are no more conspicuous than the French or German travelers who flock there.

Objection No. 2: "South America is too primitive—there are no decent hotels there, except for the $100-a-day variety."

One of our respondents, a sweet young woman who has been overseas just once, on a high-priced, rigidly planned tour, said to us:

"But isn't South America kind of jungle-y and full of natives?"

And we replied: "Of course! Buenos Aires is all jungle—just like Madison Avenue. And Rio? As thick with natives as Miami Beach."

Certainly there are jungles, but the closest you will get to them—unless on a planned excursion—is from the window of your air-conditioned jet.

As for decent nonluxurious hotels, keep in mind that South America has a growing middle class; we have uncovered in city after city dozens of hotels that the middle-income and even the modestly wealthy businessman seeks out when traveling. The hotels we have selected for *South America on $35 a Day* are clean (virtually all have private baths), conveniently located, and moderately priced. Some even have uniformed doormen, and most are air-conditioned.

Objection No. 3: "All South American countries are the same—they don't have the romantic charm or contrasts of Europe or the Far East."

Take our word for it—every South American country has an individuality and a uniqueness that makes the continent constantly fresh and intriguing.

For example, you can swim in Caracas or Rio all 12 months and ski outside Santiago nine months annually. You dine late (after 9 p.m.) in Quito and much later (after 11 p.m.) in Buenos Aires. There is little nightlife in La Paz, while the clubs in Rio seldom open before 10 p.m. and rarely close before 4 or 5 a.m.

Variety? The cultural differences between any Paceño (resident of La Paz) and any Carioca (a local of Rio) are greater than between an Italian farmer and a Scandinavian civil servant.

You will be delighted by the differences in pace, atmosphere, and customs between South America's sophisticated eastern cities and the western coast's blend of history and rugged beauty.

Romance? The Peruvian Andes and the Inca cities of Cuzco and Machú Picchú today inspire poets as the Aegean Isles have for 2,500 years.

Uruguay's Punta del Este—the Riviera of South America—stirs lovers as the Caribbean sun islands have for centuries.

An incredible marvel is in the awesome Iguaçu Falls, on the border of Brazil and Argentina, which is 50 feet higher than Niagara Falls.

And at Lake Titicaca, the world's highest lake, you will have your first and perhaps only glimpse of an Indian tribe that never sets foot on land. They live in boats and ceaselessly cruise the giant lake in search of food.

This continent's mountains, jungles, plazas, parks, and people make it endlessly fascinating.

Conclusion: It's time you explored South America!

SOUTH AMERICA VS. EUROPE: A question that confronts us at every cocktail party and business function in the U.S. is how Rio and Buenos Aires stack up against Paris and Rome. Or more broadly, how South America rates with Europe for the "average tourist," if there is such an animal. We suppose comparisons are inevitable since so many first-time travelers to Latin America are veterans of two and even three European trips.

Let's plunge in by making one point clear immediately: South America is *not* Europe and don't expect it to be. While Buenos Aires does resemble Paris in some respects, and even New York in others, fortunately it still possesses a unique flavor of its own, stemming in part from gaucho influences and the hybrid cross-currents of its Spanish, Italian, and German migrations. Rio is Rio and really not like any other city we have seen, what with its year-round carnival atmosphere in Copacabana Beach and the city's low-key, apparently worry-free populace. Some travelers insist that Rio is much like Rome, but this, we think, is a superficial view emanating largely from climate similarities (both are extremely hot in summer) and the leisurely pace of living in both cities. More to the point, it seems, is the Roman's immersion in his proud history and his tendency to look back rather than ahead. The Carioca seems to look neither back nor ahead, but instead focuses on the present.

Then there is Lima, which offers a fascinating glimpse of the 20th century in collision with a conservative Spanish colonial culture (like Spain, perhaps) and with an equally unyielding Indian culture (not at all like Spain).

And let's look at La Paz, where the 2½-mile-high elevation affects the way you walk, breathe, and just plain exist. Like some areas in Switzerland? Not really, since half of this city's population is proud Indian.

Even Montevideo, often likened to Geneva, has been undergoing an inflationary surge that the well-ordered Swiss just would never tolerate.

Quito, gentle and quiet like Copenhagen, is far more beautiful and its people more earnest about life.

The point we are making is: Every major South American city is distinctive and unique, yet some cities there are cosmopolitan enough to resemble in some ways communities in Europe and even the United States.

Several other differences should be stressed:

1. Europe is far more mature economically than the still-developing South American countries. Thus one major difference is the relative stability of European currencies compared to those of Brazil, Peru, Bolivia, Uruguay, and Chile. The purchasing power of U.S. dollars may fluctuate drastically at times.

Therefore, *don't try to anticipate exact prices.* Read our currency section below carefully and do your homework.

2. South America, unlike Europe, simply is not equipped to cope with annual floods of tourists. The continent does not yet have enough hotels, pensions, or restaurants. Fortunately for you as a visitor, however, South America is still relatively virgin travel terrain, and you do not run into old college classmates on the streets of Cuzco as you might in Nice or Naples—at least not yet. And while there are fewer hotels, almost all offer rooms with private bath, even many rock-bottom budget hotels. The South American would not hear of it otherwise.

3. And finally, don't expect much help from travel agents regarding South American budget travel. While agents are well informed about Europe, those whom we have talked with in the U.S. and south of the border really know little about nonluxury travel in South America.

$35 A DAY—WHAT IT MEANS: The goal of this book is to show you how to live comfortably on a South American trip for $35 per person per day. Let us hasten to add that this is a budget for your *basic* expenses only—that is, the

SOUTH AMERICA

cost of your hotel and three meals a day. Transportation—perhaps your biggest expense—is *not* included in this budget; nor are nightclubs, tipping, tours, or shopping sprees. Of course, those things are just as much a part of your vacation as a hotel room, so we've devoted large sections of this book to the best methods of keeping these added costs to a minimum—while still having a thoroughly good time.

The $35-a-day budget breaks down as follows: $17 per person for a hotel room (based on double occupancy), $2 for breakfast, $5 for lunch, and $11 for dinner. In some places in South America you'll find that $35 a day is enough to live semi-luxuriously; in others (notably Buenos Aires and Caracas) you will be comfortable. Period.

We have also included some hotels and restaurants that push costs above the $35-a-day budget—at the request of many readers, who'd like to keep their costs as low as possible and get the best values for their money, but can spend a few extra dollars daily for more comfort in their rooms or who enjoy food enough to consider gourmet meals an important part of their trip.

We have tried to broaden the listings so you have a wider range of choices. You can then decide to scrimp in one place so you can really live it up in another. Any way you want to do it, it can be done.

2. GETTING THERE

The only practical method of getting there—and of traveling about once there—is by air, and the reasons are obvious: South America is a huge continent, roughly the combined size of the United States and Canada. And within that massive area, the principal cities are widely scattered and distant from each other: Rio, for example, is 1,000 miles from Buenos Aires; Lima is 1,500 miles from Santiago. Complicating things even further is the awesome Andes mountain range which splits the entire continent from north to south—another factor making land travel slow and arduous.

It is, of course, possible to travel to South America by ship, but only if you have two or more weeks to spare on transportation, and are willing to pay extra for air transportation within the continent. New York to Rio, for example, is 4,700 sea miles and the cruise takes two weeks; traveling by sea to Chile will take you longer.

By contrast, there is frequent service including nonstop flights on Eastern Airlines from New York and Miami to many cities on the western coast of South America. Pan Am and Varig flights that leave New York at night will bring you to Rio by early the next morning. Pan Am and VIASA will wing you to Caracas from New York in less than 4½ hours.

THOSE FABULOUS MULTIPLE STOPOVERS: An equally important reason for traveling to South America by air is the multiple-stopover privilege that air travel affords. In effect air travelers can stop, without extra charge, at two stops on the way down and two additional stops on their way back. Thus on a round trip to Buenos Aires (we strongly recommend the Argentine capital as your farthest destination point), you can stop free at several other cities at no additional cost.

BASIC AIR FARES: In our prior editions we listed charts indicating the basic and excursion fares from major U.S. and Canadian cities to the principal capitals of Latin America. However, recent changes in fares make it ludicrous to list fares and regulations which no doubt will change by the time you read this book. Needless to say, your best bet is to check with your airline or with your travel agent regarding current fares and any special fares that may save you money. At this writing, in addition to the regular air fares, there is an APEX fare, an individual tour inclusive fare (which includes land arrangements), and a 28-day excursion fare. In addition, charters have become a popular means of saving airfare money, when heading to a particular destination. Check these out before departing.

THE AIRLINES: The major U.S. carriers are **Eastern Airlines** and **Pan American World Airways,** which just about split South America in half—Pan Am concentrates on the east coast and Eastern on the west. Pan Am, offering extensive service between the U.S. and South America, flies from San Francisco, Los Angeles, Houston, Miami, and New York. The Los Angeles, San Francisco, and Houston flights stop en route in Panama. Best of all, Pan Am has frequent flights to Brasilia, Georgetown, Montevideo, and Buenos Aires. Eastern, flying from New York and Miami, has frequent service to major cities in Colombia, Ecuador, Peru, and Argentina. They fly their new jumbo jets and offer in-flight movies as well as excellent service on board.

   Canadian Pacific offers service to South America from Canada.

   Many of the South American national airlines fly worldwide and are renowned for their excellent service, with routes from North America and within South America. **Varig** (Brazil's flag carrier) has for years been referred to by frequent travelers as "the Swiss Air of South America," in recognition of its superb, award-winning service, reliability, and spirit of its employee-owned airline.

   Other carriers are **VIASA** and **AVENSA** (Venezuela), **L.A.N.** (Chile), **Aerolíneas Argentina** (Argentina), **Avianca** (Colombia), and **Aero Perú** (Peru). Their equipment is modern and each line adds a touch of its homeland to your flight.

3. USEFUL INFORMATION

   The weeks before any overseas trip should be an exhilarating period of readying your clothes, your luggage, your documents, and yourself for the journey ahead. But some travelers seem to make it a time of aggravation by ignoring method in their planning and allowing irrational decisions to affect their arrangements—perhaps because they don't have sufficient background information.

   To smooth these weeks and free you of panic-button pushing, we've set forth a series of suggestions that should guide you through and around pre-trip details with minimum fuss.

DOCUMENTS: The only official papers you'll need in order to travel in South America are a valid United States or Canadian **passport,** required by all countries there; **Tourist Cards,** required by some countries; and **visas,** required by Argentina and Brazil.

   These are all simple to obtain and, if you allow enough time, should be no problem at all.

Passports

   Arranging for a passport is routine. Pick up your application at the State Department Passport Office (or at designated post offices and county courthouses) in any good-size city. The fee is now $42 for a new passport, $35 for a renewal, but the passport will be valid for ten years. You will need two 2½- by 2½-inch passport photos. The wait for your passport is at least two weeks from the date of application.

Tourist Cards

These visa-like cards are easily arranged for through your airline when you purchase your ticket. Most are free but some countries charge $2, and some require small photos. You may also pick up Tourist Cards in South America from your airline prior to departure for your next destination. *Tip:* Always carry extra photos (small ones) with you.

The following chart is a handy guide to country-by-country Tourist Card requirements. Since these are subject to change, check with your airline before departure.

Argentina and Brazil require visas rather than Tourist Cards.

Country	Tourist	Card Photos
Bolivia	yes (free)	no
Chile	yes (free)	no
Colombia	yes (free)	2*
Ecuador	no	no
Panama	yes ($2 charge)	no
Paraguay	yes ($1 charge)	no
Peru	no	no
Surinam	no	no
Uruguay	no	no
Venezuela	yes (free)	no

*None needed if stay is less than 90 days and you enter Colombia directly from the U.S.

Visas

Brazilian Visas: U.S. citizens need a visa to visit Brazil. A visa can be obtained from any Brazilian Consulate by mail or in person. In order to obtain a visa, you need a round-trip ticket (or a letter from a travel agent, giving the dates of arrival and departure), a photo, and a valid passport. The visa must be used within 90 days from its date of issuance and is good for 90 days from the first day it is used, and allows multiple entries within that period. Canadian citizens do not need a visa.

Argentinian Visas: Argentina, like Brazil, requires a visa. The Argentine visa is valid for four years and permits multiple entries within that period of time. You can obtain a visa from any Argentine Consulate. All you need is your passport and a photo.

Vaccination Certificates

Smallpox vaccinations are no longer required. You might consider a typhoid shot (if you normally take one) as a precaution. Readers planning trips to the jungles of Brazil or Peru should consider a yellow fever shot. A tetanus shot might also be considered as a precaution. Consult your local health department.

LUGGAGE AND CLOTHING:
The two vital rules to follow in packing—as emphasized in every $$$-a-Day travel guide—are: (1) that you take a minimum of clothing, and (2) that you make sure that what you do take is crease-resistant and/or wash-and-wear.

These rules are reemphasized here. Strongly. After each of our overseas trips we've vowed to take less luggage the next time. Each time we did take less and each time what we took was more than we needed. We think at last we have it down to a fine science. Which we plan to share with you.

Life will go much smoother if you take only one suitcase per person—24-inch or 26-inch—plus a small airline bag. This will automatically limit the amount of clothing you can take along. If you follow this basic piece of advice, you will find yourself delightfully portable, liberated from hours of packing and unpacking, and seldom arm-weary should taxis and airport porters be hard to find.

If you have luggage that is rugged and lightweight, stay with it; don't buy any additional bags. If, however, you plan to purchase luggage for this trip, then by all means pick up the zippered cloth or canvas-type bag sold at all large department and discount stores.

If you are a couple traveling together, consider taking one 26-inch case plus a hanging bag, instead of two suitcases. We always travel this way and find that the hanging bag keeps our clothes wrinkle-free. Moreover, we don't have to unpack it since it hangs in the closet just as is. Unzip it and your clothes are ready for you.

The airline totebag and/or large handbag that you should include can be carried personally aboard the plane and will not count in your luggage weight. These bags are ideal for cameras, books, cosmetics, maps, and odds and ends.

Note: The maximum luggage weight you are permitted by some airlines is 44 pounds per person, while others allow two bags per person regardless of weight. Expect to pay about $2.25 per pound for any extra weight.

Another reason for taking minimum clothing and gear is that you will need room for the gifts, maps, and books you certainly will be purchasing in South America. Therefore expect your bag to get heavier as you travel.

Besides, in the unlikely event that you find you have forgotten something, you will be able to pick up whatever you need in Rio, Buenos Aires, Santiago, Lima, or any other large city in South America. The department stores in these cities would be keen competitors of Macy's and Marshall Field's in any U.S. city.

Actually, careful planning will allow you to leave behind some necessary clothing. A good example is a warm sweater—a must item in your packing. Since you can buy a good-quality sweater in Buenos Aires at bargain prices, why take one along? The only reason for doing so would be if the cities preceding Buenos Aires on your itinerary were cool in climate. But if you're heading to Rio first—a semitropical city—and then to Argentina, a sound idea would be to leave your heavy sweater home and buy a new one in Buenos Aires.

This leads to one of our travel tips: compare our packing list below with our shopping suggestions in each city that you plan to visit. Where there are clothing items you definitely plan to buy, reduce your travel wardrobe accordingly.

Following are the packing essentials, grouped by sex and season:

For Women

When we first started traveling in South America, pants were something women wore going to climb ruins and they were rarely seen in big cities, especially at night. Now, of course, the dress code has been totally relaxed and you'd be hard put to pick out Americans from the "natives." Pants suits, culottes, and even jeans are acceptable everywhere, providing you use common sense.

Tips: Try to coordinate your clothing so that shirts and sweaters can be worn with several pants outfits. Always have comfortable walking shoes—even at night. Espadrilles and sandals may sound great, but aren't for real walkers. The weight of your clothing will depend on the season you go in. Take wools or heavy cottons May through October, and lightweight clothing November through February. (Check each chapter if you are uncertain of season.) You don't need fur coats or even a heavy winter coat—stick to a heavy sweater and a lined raincoat except for skiers or those camping out. A suggested list might include:

2 outfits for evening wear (dresses, long skirt and top, or pants outfits)
1 skirt or culotte
2 pairs slacks (jeans, corduroy, or polyester)
2 shirts
2 sweaters
1 heavy sweater (jacket type)
1 raincoat (with removable lining)
Pantyhose
Bras and panties
1 bathing suit (bikinis are worn everywhere)
1 pair pajamas
1 pair comfortable walking shoes
1 pair comfortable evening shoes
1 rain scarf

For Men
Dress codes for men have also relaxed and, where once jacket and tie were musts, a jacket is acceptable. Turtlenecks are very common, as are ascots. Sport jackets and slacks can be worn in place of suits.

1 suit for evening (or conservative sport jacket and slacks)
1 pair dark slacks
2 pairs daytime slacks
2 wash-and-wear shirts
2 polo shirts (acrylic)
1 heavy sweater
1 raincoat (with removable lining)
1 pair pajamas
1 bathing suit
2 pairs comfortable shoes (1 for evening)
1 tie (for a special occasion)
3 hankies
3 pairs socks
3 T-shirts
3 pairs shorts

Tips: Remember to coordinate your shirts or sweaters with your slacks and jacket. Take the most comfortable shoes you own. You can always buy another pair in an emergency.

Packing Tips
And now some helpful suggestions:

To prevent suits and dresses from wrinkling in your suitcase, place tissue paper between garments.

Transparent zippered plastic bags, sold at five-and-dime stores, are ideal for separating such articles as lingerie, cosmetics, shoes.

Carry all liquids, shampoos, lotions, and the like in plastic bottles only. Breakage can ruin your clothes and your luggage. Plastic bottles are available at variety stores.

Remember, you will be doing your own laundry as you go (laundry service in most South American cities is expensive and slow), so be sure to carry cold-water soap packets. One packet will do several items in your hotel sink. A small clothesline, with suction cups, is handy for hanging up your wet wash-and-wear clothes.

U.S.-manufactured drugs and sundries are widely available in South American cities, so don't load yourself down—as many travelers do—with assorted pills and remedies, but do bring your own prescription drugs. Packets of towelettes, which are ideal for a fast freshening-up while touring, are one sundry item you should bring.

Many travelers use portable wheels on their luggage as an aid. We find them more trouble than convenience since the wheels often slip off. But perhaps you'll have better luck.

South American hotels in general are generous with towels, soap, and toilet tissue. Therefore don't become a walking bathroom.

A travel alarm clock and travel iron are items that friends of ours carry on long trips. We're not sure they are necessary. Most hotels we recommend have wake-up service, and if you stick to wash-and-wear clothes, you shouldn't need an iron.

MEDICAL AID FOR TRAVELERS: The **International Association for Medical Assistance to Travelers (IAMAT)** is a nonprofit organization providing travelers in 450 cities in 120 countries with English-speaking doctors familiar with North American medical techniques. Membership is free, but members are charged a moderate fee by the treating physician abroad. We recently received a letter from IAMAT's president and founder, Dr. Vincenzo Marcolongo, which explains some of the benefits of membership in this fine organization:

"In enclosing an edition of our *Directory,* I would like to call your attention to the 'World Climate Chart.' This is a new series of eight publications which detail specific climatic and sanitary conditions of the areas of the world most visited by tourists.

"The section on South America capsulizes all the conditions that one should know before one travels to that destination. For instance, if one is going to Buenos Aires in January, he need only consult the chart to see that the highest average temperature is 29°C/85°F, the lowest average temperature 12°C/65°F, while the mean relative humidity is 71%. The average number of rainy days is seven. The conditions of the drinking water, milk, dairy products, and clothing to be worn are also included.

"In addition to supplying the 'World Climate Chart' to those who make a specific request for the area to be visited, each IAMAT member automatically receives the *Directory,* a 'Traveller's Clinical Record,' and a 'World Immunization and Malaria Risk Chart.'

"The pocket-size *Directory* lists IAMAT centers abroad in 450 cities in 120 countries. The individual English-speaking physicians associated with IAMAT centers are trained for the most part in internal medicine. Each doctor has had a period of postgraduate training in the U.S.A., Canada, or the United Kingdom, and has agreed to a fixed schedule of fees for his services.

"The 'Traveller's Clinical Record' is designed to record the traveler's medical history and any treatment during his journey.

"The 'World Immunization and Malaria Risk Chart' lists all required and recommended inoculations for all countries. Countries with a risk for malaria are noted as well.

"Anybody may join IAMAT by just writing to 736 Center St., Lewiston, NY 14092, or 123 Edward St., Suite 725, Toronto, Ontario M5G 1E2.

"IAMAT is a nonprofit foundation financed by voluntary donations from its members. All donations are tax exempt in both the U.S.A. and Canada. The funds are used for research into the medical aspects of travel."

FOOT CARE TIPS FOR TRAVELERS: Travel can be tough on the feet, especially when you spend all day sightseeing or playing sports. It's important to give your feet special care before, during, and after your trip—because paying attention to your feet now can help prevent serious problems later.

Here are some foot-care tips for travelers from Dr. Steven Baff, a well-known podiatric physician who has seen hundreds of travel-related foot ailments in his New York office:

1. Choose good walking shoes.
2. Exercise your feet.
3. Keep your feet clean and dry.
4. Handle blisters with care.
5. Cool hot feet.

SHERATON HOTELS: If you are on business, or plan to splurge, Sheraton operates hotels within South America. The Caracas, Rio, Buenos Aires, Santiago, and Lima Sheratons are each deluxe, and unlike other hotel chains, each offers a touch of the national flavor in design and service. The U.S. toll-free number— 800/325-3535—will confirm reservations for you.

HILTON HOTELS: Hilton boasts the continent's newest luxury hotels. In Caracas, Bogotá, and Panama, they are the perfect stops for business travelers since they are centrally located and offer a variety of services, such as Telex machines and direct-dial phones. In Cartagena and Margarita, the Hilton offers resort-hotel luxury. Reservations can be made from your hometown by calling 212/594-4500 or your local agent.

CURRENCY CONFUSION: As in Europe, every country in South America has its own currency with its own value in relation to the U.S. dollar. But unlike the more stable European moneys, many South American currencies tend to fluctuate in value, sometimes sharply, and sometimes almost overnight. This can make travel-guide research hazardous since hotel and restaurant prices can move up (or down) suddenly.

To our chagrin this has happened at various times in Chile, Colombia, Peru, Argentina, and Brazil. As a result, in the past some of our quoted prices in these countries were out of date virtually as soon as our book was published. The cause, simply put, was an inflationary explosion that catapulted prices up. While it was true that the dollar often increased in value and therefore tourists were able to purchase more cruzados, soles, sucres, and pesos, nevertheless price jumps generally outran the boosts in dollar purchasing power.

To confuse things a shade more, some countries (for example, Peru) occasionally counterbalance inflation by devaluing their currency. In other words, prices shoot up due to inflation, but a devaluation of the local currency in relation to the dollar more or less corrects the price "deviation" for U.S. visitors.

The Parallel Currency Market

An intriguing phenomenon has emerged in recent years—the "parallel market" in currency exchange. In short, this means that for many Latin currencies there are two money-exchange rates, the official rate and the unofficial (parallel market), the latter offering a better exchange rate for your dollar.

The official rate is the rate you receive in the host country during your stay. The parallel-market rate, which can and does change suddenly, is at times available in Latin America, in the host country, and in the U.S. through major international banks or currency dealers. While a parallel market does not always exist for all countries, it is worth checking before your departure and upon arrival in South America. It could make all the difference in your budget. To wit: in early 1989 the official exchange rate in Brazil was 700 cruzados to the U.S. dollar; the parallel-market rate was 950 to the dollar!

Warning: Some Latin countries consider the parallel rate a "black market" and strongly discourage its use. Obviously this guide does *not* recommend that you participate in black-market activities, but we believe you have a right to be informed of practices that are common in some areas.

Now that all this is said, the question remains: How do you, the traveler to South America, guide yourself through this intricate money maze so that you are protected from unpleasant price shocks? Complete protection is impossible, but the following precautions should prove helpful:

1. Do not accept any currency information as gospel, even the data in this guide. Changes take place too abruptly. Therefore you must check with a dealer or the international section of a large bank for the latest information just before your departure. (In New York, Citibank is particularly knowledgeable since it has many South American branches.)

2. We have noted all prices in dollars instead of the local currency. Thus we avoid the confusion that arises if the price in pesos (or any other currency) jumps but the real price to you remains the same due to devaluation of that local currency.

3. Where appropriate, we have listed the upper range of all budget prices charged by hotels and restaurants. The hope is to reward you occasionally with lower-than-expected bills.

4. We have included a currency section in each chapter which reviews that country's recent money history, including price and exchange-rate fluctuations. Study these carefully, particularly in the Rio, Santiago, Bogotá, Lima, and Buenos Aires chapters.

Some final suggestions: Traveler's checks are a must, of course, and those sold by Barclay's Bank are free, as opposed to the standard 1% fee charged by most others.

To cover tipping and incidentals in each city as you arrive, it's a good idea to buy a few dollars of that country's currency in advance. A Brazilian taxi driver would be as appreciative of your half-dollar as a New York cabby would be of a cruzado.

The Exchange Rates

Here are the country-by-country exchange rates as of early 1989. Remember that *each is subject to sharp changes.*

Argentina: The basic monetary unit is the **austral;** in early 1989 there were 16 australs to $1 U.S.

Bolivia: The new **Boliviano** is 2.5 to the U.S. dollar. But read carefully the currency section in the La Paz chapter (Chapter VII).

Brazil: Since January 1989, the new currency unit has been the **novo cruzado** ("new cruzado"). The official exchange rate is 1 novo cruzado to the dollar. However, the parallel-market rate varies frequently and should be checked. As we go to press, banking sources are still unclear as to whether or when novo cruzado notes will be printed, so be aware that each old 1,000 cruzado note is equal to 1 novo cruzado (just cancel out the last three zeros). Read carefully the currency section in the Rio Chapter (Chapter III).

Colombia: The currency unit is the Colombian **peso,** and there are 294 pesos to the U.S. dollar.

Chile: The basic currency unit is the Chilean **peso,** valued at 250 pesos to the dollar.

Ecuador: The primary unit is the **sucre,** made up of 100 centavos. In early 1989 there were 500 sucres to the dollar.

Panama: The basic unit is the U.S. dollar, which in Panama is called the **balboa** and, as in the U.S., is divided into 100 cents. The coins are different but the denominations are the same as in the U.S., from the penny through quarters, half dollars, and a few silver dollars.

Peru: The currency unit is the **inti,** introduced in 1985, which is valued at 1,400 to the U.S. dollar. The inti is worth 1,000 soles, the former unit of currency.

Paraguay: The basic unit is the **guarani,** valued at 600 to the U.S. dollar.

Uruguay: The currency unit is the Uruguayan **peso,** which has steadily eroded in value and at this writing stands at 450 to the dollar.

Venezuela: The monetary unit is the **bolívar,** for decades a sturdy currency, divided into 100 centisimos. The bolívar stood at 4.3 per $1 U.S. since our first edition in 1965 until 1984 when the world price of oil dropped. So did the value of the bolívar—from 4.3 to 14 per dollar within just a few months. Since then it has continued its fall and at this writing sways between 37 and 39, making Caracas—for the first time—a moderately priced city. How long will it last? *¿Quién sabe?*

WEIGHTS AND MEASURES:
South Americans use the metric system of weighing and measuring, and if you are prepared for it, you can avoid confusion. Here's a quick rundown on equivalencies:

Length
1 millimeter = 0.04 inches (*or* less than $\frac{1}{16}$ in)
1 centimeter = 0.39 inches (*or* just under ½ in)
1 meter   = 1.09 yards (*or* about 39 inches)
1 kilometer = 0.62 mile (*or* about ⅔ mile)

To convert kilometers to miles, take the number of kilometers and multiply by .62 (for example, 25 km × .62 = 15.5 mi).

To convert miles to kilometers, take the number of miles and multiply by 1.61 (for example, 50 mi × 1.61 = 80.5 km).

Capacity
1 liter = 33.92 ounces
     = 1.06 quarts
     = 0.26 gallons

To convert liters to gallons, take the number of liters and multiply by .26 (for example, 50 l × .26 = 13 gallons).

To convert gallons to liters, take the number of gallons and multiply by 3.79 (for example, 10 gal × 3.79 = 37.9 l).

Weight
1 gram   = 0.04 ounces (*or* about a paperclip's weight)
1 kilogram = 2.2 pounds

To convert kilograms to pounds, take the number of kilos and multiply by 2.2 (for example, 75 kg × 2.2 = 165 pounds).

To convert pounds to kilograms, take the number of pounds and multiply by .45 (for example, 90 lb × .45 = 40.5 kg).

Area
1 hectare (100m²) = 2.47 acres

To convert hectares to acres, take the number of hectares and multiply by 2.47 (for example, 20 ha × 2.47 = 49.4 acres).

To convert acres to hectares, take the number of acres and multiply by .41 (for example, 40 acres × .41 = 16.4 hectare).

Temperature

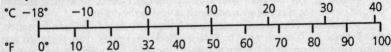

To convert degrees C to degrees F, multiply degrees C by 9, divide by 5, then add 32 (for example 9/5 × 20°C + 32 = 68°F).

To convert degrees F to degrees C, subtract 32 from degrees F, then multiply by 5, and divide by 9 (for example, 85°F − 32 × 5/9 = 29°C).

CUSTOMS REGULATIONS: Before deciding what to buy in South America, keep in mind the current Customs regulations, which permit U.S. citizens to bring back up to $400 in duty-free merchandise per person (including children). Keep in mind that many articles made in some of these countries are not subject to duty. (See the shopping sections for each country for specifics. You may also bring in one quart of liquor if you are over 21 years of age.

THE COST OF SHIPPING IT HOME: No matter what you purchase, if you plan to ship it instead of carrying it with you, then carefully add in the costs of air or ocean freight, the cost of using a Customhouse broker (say $40 or so), plus the cost of having the merchandise delivered from the airport or dock to your home. It cost us $38 to have some light furniture delivered from JFK Airport to Manhattan.

Incredibly, your overall cost can double depending on what you purchase. You can save by acting as your own Customhouse broker (which can take half a day of your time), carting the stuff home in your station wagon, and by using ocean freight instead of air freight.

The point of all this is to avoid surprises by calculating in advance what it actually will cost you to get that table or alpaca rug from the store to your living room. Don't let the merchant put you off when you ask about freight charges. He knows, or certainly can find out quickly, what the freight cost approximates. As a guide, just remember that it will cost you $62 to ship by air 90 pounds of furniture from Peru to JFK Airport; and $28 to ship 22 pounds from La Paz to JFK. Ocean freight charges run somewhat less.

AN INVITATION TO READERS: Throughout the pages to follow you'll notice "Readers' Selections" and "Readers' Suggestions"—hotel and restaurant finds, sightseeing tips and suggestions, and important comments from previous users of this book. To our mind there is no advice more valuable than yours, and we therefore urge you to share it with us and future readers. Send your letters to Arnold and Harriet Greenberg, c/o Frommer Books, Prentice Hall Press, 1 Gulf + Western Plaza, New York, NY 10023.

4. THE DOLLARWISE TRAVEL CLUB—HOW TO SAVE MONEY ON ALL YOUR TRAVELS

In this book we'll be looking at how to get your money's worth in South America, but there is a "device" for saving money and determining value on *all* your trips. It's the popular, international Frommer's Dollarwise Travel Club, now in its 28th successful year of operation. The club was formed at the urging of numerous readers of the guides, who felt that such an organization could provide continuing travel information and a sense of community to value-minded travelers in all parts of the world. And so it does!

In keeping with the budget concept, the annual membership fee is low and is immediately exceeded by the value of your benefits. Upon receipt of $18 (U.S. residents), or $20 U.S. by check drawn on a U.S. bank or via international postal money order in U.S. funds (Canadian, Mexican, and other foreign residents) to cover one year's membership, we will send all new members the following items.

(1) Any *two* of the following books

Please designate in your letter which two you wish to receive:

Frommer Guides
- Australia
- Austria and Hungary
- Belgium, Holland, & Luxembourg
- Bermuda and The Bahamas
- Brazil
- Canada
- Caribbean
- Egypt
- England and Scotland
- France
- Germany
- Italy
- Japan and Hong Kong
- Portugal, Madeira, and the Azores
- South Pacific
- Switzerland and Liechtenstein
- Alaska
- California and Las Vegas
- Florida
- Mid-Atlantic States
- New England
- New York State
- Northwest
- Skiing USA—East
- Skiing USA—West
- Southeast and New Orleans
- Southeast Asia
- Southwest
- Texas
- USA

(Frommer Guides discuss accommodations and facilities in all price ranges, with emphasis on the medium-priced.)

Frommer's™ $-A-Day® Guides
   Europe on $40 a Day
   Australia on $30 a Day
   Eastern Europe on $25 a Day
   England on $40 a Day
   Greece on $30 a Day
   Hawaii on $50 a Day
   India on $25 a Day
   Ireland on $35 a Day
   Israel on $30 & $35 a Day
   Mexico (plus Belize and Guatemala) on $25 a Day
   New York on $50 a Day
   New Zealand on $40 a Day
   Scandinavia on $60 a Day
   Scotland and Wales on $40 a Day
   South America on $35 a Day
   Spain and Morocco (plus the Canary Is.) on $40 a Day
   Turkey on $30 a Day
   Washington, D.C., & Historic Virginia on $40 a Day
($-A-Day Guides document hundreds of budget accommodations and facilities, helping you get the most for your travel dollars.)

Frommer's™ Touring Guides
   Australia
   Egypt
   Florence
   London
   Paris
   Scotland
   Thailand
   Venice
(These new, color illustrated guides include walking tours, cultural and historic sites, and other vital travel information.)

Gault Millau
   Chicago
   France
   Italy
   London
   Los Angeles
   New England
   New York
   San Francisco
   Washington, D.C.
(Irreverent, savvy, and comprehensive, each of these renowned guides candidly reviews over 1,000 restaurants, hotels, shops, nightspots, museums, and sights.)

Serious Shopper's Guides
   Italy
   London
   Los Angeles
   Paris
(Practical and comprehensive, each of these handsomely illustrated guides lists hundreds of stores, selling everything from antiques to wine, conveniently organized alphabetically by category.)

A Shopper's Guide to the Caribbean
(Two experienced Caribbean hands guide you through this shopper's paradise, offering witty insights and helpful tips on the wares and emporia of more than 25 islands.)

Beat the High Cost of Travel
(This practical guide details how to save money on absolutely all travel items—accommodations, transportation, dining, sightseeing, shopping, taxes, and more. Includes special budget information for seniors, students, singles, and families.)

Bed & Breakfast—North America
(This guide contains a directory of over 150 organizations that offer bed & breakfast referrals and reservations throughout North America. The scenic attractions, and major schools and universities near the homes of each are also listed.)

California with Kids
(A must for parents traveling in California, providing key information on selecting the best accommodations, restaurants, and sightseeing attractions for the particular needs of the family, whether the kids are toddlers, school-age, pre-teens, or teens.)

Dollarwise Cruises
(This complete guide covers all the basics of cruising—ports of call, costs, fly-cruise package bargains, cabin selection booking, embarkation and debarkation and describes in detail over 60 or so ships cruising the waters of Alaska, the Caribbean, Mexico, Hawaii, Panama, Canada, and the United States.)

Dollarwise Skiing Europe
(Describes top ski resorts in Austria, France, Italy, and Switzerland. Illustrated with maps of each resort area. Includes supplement on Argentinian resorts.)

Frommer's Belgium
(Arthur Frommer unlocks the treasures of a country overlooked by most travelers to Europe. Discover the medieval charm, modern sophistication, and natural beauty of this quintessentially European country.)

Guide to Honeymoon Destinations
(A special guide for that most romantic trip of your life, with full details on planning and choosing the destination that will be just right in the U.S. [California, New England, Hawaii, Florida, New York, South Carolina, etc.], Canada, Mexico, and the Caribbean.)

Marilyn Wood's Wonderful Weekends
(This very selective guide covers the best mini-vacation destinations within a 200-mile radius of New York City. It describes special country inns and other accommodations, restaurants, picnic spots, sights, and activities—all the information needed for a two- or three-day stay.)

Manhattan's Outdoor Sculpture
(A total guide, fully illustrated with black and white photos, to more than 300 sculptures and monuments that grace Manhattan's plazas, parks, and other public spaces.)

Motorist's Phrase Book
(A practical phrase book in French, German, and Spanish designed specifically for the English-speaking motorist touring abroad.)

Paris Rendez-Vous
(An amusing and *au courant guide* to the best meeting places in Paris, organized for hour-to-hour use: from power breakfasts and fun brunches, through tea at four or cocktails at five, to romantic dinners and dancing 'til dawn.)

Swap and Go—Home Exchanging Made Easy
(Two veteran home exchangers explain in detail all the money-saving benefits of a home exchange, and then describe precisely how to do it. Also includes information on home rentals and many tips on low-cost travel.)

The Candy Apple: New York for Kids
(A spirited guide to the wonders of the Big Apple by a savvy New York grandmother with a kid's-eye view to fun. Indispensable for visitors and residents alike.)

The New World of Travel
(From America's #1 travel expert, Arthur Frommer, an annual sourcebook with the hottest news and latest trends that's guaranteed to change the way you travel —and save you hundreds of dollars. Jam-packed with alternative new modes of travel that will lead you to vacations that cater to the mind, the spirit, and a sense of thrift.)

Travel Diary and Record Book
(A 96-page diary for personal travel notes plus a section for such vital data as passport and traveler's check numbers, itinerary, postcard list, special people and places to visit, and a reference section with temperature and conversion charts, and world maps with distance zones.)

Where to Stay USA
(By the Council on International Educational Exchange, this extraordinary guide is the first to list accommodations in all 50 states that cost anywhere from $3 to $30 per night.)

(2) Any *one* of Frommer's™ City Guides
Amsterdam
Athens
Atlantic City and Cape May
Boston
Cancún, Cozumel, and the Yucatán
Chicago
Dublin and Ireland
Hawaii
Las Vegas
Lisbon, Madrid, and Costa del Sol
London
Los Angeles
Mexico City and Acapulco
Minneapolis and St. Paul
Montréal and Québec City
New Orleans

New York
Orlando, Disney World, and EPCOT
Paris
Philadelphia
Rio
Rome
San Francisco
Santa Fe and Taos
Sydney
Washington, D.C.

(Pocket-size guides to hotels, restaurants, nightspots, and sightseeing attractions covering all price ranges.)

(3) A one-year subscription to *The Dollarwise® Traveler*

This quarterly eight-page tabloid newspaper keeps you up to date on fastbreaking developments in low-cost travel in all parts of the world bringing you the latest money-saving information—the kind of information you'd have to pay $35 a year to obtain elsewhere. This consumer-conscious publication also features columns of special interest to readers: **Hospitality Exchange** (members all over the world who are willing to provide hospitality to other members as they pass through their home cities); **Share-a-Trip** (offers and requests from members for travel companions who can share costs and help avoid the burdensome single supplement); and **Readers Ask . . . Readers Reply** (travel questions from members to which other members reply with authentic firsthand information).

(4) Your personal membership card

Membership entitles you to purchase through the club all Frommer publications for a third to a half off their regular prices during the term of your membership.

So why not join this hardy band of international budgeteers and participate in its exchange of travel information and hospitality? Simply send your name and address, together with your annual membership fee of $18 (U.S. residents) or $20 U.S. (Canadian, Mexican, and other foreign residents), by check drawn on a U.S. bank or via international postal money order in U.S. funds to: Frommer's Dollarwise Travel Club, Inc., Gulf + Western Building, One Gulf + Western Plaza, New York, NY 10023. And please remember to specify which *two* of the books in section (1) and which *one* in section (2) you wish to receive in your initial package of members' benefits. Or, if you prefer, use the order form at the end of the book and enclose $18 or $20 in U.S. currency.

Once you are a member, there is no obligation to buy additional books. No books will be mailed to you without your specific order.

CHAPTER II

CARACAS, VENEZUELA

□ □ □

1. WHERE TO STAY
2. DINING IN CARACAS
3. CARACAS BY DAY
4. EXCURSIONS AND TOURS
5. CARACAS AFTER DARK
6. THE BEST SHOPPING VALUES
7. TRANSPORTATION NOTES AND ASSORTED MISCELLANY

When we wrote the first edition of this guide in 1965, visiting Caracas on $5 a day was impossible. Caracas's prices were infamous—hotel and restaurant prices here were equal to or higher than those in New York or Paris. That remained consistently true and was not the result of inflation. By the mid-1970s Caracas was one of the world's most expensive cities. However, in the last few years economic problems have hit hard here as they have in other oil-producing countries, and prices have tumbled. If there was ever a time for a budget traveler to visit Caracas and to explore this beautiful country, this is it! While Caracas is still one of the continent's most expensive cities, you can certainly live quite comfortably and cleanly here for $35 a day. As an example of how prices have fallen, a taxi ride from the airport at Maiquetía to your hotel will run about $8 rather than the staggering $30 it was just a few years ago. If you must exceed your budget slightly, it's a small price to pay to enjoy this dynamic city with a terrific climate whose skyline is constantly in motion.

Hotel rates are on a par with those in Buenos Aires and Lima and there are decent accommodations in the $20 to $40 range for a double. There are good-value moderately priced restaurants around town and many fast-food (Latin- and American-style) establishments where you can eat three meals and still stay on a budget. Though Caracas's elegant restaurants (and there are many of them) are still above budget level, you can dine in some if you select carefully from the menu and keep down your alcohol intake.

As for transportation, cab fares are lower, there is a metro, and low-cost jitney and bus alternatives are available. What we're saying is that by choosing accommodations, meals, etc., with care, your living expenses in Caracas can be held to manageable levels.

Caracas is an important stop on your itinerary, for climate (warm and sunny much of the year), sophistication, jumping nightlife, and the warmth of its residents (called Caraqueños). It's a different side of Latin America.

A CAPSULE HISTORY:
Caracas, more than all other South American cities, recalls vividly the liberation era of Simón Bolívar in the profusion of the parks, plazas, and statues commemorating the "George Washington of South America."

Simón Bolívar was born in Caracas in 1783 to a wealthy aristocratic family. He, together with Francisco de Miranda and Antonio José de Sucre, led the fight for freedom from Spain. In 1817 he captured Caracas, earning the name El Libertador. He was also responsible for freeing Ecuador, Colombia, Panama, and Peru, and for founding Bolivia, which bears his name. The colonies joined into a federation called Nueva Grenada, and Bolívar became the president. Thirteen years later the federation fell apart, and a disappointed Bolívar retired to a friend's home in Santa Marta (Colombia), where he died in 1830. Streets, plazas, mountains, schools, parks, the airport, and even the currency throughout Venezuela—all bear his name. His memory throughout the country is revered as in no other single country.

CARACAS TODAY:
Only 2½ hours from Miami and 4½ hours by jet from New York, this gracious, sophisticated city of over four million people has probably the highest standard of living of any Latin American city, including Mexico City. Sprawling like Los Angeles for almost ten miles, Caracas incorporates an estimated score of separate communities, including several popular with North Americans. High-rise office buildings, apartment houses, and residential co-ops speckle the ever-changing skyline.

When you arrive in the Venezuelan capital, you'll probably be struck by the strong U.S. and Canadian influence in food, architecture, and in the skillful merchandising techniques of the city's shopping centers, specialty shops, and dazzling boutiques. Many corporations are structured along North American lines, and English is the second language—you'll hear it in hotels, stores, even in the streets.

Caracas is an epicure's delight, what with dozens of first-rate French and Argentinian as well as North American–style restaurants. Thousands of U.S. and Canadian citizens—employed here by North American companies originally drawn to Venezuela by the rich oil finds in Maracaibo—throng the international restaurants and nightclubs. The disco-type clubs are the best we've found in South America, and the relatively well-paid young locals, eager for a taste of "La Dulce Vida"—Caracas style—keep the town jumping day and night.

Venezuelans are well dressed, and fashions imported from Italy, France, and the United States are de rigueur in restaurants, discos, and theaters. Only in the most exclusive French restaurants are ties required, although men do wear jackets at night.

Symbolic of Venezuela's wealth are the number of autos in the city. The city is intersected by several modern highways but the traffic problem rivals that we've seen anywhere.

The new metro helps alleviate this problem a bit. The first leg of the subway from Propatria in the west to Chacaíto (which is central) went into operation in 1983. Air-conditioned cars carry approximately half a million people daily. As new tunnels are constructed to other parts of the city, whole blocks are torn up, which makes traffic worse. However, if Sabana Grande is typical of what happens after the tunnel is completed, then it will be worthwhile. The Sabana Grande, formerly a traffic-clogged shopping street, has been transformed into a strollers-only mall filled with cafés and plants. The metro line runs under the Sabana Grande.

GETTING TO CARACAS: The best way to get to Caracas is via **VIASA** (Venezuelan International Airways) or **Pan Am.** Flying modern jet aircraft and featuring good service, excellent food, and in-flight films, both offer frequent nonstop flights from New York and Miami. **AVENSA,** Venezuela's major domestic carrier, has recently inaugurated service from New York. Check with these airlines for special fares. VIASA also offers a Saturday-to-Saturday package tour, year round, nonstop to Margarita Island. **American Airlines** has service to Caracas via Puerto Rico, and **Eastern** has service too.

A WORD ABOUT CLIMATE: Nestled in the Andes 3,000 feet above the Caribbean, Caracas has ideal weather almost all year round, with sunny afternoon highs in the 80s and the nights cooling down into the breezy 60s. However, in the fall and winter—October through February—you might expect a light shower many afternoons. Swimming, of course, is a year-round sport.

There are no beaches in the city since Caracas is inland. To swim in the ocean, you must take a bus, jitney, or the cable car (not in operation at this writing) to the beach area, 40 minutes away. There are many public beach areas that rent cabañas for the day.

UPON ARRIVAL: When you exit from your plane at **Simón Bolívar International Airport,** the first hot and humid blast of sea-level air is enough to drive you back into the jet. But cheer up: the airport in the coastal city of Maiquetía (pronounced mai-ke-*tee*-ah) is only 13 miles and 30 minutes from the cool breezes of Caracas.

In a few moments you will be entering the modern, air-conditioned terminal building. Customs and Immigration are mere formalities; the officials are efficient and polite. After a stop at the bank to change your dollars, and the terminal tourist office to pick up maps, you are ready to head to Caracas. Cabs leave from just outside the Customs area, so that unless you're loaded with baggage you can easily make it without a porter. If you come by ship, the boat will dock at **La Guaira,** a port adjacent to Maiquetía.

The nearby airport you pass on your way to Caracas (in Maiquetía) is used for domestic flights.

From the Airport to Downtown Caracas

The least expensive method is by **bus.** It runs from the airport to the Parque Central near the Caracas Hilton Hotel but not near most of our inexpensive choices. The cost is $1.75 for you and 50¢ for each bag. It's scheduled to leave every half hour but is irregular. It is not air-conditioned and takes about one hour. You then must take a cab or por puesto (group cab) to your hotel. Purchase bus tickets at the terminal.

Check at the tourist counter to see if **por puestos** are available. They are at some times, but were not being used at this writing. When they were permitted, the cost was $2.50 for each person (five in a cab) to downtown, and for 75¢ more you can ask to be dropped at your hotel.

A **taxi** from the airport is $8. They zip into Caracas along the superhighway (called the Caracas–La Guaira Autopista) in a half hour. Steaming at the beginning, the trip gets gradually cooler as you reach higher altitudes.

A QUICK ORIENTATION: Situated in a valley surrounded by the higher reaches of the Andes, Caracas is a long, narrow city that extends for miles east to west. You will enter the city from its older, western section dotted with poor homes, markets, shops, and commercial buildings. You cannot help but notice the clusters of shacks clinging to the mountainsides, much like the favelas of Rio. These are the homes of squatters from other parts of Venezuela and Colombia who've come to Caracas to eke out a living. The government is building low-income projects for these people, but has been unable to keep up with the demand. As you move eastward, you see more modern skyscrapers (20 stories), lovely parks, and upper-middle-class homes. As you move vertically from the highways the neighborhoods increase in wealth. Within this east-west/north-south breakdown are numerous subcommunities called *urbanizaciones* (quarters). Wide, tree-lined boulevards and three major highways cut through the city —the **Autopista del Este, Avenida Libertador,** and the **Cota Mil** (also called Avenida Boyaca).

Major Urbanizaciones

Most urbanizaciones are residential and filled with apartment dwellings, shopping centers, and schools. But there are 12 districts that are important for the traveler to know. These are the areas where hotels, restaurants, and night activities are clustered.

El Silencio and **Altagracia:** These districts are adjacent to each other in the city's older west-side section. El Silencio is highlighted by twin 32-story buildings called the **Centro Simón Bolívar** (Simón Bolívar Center), housing government offices, shopping arcades, and the city's commercial center. These are the structures most featured in skyline photos. Altagracia, immediately to the north, is near the famous **Plaza Bolívar** along with the National Congress building and the National Library. Key streets are **Avenida Urdaneta,** which runs west to east, and **Avenida Baralt,** which runs north and south.

Parque Central: This is a modern complex which houses the deluxe Hilton Hotel (and the Residencias Anauco), the contemporary Art Museum, a trilevel shopping center, a fabulous cultural center, and luxurious condominium apartments.

San Bernardino: Situated in the higher, northern section, San Bernardino is a respectable middle-class section where several of our moderately priced hotels, restaurants, and nightclubs are to be found, along with the fine luxury hotel, the Ávila. The important thoroughfares are **Avenida Vollmer** and **Avenida La Estrella.**

Sabana Grande and **Chacaíto:** This key area has undergone a tremendous facelift which has transformed it from a traffic-clogged street into a pedestrian mall. It has benches, greenery, tables for chess and checkers, and lots of fast-food stops. The Sabana Grande, formerly lined with chic boutiques and good eating spots, has become a middle-class shopping street (the boutiques are moving to the new upscale shopping centers which have proliferated in the eastern parts of town). The traffic that once clogged the Sabana now snakes through the two adjoining thoroughfares, **Avenida Lincoln** and **Avenida Casanova.** Chacaíto, the city's first shopping center at the end of the Sabana, is still a mecca for shoppers and revelers. It has good shops, lots of inexpensive dining options, and several popular nightspots.

El Rosal: Adjoining Chacaíto on the east is the small El Rosal section which is a center for restaurants and small nightclubs in Caracas. Virtually every street in the four-block area has several restaurants and nightspots. Don't miss this area. The major street is **Avenida Tamanaco.**

Las Mercedes: In the southeastern area of Caracas is the North American quarter, where employees of U.S. and Canadian companies live in comfortable surroundings that would fit nicely in Dallas. Note the kids on bicycles, and look for the famous Tamanaco Hotel, the city's best-known luxury hotel. An estimated 20,000 North Americans reside in Caracas. Relations are excellent with the Caraqueños. Also in this section is the modern **Paseo Las Mercedes** shopping complex, which also houses the Paseo Las Mercedes Hotel.

La Castellana and **Altamira:** Heading farther east, you come to these two upper-income sections, a few blocks apart, where the night people congregate in late-opening discos, clubs, and after-midnight restaurants. The boulevard that cuts through both of these swank areas is **Avenida Francisco de Miranda.**

Los Palos Grandes: Just east of these areas is the Palos Grandes section, where the American Embassy is located. The shopping center in this area is a big singles meeting place.

Mariperez: From this northern working-class section of Caracas, the "teleférico" (a cable car) begins its 4,000-foot ascent to Mount Ávila, a sightseeing must. On cloudless days the view of the city is magnificent. At one point it was possible to go from Caracas over the mountain range to the beachfront communities by two cable cars. At this writing only the line from Caracas to the peak of Mount Ávila is in operation (this line, too, was inoperational for several years). They are working on the line to the beach, so check with your hotel clerk to see if it's working yet. It is certainly the best way to get to the beach.

Confusion in the Streets

For some reason the locals don't bother with street numbers, which can make things "muy difícil" for the traveler. Caraqueños assume that the street and the section (and at times the corner, "esquina") is enough for anyone. The address for El Carrizo Restaurant is simply Avenida Blandin, La Castellana, which tells you only that this recommended steak place is in the Castellana section of Caracas on Avenida Blandin. But this street runs for many blocks. Fortunately, hotels will list the corner as their address along with the street name. Even better, cabbies and jitney (por puesto) drivers unerringly know exact locations. So the problem is minimal—unless you're a walker, as we are, in which case you'd best have your hotel clerk estimate distances for you.

A MONETARY NOTE: Venezuela's currency, which for many years held fast at 4.3 bolívares to the U.S. dollar, was devalued in February 1983 to 14 bolívares to the dollar. When we revisited the city to update this 13th edition, the bolívar, which fluctuated daily, had reached a record 39 to the U.S. dollar. There was a lot of talk that the government would step in and fix the rate at 20 bolívares, but that hasn't materialized. Check to see what has happened before you leave. For the purposes of this guide we have pegged our prices at 39 bolívares to the dollar. Bolívares, abbreviated to Bs (and pronounced "bees"), are now worth about 2½¢. There are 100 centimos to the bolívar. Centimo coins come in units of 5 (a puya), 25 (a medio), 50 (a real, pronounced "ray-al"), and there are 1-, 2-, and 5-bolívar coins too. Bills come in denominations of 10, 20, 50, and 100 Bs. Cambios (places where you can change money) are readily available and all banks will offer the official exchange rate for your dollars. Shops, too, will gladly exchange your dollars for Bs with no discount. *Note:* Try to avoid exchanging dollars at your hotel, which will invariably offer less for your money.

TELEPHONE AREA CODE: The area code for Caracas is 02.

1. WHERE TO STAY

Caracas has many fine hotels in all categories. They range from deluxe to basic, but the majority are in the middle range. Because of the extremely favorable monetary exchange in effect at this writing, almost all the hotels, with the excep-

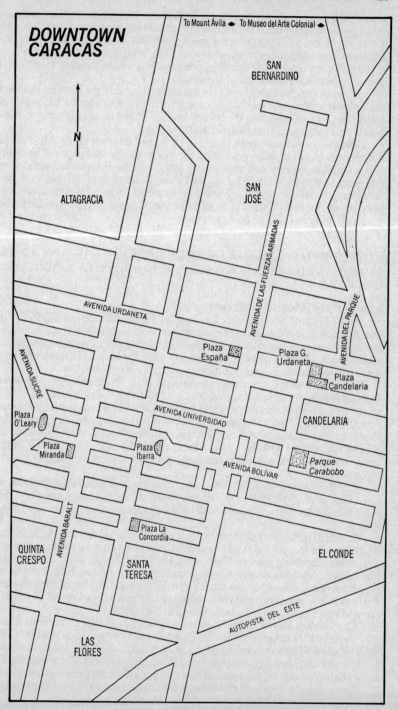

DOWNTOWN CARACAS

N

To Mount Ávila ← To Museo del Arte Colonial ←

SAN BERNARDINO

ALTAGRACIA

SAN JOSÉ

AVENIDA DE LAS FUERZAS ARMADAS

AVENIDA DEL PARQUE

AVENIDA URDANETA

AVENIDA SUCRE

Plaza España

Plaza G. Urdaneta

Plaza Candelaria

Plaza O'Leary

AVENIDA UNIVERSIDAD

CANDELARIA

Plaza Miranda

Plaza Ibarra

AVENIDA BOLÍVAR

Parque Carabobo

AVENIDA BARALT

Plaza La Concordia

QUINTA CRESPO

SANTA TERESA

EL CONDE

LAS FLORES

AUTOPISTA DEL ESTE

tion of the deluxe five-star hotels, are within our budget limits. All hotels are rated by the government, from one to five stars. Hotel prices are in tandem with the rating. Rates are also set by the government for all one- to four-star hotels (only five-star hotels can charge what they like). Four-star hotels are limited to about $30 for a double. Unless things change, you will be delighted with hotel prices in Caracas and throughout Venezuela.

For example, the Hotel Paseo Las Mercedes (formerly the Holiday Inn) and the Ávila, both fine four-star hotels, currently have rates of about $30 for a double. When oil was king, and the bolívar was 4.5 to the dollar, the rates at both hotels were the equivalent of almost $100 per day.

The majority of our hotels are in the three- and four-star range. Most of the hotels in this guide offer private baths, many rooms are carpeted and air-conditioned, and all are well maintained. You'll find the government-authorized rate posted on your door and no hidden extras. To simplify your hotel search we have grouped our selections geographically by section of the city. A catch-all category covers luxury choices, plus selections in other areas. Unless otherwise noted, all multistory hotels have elevators.

Note: For hotel choices at the beach, see "El Litoral," in Section 3.

HOTELS IN THE SABANA GRANDE AREA: Easily the most desirable for travelers is this centrally located district, which is right in the middle of town. Consider it first.

Moderately Priced Selections

Hotel El Condor, 3 Avenida Las Delicias Sabana Grande (tel. 72-9911), is near Avenida Solano and just a two-minute stroll from Chacaíto. It has 72 rooms and all are air-conditioned and have private baths. Rooms are comfortable in size and in décor. Doubles are under $20 while singles are under $18, both of which seem like good buys. Its great location makes this a terrific choice.

Without hesitation, we suggest that you head for the modern, 50-room **Kursaal Hotel,** Avenida Casanova, corner of Calle El Colegio (tel. 72-5714), where two elevators service the eight floors. You will be impressed by the carpeted floors, the private tiled baths (with shower and bidet), and fairly new desks, chairs, and bureaus in all rooms. The spacious, airy rooms, most with a red or blue motif, rent for $18 double with bath, and $16 single. There's a TV in the lobby, and an attractive bar and restaurant are on the premises. Highly recommended.

Another good selection in this category is the 39-room **Hotel Escorial,** at Calle El Colegio (tel. 71-9621), near the Kursaal Hotel. Doubles at the eight-story Escorial are $16 and singles are $14. Some rooms without air conditioning are less.

Located in the heart of this district is the 33-room **Hotel Royal,** Calle Real de Sabana Grande (tel. 72-1904), near the Centro Commercial del Este (a major downtown shopping center). Opened in 1965, the Royal, while certainly not luxurious, does offer roomy accommodations, with private bath, telephone, draperies, and sliding-door closets, for $13, single and double; air conditioning is $1 extra. The hotel is a good value, but the area tends to be crowded during the day and street noises may be a factor for you to consider.

One block from the Hotel Royal on Avenida Las Acacias is the white-hued, 32-room **Hotel Tiburon** (tel. 782-8987), which offers surprisingly small doubles for $18 and up (with shower, piped-in music, bidet, and telephone), and singles for $16; air conditioning comes with the higher-priced rooms. The best feature is the stunning view of the mountains from the upper floors of this six-story choice.

You might also try the **Hotel Odeon,** which opened in 1968 on Avenida Las

Acacias (tel. 782-1823). This 54-room hotel, on nine floors, rents doubles for $16 and singles for $14, all with bath (shower) and air conditioning. Free parking, piped-in music in the rooms, and good service are bonuses here.

The nearby **Hotel Tanasu**, on Sur Avenida Las Acacias (tel. 782-9021), has 28 rooms spread over four floors. The rooms are small but carpeted, and some have tiny balconies overlooking noisy Avenida Casanova. Doubles here are $15 and singles run $13. It's a good buy.

Want something cheaper? Try the six-story **Hotel Sava**, Avenida Lima near the Teatro del Este (tel. 781-1718), which features terraces and a fine view of the surrounding Andes with most of its 33 rooms. Soft leather chairs, modern dressers, and piped-in music make the rooms most comfortable; doubles, with bath and telephone, are a bargain (for Caracas) at $15. Singles are $12. The restaurant and bar are very popular—a fine-value hotel.

If you don't mind hoteling-it in an area known for its ladies of the evening, then look into the 30-room **Cristal Hotel**, three blocks from the Royal, on the Calle Real de Sabana Grande, corner of Pasaje Asunción (tel. 71-9131). Featuring shower stalls and radios in most rooms, the six-story Cristal offers roomy doubles for $16 and singles for $13. We were impressed by the neat, clean, modern furnishings. The entrance to the Cristal is on bustling Pasaje Asunción.

Adjacent to one of our recommended French restaurants (the Coq d'Or) is a lovely hotel, the **Jolly Inn** (formerly the Hotel Kipolo). Recently refurbished and enlarged, the 30-room Jolly Inn is on Avenida Francisco Solano, a block from the Sabana Grande on the side of the Galería Bolívar (tel. 71-4887). Doubles with private tiled bath, large mirror, venetian blinds, draperies, and spruced-up furnishings run $16; singles are $13.

At the end of Avenida Casanova, near Chacaíto, behind the Broadway movie theater, is the good-value **Hotel Broadway** (tel. 72-0838). The tall white building offers 40 rooms. Doubles and singles go for $17. All rooms come with air conditioning.

Another choice in this category is the popular **Hotel City**, Avenida Sabana Grande at Avenida Bolivia in Los Caobos (tel. 782-7501). The small but comfortable rooms rent for $18 double and $14 single. The 40 rooms are spread over eight floors. Add $2 for air conditioning.

A six-floor, 60-room choice is the **King's Inn**, Calle Olimpio in the Sabana Grande area (tel. 782-7037). Rooms are carpeted and air-conditioned, with TV sets. The hotel's location makes it convenient to the shopping mall and Chacaíto shopping center. Expect to pay about $30 double and $20 single.

If you're on business and have to entertain in your room, try the **Hotel Crillon**, Avenida Libertador in the Sabana Grande area (tel. 71-4411). All 80 rooms are air-conditioned and have a small sitting area, refrigerators, and terraces. All are individually furnished with modern furniture, very comfortable. Expect to pay $30 double and $20 single.

Less Expensive Choices

Three hotels in the Sabana Grande that come close to true budget levels are the Hotel Myriam, Hotel Los Caobos, and Hotel Pension Villa Verde. Unfortunately, the value of the real estate in this area is growing and these hotels may be knocked down in favor of high-priced condos (as was the Hotel Ibiza, formerly on this street). The 15-room, two-story **Hotel Myriam** (tel. 71-3311) resembles a private home with a small garden in front. Clean and neat, the rooms are modestly furnished and offer good value at $12 for doubles with bath and $10 for singles. An extra touch is the tiny TV in the tiny lobby.

Hotel Mari, Avenida Casanova in Bello Monte (tel. 71-7441), is a recently opened budget choice. It has only 28 rooms on three floors. Rooms are small and not air-conditioned, but have a clean bed, shower, and mirror. Doubles are $10 while singles are only $8.

Hotel Bruno, Avenida Las Acacias, Sabana Grande (tel. 781-8324), is far larger, with 100 rooms on ten floors. Rooms here are well worn but well maintained, and all have private baths and are air-conditioned. The price is right at $12 double and $10 for a single room.

The **Hotel Los Caobos,** on Avenida Bogotá between Plaza Venezuela and Avenida Libertador (tel. 781-6322), has comfortable doubles for $13 and singles for under $10. Resembling a Spanish home, it houses 15 large rooms with bath. Basic.

At 2a Avenida Las Delicias de Sabana Grande, the 40-room, two-story **Villa Verde** (formerly the Hotel Los Pinos) was recently reconditioned and enlarged into two buildings, one with a front-garden-cum-pergola where you can breakfast or snack at any hour of the day, the other with a front restaurant serving home-cooked Italian food. Prices run downward from $15 for a double with private bath to $13 for a single with bath, to $10 for a single room with shared bath. The location is near the luxurious Savoy Hotel.

Basic Choices

Two inexpensive pension-type hotels on the basic side are the **Pension Cantaclaro** at Calle Guaicapuro in El Rosal (tel. 71-7273) and the nearby **Hotel Rora,** also on Calle Guaicapuro (between Pichincha and Mercedes). Each is set in a private home, and the Cantaclaro even boasts a garden. The 40-room Rora gets a slight nod. Doubles are $14; singles start at $10. The Cantaclaro's rates are $2 less.

Splurge Choices

A semiluxury buy in this area is the jazzy 72-room **Hotel Las Americas,** on Calle Los Cerritos, two blocks off the main street (tel. 951-7387). A small outdoor swimming pool (relatively rare in Caracas) on the eighth floor highlights Las Americas, as do the plush, air-conditioned rooms that go for $26 double and $23 single. Panoramic windows in the eighth-floor bar offer brilliant views of the city, and more pluses are the restaurant, gift shop, barbershop, and cab service.

A block from Las Americas is the yellow **Hotel Montpark,** at Calle Los Cerritos in Bello Monte (tel. 71-5964). Rooms are similar to the Coliseo; some have small balconies, and all have piped-in music. Doubles are $20; singles cost $15. This 48-room hotel is near the Las Americas Hotel. For $5 you can have a TV in your room.

A longtime favorite one block off the Sabana Grande is the **Savoy Hotel,** at 2a Avenida Las Delicias de Sabana Grande (tel. 72-1971). This 100-room hotel near the Centro Comercial Chacaíto has small carpeted rooms with piped-in music and fine service. Rates are under $20 for a double. Try for a terraced room overlooking this bustling area.

Back at the beginning of Sabana Grande is the slightly more expensive eight-story **Hotel Luna,** Calle El Colegio (tel. 72-5851), behind the Hotel Kursaal. This ultramodern 67-room hotel, completed in 1964, leans to Scandinavian décor in the large, airy rooms. Doubles with piped-in music, tiled bath (shower only), large dressers, and mirrors, run $25; singles are $20.

Across from the Jolly Inn Hotel on Avenida Solano is the **Hotel Tampa** (tel. 72-3771). The original 90 rooms in an eight-story building had TV, air conditioning, and music. The furnishings were modern. Fifty new rooms have been added, and these are rather more comfortable, albeit more expensive. Doubles are about $22 and singles are $19. Look for the large neon sign.

The **Hotel Plaza Venezuela,** in the Plaza at Avenida La Salle (tel. 781-7811), one of the newer hotels in Caracas was completed in 1974. A double will cost you $21; singles are $6 less. Fine choice.

There's also the **Hotel Coliseo,** at Avenida Casanova between Calle Coromoto and 1st Calle Bello Monte (tel. 72-7916). Open since early 1975, its 42 rooms are carpeted, draped, and colorful. Doubles start at $20 and singles at $16.

A HOTEL IN THE PLAZA BOLÍVAR AREA: The older west-side district is noted for the Centro Simón Bolívar, an office-building complex that is the commercial center of Caracas and also houses government offices. The Plaza Bolívar (not to be confused with the Centro Bolívar) is technically in the Altagracia (Catedral) section, a few blocks from the Centro (itself in the El Silencio section). We would suggest that this district be your last choice, only because it is not as convenient to nightlife and restaurants as the areas noted above, and because of the heavy traffic in this old part of town.

Opened in the fall of 1980, the charming **Plaza Catedral Hotel** is on Boulevard Plaza Bolívar (tel. 563-7022). The orange-carpeted rooms are all air-conditioned, with a bath and shower, and telephone. There is a small TV. Rooms on the first and second floors have small balconies overlooking the lovely plaza. On the top floor is an excellent Swiss restaurant. The owners are Swiss, and the hotel and restaurant are spotless. Doubles are $25 and singles run $20.

HOTELS IN THE SAN BERNARDINO AREA: This upper-middle-class residential district in the higher, northern portion of Caracas is known to tourists largely because the luxurious Hotel Ávila is located here, as are several good restaurants and nightclubs. But it's also a good area for nonluxury hotels.

Moderately Priced Selections

We're fond of the pale-white **Hotel Waldorf,** on Avenida La Industria across Urdaneta (tel. 571-4733), a three-story edifice noted for its large, comfortable, informal rooms and good lobby-level restaurant. Wide, inviting hallways lead to linoleum-floored doubles with shower-bath at $19, singles at $14, and suites that can sleep three at $30. Desks and large closets are standard equipment. Definitely worth a look.

If the Waldorf is booked, you might try the **Hotel Eraso** (tel. 51-7719), on Avenida Caracas at the Plaza Estrella, a key intersection. The 18-room, two-story Eraso offers fair doubles (with bath, music, and phone) for $14 and singles for $9—somewhat high for what you get. The yellow building with a garden out front resembles a private home. Good location, but the rooms are small and the furnishings only adequate.

A Less Expensive Hotel

Far older in furnishings and décor is the aging 15-room **Hotel Las Mercedes,** Avenida Vollmer 11 (tel. 52-3148), in front of the Hospital de Niños (Children's Hospital). A double with bath (but minimal furnishings) is $10, while a single runs $6. A very basic choice.

Splurge Choices

A favorite luxury hotel in Caracas is the **Hotel Ávila,** Avenida J. Washington (tel. 51-5155), which is known in the city as a site of posh social affairs and home to international celebrities. Stressing a Spanish motif, the comfortably furnished rooms are a paean to relaxation, with area rugs, plush beds and dressers, and small terraces. Set in a 14-acre garden park with tropical birds and a pool, and housing a first-class restaurant and bar, the Ávila (accent on the first syllable) is a hotel equal to any we've seen in San Juan or St. Thomas. Prices are high but represent solid value: doubles are $30; singles cost $25. Even if you don't stay here, stroll through the Ávila at least once and note the magnificent vegetation and floral displays throughout the hotel and its grounds.

Note: The Ávila charges the same rates year round and is a perfect spot for a winter vacation. When you consider what you'd pay for an equivalent hotel in San Juan or Acapulco in December, you'll understand why we feel justified in recommending this hotel in our budget guide. Remember, there is 12-month swimming here.

Not far from the Ávila, still in San Bernardino, is the new **Aventura Caracas,** on Avenida Francisco Fajardo (tel. 51-4011). This is a great-value four-star hotel with services that include a pool, a spa, a fine bar and restaurant, and satellite TV. The 93 rooms rent for about $25 double, $20 single. Good location near the cable-car terminal.

SPLURGE HOTELS AROUND TOWN: The 900-room **Caracas Hilton,** located in the Parque Central area near El Silencio (tel. 574-1122), is the city's social center and virtually every night Caracas's beautiful people gather here at lavish parties. Many professional seminars and government conferences are held here as well. The hotel has doubled in size since it was originally built. With tennis courts, a small pool, several restaurants (including the rooftop Cota 880), and a small but interesting shopping area, the Hilton is a terrific choice if you're on an expense account or it's a special trip. Rates are $90 for a double and $80 will get you a single room.

Caracas's other renowned stop is the **Hotel Tamanaco,** on Avenida Principal de Las Mercedes (tel. 208-7000). Part of the Intercontinental hotel chain, the Tamanaco sits on a hill overlooking central Caracas. More of a resort hotel than the Hilton, the Tamanaco has a large swimming pool surrounded by a grassy sunning area. It has tennis courts too. Its shopping arcade has fine shops and it has a popular discothèque. Rates are comparable to those at the Hilton.

Two other hotels in this category, new to this edition and to Caracas, are the **CCCT Hotel,** in the city's finest shopping center, the CCCT Shopping Center (tel. 92-6122), and the **Eurobuilding,** on Calle Amazonas in the Chuao District (tel. 92-3470). Both are deluxe establishments. Rates are comparable to those above. The Eurobuilding has tennis courts, a pool, and a spa. The CCCT hotel has been open for a short while; the Eurobuilding's inauguration was early 1989.

The **Paseo Las Mercedes Hotel** is part of a lovely small shopping center on Avenida Principal de Las Mercedes (tel. 910-444). With 198 rooms, this is a four-star choice. Rooms are air-conditioned and carpeted, and have private baths. A small pool is a bonus. Doubles are $30 and singles run $27.

The 77-room **Hotel Continental Altamira,** Avenida San Juan Bosco, Altamira (tel. 262-0243), is located in an attractive area that is very residential but has many restaurants. This is an affluent part of town and many of the dining spots here are far above our budgets. Rooms at the Continental are large, air-conditioned, with private baths, and brightly and attractively furnished. The restaurant is a good one and there is a bar and small pool. Doubles are $25 while singles are $20. A good choice for night people.

In the upper-income, eastern side of town, in the Altamira section, is the **Hotel Residencia Montserrat,** Sur Plaza Altamira (tel. 284-3111), a great buy —with one restriction: you must stay at least one week. If you plan a seven-day stay in Caracas, by all means check the Montserrat, which features large, well-furnished studio apartments with full kitchen and bath for $26 a day (double occupancy). The tab is $32 for triples. A refrigerator, stove, sink, and glass serving window highlight the modern kitchen, and with the abundance of supermarkets all over Caracas, you can cut the cost of your stay substantially by eating in.

Anyone for a suite? Not far from the Montserrat is the relatively new, and expensive, **Hotel La Floresta,** Avenida Ávila at the Sur Plaza Altamira (tel. 284-4111), which features 83 suites, each with a bath and a small refrigerator. Black leather couches, draperies, thick carpeting, and upholstered chairs highlight the décor, and most units offer good views of the private La Floresta Park. More? Does a telephone in the elevator do anything for you? The price is right (for what you get) at $26 double and $22 single.

FOR FAMILIES ONLY: A new dimension in hotel accommodations in Caracas is the 317-unit **Residencias Anauco Hilton** (tel. 573-4111), offering first-class accommodations ranging from studios and two-bedroom suites to multi-bedroom duplexes. They're perfect for the long-staying traveler or families. Residencias Anauco is part of Parque Central, an urban complex (virtually a "city within a city") with several hundred shops, fine restaurants, and a theater. Apartments are attractively appointed in contemporary style, and most have balconies overflowing with leafy plants. All apartments have a refrigerator and sink, and for monthly tenants there are full kitchen facilities, including a clothes washer/dryer. Also, there's a rooftop club with a swimming pool, a gymnasium, and a lobby bar. As an added bonus, guests of the Anauco can also use all the facilities of the Caracas Hilton, which is connected to Parque Central by a bridge and tunnel. With a modern (Cada) supermarket nearby, you can cut your food costs enormously by occasionally eating in. Studios are $35 to $45; two-bedroom suites, $60; and three-bedroom suites, $65 and up. Highly recommended.

In this same category, but much smaller, is the **Hotel Santa Fe Suites,** on Avenida José Maria Vargas in the Santa Fe Norte district (tel. 979-8355). Most of the accommodations are four-room suites with kitchens and two or three baths. There is a pool and restaurant on the premises. Rates start at $40 and the accommodations go quickly. The hotel is located between the Hotel Tamanaco and Prado del Este.

2. DINING IN CARACAS

This graceful city justifiably prides itself on its fine international cuisine (including some quite good North American dishes). Caraqueños eat out often, insisting always that the restaurant be clean, somewhat imaginative in its menu, and, as in all of South America, attentive to good service. The restaurants that survive these demands for any length of time therefore must be well above average—and they are.

Before we tour our French, Italian, German, U.S., and Venezuelan recommendations, we should describe some popular local dishes. **Pabellon criollo** is a tangy main course consisting of shredded beef in a spiced tomato sauce, served with fried plátanos (a type of banana), black beans, and white rice. Some restaurants serve this dish as a casserole. Equally popular here is **hallaca,** which is usually pieces of beef (sometimes turkey or chicken) mixed with onion, pepper, raisins, and chickpeas, and wrapped in banana leaves before being boiled in water —delicious. **Arepas** are tasty hard-crusted buns made of cornmeal. Before your meal, try the domestic rum, inexpensively made from local sugarcane (our favorite brand is Ron Anejo Colonial Santa Teresa). The two widest-selling Venezuelan beers are Polar and Zulia; both are excellent.

Note: Most restaurants are open from 11 a.m. to 3 p.m. and 6 to 11 p.m., with the 8 to 10 p.m. period the most popular. A 10% service charge is added to all bills. Men need wear jackets and ties only in the very expensive dinner restaurants. Women may always wear pants. Menus are posted on the door in front of the restaurant so you can check prices and specials before entering.

Money-Saving Tip: Avoid eating breakfast in your hotel—the prices generally are high. More important, for maximum-value lunches and dinners, look for fixed-price, multicourse meals, identified by the word "cubierto" (cover) on the menu. Now to our selections:

THE SNACK PLACES (BREAKFAST AND LUNCH): Caracas has scores of fast-food stops that are perfect for inexpensive but satisfying breakfasts and lunches. Familiar names such as McDonald's, Burger King, Pizza Hut, Dunkin' Donuts, and Kentucky Fried Chicken, plus Venezuelan versions of the above, are scattered throughout the city. Better still are **fuentes de soda,** which are neighborhood counter- and table-service coffeeshops, and these seem to blossom on every block. While not uniformly acceptable, they serve wholesome food.

Another choice for an inexpensive yet satisfying breakfast is to pop into a **panadería.** These are bakeries and they serve hot breads, rolls, pastries, and tea or coffee. Many are counter only, but several we've seen have a few tables. Breakfast "continental" style in a panadería can keep this meal under $1.50. Tables must tip 10%.

Probably the most colorful and attractive fuente in Caracas is the bright **Papagallo,** a large eatery located on the main level (center area) of the Chacaíto Shopping Center on Avenida Lincoln, Sabana Grande district. Premiering in 1968, the Papagallo, whose tables face a fashionable shopping arcade, became immediately popular because of its king-size cheeseburger (served with French fries and lettuce and tomato for $2 and its pizza for $2 to $3). The Papagallo attracts late-afternoon shoppers and office workers, who stop here for coffee (café) before trekking home. Breakfast, served from 7 to 11 a.m., ranges from $1 to $3. Highly recommended.

Doña Arepa, with several locations in town (near Chacaíto and Capitolo metro stop), is a Venezuelan fast-food chain. They serve arepas, pabellon, batidos, and great coffee. Service is quick and they are very clean. A quick lunch shouldn't cost more than $1.50.

One lovely alternative in the Chacaíto Shopping Center is the **Ovni,** nestled in the upper level of the center. Umbrellas shade the outside tables, where you can get hot platters, from ham and eggs for $2 to a filet mignon for $4.50. A chicken sandwich with lettuce and tomato is $3, and very tasty. Pizza, sandwiches, and Italian dishes are good sellers too.

Another is **El Coco,** a fuente on the same level as Papagallo. With a small indoor dining area and several outdoor tables, Coco's specialties include freshfruit platters, and drinks, sandwiches, and fresh fish.

Caracas has a **fast-food row** under the El Beco shopping arcade at the end of the Sabana Grande. Head downstairs under the Multi-Cine and you'll find Burger King, Pizza Hut, Well-Well (Chinese foods), a pastry counter, plus a deli and wurst counter. Pick up your food at one of the counters and head to a nearby table to enjoy. Inexpensive and lots of options.

Probably the best fast-food complex is the **Plaza Broadway,** near Chacaíto and the Sabana Grande. This complex includes, among others, a Pizza King, Tropiburger, Lung Fung (for Chinese delights, as you probably guessed), and great wurst at La Alemanita.

Charcutería Colonia Tovar on the Sabana Grande serves delicious delicatessen food. Pick up your food at the counter and head to one of the nearby counter tables. Salami, ham, and pork sandwiches are only 75¢, while a burger platter or wurst platter will cost $1.25. Good salads too.

If you find yourself in the Parque Central at lunchtime, head to the **Fiesta del Parque.** Much like the fast-food row on Chacaíto, you'll find counters serving burgers, pizza, wursts, pastry, coffee, and sandwiches. Tables are available.

For inexpensive hamburgers, **Tropiburger** is tops. Two popular locations: Avenida Las Mercedes and the Los Palos Grandes Shopping Center. Try the guapo, a whopper of a burger for $2.

If you've eaten a large breakfast and feel like a light lunch, you'll find that the frankfurters sold by the sidewalk vendors are satisfying. A salad with dressing on it (like coleslaw) will cost only 50¢. The signs on the pushcarts say "perros calientes."

FIXED-PRICE MEALS (LUNCH AND DINNER): Here we'll list a number of good-value restaurants that offer a cubierto (fixed-price special) daily. If you're hungry, and on a tight budget, these undoubtedly should be the mainstays of your Caracas dining.

Cervecería Berlin on the second level of Centro Comercial Unio (Chacaíto) is a delightful stop for either lunch or dinner. The chalet-style eatery serves a fixed-price lunch for $2.50. It features a hardy soup, a choice of main course from three offered, and a dessert. À la carte dishes include several types of wursts, burgers, and meats.

Smarty, on Avenida Casanova, is a bright, cheerful spot for either lunch or dinner. Italian foods are the specialties here, with hero sandwiches very popular at lunch. Smarty has a cubierto for lunch, with a two-course meal running $2.25. At dinner the pasta, chicken, and veal dishes are well within budget range. Friendly staff.

El Pollo Italiano, across from El Beco, opens for lunch at 11:30 a.m. and stays open till midnight seven days a week. El Pollo has wooden tables placed in one large rectangular dining area and not much décor, but it has a delicious salad bar and very good barbecued chicken. Half a chicken is $1, as is the spaghetti bolognesa. Pizzas are very popular at lunch and they run $1 to $4, depending on the toppings. Not a fancy eatery, it's nonetheless a great value stop.

In the Plaza Bolívar area, at Avenida Urdaneta near Avenida Veroes, is the clean and cheerful **Gaggia,** replete with recorded music, air conditioning, and possibly the widest choice of dishes in Caracas—served cafeteria style from 11 a.m. to 3 p.m. and with waiter service from 3 to 11 p.m. For your meal, consider the fixed-price special (about $4), usually featuring a small steak, chicken croquettes, or a generous salad plate. Or try the pollo en su jugo, a tasty à la carte chicken dish for $2.50. A fine place to laze over late-afternoon coffee or tea.

Like wine or beer with man-size meals? Then look in on **El Submarino,** on the basement level of the south (sur) tower in the Centro Simón Bolívar near Pasaje Río Caroni, El Silencio district. Catering to middle-rank government workers in the Bolívar center, the Submarino is rather high-priced (and plain), but quantity and quality are substantial. The $6 cubierto entitles you to juice or consommé, a main platter of beef, fish, or chicken, ice cream or pastry, coffee, and beer or wine. There is a large à la carte menu as well; closed Sunday.

In the same building as El Submarino but on the street level are **El Chicuelo** and **La Violeta.** They cater to area businessmen and government workers who eat lunch and while away the siesta hours playing cards, dominos, and darts. Omelets are $3, hamburger platters are $1.85, and ice cream runs $1.

Pernil al Pincho, on Avenida Casanova at the diagonal, is an excellent stop for a stand-up or even a sit-down lunch. There are ten tables in the patio, and a three-course lunch for $6 consists of soup, main dish, rice, and salad, plus a drink is served daily. There is also an à la carte menu. Sandwiches, hamburgers, and hot dogs are popular counter choices.

BEST-VALUE DINNER RESTAURANTS IN CARACAS: As we said earlier, Caraqueños love to eat out. Locals pride themselves on the variety of good-quality "foreign" restaurants available in Caracas, and since employment and wage levels are relatively high, the better restaurants are usually crowded with well-dressed and well-heeled patrons. Even if your budget is tight, you can dine at most of the following choices by selecting carefully. One more point—don't be deterred by distances. Only a few of our recommendations are likely to be within walking distance of your hotel, but the others are easily reached by public transportation.

Sundaes and the Singles Scene

Liberty's, in the lower level of the Paseo Las Mercedes Shopping Center, is a popular meeting spot for singles. It's informal with stained-glass windows, Tiffany-style lamps, and booth and counter service. There is a fresh salad bar plus burgers of all kinds, sandwiches, ice cream, and alcoholic beverages.

Another fine choice would be **City Rock Café,** in Centro Comercial Chacaíto. Try the jumbo franks or the delicious pastry and coffee at the stand-up counters in the front. There is a T-shirt shop, a book and card store, and other tiny shops inside.

For Pasta-Lovers Only

Again in the Sabana Grande district is a top-value, southern-Italian-style restaurant called the **Sorrento,** located on Avenida Mariscal Francisco Solano, near the Coq d'Or. You may dine in any one of three rooms, all comfortably informal and similar in style to a Greenwich Village restaurant. The popular Sorrento attracts a large clientele, returning regularly for the tasty fare. You really can't go wrong with any of the main dishes, most of which run about $5 to $10. Try the cotolleta à la Boloñesa (veal and cheese) for $4.75, the escalopa de lomito (steak) at $5.25, or, perhaps your best bet, the $6 daily cubierto.

In Las Mercedes, the attractive **Mamma Mia,** on Avenida Las Mercedes between Calles Monterrey and Mucuchies, draws the locals to both the indoor air-conditioned or terrace tables. The pizza is king here and prices range from $5 to $7. Popular, too, are the fettuccine at $3 to $5, and ravioli dishes at $3. Gerente Mario without hesitation advised us that the specialty here is "pasta e pizza."

Da Peppino is an informal family restaurant that reminds us of a U.S. pizzeria, but it is quite large and attractively decorated. Crisp pizzas with sausage and olives are $4.50, and each additional ingredient is 75¢. Fettuccine, spaghetti with a variety of sauces, and lasagne are under $5. Meat dishes are a bit higher, but with prudent selection you can stay within your budget here. It's located on Avenida José Felix Josa in the La Floresta district (near Altamira).

La Strada del Sole, on Calle Madrid at Calle Caroni in Las Mercedes, is the most attractive restaurant of this group, and the most expensive. The outdoor tables are on a covered atrium with a large tree in the center. The indoor dining area is not air-conditioned. The walls are covered with chianti bottles and hanging garlic and ceramics. There are price-fixed dinners that change nightly, pasta dishes, and a variety of pizzas.

Pizza House, Avenida Tamanaco, El Rosal (look for the waterfall), is a bright, cheerful spot that looks like a greenhouse. The pizzas here are thick and doughy and are offered with a score of topping choices. Sizes range from a mini-pie for one to a large pie with eight slices. A large pie with cheese and tomato sauce is $5. Pasta dishes, a large salad bar, and daily specials are all worth examining further. When your meal is done you might like to head next door to the Red Parrot, the hottest club in town (see "Caracas After Dark").

Spanish Restaurants

Don Comodo, at Puerto Yanes, advertises "the best paella" in Venezuela and, what's more, delivers. For $5.50 you get a huge mound of richly seasoned rice, clams and gigantic shrimp, and chunks of chicken. Don Comodo is in the basement. Take the metro to the Plaza Carabobo station.

Another restaurant for fine Spanish dishes in a nautical setting is **Las Rocas,** on Avenida F. Solano in Sabana Grande, near the Savoy Hotel, featuring highback couches, beamed ceilings, a fine bar, and white stucco walls. The Spanish dishes are tasty and relatively inexpensive. The paella Valenciana is $12 (for two), and the camarones ala ajillo (shrimp with garlic sauce) is $6.75. There is a daily special.

Restaurant Nueva Esparta, on Avenida Los Manguitos near Francisco Solano, is an attractive Spanish-style restaurant. Its white stucco walls and low wooden ceilings make for a cozy atmosphere. The menu is varied, with many meat and fish dishes. Meats start at $6.50 and chicken at $5.50.

La Sarten de Plata, at the Final de Francisco Solano (near Galería Bolívar), is a basic eatery whose white-and-green-checked tables have glass tops. Soups at $1.50, pasta dishes at $2.25, and meat dishes at $3 make this a good choice if not an exciting one.

Cervecería Juan Griego, at Calle Coromoto and Avenida Casanova, has as large a selection as we've seen anywhere. Many fish selections, as well as meats. There is a price-fixed dinner that runs $8.

Parrillada Restaurants

Parrilla means "grilled," and these restaurants feature grilled meats, sausages, and poultry. Your order is brought to your table in a small charcoal oven, where it stays hot through the entire meal. These restaurants are very popular in Caracas and there are many good ones.

The **Tropical Room,** on Avenida Casanova at El Colegio, is a very well-known parrillada. It was recommended in our early editions but then burned down. It has since been rebuilt and is booming, especially for lunch. The two large dining rooms with red-and-white-checked cloths and red wicker chairs are open till 11 p.m. The grilled half chicken is $4.25, and the half steak runs $5.75. An order of fried potatoes is $1. There are inexpensive pasta dishes starting at $3 and salad platters (enough for a meal) at $4.50. Highly recommended.

Another fine parrillada restaurant is **Parrillada Onassis,** located on Avenida Casanova at the corner of Baldo in Bello Monte. While rather basic and raunchy in décor, the Onassis serves two fine specialties, the parrilla mixta Argentina ($8 for two) and the parrilla especial de la casa ($10 for two). The marisco dishes are popular too.

A third parrillada with rather the same dishes and prices is **La Cazuela,** at Avenida Francisco Solano and Calle Apamate. It's air-conditioned.

A newish entry into the parrillada wars here is **Bamboche,** Avenida Tamanaco, El Rosal, open for both lunch and dinner. You can see and smell the meats grilling as you enter. Most plates will run $6 to $7.

Drop into **El Tinajero de los Helechos,** on Avenida Río de Janeiro in Las Mercedes. Good piano music and dim lighting enhance the superb steak and grilled chicken platters. Prices are a shade higher, but you dine here rather than eat.

Sauerbraten in the Andes

If your palate tingles at the thought of red cabbage and apple strudel, head to the **Rincón de Baviera,** Avenida Gamboa and Avenida Panteon, in the San Bernardino district. The delicious sauerbraten is $4.50; veal escaloppe à la Vienesa is $5; a splendid strudel, 75¢; liederkranz cheese, $2. The sour pickles are incredibly good. The two small dining rooms are conservatively and tastefully furnished; hours are noon to midnight.

For delicious bratwurst, eisbein, or goulasch soup, head directly to **Fritz & Frans,** on Avenida Naiguata in El Rosal, with both indoor and outdoor eating at the attractive wooden tables, in a Bavarian setting. The bratwurst runs about $2.75 and includes a salad. Fine apfelstrudel is $1. A stein of beer runs $1.25.

Die Hutte, on Avenida Tamanaco in El Rosal, boasts a menu featuring Greek, Russian, and German dishes. Sausage platters are $3, and shashlik (shish kebab) is $4. There are several dining areas in this eatery and it is very popular.

A Chinese Choice

Our favorite place for Oriental cuisine in Caracas is **El Dragon Verde** ("The Green Dragon") on Avenida Maturin in Los Cedros. The eggrolls (lumpias), sweet-and-sour shrimp, and spareribs are superb. Prices are not low but the value is there. Highly recommended.

A Peruvian-Mexican Choice

Perched in the Centro Comercial Bello Compo is **El Tizon,** a rather small restaurant that brings a touch of Lima to Caracas. You will find the likes of ceviche (marinated fish) and anticuchos de corazon (marinated chunks of heart) interspersed amid Mexican fare. We suggest that you stick to the Peruvian food and sip a pisco sour.

A Tex-Mex Choice

Spicy guacamole, tamales, and frijoles are specialties at the tiny Tex-Mex eatery, **El Tizonrito,** in the rear ground level of the Paseo Las Mercedes Shopping Center. There's a small counter for eating inside the restaurant, but if you sit at one of the arcade tables there is waiter service. Very inexpensive and delicious.

Middle Eastern Food

For a different dining experience, head to **Kibbe,** on Calle Madrid in Las Mercedes, an attractive restaurant which serves Middle Eastern and vegetarian foods. The Kibbe's décor resembles a Bedouin tent with flowing gauze fabrics overhead and mosques and minarets painted on the walls. Undulating music is piped in at lunch but is live at dinner. Lentil soup, baba gannoush, and hummus are on the menu, as well as grilled meats. Kibbe has a three-course cubierto at lunch for $2.50.

Japanese Food

Shogun Restaurant, Avenida Tamanaco in El Rosal, is a lovely Japanese dining spot with a sushi bar on your left as you enter. The décor is beautiful, with lots of mats, light woods, and stone floors. The daily menu, which includes soup, salad, main course, and coffee, is $4. Teppanyaki, tempura, and sukiyaki are a bit higher.

A Korean Restaurant

Venezuela's, and probably South America's, first Korean restaurant is **Seoul,** on Avenida Francisco Solano in Sabana Grande. If you cannot live another day without ji bog um oz (octopus) or tang soo yook (meat in sweet-and-sour sauce), make a beeline to this restaurant. You can eat lunch or dinner here for about $4 or $5, depending on what you order for a main course. You'll like it.

French and Continental Restaurants

With the current strength of the U.S. dollar vis-à-vis the bolívar, it is now possible to dine in Caracas at fine French restaurants at prices that won't break you. So we have decided to include a few that are excellent, new, and worth the extra bolívars. By choosing carefully, you can limit your bill to $10 per person for dinner and an evening's entertainment.

Probably our favorite in this category is **Gazebo,** on Avenida Río de Janeiro in Las Mercedes (tel. 92-5568). The fare here is nouvelle cuisine in elegant surroundings. There's no menu, but the maître d' will explain the menu to you in English. Silver plates and candles on the table set the mood. Try any of the fresh fish dishes. Reservations are suggested, especially on weekends.

Girafe, on Avenida Venezuela in El Rosal (tel. 261-8218), has wonderful French food, live music, and elegant surroundings. The duck is fabulous. It's not easy to find since it is in an apartment house, but tell the driver to stop in front of the Edificio Venezuela.

Finally, you should try **Petite Bistro de Jacques,** in Los Mercedes next to the Banco de Venezuela. This is a typical French bistro that will have you convinced you're back in Paris. The menu is on the mirror and this small place is usually packed.

Venezuelan Dining

Los Plones, Avenida Pichincha in El Rosal, is a criolla restaurant with Spanish colonial décor, whitewashed walls, and wrought-iron grillwork separating the various dining rooms from one another. Ask for a booth, which has high wooden backs. Sliced tomato and onion salad with a tangy vinaigrette dressing is $1.25, while a thick steak with a fried egg atop (a caballo) is $4. Chicken in the basket is $2.50.

Save at least one evening for dinner at the popular **El Jardin II** ("The Garden"), Avenida Panteon and Avenida Alameda in the San Bernardino district, generally acknowledged as having the best local cuisine. Try the pabellon here (shredded meat, rice, beans, and fried bananas), a good value at $5.25, or the solomo (sirloin steak, arepas, black beans, in a spicy sauce) for $4.50. Large and attractive, El Jardin appropriately bedecks its indoor and outdoor tables with fresh flowers. Try for an outdoor table.

Then there's **La Tinaja,** a criolla (Venezuelan) choice on Avenida Sabana Grande near Cine Radio City (movie house). Here is the place to try such criolla dishes as pollo deshuesado (boned chicken), pabellon criollo, or the punta trasera—about $5 to $9 each. Daily specials are offered.

El Tejar, with a branch on Avenida Tamanaco, is well known for its criolla cooking. Sample the sancocho or the arroz con mariscos. Delicious.

Up from the Sea

For superb garlic-flavored shrimp ($4.25) or succulent clams ($4.50) and up), look no further than **Cervecería Maracaibo** in the Sur Plaza Altamira shopping center, Altamira district. The front is shaped like a huge face; you'll enter the dining room, usually crowded with area workers and shoppers, through its "mouth." The garlic shrimp (camarones ajillo), like nearly every dish here, are flown in daily from Lake Maracaibo. Other recommended choices are the paella ($10 for two) and the pargo gratinado al lago (a red snapper dish; just over

$5.50). A big seller, too, is the squid (calamares), but you're on your own here—we haven't tried it. Open from 11 a.m. to 1:30 a.m. every day but Sunday.

Bodegon del Bogavante Marisquería, on Avenida Venezuela in El Rosal, is a mighty attractive restaurant which resembles a whaler's inn. Naturally the specialty of the house is seafood, well prepared and interestingly served. The sauces are light and delicate. Avoid the shellfish dishes which are astronomically priced and you can eat reasonably. Look for the sail out front.

Higher-Priced Choices

A number of good restaurants in Caracas fall between moderate and big splurge in cost. Let's start with a popular Venezuelan dinner choice in the city (a true favorite of ours)—**El Carrizo,** on Avenida Blandin, La Castellana district. Portuguese-born David Gomez and his Italian partner, Mario, are usually around to tend to your every whim. Try the steaks (punta trasero is our favorite), $5—enough for two. An excellent appetizer is the cocktail de aguacate (avocado). A luncheon special of juice, salad, steak, and coffee is $5. The rustic bamboo setting is a delight. Highly recommended.

Lee Hamilton Steak House, a typical U.S.–style restaurant in a converted private home, is on Avenida San Felipe, Castellana district. The Hamilton family continued to run this landmark here after Lee's death, but sold it to new owners. They have remodeled it and added scenes from U.S. history and named each dining area for a state. The food remains first-rate, with steaks ($6 to $8 per platter), roast beef, shish kebab, and a tempting half chicken—potato and garlic bread included. You get beef second only to Argentina's, a garden setting, piano entertainment, choice of a main dining room or two smaller, more intimate rooms, and a touch of the U.S.A.

Argentines in Caracas flock to **La Estancia,** named after the famous ranches in Argentina, on Avenida Principal, one block north of Francisco de Miranda, Castellana district. Parrillada (mixed grill cooked on individual skewers), for $8, is the thing here, and per tradition, it's served on a small stove at your table. Be sure to sample the two dishes placed on all tables: one is hot red pepper and onion; the other, green pepper and onion—delicious. Not in the mood for parrillada? Try the bistec de churrasco (steak) for $7, or the pollo à la parrilla (chicken that is boned by the waiter and served on a wooden platter) for $6. La Estancia is open from noon to 3 p.m. and 7 p.m. to midnight every day but Sunday. La Tapera, a lovely cocktail lounge, is in front of the restaurant—a nice place for a drink before dinner.

One of Caracas's more attractive dining spots, with prices a bit over budget but not out of sight, is **La Mansion,** on Avenida Tamanaco in El Rosal. It's woodpaneled walls contrast with the central open courtyard filled with greenery and gently shooting fountains. Meats are featured here and a perfectly grilled filet mignon will cost $4. Of course other items are less, but it adds up—everything is à la carte. You can dine here for $10 if you're selective.

Best Bets

For a fun way to spend an evening, stop by at **El Porton,** at 18 Avenida Pichincha in El Rosal (tel. 71-6071), where a five-piece combo plays folk music nightly (except Sunday). Although the criolla food has won gourmet awards, prices are surprisingly not astronomical. Most platters are $9. Try the hallacas, yucca (manioc), and nata (a sour cream–type spread) which come with all meals. Reservations are suggested on weekends.

A fine neighborhood restaurant (few tourists dine here) is **La Caleta,** on Avenida Las Acacias (next to Cine Las Acacias). Specialties here are the shellfish (mariscos) and paella dishes. There is a full à la carte menu, but stick to the Spanish platters.

Weekends, on Avenida San Juan Bosco in Altamira, a recommended nightspot, is a great place for a burger or sandwich reminiscent of home. It's a restaurant-nightspot on three floors, full of young people.

Castellino, on Avenido F. Solano, near the colorful Vecchio Molino restaurant, has a bargain cubierto (Monday through Saturday) for $5, which usually includes an Italian main dish. Here the à la carte menu is not too steep and you can get fine pasta dishes for $3.50 to $6, fish dishes for under $4, and most meat dishes start at $5.50. Head to the main dining room in the rear, beyond the open-sided foyer. This is a colorful, attractive restaurant, which we highly recommend.

A LATE-NIGHT ESPRESSO: For an after-theater dessert, drop by the **Café Memphis,** a sidewalk café in the Galería Bolívar, Sabana Grande district. Here's where, on a weekend evening, the partygoers and night people of Caracas congregate for cappuccino and music from strolling singers.

READER'S CAFÉ SELECTION: "Checheres, Local B (upstairs) la Calle, Bello Monte, Sabana Grande (tel. 72-3549), is a European-style café opened about 15 years ago by Noris Ugueto, a young Caraqueño who is also a professional folk dancer. There is a menu which changes daily and the 'home-style' cooking features criolla (typical) dishes. For $4.75 you get soup, main dish, bread and butter, and coffee. Extras are natural fruit juices and home-baked pastries. Occasionally wine and cheese nights draw an international crowd. Open from 11 a.m. to 1 a.m. Monday through Friday" (Judith Blythe, Caracas, Venezuela).

3. CARACAS BY DAY

Since we're inveterate walkers, we always recommend a strolling tour as the fastest way to get to know a city and its people. With this, you can combine a quick visit to most major museums, monuments, and shopping areas, then decide later on what looks like it's worth a return trip.

CARACAS IN THREE STROLLS: Since Caracas is so sprawling, we've divided your footwork into one long amble and two "quickies."

A Stroll Through El Silencio

This section of Caracas houses the major historical sites of the city. Ask your hotel clerk for the nearest bus stop, then take the bus marked "El Silencio," which will drop you at the **Centro Simón Bolívar** (twin office buildings) on Avenida Baralt. This wide north-south street is the heart of the older (and poorer) Silencio district, easily the city's most teeming and most photographed area.

Once there, poke around the magnificent Centro Simón Bolívar, which houses government and commercial offices as well as shopping arcades. Then head north (left, as you face the 32-story Centro), and turn right on Avenida Universidad, two blocks up; on your right is the impressive National Library **(Biblioteca Nacional),** housing 300,000 volumes, many from the 16th, 17th, and 18th centuries. Opposite the library is the golden-domed **El Capitol,** the national congress. The exotic vegetation and fountain in the courtyard are worth a look. On your left, the elliptical building decorated with native Venezuelan art is the **Assembly.**

Head right as you leave the congress to Esquina Padre Sierra, then right again for one block and you'll be in the **Plaza Bolívar,** traditional center of Caracas. This is a restful spot, graced with fountains, lush foliage, trees, benches, and a huge equestrian statue of Simón Bolívar, a copy of which stands on New York's Central Park South. A rich variety of activities will occupy your attention: if it's a

Sunday (or holiday) afternoon, you can join the throngs of Caraqueños happily munching snacks and listening to the outdoor concerts; you can browse through the fascinating underground gallery, where you'll see old photos and newspaper clippings of the plaza's history; or if it's nighttime, you can simply admire the floodlit architecture. Before the revolution of 1821 this was an execution arena.

City dwellers, used to parks with nothing more exotic than a squirrel or two, might be unnerved by the peresas, small monkeys that casually swing from the trees here. Don't worry—they're harmless, and once you get used to them they won't distract you from the impressive changing-of-the-guard ceremony that takes place every hour on Sunday (and holidays) in front of the Bolívar statue.

That impressive building on the plaza's east side is the late-16th-century **Catedral de Caracas,** the city's oldest church, twice rebuilt after earthquakes. Inside are the family vaults of the Bolívar family, as well as several notable works of art, including a Rubens and a Murillo. The large yellow edifice on the south side of the plaza is the Municipal Building **(Edificio Municipal),** an outstanding example of colonial architecture. Ask the guard to let you see the conference room with its beautiful ceiling frescoes.

Now we'll head east (to the right, if you're facing the plaza) and walk to the intersection of Avenida San Jacinto (one block). Look for the **Museo Bolívar** (near the bank displaying the coats-of-arms of those nations freed by him), dedicated to Bolívar's career, and the nearby **Casa Natal,** a reproduction of the adobe house in which Bolívar was born. (We'll have more to say about this in our sight-by-sight section below.) Now stroll back past the plaza, then five blocks farther along Avenida Veroes to the magnificent **Panteon Nacional,** a former church and now the resting place of Bolívar and many other Venezuelan heroes. Men need jackets here; open daily from 8 a.m. to noon and 3 to 6 p.m.

A Stroll Through Sabana Grande

The Sabana Grande is a mile-long galaxy of boutiques, theaters, and discos running from the Plaza Venezuela along Avenida Lincoln to the **Centro Comercial Chacaíto.** Recently modernized, the Sabana Grande's main street, **Avenida Lincoln,** has been made into a shopping mall—no traffic! You can stroll along the cobblestone street, window-shop, nosh, and rest on benches along the route.

An Excursion to a Residential Area

To see how the upper middle class of Caracas lives and plays, save an afternoon to explore the Altamira and La Castellana sections. Any por puesto going along Francisco de Miranda will take you there. Start at the **Plaza Castellana,** surrounded by nightspots and restaurants, and walk two blocks to the **Plaza Altamira.** This is a pleasant place to pause and admire the apartment houses, restaurants, and clubs. A few blocks off Avenida Miranda (to the north) are the fine mansions of wealthy locals and the Caracas Country Club. The exact streets you choose to walk on are not important; it's the general impression of the area that you get on foot. We think you'll find it interesting.

CARACAS, SIGHT BY SIGHT: Time now to consider the specific sights of Caracas, starting at the top . . . literally.

Mount Ávila Peak

The most spectacular sight in Caracas is undoubtedly Mount Ávila, the 7,000-foot peak that rises majestically behind the city. The summit is reached by cable car from the terminal in the northern Mariperez section. The "teleférico," back in operation after a hiatus of several years, operates Tuesday through Sunday from 8 a.m. to 8 p.m. The last car from the peak descends at midnight. Round-trip fare is $1.50. Try to avoid a weekend trip when the long line snakes around Mariperez Terminal. Each car carries 24 people. Get a rear seat and you'll watch a magnificent panorama unfold as the car starts its ascent up the sheer cliffs of Áv-ila. Houses, churches, and great office and apartment buildings gradually dimin-ish in size; small wispy clouds brush past the car. From time to time the car stops in mid-passage, and your heart will probably skip a beat as you dangle thousands of feet above sprawling Caracas; don't worry, it always starts again.

Finally you'll reach the top, and the view alone is worth the air fare to Vene-zuela. You'll peer down between the clouds at the impressive expanse of Caracas, 4,000 feet below; if it's clear you might catch yourself straining to see Miami. In addition to the breathtaking views, the peak offers an ice-skating rink (it's 10° cooler up here), a children's playground, a snackbar, and an informal restaurant. But of course the main thing here is the view. A good suggestion is to schedule an afternoon ascent to the summit so that you can watch the soft approach of the South American evening, have dinner at the restaurant as night falls, then take a leisurely stroll along the parapets to admire the vista of Caracas by night when the city is transformed into a shimmering, multicolored bed of jewels nestled in the dark Andean slopes. When you've lingered with romantic thoughts long enough, catch the teleférico back to town. Sit in the front of the car this time and watch the city gradually grow in size until it enfolds you in its noise and lights.

Museo del Arte Colonial

This perfectly preserved colonial estate reflects Venezuelan life of 100 years ago. Once owned by a marquis, the estate embraces gardens, stables, a chapel, and a mansion that features a sunken bathtub fed by fresh stream water. It's located at Quinta Anauco and Avenida Panteon in the San Bernardino district, and you can walk there from anywhere in this section. Otherwise a cab is best (about $2.50). Open Wednesday, Thursday, Saturday, and Sunday from 9 a.m. to noon and 3 to 5 p.m.; admission is 5¢.

University City

Located in 400 acres in the heart of Caracas near the Plaza Venezuela is the **University of Venezuela.** Originally the site of a colonial sugarcane plantation, the university today houses one of Latin America's most extensive libraries, as well as 174 acres of magnificent **Botanical Gardens.** The gardens include a mini-ature rain forest, waterfall, lily ponds, and cactus plantings, and are open daily from 8 a.m. to noon and 2 to 6 p.m. The buildings, by the way, remind us of the university in Mexico City with their multicolored murals and modern architec-ture. Many of the city's important sports events take place at the university's sta-diums.

The Bolívar Museum

This is the home of military, artistic, and literary remembrances of the life and times of Simón Bolívar, and the three-story museum is itself a fascinating tour through Venezuela's independence era (early 19th century). Most interest-ing is the main floor, where cannon and armor are displayed, as are copies of the famous newspaper, *Correo del Orinoco,* which inspired the revolution. The sec-ond floor is an art gallery; see the interesting painting which depicts Bolívar signing the Declaration of Independence from Spain. The top floor is devoted to Bolívar's personal papers and the golden altar on which his body was carried to the Panteon in Caracas. You'll find the museum one block east of the Plaza

Bolívar, between Avenida San Jacinto and Avenida Traposos. Hours are 9 a.m. to noon and 3 to 6 p.m.; admission free; closed Monday and Saturday.

Adjacent to the museum is the **Casa Natal,** a 1920s reproduction of Bolívar's birthplace (the original adobe home was destroyed by an earthquake). Inside you'll see personal belongings, original furniture, and a painting of his marriage in Spain by Tito Salas. The museum is open on Saturday and Sunday from 10 a.m. to 1 p.m. and 3 to 6 p.m., and Tuesday through Friday from 9 a.m. to noon and 3 to 5 p.m.; closed Monday; admission free.

Museo de Bellas Artes

The Fine Arts Museum in the Parque Central has everything from modern art to old masters, many on loan from private collections. During our last visit we saw works by Chagall, Picasso, Miró, Klee, and Gauguin, as well as native Venezuelan art spanning the 19th century to present times. The museum also has an antique Chinese art collection, a movie theater, a cafeteria, and a charming lily pond. It's open Tuesday through Saturday from 9 a.m. to noon and 3 to 5:30 p.m., on Sunday from 10 a.m. to 1 p.m. and 3 to 5:30 p.m.; closed Monday. There is a small admission charge.

Museo de Ciencia Natural

Located in Los Caobos Park, the Museum of Natural History contains pre-Columbian ceramics and stuffed wildlife, and has extensive sections devoted to geology and entomology. Open Tuesday through Friday from 10 a.m. to noon and 3 to 5 p.m., on Sunday from 10 a.m. to 5 p.m.; closed Monday and Saturday. There is a small admission charge.

SPORTS IN CARACAS: Like most other South American countries, Venezuela's most popular sport is futbol (soccer). Major international matches can be seen in Caracas at the 50,000-seat **University City stadium,** where prices range from $5 to $12 for championship contests. Check the *Daily Journal,* the English-language newspaper, for schedules.

For some reason, U.S.–style baseball—called "beisbol"—has caught on big in Caracas. Helped along by the publicity generated by Venezuelan-born stars (like Luís Aparicio, former White Sox shortstop), local games draw up to 45,000 fans in the University City beisbol stadium. Many U.S. major leaguers play winter ball in Caracas. Tickets are $2.50 to $4; the season is from October to February; never on Monday.

The Turf

Track aficionados should head without delay to the magnificent **Hipodromo Nacional de la Rinconada** in the southern suburb of El Valle. Even though off-track betting is legal in Venezuela, the track is packed most Saturday and Sunday afternoons (admission is 25¢; minimum bet, 50¢). The Hipodromo offers several ingenious ways to relieve you of your money, one of the riskier being the "cinco y seis 5/6." This means you must pick at least five of the last six winners.

Toreador!

Scheduled irregularly, bullfighting does not have the hold that it does in Mexico. Depending on the reputation of the toreador (many are imported), prices range from $3 to $20. Check the *Daily Journal* or your hotel clerk for schedules at the **Nuevo Circo** arena in downtown Caracas. Most events are on Sunday from September to February. Bullfighting also takes place in Maracay (see below).

Boxing

Prizefighting is big business in Venezuela. A new arena, the **Poliedro** was inaugurated for the Norton-Foreman fight. Most events, however, are held in the **Nuevo Circo** bullring on Saturday nights.

EL LITORAL—THE BEACH AREA: If you crave sandy beaches along with
the Venezuelan sun, head to El Litoral, the Caribbean coastal area about three-quarters of an hour from downtown Caracas. You'll find calm waters and weather perfect for swimming, and a background of mountains reaching toward Caracas.

Where to Stay

By all means, stay at one of El Litoral's hotels. The **Macuto Sheraton** (tel. 031/9-1801)—deluxe in class and cost—has long dominated most tourist brochures. If you can afford it (doubles average about $60), go right ahead and book a room.

The most expensive hotel on the beach is the **Melia Caribe** (tel. 031/9-2401), opened in 1978, a deluxe choice with deluxe prices ($60 and up for doubles).

If you decide to stay at the beach and are not willing to pay the tab at the Macuto Sheraton or Melia Caribe, your first choice should be the **Hotel Las Quince Letras,** which is located on Avenida La Playa in Macuto (tel. 031/4-5821). Renowned as having one of the best seafood restaurants in Venezuela (see below), the hotel was opened in 1974 and immediately became a popular weekend favorite. Rooms are air-conditioned and include private bath and TV. Doubles are $25; singles run $18. An enormous bonus is being across the road from the restaurant, where you will never tire of eating.

Among the better choices remaining would be the **Hotel Macuto,** on Avenida La Playa in Macuto (tel. 031/4-4561), where doubles are $28. The hotel features a pool and a fine restaurant, air conditioning too.

Nearer to the Macuto Sheraton, in Carabelleda, are the **Hotel Royal Atlantic** (tel. 031/9-1250), with doubles at $20; the **Hotel Villamare** (tel. 031/9-1691), with doubles at $21 and featuring a pool; and the **Hotel Fiore** (tel. 031/9-1535), with doubles at $18. These three hotels are all within walking distance of the Macuto Sheraton Hotel and the nearby beaches.

Where to Eat

One of our favorite Venezuelan restaurants is located on Avenida La Playa in Macuto—**Las Quince Letras,** jutting out on a peninsula into the Caribbean, with Simón Bolívar Airport in full view. As you dine on some of the best seafood this side of North America, you can observe jets taking off and landing, cruise ships passing, waves beating against the nearby rock formations. A full dinner should run about $10. Make it a point to have at least one meal, preferably dinner, here.

Timotes, with a branch on the main street of Carabelleda beach and another in the Cada shopping center in Maiquetía, is one of the beach strip's finest restaurants. Specialties here include Venezuelan and seafood dishes. The freshly caught fish are prepared in a multitude of fashions. The branch on Carabelleda is the more attractive, for it's located in a Spanish colonial house. There are several dining rooms and they are decorated with swords and bullfighting paraphernalia. You can eat a three-course meal for under $10 here.

Nearby, **Hong Kong Chef** serves chop suey and chow mein, beef in oyster sauce, and shrimp in curry sauce. They season to taste. Main dishes will run under $3.

A newcomer on the beach, **The Cookery,** on Carabelleda, is the most attractive and expensive eatery here. Candlelit tables with sparkling white cloths and fine service make this an option, if a slightly more expensive one. Stick to the pasta, chicken, and fish dishes and you won't break the bank.

Avenida Playa, the main street in the Carabelleda district, is lined with many **open-air eateries,** serving the likes of pizza, fried chicken, hamburgers, and milkshakes. Typically, pizzas start at 75¢; half a fried chicken, $2.25; hamburger, 65¢; and hot dogs, 35¢. Our two favorites are Tomaselli and Cream Paraíso.

A McDonald's-type hamburger can be found at **Tropiburger** nearby. The prices are low.

If you're in the mood for Italian food, you have your choice of dining at the fine restaurants at either of the **Hotels Fiore** or **Royal Atlantic.**

The Beaches

There are many beaches and towns along the miles-long stretch of El Litoral. But the quality of the beaches varies greatly. **Macuto Beach,** nearest to the cable-car terminal, is a popular one, accessible by bus marked "Macuto," which leaves from the terminal. Macuto Beach is jammed on weekends. There are many ultra-basic hotels in this rather raunchy area. Several have open-air restaurants, where you can dine if you choose to spend your day at the beach. Better still, bring sandwiches. By all means use the hotels to change clothes.

Most Americans head for the **Playa Sheraton,** next to the Macuto Sheraton Hotel, while most organized tours head for **Marina Grande,** the beach closest to downtown Caracas. Many readers have written about **Los Angeles Beach,** about three miles beyond the Macuto Sheraton Hotel; take the bus marked "Los Caracas." Look for the **Camuri Yacht Club,** which is next to Los Angeles Beach.

Finally, consider the **Camuri Chico Balneario,** about one mile from the cable-car terminal. You can rent lockers and chairs, and there is even a cafeteria on the premises.

Besides buses, por puestos ply the main beachfront avenue, so getting around is no problem.

Getting to El Litoral

A delightful excursion combines a trip to Mount Ávila with a teleférico ride 7,000 feet down the other side of the mountain to the warm Caribbean coastal region. The view during the descent to the blue waters of the Caribbean is so stupendous you probably won't even notice the rising temperatures. The total price is $3, but only when it's working (which it isn't at this time). If you have a group of five, split the $20 cab fare. Otherwise take a por puesto to La Guaira. Buses run from behind the Centro Comercial Chacaíto (at OVNI) and the El Silencio Bus Terminal. The cost is $2.25.

4. EXCURSIONS AND TOURS

MARACAY: Some 70 miles west of Caracas in what is called the "interior"— Caraqueños call everything outside the capital "the interior"—is the state of **Aragua.** You'll spend most of your time here in Maracay (pop. 150,000), the favorite home of former dictator Gomez, and known for its well-stocked zoo and a lavish bullring, a replica of the one in Seville, Spain. But what makes the trip particularly worthwhile is the **Hotel Maracay**—truly a total resort city. Operated by Conahotu, the 156-room government-owned Maracay offers tennis courts, horseback riding, a free (to guests) golf course, huge free-form pool, a film theater, disco nightclub, and a first-class restaurant and coffeeshop. In case you want to stay overnight, doubles start at $40 and singles at $30.

There are other things to keep you busy in Maracay. If old airplanes do something for you, check the **Museo Aeronautico,** located on the outskirts of the city and open each weekend. Also, one of South America's most beautiful beaches, **Playa Cata,** is a 1½-hour drive over the Andes from Maracay. You must rent a car in town to get there, and the drive along the winding road will take you through an exotic rain forest, complete with waterfalls—better not try it at night, though.

Getting to Maracay is an easy matter. Buses ($6 per person) and por puestos ($8 per person) leave regularly from the El Silencio district; check with your hotel clerk for precise departure locations. On the way down (via a modern six-lane highway), you'll see miles of sugarcane fields, royal palm trees, and gadzooks!—a Kellogg factory.

COLONIA TOVAR: Anyone for a detour to Bavaria? Just 90 minutes, 40 miles, from Caracas is the authentic southern German mountain village of Colonia Tovar, where the architecture, language, and food are much like you'd have found in the Black Forest in the 1860s. Settled well over 100 years ago by South German immigrants, the area has retained the customs and culture of Germany and boasts excellent restaurants, quaint hotels, and blue-eyed blondes and blonds galore. By all means pick up some homemade jelly, which is delicious— and don't forget to bring a jacket, since the mountain air is chilly.

Unfortunately, there's one hitch. There is *no* public transportation to this area, so if you don't rent a car or thumb a ride, you can only go by organized tour. Every operator in the city runs one—but the price averages $35 per person. **Candes** (see below) provides an 11-passenger minibus, lunch, a visit to a ceramics factory on the way, and coffee at a country club for this price. The cost makes this trip a low-priority option, unfortunately.

MARGARITA ISLAND—WHERE THE LOCALS GO: Until 1970 Margarita was a quiet, 300-square-mile jewel, a budget traveler's Caribbean paradise with terrific climate, endless beaches, inexpensive hotels and restaurants, and a score of picturesque fishing villages to explore. In 1970 the Venezuelan government declared Margarita a duty-free port. Virtually overnight chic shops and boutiques stocking imported clothes from France, Italy, and the U.S. sprang up in Porlamar, the island's capital city. The shops lured Venezuelans in droves on weekends and it seemed that the island's character would be forever lost. We are happy to report that it isn't so. Of course, parts of Porlamar have changed dramatically, but the changes have improved services and the island isn't "ruined." In fact you'll enjoy the newer budget hotels, far more interesting dining spots, and even the surprising nightspots which, combined with the perfect weather, unspoiled beaches, and gentle, warm Margariteños, make the island a delight. What it does mean is that you'll need reservations on weekends year round and during such peak holidays as Christmas and Easter.

Getting There

Your best bet is by air from Caracas. There are several flights daily by both AVENSA and Aeropostal, Venezuela's domestic carriers. At this writing, the 35-minute nonstop flight will run under $25 round trip. You will land at Aeropuerto Internacional del Caribe, a 15-minute, $5 cab ride from downtown Porlamar where most of the island's hotels and restaurants are located.

The hydrofoil that once linked La Guaira, Caracas's port, with the island is no longer in service. You can take a bus from the Nuevo Circo Bus Terminal (downtown Caracas) to the mainland ports of Cumaná and Puerto La Cruz and then ferry across to Margarita's Punta Piedras. Ferries from Puerto La Cruz run six times a day and have both first class and tourist class. Tourist class costs under $5 one way. The ferry from Cumaná goes twice daily and the fare is also under $5.

A Quick Orientation

Porlamar has retained its colonial flavor while refurbishing the modern commercial center. The traditional heart of town is the **Plaza Bolívar.** It's marked by the **Cathedral of St. Nicholas,** whose huge dome is visible from all parts of town. The busy plaza is enclosed by small homes, schools, and shops that serve the daily needs of the locals. The commercial center has two major streets: **Avenida 4 de Mayo** and **Avenida Santiago Mariño.** These thoroughfares and the streets adjoining them are lined with chic shops, hotels, restaurants, and nightspots.

Where to Stay

There are a great many hotels here and we have selected only a random sampling. If you don't pick a peak time, such as Christmas or a weekend, you can come sans reservation.

The **Margarita Concorde,** on Avenida Raul Leoni (tel. 095/61-3333), is the island's only five-star hotel. It has a private beach, tennis courts, and a marina. The rooms are disappointing, but the hotel offers a true resort atmosphere with several dining options and evening activities. There is a large pool and sundeck. Expect to pay $65 for a double room and $40 for a single.

The **Bella Vista,** Avenida Santiago Mariño (tel. 095/61-4157), is a delightful in-town choice. Run by the government, this four-star hostelry has a large pool and sun area, plus the nicest beach in Porlamar. The 250 rooms are in two buildings, one more modern than the other. Doubles are $45; singles are $8 less.

Hotel For You, Calle J. M. Patino (tel. 095/31-995), is a good choice for it's right in the heart of the commercial center, surrounded by good shops and restaurants and a ten-minute stroll from the beach. Rooms are air-conditioned and carpeted, and have mini-refrigerators. Doubles are $25 while singles cost under $20.

Hotel Colibri, Avenida Santiago Mariño (tel. 095/32-567), has 64 rooms and these, too, are air-conditioned and have private baths. Rooms are small but clean, and the furnishings are minimal. Doubles at the Colibri run $15 and singles are only $1 less.

Other budget choices you might consider are the **Hotel Maria Luisa,** Avenida Raul Leoni on El Morro (tel. 095/61-7964); the **Hotel Boulevard,** Calle Marcano, near the Plaza Bolívar (tel. 095/61-0522); and the **Hotel Flamingo,** on Avenida 4 de Mayo (tel. 095/61-6301). These are small hotels with air-conditioned rooms, and each is comfortable and clean.

In early 1989, the new **Margarita Hilton International** is scheduled to open. You can make reservations in the U.S. or in Caracas at the Caracas Hilton. The hotel is deluxe, with its own beach, pool, and disco.

Where to Dine

The food in Margarita is not as good as that in Caracas, but they have taken giant steps from the culinary wasteland of just a few years ago. Many lovely restaurants have opened and the service has improved as well. Seafood is very much the thing here, and of course the catch of the day is just that. Remember that most Margariteños earn a living as fishermen. You'll enjoy Caribbean lobster (no claws), shrimp, clams, and crayfish. Prices are very low: a lobster dish, which is invariably the most costly item on the menu, is $10. The island's specialty is a tiny clam called chipi-chipi, usually served in a delicious broth. Popular, too, is a shellfish stew called zarzuela or cazuela, with a tomato-based sauce. All restaurants here are informal, but most men do wear jackets to dinner.

El Yate, Calle J. M. Patino, one of the newest and most attractive eateries here, is owned by an Italian. You'll be welcomed aboard by the sounding of the ship's bell and served excellent seafood, especially the lobster dishes. Try the carpaccio to start.

El Chipi, on Calle Cedeño, is an institution here, having emerged in a lovely modern new building. Look for the flags flying out front. Try the chipi-chipi chowder and the pargo meunière or grilled bass. These make a delightful low-calorie meal. Most fish dishes are $4. The restaurant is being renovated following a fire.

Los Tres Delfines, across the street, is the place to head if you like shrimp. They are prepared here in several ways and all are delicious, but our favorite here is the seafood paella—it's enough for two. Shrimp dishes run about $6, though others are less.

Delis, on Avenida 4 de Mayo, is a less formal eatery with both indoor and outdoor seating. Pizza, grilled meats, and sandwiches are the most asked-for items. Prices are low.

El Viñedo, on Avenida Santiago Mariño, is another informal dining choice with red-and-white-checked tablecloths and a huge menu. Try the grilled meats, the pastas, or the three-course cubierto which costs only $3.75. You can't beat that.

Pastissima, on 4 de Mayo, is a self-service eatery which we recommend for all three meals. There is a bilingual menu and tables inside.

Paris, on Santiago Mariño near the Bella Vista Hotel, is a delightful sidewalk café which is perched under bright-yellow awnings. Great for breakfast, lunch, or a late-night cappuccino.

A COUPLE OF INTERNATIONAL RESTAURANTS. The only French restaurant on the island is **L'Été,** on Avenida 4 de Mayo. This is a formal restaurant with a classical French menu that includes pâtés and mousses. The truite farcie au champagne (trout dish) is excellent.

In this category we can also suggest **La Gran Piramide de la Buena Suerte,** on Calle Malave, which features international dishes, highlighted by the red snapper (pargo) and steak platters.

Margarita by Day

Obviously, as with any resort blessed with magnificent beaches—there are 18 officially listed in Margarita, but we've counted a dozen more—you will while away many an hour on the warm, thick sands. Not a beer can or candy wrapper pollutes your vision, and the sea is always a clear blue no matter where you swim. Palm trees sway in the background to ever-present breezes. Waters are generally calm, although there are beaches, especially in the El Tirano section, where swimming can be a battle against the waves. Larger beaches offer lockers and snackbars. In sum, as we've told our friends as often as they'll listen, Margarita offers a more inviting collection of beaches than we've seen anywhere else—including Puerto Rico, the Virgin Islands, even the French or Italian Rivieras. But besides beaching it, we urge you to explore the island to discover your own personal hideaway areas.

Now for the best beaches, counterclockwise around the island.

THE BEST BEACHES. In Porlamar, the main swim area is **Bellavista Beach,** a wide white expanse that extends from the city center beyond the Bella Vista Hotel to Punta El Morro. Rarely crowded, the beach is best for swimming in the morning. By late afternoon, waters can get choppy.

Heading east, you reach the small but lovely **Playa Moreno,** near Pampatar, a beach distinguished by unusual rock formations and the angel that overlooks the sands. Calm waters.

In Pampatar, a fishing village seven miles from Porlamar, there is the scenic **Pampatar Beach.** Boats line the bay and in the background are the fishermen's hillside homes. A restaurant caters to swimmers.

Incredibly beautiful is the mile-long **Guacuco Beach,** near the town of Asunción, three miles beyond Pampatar. The waves, which are swimmable until late in the day, gently lap against the spotless uncrowded sands. Lockers and a restaurant are available. Highly recommended.

Continuing in the same counterclockwise direction, we come to another favorite of ours, the lovely **El Agua** beach, in the section of that name. Despite waves that are truly formidable, snorkelers seem to congregate here. Huge coconut trees lend a tropical look to El Agua. There are lockers and a restaurant.

In the island's most northerly portion is the quiet **Manzanillo Beach,** where you might like to picnic in seclusion. While calm, the waters are a shade cool in winter.

And finally, in the town of **Juan Griego** is a tiny picturebook beach.

EXPLORING MARGARITA. When you've had enough of beaches, you should spend a couple of days exploring the island's colonial fortresses, religious shrines, fishing villages, and out-of-the-way, unmapped inlets and coves. For this you will need a car, which we recommend that you rent. Roads are generally excellent throughout the island: most are asphalt, and road signs are large and easy to read. And by following our suggestions you won't need a guide. You must be 21 to rent a car and must show a valid license (U.S. and Canadian licenses are fine). Rental costs are reasonable. **Volkswagen** and **Mercedes** are located at the airport or on Avenida 4 de Mayo (near the old airport). Rental costs are $10 per day plus 6¢ a kilometer for the VW. There is a **Jeep Rental** at Avenida Santiago Mariño and Calle Marcano, and a **Fiesta Rental** at the airport and on Calle 4 de Mayo. You might want to rent a bike at **Bici-Rent** on Avenida Santiago Mariño. All rentals can be made through your hotel.

Or you might prefer the convenience of a cab, with the driver acting as your guide. The cost runs $18 a day—be sure to establish the fare and trip hours in advance. A bit of bargaining sometimes helps, depending on how busy your cabbie is that morning.

Remember that the Margariteños are invariably friendly to Norte Americanos, so don't hesitate to ask directions from a man astride a donkey or from a woman carrying well water in buckets.

Only 15 minutes northwest of Porlamar in the village of **El Valle** is the island's most revered shrine, a pale-blue church housing a statue of Mary, reputed to have been found in a nearby cave by a Guaiqueri Indian. Today the statue is the patron of all fishermen and sailors in Venezuela and thus many families make pilgrimages here. In the parish house next door is a famous pearl. Legend has it that a pearl diver, stung in the leg by a deadly stingray, offered the next pearl he found to the Virgin if she would save him. He raised himself up and found his leg healed. His next pearl, shaped like a leg and with a mark on it said to resemble a stingray's sting, is now on display.

Seven miles from Porlamar is the lovely fishing village of **Pampatar,** the island's main port. Overlooking the harbor is the famous **San Carlos Fortress,** now a museum housing Spanish colonial paintings, and armor and weapons dating back to the 17th century. The best site for photos is the drawbridge, where you can look out over the fishing boats in the bay (try to catch the colored balloons affixed to the boats for luck). Open until 5 p.m. every day; closed Wednesday. Also take a look at the colonial-style church opposite the museum, which features a statue called *Christ of the Happy Voyage.* Originally destined for Peru, the statue was unloaded because the ship carrying it from Spain couldn't weigh anchor with the statue on board. Beaches here are nice indeed.

Your trip should include a stop in the state capital of **Asunción** (pop. 6,000), six miles from Porlamar, which, architecturally, is the most authentically colonial town in Margarita. Look in at the **Santa Rosa Fortress** which overlooks most of the island. A local heroine of the revolution, Luisa Arismendi, was imprisoned here; a statue of the lady stands in the city's main plaza amid lush tropical plants and flowers. Check the **Museo de Nueva Esparta** in the Plaza Bolívar for a topographical understanding of Margarita and its two sister islands. Open daily from 8 a.m. to noon and 2 to 5 p.m.

Couples in love and other hopeless romantics should drive to the opposite end of the island from Porlamar to the village of **Juan Griego,** where sunsets are magnificent. The sky is filled with beautiful colors and blends with the bay and surrounding mountains. A ruined hillside fortress, the **Galera,** outside the town, offers the best panorama.

La Arestinga Lagoon, an inland waterway, is one of the few places we know to get away from smog, pollution, and noise simultaneously. Only the sounds of nature are heard. The area has unusual bird life, a good beach, thick mangrove trees, as well as water sports. An added plus is the oyster beds—you may even find a pearl. The lagoon is located off the highway to Punta de Piedras on the narrow strip that connects the two parts of Margarita.

Margarita by Night

Margarita is not an island for night folk. There are not many nightclubs, and those that do exist are tame in comparison with those of Caracas. However, new discothèques have opened recently, and with the influx of tourists this situation may change.

For those who love gambling, there is the **Canodromo** (dog track) on the road from Porlamar to Pampatar. The greyhounds race every Thursday, Friday, and Saturday night in an open-air stadium. Check with your hotel concierge for details and tips.

There are a few discos, the best being **Doce 34,** on Avenida 4 de Mayo, and **Maximo,** on the same block next to the bowling alley.

There are attractive **piano bars** at the Hotels Concorde, Bella Vista, and Guaiqueri.

Bowling is available at the **Margarita Bowling Club,** on Avenida 4 de Mayo near the airport.

Shopping

The major shopping streets, Avenidas Santiago Mariño and 4 de Mayo, are lined with boutiques. The clothing is imported from Europe, the Far East, and the U.S. Items seemed expensive but were less so than in the U.S.

Margarita does have two excellent handcraft shops. **Galeria del Arte Del Bellorin,** on Calle Cedeño, is filled with primitive paintings, lovely wall hangings, and woodcarvings. Nearby, **Los Makiritares,** on Calle Igualdad (upstairs), is more típico with ceramic and wooden masks, straw baskets, and lovely woven hammocks.

MERIDA: This city, as famous for its university as for its fishing, is nestled in the Andes at 5,400 feet. Venezuelans flock here for peace and quiet and the chance to ride the world's highest cable car—to a height of almost 16,000 feet. Locals claim the trout fishing in the nearby lagoons is the world's best.

The cable-car journey, via four separate cars, will take you to **Pico Espejo,** 16,000 feet above sea level, the highest point of the Venezuelan Andes.

You can get here via AVENSA or Aeropostal in about an hour from Caracas.

There are excellent restaurants and fine hotels, all at bargain rates. Our first choices would be the **Hotel Pedregosa** and the **Park Hotel.**

The **teleférico** (cable car) runs daily except Monday and Tuesday, so make sure you don't arrive only on those days. It's an incredible one-hour trip that all by itself will make the Merida excursion worthwhile.

READERS' TOURING TIPS: "We visited Angel Falls, Canaima, Margarita Island, and Merida within a six-day period; of all the places visited, including Caracas, I was delighted with Merida, the City of the Caballeros. Nestled in a quiet, clean valley in the snow-capped Andes, this university town of about 100,000 people has a long, narrow park lining the Pan American Hwy., which runs through the outskirts of the town; busts honoring Venezuelan poets dot the green park shaded by tall trees. Planes land only in the forenoon and early afternoon before the clouds cover the airfield, so we had to stay overnight here at the **Hotel Belensate,** which has a restaurant and bar and is built like a southern ranchero. We visited the parks, cathedrals, and museums of Merida and were especially charmed by the large flower clock (like those in Switzerland) and the Carillon/Glockenspiel honoring Beethoven built in the park in front of the Museum of Modern Art. We hired a taxi and went into the mountains where we found a small shop run by Andean Indians and bought some beautiful hand-woven ponchos for about half what they cost in Caracas. Hope to visit Merida again some day and ride that cable car" (Ruth Y. Hashimoto, Albuquerque, N.M.).

"The incredible teleférico there makes it well worth the trip. The ride and the views are spectacular. The teleférico, located at Avenida 8 and Calle 24, about a ten-minute walk from the main plaza in the center of town, runs only from 8 a.m. to noon Wednesday through Sunday (clouds cover the peaks by noon). Long lines form, especially on weekends and when Venezuelans have vacations. The trip takes 1¼ hours each way. The round-trip cost is 50 Bs, but the day I went up, a weekday in low tourist season, everyone got on for the student charge of 25 Bs, certainly one of the best bargains in Venezuela. You can fly to Merida, of course, or take the bus, a 12-hour trip from Caracas. Have a heavy sweater handy when you get into the high altitudes, both on the teleférico and on the bus ride to Merida" (Violet Lane, Pa.).

CANAIMA AND ANGEL FALLS: A visit to **Canaima,** carved out of the

jungle in an effort to draw tourists to the interior, is an experience to consider. Some 500 miles southeast of Caracas are two camps that will enable you to experience Venezuela's teeming wilderness and natural beauty.

The memorable 2½-hour flight to Canaima passes **Angel Falls** with its record 3,200-foot drop. If time permits, definitely consider making Canaima a part of your itinerary.

ORGANIZED TOURS: The best-value tours in Caracas are offered by

Agencias Candes, Edificio Roraima, Avenida Francisco de Miranda, beyond Chacaíto (tel. 33-5773). Local offices are at most major hotels. Trips can be arranged to Colonia Tovar, Margarita, Merida, and Angel Falls; day and night tours are offered.

5. CARACAS AFTER DARK

Like Rio and Buenos Aires, Caracas is for night people, insomniacs, and all others who come alive when the sun goes down. The posh restaurants, classy nightclubs, swinging discos, and plain old saloons are thronged with late-to-arrive, late-to-exit youngish couples. Yes, couples—in Caracas, as in much of Latin America, unescorted women and even single men are discouraged from entering most clubs. But there are exceptions, fortunately, as you will see below.

THE BEST IN LIVE MUSIC: If you ask any (with-it) local where you can find the best nightspot, the answer will invariably be the jumping **Hipocampo,** in the Centro Comercial Chacaíto (that's the huge modern shopping center at the end of the Sabana Grande). Climb to the upper tier, local 215, where three bands—Latin, mild pop, and mad rock—pound out the beat from 10 p.m. to 5 a.m. every night. Tiny tables ring the roomy dance floor and a red-hued ceiling covers the clinched couples. The lighting is subdued, and even if you don't like to dance, you'll soon become infected with the contagious spirit. The bar, our favorite in Caracas, manages to convey an air of intimacy, and it's here that the singles of Caracas gather faithfully. Best of all is the cost—no cover, and one drink can be nursed through most of the evening. *Caution:* Occasionally, on weekends particularly, the Hipocampo offers rather elaborate floor shows. The tab then is a stiff $10 cover charge—so check before entering. Jackets are necessary for men.

Another great place is **Fedora,** on Calle Madrid in Las Mercedes. Designed like a ship, Fedora offers both live and DJ music nightly. The bar is enormous and the place is crowded with with-it Caraqueños.

Finally **Cota 880,** on the top floor of the Hilton Hotel, offers dancing to two orchestras while providing a panorama of the city.

THE BEST DISCOS: For a lovely evening of imbibing and dancing, head to the newest in spot in town, the **Red Parrot,** on Avenida Tamanaco in El Rosal. Mirrored walls, comfortable tub chairs, and a sleek chrome bar plus the raucous music make this a special spot. When the disco is quiet, the beat is taken up by the piano player and the piano bar which is center stage here. Couples only. Men must wear jackets. No cover or minimum. Drinks are $3.

Café L'Attico, in Altamira on Avenida Luís Roches, has video discs that keep it packed. This is a singles hangout, noisy and fun.

Previously mentioned in the restaurant section is **Weekends,** nearby in Altamira at San Juan Bosco. You will find booths and tables with huge video screens all over the trilevel establishment. The bar is among the best in town and is a great meeting place.

Young couples, drawn by the swing-type love seats and the jungle motif, flock to **La Jungla,** on the Plaza La Castellana, near La Estancia Restaurant. Tarzan-like films flash on the walls periodically and stuffed animals line the entrance area. Completing the jungle mood are animal skins, prints, spears, and native masks that almost growl from the walls. The waiters, in tiger-skin vests, look right at home. La Jungla is packed most evenings from 6 p.m. right up to its 4 a.m. closing, 5:30 a.m. on weekends. Drinks are $4.50 and women can wear slacks, but manager Manolo Diego tells us that singles are discouraged. Oh yes, the music—it roars out at ear-shattering pitch.

A club dedicated to the charms of women and the complications caused therefrom is the wild **Eva's,** located on the lowest level of the Centro Comercial Chacaíto (Hipocampo is upstairs in the center). Statues of women occupy the red velvet couches; do note the ceiling over the dance floor, which can be maneuvered to create effects you'll see nowhere else. Owned by a Portuguese couple, the disco is open from 8:30 p.m. until 5:30 a.m. (closed on Sunday). Prices at the bar are $5 per drink, and at tables $5.50; add 10% for service. No cover or minimum; single men are admitted, but women need escorts. Remember, you enter *below* the main floor.

An attractive disco, **Dog and Cat** is on Avenida Río de Janeiro, Las

Mercedes. There is a pub on the lower level and a disco above. Drinks are about $3 each and the club is open until 4 a.m.

There are several discos in La Castellana on the main Avenida Principal. You can easily walk from one to the other. **Number Two,** a couples-only club, the **Sun Set,** and the **Flower** are just a few. **Pop 68,** Avenida Naiguata, El Rosal, features Salsa music at its small dance floor. Only a dozen tables, but there's action at the bar.

BIG NIGHT OUT: One of the most attractive clubs we've seen anywhere is 1900 Mx Way, in the C.C.C.T. shopping center (tel. 92-1010). This is actually a private club. Men need jackets. The place opens at 10 p.m. and has both live and disco music. Mirrored ceilings, hanging plants, and a large bar area make this one special. Drinks are a steep $6—but the atmosphere is worth the extra $1.

COCKTAIL LOUNGES: Caracas is renowned for its intimate clubs where relaxation and conversation are the rule. Several favorites are in El Rosal. **El Coche de Isidoro Piano Bar,** on Avenida Venezuela, features three combos in a colonial setting. A block away on Avenida Tamanaco, **Feelings,** has caught on with the younger set. Both clubs are packed on weekends.

The **Juan Sebastian** bar on Avenida Venezuela admits singles and jazz is featured. **El Decamaron,** on Avenida Venezuela in El Rosal, is one of the city's nicest piano bars. The music is delightful and ranges from pop to show tunes and even a little Latin beat. The seating is comfortable and the lighting dim. What more can you ask for?

SMALL AND INTIMATE (NO MUSIC): For a marvelously relaxing cocktail hour in intimate alcoves, try the **Bar Cacique** in the Hotel Tamanaco, Avenida Las Mercedes. Stroll onto the adjoining terrace for a marvelous view of the city below. Most drinks are about $4, but you should try the Coctel Zorba ($3.50), a secret concoction that has won awards, we're told.

Another plush cocktail retreat is **La Ronda Bar** in the lobby of the Caracas Hilton Hotel. Cocktails range from $4 to $5. A stop here should be combined with a nonorganized tour of the hotel, which is almost a city unto itself. Remember, you need a jacket after 7 p.m.

El Trapiche Bar in the Holiday Inn offers live entertainment evenings. Take the elevator to the "PP" level. A $2 cover is added to your bill. Drinks are $5.

Like informal outdoor cafés? Stop at the **Café Memphis** on Avenida Sabana Grande, opposite the Cristal Hotel, where you can sit for hours and gaze at the pedestrians. The sandwiches and light desserts are quite good. The Memphis is a big meeting place for single people. Occasionally a group of sidewalk musicians serenades you for a few centavos. The street is closed to traffic and the tables are placed on the mall.

THEATERS: The best in opera, ballet, and theater appear at the **Teatro Teresa Carreño,** a new cultural complex that can rival Lincoln Center in New York. Local and touring companies often perform here. Every seat in the theater is comfortable and affords unobstructed views. Prices are low—$10 is on the high side for an opera or ballet.

The *Teatro Municipal,* Plaza Municipal, still hosts touring companies. Other live theater productions can be seen in the **Teatro Nacional,** Esquina Cipreses in downtown Caracas, and at **Aula Magna,** in the Ciudad, Universitaría. There are also occasional English-language performances at the Caracas Theatre Club, near Las Mercedes. Check with the local *Daily Journal* for details.

CINEMAS: Caracas has many good movie theaters, complete with soft seats, air conditioning, and English-language films that are still in first-run New York theaters. There are also numerous drive-in theaters for those who've rented cars.

Tip: For schedules, check the *Daily Journal,* the English-language newspaper published here. Movie schedules are printed daily along with capsule film reviews. The paper's "Calendar of Events" also notes major social and cultural activities.

6. THE BEST SHOPPING VALUES

While the shops of Caracas are as chic and posh as any in North or South America, few offer the unusual values that we like to recommend. The boutiques would be at home in Palm Beach, but that doesn't help much if you're out looking for that bargain in wool or wood jewelry. Caracas simply is not the place for that typical tourist-type shopping where you load up your luggage with those inexpensive but quaint items for Uncle Harry and Aunt Sophie.

Now, after saying all that, we'll cite the two possible exceptions—pearls from Margarita Island, which are widely available in bracelets and necklaces, and are certainly the best value in town, as well as ladies' shoes. And who knows, you might stumble on a "find" among the rusty swords and other knickknacks touted by local shops. Most stores, by the way, are open from 9 a.m. to 1 p.m. and 3 to 7 p.m., including Saturday.

A Word About Ladies' Shoes: At this writing, shops all over Caracas are selling locally made ladies' leather shoes in beautiful styles for a fraction of their U.S. price. A good pair of shoes costing $150 and up in the U.S. was under $50 in Caracas. The finest shops selling shoes were located in the C.C.C.T. shopping center.

SHOPPING CENTERS: Caracas is studded with magnificent shopping centers filled with a great variety of boutiques, restaurants, and entertainment areas —certainly worth at least a browse. New ones open constantly, but we still prefer the **Chacaíto Shopping Center** in Sabana Grande; **Concresa,** the largest in the city, in Prados del Este; the **Paseo Las Mercedes,** where the Holiday Inn is located; and the **Centro Ciudad Comercial Tamanaco (C.C.C.T.)** near La Carlota airport.

Chacaíto is crammed with the specialty shops that draw the well-heeled matrons of Caracas and whose names are found along Fifth and Madison Avenues—Charles Jourdan, Gucci, Yves St. Laurent, and Pierre Cardin. Styles and prices are much the same as in New York. You might try **Biki Bou** for bikinis, **King's Row** for ladies' sportswear, and **España** for handbags and belts.

The **Paseo Las Mercedes Shopping Center** is another trilevel shopping center with fine shops in all categories, similar to Chacaíto. Some of our favorites are **Elena,** next to the Holiday Inn, which has magnificent papier-mâché figures; **Copenhague,** a gourmet food and deli shop; and **El Taller de la Esquina,** which has lovely rugs, ceramics, and hanging plants.

The **Concresa Shopping Center** is a huge trilevel complex in Prados del Este, a relatively new section. Within Caracas you will find every type of shop, movie theaters, bars, restaurants, nightclubs, and a supermarket. Worth a visit just to browse.

Avenida Lincoln, the principal avenue of La Sabana Grande, is something of a shopping center itself. This one-mile stretch holds hundreds of shops, and you'll find here examples of all the city has to offer.

VENEZUELAN HANDCRAFTS: In our view, the following three stores have the best buys in the city. All offer unusual, decorative, and well-made wares.

Artesanías Venezolana, Calle Real de Sabana Grande in the Palacio de las Industrias building, is the best place to browse. Vases, ashtrays, carvings, sculptures, hammocks, ponchos, straw bags, religious items, and jewelry are just some of the items to be found here.

A smaller selection, but with interesting items, is **El Porton de Plaza** in the Paseo Las Mercedes Shopping Center. Particularly good here were the rugs.

The handcraft shop in the **Hotel Tamanaco** is another excellent source. Prices here were competitive and in some cases lower. They had lovely woodcarvings of toucans and other tropical birds that swing on a trapeze. These make terrific gifts.

ANTIQUES 'N' THINGS: Every city seems to have a flea market, and Caracas is no exception. The local version, **Manuel Herrera,** is located behind the Red Cross building on Avenida Urdaneta, San Bernardino district; look for the sign saying "Cerveceria a Pandero." The market has two floors stuffed with swords, paintings, utensils, clocks, telescopes, mirrors, furniture, vases—all very old and all an irresistible lure for Caraqueños. Prices range from pennies up to $100.

If you'd like to pick up reproductions of Spanish colonial furniture and accessories, take a cab to **A. E. Limes,** Calle Gerosal, Prado del Este section (a newly developed area of Caracas). Prices start at $15. Another A. E. Limes outlet is in the Paseo Las Mercedes Shopping Center.

JEWELRY: Pearl jewelry from Margarita is sold at every jewelry store in the city. Your best bet is to comparison-shop along Sabana Grande for style and price (18-karat gold pins with a small pearl start at $25).

South America's leading jewelry concern, **H. Stern,** has four outlets in Caracas, at the Tamanaco, the Eurobuilding, and Hilton Hotels. In addition to gemstones, typical Cochano jewelry of gold and natural pearl are for sale. We also recommend the 22-karat gold coins available. A small H. Stern shop is located at the international airport.

Another shop where you can pick up Cochano jewelry with pearls from Margarita is **Walter Peter,** on Avenida Francisco de Miranda.

FABRICS: For good value in imported European fabrics (silk and polyesters), try any of the **Raymar** branches. Most convenient is the shop in the Chacaíto Shopping Center.

PIÑATAS: For great gifts for youngsters, make sure to pick up a piñata (papier-mâché figure), which you stuff with small toys and candy. Traditionally the figure is broken at birthday parties by a blindfolded child who hits it with a stick. For the best in piñatas and stuffings, stop at **La Piñata** in Centro Comercial Chacaíto, near Le Drugstore.

Another fine piñata shop is **Piñatas Mary Silvia,** at Centro Comercial Paseo Las Mercedes (upper level). Prices are comparable.

HAND-WOVEN RUGS: For fine rugs, woven by Guajiro Indians, shop at **Tere,** in the Centro Ciudad Comercial Tamanaco. Prices for small rugs start at about $50 and range upward. The quality is super and they are original works of art. (We have two rugs displayed in our apartment.)

ARTISTS AND HIPPIES: An outdoor hangout for Caracas's hippie artists is on Avenida Casanova at the corner of Calle Coromoto. Note the walls painted in bright orange, yellow, and purple in fine cubist style. Whether you pass here day or night, you will find several artists offering their works at all price levels. Some of the art is quite good, but be prepared to bargain.

7. TRANSPORTATION NOTES AND ASSORTED MISCELLANY

BUSES, POR PUESTOS, AND TAXIS: Buses are the cheapest (10¢) way to get around town, while the jitney-like autos called por puestos (about 75¢) are the quickest. Buses are clean and generally in good condition; enter from the front and exit through the rear. The por puestos, which are standard sedans, zip along the main thoroughfares picking up and dropping off passengers constantly. Look for the "por puesto" sign and the destination. Raise your hand to hail a por puesto and the driver will respond with his hand. For 30¢ you can get a bus from Nuevo Circo to the beach. Check with your hotel clerk for exact locations.

Taxis are plentiful and are equipped with meters that start at 30¢.

THE SUBWAY: The metro, built to resemble the Paris Métro, is efficient and clean. The stations are marked by the big orange "M" and the ticket system is similar to that of Paris. Buy a ticket from a booth or from a ticket machine. The ticket you receive is necessary to get in and exit. Put it in the slot on the turnstile, and at the entrance it flips out back to you; at the exit it doesn't. The main line runs from east to west, from Propatria to Parque del Este. It is open from 5 a.m. to 11 p.m. The cars are also air-conditioned.

RENTING A CAR: Because of the fine highway system and the reasonable price of gas, this is one of the few Latin cities where we suggest that you consider car rentals. **Avis, Budget Rent-A-Car,** and **Hertz** have bustling outlets here, and rates are comparable at each. Your hotel clerk is your best bet for making arrangements. Advance reservations are usually unnecessary.

MISCELLANY: Here follow some helpful odds and ends:

Reading Matter: The *Daily Journal,* published daily, is the best English-language paper in South America. Coverage includes stocks, sports, theater schedules. One-day-old editions of the *New York Times* are often sold at the Ávila, Tamanaco, and Hilton hotels for $1.75. *Time* magazine's Latin American edition ($1.20) is available Wednesday at most newsstands.

Government: Venezuela is a democracy with an elected president and congress.

Ice Cream: The best-known local brands are **Tío Rico** ("Rich Uncle") and **EFE**—both quite good.

Post Office: The main office is on Avenida Urdaneta, corner of Carmelitas, diagonally opposite the Central Bank of Venezuela.

Population: Venezuela has over 18 million residents. Caracas has more than 4 million.

Telephones: Easy to operate: just wait for a dial tone, deposit a *ficha* (token) and dial.

English-Language Radio: Radio Libertador broadcasts in English for several hours daily. Check the *Daily Journal* for program information.

U.S. Embassy: Located on Avenida Principal La Floresta (tel. 32-5287).

Venezuela: The name "Venezuela" is credited to Amerigo Vespucci. Supposedly, when he first observed the native homes along Lake Maracaibo, he was reminded of his native Venice ("Venezia" in Italian); hence the diminutive "little Venice"—"Venezuela."

Duty-Free Shop: You can pick up perfume, liquor, cigarettes, etc., in the terminal building before departure.

Airport Tax: North Americans pay $5 tax upon leaving Venezuela.

CARACAS ALIVE: An in-depth guide to Caracas and other parts of Venezuela, *Venezuela Alive* (by the same authors) is for nonbudget visitors who are looking for good values. It's available from Alive Publications, 32 E. 57th St., New York, NY 10022, for $10.95.

READER'S TOURING TIP: "Anyone who wants unusual insight into very típico South American life and at the same time wishes to save air fare should consider going from Caracas, Venezuela, to Bogotá, Colombia, by bus. The bus leaves Nuevo Circo in the heart of downtown Caracas at 6:30 p.m., and arrives at San Antonio at the Venezuelan border at around 7:30 a.m. the next morning. Bus reservations are imperative, and may be made at the bus station at window 7. To be safe, book the day before, and make certain to ask for a ticket to San Antonio and not Bogotá (no through tickets are sold). From San Antonio a cab will be needed (about five miles) to make the 8:30 a.m. bus from the border town of Cucuta, Colombia, to Bogotá. Make certain to tell the cab driver you need to stop at the border check to have your passport stamped. If there's a backup there, this can also be done at the D.A.S. office in Cucuta; it's located about five blocks from the bus terminal and on the way. Without a properly stamped passport, it will be impossible to buy a bus ticket, or for that matter, to obtain a hotel room anywhere in Colombia. All this might be in vain if you arrive at the bus terminal in Cucuta without Colombian pesos or American dollars, as it's impossible to change traveler's checks there. The 8:30 bus from Cucuta arrives in the terminal in Bogotá between 11 p.m. and 2 a.m., but cabs are available to bring you to a hotel that remains open all night. Hotel El Dorado at Calle 18 no. 10–69 (tel. 242-6419), charges $9.50 for a single with private bath. Total cost from Caracas to Bogotá, around the breathtaking Andes, cab fares included, is about $42" (Michael Romano, New York, N.Y.).

CHAPTER III

RIO DE JANEIRO, BRAZIL

□ □ □

Rio is an exciting introduction to Brazil—it has a beat and a beauty all its own. The breathtaking appearance of the city, which you first glimpse as your plane glides in low over blue Guanabara Bay, is the perfect prelude to this capital of the samba, of nightclubs that never seem to close, and of futebol (soccer) matches that rival the World Series in spectator fervor.

From the moment you step off the plane at Galeão International Airport, you'll sense a tempo and an aliveness in the air. There is no languor here, despite the fact that Rio is a semitropical city whose Copacabana Beach is an attraction in June as well as January. The pace is fast and the residents have a zest for living and life. It is no place to rest. Rio is truly one of the world's great cities.

ENTRY REQUIREMENTS: U.S. citizens need a visa, valid for 90 days (you must leave the U.S. within 90 days of obtaining the visa), in order to visit Brazil. You can get your visa the same day upon presenting to the Brazilian Consulate a completed form with photo and round-trip airline ticket.

THE AIRPORT: You will arrive at **Galeão International Airport,** a modern, air-conditioned, well-organized facility with a duty-free shop. After you pick up your bags, head to the Customs area. There you will press a button lighting either a green light or a red light—it's random. If it's green, just proceed; if it's red, a polite spot search of your bags will follow. Stop at the duty-free shop where you can purchase $300 of duty-free cigarettes, liquor, perfumes, radios, and the like.

Next, step outside where two rival **taxi** companies (Cootramo and Transcoopass) provide cab service to Copacabana for about $15 and to Leblon or

Gavea for about $20. (You purchase taxi tickets at the airport terminal as you exit and give your ticket to the waiting cabbie.) Or if you're unencumbered by luggage, you can take **bus** no. 322, 324, or 328 downtown for a fare of about 50¢.

There are two special buses leaving the international airport. One heads to Santos Dumont Airport and the other heads to the Barra area, each for under $1.50. Look for the bus marked "Aeroporto Internacional–Alvorada."

THE FIRST IMPRESSIONS: During the 40-minute taxi ride from the airport your eyes will be filled with exotic sights and shapes, ranging from the teeming favelas (hillside homes of the poor) to ultramodern buildings that could fit comfortably on Chicago's North Side to the jam-packed sidewalks in "center city" where you expect to see pedestrians break into a samba. And at carnival time they do.

Dominating the southwest side of the city and guarding the entrance to Guanabara Bay is the famous **Pão de Açúcar** (Sugarloaf) mountain, which is shaped like a giant brown gumdrop. Look for the 1,230-foot-high peak—at the end of the beach area—as your plane circles before landing. And if you are a climber, try scaling it. A British woman was the first to do it—150 years ago. You can also reach the top by cable car, an excursion that we describe in detail in Section 3, "Rio by Day."

Prepare, incidentally, for traffic jams comparable to those in Rome or Paris. The taxi drivers here have a certain originality in their mode of driving that makes New York cabbies seem inhibited. Driving the 40 minutes from the airport into center city, where you may want to stay, will quickly orient you to driver and pedestrian idiosyncrasies.

Clothes will be no problem in Rio since the Cariocas (as residents of Rio are called) dress informally day and evening. The only exception to this is in the high-priced hotels and restaurants, which hardly concern us.

Dominating everything here is the beauty of the surrounding bay, the superb backdrop of mountain, and the sultry women who are slender and dark—"stunning" is the word.

A GEOGRAPHICAL ORIENTATION: There are six important sections of Rio you need to know: **Center City,** where the better budget hotels and restaurants are located; **Flamengo Beach,** a small, charming stretch of beach along Guanabara Bay, where there are several budget hotels but few restaurants other than those in the hotels; world-famous **Copacabana Beach** beyond Flamengo Beach, where there are a number of good-value hotels and restaurants a block or two from the glitter of the beachfront and its $100-a-day establishments; and **Ipanema, Leblon,** and **Gavea,** adjoining beach communities which are the newest commercial and residential areas.

Your best bet for movies, theaters, shopping, and sightseeing is downtown Rio. If, however, you crave quiet and calm, try a Flamengo hotel; if you like hectic nightlife and rubbing elbows with the wealthy, then by all means stay at one of our beach choices. It's all up to you—since budget-hotel rates are roughly the same in all of these sections.

Personally, we prefer staying in Copacabana; it's somewhat less crowded than downtown, the restaurants are generally better—and ah, those omnipresent beaches. In summer (December to February) it's a shade cooler out here too. But read on and make up your own mind.

Center City

To orient yourself rapidly to downtown Rio, familiarize yourself first with the important **Avenida Rio Branco,** a wide thoroughfare that extends from the

Praça Mauá (dock area) just over a mile south to **Guanabara Bay,** not far from Flamengo Beach; most of our center-city hotel and restaurant selections are within walking distance of Avenida Rio Branco. During the day traffic here is extremely heavy—mostly Volkswagens, it seems—and the sidewalks are crowded with office workers and shoppers. At nearly every corner there's a Bahian woman selling baked goods. Everyone moves briskly. The pace is much like that of New York.

Strolling around downtown, you will be conscious of the tremendous building boom taking place in Rio. Almost every block is the site of a construction project, and the sidewalks and streets seem under endless repair.

At night, quiet suddenly descends—as the cars and pedestrians head for home. The only downtown area alive after dark is the movie district **(Cinelandia)** near the **Praça** (plaza, pronounced "prahsa") **Mahatma Gandhi.**

Wondering where Rio nightlife really jumps? Look toward Copacabana, Ipanema, and Leblon, a short 20-minute bus ride away.

There are several other center-city streets and areas important to know. First, five blocks from the Praça Mauá, heading down Rio Branco, is **Avenida Presidente Vargas,** a major transportation artery where buses leave for the beaches and for several excursion trips we'll recommend.

Continuing down Rio Branco for four more blocks, you come to **Rua Ouvidor,** Rio's main shopping street, that is closed to traffic most of the day.

Near the end of Avenida Rio Branco, off to the right, is the above-mentioned Praça Mahatma Gandhi, locally known as Cinelandia. This large plaza, considered by many the heart of downtown Rio, is the hub of several bus lines. Nearby are the movie district and the best budget hotels and restaurants in the city. The key street here is **Rua Senador Dantas,** which runs from the plaza to Avenida República do Chile.

And finally, you should be familiar with **Avenida Mem de Sá,** in the higher-altitude section of Rio several blocks west of Praça Mahatma Gandhi, behind the site of the new cathedral of Rio de Janeiro. This is the older section of the city, and we have a number of good budget hotels here.

A NOTE ABOUT STREET NAMES. Streets in downtown Rio—as throughout South America—are named after famous people, events, and dates. And the people so honored are not limited to Brazilian heroes. Don't be surprised when you come across streets named after Woodrow Wilson, Franklin D. Roosevelt, and even Medgar Evers, the slain U.S. civil rights leader.

Street signs at each corner note both the name of the avenue plus the house numbers on that block, with an arrow indicating which way the numbers run.

Flamengo Beach

The bus that carries you from center city to Flamengo Beach—in under ten minutes—winds its way along **Avenida Beira Mar,** a scenic bayfront drive that has 150-foot-high royal palms on either side. This tiny but attractive community houses the famous Gloria Hotel as well as a number of budget hotels. The beaches are free and open to the public.

Copacabana Beach

A most exclusive and modern section of Rio is Copacabana Beach, a must in your sightseeing. And if you have time, slip in for a swim—it's free. The cool water is a deep blue and as you thrash around in the ocean, glancing now and then at the plush beachfront hotels, you'll feel for an instant like one of the millionaires strolling along **Avenida Atlantica.**

Copacabana is less than 20 minutes from downtown Rio by bus, which you

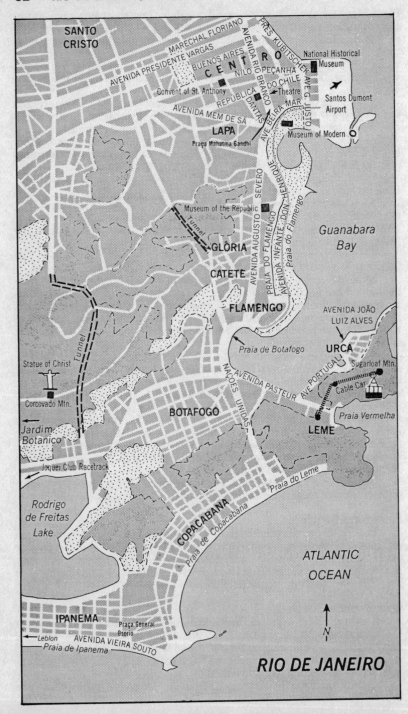

can catch at the intersection of Rio Branco and Vargas, or at the Praça Mahatma Gandhi. The fare is under 25¢. It's an enchanting drive: the bus follows the bayfront, in and out of tunnels, the blue of the Atlantic on the left, the splendor of the royal palms on the right.

For budget-hotel-hunting here, stick to **Avenida Copacabana,** one block from the beach. Throughout the area you'll find most of our restaurant and nightclub selections, as well as the largest stores in this area.

Ipanema and Leblon

Just beyond Copacabana is the modern beach community of Ipanema. The main streets to remember are **Avenida Vieira Souto** on the beachfront and **Visconde de Pirajá** two blocks inland, where some of the city's finest shops are located. Two popular meeting points are the **Praças General Osorio** and **Nossa Senhora de Paz.**

Leblon, the next beach area, is separated from Ipanema by a canal. **Avenida Delfim Moreira** is the beachfront street, while **Ataulfo de Paiva** is the principal commercial thoroughfare.

Gavea

Just south from Leblon is the beach community of Gavea, which houses three of Rio's most elegant hotels: the Sheraton (closest to Leblon), the Intercontinental, and the Nacional. The beachfront street is **Avenida Niemeyer.** Beyond Gavea lies **Barra da Tijuca,** a lovely beach area rapidly being developed as a residential and commercial hub.

The Lagoon

The center of Rio houses **Lagoa Rodrigo de Freitas,** which is particularly lovely at night. Located behind Ipanema and Leblon, the Jockey Club Racetrack and Tivoli amusement park are landmarks.

WARNING: The beaches of Rio are for pleasure. To assure that, don't bring your valuables with you. Okay?

CURRENCY BRIEFING: For the past decade the Brazilian currency, the cruzeiro, tended to decline in value in relation to the U.S. dollar. In a superficial sense, the traveler has benefited by being able to purchase more Brazilian money for his or her dollar. But in reality the galloping inflation tended to erode the cruzeiro's purchasing power. Prices were totally unpredictable, since your costs were affected by the swing of the currency devaluation versus inflation rate. Further complicating the situation was the frequent variance between the official rate and the world (parallel-market) rates of exchange. The variance could be as much as 30% to 40%.

In early 1986 the cruzeiro soared to as much as 17,000 per $1 U.S., with the parallel market over 20,000. In late 1986, under Brazil'a new president, José Sarnay, a bold new economic policy was inaugurated. The **cruzado** replaced the cruzeiro, with each new cruzado worth 1,000 old cruzeiros. Prices, wages, and inflation were frozen and the economic situation improved overnight. However, by early 1989 the situation had again reversed and Brazil introduced a new monetary unit, the **novo cruzado,** with each novo cruzado worth 1,000 old cruzados. At this writing, new bills have not been issued so be alert that each old 1,000 cruzado note is equal to 1 novo cruzado (just cancel out the last three zeros). We recommend that you only change small amounts of dollars into novo cruzados on an as-needed basis as exchange rates might not be favorable for changing your left-over Brazilian money back into dollars.

What will the future hold? There is no way to predict what conditions will prevail when you arrive, so make it a point to *check the exchange rate prior to your visit.* That way you'll have a better idea how far your dollars will stretch. And stretch they will, despite all this unpredictability—better than in Paris or Rome.

Also make sure you purchase your novo cruzados at the parallel-market rate (which will cut your cost enormously), and pay your bills with novo cruzados, not dollars or credit cards.

By the way, the dollar sign is widely used in South America, and you should not assume it refers to U.S. dollars. More likely it indicates pesos, soles, sucres, or cruzados.

HELPFUL TIP: Refer to this city as Rio, *never* as Rio de Janeiro. The longer version is never used by Cariocas and is seldom used in other parts of South America. Rio is enough—and easier to say.

THE CLIMATE OF RIO: Semitropical Rio is warm enough for swimming all year round. In many respects the climate resembles Puerto Rico's. The best period for travelers is April through November, which is the dry winter season when afternoon temperatures hover around 80°. Evenings then are delightfully cool. The summer rainy season (December to March) is only slightly warmer but far more humid. The mercury seldom rises above the mid-80s. Remember that this latter period is vacation time in South America, and Brazilians and other nationals flock to Rio—especially during the frenetic carnival season in February.

LANGUAGE: Portuguese is the national language of Brazil, with Spanish readily understandable, particularly in the south. Many Brazilians understand some English. All hotels have English-speaking staff, and many restaurants have menus in English and Portuguese. The Carioca Portuguese is unique to Rio, and is difficult even for Brazilians from other parts to comprehend totally. If you speak some Spanish, use it!

TELEPHONE: Rio's telephone area code is 021.

1. WHERE TO STAY

Because of inflation, particularly since 1978, the great luxury-hotel bargains once available in Rio have passed from the scene. The $10-a-day air-conditioned double with bath in a five-star hotel is now $150 and up. Nevertheless we've found a good number of acceptable and clean hotels in center city and the nearby beach communities that offer good value at moderate cost. A filling breakfast is an extra bonus at most of our choices.

Tip: For variety, you might consider dividing your stay between a downtown hotel and a beach choice. In this way you experience two distinct aspects of Rio and also learn which suits you best for future visits.

All rates, unless otherwise noted, include a three-course breakfast (cheese, fruit, rolls, and coffee) or a continental breakfast, and the hotel tax. And rates are based on the *official* exchange ratio.

Hotels are rated by the Brazilian government on a star basis from one to five, with five being the top. We have omitted the ratings in this chapter for the most part.

IN CENTER CITY: Undoubtedly the best downtown budget hotel buys are on or near the one-mile stretch of Rio Branco between the Praça Mauá (dock area) and the Praça Mahatma Gandhi near Guanabara Bay. In our listings we'll start at the northside dock area and work south toward the bay.

Hotels Near Praça Mauá (Dock Area)

If you arrive by ship you will dock here. Not far from the plaza is the 300-room **Grande Hotel São Francisco,** Rua Visconde de Inhauma 95, corner of Rio Branco (tel. 021/223-1224), a good big-splurge choice where an enormous breakfast is included in the rate. This clean, 17-story, elevator-equipped hotel charges $37 for huge doubles, with throw rugs, radio, draperies, and spotless private bath. There are a few bathless doubles starting at $27, while singles are a high $34. Air conditioning, a must between December and February, is $5 extra. A first-class restaurant is on the premises. The treat here is breakfast in bed. And what a breakfast! You get a boiled egg with cheese slices; an orange, banana, and a mamão (papaya); rolls and bread with butter and marmalade; and coffee, tea, milk, or hot chocolate. One thrifty traveler we once met here saved the cheese, bread, and fruit for lunch. Breakfast is served until 10 a.m. and all you need to do is pick up your phone and order it. It arrives within ten minutes.

Want an even better value? Walk to the corner of Rio Branco and Presidente Vargas and turn right. Half a block up on your right is a truly outstanding hotel by any standard—the first-class **Guanabara Palace,** Avenida Presidente Vargas 392 (tel. 021/253-8622). This 304-room, 22-story hotel, furnished in old-world style, is comparable to any $50-a-day Paris hotel we've seen. The Guanabara Palace offers large airy doubles, all with private bath and parquet floors, for $30 and up, singles for $25 and up—mammoth breakfast included. Add $8 for each additional bed. Some rooms even have anterooms, and all accommodations come with radios, telephones, bureaus, and large closets. Breakfasts are comparable to those at the São Francisco. Well located within easy walking distance of our recommended shopping streets, this area is relatively quiet at night and not too populated. Morning traffic can, however, be a problem if you have a room facing Avenida Vargas. Although meals are available in the rooms, there is no actual restaurant on the premises.

Our final choice in this area is the **Hotel Center,** at Avenida Rio Branco 33 (tel. 021/296-6677), where roomy doubles are $23; singles, $18.

NEAR "GREENWICH VILLAGE". A favorite of ours in this area is the **Grande Hotel Presidente,** Rua Dom Pedro I 19 (tel. 021/297-0110), which you reach by walking from bustling Largo da Carioca along Rua Carioca until you come to popular Tiradentes Plaza (the "Greenwich Village" of Rio). Turn left for one block, and on your left is the Presidente. This 206-room structure (all rooms have bath and telephone) charges $21 for clean, roomy doubles (with continental breakfast), $19 and up for singles. There are two elevators for the 12 stories, and the handsome lobby is air-conditioned. Most rooms offer splendid views of the hills in and around Rio, including Corcovado, and the accommodations are highlighted by attractive desks, vanity tables, bureaus, and highly polished wood floors. A modern bar, writing room, and barbershop are located off the lobby. This is one of your best choices, with a management extremely eager to please. Most comfortable and recommended.

LOWER-PRICED HOTELS. Three similar choices in this area, on the same street, are the **Hotel Paulistano,** at Rua Visconde do Rio Branco 28 (tel. 021/222-3483); the **Hotel Barão do Rio Branco,** Rua Visconde do Rio Branco 47 (tel. 021/252-9300); and the **Hotel Belas Artes,** at Rua Visconde do Rio Branco 52 (tel. 021/242-1707). Each offers good-value doubles for less than $10, and singles for $7,

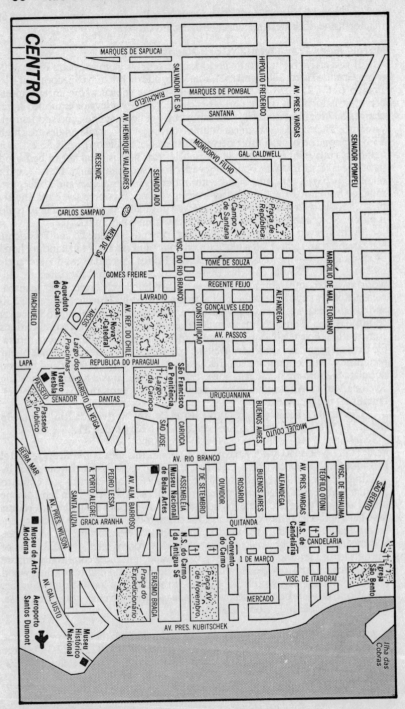

for tidy but sparsely furnished rooms that are ideal for students and others young in spirit.

IN THE SHOPPING AREA. For a much cheaper room in the downtown shopping area, where three meals are an available option, you'll want to consider the 110-room **Hotel Globo,** at Rua dos Andradas 19 (tel. 021/221-6602). While accommodations here are only a cut above the basic, still the $15-per-person charge for a bathless double *with full board* (all three meals) is an unusually good value. Meals are served in the bright 50-table restaurant located just beyond the lobby. Doubles without bath, and with breakfast only (egg, fruit, bread, and coffee), are $12; singles run $10. Remember that this is the heart of the shopping district and there is a good deal of morning traffic, although the nights are quiet.

Hotels Near Praça Mahatma Gandhi

This area, adjacent to a large park and numerous movie theaters (Cinelandia district), is physically the most attractive section of center city. The streets, wide and tree-lined for the most part, are busy with fast-moving traffic. Yet the tempo picks up even more in the evening when the area is thronged with movie-goers; sidewalks are jammed and the section is anything but restful.

We'll begin with one of Rio's best downtown hotels, the handsome **Ambassador,** Rua Senador Dantas 25 (tel. 021/229-9783), half a block from the plaza. Marked by a circular driveway in front and a uniformed doorman, the Ambassador features spotless doubles with private bath, telephone, and radio for $39, singles for $35. Add $5 for air conditioning. While rooms are relatively small, they are most comfortable, with attractive draperies. The bar on the premises, Juca's, is packed with locals most evenings. And the second-floor barbershop is highly recommended.

A more modestly priced selection is the attractive eight-story **Hotel Nelba,** a short walk from the Ambassador at Rua Senador Dantas 46 (tel. 021/262-7002). Here, airy, carpeted doubles, without bath but with a filling breakfast, range from $15; singles begin at $12. Add $4.50 for private bath, $3.50 for air conditioning. Many rooms come with terraces. One of our top budget restaurants, Mon Jardin, is adjacent to the Nelba, and the hotel has an ideal location.

Opposite the Ambassador Hotel is the outstanding 16-story, 180-room **Grande Hotel O.K.,** Rua Senador Dantas 24 (tel. 021/292-4114), where attractive doubles with bath, radio, and generous breakfast are under $28. Singles are a high $21, but for that you get a good-size room. An air conditioner will cost you $2 additional. Although furnishings are well used, and the hotel is starting to show its age, this is still a good value. A bar is off the lobby, and a highlight for guests is the top-floor sundeck which overlooks the bay.

Several hotels are within a few steps of each other on Rua Alvaro Alvim, a small street that runs between Rio Branco and Senador Dantas. The best of the lot is the 180-room **Itajuba,** at Rua Alvaro Alvim 23 (tel. 021/240-9942), which features cozy double rooms with parquet floors and private bath for about $27, singles for $21. While unimpressive from the outside, the 15-story Itajuba is clean and tidy inside. Plush leather chairs and a TV mark the second-floor lobby area. No air conditioning, however—keep that in mind.

Hotels Near Avenida Mem de Sá

While somewhat out of the way, the high-altitude Avenida Mem de Sá section does offer a number of advantages to the traveler. It is, to begin with, somewhat cooler than other center-city sections, and certainly it is quieter. And this district—site of the new cathedral of Rio—has a subdued charm all its own that endears it to many travelers who would not think of staying anywhere else in Rio. To reach the area, walk west from Rio Branco along Avenida do Chile or Avenida Mem de Sá.

Some Cariocas maintain that the hotels here do not compare with other downtown selections. But to our mind there are several outstanding choices here.

Certainly one of the best is the 97-room **Marialva,** Avenida Gomes Freire 430 (tel. 021/221-1187), corner of Avenida do Chile, a new street built through Morro St. Angelo, a hill that was leveled to provide a site for the new cathedral. You start your day at the Marialva with an enormous breakfast of bananas, oranges, bread, fruit, and coffee, which is included in the rate of $19 for a double with bath, $14 for a single. It's a modern hotel, with two elevators serving its 11 floors; rooms are large and bright, with not a speck of dust. Service is excellent, and you will feel right at home immediately. In all, a superb value.

Another favorite of ours is the homey, 113-room **Hotel Bragança,** Avenida Mem de Sá 117 (tel. 021/242-8116), not far from Rua dos Invalidos. If not for its slightly out-of-the-way location, the Bragança would be a "Best Buy." As it is, you'll find the room spotless and extremely cheerful (many come with balconies). The rates make this a good value. Doubles, with bath, telephone, and filling breakfast, are $15, with singles renting for $10. The Bragança's maids are worth a descriptive word or two: garbed in charming blue uniforms and white aprons, and carrying huge featherdusters, these women are invariably pretty, neat, and polite.

A third budget hotel in this vicinity is the white-brick **Hotel Nice,** at Rua Riachuelo 201 (tel. 021/297-1155), with two elevators and 11 floors. You'll find the accommodations light, clean, airy, and quiet. All rooms come with bath, telephone, and relatively new furnishings. Doubles, with breakfast, are $17, and singles run $15. A top-floor sundeck is made inviting by shrubbery and benches. One disadvantage: The hotel is six long blocks from the Cinelandia district.

Finally in this area consider the **Hotel Granada,** at Avenida Gomes Freire 530 (tel. 021/224-6652), a three-star hotel where doubles are a reasonable $20 and singles run $15, continental breakfast included. Rooms are spacious and offer a fine value.

Other Downtown Selections

There are two other choices you should consider downtown. The **Hotel Aeroporto,** on scenic Avenida Beira Mar at no. 280 (tel. 021/262-8922), has comfortable doubles starting at $28. Singles start at $20. The **Hotel Pouso Real,** at Rua do Resende 35 (tel. 021/224-2757), has good-value doubles for as little as $16 (and up) and singles for $12.

An even better choice is the **Hotel Ambassador Santos Dumont,** at Rua Santa Luzia 651 (tel. 021/210-2119), where doubles are a hefty $33; singles, 10% less. But rooms are well appointed and the service first-rate.

If price is a consideration, try the **Pousada Estacio,** at Rua do Bispo 83 (tel. 021/293-3112), where doubles are only $12.

HOTELS NEAR FLAMENGO BEACH: This quiet, elegant beach area, 15 minutes by foot from Praça Mahatma Gandhi, is the home of the world-famous Gloria, a luxury hotel that attracts frequent international conferences. It is also home to several budget hotels, a block or two off the beach. But keep in mind that Flamengo Beach has two minor disadvantages: first, there are few restaurants here, other than in the hotels, and most of these run somewhat high; second, for excursions and sightseeing you'll still have to use center city or Copacabana

Beach as your departure point. Nonetheless, many travelers prefer the quiet evenings of Flamengo Beach and the splendid beaches.

The best hotel near the beach, apart from the Gloria, is the first-class, 240-room **Grande Hotel Novo Mundo,** Praia do Flamengo 20 (tel. 021/225-7366), facing the sea and not far from the Gloria and the Museum of the Republic. Here, large air-conditioned doubles, with modern furnishings, bath, telephone, and full breakfast, run $36 and up, while singles are $32 and up. For an enchanting interlude, gaze at Sugarloaf Mountain and the surrounding beaches and giant palm trees from in front of the hotel at twilight. After you've forgotten much else about your travels, you will recall those sights. The 12-story Novo Mundo features a North American–style bar and restaurant, barbershop, and beauty salon.

A cut below the Novo Mundo, but a truer budget buy, is the handsome 130-room **Regina Hotel,** Rua Ferreira Viana 29 (tel. 021/225-7280), where attractive airy doubles, with modern furnishings, bath, and breakfast, range from $30. Small, comfortable singles are $25, and triples are $36. Located less than a block from the beachfront, this six-story hotel is carefully maintained and service is outstanding. Breakfast is served in the top-floor dining room.

Note: Rue Ferreira Viana houses five of our hotel selections as well as numerous high-priced apartment houses.

Another fine first-class hotel is the 200-room **Florida,** located down the block from the Regina at Rue Ferreira Viana 81 (tel. 021/245-8160). Roomy doubles, with private tiled bath, parquet floors, and man-size breakfast, are a good value here for under $20. Singles run from $15, and triples are $26. An intimate bar and TV room are situated off the spacious lobby where red-jacketed bellhops abound. Four elevators service the seven floors, and the rooms, as you might expect, are modern and bright. Worth checking.

Partial to a newer hotel? Then definitely consider the well-regarded **Hotel Flamengo Palace,** Praia do Flamengo 6 (tel. 021/205-1552), a 60-room, 15-floor hotel that opened its doors in 1974. Doubles are under $35 and singles for around $30, and these rates include air conditioning, TV, refrigerator, and telephone. A coffeeshop is on the premises.

The **Imperial Hotel,** at Rua do Catete 186 (tel. 021/205-0212), offers 58 air-conditioned rooms with modern furnishings and piped-in music for $22 double, $18 single. Free parking and TV are bonuses.

Another highly regarded choice would be the 40-room **Hotel Inglês,** just up from Novo Mundo at Rua Silveira Martins 20 (tel. 021/265-9052 or 265-7797). Small, comfortable doubles, with polished wood floors and large closets, range from $20 (rear room) to $25 (front), all with private bath and continental breakfast. Singles cost $16. Most rooms come with circular floor fans, some with private terraces. It's a good value, especially since off-season rates are a third cheaper.

Back on Rua Ferreira Viana, at no. 58, opposite the Florida, is a good budget choice, the 32-room **Ferreira Viana** (tel. 021/205-7396 or 205-7840), which offers clean doubles, without bath but with light breakfast, for only $12, and singles for $8. Rooms, while plainly furnished, are tidy. Add $3 for private bath.

A rather basic choice on this street, opposite the Regina, is the 12-room **Antabi,** at no. 20 (tel. 021/265-6070), where the eight rooms are small but neat and the breakfast unusually generous. Bathless doubles, plainly furnished, run $11, and singles, $6; doubles with bath go for $14. A guest bonus is free transportation from the airport—if you have advance reservations. A station wagon is available to groups at reduced rates.

ON RUA CORREIA DUTRA. Three final and equally plain choices are on Rua Correia

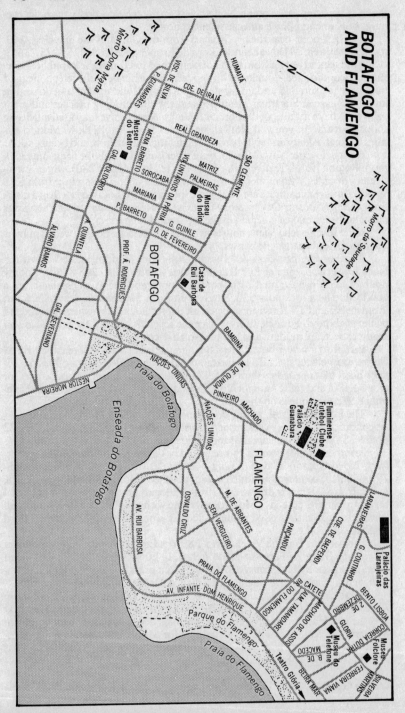

Dutra, within a block of Praia do Flamengo (beachfront), one block from Rua Ferreira Viana. Best of the trio is the **Hotel Mengo,** at no. 31 (tel. 021/225-5911), where clean doubles with bath, bidet, and breakfast will run you $14; bathless doubles are $10 and singles run $9. The rooms with bath have showers rather than tubs, and there is no elevator here. The floors are bare wood—notice how clean they are.

The other two are the **Hotel Cambuquira,** at no. 19 (tel. 021/245-4323), and the **Hotel Caxambu,** at no. 22 (tel. 021/265-9496). Neither serves breakfast. The 32-room Cambuquira charges $15 for doubles with bath, $10 for singles, while bathless doubles are $10, and singles, $7. The sparsely furnished rooms are quite small. A narrow staircase leads to the second-floor lobby. More attractive is the Caxambu, across the street. Doubles with bath are $15, and singles, $10; bathless singles are $7. This 35-room, two-story hotel is clean and well maintained. Adjoining the lobby is an outdoor covered courtyard with several highback chairs for guests. Two parakeets and fish brighten the lobby. Good value.

Big Splurge

We would be remiss if we failed to describe the 700-room **Hotel Gloria,** Rua do Russel 632 (tel. 021/205-7272), one of the best-known hotels in all South America. The décor is classic throughout, and the lobby and the rooms are smartly furnished in traditional style. Many rooms overlook the bay. The kidney-shaped swimming pool is popular all year round with guests, who seem to prefer it to the nearby beach. On the premises are a drugstore, beauty salon, barbershop, and sumptuous bar and restaurant.

Rates, of course, are high. Occasionally you can get a non-air-conditioned double for $70, although most doubles range from $80 per day; singles run $60 and up. All rates include breakfast, served in your room or in the plush dining room.

Make it a point to stroll through the lobby and pick up maps, brochures, and car-rental and excursion information. You can buy U.S. cigarettes here—not easy to find in Rio. There is a coffeeshop on the premises. Technically the Gloria, within walking distance of the Praça Mahatma Gandhi, is not in Flamengo but in the adjoining community of Gloria. Still, most Cariocas consider the hotel the starting point of Flamengo, so we shall too.

Additional Budget Choices

Three lower-priced hotels you should consider are located near each other in Flamengo. The **Hotel Paysandu,** at Rua Paysandu 23 (tel. 021/225-7270), spreads 75 rooms over its seven floors and offers them at $20 double and $17 single, all with bath, air conditioning, and telephone. Look for the colorful canopy outside. Across the street is the basic **Hotel Venezuela,** at Paysandu 34 (tel. 021/205-2098), where doubles are $15. Despite the attractive exterior, keep in mind that the rooms are quite basic.

Nearby, at Rua Cruz Lima 30, is the five-floor **Hotel Argentina** (tel. 021/225-7233), a 71-room choice where doubles are $26. The Argentina is located on a small street off the main drag, and bath and air conditioning are standard.

Another selection of ours is the **Hotel Serrano,** at Rua Gago Coutinho 22 (tel. 021/285-3233), where doubles are only $17, for which you get a sparsely furnished room, breakfast, good service, and convenient location.

HOTELS NEAR COPACABANA BEACH: The hub of Rio, Copacabana
Beach is lined with high-priced private homes, apartment buildings, and of

course, luxury hotels. The question is obvious: In this setting are there any acceptable budget hotels? We have been told flatly by several well-traveled Cariocas in downtown Rio not to waste our time trudging the streets of Copacabana Beach. "You will find expensive hotels and unlivable hotels—that's all," one center-city hotel manager told us. Nonsense—we've uncovered half a dozen clean, perfectly livable budget hotels in this community of 400,000, bounded on one side by the mountains, on the other by the ocean.

The key rule here is to avoid the beachfront (Avenida Atlântica), and concentrate on streets a block or two from the water.

Note: Copacabana Beach is only 20 minutes from center city by bus, which you can catch at Rio Branco and Presidente Vargas, or at Praça Mahatma Gandhi.

One additional point: Copacabana and Rio's other beach communities are packed in the Brazilian summer (December to February), only moderately crowded the balance of the year. We prefer coming here between April and October, when the humidity is lower and hotel rooms are more easily available.

Now for our selections:

We'll begin with a favorite nonluxury hotel in Copacabana Beach—the 63-room **Hotel Canada,** Avenida Copacabana 687 (tel. 021/257-1864), near Rua Santa Clara. This first-class hotel—spotted by its awning outside—has cheerful doubles with private tile bath and breakfast for $27 and up, and singles for $21 and up. Two elevators service the ten floors, and the rooms are brightened by print bedspreads and piped-in music. If you're a late sleeper, ask for a room that doesn't front on traffic-jammed Avenida Copacabana. The desk clerks, who speak some English, are eager to offer dining and nightclub suggestions within budget limits.

Equally attractive and well regarded is the impressive 50-room **Hotel APA** (pronounced "ahpa"), at Rua República do Peru 305, corner of Copacabana (tel. 021/255-8112). Handsome inside and out, the seven-story APA features rooms with red linoleum floors and rather startling black-tile bathrooms—most comfortable. Doubles, with radio, telephone, club chairs, huge closets, and of course, bath, run $33, and that includes a filling breakfast. Triples are $38. Air conditioning will cost you an extra $3, and in summer (December to February) is well worth it.

Bedrooms large enough to serve as sitting rooms can be found at the **Hotel Castro Alves,** Avenida Copacabana 552 (tel. 021/257-1800), corner of Rua Sequeira Campos. Another highly recommended choice, the 78-room Alves has two elevators servicing its 12 stories. Accommodations feature large private bathrooms with separate shower stall, wall-to-wall draperies over the windows, a writing table, bureau, and twin beds. Doubles with breakfast start at about $47 and singles at $41. If it were located on the beachfront the Alves's rates would run much higher, as is true for its sister hotels on Avenida Atlântica—the Olinda, Lancaster, California, Trocadero, and Leme Palace, all under the same management.

At the 60-room **Toledo Hotel,** Rua Domingos Ferreira 71 (tel. 021/257-1990), a half block from the beach near Santa Clara, the 48 doubles rent for under $30, the 12 singles for $25, breakfast included. The manager, Antoine Georges Albanakis, is of French extraction and speaks seven languages including English. You will find him a wonderful host, spilling over with sightseeing tips and restaurant suggestions. The rooms are large and comfortable. *Note:* Rua Domingos Ferreira is a small street—between Avenidas Copacabana and Atlântica.

Our final recommendation in this category is the 22-room **Hotel Praia Leme,** on the beach at Avenida Atlântica 866 (tel. 021/275-3322). First-class doubles start at $25 and range up to $35. Singles start under $20. Service is excellent.

Less Expensive Choices in Copacabana

The best true budget buy here is probably the 30-room **Hotel Copa Linda,** Copacabana 956 (tel. 021/255-0938), near Rua Bolívar, where doubles, without bath but with breakfast, will run you $20, and singles, $14. While rooms are small they are relatively tidy, and each has a sink and mirror. You can't miss the Copa Linda—it's opposite the Cine Roxi cinema.

Most maps do not list a tiny street called Travessa Angrense, located off Copacabana (heading away from the beach) between Santa Clara and Raimundo Correa. At the end of this narrow street, at no. 25, is the 33-room **Hotel Angrense** (tel. 021/255-0509), a three-story walkup. Bathless doubles, with breakfast, are $21, and singles are $14; a few with-bath rooms are available at higher rates. While accommodations are only a shade above the basic, still the Angrense is unusually quiet for Rio, due to its location. Some rooms come with terrace. Definitely worth considering.

Probably the best hotel in this category is the **Praia Lido,** at Avenida Copacabana 202 (tel. 021/541-2097), where all rooms include air conditioning, radio, and TV. The 50 rooms are spread over six floors and doubles are $40, while singles cost $35. Breakfast is included in the rate. Head up one flight to the usually crowded lobby.

Lower in price, and service, is the **Martinique Hotel,** at Rua Sá Ferreira 30 (tel. 021/521-4552). A rather old hotel, no better than basic, the 44 rooms are sparsely furnished and rent for $30 double, $21 single.

Behind the deluxe Othon Palace Hotel on Copacabana Beach is the 29-room, ten-floor **Biarritz Hotel,** at Rua Aires Saldanha 56 (tel. 021/255-6552). All rooms are air-conditioned; the rates are a steep $30 double, $27 single.

A 17-room hotel with an unfortunately gloomy entrance stairway is **Hotel Copamar,** Rua Santa Clara 116 (tel. 021/237-8382), half a block from Avenida Copacabana (away from the beach). Attractive doubles are $45 and singles run $36, including bath and continental breakfast. One advantage: The Copamar is located a few steps from Rio's fine budget luncheonette—the Arosa (see below).

The parade of hotels in this category continues. A popular choice is the **Hotel Acapulco,** Rua Gustavo Sampaio 854 (tel. 021/275-0022), where spacious doubles are $38; singles, $34. Less expensive is the **Hotel Bandeirante,** Rua Barata Ribeiro 548 (tel. 021/255-6252), two blocks from the beach, where doubles are $37. A three-star selection near the Meridien is **Hotel Rio Copa,** Avenida Princesa Isabel 370 (tel. 021/275-6644), with doubles in the $40 range.

Other Splurge Choices in Copacabana

The **Hotel Astoria,** Rua República do Peru 340 (tel. 021/257-8080), opened in July 1974. For the prices of $39 double and $27 single, guests are entitled to air conditioning, refrigerator, music, and TV. Next to the Hotel APA.

Coming from center city, the first major street in Copacabana you reach is Princesa Isabel, and at no. 263 is the top-notch **Plaza Copacabana Hotel** (tel. 021/275-7722), which offers doubles for $45, with breakfast and bath. This huge (220 rooms spread over 17 floors) hotel features wall-to-wall carpeting, vanity tables, club chairs, air conditioning, and tile bath in all rooms. The mammoth lobby is a showplace, with plush sofas, deep chairs, and pile carpeting in a sunken area. Cocktails are served from a bar tucked discreetly in the rear.

Back now to the beachfront, where you'll find the **Hotel Riviera** at Avenida Atlântica 4122 (tel. 021/247-6060). It has some doubles for $45; others are

$55. Singles start at $35. Most rooms cost more, though. Write ahead and ask to reserve one of the "cheaper" rooms.

HOTELS IN IPANEMA AND LEBLON: There are three hotels in this area under the same management, all offering uniformly excellent accommodations with fine service. All, too, are a couple of blocks from the beach, and all are similar in appearance. The **Hotel Vermont,** at Rua Visconde de Pirajá 254 (tel. 021/ 521-0057), charges $30 and up for carpeted, air-conditioned doubles, $23 for singles. A few blocks away is the 56-room **Hotel San Marco,** at Rua Visconde de Pirajá 524 (tel. 021/239-5032), which charges about the same as the Vermont. In Leblon, try the 46-room **Hotel Carlton,** Rua João Lira 68 (tel. 021/259-1932). Which one to choose? Doesn't really matter. Remember, though, that Leblon is farther away from Rio's center than Ipanema.

Two other hotels in Ipanema under the same management are the **Arpoador Inn,** at Rua Francisco Otaviano 177 (tel. 021/247-6090), and the **Ipanema Inn,** at Rua Maria Quiteria 27 (tel. 021/287-6092). Located at the beginning of Ipanema just off the beach, the quaint (50 rooms) Arpoador features air conditioning, refrigerator, piped-in music, and comfortable rooms with bath. The newer Ipanema Inn (opened in 1976) is similar, and boasts a pool. Prices for doubles start in the $40 range. Good choices.

YOUTH HOSTELS: Youth Hostels aren't necessarily for "young" travelers only, although it does help to be young in spirit. They are far cheaper than hotels and pensions. Plus, staying in a hostel is a great way to meet other travelers.

There are five hostels scattered throughout Rio. The **Albergue da Juventude Bello** in Gloria is at Rua Santo Amaro 162 (tel. 021/222-8576); the **Albergue da Juventude Copacabana** in Copacabana is at Rua Emilio Berla 41 (tel. 021/236-6472). Then there is the **Casa do Estudante do Brasil,** on the Praça Ana Amelia 9 in Castelo (tel. 021/220-7123 or 220-7223); the **Pousada do Garuda,** at Rua Almirante Alexandrino 2840 in Santa Teresa (tel. 021/225-0393 or 326-1419); and finally the **Albergue da Juventude Barra Sol,** at Avenida Grande Canal 301 in Barra (tel. 021/399-0659).

Young people of all ages who are planning to stay in hostels when traveling abroad would do well to contact the youth hostel organization in their own countries first for membership and information on travel benefits available. In the U.S. it's the **American Youth Hostels Association,** in Delaplane, VA 22025 (tel. 703/592-3271). Members of the Federation of International Youth Travel Organizations can contact **International House,** Rua Visconde de Caravales 1, Botafogo (tel. 021/266-0890).

RESIDENTIAL HOTELS: Rio has several decent apartment hotels which a family or group of three to six people might consider. A good choice is **Apart-Hotel,** at Rua Barata Ribeiro 370 (tel. 021/256-2633) in Copacabana. All 70 apartments have their own cooking units. In Leblon the larger **Rio Flat Service,** at Rua Alm. Guilhem 332 (tel. 021/274-7222), has 103 apartments with kitchen facilities holding two to four guests. Rates at both are about $200 per week. If they're not busy you might negotiate a daily rate, but minimum stay is normally one week.

2. DINING IN RIO

Rio has an abundance of inexpensive U.S.–style snackshops ideal for quick lunches and late-afternoon coffee and pastry. At those we have selected, you will find the food tastefully prepared, the service efficient, and the prices well within our budget limits.

Cariocas, you should know, generally eat a heavy breakfast, a light lunch between noon and 2 p.m., a late-afternoon tidbit between 4 and 6 p.m., and dinner quite late by U.S. standards.

Food specialties vary from state to state in this mammoth country, which is larger than the continental U.S., but there are three dishes and one alcoholic drink that are universally popular.

One specialty is the **frango com arroz,** which is boned chicken and rice mixed with chopped olives, hard-boiled eggs, green peas, and other vegetables. Then there's **churrasco,** beef steak grilled over an open fire. A variation of this is **bife de panela,** a thin steak grilled with onions and tomatoes. A much tangier dish is **feijoada,** black beans and rice cooked with sausage or tongue, bacon, tomatoes, onions, and hot spices. And that ever-popular drink is **batida,** a potent sugarcane extract served in fruit juice. Ultra-sweet, this beverage has a kick, so watch it!

Tips: It is perfectly acceptable in Rio for two people to share one order, so if you're not too hungry, or short of cash, tell the waiter to bring one main dish and two settings.

Many restaurants charge a "couvert," a cover (which might include celery, cucumber, radishes, quail eggs, etc.). Prices range from $1 to $3 per person. To save this charge, tell the waiter "No couvert, please."

MEALS IN CENTER CITY: We'll first review the snackshops of Rio (where you'll want to have lunch), then move on to the full-fledged restaurants (for dinner).

The Snack Places

A chain of ten stand-up snackbars called **Bob's** are scattered throughout downtown Rio. Convenient for shoppers is the one on Rua São José in Largo da Carioca, a park-like plaza in the shopping district. The branches we've seen are all spotless and tidy, the waiters polite, and the service rapid. Resembling the Chock Full O'Nuts chain, Bob's has good burgers for under $1 and thick milkshakes for 90¢. Ham and eggs will cost you $1.25. The chain, originally owned by Bob Falkenberg, brother of show-business personality Jinx Falkenberg, also does a booming take-out service for lunch.

In the Praça Mauá area, try the small but clean **Lanches Cerejinha,** on Presidente Vargas and Uruguaiana, near the Guanabara Palace Hotel. Fried shrimp is recommended here, and sandwiches all cost under $2.

Nearby is the much larger **Insalata,** Rio Branco and Rua Inhauma, opposite the São Francisco Hotel. Counter service only. In this eatery you pay first and order later. We enjoy the ham and eggs here at $1, and the ice cream is as good as any we've found outside Italy and the U.S. Try an ice-cream cone (sorvete) for 50¢. Hot dogs (60¢), served with tomato and relish, are also quite tasty.

Lunch and Dinner Restaurants

What follows now are the "real" restaurants of downtown Rio, each with extensive menus and table service only.

We'll begin with the small **Leiteria Mineira,** Ruada Ajuda 35A, a block and a half east of Rio Branco (away from Largo da Carioca), recommended to us by no less a figure than the former secretary of tourism. He says he eats lunch here regularly. The restaurant is spotless and the jacketed waiters are prompt with bread, butter, and water. The "Sugestões do Dia" (suggestions of the day) on the upper left-hand side of the menu are your best bets: platter prices rarely exceed $5. Or try the risoto de frango, a chicken dish that's an inexpensive $2.50, the fish stew for $2.25, and the steak dishes, about $4. The chef of this 50-year-old restaurant

—open from 8 a.m. to 8 p.m. every day except Sunday—heartily recommends a Brazilian dish called tutu a mineira, made of beans mixed with manioc flour and served with pork chops. Recommended, too, is the camarão com arroz (shrimp and rice) for $3.50.

For the best in Bahian food (at moderate prices) head for **Oxalá,** downtown at Rua Alvaro Alvim 36A, inside the gallery in Cinelandia. By all means try any of the numerous shrimp dishes ($5 to $8). Air-conditioned, usually crowded, and not known for its décor, the Oxalá offers true value for your cruzado.

If you enjoy beer with your meals, by all means try the **Restaurant Cervejaria Capelão,** Rua Senador Dantas 84, decorated like a beer hall, with wood-paneled walls and garden complete with waterfall. The $3.50 daily menu usually includes beer, dessert, and a large main course (fish or meat). À la carte fish dishes range from $1.75 to $3.25. It's not plush, but the service is good and the atmosphere just fine. Highly recommended for lunch.

For a tavern-like setting, you can head for the **Taberna Azul,** Rua Senador Dantas at Praça Mahatma Gandhi. Here you can try the $4 fixed-price four-course lunch; it might include frango, a potato or rice dish, a beverage, and dessert. Wood-paneled lanterns, clothed tables, and well-dressed waiters add to the décor. Look for the chicken grilling in the window.

For superb steaks, roast beef, or feijoada at moderate prices, head directly for **Churrascolandia** ("Steak Land"), located opposite the Nelba Hotel at Senador Dantas 31, near Praça Mahatma Gandhi. You pass a number of beer barrels serving as tables in the bar area and enter the attractive dining room. Popular dishes include feijoada completa ($5), roast beef with potato and salad ($4.50), and the churrasquito with rice ($3.50). Chicken dishes are available too, and many customers partake of the take-out service.

For some of the best chicken in Rio, try the **Chicken House,** located in the shopping district at Rua Miguel Couto 36, which is a small street between Rio Branco and Gonçalves Dias. Open until 10 p.m., the Chicken House features a large rôtisserie filled with chicken quarters in the window. Chicken dishes, listed in the upper right-hand corner of the menu, range in price from $2.50 to $5, with the other daily specials going for the same price. If you're on a tight budget, consider the egg platters for $1.50 and up. Brightening the décor here are the pert, yellow-uniformed waitresses. Recommended.

If Italian food is a favorite of yours, as it is with us, then try **Paisano,** Avenida Rio Branco near Avenida Presidente Wilson, next to the SAS office. A lunch special for $3 is noted in the window each day, and it includes a main dish such as lasagne, ravioli, or gnocchi, plus dessert. À la carte prices range from $2 to $5 per dish, and quality is generally high.

Spaghettilandia, opposite the Hotel Itajuba near Cinelandia, serves excellent spaghetti dishes. Try the cannelloni and ravioli dishes too. Table or counter service.

Pizza? At **Pizzalandia,** Rua Senador Dantas 23A, heading away from the plaza, you can get a pie with the works—sausage pieces, anchovies, and other goodies for around $3. Or try **Mister Pizza,** on Rua 13 de Maio near the Teatro Municipal. Here, $1.50 will get you a pizza, hot dog, sandwich, or salad. Beer and fruit juices are available too.

A Special Luncheon Treat

You owe it to yourself to have one lunch at the **Café do Teatro,** located in the Teatro Municipal (theater-opera house) on Avenida Rio Branco (tel. 262-6322). The restaurant replaced the theatrical museum previously here. The tiled walls and columns resemble a scene from *Aïda.*

Open from noon to 3 p.m. Monday through Friday, the restaurant serves a fixed-price $10 four-course luncheon, including soft drinks or beer. But come here for the atmosphere, casually elegant and relaxing. Some 200 diners, mostly businessmen, crowd into this popular luncheon retreat.

Vegetarian Choices

In the heart of the downtown area is a favorite vegetarian choice, aptly named **Restaurante Vegetariano Green,** at Rua do Carmo 38 (tel. 252-5356). Head up one flight for a self-service delight in the vegetarian tradition. Start with a nonalcoholic drink, then choose a salad, fruit juice, soup, a hot plate (rice, vegetables, etc.), and dessert—the whole meal will cost under $3 total.

You should also consider **Health's,** at Rua Beneditinos 18, near Praça Mauá and on Rua Senador Dantas, downtown.

If you are spending the day at the beach, you may want to try **Dietas e Delícias,** Ataulfo de Paiva 196 in Leblon. **Natural,** at Barrao da Torre 171 in Ipanema, is another good choice.

Some Final Choices

A wonderful churrascaria downtown is **Cruzeiro do Sul,** at Rua do Riachuelo 19. You can stuff yourself here for $3. If German cuisine is on your mind, head to the **Bar Luíz,** at Rua da Carioca 39. It's not fancy, not expensive, but good.

A restaurant with excellent German dishes is **Ficha,** at Rua Teofilo Ottoni 126, near the Praça Mauá, where tables are a rare commodity at lunchtime. Check out the daily specials.

In the shopping district at Rua do Ouvidor 14 is **Esquina-Sabor Brasil,** where a couple can dine in comfortable surroundings for less than $10.

Confeitarias

A late-afternoon tradition in Rio is the tea and cocktail hour, a rite celebrated in establishments known as confeitarias, loosely translated as confectionery shops. The better ones remind us of old-world European cafés where one sips coffee, nibbles a pastry, and observes what's going on at the next table.

The most elegant confeitaria in Rio is the huge **Colombo,** Rua Gonçalves Dias 36, near Rua 7 de Setembro—really stunning. Large, old chandeliers dangle from the high ceilings, and enormous breakfronts, filled with odd-shaped liquor bottles, line the sides. Smartly jacketed waiters scurry about the block-long dining room and the second-floor balcony catering to sophisticated matrons simply exhausted after a day of shopping. Well-dressed men who look as if they just arrived from Madison Avenue make up another sizable customer segment. Strains of Portuguese, Spanish, French, and English waft about you as you thread your way through the ever-crowded dining room looking for your table. At last you are seated—and within minutes a tray loaded with tarts, napoleons, eclairs, and other pastries is placed before you by quick-as-a-cat waiters. Order coffee, tea, or a cocktail and prepare to relax for an hour or two in an atmosphere reminiscent of Vienna. Surprisingly, prices are quite low—if you avoid the regular menu. We recently paid $3 for four pastries and two pots of coffee. (You are charged for what you eat from the pastry tray, which is left on the table.) Some hot dishes on the menu are also reasonably priced. If you're in a hurry, try some stand-up empanadas, croquettes, and a soft drink.

Note: A sister confeitaria—same name—is in Copacabana Beach, Avenida Copacabana 890.

One other attractive confeitaria is the **Casa Cave,** corner of Uruguaiana and

7 de Setembro. It resembles an old-fashioned U.S. ice-cream parlor, but the pastries are pure Rio. Prices are a cut below the Colombo, and the take-out shop on the premises is invariably crowded. Most enjoyable.

DINING IN FLAMENGO: There are few acceptably priced restaurants for you to consider in this area. However, if you are staying here, you might stop at **Aurora** in Botafogo at Rua Capitão Salomão 43, at corner of Rua Visconde de Caravelas. A hangout for artists, this eatery was suggested to us by an executive of Varig who eats here regularly. The menu is varied and the prices are low.

A good churrascaria in this area is **Parque Recreio**, at Rua Marquês de Abrantes 92 (Flamengo). Usually crowded (especially on weekends), the meat is tasty and prices are reasonable.

Another popular spot in Botafogo is **Bismarque**, at Rue São Clemente 24. Enter through the swinging bar, passing the counter stand-up service area, and enter the small restaurant in the rear. Daily specials such as badejo frito at $4, or liver with onions at $3, are usually generous in size.

In this area, too, are **Janina**, at Rua Senador Correia 10, near Praça São Salvador, where you can dine for about $4 including dessert; and **Amazónia**, at Rua do Catete 234, which is even cheaper. Fine steaks are available at the churrascaria **Majorica**, Rua Senador Verqueiro, nearby.

Probably your best bet in Botafogo is **Gosto Bom**, situated in a private house at Rua Teresa Guimarões 62, a quiet block. Popular with students and student-types, the daily specials (about $4) might include bacalhau or even feijoada. The high ceilings and tile floors add to the décor.

A landmark in this area is the 110-year-old **Café Lamas**, at Rua Marquês de Abrantes 18 in Flamengo. It's open until 4 a.m., and usually packed. On our last visit we stopped in on a Tuesday night at 2 a.m. and had to wait for a table. The carne assado at $3 is a good buy, as is the perú (turkey) with rice at $2.50.

Nearby is the **Taberna da Gloria**, at Rua do Russel 32, a bar and pizzeria. Frango dishes ($3) are popular too. You can choose between indoor (air-conditioned) or outdoor tables. Open late.

The most American bar and grill in Rio, **Neal's**, at Rua Sorocaba 695 in Botafogo, offers good barbecued ribs and hamburgers, as well as videos on both levels. Photos of celebrities and Broadway show posters decorate the walls. For all its New York glamour, Neal's, situated in a private house, has intimacy. We were very happy with the oven-roasted chicken, the shrimp, and the ribs. There is a Neal, and he hails from Canada.

A Big Splurge

By far your best scenic dining spot in this area is **Rio's**, in Parque do Flamengo on the bay. It's part of a complex that includes a disco, bar-restaurant, and outdoor snack area. The restaurant offers great views of Sugarloaf, Guanabara Bay, and the yacht club. Chicken dishes run $8, fish is about $10, and meat dishes, about $12. The restaurant is located between Botafogo and Flamengo Park on the right as you head downtown. Look for the conical pyramid as a landmark.

DINING IN COPACABANA BEACH: Despite this area's reputation for high prices, there are a number of budget choices well within our limits. First the snackshops, then the dinner restaurants.

Snackshops

The best-value all-around eatery in the Rio area is the counter-only **Arosa Lanchonette,** located at Santa Clara 110, near Barata Ribeiro, where you can get a filling fixed-price lunch (or dinner) for $5 and up. Open daily from 11 a.m. to midnight, the Arosa offers one-price selections from three columns—including one hot dish (such as chicken or beef), three side dishes (vegetables and salads), dessert, and beverage (you may even choose an excellent Brazilian beer at no extra cost). Packed with shop and office workers at lunchtime, the Arosa also features numerous pizza selections ($1.75 and up), and a lengthy sandwich list. Portions are absurdly large and the place is immaculate. Unbeatable values.

Another highly recommended Arosa-type eatery is **Michel's,** on Avenida Copacabana at Rua Sara Kubitschek. Prices are similar to Arosa's, and sandwiches here range from $1.50 to $2.50. Remember, counter service is the rule here, although there are a few tables.

Copacabana has several fast-service stand-up eateries similar to Bob's downtown. Favorites of ours are **Boninos,** on Avenida Copacabana near Rua Bolívar; **Bonis,** on Avenida Copacabana near Rua Siqueira Campos; and **Gordon,** near the Bonis and famous for its crêpes. In each, purchase a ticket before you order.

For tasty burgers, sandwiches, and inexpensive meat platters, try **Top Top** at Rua C. Ramos near Avenida Atlântica. Look for the large orange sign.

Nearby at the Woolworth-type **Lojas Americanas,** one can enjoy inexpensive dishes at the counter. Sandwiches start at 75¢; beef dishes range from $3 to $5; a soft drink will cost you 25¢.

Other good choices nearby are **Adega Perola,** Rua Siqueira Campos 135; **Cervantes,** Rua Prado Júnior 335; and **Cupim Minas,** at Avenida Copacabana 895. All are similar in menu and décor.

Note: We haven't made breakfast recommendations for good reason—virtually all hotels include this meal in their room rate.

The Dinner Restaurants

Our favorite dinner restaurant in this category in Copacabana is the huge—and invariably jammed—**Churrascaria Jardim,** Rua República do Perú 225, a few steps off Avenida Copacabana walking away from the beach. No fewer than four chefs grill the wonderful steaks and chops on a blazing hearth at the left side of this beef oasis.

Don't be misled by the exterior, which resembles a private home. To the left outside is a walkway covered by a canopy of branches, leaves, and lanterns. Part of the dining area is outside and covered by the same natural "ceiling"; the other half is indoors. (In the evening the outdoor area is quite romantic, but you might feel a sprinkle or two should it rain.)

The dishes here come close to equaling a good Argentine parrillada, and there's no higher compliment than that. Co-owners Eugene Gudman (Hungarian) and James Brager (German) are justifiably proud of their filet mignon platters ($5) and mixed grill ($7). Vegetables are an extra 70¢ per portion. Most tempting, too, are the superb maminha de alcatra (baby beef) for $6, and the cordeira (lamb) for $4. Incidentally, the mixed grill (churrasco mixto a Jardim), a house specialty, is a feast of steak, liver, and sausages. It's enough for two. Domestic wines are only $3 per bottle. Open from noon to 1 a.m., seven days a week, the Jardim attracts a cosmopolitan crowd—both the well-dressed and the casual beach weekender. Highly recommended.

For perhaps the largest T-bone steak served anywhere in Rio, you might like to try the **Rian,** located just off the beach at Rua Santa Clara 8A. On our last visit the T-bone steak spilled over the plate and was easily enough for two. The price: $7. Actually noted for its Italian food, the Rian offers outstanding pizzas ($2 to $4); also recommended is the shrimp en brochette with Brazilian rice ($6), called brochettes de camarão com arroz a grega. Small and cozy, the Rian has a good wine and liquor stock too.

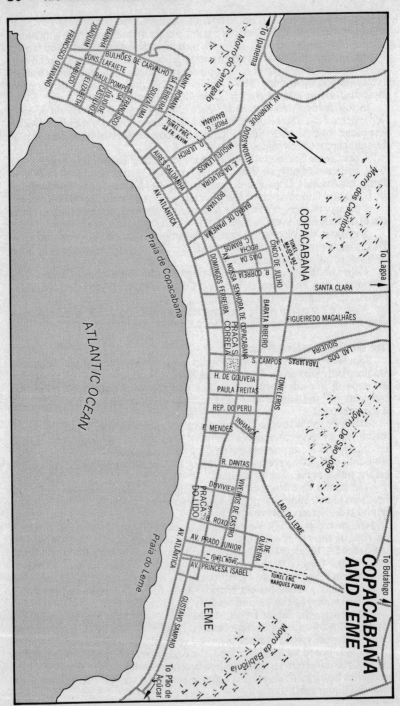

COPACABANA AND LEME

One of the local churrascaria favorites is **Márius,** in Leme on the beachfront Avenida Atlântica 290. Here for $8 you can enjoy an endless supply (all you can eat) of sausage, chicken, turkey, and steak, tomato, salad, heart of palm, and potato salad. Empty liquor bottles line the wall of this bilevel eatery. It's open from 11 a.m. to midnight, and you'll enjoy this place.

If scenic outdoor dining is your cup of café, then the bayfront **Mondego,** Avenida Atlântica 2936 at Rua Constante Ramos, where you can dine at an outdoor table on a raised platform overlooking the beach, will attract you. The Mondego is best for light dancing. The grilled meat sandwiches ($3) are good values, as are the pizza dishes. The atmosphere is leisurely, and bathing suits are commonplace during the afternoon, so feel free.

Seafood fans should try the **Restaurante a Marisqueira,** Barata Ribeiro 232, off Rua República do Perú near the Uruguay Hotel, where the house specialty is peixe frito a marisqueira (fried fish filet) for $6.

A brother-and-sister team, René and Irene Brulhart, are currently the talk of Copacabana with their fine Swiss and French cuisine at **Le Mazot.** Located at Rua Paula Freitas 31, it's a classy, though small, dinner club with both outdoor and indoor dining. Any of the blue-jacketed waiters will tell you that the fondue bourguignonne ($7) is a superb delicacy. We heartily concur, but we enjoy the filet de sole meunière ($6) almost as much. Frequently jammed in the evening, Le Mazot would be a good lunch choice; it opens at noon and closes at 1 a.m. The 90¢ cover and 10% service charge boost the prices somewhat, so if you're watching your pennies, watch carefully.

How about a Polish restaurant? Well, the **Restaurante A Poloneza,** on Rua Helário de Gouveia in Copacabana, is a good choice. A small eatery owned by a Polish woman, it serves the best beef Stroganoff ($6) this side of the Amazon. This is a family-run restaurant; the cook and waiters are all related.

Also recommended highly is the **Restaurante Oriento,** on Avenida Copacabana at Rua Bolívar. Head up one flight. The soups (enough for three) are delicious and cost only $3.

For fine steaks at bargain prices, try **Churrascaria Copacabana,** at Avenida Copacabana 1144 near Alm. Gonçalves. Fine baby beef is only $5; filet mignon is $6; and delicious galeto (baby chicken), $4. Attractive mirrors and red-brick walls brighten the surroundings.

More attractive, and sporting slightly higher steak prices, is **Churrascaria Beliscão,** on Rua Siqueira Campos off Avenida Atlântica. Recommended are rump steak (alcatre; for $6), churrasco, and frango desassado (boneless chicken). A mixed-grill barbecue is $8. Note the electric-eye sliding entrance door.

Finally there's the **Restaurant Moenda,** Avenida Atlântica 2064. The muqueca de peixe at $9 is a must. A bonus here is the scenic view. A $1 cover charge puts Moenda in the splurge category. Try it—if you're willing to pay the tab.

A popular hangout is **La Mole,** at Avenida Copacabana 552 next to the Castro Alves Hotel. Here, the massas (pasta) dishes at $2 are in demand. The steak ao pouvre ($3) is delicious. The branch in Leblon, at Rua Dias Ferreiera 147, is even more crowded and newer.

The **Cantina Bella Roma,** at Avenida Atlântica 928, is a fine Italian restaurant with an ocean view as a bonus. In a private house setting, spaghetti is king here ($3 and under). Pizza and frango are in the same price category, and a favorite of ours is the gnocchi a blonhesa (meat with tomato sauce).

Finally, you should try the **Terraço Atlântico,** at Avenida Atlântica 3432, primarily for the spectacular view of the beach and ocean. Head up to the second floor next to the Help Discothèque. Vie for one of the outdoor tables. You can also dine indoors in air-conditioned comfort. Choose from an enormous menu and enjoy the pasta, fish, meat, and typical Brazilian dishes. Most platters are under $8.

Galeto Restaurants

Some of the least expensive restaurants are those establishments featuring barbecued chicken. You'll be presented with a choice of either galeto, a small chicken, or frango, a larger version.

A delightful eatery is the colorful **Rei dos Galetos,** on Rua Senador Dantas in the Praça Mahatma Gandhi area. A whole galeto (small chicken) will cost $2 and drinks are an extra 30¢.

Nearby on Rua Senador Dantas is **Pizzeria Nova Cinelandia,** not far from the OK Hotel. For the same $2 you get a small pizza. Add dessert and beverage and your lunch will still be under $3.

DINING IN IPANEMA AND LEBLON: There are a number of eateries offering tasty repasts in these two sections of Rio, from low-budget, fast-food establishments to the super-splurge.

The Snack Places

Our favorite fast-food stop in this part of town is **Chaplin,** at Visconde de Pirajá 187, near Farme de Amoedo. Murals of the tramp in Chaplin's classic films line the walls. Purchase tickets at the cashier and enjoy magnificent crêpes (70¢), delicious ice cream, or tasty sandwiches.

Nearby is **Gordon,** on Visconde de Pirajá opposite Praça Gen. Osorio, a similar type of establishment. Recommended here are the submarine sandwiches ($1 and up) and the super hot dogs.

Finally, for some of the best freshly squeezed juices south of the equator, try **Polis Sucos,** Visconde de Pirajá at Teixeira del Melo, opposite Gen. Osorio Plaza.

A number of fine fast-food eateries are on Rua Visconde de Pirajá in Ipanema. Try **Bob's,** at no. 463, opposite the H. Stern building, and sample a delicious hot dog for 40¢ or a tuna sandwich (75¢). Look for the red-and-white sign. **Bonis,** at no. 595C, is a stand-up fast-food sandwich shop with fine milkshakes (50¢). **Chaika,** at Visconde de Pirajá 321, has stand-up service in front and booths in the rear (extensive menu). Finally, the ubiquitous **McDonald's** is at Visconde de Pirajá 206—and just like at home.

A KOSHER CHOICE. Rio's only "Judaica" restaurant is **Delicat's,** at Avenida Henrique Dumont 68, a small counter-service (or take-out) spot where you can stuff yourself on the likes of a kosher salami or pastrami sandwich ($1.50 to $2), knishes (35¢), or gefilte fish. On Friday, chicken soup with kneidlach is the draw. Come early; it closes at 8 p.m., at sundown on Friday.

Lunch and Dinner Restaurants

This newer section of town is home to some of Rio's best restaurants. We have chosen not the most renowned eateries, but those neighborhood-type restaurants where local residents eat on Tuesday nights.

For the best sandwiches this side of Copenhagen, direct your feet to Leblon, where **Helsingor,** at Avenida Gen. San Martín 983, corner of Artigas, serves 66 sandwiches (order by number, please) in a Danish home setting. You might start with the shrimp salad with asparagus ($6) or the chicken, cucumber, and tomato sandwich. With beer, tea, and cookies, you will enjoy a filling lunch or late-afternoon snack.

Two Argentine-type confeiterias offer fine food and drinks in old-world setting. **Le Coin,** at Ataulfo de Paiva 658 in Leblon, is our first choice. It's bustling and noisy and customers sit for hours, enjoying sandwiches, tea, coffee, and whisky. Hot plates (frango, $3.50; or steaks, $5) definitely take a back seat.

Alvaro's Bar, at Ataulfo de Paiva 500, corner of Cupertino Durão, is more a "whiskeria" than a confeiteria. Hot plates, sandwiches, and pizza are available, but beer, wine, and whisky are bestsellers. Lots of fun.

In Leblon we like **Gordon's,** at Rua Dias Ferreira, near Final do Leblon. Sidewalk tables and indoor seating vie for customers. Huge kangaroo toys attract the small fry. Buy tickets at the counter and pick up your 75¢ hamburger, egg-salad sandwich ($1), or tuna (90¢).

Health-Food Restaurants

Two health-food restaurants we highly recommend are in Leblon. The larger of the two is **Sabor Saude,** Avenida Ataulfo de Paiva 630, and the other is **Celeiro,** Rua Dias Ferreira 199. Both feature such items as eggplant, salad bar, pure juices, quiche, and vegetable meat-type dishes. Sabor Saude is open from 7 a.m. to 10 p.m.; Celeiro, from 10 a.m. to 7 p.m.

Big-Splurge Restaurants

A wonderful restaurant in a nautical design is **Del Mare,** at Rua Paul Redfern 37 (tel. 239-1842), in Ipanema. Hanging wine bottles set the mood for the fine seafood dishes that are available.

Excellent seafood along with Italian dishes are the thing at **Grottammare,** an almost always packed restaurant at Rua Gomes Carneiro 132, at the beginning of Ipanema. The peixe ao Grottammare special is enough for two, and the sauce is spectacular. Try for a table on the terrace.

Probably Rio's most popular Bahian restaurant is **Chalé,** at Rua da Matriz 54 in Botafogo. Set in an 1884 home, Chalé has waitresses in traditional Bahian dress. Here is where you should sample the likes of xinxim de galinha and moqueca de peixe.

Also in Botafogo, and on the same theme, is **Maria Thereza Weiss,** at Rua Visconde Silva 152. Maria Thereza Weiss, the owner, is a famous cook and author, and the vatapá dishes are fabulous.

A pizza restaurant with an enormous menu is **A Grelha,** at Rua Garcia D'Avila 73 (tel. 239-6045), a half block from Visconde de Pirajá. Pizzas are $2 and up; frango, $2 to $3; fish platters, $3 to $5. The décor is just above plain.

Individual pizzas are the featured selection at **Il Capo,** at Rua Visconde de Pirajá 276. Seafood dishes are also good here, as is the pasta. Prices are moderate.

A bilevel steakhouse in Ipanema is **Alberico's,** at the beachfront Avenida Vieira Souto 236 (tel. 267-3793). Try the steak ao sal grosso (filet mignon) for $5 or the churrasco na brasa (steak) at $6. There are several dining rooms in this eatery resembling a private home.

Another fine Italian choice is **Rio Napolis,** Rua Teixeira de Melo 53, where pizzas, spaghetti bolonhês ($2), and cannellone ($3) are featured.

The **Porcão Churrascaria,** at Rua Barão da Torre 218 (tel. 521-0999), has a $7.50 fixed-price all-inclusive menu. The food is delicious and more than you can handle. Look for the pig logo on the sign.

If Rio's prettiest Chinese restaurant set in a lovely lagoon backdrop is your cup of tea, head to **Centro China,** Avenida Epitácio Pessoa 1164. The fried wonton is $2, shrimp dishes run $8, beef is $5, and chicken, about $4. It's like dining in a private home.

You will be well taken care of by owner David Zee at **Mr. Zee,** Avenida General San Martín 1219 (tel. 294-0591). David, a Hong Kong native educated in the United States, left a career in banking to open one of Rio's finest Chinese restaurants, attracting a well-to-do clientele. Among the delights on the menu are

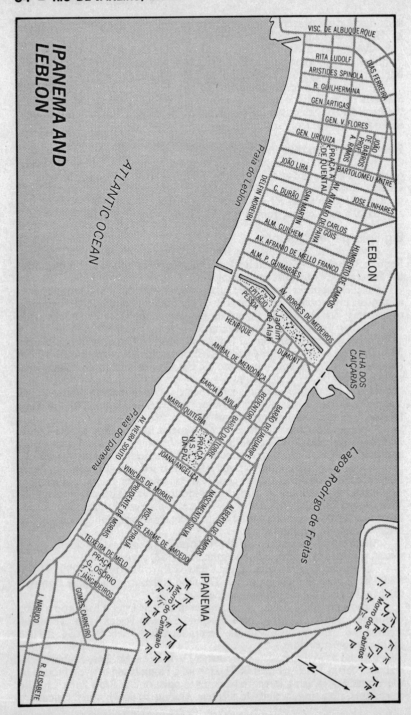

IPANEMA AND LEBLON

ATLANTIC OCEAN

LEBLON

IPANEMA

VISC. DE ALBUQUERQUE
RITA LUDOLF
ARISTIDES SPINOLA
R. GUILHERMINA
GEN. ARTIGAS
GEN. V. FLORES
GEN. URQUIZA
JOÃO LIRA
C. DURÃO
ALM. GUILHEM
AV. AFRANIO DE MELLO FRANCO
ALM. P. GUIMARÃES
AV. BORGES DE MEDEIROS

DIAS FERREIRA
JOÃO DE BARROS
PROF. A. RAMOS
BARTOLOMEU MITRE
JOSE LINHARES
HUMBERTO DE CAMPOS
AV. ATAULFO DE PAIVA
AV. PAULO DE GOIS

Praia do Leblon
DELFIM MOREIRA

PRACA ANT. DE QUENTAL
SAN MARTIN

IGNACIO PESSÔA
Jardim de Alah
HENRIQUE DUMONT
ANIBAL DE MENDONÇA
GARCIA D'AVILA
MARIA QUITÉRIA
REDENTOR
BARÃO DA TORRE
BARÃO DE JAGUARIPE
PRACA N.S. DA PAZ
JOANA ANGELICA
VINICIUS DE MORAIS
NASCIMENTO SILVA
ALBERTO DE CAMPOS
PRUDENTE DE MORAIS
VISC. DE PIRAJÁ
PRAIA DE FARME DE AMOEDO
TEIXEIRA DE MELO
PRACA G. OSÓRIO
JANGADEIROS
GOMES CARNEIRO
J. NABUCO
R. ELISABETE

Praia de Ipanema
AV. VIEIRA SOUTO

ILHA DOS CAIÇARAS
Lagôa Rodrigo de Freitas

Moro do Cantagalo
Moro dos Cabritos

N

Beijing duck, sweet-and-sour spareribs, and squid with onions and black-bean sauce, all served on beautifully decorated plates, and for dessert caramel-fried bananas with ice cream and honeyed pears with crème de menthe sauce.

For the best in Mexican food, try **Lagoa Charlies,** Avenida Epitácio Pessoa at Maria Quiteria 136, open for dinner only. The three Mexican owners operate three restaurants in their home country. We enjoy dining on the outdoor terrace, particularly on warm nights. Try the guacamole salad for $3 and the pollo curry for $5. Humorous Mexican posters adorn the festive indoor dining room. Strolling musicians too.

For an elegant meal with an apple motif, try **Pomme d'Or,** at Rua Sá Ferreira 22 in Copacabana (tel. 521-2548). Stick to the chicken and veal dishes to avoid a too-high tab. The mirrored walls and booths are inviting and you should try the cotelette de volaille Kiev or escaloppines de filet au roquefort ($6 to $7). The couches in the bar area are usually crowded.

For the finest in Portuguese cuisine, especially seafood, **Antiquarius,** at Rua Aristides Espióla 19 (tel. 294-1496), is a definite must, as long as your pocketbook can handle it—prices are on the steep side. But the attractive interior of this elegant dining choice is worth a look. Both floors are filled with antiques, and from the dining areas you can see the sculptures in the garden. Antiquarius is filled with fashionable people who entertain here at lunch. Upstairs there is a collection of valuable antiques, which are for sale. Small private alcoves make for intimate dining.

Our final choice in this category is **Final do Leblon,** at Rua Dias Ferreira 64 in Leblon. The young crowd takes to this bustling restaurant where the sidewalk tables are at a premium. Sit and enjoy the Cariocas at play. Prices are reasonable: milanesa is $3; churrasco, $5. There is a daily special for about $3.50 to $4. The menu is varied. There is also indoor dining for those preferring a quieter backdrop.

Big Splurge with a View

For a truly special big-splurge night out, head downtown to **La Tour,** at Rua Santa Luzia 651 (34th floor), a restaurant located in the tower of a downtown office building. The restaurant revolves, taking about one hour to go full circle. The views of the city are spectacular. While the restaurant could get away with inferior food, in fact the food is excellent. Expect to spend at least $15 to $20 per person.

3. RIO BY DAY

Now for the sights of Rio. To familiarize yourself with a strange city, nothing is better than a quick walking tour.

A STROLL THROUGH RIO: We suggest that you begin your stroll through center city at the **Praça Mauá,** the northside dock area of Rio Branco—the city's main thoroughfare.

As you walk south on this bustling street, note the enchanting sidewalk mosaics. Some blocks have animal or bird designs imbedded in the concrete. Other sidewalk areas are decorated with undulating lines that resemble abstract paintings.

Four blocks down is **Avenida Presidente Vargas,** a wide thoroughfare that is a main transportation artery for buses heading to the beaches and to suburban districts. Two more blocks and you'll find yourself at **Rua Buenos Aires,** where a wooden sign with an arrow pointing to the right indicates the **Mercado das Flores** (flowermarket) in the nearby Praça Olavo Bilac. The outdoor shops sell beautiful flowers, and orchids are a specialty.

Praça Olavo Bilac is at the beginning of Riio's shopping district, where traffic is barred much of the day. Alongside is the **Rua Gonçcalves Dias,** which is lined with hundreds of shops. Browse through the alligator goods and the native handcrafts. Some of these shops are noted in our shopping section below.

The **Largo da Carioca,** a park-like plaza, is your next destination. Follow Gonçalves and you'll find it. On a small hill is the **Convento de Santo Antonio,** a convent and church which you might like to visit.

A small overhead two-car railway runs from here toward the Corcovado district, where the famous **Christ the Redeemer statue** is located. The fare is only $3 round trip.

The new tree-lined thoroughfare here is **República do Chile,** built as part of the reclamation program. Turn left on Chile for one block and you are back on Branco. Continue along that street for two blocks until you reach Rua Araujo, **Porto Alegre.**

On your left, across Rio Branco, is the **National Museum of Fine Art** (open Tuesday through Friday from 1 to 5 p.m., on weekends from 3 to 6 p.m.; admission is free). Adjacent to the museum is the **National Library,** where browsers are welcome.

On your near right is the elegant **Municipal Theater** (see our "Rio After Dark" section), which is a small replica of the Paris Opera House. On the theater's lower level is a restaurant.

The front of the theater faces **Praça Floriano,** which is the start of **Cinelandia** (movie) district. The area is noted for good budget restaurants as well. The street leading from Floriano winds up at the **Praça Mahatma Gandhi,** considered the heart of downtown Rio.

From here you can stroll to **Flamengo Beach** (a 15-minute walk) by heading to the bay and making a right on **Avenida Beira Mar,** a wide, winding bayfront drive that leads into Flamengo's center. It's a lovely walk, with the bay and Sugarloaf peak on the left, landscaped gardens on your right.

To reach **Copacabana Beach** from Flamengo, take any bus from Praia Flamengo, the main street, heading in that direction. We recommend this scenic ride. Direct buses will return you to downtown Rio in only 20 minutes or so.

JARDINEIRAS: Probably the best way to orient yourself to Rio's sights is via the jardineiras, a trolley bus that runs along the beachfront from Praia Vermelho (near Sugarloaf) to São Conrado (near the Intercontinental Hotel) in about 1½ hours. The trolley costs about 50¢ and glides slowly along the beachfront. Posts marked "Jardineira" are clearly visible and indicate stops. We suggest you board at Leme for best viewing.

RIO, SIGHT BY SIGHT: Now we'll take them one at a time, beginning with:

Sugarloaf

Vying with Corcovado as Rio's major tourist draws is the **Pão de Açúcar** (Sugarloaf Mountain), to the southwest of center city in the bayfront community of **Urca,** near Botafogo. This world-famous gumdrop-shaped peak, which overlooks Guanabara Bay, offers a stunning view of Rio.

To reach Sugarloaf, you must take two cable cars—one carries you 700 feet up to Urca, the lower mountain adjacent, while a second car lifts you the additional 500 feet to the 1,230-foot peak. After disembarking at Urca, stroll about and then pick up the second car at the area's far side, beyond the restaurant. At several points in the ascent the 75-passenger car appears to be rising vertically, and it just about is. Besides the stupendous view, there are lovely winding paths and unusual vegetation at both levels. Bring your camera, and a sweater if the day is cool.

(Prepare, however, for a wait on weekends when Brazilians from other cities as well as foreigners throng here. It's worth the wait.)

To reach Sugarloaf from center city or Copacabana Beach, take any bus marked "Lins-Urca" and ask to be dropped at **Praia Vermelha** (the end of Avenida Pasteur, near the cable-car entrance), a 25-minute ride from Praça Mahatma Gandhi. (From center city, bus 442 is your best bet.) The cable cars leave frequently, beginning at 8 a.m. and continuing until 9 p.m.; the round-trip cost is $2. If you're going only up to Urca, the cost is $1.

Corcovado

Fifteen miles from center city is another legendary landmark—the 2,300-foot Corcovado (Hunchback) Mountain. At its peak is the famous 130-foot-high **Statue of Christ the Redeemer,** built as a peace symbol, the figure's outstretched arms welcoming all travelers.

Families live in small favelas along Corcovado's hillside, and the 50-passenger train makes a number of stops in its ascent. At each station shoeless children throng around the visitors, selling bags of roasted peanuts for 15¢. The vegetation is exotic and worth a picture or two.

Before beginning the fascinating 227-step climb to the peak, fortify yourself with an ice cream (40¢) sold at a stand near the train exit. As a thirst quencher, pick up a fresh orange (10¢) too. You can rest during the climb at a midpoint café that has an outdoor dining area jutting out from the mountain. At the top, stroll along a winding uphill path that carries you to the foot of the Christ statue. The inevitable souvenir stands (prices are high) dot the scene. From the lookout balconies you can spot the famous Maracanã soccer stadium, the Joquei Club racetrack, and the Botanical Garden palm trees. And look for Sugarloaf, which dominates the bay side. At night the statue is floodlit, an awe-inspiring sight.

Any bus marked "Cosme Velho" will drop you at the Corcovado train station, including buses 422, 497, and 498 from center city, and 583 from Copacabana. The fare is 30¢.

The open-sided train departs every hour beginning at 8 a.m. on weekdays and every half hour on weekends. The last train leaves for the top at about dusk. Round-trip fare is $2.50.

Rio's Museum of Modern Art

A beautiful sight in Rio is the small, exquisitely designed Museum of Modern Art, on Avenida Beira Mar, at the bayfront within sight of the Praça Mahatma Gandhi, and not far from Santos Dumont Airport. Landscaped gardens and illuminated fountains make the exterior a rival of the interior for visitor attention. Virtually all glass, the museum was designed by the famous Brazilian architect A. E. Reidy, who shrewdly planned a broad expanse of window for the Sugarloaf view. The two new wings house an art school and a small theater; the main building is for exhibitions.

Admission is only 50¢ (free on weekends), and the museum is open Tuesday through Saturday from noon to 7 p.m., on Sunday and holidays from 2 to 7 p.m. To reach the museum on foot, use the Presidente Wilson overpass, which bridges busy Beira Mar.

Monument to World War II Heroes

Near the art museum on the bay is an impressive monument to Brazilian World War II heroes, visible from the Praça Mahatma Gandhi. This awesome structure has a portico resting on two 150-foot-high concrete pillars. Three sculptured military figures protect the monument, and an eternal flame burns at the base.

A small museum here houses a collection of World War II weapons (mostly submachine guns and automatic rifles) as well as brilliantly colored war murals. The mausoleum under the monument is moving. Even if you usually avoid monuments, try to visit this one.

Museum of the Republic

Ever wear slippers in a museum? Well, to tour the Museum of the Republic, on Praia do Flamengo in Flamengo Beach, you'll have to don them to protect the 100-year-old wooden floors in this handsome structure, which was once a palace. Every room here, with varying colors and décors, represents a different era of world history.

Equally interesting is the garden, dotted with 120-year-old royal palm trees that soar 150 feet in height. And there are lily ponds here bridged by wooden walks. Enchanting. The entrance is on Rua do Catete, one block from the beachfront, off Silveira Martíns. Open Tuesday through Friday from 1 to 6 p.m., on Saturday and Sunday from 3 to 6 p.m.

Other Museums

Three other museums worth visiting are the **Folklore Museum,** at Rua do Catete 181; the **Indian Museum,** at Rua do Palmeiras 55; and the **Museum of National History,** at Praça Marechal Ancora. The National History Museum has interesting collections of porcelain, crystal, silver, weapons, coaches, and imperial coats-of-arms. Admission is free at all three, and hours are Tuesday through Friday from 10 a.m. to 5 p.m.

For a nostalgic look at the 1940s, head to the **Carmen Miranda Museum,** at Rua Barbosa 560 in Flamengo. Closed Monday; admission is free.

Hippie Fair

Every Sunday, Praça General Osorio in Ipanema is host to a fair that draws thousands of locals. Youthful vendors display their wares, and prices range from under $2 to several hundred dollars. The most popular items for sale are paintings, leather goods, inexpensive jewelry, unique clothes, etc. Hours are 11 a.m. to 6 p.m.

Favelas (Shantytown)

Rio's rock-bottom poor—estimated at one million people—live in shacks clustered in steep hillside communities that are called favelas. In all there are 100 favelas scattered through the city's hills. The largest is probably **Rocinha** (near Gavea), which houses thousands. *Black Orpheus,* a brilliant movie filmed in the Pasmado favela (which no longer exists), beautifully captured the spirit of favela life during carnival time.

There are tours that include favela visits for $20. While we're on the subject, there's an extensive city bus tour, another that includes dinner and a macumba—black magic—show at a nightclub. *Note:* It makes us uncomfortable to recommend entering a favela even with a tour, and it certainly is not advisable to enter a favela on your own.

The Beaches

Flamengo and Botafogo, which front on Guanabara Bay, are sometimes polluted and, therefore, we strongly advise against swimming there. Head for Lemme and Copacabana Beach which are the closest beaches to center city. Rio is blessed with a number of other ocean beaches beyond Copacabana. Among these are **Ipanema** (you remember "The Girl from Ipanema"?), where some of our top nightclub recommendations are located, and **Leblon** and **Gavea.** All are open year round. More on Ipanema later.

In general the waters are calmest earlier in the day; the waves tend to build as the day wears on, and by late afternoon you can have a vigorous battle on your hands trying to swim.

As we pointed out earlier, Flamengo is nearest to center city and Copacabana is beyond it, as are the other beaches. A highlight in Copacabana is the imaginative, bird-shaped papagallo kites flown by nearly every youngster on the beach.

To reach any of the nearer beaches, take bus 415, 438, 464, or 472 from Avenida Presidente Vargas and Rio Branco. Or from Praça Mahatma Gandhi, take any of these buses: 119, 121, 122, 128, 132, 175, and 179. From the Praça Mauá, bus 121, 123, 128, or 173 will get you there. The fare is always under 30¢ to the farthest point.

National Museum

Just outside center city, near Maracanã Soccer Stadium, is a large park—**Quinta de Boa Vista**—that houses the National Museum, a zoo, and an aquarium. Open from 10 a.m. to 5 p.m. every day except Monday, the museum exhibits Indian weapons, clothing, and utensils, a six-ton meteorite (largest ever to hit the earth), and other relics from Brazil's past. Admission is free.

A variety of South American animals and birds can be seen at the nearby zoo, along with Asian and African species.

Getting here is simple. From Avenidas Presidente Vargas and Rio Branco, and Copacabana, take either bus 472 or 474 and get off at Cancela. From Cinelandia (Praça Mahatma Gandhi), catch bus C4, and from the Praça Mauá, bus 312. The stop is the same.

A DAY AT THE RACES: Fifteen miles from downtown Rio, in the Corcovado district near the Botanical Gardens, is the famous and aristocratic **Joquei Club** racetrack. A handsome oval track, it charges only 10¢ for admission. And betting windows range from 60¢ and up. To get here, take bus 172 or 178 from Praça Mauá, or bus 438, 558, or 592 from Presidente Vargas and Rio Branco. The latter three buses also run from Copacabana Beach, along with 592.

Near the Joquei Club are the **Botanical Gardens** (admission is 15¢), called Jardin Botánico, which are located on 120 acres dotted with 7,000 species of trees (including 100-foot-high royal palms) and 600 varieties of orchids. On the grounds also are a museum, library, and aquarium. We recently combined a visit here with our trip to the track. Hours are daily from 8 a.m. to 5 p.m.

SANTA TERESA BY TROLLEY: For a pleasant afternoon, why not head to Santa Teresa, one of Rio's oldest areas, via one of the few remaining trams in the Western Hemisphere. For 20¢, the *bonde,* a trolley with open sides, will take you up the mountain to Santa Teresa. Be sure to take the one that says "Dois Irmões." The views are spectacular and getting there is almost an adventure. You can take the same trolley back or stroll around and catch the next one. Along the way you pass **Chacara do Ceu Museum.** The bonde station is located downtown near the new cathedral and the foot of the old aqueduct. It's open Tuesday through Friday from 2 to 5 p.m.

Warning: You should be careful not to bring cameras or other valuables with you on the trolley. Thieves have been known to frequent the route.

THE COUNTRYSIDE: Numerous wealthy Cariocas live in the state of Rio de

Janeiro, just outside Rio. A popular suburb in the mountains about 40 miles from center city is Petrópolis, where the Brazilian emperors once lived. The **Imperial Museum** is located here, not far from a venerable old hotel, the **Quitandinha** (now a country club). Buses leave for Petrópolis every 15 minutes from the Rodoviária Novo Rio. The fare for the two-hour ride is $1 each way.

Closer to Rio is **Tijuca Forest**, a lush tropical area, floodlit at night, where the famous **Cascatinha** (waterfall) can be seen amid grottoes and caves in the area. To reach the forest, take bus 233 or 234 marked "Rodoviária–B. Tijuca" from the Praça Saenz Pena. The main square **(Praça Saenz Pena)** in the village of Tijuca is where you pick up bus 640 (marked "Saenz Pena–Barra da Tijuca"), which passes within walking distance of the waterfall. A cab will cost you $8 from center city.

Inexpensive tours to Petrópolis and Tijuca are widely available.

READERS' SUGGESTED TRAVEL TIPS: "(1) The modern intercity bus system is a delight to travel. I rode from **São Paulo** to **Brasília,** with an overnight stop in Belo Horizonte and a side trip to Ouro Preto, in comfort. There was a rest room on board, free soft drinks, and pleasant roadside stops in the jungle. Seats are reserved in advance. Schedules are adhered to. (2) Avoid broken-down, beat-up taxis. Most meters work. No tipping. Secure the price of your trip if the meter is inoperative. If the taxi driver goes wild, say, 'Na esquina proxima' ('Next corner, please'). He'll stop and let you out. (3) Brazilians hate to admit that Spanish is 'just like Portuguese.' If you speak Spanish, always ask first: 'Fala inglês?' If they say 'Não,' ask if they *mind* if you speak Spanish. It works. (4) Anywhere in South America, carry a small penlight. One saved my life several times during power failures on an elevator or in a theater when power outages occurred. (5) Customs hint: Always look for the oldest Customs officers, if you can. They are ready to retire, or are bored with their job, and are usually friendly and helpful. (6) Rio is great, but São Paulo is one of the most sophisticated cities in the world, with fantastic restaurants" (A. Oreb, Jr., Ventura, Calif.).

"In Rio de Janeiro, Brazil, an interesting side trip is to **Niterói** via the Costa da Silva Bridge, longest in South America. A bus can be picked up on the south side of Praça Mahatma Gandhi. It is line 999, marked 'São Francisco'; fare one way is about 25¢. Termination is in São Francisco, adjacent to the neighborhood of Icaraí. In the latter, the beach overlooks Sugarloaf (and the fort opposite on the bay) and Corcovado. Return may be by the same line (or other buses marked 'Barcas' to the docks of the ferry boats, for a 20-minute view of the harbor). The return bus 999 is marked 'Largo de Lapa.'

"Also in Rio, the Santa Teresa 'bonde,' the last remaining streetcars, can be taken at the base of the Petrobras Building near Rua Senador Dantas and República do Chile. The end of the longer line, 'Dois Irmões' (at the fare station), provides a spectacular view of Sugarloaf. Fare is about 10¢ each way. (Both lines go over the Roman-style aqueduct arches.)

"Bus line 553 in Rio has been changed and now runs from Hotel Nacional in São Conrado along Avenida Atlântica to Leme. Visitors to Copacabana can take it along the beach and the spectacular views going around the base of Dois Irmões Mountain via Avenida Niemeyer. End of the line is at the Hotel Nacional where the return bus, marked 'Lem,' may be caught" (Robert Daus, Falls Church, Va.).

4. EXCURSIONS FROM RIO

PAQUETÁ ISLAND: In Guanabara Bay, just off Rio, are dozens of lovely islands used as weekend retreats and as stations for the thousands of yachtsmen and sailors here. Many Cariocas consider Paquetá Island the most enchanting of these for swimming and boating. Horse-drawn carriage tours around the island are available and recommended, and there are cabins for changing at the beaches.

The cheapest way ($1 round trip) to make the trip is via an aged ferry that takes 80 minutes (a motorboat might do it in 30 minutes). Departure times vary with the season, but the first boat invariably leaves at 5:30 a.m. from Estação 1 in the Praça 15 de Novembro ("Praça Quinze"), and there is usually a boat at about

7 and 10:15 a.m., and 1:30, 3, 5:30, 7, and 10 p.m. The final boat back to the mainland leaves at 8:30 p.m. nightly. To reach Praça 15 de Novembro, walk four blocks east from Rio Branco and 7 de Setembro toward the Imperial Palace.

If you prefer to travel in greater style, consider taking a tour package for about $25 (tourist class) that includes a 30-minute yacht cruise to the island, an island tour, and swimming. For an additional $3.50 you will be picked up at your hotel by limousine and you travel first class. Make arrangements through your hotel.

On the way you will pass the **Costa da Silva Bridge,** longest in South America, which joins Rio with Niterói.

AN AFTERNOON IN GAVEA: A quiet beach area that is home to three of

Rio's most lavish hotels in Gavea, located just beyond Leblon. Nearest to Leblon is the **Sheraton,** with its excellent restaurants, clubs, and swimming pools. A mile or so farther out, and next to each other, are the **Nacional** and **Intercontinental.** Don't leave Rio without dropping by. While here, note **Rocinha,** Rio's largest favela, near the Nacional Hotel.

BATEAU MOUCHE: A popular half-day or even day-long water excursion is a

yacht cruise around Guanabara Bay. The all-day bateau mouche (or boat cruise) stops for swimming at **Jurujuba,** then proceeds on to Paquetá Island, where first-class passengers get a horse-drawn-carriage tour. (Everyone gets a superb look at the Rio skyline and at nearby communities.) Tourist-class fare is $30 all day with lunch, while half-day tours run $21. Tourist passengers must be at the Sol e Mar dock in Botafogo 20 minutes before departure time. First-class passengers are picked up at their hotels.

Another recommended cruise operator is **Barracuda Rio,** at Marina da Gloria, which operates boats Tuesday through Saturday in various price categories. For information, call 285-0946 or 265-3997. Your hotel clerk can assist you.

COSTA VERDE CRUISE: If you need a few days to catch your breath after the

hectic pace in Rio, you may want to look into a Costa Verde Cruise. The weekend cruise, which sets sail on Friday and returns on Sunday, will take you to Itacuruca and Ilha Grande. There is also a four-day cruise, from Monday to Thursday, which goes to Itacuruca, Ilha Grande, Ilha Sandri, and Paquetá Island. The weekend cruise is $300 and the four-day cruise is $600. Both include breakfast and dinner. For more information contact **Camargo Yachting in Rio,** Avenida Prado Júnior 160, Copacabana (tel. 275-0643).

A TRIP TO BRASILIA: In a bold plan to develop Brazil's interior, former

President Juscelino Kubitschek implemented the 200-year-old idea of carving a new city out of the wilderness. A site 575 miles west of Rio was chosen for its low humidity, relative coolness, and the fact that it could be reached by air from Rio in 1½ hours.

Kubitschek insisted that the city become the official capital of Brazil to attract international attention and commerce and industry. And thus in 1960 Brasilia became Brazil's seat of government. It is today a sleekly modern city with a population that has grown to well over a million.

The architecture of Brasilia is truly dazzling. Lúcio Costa designed the city along two main highways that intersect at the city's center. Along the east-west axis are the government buildings, designed by internationally famous Oscar Niemeyer (he designed the U.N. building).

At the end of this axis **(Eixo Monumental)** is the most famous Brasilia landmark, the spacious Plaza of Three Powers **(Praça dos Três Poderes),** where the executive, legislative, and judicial branches are housed in separate buildings. Note the center **Congress** building, with its twin towers set in a "bowl" and "saucer." The House of Representatives meets in the bowl, while the saucer structure is home to the Senate. To the left is **Planalto Palace,** the executive office building; to the right is the **Palace of Justice,** where the Supreme Court meets.

An artificial lake was created inside the city; on its far bank is the **Palácio da Alvorada** (Palace of Dawn), the residence of the president. Nearby is "Embassy Row," also worth a visit for its architectural diversity.

Note: Most of Brasilia's hotels are in the southern and northern sections, near each other, and not far from Eixo Monumental. Rates are not high.

Several tours are available through Rio travel agencies. In addition, there are frequent flights from Galeão Airport for $180 round trip.

Tip: Some airlines allow you to include Brasilia in your U.S.–to–South America air fare at no extra cost. One way is to fly from New York to Brasilia and then on to Rio. Check your airline for multiple-stopover itineraries that include Brasilia for no additional fare.

There are five hotels you can consider in the budget category: **Hotel Aristus** (tel. 061/223-8675); **Brasilia Imperial Hotel** (tel. 061/223-7252); **Byblos Hotel** (tel. 061/223-1570); **Itamaraty Parque Hotel** (tel. 061/225-6050); and **Mirage Hotel** (tel. 061/225-7150). All charge under $25 for a double.

The most popular hotels are probably the **Carlton** (tel. 061/224-8819), the **St. Paul Park** (tel. 061/226-1515), and the **Nacional** (tel. 061/226-8180). Each charges under $50 for a double.

SALVADOR (BAHIA):

SALVADOR (BAHIA): Perched on the Atlantic 1,000 miles northeast of Rio, exotic Salvador is an all-year tourist mecca. What draws over half a million travelers to this capital of the state of Bahia? For openers, it has 40 miles of magnificent beaches in year-round use and a bay that rivals Guanabara for sheer hypnotic beauty. Next, it has a colonial history (it was founded over 400 years ago and was Brazil's first capital and the center of Portugal's New World colonies) with some of South America's finest colonial architecture and museums. Add a population of African origin, which retains the folklore of Candomblé (a mystic form of voodoo) in its everyday culture, plus local Bahian dishes which make dining here a delight, and you can understand why we strongly recommend (time permitting) that you make Salvador a must stop.

Climate

Like Rio, Salvador has year-round swimming and warm temperatures. Salvador actually can get even warmer than Rio, which is understandable since it's nearer to the equator. The hottest months are during our winter season (December to March). From May through September you can get occasional rainy days, with mild afternoons.

Arrival

You will no doubt arrive by plane at modern **Dois de Julho Airport** after a 1¾-hour flight from Rio via modern jet aircraft. Your best bet is to take a cab ($15) to the center city 20 miles away. Use the buddy system since cabs hold four to five passengers for the same fare.

Hotels

Salvador has several deluxe hotels in the $50 to $80 range which rival the finest hotels in Rio. Among the best are the Meridien Bahia Hotel, in the Rio Vermelho Beach area; and the Bahia Othon Palace and the Salvador Praia Hotel, both in the nearby Ondina Beach area, and the Hotel da Bahia, downtown. Each has its own pool and first-class service and accommodations. The Meridien even has tennis courts and a sauna.

Don't be discouraged, however; there are several fine hotels in the $20 to $35 range (doubles). Typically they offer comfortable rooms with bath, telephone, and piped-in music, and air conditioning is either available or standard. Unfortunately, none of these hotels has a pool.

A good first choice would be the **Barra Turismo Hotel**, at Avenida 7 de Setembro 502 (tel. 071/245-7433), in the Barra section. This 60-room hotel has doubles starting as low as $32 and singles under $27, all with air conditioning. There is no pool and the hotel is located on one of the main streets leading to the downtown area. On the same Avenida 7 de Setembro, at no. 106, is the good-value **Hotel Bahia de Todos os Santos** (tel. 071/243-6344), a 93-room hotel slightly more expensive than the Barra Turismo Hotel, where doubles start at $38 (singles are about $25 and up). This colonial-style hotel has air conditioning and a bar but no pool. If possible, try for an upper-floor room, which has stunning views of the bay. A third choice would be the **Hotel Bahia do Sol**, also on Avenida 7 de Setembro at no. 2009 (tel. 071/247-7211), downtown in the Vitoria section. Doubles at this 91-room hostelry range from $38 upward. Singles are $29. Add $4 for a triple.

If you are traveling with the family, you would do well at the **Suites Sabre** on Rue Helvecio Carneiro Ribeiro (tel. 071/247-3450), in the Ondina Beach area near the Othon Hotel. The Sabre offers apartment-style accommodations for about $35, but four or more people could comfortably live here. A bonus is the kitchenette which permits dining "at home." A good family value. In the Barra section you should consider the **Vila Romana Hotel**, Rua Lemos de Brito 14 (tel. 071/247-6522). This small hotel (56 rooms) has doubles for as little as $28, singles for $23. Add $3 for air conditioning and $3 for an extra bed. Worth the money.

Back on Avenida 7 de Setembro again, at no. 2998, is the **Hotel Solar da Barra** (tel. 071/247-4917), a small 18-room choice. Here doubles are a good value at $21, and singles at $16. Air conditioning is $2 extra. Another choice in this category is the **Hotel Pelourinho**, at Rua Alfredo Brito 20, near the famous Pelourinho Square (tel. 071/242-4144). This is a charming renovated colonial house, retaining much of its former character. Prices are equivalent to our prior selections, doubles for $25 and singles for $19.

You can also consider the **Hotel Marazul**, Avenida 7 de Setembro 3937 in the Barra section, fronting the sea near Porto da Barra (tel. 071/235-2110), with rates about $40 to $50 double. Another good choice would be the **Hotel Quatro Rodas**, Rua da Passagarda, Praia Farol de Itapão (tel. 071/249-9611). It is situated in a large area and has a pool, tennis court, and sauna. It's a deluxe hotel with 195 apartments, 200 yards from the beach, near the airport. Rates are about $60 double.

Special mention should be made of the **Pousada do Carmo Hotel**, formerly a Carmelite convent, which still retains much of its original charm. Located at Largo do Carmo 1 (tel. 071/242-3111), the 70 rooms are air-conditioned and include a refrigerator, TV, and piped-in music. A pool is a welcome bonus in tropical Salvador. The sauna gets less use. Doubles are in the $45 range.

Restaurants

Derived from Africa, Bahian cuisine includes those typical dishes with which Brazilian food has come to be associated. Such exotic dishes as **vatapa** (a fish, nuts, onions, pepper, and coconut-milk combination), **xinxim de galinha** (a chicken stew in a mild sauce), and **frigideira** (shrimp or crab boiled with eggs, coconut, and oil), are delightful examples. While these dishes are uniformly

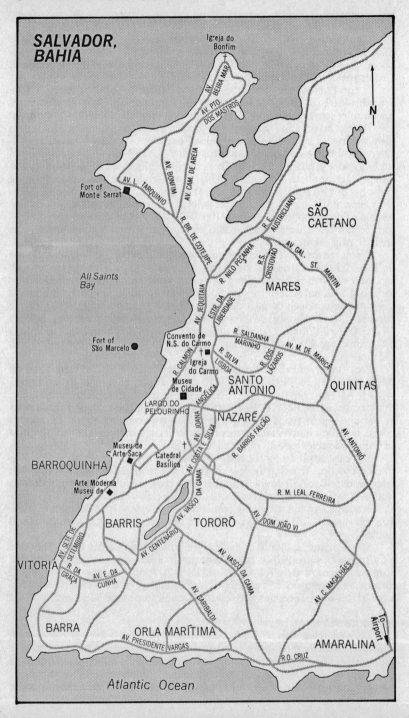

SALVADOR, BAHIA

N

Igreja do Bonfim

AV. BEIRA MAR

AV. PTO. DOS MASTROS

AV. CAM. DE AREIA

AV. BONFIM

AV. L. TARQUINIO

Fort of Monte Serrat

R. BR. DE COTEJIPE

SÃO CAETANO

R.E. AUSTRICLIANO

AV. GAL. ST. MARTIN

R.S. CRISTOVÃO

R. NILO PEÇANHA

AV. JEQUITAIA

ESTR. DA LIBERDADE

All Saints Bay

MARES

Fort of São Marcelo

Convento de N.S. do Carmo

R. CALMON

Igreja do Carmo

R. SALDANHA MARINHO

AV. M. DE MARICA

R. SILVA LISBOA

R. DOS LAZAROS

Museu de Cidade

AV. JOANA ANGELICA

SANTO ANTONIO

QUINTAS

LARGO DO PELOURINHO

NAZARÉ

AV. COSTA E SILVA

R. BARROS FALCÃO

AV. ANTONIO

Museu de Arte Saca

Catedral Basílica

BARROQUINHA

AV. VASCO DA GAMA

R. M. LEAL FERREIRA

Arte Moderna Museu de

AV. DOM JOÃO VI

BARRIS

TORORÓ

AV. CENTENARIO

AV. VASCO DA GAMA

AV. SETE DE SETEMBRO

VITORIA

R. DA GRAÇA

AV. E. DA CUNHA

AV. GARIBALDI

AV. C. MAGALHÃES

To Airport

BARRA

ORLA MARÍTIMA

AMARALINA

AV. PRESIDENTE VARGAS

R.O. CRUZ

Atlantic Ocean

good throughout Brazil, in Salvador they are truly special. Definitely make it a point to have at least one typical Bahian meal here.

For an enjoyable evening out, why not dine at **Senac** in Largo Pelourinho, on the third floor of the Teatro Senac? Here you can dine buffet style on a wide assortment of Bahian dishes for about $7 per person, all you can eat. Set in a colonial house, this area has perhaps the most intriguing architecture in Brazil. There is a nightly open-air samba show starting at 8:30 p.m. on the second floor. The restaurant is one flight up. Dress informally. The atmosphere is definitely earthy.

Another good choice for Bahian dishes is **Casa da Gamboa,** at Rua da Gamboa de Cima 51, in the downtown area. Much more attractive than Senac, the Gamboa is a true restaurant with several dining rooms in a handsome setting. Here you can feast your palate on all of the typical local dishes.

You should also try **Bargaço** (tel. 231-5141), in Pituba, a residential area of Salvador. Definitely try the sopado and soft-shell crabs in the open-sided, award-winning restaurant.

For fine steaks, try **Churrascaria Alex,** on Avenida Otavio Mangabeira, in the Boca do Rio Beach area. Here, in an attractive setting you can dine on delicious Brazilian barbecued steaks for $5 to $7. As in Rio, most platters are usually served with a sausage appetizer.

Other Bahian restaurants serving typical cuisine in the $5 range are **Yemanja,** Avenida Otavio Mangabeira (Praia da Armacão), and **AGDA,** Avenida Otavio Mangabeira (Praia Boca do Rio). Less expensive are **Rincão Gaucho,** Avenida Otavio Mangabeira (Praia da Armacão), and **Laçador,** Avenida Otavio Mangabeira (Praia Pituba).

Boasting a population of over a million, cosmopolitan Salvador has fine seafood, Italian, French, and Chinese restaurants scattered throughout the city. We have confined our recommendations to those specializing in Brazilian dishes in the hope that this will convince you to try them.

Seeing Salvador

To best orient yourself to Salvador, you must first understand that it is a large city of over one million, bounded on the south by the Atlantic Ocean and on the west by the scenic All Saints Bay. Next, note that it is a bilevel city, with the center area separated into "lower city" and "upper city."

Let's start at **Rio Vermelho** on the south (Atlantic Ocean) side. This beach area is the site of the Meridien Bahia Hotel, with several charming inlet bays, ideal for swimming. Heading west along the Atlantic from here is the main oceanfront avenue, Avenida Presidente Vargas. We next come to the **Ondina** area, after passing the zoological park. Ondina Beach is here and you couldn't expect a finer place to swim. The Othon Palace and Salvador Praia Hotels are here. Back on Vargas again, we pass **Morro do Cristo,** a fort jutting into the ocean, and continue until we reach **Farol da Barra,** marked by the lighthouse that is at the entrance to All Saints Bay **(Bais de Todos os Santos)** on Salvador's west side. At this point the Atlantic Ocean and the bay meet. Nearby is the 17th-century fortress (Brazil's oldest) of **Santo António,** which extends into this ocean-bay area. From here the main bayfront thoroughfare is **Avenida 7 de Setembro,** and we are now heading north toward center city, with the magnificent bay on our left. Just ahead is the **Santa Maria Fortress** (also 17th century), and just beyond is **Porto da Barra,** a beach area offering spectacular views of the bay as well as elegant boutiques and shops. A top hotel, the Praiamar Hotel, is here too. This section is referred to locally as the **Barra** section.

Continuing toward center city (north), we pass the **Costa Pinto Museum,**

Avenida 7 de Setembro 2490. This museum is known for its fine silver, china, jewel, furniture, and art collections, and was originally owned by Senhor Carlos Costa Pinto as his home. It was donated to the state of Bahia by his widow after his death in 1946. The museum opened in 1969. Just beyond, on the bay, is the **Vitoria** section. At this point, Avenida 7 de Setembro continues downtown through the heart of Salvador. A parallel street downtown is **Rua Carlos Gomes,** the main shopping thoroughfare. On Carlos Gomes you will find such department stores as **Mesbla** and **Casa Sloper.**

From here the bayfront avenue is **Avenida do Contorno,** which continues downtown toward the lower city, passing near the famous **Museum of Sacred Art** at Rua do Sodre 24. This classic structure contains religious treasures, including paintings, murals, and sculpture. Definitely worth a visit. Note the art derived from the Peruvian School of Cuzco.

We now are in the heart of the downtown area in the "lower city." As indicated above, Salvador is divided into two sections, the "lower city" with its old shops, streets, and commercial establishments, and the "upper city" with its contrasting modern apartment buildings, colonial architecture, and churches. To get to the upper city you can drive, walk, or go via elevator or funicular. By all means take the **Elevador Lacerda,** a 100-year-old elevator, originally built to tote whale oil, which in about one minute will transport you to the upper city.

Cidade Baixa (lower city) was the commercial center of colonial Salvador, and you will find the fascinating outdoor market **Mercado Modelo,** with its endless stalls, shops, and cafés jam-packed with Bahians and merchandise. A must stop is a visit to **Largo do Pelourinho** (Torture Square), which contains in its streets and buildings the best example of colonial (18th century) architecture in Brazil and perhaps in all of South America. It was here that Africans and political prisoners were tortured. Historians note that "proper" ladies donning their finest clothes would peer down from their elegant balconies to observe (and presumably enjoy) the whippings. Visit the **Igreja do Rosário dos Pretos,** a church in the square housing a black order. Note the rococo architecture. Head to the third floor and, in a room on the right, view the Candomblé saints, all bearing Christian names.

Try heading to the upper city via **Santo António,** one of the oldest residential sections of Salvador, with steep hills and charming cobblestone streets, offering memorable views of the bay.

Other Sights and Activities

Before leaving Salvador, be sure to visit the **São Francisco Church,** located in the Praça Terreiro de Jesus, often called the "Golden Church." It was built out of chipped stone. Also, the **Bonfim Church** is visually stunning, in both external and internal viewing. Completed almost 200 years ago, the imported-marble construction is truly magnificent.

Bahia is famous for its art, artists, and handcrafts, and you should browse the many shops here featuring these items. If you are fortunate enough to be here on Sunday, be sure to visit the **Hippie Fair** in the upper city a Praça Terreiro de Jesus (near the Praça da Sé). Here you will find a great assortment of Bahia's arts and crafts such as bracelets, jewelry, leather goods, carvings, art, tapestries, pottery, and much more.

For the finest in gemstones, **H. Stern** has three shops in Salvador. They are located at the Meridien Hotel, the Othon Palace Hotel, and at the airport.

Itaparica Island

This lovely island, visible from the bay, is a 45-minute boat ride from Salvador. Time permitting, you should plan to spend one day viewing this island and roaming its beaches. Ferries leave all day, and you can even go by car. The boat ride offers incredible views of Salvador and its bay. Check with your hotel clerk for latest details.

While there is much to see (the São Lourenço Church and Fortress, for example), come for the beaches and tropical fruits. The island does house acceptable hotels and pensions if you wish to join the Bahians for an overnighter. For example, the **Grande Hotel de Itaparica** has 60 rooms and charges $50 for doubles; singles are $40.

CLUB MÉDITERRANÉE, ITAPARICA. During the summer of 1979 the club's first Brazilian village opened on Itaparica, at the entrance to All Saints Bay. Built in a lush palm grove facing the Atlantic Ocean, the village has fresh sea breezes all year round. A fine white sand beach and reef-protected waters invite swimmers and beachcombers alike. Brilliantly colored hammocks swing gently. A freshwater river flows through the coconut-studded grounds, forming a natural lake around which the bungalows and activities complex have been nestled.

The club is set in an 86-acre palm grove facing the bay and the modern, white skyline of Salvador. The winding beach and warm reef-protected waters combine to make this Franco-Brazilian spot ideal for both an active or relaxing vacation.

Some 600 members are accommodated at the club in two-story, ochre-colored stucco bungalows topped by red-tile roofs. Some of the rooms face the sea, while others are tucked around and over an artificial lake formed by a river flowing through the grounds. Each twin-bedded room is air-conditioned and decorated with green-and-white thick cotton bedspreads. The floors made from highly polished wooden planks are invitingly cool to the touch. All rooms have a large private tiled bathroom with built-in shower.

Abstract mosaic walkways inspired by the sidewalks of Rio and Bahia lead to the southern section of the village where there are 12 tennis courts, plus two paddle tennis courts, a horseback-riding center, and a covered open-air gymnasium with adjoining sauna. Nearby, the small churrascaria (barbecue) restaurant and bar provide an intimate setting for a typical Brazilian dinner under the stars. At the stroke of midnight, the pace changes and this area turns into the setting for some high-spirited al fresco disco and samba.

Sports activities offered with free equipment and group instruction include tennis, paddle tennis, windsurfing, indoor and outdoor soccer, volleyball, basketball, Ping-Pong, swimming (pool and ocean), calisthenics, yoga, and unsupervised sailing. Horseback riding is available at a stable of 20 fine Argentinian horses (small extra charge for riding). Members can also sample sailing trips around All Saints Bay and day-long picnics to secluded beaches.

The younger set will find a special world, created just for them, at the Mini Club. The Mini Club has its own kiddies' pool, and youngsters can participate in sports activities and outings geared to their particular interests.

Weekly group departures via Varig Airlines to Club Méditerranée–Itaparica leave on Sunday from both New York and Miami. A one-week stay at Itaparica is about $800 per person from January 4 to April 26. This includes double-occupancy-only accommodations; three daily meals featuring French, continental, and Brazilian specialties, plus unlimited wine; use of all sports and recreational activities; plus nightly entertainment. *Tipping is always prohibited.*

For more information, phone toll free 800/528-3100 in the U.S.

Folklore and Religion

The African influence is still strong in Bahia in religion, music, food, and customs, and why not? After all, 300 years ago many of Bahia's ancestors were brought here in captivity to work the plantations. Their culture strongly influenced the indigenous Indians and the Portuguese settlers so that today Bahia, unlike the rest of Brazil, retains a mixed culture, blending the African, Indian, and Portuguese influences.

The African religion was originally suppressed by the Portuguese, with the result that the slaves surreptitiously conducted their ceremonies in out-of-the-way locations. When the Catholic church sought to convert the slaves and destroy their religion, the Africans shrewdly renamed their gods with equivalent Christian and biblical names. Slowly but surely, however, ceremonies and traditions of the Africans mingled with those of the native Indians and Christians until today they are a far cry from their African origin. In Bahia, a form of voodoo called Candomblé is practiced in scattered houses of worship called **terreiros.** The Catholic saints are in integral part of the religious ceremonies. The worshippers, attired in bright costumes, hypnotically move to the beat of drums until apparently lost in a trance. The altars and statues bear a resemblance to those normally seen in Catholic churches, yet you are aware of differences. To witness the ceremonies, you had best check with your hotel clerk to make arrangements. Few terreiros have precisely scheduled services.

There are two important religious festivals held in Salvador that we think you would enjoy viewing. On January 1, the **Festival of Our Lord of the Seafarers** begins with a procession of boats crossing All Saints Bay. What follows is a frenetic festival of music and dancing, lasting into the wee hours. On February 2, the **Ceremony of Iemanja** is held in Rio Vermelho. Small fishing boats head out to the beautiful goddess who lives under the sea and "steals" fishermen. Each wife throws gifts (flowers, perfume, makeup) to the vain goddess, praying that Iemanja will not steal her husband. Parenthetically, when a fisherman drowns, it is commonly said that he has gone to Iemanja.

Capoeira

When the African slaves were brought to Bahia, they brought with them their dance and a self-defense technique called capoeira, which is actually a system of body movements, often done in pantomime style. On holidays, a musical instrument (berimbau) sets the rhythmic beat. In order not to miss this exotic activity, check with your hotel clerk as to where you can view a capoeira show, which you will long remember.

Salvador by Night

Salvador's nightlife ranges from the earthy to the elegant. At the latter end you have **Le Zodiaque** disco at the Meridien Hotel. This plush, expensive private club admits tourists, but the tab is high—$5 to $8 a drink.

Hippopotamus at the Bahia Othon Palace Hotel is also a first-rate disco, and the Salvador **Praia Hotel Champagne Bar** features live music and dancing.

For a pleasant evening, take a cab to **Bual'Amour** in Praia do Corsário (tel. 231-9775), where nostalgic music alternates with rock, and it's usually crowded with local youths.

FOR MEN ONLY. Unescorted men on the prowl can try **Holiday,** on Rua Chile, which is similar in all respects to the club of the same name in Rio. You are on your own here. The bar girls will eagerly join you for a drink, invited or not.

Tip: Any cab driver will gladly drive you to the many establishments in the old city that admit single men.

BELO HORIZONTE: The capital of the state of **Minas Gerais** is Belo Horizonte. At about the midpoint between Rio and Brasilia, Belo Horizonte is

an industrial city, located near some of Brazil's most important historic areas. The city of **Ouro Preto** is preserved as it was centuries ago. You can get here in about two hours by bus from Belo. Exceptional values are available in unset gemstones, inasmuch as Ouro Preto is also a mining center.

A planned city, Belo Horizonte was founded in 1897 and is a good base from which to visit Ouro Preto, as well as Mariana, 70 miles away, and Congonhas which is even closer.

Your best bet is to stay at the **Hotel Normandy,** Rua Tamoios 212 (tel. 031/ 201-6166), which is downtown and boasts a fine restaurant. A fine alternative is the **Hotel Savassi,** Rua Sergipe 939 (tel. 031/212-3266). A new hotel, it's located near the government ministries in the Praça da Liberdade. This plaza is also the site of several local food and handcraft fairs. Doubles at these choices are in the $20 range, with singles a bit less.

Two recommended restaurants are **Yun Ton,** at Rua Santa Catarina 946, which serves delicious Chinese specialties; and for Italian specialties, drop in at **Buona Tavola,** Rua Alagoas 777. Dinner will run about $5, sans alcoholic beverages.

SÃO PAULO—BRAZIL'S LARGEST CITY: One hour from Rio via air

shuttle—**Ponte Aerea** (and a free stopover on most flights in and out of Rio)— is the modern, booming metropolis of São Paulo. Skyscrapers, luxury apartment houses, and superhighways combine to make this city representative of South America's industrial potential. A popular line here is: "We work hard, so we can play in Rio."

Whenever heading to São Paulo we always look forward to visiting the world-famous **Butantan Institute and Snake Farm** (where antitoxin research is the thing), and the Sunday **Hippie Fair** in the Praça da República. While there, plan to spend a few days at the magnificent resort of **Guaruja,** just off Santos.

Getting around São Paulo is very easy: there are many taxis, and there's a clean, efficient subway too.

Hotels in the city tend to be posh and above our budgets for they cater primarily to the business traveler on an expense account. There are two Hiltons in town, as well as a Caesar Park. But obviously in a city this size there are lots of moderately priced stops as well. When you arrive at the airport, head to the **hotel reservation desk.** The staff is English-speaking and they'll help you find a hotel that meets your needs and budget.

Two hotels we often stay at are the **Bristol,** at Rua Martins Fontes 277 (tel. 011/258-0011), and the **Bourbon,** at Avenida Vieiro de Carvalho 99 (tel. 011/ 223-2244). Doubles are in the $30 range.

Excellent steakhouses are the three branches of **Dinho's Place,** and **Bassy,** at Rua 13 de Maio 334. Naturally in a city this size, and with so many ethnic groups, you'd expect many ethnic eateries—and you won't be disappointed.

Two nightclubs we heartily recommend are **Clydes,** at Rua Mata 70, and **Roof,** at Avenida Cidade Jardin 400. Both are singles watering holes.

For a romantic view of the city, dine and dance at **Terraço Itália,** at Avenida Ipiranga 344. Head for the 41st floor.

IGUAÇU (IGUASSU) FALLS: When listing "must" places to visit in South

America, many people would put Iguaçu Falls near the top. The waterfalls on the Iguaçu River mark the border of Brazil and Argentina; 18 miles farther downstream, at the confluence of the Iguaçu and the Paraná rivers, Argentina, Brazil, and Paraguay meet. You can visit the falls from Brazil or Argentina, but the Brazilian side is the most developed for tourism.

Getting there requires a two-hour flight from Rio to São Paulo. Varig has daily 737 and DC-10 flights to Iguaçu from Rio via São Paulo. The plane lands at an airport located midway between the falls and the nearby town of **Foz do Iguaçu.** Buses run from the airport to Foz, which has a population of 200,000, over 50 hotels, and not much else. If you visit in December, January, or February, *you must have a reservation.*

Where to Stay

Try the **Hotel Salvatti,** Rua Rio Branco 951 (tel. 0455/74-2727). It has 100 rooms spread over 14 floors, and some rooms are air-conditioned. Doubles are $30 and singles run $27; up the ante 10% December through February.

Another hotel to consider is the 140-room **Hotel Foz do Iguaçu,** Avenida Brasil 99 (tel. 0455/73-2511). Doubles are $20 and singles run $27, all with air conditioning.

Since this is a resort area, you might want to spend a little more and have a pool and other more resort-like amenities. Several such hotels are located on the 14-mile stretch between Foz and the falls. Among them are the **Hotel San Martin** and the **Hotel Carima** (tel. 0455/74-3377), each with restaurants, lounge areas, bars, pools, and tennis. Doubles are $30; singles, $25.

Hotel Das Cataratas (tel. 0455/72-2666) is directly across the road from the falls, in the national park of Iguaçu. A pink E-shaped building with lovely grounds, it has plush sitting rooms with fireplaces, pool tables, good food, a swimming pool, even a menagerie. Doubles are $50; singles, $41; and front rooms offer a fine view of the falls.

The 150-room **Hotel Panorama** at Avenida das Cataratas, km 12 (tel. 0455/74-1200), has doubles starting at $30 and is a comfortable hotel with a coffeeshop and bar. Singles run $21.

Finally, in town on Avenida Brasil is the **Bogari** (tel. 0455/73-2411), where comfortable doubles rent for $27. All rooms are air-conditioned with piped-in music. A bar is on the premises.

THREE BIG-SPLURGE CHOICES. Perhaps the best hotel in town is the **Hotel Bourbon,** at Avenida Das Cataratas, km 2.5 (tel. 0455/74-1313). This is a lovely five-star hotel with 150 rooms. Doubles will run under $50, with singles at $32.

In the center of the city is the five-star **Hotel Internacional** (tel. 0455/73-4240), a 214-room hotel featuring a pool and a churrascaria restaurant. Doubles are $50; singles, $38. You might also consider the four-star **Hotel Rafain-Palace** (tel. 0455/73-3434), on the outskirts of the city at km 727, a 96-room establishment with pool and bar. Doubles are a reasonable $35; singles, $28.

Where to Eat

Eat at least one meal in the dining room of the **Hotel Das Cataratas.** Price-fixed dinners are about $5, and the first-course smörgåsbord could be an entire meal by itself. **Restaurant China,** on the highway, features Chinese and Brazilian food and an English menu. The **Restaurant Rafaian** and **Cabeça de Boi,** Avenida Brasil 1291, are good choices for beef and grilled meats. The **Bottega Churrascaria,** on the highway near km 6, is recommended, along with the **Napolitana** on Rua Rio Branco. As the name suggests, the Napolitana specializes in fine Italian fare.

Visiting the Falls

Buses run to Iguaçu Falls from Foz hourly, and the ride (14 miles) takes 30 minutes. Unlike, say, Niagara Falls, the falls here are not continuous, nor are they uniform in size or water volume. Still, the average drop into the river is about 1½ miles, and the sheer amount of water spilling over is truly astonishing. You walk along a path, stopping at various lookout points, each at a different height and with its own magnificent view.

The most spectacular fall is the U-shaped Devil's Throat **(Garganta do Diablo).** Don the slicker you'll be offered and walk right into the center of the U. The roar is deafening, the spray drenching, and it's slightly scary (but not dangerous). For excellent photos, take the elevator over Devil's Throat.

Since 85% of the falls are on the Argentine side of the river, they are best viewed from the national park on the Brazilian side. The park, by the way, offers plenty of good scenery—a fine place for a picnic.

You can easily visit Argentina or Paraguay from here. There are small towns nearby, and many people go to Paraguay at night to gamble at the casino. Many of our readers have in fact come here from Argentina and Paraguay. Since the falls are closer to Buenos Aires and Asunción, it will be cheaper to come from there, but the nearby towns have nothing to offer so we suggest staying on the Brazilian side.

To cross to Argentina, use the Tancredo Neves Bridge. Its 380 yards span the Iguaçu River after the falls to reach the Argentinian city of Puerto Iguassu.

Itaipú Dam

It always seemed incredible to us that the great energy produced at these falls was never harnessed. That omission was rectified with the construction of the Itaipú Dam and hydroelectric plant. The plant is 20 miles from the falls and can be visited. The dam, the largest in the world, was a joint effort between Brazil and Paraguay under a treaty signed in 1973.

Construction started in 1975 with the artificial diversion of the waters of the Paraná River. The length of the dam is almost five miles and it's as tall as a 62-story building. The project was such a massive undertaking that a company town was established nearby. It houses 9,000 people and has schools and a hospital. At peak periods during the construction process over 40,000 workers were employed here. Four generators are operational (18 are planned) and it's amazing to learn that a third of the energy produced by one of these generators supplies all of Paraguay's electrical needs.

There are four daily tours of the dam and each is preceded by a film which explains the construction and the operation of Itaipú. Don't miss it!

READERS' TRAVEL SUGGESTIONS—IGUAÇU FALLS: "On certain days of the week it is possible to fly into Iguaçu Falls on the Argentine side in the morning and leave from the Brazilian side in the afternoon. This is heartily recommended since walking the catwalks and the circular hike below on the Argentine side can be accomplished within a few hours. First, Argentinian Airlines circled the falls so passengers on both sides could get a good view (I've never experienced an airline so accommodating before). A bus was waiting just outside the airport to take passengers to the Hotel de Cataratas de Argentina. We boarded the bus (cost, about 40¢) and were driven to the hotel, about a 15-minute drive. The bus stops along the way at the entrance to the National Park in order that nontour passengers can purchase admittance passes (cost, about 25¢). We made arrangements with a taxicab driver at the hotel to hold our luggage and drive us to the border at 3 p.m. for a cost of $7. We then hiked around the park, stopping for Cokes at the refreshment stands scattered about the park. (It can get up over 100° during November to January.) We met our driver as arranged and reached the border in about 20 minutes. After passing through Argentine Customs, we boarded a small wooden launch which ferried us across the river to the Brazilian side. After having our passports stamped and exchanging money at the adjacent office, we boarded a bus that goes to the central bus station. Here one changes for a second bus to the airport. The cost was 25¢ versus $9 for a taxi from the boat dock" (Barbara Mueller, Texas).

"The Iguaçu Falls are the most spectacular natural sight in South America. They surpass Niagara Falls and even are more exciting than the trip to Machú Picchú. Without doubt the Brazilian side is the better for viewing, especially if one takes the canoe trip to Garganta do Diablo, but a trip to the Argentine side is likewise indispensable. To truly see the falls, however, requires two days: it is virtually impossible to see the falls from both sides in one day. Expensive guided tours abound in the area, but economical means are also available. First, for accommodations, one should stay on the side which is the country of the traveler's next destination. Since luggage becomes a real problem here, particularly when crossing the river between Argentina and Brazil, make it easy on yourself. Reasonable rates are available on all three sides—Argentina, Brazil, Paraguay—while the Brazilian side offers more hotels and nightlife. Second, trips to both sides of the falls are distinct—one cannot go directly from one side to the other without backtracking to the starting point. The starting points are the towns of Foz do Iguaçu, "Cataratas," or "Parque Nacional" from the bus station (by the Hotel Foz do Iguaçu) in Foz do Iguaçu, Brazil, for the 45-minute trip. Buses always leave on the even hour and return on the odd hour. The bus passes the airport and also several luxury hotels outside the city. To see the Argentine side, there is public bus service from the bus station and main street in Puerto Iguazu, Argentina, for the 30-minute ride to the Hotel Cataratas, the disembarkation point for the long walk to the Argentine falls. There is no need to hurry—the first afternoon return bus from the Hotel Cataratas to Puerto Iguazu does not leave until 3:30 p.m. Finally, to reach Puerto Iguazu, Argentina, from Foz do Iguaçu, Brazil, you leave from the Foz do Iguaçu, Brazil, bus station on a local bus marked 'Porto Meira.' At Porto Meira you cross the river by ferry to Argentina. On the Argentine bank you take a local bus, or walk the three-quarters of a mile by taking a shortcut up the steep hill behind the pier, to the bus station in Puerto Iguazu. Conversely, if going from Puerto Iguazu to Foz do Iguaçu, take the ferry across the river to Porto Meira, from which all local buses go to the Foz do Iguaçu bus station. And if you're going to or coming from Puerto Stroessner, Paraguay, use Foz do Iguaçu, Brazil, for connections" (Robert D. Klock, Austin, Tex.).

"This was the highlight of our trip. The Cruzeiro airlines flight circled the falls and then landed. We got a room booked by the tourist office at the Hotel San Martín, although the rates on the brochure were incorrect. I urge all people to check the room rate before accepting the accommodations. Nevertheless, we did enjoy the swimming pool, and the close proximity to the falls was an added advantage. The hotel cost about $50, and breakfast was included. Although we only saw the falls from the Brazilian side, we went twice and loved the sight—tons of brown water and roaring streams, constant mist and morning rainbows. We even saw some native animals on the path, and an armadillo in the bushes. A beautiful place" (Rod and Kay Sims, Newport, Australia).

5. RIO AFTER DARK

THE SPORTING LIFE: Brazilians are mad about athletics and athletes. Night after night—there are few daytime events because of the warm sun—huge crowds flock to basketball, boxing, and horse-racing events in and around Rio.

But for the South American, and particularly the Carioca, there is only one special hero and he is the futebol (soccer) star, for futebol is the national sport (Brazil has won three of the last eight world cups) and much more a part of life here than even baseball is in the U.S. Futebol is played everywhere by youngsters and even oldsters—on the beaches, in the streets, in the parks, and (via television) in the living rooms and basements of private homes.

This year-round devotion pays off. Every year at least one of Brazil's many teams reaches the international soccer playoffs.

You should not miss seeing a futebol match here. Whether you are a sports fan or not is immaterial. You will be roused to a fever pitch of partisanship for one team or the other in the emotional storm that will swell around you from the grandstand regulars.

On one of our recent visits to magnificent **Maracanã Stadium**—a mammoth, oval amphitheater completed in 1950 which has an official seating capacity of 150,000 but squeezes in 200,000 for major matches—we found ourselves shouting for the Vasco da Gama team as if we were veteran fans. Not that we'd ever seen them play before. . . .

When the main match started—at about 9:15 p.m.—it seemed that every spectator had a small transistor radio pressed to an ear to catch the broadcast of the contest. The Brazilians take their futebol quite seriously. If you have the chance, catch the most famous players in the futebol world who star for the Brazilian teams.

Tickets for Maracanã Stadium matches can be purchased in advance at the Municipal Theater box office or at the park. For important weekend matches you should reserve ahead; otherwise it isn't necessary. Reserved-seat prices range from $25 for an upper-tier midfield location to $10 for a lower-deck ticket. An unreserved bleacher ticket will cost you $3, and you can stand for $1.25.

Unlike the fare at many U.S. stadiums, food is cheap here. Sandwiches run about 75¢; a can of beer, about 50¢; and soft drinks, 25¢.

All teams are owned by private social clubs. There are several matches a week in Rio. For schedules, check the *Daily Post,* an English-language daily, or your hotel clerk.

To reach the stadium, take bus 234 or 241 from Praça Mauá, or bus 434 from Copacabana Beach. A cab from center city costs about $2.50.

Near Maracanã Stadium is a 50,000-seat indoor arena, **Maracanazinho Stadium,** which features boxing and basketball.

TEATRO MUNICIPAL: The cultural center of Rio is the **Municipal Theater,** a regal 2,200-seat structure located on Rio Branco at Praça Floriano. At carnival time this was the site of exclusive masked balls. In other seasons you can see domestic opera, ballet, concerts, and Portuguese-language theater, at prices ranging from $5 to $12.

Often, international companies appear at the Municipal Theater at somewhat higher prices. For example, we recently paid $5 per ticket to see a performance of *Rigoletto.* For the Hungarian Ballet, tickets ranged from $8 to $15. For the San Carlo (Naples) production of the opera *Otello,* tickets ranged from $7 to $15.

In the theater's basement, by the way, is a fine restaurant open for lunch.

CINEMA: The movie district—**Cinelandia**—is on Rua Senador Dantas off Avenida Rio Branco, not far from the Praça Mahatma Gandhi. Tickets, all unreserved, are much in demand: for popular films, be sure to pick up your ducats the morning of the day you plan to go. Prices at the best theaters run no higher than $2, while at others admission is as low as $1. Before performances, queue up early, because there's a mad scramble for seats when the doors open. And contrary to what you may read in travel brochures, you may dress informally.

Other good cinemas are in Copacabana, Ipanema, Flamengo, Leblon, and at the Barra Shopping Arcade and São Conrado Shopping Mall. Most English-language films are in English and not dubbed into Portuguese. Porno films are shown at certain cinemas, and are advertised as such.

RIO AFTER MIDNIGHT: Cariocas come alive in the wee hours. If you are a night person in this world of day people, waste no time in center city. Shoot immediately for Copacabana or Ipanema, where the later the hour the wilder the beat of the bossa nova and the latest hip-action step.

The rage of Rio's younger set is the mammoth (600 tables) **Canecão,** the wildest—and least intimate—nightspot we've seen anywhere. Opened in early

1967 in Botafogo on Rua Lauro Muller 1 (bayfront), Canecão caught on instantly. On weekends, 2,400 guys and gals (many stag) pack the joint from 7 p.m., when it opens, until the last music note fades away in the early morning. The go-go girls probably wouldn't make it in San Francisco, but who cares? The ear-shattering music—emanating from two rock 'n' roll quartets and one bossa nova combo—nearly shakes the murals (by Ziraldo) from the walls. Many post-teen Cariocas seem also to have found a home in the football-field-size club, which has a $9 (and up on weekends) cover, but charges only $1.25 for a stein of good domestic beer, $2.50 for Brazilian whisky, and $3 for gin and tonic. You enter through a courtyard, which serves as a screening area to keep out the underage and also acts as a waiting area on weekends, when tables are at a premium. The interior has a large reception area with pretty hostesses who guide you to a table located several steps down on a lower level. The elevated bandstand—in the center of the oval-shaped room—is surrounded by the dance floor, which in turn is encircled by tables. The designer's best touch was to have the band rise up from below on a moving platform and when finished depart the same way, only to be replaced by the next combo. Through the use of colored lights, the effect is pleasingly theatrical. For a quick look at Canecão from the highway, keep your eyes to the left when heading out to the beach area from center city. Just past Flamengo, and immediately before your bus passes through the Botafogo tunnel you'll see the huge club. This is a must. Closed Monday.

Let's move now to Copacabana Beach proper.

A more intimate club, in its way a kind of Europe in the tropics, is **Le Terrazze do Lido,** Rua Ronaldo de Carvalho 55, half a block from Avenida Atlântica (beachfront). This German-style restaurant and nightspot is infused with a gemütlich atmosphere that makes you feel at home instantly. Pianist Harry Hochmayer, an urbane Londoner now living in Rio, has a way with standards like "Mack the Knife" and "Volaré" that has the customers dancing and singing along. It's an experience to hear "I Love Paris" rendered in Portuguese, Spanish, English, German, and French simultaneously. That's how international the crowd is. Owner Adolf Jacobsohn, who retains his Berlin accent although he's lived in Rio since 1933, has combined the best of Brazil and Europe in his charming café. The balcony area is ideal for dining since it overlooks the dance floor. We recommend the pasta ($3) and the wienerschnitzel ($4). A stein of excellent beer is only $1. There's a cover charge, however, of $5 in the upper-level nightclub. Open from 7 p.m. to 4 a.m. seven days a week, the Terrazze do Lido is highly recommended.

The **Café do Teatro,** a must lunch stop, is perfect for an early cocktail from 3 to 8 p.m. Drinks are only $2 to $3, and you can enjoy the opulent décor of this former museum in the Teatro Municipal (the city's cultural center). Enjoy your drink along with the Cariocas awaiting the evening's performance. Note the tiled walls and columns.

For disco music with incredible views, head to **Rio's,** in Flamengo Park, and gaze at Guanabara Bay, Sugarloaf, and the like. Head for the romantic piano bar at the **Boite** nightclub with its live combo group. The Pub is open from 7 p.m. The views are spectacular. Note the old photos of Rio in the 1920s.

Café Un Deux Trois, at Avenida Bartolomeu Mitre 123 in Leblon (tel. 239-0198), a wine-and-cheese restaurant, has a fantastic piano bar upstairs that's open until 5 a.m. daily. Fernando Gallo, a worldly pianist, heads a three-piece combo and no request will be denied. Stop by and let him know your favorites. You can drink and/or dine at this friendly oasis. A $4 minimum.

Another fun place is **Amigo Fritz,** at Barão da Torre 472 (a block beyond Pirajá). This small Bavarian house is actually a restaurant, but feel free to enjoy the festive German ambience sipping your beer (75¢). The owner (no doubt a Mascagni opera fan) converted his private home into a student hangout. *Note:* There is a $4 minimum on weekends. If you're hungry, try the sausages with sauerkraut ($4).

To really understand the working-class Cariocas, why not join them at one of their clubs where on weekends they let it all hang out to the beat of the samba. There are many similar clubs, but one we particularly enjoy (Saturday night only) is **Club Renascenca,** at the Gimnasium of Maxwell Sports Club, Rua Maxwell 174 in Vila Isabel. The entrance fee for men is $3 (women are free if accompanied by an escort). You can stand free or pay $1 for a table with waiter service. Take your place and wait for the music to blast off. Within seconds the crowd is in a samba frenzy. The dance floor and aisles are filled with dancing and singing bodies. You'll need a cab to get there.

Check with your hotel clerk to make sure which clubs are open. Remember —dress informally.

A Couple of Spots for Singles

One of the most popular clubs is **Lord Jim,** a British pub at Rua Paul Redfern 63 in Ipanema, which is open from 6 p.m. to 2 a.m. Lord Jim tends to be standing room only in the downstairs area where singles congregate to drink. By all means join the dart games. If you're hungry, head upstairs where fish and chips ($5), shepherd's pie ($4), and steak-and kidney pie ($6) are popular.

Another good meeting place is **Biblos,** at Epitácio Pessoa 1484, facing the lagoon above the Rive Gauche restaurant. There is live music, usually jazz, and the drinks are under $3. The clientele are usually well-dressed businesspeople out for fun. Next door is **Chiko's Bar** at Epitáio Pessoa 1560, where the prices, clientele, and ambience are the same.

Live Music Shows

Rio has several restaurant clubs open late featuring live shows that draw tourists as well as some locals. One of the newest is **Scala,** in Leblon at Avenida Afaranio de Melo Franco 296. The club features a two-hour show with samba performances of singing and dancing and lovely ladies. The show starts at 11 p.m. There is a $15 admission charge and the show has been compared to that at the Lido in Paris. If that type of entertainment is your cup of tea, you will enjoy Scala.

A popular—and, we think, a bit of touristy—show that lures visitors, particularly those on package tours, is **Oba-Oba,** at Rua Humaita 110 in Botafogo. Here the draw is the stunning mulatas. Stunning may be an understatement, and the variety show is fine for what it is. Another club catering to those with similar taste is **Plataforma,** in Leblon at Rua Adalberto Ferreira 32. The lower level is a restaurant (high-priced churrascaria). Upstairs, starting at 11 p.m., is a carnival-mulata show.

Picking up the tempo a bit, you might want to drop in at **Zoom,** on Rua Rodolfo Dantas, off Barata Ribeiro, a rock 'n' roll disco that could comfortably fit into Greenwich Village. Psychedelic lighting and color give the club a contemporary air. Open until 5 a.m. on weekends; there is a $9 minimum on weekends per couple. Drinks are about $3 each.

Another popular club downtown is **Asa Branca,** at Avenida Mem de Sá 17, where there are two shows nightly and a $10 minimum. You can drink or eat here. A similar show is held at the **Café Nice,** downtown at Rio Branco 277 (tel. 240-0490), where popular local singers and dancers perform nightly.

Popular, too, is **Carinhosa** in Ipanema at Visconde Pirajá 22, a restaurant with dancing and live music, where, for an additional $3 cover, you can be entertained while you dine.

City View

For the best panorama of Rio, head to the 37th floor of the Hotel Meridien, where the bar overlooks Rio. The mountains, ocean, Sugarloaf, and Corcovado are your backdrop. Similar, too, is the view from the bar atop the Hotel Othon Palace.

NIGHTLIFE IN IPANEMA:

Three clubs we like here are popular with Cariocas. Start at the **Barril 1800,** which can hold close to 500 guests. For informal dining, choose an outdoor patio table, where you can have pizza ($4 per pie) or any one of two dozen platters ($3 to $6).

Varanda de Ipanema, Rua Vinicius de Moraes 39, near the beach, attracts a young following who stop by for a late snack and a chance to watch the passing scene.

By the way, across from Varanda is **A Garota de Ipanema,** a youth hangout where the song "The Girl from Ipanema" was inspired (Garota de Ipanema means "Girl from Ipanema").

Nightlife in Leblon

One of our favorite spots in Rio is **People,** Avenida Bartolomeu Mitre 370 (tel. 294-0547), a bar and restaurant with live music ranging from pop and jazz to Dixieland and old movie favorites. The show starts at 12:30 a.m., but we particularly enjoy the pianist who precedes it at 9 p.m. You can eat or drink here. The bar is crowded with the sing-along patrons whose requests are always honored. Nearby in Leblon is **Harry's Bar,** at Rua Bartolomeu Mitre 450 (tel. 259-4043). While it's advertised as a steakhouse, come here for drinks and the live piano music.

For Men Only

Two clubs that offer erotic sex shows, nude go-go dancers, female companions, and an attractive setting are **Assyrius,** downtown at Avenida Rio Branco 277, and **Erotika,** in Copacabana at Avenida Prado Júnior 63. Both have a $10 minimum, and drinks are about $3 to $5. Don't be surprised when you spot many couples who come for the show.

Two expensive Copacabana clubs that feature good-looking dance hostesses are the **Bolero,** Avenida Atlântica 1910 (upstairs), and the **Holiday,** at Avenida Atlântica and Rua Ronaldo Carvalho. You're on your own here.

Off Avenida Atlântica between Ruas Belfort Rojo and Ronaldo Carvalho are a series of clubs catering to the stag male. Sporting names the likes of **Pussy Cat, Bar Man,** and **Scheherazade,** the clubs feature attractive, unattached young women at the bar eager to join you for a drink. Once there, you're on your own.

Popular also is **Mikado,** at Rua Ministro Viveiros de Castro 127 in Copacabana. Head downstairs where the ladies are anxiously awaiting your arrival.

Gay Clubs

Rio has a sizable gay population. One of the most popular hangouts is in the **Galeria Alaska** in Copacabana, where there are clubs and shows featuring transvestite male strippers. There is usually a minimum, but no cover for entering. Other gay clubs include **La Cueva,** in Copacabana at Rua Miguel Lemos 51, and **Zig-Zag,** Avenida Bartolomeu Mitre 662 in Leblon. Another popular hangout is **The Club,** at Travessa Cristiano Lacorte 54 near Rua Miguel Lemos in Copacabana.

6. CARNIVAL TIME

Ever been in New Orleans during Mardi Gras? Well, multiply the frenzy there by several times and you will come up with an approximation of what happens in Rio each year during the three days and four nights preceding Ash Wednesday, the beginning of Lent.

This is a period when the life of Rio is devoted only to carnival. Business is suspended; commercial life stops. Hundreds of costume balls are held throughout the city, and the Carioca talks, walks, and breathes in time to the samba, Brazil's national dance. The streets are filled with dancers, small Latin combos, confetti, strong perfume, and endless parades organized by the many private samba schools in Rio.

Prelenten celebrations are traditional in most Latin countries. Each country puts its own special stamp on its carnival or Mardi Gras. In New Orleans the beat is jazz, in Trinidad it's steel bands, and in Rio the beat is the samba and it's everywhere—on the radio, blasting out of record shops, and in improvised groups along the beaches. Rio's carnival celebration lasts four days and nights (from Saturday until Ash Wednesday) without, as we said, let-up, and its frenzy, excitement, and gaiety are infectious. You'll find yourself moving with a lighter step and caught up in the beat of the samba bands along the streets. There is dancing the length of Rio Branco, from President Vargas to Cinelandia. Everyone is in costume, some elaborate, and you'll feel more comfortable in one too.

Every evening the specific carnival events take place at the Sambadroma. Buy grandstand tickets for best viewing, and be sure to be in your seat Sunday night for the most famous event—the **March of the Samba Schools (Escolas de Samba).** It lasts till the next morning. Each of the ten schools has a theme and a song (samba, of course). It may have anywhere from 1,000 to 2,500 costumed people dancing down the street to its own band. The people in the stands join in the singing and it's a thrilling experience.

There are also balls in some hotels and theaters. They're expensive and not worth the money. Instead, go to Canecão and dance on the tables all night.

The carnival season formally begins at midnight on New Year's Eve, when sedate orchestras in the hotels and at private balls give way to the frenetic rhythms of native bands. We're told that South American visitors planning to come to Rio for Carnival Week come here on New Year's Eve "to train" for the sleepless stretch ahead. Anyone who saw *Black Orpheus,* a marvelous movie filmed during Carnival Week, will have an idea of the atmosphere.

7. A SHOPPER'S GUIDE TO RIO

In many ways Rio is a bargain-hunter's paradise, since the city offers superb buys in semiprecious stones and jewelry, woodcarvings, wooden trays, handcrafted native goods, natural stone ashtrays and pendants, and alligator and leather handbags and wallets. The **Largo da Carioca** area is in the heart of the downtown shopping district. Outstanding shops are found on **Rua Gonçalves Dias** and **Rua Ouvidor,** both narrow streets that are closed to traffic. Another good shopping street in this area is **Uruguaiana.** Gonçalves Dias runs parallel to Rio Branco and intersects with Ouvidor. (Incidentally, our favorite confeitaria, the Colombo, is near here on Gonçalves, and is ideal for a meal or quick snack.)

For the best in rings, necklaces, bracelets, and other jewelry made with Brazilian gemstones (topaz, tourmaline, aquamarine, emerald, and amethyst), you will do no better anywhere than at the string of shops operated by **H. Stern.** This brilliant naturalized Brazilian has been purveying his wares since 1946. These days he operates over 150 retail outlets in Latin America, Western Europe, and the United States (he has a shop in the Olympic Tower on New York's Fifth Avenue), which means he's one of the world's largest gemstone dealers. We strongly urge you to visit the company's main office and workshop at Rua Visconde de Pirajá 490, in its own building, where you will get a free plant tour for which English language cassette-tape guides are available. You will witness the entire process whereby a stone is chosen, cut, shaped, and placed in a setting. And you don't have to buy a thing. Since Brazil is the largest producer of colored gemstones, prices are quite reasonable; we recently purchased a small pendant with a tourmaline stone and 18-karat gold setting for $95. The main showroom is red-carpeted and wood-paneled and the soft-sell personnel make us feel like aristocrats (coffee and soft drinks are served). Every design is unique—no duplications. If you can't make it to the main office, browse through the H. Stern shop at Galeão Airport (open 24 hours a day), at the Copacabana Beach outlet at Avenida Atlântica 1782 near the Excelsior Hotel, or in many of the major hotels. You will find additional outlets at the Touring Club do Brasil in the Praça Mauá and at Santos Dumont Airport, as well as in most South American cities. *Note:* All sales are refundable within one year—regardless of reason for return. Ever see a guarantee like that? The New York outlet will gladly accept the returned merchandise and either exchange it or refund your money.

Also at the H. Stern Building on the second floor is the **Casas do Folclore,** which is crammed with woodcarvings, trays, and native handcrafts. Best buys are the Indian figures fashioned from jacaranda wood (rosewood, a hard dark variety), which sell from $10 to $30. Butterfly trays range from $5 to $50; handsome native dolls are as low as $10. Inexpensive native drums, masks, and headpieces are interesting gift ideas.

We've been happy, too, with our batik and jewelry purchases. Readers' comments confirm our opinion that Folclore is your best-value shop for folkloric items. Other Folclore branches are located in the Sheraton, Inter-Continental, Leme Palace, and Gloria hotels.

An interesting shop featuring handmade and painted crafts is **O Sol,** Rua Corcovado 213. We particularly like the brightly painted wooden treasure boxes, $12 and up. This nonprofit outlet offers a wide variety of attractive, low-priced items.

We also recommend **Les Griffes,** Rua Garcia D'Avila 108, in Ipanema, with a branch at Avenida Atlântica 1702, in Copacabana. These shops are popular for the famous designer-label handbags, wallets, wearing apparel, accessories, and other fine leather goods. Also gift items and linens.

For inexpensive alligator belts and wallets, drop in at the **Souvenir de Rio,** Rio Branco 25 (near the Praça Mauá), where prices start at $10. Dolls, beads, and keychains are also low-priced.

Woolworth-type variety stores where you can pick up inexpensive children's gifts are **Lojas Americanas,** on Visconde de Pirajá between Garcia D'Avila and Anibal de Mendosa, and **Lojas Brasileiras,** on Gonçalves Dias near Ouvidor. Best buys here are the necklaces fashioned from Brazilian nuts—all for $1.

Rio's equivalent of Macy's is **Mesbla,** an 11-story department store located near the Praça Mahatma Gandhi, where you can find clothing, records, sports equipment, and even an elegant theater on the 11th floor.

A **Sear's** outlet is located in Botafogo.

The best bookstore for English-language reading material is the **Livraria Kosmos,** Rua Rosario 135-137, which charges about 50% above U.S. prices for paperbacks. If you're in Rio during carnival season, pick up a copy here of *Escolas de Samba* ("The Samba Schools"), a good background study, in English, of this local phenomenon ($3). You can buy English-language books at the airport shop, too, along with copies of *Time* and *Newsweek.*

If you're partial to chocolate, hustle into one of the **Chocolate**

Kopenhagen branches scattered throughout Rio. Manufactured in São Paulo, this delicious chocolate comes in jars and boxes at prices starting at $1. Other branches are at Rua Ouvidor 147, between Avenidas Rio Branco and Gonçalves Dias; Rua Visconde de Pirajá 250, in Ipanema; Senador Dantas 24B, opposite the O.K. Hotel; and at Avenida Rio Branco 181.

If you're interested in Macumba artifacts, try **Casa Sucena,** at Rua Buenos Aires 96.

SHOPS IN COPACABANA BEACH: The main shopping street of Avenida

Copacabana houses branches of many center-city stores, so some shop names will seem familiar.

One unusual store here is **Liane Souvenirs,** Rua Santa Clara 27, between Copacabana and Avenida Atlântica, where the Indian masks of palm and straw are good buys at $8 and up. Wooden art pieces, Bahian dolls, and stone ashtrays are interesting gift items too. A sister store is located downtown at Rio Branco 25 (17th floor).

Two other stores you might look in on are across the street from each other. **Thompson,** Avenida Copacabana 371A, specializes in wooden items, leather bags, dolls, and beads. At **Iviotici,** in the Cassino Atlântico Shopping Center, we suggest you look at the ceramics and paintings. All the other traditional items are available here too.

For fine leather items such as hassocks, wallets, and belts, try **Copacabana Couros e Artesanatos,** Rua F. Mendes at Avenida Copacabana. All items sold are made on the premises and prices are right. We recently purchased a cowhide beanbag chair here that is stunning. We have never seen anything like it in the U.S.

Another fine leather shop is **Lido Bags,** at Avenida Copacabana 267. Featured are wallets, cigarette cases, travel bags, and other novelty items.

For artesanias from other Latin American countries, try **Artezania** in the Vitrine de Ipanema gallery in Ipanema, at Visconde de Pirajá 580, Loja 111. Here you can find puno bulls from Peru, gourds from Ecuador, Guatemalan handcrafts, and many items from Bahia. Great for browsing.

Shopping Centers

Rio has three excellent shopping centers where you can get just about anything. Two are large, multilevel, and centrally located. The larger of the two is the modern **Rio Sul** shopping center, located in front of the Canecão Club in Botafogo. This trilevel arcade features a Mesbla department store on the mall level, an H. Stern outlet, boutiques, music, men's shops, toys, and lots more— excellent for browsing.

The other convenient center is the **Cassino Atlântico,** adjacent to the Rio Palace Hotel in Copacabana and connected by a passageway. Both are centrally air-conditioned, with escalators.

The newest shopping center is the **Barra Shopping Center,** at Avenida das Americas 466, way out beyond Gavea in Barra da Tijuca, a growing community. Unless you happen to be in the area, forget about this one.

Additional Ipanema Shops

For sporting outfits that are different, try **Amor Perfeito,** Rua Visconde de Pirajá 371, a popular shop for Cariocas.

Brazil is a major manufacturer and exporter of shoes and a fine shop to browse in **Rotstein,** Rua Visconde de Pirajá 371.

There are many shopping arcades and boutiques on and adjoining Rua Visconde de Pirajá in Ipanema. It is on a long street and you can easily walk from one end to the other and sample the many shops (bikinis are an excellent buy here), men's and women's boutiques, shops for bags, belts, and other leather items, sports outfits, all in bright colors. Don't be afraid to try the clothing you are considering. Shop owners expect you to do so and will ordinarily offer you coffee while you wait.

8. TRANSPORTATION NOTES AND ASSORTED MISCELLANY

BUSES: The best way to travel around Rio is via bus—cheap (about 20¢), quick, and plentiful. You enter in the rear, pay, and receive a token, the color varying with your destination. Since the exit door is in front, gradually work your way forward to avoid a last-minute crush. Incidentally, no matter how hot and crowded the buses are, the even-tempered Carioca is invariably calm and polite. However, on a crowded bus, here as elsewhere, beware of pickpockets.

Important bus stations are at the Praça Mauá, on Presidente Vargas just off Rio Branco, along Rio Branco, and at the Praça Mahatma Gandhi.

The major bus terminal is the **Rodoviária Novo Rio,** located near the start of Avenida Brasil. Bus 123 will get you there. Buses leave hourly from here to São Paulo (seven hours; the fare is $8); to Petrópolis ($1) every 15 minutes; and even to Brasilia.

TAXIS: Taxis (usually VWs) are easy to come by (just wave your arm) and they are cheap enough. Rates jump 20% between 11 p.m. and 6 a.m. A cab from the Praça Mahatma Gandhi to Copacabana Beach should run you $5 during the day and $7 after 11 p.m. Taxis are required to post an accurate rate chart but frequently do not do so. If you feel you are being overcharged, ask to see the driver's rate charge.

CAR RENTALS: If you want to rent a car, try **Hertz,** Avenida Osvaldo Cruz 61 (tel. 285-1249), in Flamengo. A VW will cost you $30 a day plus 10¢ a kilometer. A Super VW goes for $30 per day and 15¢ per km.

MISCELLANY: Herewith some information that could prove helpful:

Thumbs Up: When saying hello or good-bye in Rio, the standard gesture is "thumbs up," which means all is well. Or sometimes "thumbs down," which of course means the reverse.

The Press: The *Daily Post,* an English-language daily published here, is your best bet for keeping up on U.S. news, local sports, and entertainment events (60¢). *Newsweek* is $1.50, and *Time* (Latin American edition) is $1.20.

Emergencies: Doctors are available, night and day, at 236-2887.

Drugstores: U.S. drugs are sold all over Rio. One store popular with North American travelers is the **Farmácia Mundial,** Senador Dantas 118D, in Cinelandia, near Praça Mahatma Gandhi.

Post Office: You will find the main building on Rua México 148. The Portuguese word for stamp is "selo." An airmail letter to the U.S. is 40¢. In Copacabana, the post office is at Avenida Copacabana 540A, near Rua Siqueira Campos; in Ipanema it's at Rua Visconde de Pirajá 452.

Street Signs: These often include mention of an important restaurant or store in that vicinity, with an arrow.

Telephones: Many stores and restaurants will allow you to use their phones at a cost of about 10¢. If the shop has a public phone, buy a *ficha* (token) for 10¢ at the cashier. Newsstand vendors sell tokens for street booths (10¢).

Airports: When flying out of the country, your plane will depart from Galeão Airport; domestic flights usually originate at Santos Dumont Airport, within sight of the Praça Mahatma Gandhi. The duty-free shop is located one flight up. Stock up on the usual cigarettes, perfumes, etc., at duty-free prices.

Airport Tax: When flying out of Brazil, prepare to pay an airport tax of about $8 per person; flights within Brazil, $1.50.

Dr. Scholl: If your feet are tired or hurt, see the good doctor on Avenida Copacabana, corner of Figueroa Magalhoés (second floor), or downtown on Rua Buenos Aires.

Hot Dogs: Street vendors (mostly at the beach) sell delicious hot dogs for 50¢. The most popular brand is Genial.

Toys: For the children left behind, stop at **Carrousel,** Avenida Copacabana 680B. Also **Brinquedos Modernos,** at Rua Visconde de Pirajá 592.

Tipping: Cab drivers are not tipped by Brazilians and they don't expect to receive tips from tourists. Bellhops should be tipped about 50¢ per bag and waiters should be tipped about 5% above the 10% service added to your bill (the 10% service charge is for the restaurant, not the waiter).

CHAPTER IV

MONTEVIDEO, URUGUAY

□ □ □

Located between Rio and Buenos Aires, Montevideo makes a good midtrip stop on your journey to those cities—in much the same way that Switzerland offers a change of pace on a trip between Italy and France. And the comparison, we think, is apt, because the welfare state of Uruguay resembles Switzerland in its well-ordered and quiet life.

South American tourists flock to Uruguay in the tens of thousands from December through April (summer in South America) when the weather is far more temperate than in tropical Rio. (Understandably, accommodations are difficult to get at that time, so write well ahead for reservations.) Yet amazingly few North Americans come to this cosmopolitan city, surrounded by beautiful beaches, which helps to make it a superb tourist find!

IMPORTANT CURRENCY NOTE: Exchange rates for the Uruguayan **peso** shift so rapidly that it is vital that you check carefully before you leave. For example, in late 1980 the U.S. dollar could purchase approximately 9 pesos. Within the next two years the dollar gradually rose so that by late 1982 you could purchase approximately 13 pesos for the U.S. dollar. Within months a dramatic devaluation occurred and the peso had an official rate of 23.5 pesos to the dollar and a parallel-market rate of almost 27 pesos. By 1986 the exchange had risen to 180 pesos per U.S. dollar.

At this writing, you can purchase 400 pesos for each U.S. dollar, and prices, while adjusted, are quite low. Simply stated, it's impossible to know what the situation will be at the time of your trip.

URUGUAY IN A NUTSHELL: Before making our specific recommendations, let's first examine briefly some background facts about South America's smallest country.

About the size of Nebraska, Uruguay is a seacoast nation with some of the finest beaches anywhere. Within two hours from Montevideo by bus is the great playground of the rich, **Punta del Este,** the Riviera of eastern South America, where the high-stakes casino never closes.

The authentic folk hero in Uruguay—as in Argentina—is the fabled **gaucho,** who can be seen on horseback roaming the huge ranches outside Montevideo.

A semi-welfare state like Sweden, Uruguay has nationalized numerous industries. Indeed, even some banks, theaters, hotels, and casinos are government owned.

Montevideo, with over one million residents, is an aging city with wide, tree-lined thoroughfares and enormous parks. Eight beach communities lie within 45 minutes of downtown on the Río de la Plata, and the two closest— **Ramírez** and **Pocitos**—can be reached by bus in 15 minutes.

ARRIVAL IN MONTEVIDEO: The modern **Carrasco Airport,** about 13 miles from center Montevideo, functions efficiently and is equipped to assist the arriving traveler. The government tourist office in the arrivals area will gladly confirm hotel reservations if you haven't already done so. Head for the "Ningun Bien a Declara" ("Nothing to Declare") exit sign and you will find a cambio offering a fair rate of exchange. Nearby are several auto-rental agencies. Rates for rentals are extremely low by U.S. standards and you might consider an auto rental.

Take an airline bus for $4 or a taxi for $16 into the city. You will drive along the attractive beachfront, and then inland a bit through the rolling ranch and dairy farmland that surrounds the capital city. (Try to get a group of five to keep your cab costs down.) There are also regular buses from the airport to the city— but they won't take you with luggage.

MONTEVIDEO ORIENTATION: For a quick orientation in downtown Montevideo, familiarize yourself with three key plazas: **Constitución,** in the older west side of center city; **Independencia,** in the center; and **Libertad** (also called **Plaza Cagancha),** in the newer, east side. The important **Avenida 18 de Julio** links Plaza Independencia with Plaza Libertad. These three plazas fall within a rectangular area that's about a mile long and a quarter of a mile wide. In and around the rectangle are most of our recommended hotels and restaurants. The only ones missing are those found in the beach communities a mile or so to the south.

The older section of Montevideo, around Plaza de la Constitución, has narrow, winding streets with well-preserved 18th-century buildings. The more modern areas, in the vicinity of the other two plazas, are marked by large parks, smart shopping arcades, and wide streets with statues all about.

Plaza de la Independencia is the city's social hub and the center of government buildings, theaters, shops, and luxury as well as budget hotels. Heading away from this plaza is Avenida 18 de Julio, which is lined with restaurants, hotels, shopping arcades, and motion picture theaters. At the end of it—beyond Plaza Libertad—is beautiful **Batlle y Ordóñez Park.**

Playa Ramírez, ten minutes from 18 de Julio by bus, is the nearest beach area. In one of our budget choices here—the Parque Hotel—is a famous casino. Nearby is **Parque Rodo,** a huge park that houses an open-air theater, amusement center, and lake.

The newer **Playa Pocitos,** our other nearby recommended beach community, is a mile farther away from center city and is the site of several fine restaurants and hotels, within our budget range only because of the peso's declining value in relation to the dollar.

Continuing from Pocitos, along the **Rambla** (beachfront avenue) and heading toward the airport you pass the beach communities of **Puerto del Buceo** and **Playa Buceo** before reaching **Malvin.** Then comes **Playa Honda, Playa Carlos Gardel,** and then approximately six miles from downtown, **Punta Gorda,** the home of the fine Oceania Hotel. Three miles farther out, near the airport, is the attractive beach area of **Playa Carrasco.** There are two fine hotels in this area, the Hotel Bristol and the renowned Carrasco Hotel, which has a government-run casino. The area has lovely beaches and is surrounded by thick forest. However, this is not a convenient area for budget travelers who will be using public transportation. Still, readers who don't mind the distance have written that they have enjoyed staying in Carrasco.

Street Name Changes

Many streets have recently changed their names and looking at a map or seeing an old address can be annoying. Notably, Convención was changed to **La Torre,** and the diagonal street leading to the Capitol, Agraciada, is now **Avenida Libertador.** The main beachfront avenue, **Rambla** serves multiple duty and changes its identity as it heads toward the airport. Rambla Pres. Wilson suddenly emerges as Rambla Mahatma Gandhi, then Rambla del Perú, followed by Rambla República de Chile, Rambla O'Higgins, and finally near Carrasco Airport, Rambla República de México.

CLIMATE: Montevideo has an almost ideal climate—temperate and dry. Remember always that the seasons are reversed here, so that June through September is winter. Nevertheless, even July and August are mild, with afternoon highs in the 60s and evening lows in the mid-40s. Snow is unknown.

Summer (December to February) highs are in the low 80s, and the evenings are a delightful 60° to 65°.

1. WHERE TO STAY

The best budget hotels are found in that section of the city that stretches between Plaza de la Constitución and Plaza Libertad, passing Plaza de la Independencia along the way. Virtually all of these are within easy walking distance of one of the three plazas and also near the important Avenida 18 de Julio, which links Independencia and Libertad. We also have some choices at the two beach areas nearest downtown.

Note: The rates we quote exclude breakfast, unless otherwise noted, include tax and service, and are based on an exchange rate of 400 pesos to the dollar. All prices noted here are in-season rates (December to February); they may be lower in other months. All prices include a 20% value-added tax (IVA).

IN THE PLAZA DE LA INDEPENDENCIA AREA: Here is the heart of Montevideo, which separates the old portion of the city from the new. Famous hotels—including the posh Victoria Plaza—are located here, along with government buildings, offices, and theaters. Most of our choices will be only a short distance from 18 de Julio, the main thoroughfare that connects with Plaza Libertad. (Midway between the plazas is Avenida Agraciada, now called Avenida Libertador—a wide diagonal street that leads to the Legislative Palace.)

We'll begin with the best, and that would be the first-class, 78-room **Hotel Crillon,** Andes 1318 (tel. 920195), between 18 de Julio and San José. Here, a large, modern, carpeted double, with bath, telephone, double bed, night table with lamp, comfortable chair, and draperies, rents for $28, breakfast included. Singles are $22. And there is a bar and a doorman! Some rooms have terraces.

Another of the fine values in this city is the high-quality **Hotel Cervantes,** Soriano 868 (tel. 907991), which you can reach by strolling along Andes one more block away from 18 de Julio. This 66-room, three-floor choice (with elevator) has clean, bright doubles with breakfast, bath, and telephone that rent for $25, and singles for $15. Rooms without bath are cheaper. The management is friendly and helpful, and your stay here should be most pleasant. Take the elevator to the reception office on the first floor.

A perfectly fine choice is the 40-room **Hotel Rex,** at 18 de Julio 870 near Andes (tel. 901820). Head up one flight to the reception desk. Doubles with bath and breakfast run $24; singles are $15.

You might also try the **Hotel Español,** at La Torre (Convención) 1317 (tel. 915772), corner of San José. It's a 45-room, two-story place that charges about $18 per person for a clean room with bath and breakfast. The owners are exceptionally friendly.

A Family Selection

Back on the main thoroughfare, just beyond Rio Branco, is the renovated, 102-room **Hotel Los Angeles,** 18 de Julio 974 (tel. 920439), which is ideal for families—its manager has assured us he gives special rates to families of four or more. Doubles here, all with bath and telephone, are $20 to $25; singles run $16 to $18 (the more expensive prices for exterior rooms). This five-story, elevator-equipped hotel is extremely well maintained, and the high-ceilinged rooms are spotless and airy. You enter through a gate and the reception desk is on the second floor.

Starvation-Budget Selections

On the whole, basic hotels in Montevideo are less grim, and cleaner, than many of those we've seen in other South American cities. It is possible to live on a budget here without sacrificing comfort. These small hotels are often identified with the word "pension," as many are converted private homes. However, a word of caution: Accommodations are very, very basic. Rooms often come with a sink, bed, table, and chair—period. Private baths are usually a toilet, sink, and for a shower, simply a shower head and drain in the floor. Bring a pair of rubber thongs if you're squeamish about stepping onto a cold, bare floor to shower. On the bright side: Owners often take personal pride in keeping their hotels clean and tidy.

Most of our starvation choices are located near the Plaza Libertad. However, there is a good, basic hotel in the Plaza de la Independencia area: the **Arteneo** at Colonia 1147, halfway between the Plazas Independencia and Libertad (tel. 912630). Several rooms here do have a private bath (again, a basic shower with no stall). Bedspreads are a bit thin and mattresses do have a slouch to them. On the other hand there are nice tile floors in the hallways, and French windows and high ceilings in many rooms. Doubles with bath are $14; singles are $9. Rooms without bath are about $2 cheaper.

A Super Splurge

We cannot discuss Montevideo's hotels and ignore the magnificent 21-story **Victoria Plaza,** Plaza de la Independencia 759 (tel. 914201), which is the prestige hostelry of Montevideo. This 358-room palace charges $80 for doubles, $55 for singles.

IN THE PLAZA LIBERTAD (CAGANCHA) AREA: The most modern

section of downtown Montevideo is centered around the Plaza Libertad (Cagancha), which is due east along 18 de Julio from the Plaza de la Independencia. Dotted with nightclubs and good restaurants, this higher-in-altitude area of the capital probably has more good hotels than you'll find in any other part of the city.

You will find some first-class hotels here—some almost within our budget limits—including the Lancaster, London Palace, California, Oxford, and the Presidente.

The best is the 80-room, 12-floor **Lancaster**, right in the Plaza Libertad at no. 1334 (tel. 920029). Modern and roomy, this hotel offers large doubles with bath, telephone, radio, lamps, and writing desk for $43. Some rooms overlook the plaza. Singles are $25, and triples are $66. All rates include a continental breakfast of juice, coffee, a variety of breads, and cheese. A uniformed doorman greets you outside, and red-suited bellhops whisk your luggage up to your room. A bar and confitería (snackshop) are off the lobby. And guests are allowed free use of the golf course nearby at Playa Ramírez. Associated with the luxurious City Hotel in Buenos Aires, the Lancaster offers good living indeed.

Another excellent choice is the 100-room **London Palace Hotel**, Río Negro 1278 (tel. 920024), between San José and Soriano, where doubles with bath and all the comforts are $35, and singles cost $21. Accommodations are roomy, light, and comfortable. The traditional bar and tea room, lounges, and service make your stay here all the more enjoyable. Highly recommended.

Third choice is the 84-room **California Hotel**, San José 1237 (tel. 920408), near Cuareim. Nine stories high, this fine hotel has large airy doubles, with bath and comfortable furnishings, for about $35 and singles for $25, breakfast included. A bar, TV room, and writing rooms are off the handsome lobby.

The **Oxford Hotel**, República de Paraguay 1286 (tel. 989465), a half block from the plaza, just off San José, is an outstanding place. With 70 rooms spread over nine stories, the Oxford is blessed with a winding stairway leading from the flag-bedecked, mirrored lobby to the top floor. (Fear not, there's an elevator.) Rooms are large; come with bath, parquet floors, and modern furnishings; and rent for $36 to $43 double, depending on whether you get a front or rear location. Singles are $26. Triples are about $60, and quadruples, $70, but in these cases the management normally squeezes extra beds into a double room. (The fact that two additional cots can be added indicates the size of most doubles.) The rate here includes a continental breakfast. While the hotel is beginning to show some signs of age, it still is an excellent buy.

The **Gran Hotel America**, at Río Negro 1330, corner of Avenida 18 de Julio (tel. 906625), has 80 rooms renting for $30 double, and $20 single, breakfast included. Added frills include a garage, bar, barbershop, beauty parlor, and 24-hour room service.

A rather new hotel in this area is the 80-room, 14-story **Hotel Presidente**, 18 de Julio 1038 (tel. 982166), over the Galería Madrileña shopping arcade near Río Negro. Rooms are appropriately modern and rent for $29 double and $22 single. There are two elevators for the building, which faces 18 de Julio and Avenida Liberatador (Diagonal Agraciada). The lounge and bar on the premises are very popular, and the management is most anxious to please.

Another good choice is the very attractive **Hotel Internacional**, Colonia 823 (tel. 905794), near Calle Andes. The Internacional offers 24-hour-a-day room service, a rarity in all but the most expensive hotels as well as a mini-bar in your room. The hotel restaurant serves excellent parrilladas. Rooms are of good size and the furnishings are in good repair. Private baths in all rooms. Doubles here are $40, with singles running $10 less.

A reader tipped us off originally and we enjoy the **Hotel Klee**, at Yaguaron

1306, corner of San José (tel. 916460). Management sees to it that every guest feels at home. Doubles with bath and continental breakfast go for $36 and singles run $25. The hotel is located in the heart of the city adjoining many restaurants and bus routes, and is only a block off 18 de Julio. All rooms come with color TV and mini-bars (frigobars). There is a fine restaurant in this eight-story, 108-room hotel.

THREE SPLURGES: We are including three new hotels in this edition which, while a bit in the higher price range, are definitely worth your consideration and offer fine value for the price.

The **Hotel Embajador,** at San José 1212 (tel. 920762), is a four-star, 80-room hostelry spread over nine almost-luxury floors. While doubles are $45 (singles, $30), your room includes a color TV, mini-bar, and safe-deposit box. The lobby bar is attractive and the coffeeshop is usually crowded. There is a garage on the premises.

In the same category is the **Hotel Europa,** Colonia 1341, corner of Ejido (tel. 920045). This four-star hotel, consisting of 64 rooms on nine floors, is similar in style and services to the Embajador. Doubles are over $40; singles, about $32. Again color TV and mini-bar are standard, and there is a garage for guests.

The final choice in this category is the **Gran Hotel America,** Río Negro 1330 (tel. 920824). For $33 you get a double room with a safe, TV, and mini-bar. There are 90 rooms and you can have room service here 24 hours a day.

Less Expensive Choices

A good budget buy is the 52-room, six-story **Residencial Nuevo Uruguay,** Avenida República de Uruguay 1030 (tel. 915876), three blocks north of 18 de Julio on the near side of the plaza. All rooms here come with bath and telephone; doubles are $25 and singles run $19 (extra charge for each additional person in a room). Winter rates are slightly lower. Upgrading the Uruguay are the recently installed wooden floors, the elevator, and a cheerful U.S.–style bar with handsome wide windows that offer a fine view. Good value.

The **Hotel Iguazu,** at Gutierrez Ruíz 1296, corner of San José (tel. 920108), offers fine doubles with piped-in music for $19, singles for $13, continental breakfast included. Housed in a bright-yellow building, the hotel is conveniently located near the Plaza Libertad.

Yet another good one is the 40-room, three-story **Hotel Balfer,** Zelmar Michelini 1328, corner of 18 de Julio (tel. 920073). Plain doubles with bath are $30; singles are $22. The ONDA bus depot is only a few steps away.

The **Richmond Hotel,** at San José 1034 (tel. 917796), has 60 rooms with bath for $34 double, $24 single. Furnishings are basic.

At 18 de Julio no. 1103, corner of Paraguay, is the 70-room **Hotel Aramaya** (tel. 981060), a few steps from the Plaza Libertad. The large rooms, with drapes, basic furniture, and bath, rent for $12, singles for $8. Doubles without bath are $16; singles run $11. An elevator services the six floors of the hotel. Head up a short flight of stairs to reach the reception desk.

Something cheaper? Head for the **Hotel Windsor,** near Soriano at Zelmar, Michelini 1260, two blocks right of the plaza's far side (tel. 984019). Among the 30 rooms here are doubles with bath for $16; singles are $12. Bathless rooms are about $2 less. A coffeeshop and bar are on the premises. Basic, of course.

Another choice would be the **Gran Hotel Alvear,** Yi 1376, in the Plaza Libertad (tel. 920244), a 50-room hotel. All rooms have bath and telephone. A cafeteria and bar round out the amenities. Doubles cost $20, singles run $15, and the service is friendly.

BUDGET CHOICES ALONG AVENIDA MERCEDES: The traveler on a limited budget should head straight for Avenida Mercedes, to the long stretch running between Plazas Independencia and Libertad. The street is dotted with entranceways to small, low-budget hotels. While all of these establishments tend to look alike, we have singled out two that offer good value.

Two blocks from the Plaza Libertad, at Avenida Mercedes 1166, is the basic **Hotel Cifre** (tel. 906428). Doubles here run $15 with bath (shower only), $10 without. Singles share a communal bath and run $8. Rooms are very plain, but livable. Mattresses have valleys. On the plus side, the reception area is cheerful. Ask for a room facing the street as these have balconies and are much sunnier. The Cifre is popular with students.

One block up from the Litoral at Mercedes 924 is the very plain **Claridge.** Check in here only if the Cifre is full. Doubles with bath are a high $21, singles at $17. Without bath, the prices drop: $12 for doubles, $9 for singles. Rooms are quite large and come equipped with small heaters. There are only a few singles.

IN THE PLAZA DE LA CONSTITUCIÓN AREA: This older section of Montevideo is the heart of the financial district and is marked by colonial architecture, narrow, winding streets, and friendly residents whose families have lived here for generations. This is easily the most picturesque area of the city. The key streets for you to know are **Calle Rincón** and **Calle Sarandi,** which adjoin the plaza.

Budget Choices

Recently renovated is the elevator-equipped **Reina Hotel** (formerly the Ritz Hotel), at Bartolomé Mitre 1343, corner of Sarandi, a block from the plaza (tel. 959461), which has 40 rooms spread over six stories. Rooms are pleasant and airy, if somewhat on the small side. All have private baths (shower only). Singles are $16; doubles cost $22. The cafeteria on the fifth floor is bright and cheerful, with an excellent view overlooking the rooftops of the city. Continental breakfast is about $2.50.

If, but only if, the foregoing selection is full, then try the rather meagerly furnished **Hotel Palacio,** Bartolomé Mitre 1364 (tel. 963612), a six-floor, 26-room establishment. Doubles with bath go for $10, singles for $7. Bathless rooms are cheaper. The reception desk is located one flight up.

You might also consider the 35-room, four-story **Artigas Hotel,** across from the Palacio Hotel at Bartolomé Mitre 1361, corner of Sarandi (tel. 959563), where large, bare doubles with bath (shower) cost $14; singles are $10. Bathless rooms are cheaper. A little better than basic.

A Big-Splurge Choice

And now we come to the "class" hotel in this area of Montevideo, the 150-room **Columbia Palace Hotel,** Rambla República de Francia 473 (tel. 989364), which faces the river south of the plaza. After you allow the doorman to open the front door for you, and stroll through the plush lobby, passing the beauty salon, barbershop, bar, and restaurant, you'll discover at the desk that rooms rent for only $45 (rear view) to $50 (front view, facing the sea) double, and for $35 to $40 single. For that sum you get a carpeted room with large private bath, modern twin or double beds, dresser, vanity table, enormous closets, radio, and a uniformed bellhop at your disposal within minutes after you summon him by telephone. Some rooms come with a sitting room, and front rooms offer splendid views of the Plata River, which is another reason why this is an exceptional hotel.

To reach the Columbia Palace, go to the Plaza de la Constitución, then walk down (south) along Ituzaingo and make a right on Brecha to the hotel.

AT THE SEASIDE: If you prefer sea to city, you might consider staying at a budget hotel in one of the eight beach communities on the fringes of Montevideo. Remember, however, that in winter (June through September), these areas can be damp and possibly chilly; we recommend this area for summer stays primarily. Still, winter temperatures rarely dip below 40°, so that staying here in August can hardly be thought of as a hardship.

We have confined our hotel search to the two beach suburbs nearest center city—Playa Ramírez and Playa Pocitos—as well as several hotels in the farther beach communities, Punta Gorda and Carrasco. Most hotels here charge somewhat less during the winter months (June to September). We start with the nearest community of Ramírez, and head along the Rambla toward the airport.

Along Playa Ramírez

Closest to downtown Montevideo, this community is within ten minutes of any of the main plazas via bus 116, 117, 121, or 300. Near the Municipal Golf Club (where golf is free) and lovely Rodo Park, Playa Ramírez is less than two miles south of Plaza Libertad and faces the mouth of the Río de la Plata.

Probably your best choice here is the old and courtly **Parque Hotel Casino** (tel. 497111), which houses the government-owned casino. Facing the beach on Rambla Presidente Wilson, the aging 60-room, three-story Parque offers roomy, comfortable doubles for $35 to $40, depending on location, and singles for $25 to $29. All rooms come with bath and telephone; the furnishings are quite old but well cared for. Guests are entitled to free admission to the casino. This hotel has deteriorated somewhat over the years, but is still popular and a good value.

Along Playa Pocitos

Five minutes (by bus) beyond Playa Ramírez is a second beach community, Playa Pocitos, which is larger and more recently developed than its neighbor.

The outstanding hotel here is the modern, 100-room **Gran Hotel Ermitage,** Juan Benito Blanco 783 (tel. 704021), near Calle J. Zudanez. The bright, airy, air-conditioned doubles, all with bath and telephone, are $35 to $40; singles cost over $25. Situated on a rise 50 yards from the beach and two blocks from the main street (España), the nine-story Ermitage offers guests a fine view of the city from its upper stories. With elevator, bar, and restaurant, this hotel is an excellent value. Highly recommended. Look for the green-and-white awning (there may be no sign).

At Punta Gorda

One of Montevideo's finest hotels, the **Oceania** is located here at Mar Artico 1227 (tel. 500444). This hotel faces the beach six miles from center city and offers air-conditioned rooms with TV, and features a fine restaurant and bar. If you are driving, the hotel has a garage. Doubles run about $40.

At Carrasco

This beautiful beach area near the airport has two hotels that attract a steady crowd during the summer months of December to February. More famous by far is the **Casino Carrasco Hotel,** at Rambla República de México (tel. 501261), which sports one of the two casinos in Montevideo and ranks with the Ermitage in décor and service. The **Hotel Bristol,** nearby at Rambla República de México (tel. 500313), is smaller but features excellent service and amenities. Rates run approximately $45 double at both hotels.

The **Hosteria Del Lago,** at Arizona 9637, Lago de Carrasco (tel. 512210), in Carrasco Beach, is a beautiful colonial-style hotel. A long and low building, most rooms face the lovely lake. The rooms are air-conditioned, and have mini-bars and stereo music systems. This is a lovely stop in summer (December to March). Doubles are a very low $30.

2. DINING IN MONTEVIDEO

Uruguay is much like Argentina in that both raise what some experts claim is the best beef in the world. Enormous ranches run by gauchos are a fact of the rural life here, as in Argentina.

The result in both nations is that steak and beef are national staples—and what staples! A popular restaurant dish in Montevideo and Buenos Aires is the **parrillada,** a mixed meat grill of steak and beef chunks, organ meats, chicken, and sausage cooked over an open fire on a parrilla, or grill. Try it here for a filling, delicious treat.

Uruguayan specialties also include **carbonada,** a meat stew of rice, peaches, raisins, and pears; **carne asado,** a grilled steak; **churrasco,** a thin steak cut; and **puchero,** beef stew served with vegetables and beans. The steak sauces—particularly the tangy **salsa criolla**—should not be overlooked. And do try a **chivito,** a typical Uruguayan sandwich made with a little steak, ham, egg, tomato, bacon, melted cheese, olive, and lettuce. Very tasty! This treat can be ordered at any cafetería.

Dinner is served late—well after 9 p.m.—and you find the late-afternoon tea hour a must to hold you until that meal; it also provides a good occasion for sampling the Uruguayan pastries, which are an art here. The locals wash them down with a strong tea—**mate**—made of yerba leaves.

IN THE CENTER OF TOWN: The best budget restaurants in Montevideo are between the Plaza de la Independencia and Libertad, on and near 18 de Julio.

Note: By virtue of a recent law, the prices listed on a menu include tax and service.

For Breakfast and Lunch

You will want to have breakfast and lunch at one of the many downtown cafeterías. There are one or two on every block. Most are Swiss-like in their cleanliness, and ideal for light meals. They cater to crowds of shoppers and office workers.

You will quickly recognize a cafetería by the words "El Chana" that appear on the awnings of most. This is the name of a popular brand of coffee and tea here—the manufacturer seems to have cornered the market on awning advertising. Some cafeterías serve liquor and some have optional table service. All are wonderfully low-priced.

A typical one is **Los Chivitos,** 18 de Julio 949 at Río Branco, a very clean place where you can get an open sandwich (egg, veal cutlet, tuna fish) for $1, and a large variety of other dishes for under $2. As you enter, you'll find a long counter on your left with sandwiches in front and hot plates in the rear. A lunch special consisting of steak, potatoes, egg, and dessert will cost you $2.50.

Another, **El Chivito de Oro,** at 18 de Julio 1251, serves a great steak sandwich called a "chivito." You can adorn your sandwich with a variety of toppings, and it makes a delicious lunch with a salad or soup. Other sandwiches are made to order and there is a large selection of both hot and cold ones.

Conaprole, on Calle Eduardo Couture, will be your second home if you're staying in a hotel in Carrasco. Set in a large park, Conaprole serves breakfast, chivito sandwiches, and omelets, and gears up for dinner with huge steak platters. It's inexpensive and quite nice.

Or try the **Manchester Grill**, 18 de Julio 899, next door to Horniman's Tea Room. The Manchester is a good stop for a quick breakfast or lunch. Two small croissants and café con leche (coffee with steamed milk) will cost $2. Ham-and-cheese sandwiches are $1. Crowded at tea time. Table seating.

There are dozens of similar choices in this vicinity. Most offer good quality and bargain prices. Scout around 18 de Julio for those that look appealing to you. We've decided not to list a long series of almost identical eateries, but instead to concentrate on other types of breakfast and lunch places.

We are quite fond, for instance, of the **Cervecería La Pasiva,** next to the Hotel Alhambra, Plaza de la Constitución, one of the few budget choices west of the Plaza de la Independencia. Located on the hotel's main floor, the Alhambra has a Spanish colonial décor, including enormous chandeliers dominating the dining room. Booths, tables, and even counter service. We've enjoyed the ham-and-cheese sandwiches for $1, franks for 55¢, and the delicious beer at 60¢. Good for a quick meal.

Note: There are many **galerías,** shopping concourses, along 18 de Julio and elsewhere. Many include cafeterías where you can snack or even dine inexpensively. The **Galería de Notoriado,** at 18 de Julio 1730, on the upper level, is an excellent example.

Dinner Restaurants

Our favorite dinner restaurant in Montevideo is **Doña Flor,** at Bulevar Artigas 1034 (tel. 785751), about ten minutes by taxi from the center of town. Head up a flight of stairs in this white stucco house. There are three small dining rooms, with stained-glass windows and skylights. Each room has only three or four tables. Circular arched columns add a Roman touch to the décor. Surprisingly, prices are not out of sight. Try the champignons à la provençale ($6), the escalope de veau à la compôte d'orange (veal in an orange sauce; $8), or the steak au poivre. For dessert, the soufflé with oranges or cherries is fantastic. Doña Flor has a sibling in Punta del Este. Not to be missed.

For excellent Italian food, perhaps the best in Uruguay, try **Restaurante Bellini,** at San Salvador 1644, corner of Minas (tel. 412987). You will need a cab to get here, but the fare is worth the Fare. Try the pollo cacciatore or the excellent veal dishes. Lasagne is available and the pasta is fabulous.

A local favorite dinner restaurant is **Restaurant del Aguila,** in the Plazoleta del Teatro Solis, next to the theater. Stone archways lead to this popular spot. The white-jacketed waiters will no doubt suggest the brochette de lomo ($5), the entrecot parrilla, the chicken cazadora ($3), or the arroz valenciana ($4). For dessert, try the peaches Chantilly ($2) or the guayaba fruit ($1). Excellent food at moderate prices.

On a par with Aguila is the **Restaurant Morini,** at Ciudadela 1229, two blocks down from the Plaza de la Independencia in the Mercado Central. Open from 11:30 a.m. to 3 p.m. and 7:30 p.m. to 1 a.m., it is decorated like a ship's dining room. Try the cazuela de mariscos ($4), a delicious sea stew; suprema de pollo ($4); or the chateaubriand ($5). Many dishes are prepared at your table. Service is excellent. Highly recommended.

Perhaps the finest downtown restaurant is **Bungalow Suizo,** at Calle Andes 1427. Attractive and offering live music nightly, the Suizo serves delicious cheese fondue, which you definitely should savor. The cost is $6, but portions are enough for two. Also recommended are Swiss potatoes ($2.50).

A Luxembourg businessman who happened to be sitting next to us on a

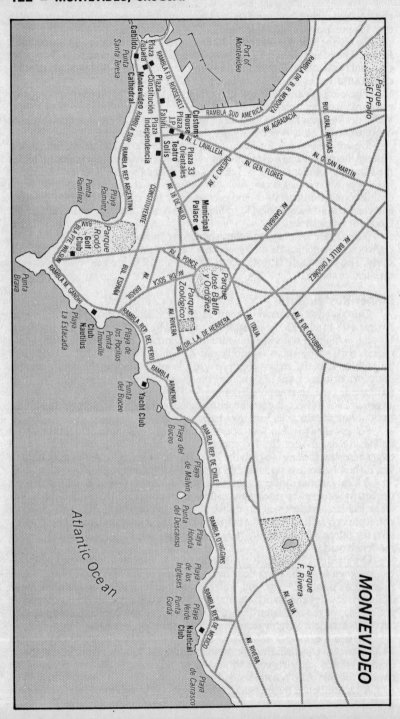

flight to Europe tipped us off to **El David,** a fine steak restaurant downtown at Rivera 2000. Far from fancy, this churrascaría serves the finest parrillada in Montevideo ($4). Also recommended is the entrecot, and the cordero (lamb). One whiff of the meat cooking as you enter will make your mouth water.

A fine restaurant for parrillada (mixed meat grill) is the homey **Las Brasas,** San José 909 at Convención, three blocks from the Plaza de la Independencia; the restaurant is part of a chain. You can see the chef grilling the succulent meats in the window. The parrillada, which is almost enough for two, is under $4.50. A steak will cost you $1.75, and a chicken platter, about $2.50. Like wine? A bottle of good domestic will run you $3. Add 50¢ for cover (bread and butter).

Another typical Uruguayan restaurant is the comfortable **El Fogon,** San José 1080, between Río Negro and Paraguay, which manages to keep two parrillas going at the same time. We like the lower-level dining area, which we have labeled the "Old West Room" because it reminds us of the living room of an old ranch house. It's quieter and more intimate than the main dining room above. Again the parrillada is the specialty. Try the entrecot Fogon, a mixed grill priced at $5.

For a taste of Bavaria, try **Otto,** Río Negro and San José, under the same management as the similar eatery in Buenos Aires. Highly recommended are the leberwurst (liver pâté) and the salchichas de Viena, both $3; excellent beer and German wines. Wooden tables and red-jacketed waiters brighten the décor.

If you're on a budget, try **Vascongada,** on Yaguaron between 18 de Julio and Colonia. Meat and fish dishes are excellent, but prices are well below the fancier restaurants a block away. There is a large TV, and waiters often get absorbed in the 8 o'clock news or Spanish programs following.

Many Uruguayans are of Italian descent and so you might expect to find many good Italian restaurants here. You won't be disappointed. One of our favorites is **Catari,** at San José 935. The lasagne here is served with a mushroom sauce—very different and delicious. Pastas come with a variety of sauces and the meat sauce has lots of meat in it. Pasta with marinara sauce with shrimp is also a fine choice. When we feel like eating pizza we inevitably head to **Hispaño Bar,** on San José at Río Negro. The pizzas here are doughy, with a generous helping of cheese and whatever toppings you choose arrayed over the bubbling top.

Candela, at the corner of San José and Yi, is another good stop for dinner. Newly remodeled, this attractive stop features fine chicken and beef dishes. Not expensive and the meats are outstanding.

Vegetarian fans should head directly to Yi 1344 near the Plaza Libertad, to the **Restaurante La Vegetariana,** where you can feast on a huge variety of dishes featuring vegetables and excellent juice concoctions. They have take-out service too. Open from 11:30 a.m. to 3 p.m. and 7:30 to 11:30 p.m. Inquire about their Scarsdale Diet.

DINING AT THE BEACH:
The better seaside restaurants are in Playa Pocitos, but there is one acceptable budget choice in Playa Ramírez—**Rodo Park,** Gonzalo Ramírez, next to the Rodo Park Hotel. Don't expect fancy décor here, but do plan on tastefully prepared food at low prices. The parrillada dishes, for example, all run under $5. The menu is extensive. Try the plate of the day (select from among ten entrees) and pay about $4.

In the Pocitos area, we're fond of the modern **La Azotea,** Rambla República de Perú at Massini, facing the beach, where the T-bone steak is nothing short of magnificent. The price? $4.50. Tossed lettuce-and-tomato salad comes with most platters. We have also enjoyed riñones (barbecued steer kidneys) as an appetizer ($2), as well as barbecued lamb for $3. The menu is bilingual and most main dishes are well under $5. Meals here would be a bargain at three times the price.

Another selection is the attractive **Le Rendezvous,** in the Hotel Ermitage, which serves a daily special of three courses (soup, meat, and dessert), plus a beverage, for $7.50. You can order a delicious filet of sole for $3.50, or a variety of à la carte choices, most under $5.

We also enjoy the **Sea Garden Restaurant,** at Rambla República de Perú 1402 in Pocitos. Sporting a lovely bar and music at night, this restaurant serves fine seafood in a romantic setting. Highly recommended, especially for those of you staying at the Ermitage.

For fine pizza, try **Las Tejas,** on Avenida Brasil near Avenida España in Pocitos.

El Entrevero, at 21 de Setiembre 2774 in Pocitos, is a good stop for those wanting to try Uruguayan foods. The meats are the highlights here, and you'll enjoy the special sauces that accompany the platters. Try the tomato-and-onion salad for openers, and if you have room, the empanadas are stuffed to bursting.

THE CONFITERÍAS: With dinner as late as it is here, the Montevidean relies on a late-afternoon tea (or more often, cocktail) hour to tide him over. This daily ritual is carried out in informal tea rooms called confiterías, which are spotted throughout the 18 de Julio vicinity.

A particularly attractive confitería, where the pastries are marvelous, is **Horniman's Tea Room,** 18 de Julio 907 (upstairs), a long, rather narrow spot which has superb strawberry tarts for $1. Add 5¢ for whipped cream. The pastries are good enough to take back to your hotel. Crowded.

Other fine pastry shops in town are **Rhin de Oro,** at La Torre and Colonia, and **Confitería Francesca,** at San José 923, near Las Brasas restaurant. There are also many take-out eateries around town. Stroll on Yaguaron between 18 de Julio and San José or around the corner on San José between Yaguaron and Cuareim.

In Pocitos, two confiterías are particularly worthwhile. **Giorgio's,** Rambla República de Perú 871, offers a view of the ocean through its glass windows. Try the nut pastry called "plancha de almendrez" ($1.25) or the sandwiches ($1.50 and up). A block farther along Perú, at no. 893, corner of España, is **Las Palmas,** another good-value confitería.

Empanadas, meat or cheese pies with many variations, are tasty and are found around town.

THE BIG SPLURGE: Two locally renowned restaurants are located in the city's best hotels—the Victoria Plaza and the Columbia Palace. Outstanding in food, décor, and service, these two places are amazingly modest in cost by U.S. standards, but much too high in price for the average Uruguayan.

At the elegant Victoria Plaza grill room, **La Rôtisserie,** Plaza de la Independencia, diners are entertained by a violinist who strolls around the thick-carpeted dining room. There is a nightly orchestra too. The tablecloths and the waiters' jackets are red and match perfectly. There are two maître d's, along with a sommelier with a gold key to the wine cellar dangling from his jacket.

Yet despite this panoply of elegance, you can have a one-inch-thick steak here —the quality is as good as in Argentina—for $5. With appetizer, vegetables, special criolla meat sauce, dessert, coffee, service, and tax, your bill will still be under $8. A special treat? Try the canard à l'orange, wild duckling with orange sauce, which will cost you $6; or for a bit more, try the superb boneless chicken au whisky or champagne. And if you are hungry at lunchtime, be sure to sample the five-course, fixed-price midday meal served here for $5. You get soup, steak, almond cake, and coffee, enough to satisfy the hungriest traveler.

Not quite as plush, but on a par in food quality, is the **Short Horn Grill** in the Columbia Palace Hotel, south of Plaza de la Constitución. North American colonial in motif, this inviting restaurant has wood paneling throughout. The imaginative hors d'oeuvres are an immediate attraction as they are carted about from table to table. Ditto the dessert cart. Favorites of ours are the chateaubriand with béarnaise sauce at $8, and the boiled fish, served Spanish style, at $5. For an extra treat, try the apple pancake dessert ($2). Open daily until 11 p.m.

Finally, the **Restaurant Panoramico,** Soriano 1375 (tel. 920666), on the 24th floor atop the lookout tower, is open for lunch and dinner, at prices in the big-splurge category. The views are spectacular and worth the extra cost.

3. MONTEVIDEO BY DAY

MONTEVIDEO ON FOOT: A do-it-yourself walking tour is the best budget way to begin your visit here as elsewhere. Depending on where you are staying, you can start either at the Plaza de la Constitución or the Plaza de la Independencia.

If you begin at the centrally located Independencia, you will be in the area of important government and office buildings, and also near the famous **Teatro Solis** (where ballet and dramatic troupes appear) and the **Museum of Natural History** (open on Tuesday, Thursday, and Sunday from 2 to 5 p.m.; admission is free). Drop in at the museum and you'll see stuffed snakes, tortoises, and alligators, shrunken heads, and mummies.

At the west end of the plaza is a tall colonial-style archway that is the starting point for a tour of the city's older section. Pass through the archway onto **Calle Sarandi** and in two blocks you'll reach **Plaza de la Constitución,** which is Montevideo's oldest square. The **Cathedral of Montevideo** is here, along with the old **"Cabildo,"** the former Town Hall. Cross the plaza to Calle Rincón. Stroll along Rincón for three blocks until you reach the **Plaza Zabala,** the city's commercial center. Nearby is the stock exchange, the National Bank, and the Customs House. The buildings on these narrow winding streets are all of 18th-century design and construction, and they stand in sharp contrast to other parts of the city.

Return now to Plaza de la Independencia on Rincón and pick up **Avenida 18 de Julio.** Walk along this lovely tree-lined street (you will be heading east) to the **Plaza Libertad (Cagancha),** site of arcades, department stores, restaurants, and hotels. Continuing on 18 de Julio four blocks beyond Plaza Libertad, you come to the **Municipal Palace,** presently the main office building for the municipality. Be sure to note the replica of Michelangelo's *David* that stands in front of this structure. And on the corner nearby is a noteworthy equestrian statue of a gaucho, Uruguay's folk hero.

Here our brief walking tour ends, but we suggest that at a later time you stroll through the beach communities of **Playa Ramírez** and **Playa Pocitos,** both only 15 minutes by bus from center city. By all means, stop at the **Mirador Panoramico** (Lookout Tower) on top of the town hall on Ejido, near Soriano. Note the two elevators outside the building. Pay 10¢ and ascend. You will glide rapidly upward as a view of the ocean expands in front of your eyes. Getting out, you can walk around all sides and enjoy a magnificent view of the harbor, some of the beaches, and a large part of the city. Inside is a large horizontal map of the city surrounded by placards with buttons, indicating the main points of interest in the city. We like it best at sunset, when the sun slowly dips into the sea and the upper arc degenerates into a straight line and then goes out. There is a confitería where you can partake of drinks and light refreshments. Not so visible is the restaurant on top, whose menu is slightly more expensive than most in the city but is still a rather charming place. It opens in the afternoon and remains open until after dark. You might enjoy watching the lights of the city twinkle on (*mirador* means "lookout").

THE PARKS: Montevideo enjoys an abundance of well-manicured parks, and one of the loveliest, a popular weekend gathering spot, is the **Parque Batlle y Ordóñez,** located at the end of 18 de Julio, about two miles from Plaza Libertad. Take any bus along 18 de Julio to get there. Inside the park is one of Uruguay's most famous monuments—**La Carreta.** Don't miss it. Remarkably clean (no litter on the grass), the park offers a bicycle path, running track, and the **Estadio Centenario,** where futbol matches are held.

Actually the city's most popular park is the huge **Parque Rodo** in Playa Ramírez, near Rambla Presidente Wilson, where you can rent a rowboat, canoe, or paddleboat, and have a remarkably idyllic time on the beautiful island-dotted lake in the center of the park. Or you can stroll over the footbridge leading onto some of the islands and watch the swans and ducks on the water. Near the lake is a band shell where open-air concerts are often staged. And there's a major amusement center here, one of the reasons for the park's popularity. While here, stop in at the **National Museum of Fine Arts,** in the park, which features works of contemporary Uruguayan artists. Admission is free, and the hours are 3 to 7 p.m. Tuesday through Sunday (closed Monday). To reach the park, use bus 116, 117, or 121.

Flower-lovers should make it a point to visit another of Montevideo's parks—**El Prado**—off Avenida La Torre (Agraciada), a diagonal street leading off 18 de Julio, between Plaza de la Independencia and Plaza Libertad. Here you can roam among 800 varieties of roses in impeccably maintained gardens.

Finally, the **Parque Zoological** houses both a planetarium and zoo; admission to the zoo is 50¢, and that includes free admission to the planetarium. The latter institution, elaborately equipped, offers shows at 5, 6, and 7 p.m. on Saturday, Sunday, and holidays, and at 6 and 7 p.m. on Tuesday and Thursday. The zoo, which has unusual camel species as well as vicuñas, llamas, guanos, and varieties of snakes, is open until sundown every day. To reach this park, which is about half a mile from Batlle Park on Avenida Rivera, take bus 141, 142, 144, or 191 from the Plaza de la Independencia or Plaza Libertad. Trolleys 63, 67, and 68 also head here. A cab will cost no more than $2.

TWO OTHER MUSEUMS: There are two other museums that we think are worth your time. **Museos del Gaucho y de la Moneda,** located downtown at 18 de Julio no. 998, at the corner of Julio Herrera y Obes, combines gaucho artifacts and history along with antique money and coins. Formerly a palace, the museum has interesting gaucho bolos, cooking utensils, horse equipment, and the like. Open Tuesday through Friday from 9:30 a.m. to 12:30 p.m. and 1 to 7 p.m., on Saturday from 3:30 to 7 p.m., and on Sunday from 3 to 7 p.m.; closed Monday.

Museo de Bellas Artes "Juan M. Blanes" is not as convenient. It's located at Avenida Millan 4015, at the corner of Mauá, in Prado.

SPORTS: As everywhere else in South America, soccer is the national sport in Uruguay. Major matches are held at the 70,000-seat **Estadio Centenario,** a stadium in the Parque Batlle y Ordóñez, at the end of Avenida 18 de Julio. Admission for nonchampionship matches is only $2; for the important contests, including international events, the top price can be anything from $3 to $10.

Bus 121 will take you to the stadium from the Plaza de la Independencia, but a taxi is quicker. Tickets can be purchased directly at the stadium.

Uruguayans are also fond of the turf, and on racing afternoons they flock to the **Hipodromo de Maronas,** on José M. Guerra, where admission is 85¢ and the minimum bet is $1. This is an exciting Montevideo activity. First race starts at 1 p.m. (weekends and sometimes on Wednesday) all year round. Trolleys 4 and 5 (from Plaza de la Independencia) will drop you at the Hipodromo, as will bus 102; from the Plaza de la Constitución take bus 5. A taxi will cost you $3.

4. EXCURSIONS AND TOURS

PUNTA DEL ESTE: The Riviera of South America is a series of beach communities about 80 miles east of Montevideo, where the Río de la Plata and the Atlantic meet at the peninsula called Punta del Este. On one side of the point is the ocean, with huge waves that challenge the most rugged of swimmers and surfers. On the inner side are the gentle waters of the bay, and here waterskiers and sailors are visible from dawn to dusk. Sea breezes keep the temperature moderate during summer, when it is very crowded.

There are many beaches in the area. The most popular is **Playa Brava.** Fishing, golf, tennis, and horseback riding are popular, in addition to the usual water sports.

Where to Stay

There are many luxurious hotels here but they are way over our budget limits, particularly "in season" (December to March) when prices virtually double. The smaller hotels that are more reasonably priced fill up quickly; in fact many regular guests reserve on an annual basis. Make sure to reserve if you're coming in season. Hotel rates here are in general a bit higher than those in Montevideo, but are lower than one would expect at such a well-known resort.

Hotels with the lowest rates are the **Brisas del Este,** at Avenida Las Delicias, Parada 25 (tel. 23554); the **Cordoba,** on Calle 27, between 20 and 18 (tel. 40003); the **Ajax,** at Parada 2 (tel. 84550); the **Arenas,** at Costera Wiliman, Parada 3 (tel. 84556); and the **Castilla,** on Calle 18, between 27 and 28 (tel. 40913). Expect to pay between $30 and $40 for a double room here.

READER'S HOTEL SELECTION: "I just returned from a trip to Punta del Este and want to give a well-deserved plug to an elegant small hotel, the **Jamaica,** Calle Santa Teresa, Parada 2 (tel. 82225). You can walk to the town and to the beach, and the friendly, English-speaking owners will lend you beach chairs and umbrellas. We paid $55 double in this elegant spot, and that included breakfast" (Chas. Soroka, Connecticut).

Where to Eat

Dining in Punta del Este is just that: there are many elegant gourmet dining spots serving fine foods, well prepared and served grandly. These are way over our budget, but if you can splurge a bit you will enjoy dining here.

The town has many small cafés and eateries where you can have an inexpensive breakfast and lunch. Along the beach there are fast-food stops for a daytime snack.

For dinner, try **Club Ciclista,** on Calle 20, which specializes in seafood and Italian dishes. Shrimp, mussels, clams, and a variety of freshly caught fish are prepared in endless ways—all seemingly delicious. The Italian dishes are also standouts. You'll have to go above budget a bit here.

Bungalow Suizo, a branch of our Montevideo selection, serves Swiss-style food, heavy on cutlets and wursts. Delicious.

For Chinese food, try **Restaurant Chino,** also on Avenida Roosevelt.

Finally the **London Grill,** on Gorlero, serves good grilled meats and fish.

Nighttime Activities

Most visitors while away the evening hours here at the two gambling casinos, both open year round from 6 p.m. to 2 a.m. The casino in the **Hotel San**

Rafael, in a chic beach area just east of town (Rambla L.B. Pacheco), gets the elegantly clad high-rollers. Jackets are required here. The in-town **Casino Nogaro** draws a younger, less affluent, but livelier group of betters. Both casinos have roulette, blackjack, baccarrat, and slot machines.

If gambling isn't your thing you can dance away the hours at any number of discos in town. Punta del Este is not a singles spot and most discothèques are for couples. Try **Le Club,** at the San Rafael Hotel, which is stunning. (If you like golf, there's an 18-hole course here.) Another good choice is **Rainbow,** at La Drega Beach.

Clubs with shows include **Casas and Cartas,** at the port, and **Mozart Piano Bar.**

Getting There
ONDA (a bus company) in Montevideo operates several buses a day (two hours each way) to Punta del Este, for a round-trip fare of under $10. ONDA is located at the Plaza Libertad, corner of Ibicuy (tel. 912333).

It has a fleet of modern air-conditioned Mercedes-Benz buses complete with washroom and toilet to whisk you in the comfortable reclining seats to Punta del Este nonstop in a little over two hours. They're not as scenic as the tour buses or local buses which tend to run along the shore, so you must make a choice. Going north from Montevideo you get the impression that Uruguay is a land of beaches and more beaches. There are no longer trains to Punta del Este.

TOURS IN AND AROUND MONTEVIDEO: Day bus tours of the city, which include a trip to the planetarium, can be arranged through the **Cot Agency,** Sarandi 699, at the Plaza de la Independencia. The cost is about $11. A night tour of the city, including a casino visit and dinner at a good restaurant, can also be arranged through Cot, this time for $28. Cot also operates organized tours to Punta del Este.

Another reliable tour agency is **Tudet,** Julio Herrera y Obes 1338 (tel. 987921), near 18 de Julio, two blocks from Plaza Libertad. Tudet runs tours to Punta del Este ($20 with lunch), city tours ($13), nightclub tours ($30), as well as inexpensive scenic tours of the coast and highlands.

Viajes Cynsa, at 18 de Julio 1120 in the Plaza Libertad, is also highly recommended. Stop by and pick up their brochure, which will list departure times and precise costs.

5. MONTEVIDEO AFTER DARK

THEATER AND MUSIC: Touring international shows, including some from the U.S. and Great Britain, appear regularly at the **Solis Theater,** Buenos Aires 678 in the Plaza de la Independencia. Performances are generally at 7 p.m. (the early, or "vermouth" show) and at 9:30 p.m., and while prices vary with the event, they seldom run higher than $5. In some cases you may be required to buy tickets for two different events—a common practice in some South American cities—so check first at the box office.

Free open-air concerts in the summer (December to February) are a delight in the **Rodo Theater** in Parque Rodo (Playa Ramírez).

TELEVISION: Uruguayan television can be worth your time, since Channel 5, the government-operated station, often screens ballets and opera. Many hotels have TV rooms; check your desk for schedules.

CINEMA: Montevideans are great moviegoers, and U.S. and British films are enormously popular. Admission is about $2. Flicks are undubbed, with Spanish subtitles.

NIGHTCLUBS: As in other parts of South America, Uruguayans like to stay up late and live it up.

A magnificent club set at the highest point in Montevideo (2,100 feet), at the foot of a lighthouse and fort, is **Parador del Cerro.** There is no cover or minimum and drinks are $5. There's a nightly show at 12:30 a.m. Step outside, let the wind rush by, and take in the panorama of the city and bay. A taxi will cost you under $5 for the 20-minute ride here. Absolutely recommended.

Another top club, this in a country setting, is **Portofino,** at Belastiqui 1325 in the beach community of Punta Gorda. The club fronts Playa Verde. The daily show at 1 a.m. features three groups and attracts a large crowd. You'll need a cab to get here—about $4.

FOLK AND ROCK: A jumping place that jams in couples on weekends is the **A Baiuca,** in Playa Pocitos at Francisco Vidal 755 (tel. 788340), corner of Juan María Perez, a dark and intimate disco where rock is very much the thing. It opens around 8 p.m. and stays open until 4 a.m. There is no minimum, and drinks run about $3 to $5. You can get here easily by taxi for about $5, or via bus 116 (get off at Juan Bianco and Juan María Perez).

CANDOMBE: Uruguay's contribution to the dance scene, akin in many respects to the tango, is candombe. The tempo can get feverish and is a joy to watch or participate in. For the best in candombe and the tango, head over any night to **La Vieja Cumparcita,** at Carlo Gardel 1181. Located on a quiet street not far from central Montevideo, the club is packed on weekends. Open from 9 p.m. to 2 a.m. nightly, later on weekends. You'll have a good time here.

FOR MEN ONLY: Montevideo has many clubs featuring live music, whisky, and women eager to join you for at least a drink. Some of these clubs are attractive, not the seedy places common worldwide. We have included several establishments that are pleasant and safe, and offer a good time if this is your cup of tea.

Probably the most popular club is **Baires,** at San José 872 (tel. 903304), where striptease is the lure along with pretty muchachas. When the live music stops, disco music sets in. Open from 8 p.m. to 4 a.m. seven days a week. The music is blasting.

Two other similar clubs are **Willy's,** at San José 1077, and **Village,** at Río Negro 1283. Each offers a large attractive bar, ample dance floor, and congenial environment. The strip shows blast off after midnight.

Another club where female companions are at the bar ready to join you—at your invitation—is **Cubilete,** in Pocitos at Gabriel A. Pereira 3106. Cubilete is open from 8:30 p.m. until 3:30 a.m. Drinks are $4. You're on your own here.

By the way, a red light in a house on a side street means just what you think. If interested, just knock on the door. It's legal.

AFTER MIDNIGHT: A club strictly for night people is the **Bonanza,** Bartolomé Mitre 1356, near the Plaza de la Constitución, where the doors swing open at midnight and slam shut five noisy hours later. No need to worry about a cover. For the price of one or two drinks ($3.50 each), you can see a floor show and dance to two alternating bands.

In the Plaza de la Independencia is **Domino,** which has shows on weekends and operates as a disco weekdays. Bar girls are here seven days a week.

An arcade off the Plaza de la Independencia near Sarandi leads to **Le Toucan,** where shows are staged until 4 a.m. Drinks are $2, and women are everywhere.

BIG SPLURGES: Our favorite place to relax in Montevideo is the elegant bar at the **Hotel Columbia Palace,** where you get a feeling of pleasant seclusion as well as a fine view of the Río de la Plata and the shore. Surprisingly, drinks need not be expensive. Domestic brandy is as little as $2.50; cocktails are about $3.50; imported scotch can cost you $4.50.

You should also have at least one drink at the **Carnival Room,** a plush cocktail lounge in the Victoria Plaza Hotel (Plaza de la Independencia), where the décor is Gay '90s complete with gaslights. The best scotch runs about $4 a drink, but manhattans are $3, and martinis, only $2.50. The room opens just before noon and closes at 1 a.m.

GAMBLING: You might like to place a modest bet or two while in Montevideo, and the place to do it is at the unpretentious **Hotel Parque Casino** in Playa Ramírez. Admission is $2 for nonguests and the minimum bet is a low 80¢, while the maximum is only $6.

There are about 30 separate tables (baccarat and roulette only), and smartly jacketed waiters circulate among the well-dressed gamblers. Hours are 6 p.m. to 3 a.m. Bus 117 in the Plaza de la Independencia will take you right to the casino, or you can get there by cab (about $1.25).

Note: Don't cash your traveler's checks here, as the rate is not nearly as favorable as you might get at a bank or cambio.

Another casino, at the **Hotel Carrasco,** near the Carrasco (International) Airport, has a similar betting scale. At each you must purchase a minimum of $8 worth of chips, which of course are redeemable whether you use them or not.

BILLIARD AND POOL: The newest craze here is the proliferation of pool halls. They are a far cry from the smoke-filled atmosphere of a Minnesota Fats–Jackie Gleason movie setting. Found all around the city, they are generally quiet, home-like places with a few tables, serving food and drink. In most, you can come in and sit down without playing, taking only a drink or some food, although many have extensive menus. However, do *not* expect to find many pool sharks. Most of the players are rank amateurs, so you can play poorly without drawing attention. There is a pool hall in the Plaza Libertad, and another off 18 de Julio at Cuareim.

6. A SHOPPER'S GUIDE

Your best buys in Montevideo are jackets, coats, wallets, and women's sport tops, all of suede, and hand-loomed sweaters with colorful folk patterns; leather handbags and wool sweaters trimmed with "nonato," the unusually soft skin of an unborn calf, are equally good buys. The all-wool skirts and sweaters will attract the shopper too.

DOWNTOWN SHOPPING: Downtown shops are for the most part clustered in small arcades called *galerías*.

The modern shopping arcades off Avenida 18 de Julio house some of our favorite shops. Particularly attractive is the **Galería Madrileña,** at Río Negro, and the **Galería Caubarrere,** at La Torre. A third gallery we enjoy browsing in is **Galería de Las Americas,** on 18 de Julio, two blocks beyond the Plaza Libertad.

As for particular shops, a fine one in Galería Madrileña is **Taborelli's,** which has a large variety of handbags in leather ($40 and up), alligator ($125 and up), and leather with suede trim ($40 and up). A branch store is at 18 de Julio 1184 at the Plaza Libertad.

La Opera, Calle Sarandi near the Plaza de la Constitución, is a large department store where you can get sweaters made of a cashmere-like wool called burma, $25 and up. Handbags trimmed with nonato, suede, or pony skin start at the same price.

Montevideo also has several leather factories where you can get good buys on ready-to-wear garments or have them made to order. A typical one is **King's,** Plaza de la Independencia 729, which maintains a large showroom for customers. Suede coats for women start at $350, and vests and unusual sport tops are only $50. Men's suede or leather jackets can also be purchased here.

More leather factories: **Leather Factory,** at San José 976, and **Athens Leather Factory,** at Andes 1341, off 18 de Julio, offer leather and suede jackets and coats. Each promises 24-hour service.

Yet another is the **Montevideo Leather Factory,** upstairs at Plaza de la Independencia 832 (tel. 916226), opposite the Victoria Plaza Hotel. Here ladies can have nutria coats, handbags, jackets, or stoles, or nonato bags and gloves custom-made; men can choose among antelope and suede jackets. There are also clothing items for children, and alligator and ostrich bags.

Ideal for gifts is **Plaza Leather,** Plaza de la Independencia 707, where you can pick up wallets from $12, purses made of calf and pony skin for $50, and gloves for $5 and up.

One of our favorite shops in town is **Pieles Victoria,** in the Hotel Victoria Plaza (tel. 914201). The store is owned by two English-speaking women, Alba and Marta (say hello to them for us), who offer excellent buys in coats, belts, and handbags. You can charge your purchases with American Express or Diners cards.

Try the **Topaz International Jewelry** gemstone outlet for the best in jewelry; it's in the Victoria Plaza Hotel. Your best bet is the local specialty, topaz. Other excellent values are the amethysts and the top-quality agates.

Another fine shop offering Uruguayan gems is **Cuarzos del Uruguay,** at Sarandi 604 (tel. 959362). The shop is well stocked and is conveniently located at the corner of J. C. Gomez, two blocks off the Plaza Independencia.

Uruguay's hand-woven sweaters have become collector's items in the U.S. They are hand-knitted and hand-woven in vibrant colors, employing folk patterns and contemporary designs in unisex sweaters. Both cardigans and pullovers are available. A fine shop is **Manos del Uruguay,** with a convenient location at San José 1111 and in the Montevideo Shopping Center. These sweaters are truly hand-knit folk art.

For women's clothing, we're particularly fond of **Rachel Boutique,** at Río Negro 1320, near San José. And we're pleased to report that the recently purchased wool sweater and coordinated slacks are wearing well. Rachel is in an arcade that houses other good-value, high-fashion shops.

Casa Mario, at Piedras 641 (tel. 962356), offers suede and antelope for men and women, sheepskin and cowskin rugs, and leather handbags—all at bargain (factory) prices. The **Amazon Leather Factory,** at Sarandi 638 (tel. 908970), is also well regarded.

THE MONTEVIDEO SHOPPING CENTER:

Not far off the Rambla, near Playa Buceo, is the Montevideo Shopping Center, a large, modern two-story redbrick shopping mall. Virtually a self-contained outlet, it's open from 7 a.m. to 9 p.m., seven days a week. You might want to wander through it to get an idea of the prices generally charged for featured items. Or you might check out the likes of the **Doña Ines** boutique, **Pierre Cardin,** and **Daniel Hechter.** In addition you'll find several fine restaurants, snack shops like **Mister Pizza** and **Bier Hot,** as well as a supermarket, music shops, pubs, etc. Stop by for a look at the Montevideo lifestyle.

7. TRANSPORTATION NOTES AND ODDS 'N' ENDS

TAXIS: Taxis are astonishly cheap here, and unless you're on a substarvation budget, you should consider traveling this way almost exclusively. The meter starts at 50¢ and jumps 15¢ every quarter of a mile. Therefore, a two-mile trip will cost you under $2. We once had a cab wait for us for 15 minutes, and the charge came to only $1.50. They seem to be all over the place. Due to rate changes, a chart will indicate the meter reading. Look for this. Although most drivers are honest, you may find an occasional one who will overcharge.

COCHES: The word *coche* literally means "car" or "automobile," but a coche always is an unmetered car whose driver can charge what he wishes. If you have to take one, ask the fare in advance. Although not so prevalent in Montevideo as in Buenos Aires, you may find coches at boat landings or wherever there is a temporary shortage of taxis. On a recent overnight boat trip from Buenos Aires to Montevideo, a driver asked us if we wanted a "coche." Noting a long line of waiting taxis and knowing that we could walk to our hotel or an area where there are always many taxis, we asked him what it would cost. He gave us a figure five times the taxi rate. Needless to say, we took a taxi.

BUS SERVICE: The bus system in Montevideo is very efficient and there is frequent service to all parts of the city. All you need to know is the bus route number, and this you can obtain from your hotel management.

However, buses go by zone and you will be asked your destination when you enter. For beach areas such as Pocitos, Carrasco, etc., this is no problem. If necessary, hold in your hand a coin larger than needed and hold onto the ticket you receive. An inspector frequently strides through, checking to see if everybody has paid. You will not be thrown off, but it can be embarrassing. Also, do not pull the cord that runs from the front to the rear. It is used for the conductor to signal the driver to start and stop the bus. As in any city, avoid the rush hour and crowded buses (as there are occasional pickpockets). Better still, try the metered taxis; they are inexpensive and plentiful, and most are honest.

Key Local Bus Routes

To Playa Ramírez and Playa Pocitos—116, 117, 121, 300.
To Parque Batlle y Ordóñez—121.
To Parque Rodo—117.
To the zoo and planetarium—141, 142.
To the stadium—121.
To the Parque Casino Hotel (for gambling)—116, 117, 300.
To the airport—209, 214.
To the Golf Club—117, 300.

Buses to the Airport

Airlines maintain shuttlebus service from downtown to the airport to coordinate with your international flight. Check with them since the rate is only a fraction of the cost of a taxi.

CAR RENTALS: If you insist on driving, try **Sudamcar, Snappy Car,** or **Avis,** which charge $20 a day plus 20¢ a kilometer for a small car. A deposit of $800 is required unless you use a credit card. Your hotel clerk will make all the arrangements.

ODDS 'N' ENDS: We'll end, as usual, with some essential miscellany.

They Speak English: The **Government Tourist Office** branch is near the Hotel Lancaster in the Plaza Libertad, and here you can load up on street maps and general information. Clerks are multilingual. The office is open weekdays from 8 a.m. to 8 p.m., on Saturday from 9 a.m. to 5 p.m., and on Sunday from 9 a.m. to noon.

Cook's: Office of Wagon-Lits Cook is at Río Negro 1356 (tel. 911426), corner of 18 de Julio. **American Express** is at Bartolomé Mitre 1318 (tel. 914823).

Telephones: To get a dial tone, deposit a *ficha* (token), currently costing 5 pesos. If you are calling from a private home and would like to repay the owner, give him 10 pesos.

Tours: Exprinter maintains an office at Sarandi 700, where you can arrange tours and exchange dollars for pesos.

Pluna: The national airline of Uruguay maintains an office on Colonia near La Torre, formerly Agraciada (tel. 916591 or 912772).

First National City Bank: A branch of this bank is located at 18 de Julio, corner of Paraguay (tel. 901981 or 986848).

Maps: The **Hotel Los Angeles,** 18 de Julio 974, has excellent maps. Ask the desk clerk for one.

Airline Offices: Most airline offices are located in the **Plaza Entrevero,** off 18 de Julio at Río Negro.

Airport Tax: Expect to pay about $3 when leaving Uruguay.

Airport Bus: The terminal is located on Calle Yaguaron, just off Avenida 18 de Julio.

Pan Am: The airline ticket office is on 18 de Julio at the corner of Rio Branco.

ON TO BUENOS AIRES: Your next stop is Buenos Aires, a wonderfully sophisticated city where the days will fly by. You can reach the Argentine capital by plane **(Aerolineas Argentinas** has regular 40-minute flights costing $49 one way), or by a combination of bus/ferryboat, bus/prop plane. The latter service is operated by Arco and costs $30 one way. It involves a 3½-hour bus trip through farmland to an airstrip in Colonia. The small prop plane, accommodating up to 44 passengers, takes another 15 minutes to arrive in Buenos Aires's Aeroparque. *Budget Tip:* The taxi fare from the Aeroparque to most of our hotel recommendations is a hefty $10 to $15. Many of these hotels are reachable by subway. Take a taxi to the Plaza Italia ($5) and subway line D to "Catedral" (15¢) and get off at Florida. (The D line connects at 9 de Julio Pelligrini with both the B and C lines.)

A second alternative travel plan from Montevideo is to **bus** it to Colonia (again, 3½ hours) and catch the **ferryboat,** which takes another three hours before docking in Buenos Aires. The trip—far more scenic—costs about the same: $31. Cars can also be transported via ferry from Colonia.

You can also head on to Buenos Aires via **Bus Hydrofoil Service.** It, too, operates via Colonia and takes about 4½ hours total, at a cost of approximately $35.

Tickets for all three services are available through **Cot,** in the Plaza de la Independencia, Sarandi 699 (tel. 984554). All three methods are much cheaper than flying. Take your pick!

CHAPTER V

BUENOS AIRES, ARGENTINA

□ □ □

The advertisements label Buenos Aires "the Paris of the Americas," and they're not exaggerating. We'd go even further and say that this enchanting place combines the sophistication of the French capital, the best of New York, and the gemütlichkeit of Vienna.

Still, Buenos Aires has never attained the fame it deserves—not even with the jet set. Perhaps its unpredictable economy has confused the traveler. At times inflation has run rampant in this fabulous city, normally one of South America's least expensive cities. Nevertheless, in our 1980 edition prices skyrocketed, tripling and quadrupling over the prior edition. Buenos Aires was, for a period of almost two years, the world's most expensive city. Fortunately for the North American traveler, on our last visit in late 1988, the strength of the dollar coupled with the devaluation of the austral made the U.S. visitor if not a king, at least a prince. A steak dinner at most fine restaurants, once again, costs only about $5.

Nonetheless, Buenos Aires, with its sultry climate, pulsating beat, and combination of sophistication and local color, is a city that you would not want to miss.

A BIT OF BACKGROUND: The second most populous city in South America, Buenos Aires is the 11th-largest city in the world, with seven million residents in its metropolitan area. In atmosphere, attitudes, architecture, and contemporary awareness, this pulsating metropolis more closely resembles a Western European capital than any other South American city. The Porteños (as residents are called) dine late, generally after 10 p.m., in fine restaurants that dot the city, browse in boutiques and specialty shops that would be perfectly at home on the rue de la Paix, and revel in the joys of wine, sport, and politics.

Yet basic to the fascinating magnetism of Buenos Aires is the startling hold exercised on the civilized urban community by the rural world of the gaucho, the pampas, and the estancias (ranches)—unchanged for a century or more—that lie within 12 miles of center city.

We shall suggest one-day excursions to gaucho country; don't pass them up.

YOUR ARRIVAL: Reaching center city from modern **Ezeiza International Airport,** where you will probably land, is simple. The Customs check is perfunctory. Your best way to get downtown is by the **Buenos Aires Tour airline bus.** You get your tickets at the "Transportes" sign. The fare is $5. (A private taxi will cost you $12.) At the same location, government clerks will call ahead and confirm hotel reservations. Give them some of our selections and you will get a sheet listing your hotel and the rate. If you need to exchange money, a cambio is nearby. Remember, however, that here you will get the official rate of exchange—so cash only the minimum amount. (Read our "Important Monetary Tip," below.) For all these services, head left as you exit from Customs, and look for the bus and taxi sign.

At the airport there is a **duty-free shop** where you can pick up inexpensive liquor, cigarettes, perfumes, and the like. You are permitted to take these purchases with you into Buenos Aires.

The airline bus will drop you at your downtown hotel in about 45 minutes. Otherwise, the bus will head to its downtown office at Carlos Pelligrini and Lavalle, about 21 miles from the airport.

A **public bus,** no. 86, leaves from in front of the International Hotel. For 50¢ it will drop you downtown in about 1½ hours. Baggage can be a problem. Private cars will then meet you at the bus station and take you to your hotel. This is a free service; however, hang onto your bus ticket to give to the driver when you are dropped off.

The other airport, **Aeroparque,** is only 2½ miles from center city. A taxi ($5) is best.

A QUICK ORIENTATION: Downtown Buenos Aires—which amounts only to a 16- by 10-block rectangular area—is the true hub of the city. Not only are the best budget hotels and restaurants located here, but all important commerce, shopping, nightlife, and posh eateries and inns are congregated in this section as well. It is the city's heart and it beats all day and most of the night.

While a few Porteños live downtown, they come here to work, eat, and play. The only major aspects of life not found downtown are the soccer stadiums and racetracks, which are within 20 minutes by commuter railroad.

There are four major center-city areas, each with its own particular attractions and each with its share of budget hotels:

1. The **Plaza de la República,** marked by a 220-foot-high obelisk that commemorates the 400th anniversary of the city's founding in 1536, is on Avenida 9 de Julio, probably the widest street in the world. The plaza fringes the entertainment and theater district that thrives particularly on two parallel streets—Calle Lavalle and Avenida Corrientes. These are the "Broadway" of Buenos Aires, and you'll find a number of good budget hotels and restaurants in the vicinity. But don't look for relaxation. This area swings day and night.

2. The beautiful **Plaza de Mayo,** considered the true center of the city, houses a number of government and office buildings; the many parades that help keep this city constantly alive often start here and head west along the Avenida de Mayo to 9 de Julio and then north to the obelisk at the Plaza de la República. We have found several good hotels in this area.

3. The posh **Plaza San Martín,** which adjoins an exquisitely manicured park

and a number of luxury hotels and shops, is the third major downtown section. Be sure to see the replica of London's Big Ben that decorates the park in the nearby **Plaza Britania.** This area, located near one of the important suburban train stations, has a number of fine hotels and restaurants well within our limits. The deluxe Sheraton and Plaza Hotels are here too.

4. The impressive **Plaza del Congreso,** a quarter of a mile beyond the far side of 9 de Julio on Avenida de Mayo, is where you will find the Roman-style National Congress building which sits amid shrubbery, grass, and benches in a restful setting. A short walk from the plaza is one of the world's great restaurants by any standard, La Cabaña (see our section on big-splurge restaurants). The deluxe Bauen Hotel is located near the plaza.

The major streets you'll need to know for orientation purposes are **Avenidas de Mayo, 9 de Julio,** and **Corrientes,** and **Calle Lavalle**—plus **Calle Florida,** a bustling shopping thoroughfare that runs from the Plaza San Martín to the Avenida de Mayo, near the Plaza de Mayo.

Note: Avenida 9 de Julio is so wide that each side has its own name—**Carlos Pellegrini** on the near (east) side and **Cerrito** on the far (west) side.

Buenos Aires's newest "in" area is **Recoleta,** home of the poshest restaurants and clubs, and a popular meeting place. **San Telma** is the oldest part of town, located near the dock area, and Avenida Necochea is the main street of **La Boca,** an old Italian section where at night you can join in some of the wildest tarantella while dining on home-cooked Italian food.

Familiarize yourself with these streets and areas, and Buenos Aires will become an immediate friend.

A WORD ABOUT CLIMATE: The Buenos Aires winter (June to September) is quite mild, with temperatures generally hovering in the 50s and 60s during the day and the 40s at night. Summer readings average in the mid-70s, with occasional sweltering afternoons. In general, Buenos Aires is milder than New York City.

IMPORTANT MONETARY TIP: Historically, the Argentine exchange rate has fluctuated sharply and suddenly—even overnight. This means, and we cannot emphasize this too strongly, you *must* check the rate immediately *prior* to your visit to Argentina.

A brief synopsis of the past decade or so best illustrates our predicament in trying to apprise you of what you will encounter. Buenos Aires, historically, was one of Latin America's best buys for the U.S. dollar. In 1974 a "parallel market" arose, creating at times an enormous variation between it and the official rate of exchange; so your exact cost was dependent on where you purchased your pesos. Either way, Buenos Aires was a traveler's dream from the point of view of costs.

In 1980 inflation soared out of sight. A cup of coffee cost as much as $5 and a cab to Ezeiza Airport was over $50.

Fortunately, since 1982 the strength of the U.S. dollar, combined with other circumstances, permitted the dollar to purchase so many pesos as to make the cost of a visit to Buenos Aires inexpensive, and Buenos Aires became one of South America's least costly cities for North Americans. Since then prices have been creeping up, but only slightly, and we can happily report that Buenos Aires is, as of this writing, an enormous bargain.

But this can change—unfortunately, even overnight—so it is possible that at the time of your visit the prices quoted in this chapter could be doubled or halved, or (most likely) somewhere in between.

In 1986 the peso was replaced by the **austral** as the unit of currency, at approximate par with the U.S. dollar. Since that time, the dollar has soared over

15-fold so that now you can purchase 15 australs with each dollar. This exchange rate keeps prices reasonable for those entering Argentina with U.S. dollars. How long will this last? *Who knows?*

We suggest, therefore, that prior to your departure you check out the situation in Argentina and if necessary purchase australs *before* you arrive in Buenos Aires. In summary, we won't say to look before you weep, but we do say to look at the exchange rate and budget yourself accordingly.

P.S. Even at three times the price, Buenos Aires is a marvelous town that deserves all the time you can spare.

THE MALVINAS: While in Argentina, you will still feel the repercussions of the 1982 clash between England and Argentina over the Falkland/Malvinas Islands. That unfortunate war has left behind scars which hopefully will fade with the passage of time. Remember that this was and still is an extremely emotional issue to Argentinians, and a word of tact to the wise should be sufficient. At this writing, negotiations to settle the dispute politically are under way between the two governments. Little progress has been made.

1. HOTELS OF BUENOS AIRES

Without fear of contradiction we can flatly state that we found fewer unacceptable hotels in Buenos Aires than in any other city in which we have traveled, be it in Europe, North Africa, Mexico, or elsewhere in South America. Unlike budget hotels in Europe, most of the less expensive Buenos Aires establishments are large, often with 100 or more rooms. Only a few (deluxe) hotels have pools.

Be aware, however, that hotel prices occasionally rise drastically and that now many of the centrally located luxury hotels are on a cost scale with deluxe hotels in major American cities.

Hotel prices are currently affected by the 16% surcharge added to the normal 24% tax and service charges. Whether this hefty bite out of the tourist pocketbook will remain, only time will tell.

Note: Prices do *not* include breakfast, unless indicated, but generally do include private bath, telephone, and the 40% tax and service charges.

ON OR NEAR CALLE FLORIDA: Many of the best budget hotels in Buenos Aires are found along Calle Florida and the blocks adjoining it. We personally prefer staying in this area, since it is quieter at night than the "Broadway" section and yet right in the heart of things.

An excellent first choice would be the wondrous old-world **Hotel Carsson,** located at Viamonte 650, between Calle Florida and Maipu (tel. 392-3551). This relatively small (for Buenos Aires), 95-room hostelry offers spotless, roomy doubles with twin beds, private bath, telephone, and radio for $45, service and tax included. Singles are a high $30, but you get a double-size room for that price. A four-story building, with bar, coffee room, and elevator, the Carsson will enchant you with its handsome lobby bedecked with soft leather chairs and deep red carpeting; we associate it with the Harvard Club in New York. And the Carsson is just as quiet. An important plus is location, half a block from the main shopping street of Florida and only two blocks from the entertainment center on Lavalle. Manager Adriano Lopez aims to please. Rooms here are highly desired by Argentinians and tourists alike. Reservations are a must. (We tried to stay at the Carsson on the spur of the moment, only to find that it was full for the week.)

On a recent trip to Buenos Aires we arrived "plumb tuckered out" at the **Eibar Hotel,** Avenida Florida 328, between Corrientes and Sarmiento (tel. 45-0969). Two cups of tea and two toasted sandwiches later, enjoyed in the hotel's comfortable cafetería, we felt completely revived. That was to be the pattern throughout the rest of our stay. While not plush, the Eibar makes you feel right at home. The friendly staff—several of whom speak a little English—are helpful, offering good tips on shopping and sights. And you can't beat the location smack on Florida. Two high-speed elevators serve the 100 rooms spread over seven carpeted floors. Rooms are modern and several doubles have comfortable sitting areas. Prices? $22 for singles, $32 for doubles, and $38 for triples (tax included). Breakfast is extra and runs about $2 for luscious croissants (medias lunas) and coffee, served in the adjacent cafetería. We had many quick meals here and found that service was top-notch and the atmosphere calming (this is an excellent place to meet friends or just linger over a pot of tea). Request rooms away from the street, as those facing Avenida Florida can be noisy, especially on weekends.

The **Camino Real Hotel,** at Maipu 572 (tel. 392-3162), offering 75 rooms spread over ten floors, is a bargain with doubles for $35, and singles for $25, with breakfast included. There's a fine confitería in front of the hotel, and the location makes the Camino Real a convenient, quiet stop.

The Big Splurge

Offering both elegance and comfort is the **Grand King Hotel,** at Calle Lavalle 560 (tel. 392-4012). This 100-room luxury establishment has central heating, air conditioning, and television in all rooms. A bar, tea room, and room service are added attractions. Rooms, ultramodern, although a little on the small side, have nice tile baths. Singles are $45, while doubles are $60. Prices include a continental breakfast of coffee and rolls. The Grand King Hotel is a bargain when compared to the Plaza, Panamericano, or Sheraton hotels, considered to be the elite among the city's hotels, where guests pay $100 and up a night for accommodations.

Less Expensive Choices

On or near Avenida Florida are three cheaper hotels which, although not as lavish as the selections above, hold their own in cleanliness and comfort.

The **Hotel Goya,** at Suipacha 748 (tel. 392-9269), is a small, 40-room hotel, basic at best, with doubles for $13, singles for $7. The hotel reception is a floor above the lobby.

The 32-room **Florencia,** a few steps from the Jockey Club at Avenida Florida 575 (tel. 32-0157), asks $13 for doubles with bath, and $8 for singles. Bathless rooms are cheaper.

The third selection here is the large, 85-room **Florida House Hotel,** at Avenida Florida 527 (tel. 32-5391), a four-story, elevator-equipped choice. Doubles are $12, bath included, while singles are $7. A good value.

IN THE "BROADWAY" AREA: We recommend these hotels, along Corrientes and Lavalle, for night people. If you stay out late, the street din won't be a problem; but if you retire early, skip this area. It's loud—until 3 or 4 in the morning.

Two excellent choices, opposite each other on Corrientes near Florida, are the **King's Hotel,** at no. 623 (tel. 392-8161), and the **Liberty Hotel,** at no. 626 (tel. 46-0261). The 50-room King's is somewhat unusual in that a continental breakfast (croissants and coffee) is included in the $35 price for a double with bath ($28 for singles). Rooms are clean and furnished simply but quite adequately. The 100-room Liberty, with piped-in music, breakfast included in the room rates, and high-speed elevators for its 12 stories, is more modern than the King's. Here, beautifully furnished doubles, with bath and telephone, are $35 and up, with singles at $29. However, we prefer the King's.

Nearby is another high-quality recommendation, the 100-room **Regis,** at

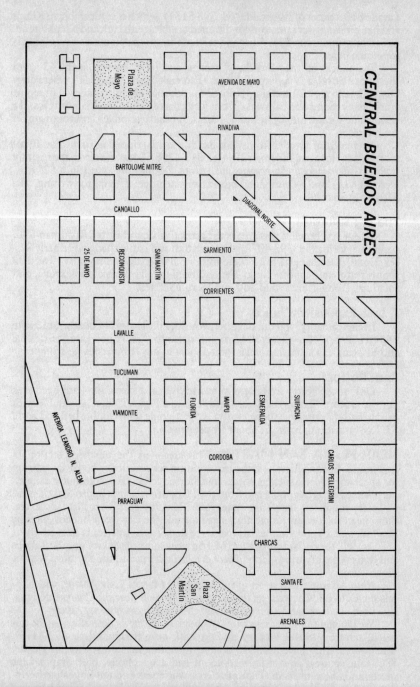

Lavalle 813, corner of Esmeralda (tel. 393-5131), which is comparable to King's and has similar lower rates. Air-conditioned doubles with bath and telephone are $28, while singles run $21. A bar and cafetería are on the premises. Everything is top-notch here.

Two blocks off the "Broadway" streets, and much quieter, is the 42-room **Viamonte Hotel,** at Viamonte 833, near Esmeralda (tel. 392-5241), where doubles with bath are $22 and singles are $16. Although slightly rundown in recent years (many rooms and hallways cry out for a coat of paint), the Viamonte is still a good value for the money in Buenos Aires. A beauty salon and tea room are on the premises.

A letter from a reader from Vero Beach, Florida, tipped us to the fine **Tucuman Palace Hotel,** at Tucuman 384 (tel. 311-2298). Ideally located, the friendly staff will offer advice and assistance at all times. Doubles are a bargain at $27 (singles run $18), and a continental breakfast is included. Thanks for writing, Mr. Richard Stockton.

The Big Splurge

A four-star hotel in this area is the attractive **Grand Hotel,** Tucuman 570, corner of Florida (tel. 393-4073). A renovation and name change (formerly Sussex Hotel) has changed this classic into an almost deluxe hostelry. The 100 rooms feature air conditioning, TV, and mini-bar. There is a pool, sauna, and solarium. Doubles are a solid $60; singles run $10 less.

A Less Expensive Choice

In this category, you can definitely consider the **Hotel El Cabildo,** at Lavalle 748 (tel. 392-6745), where the 43 rooms in this four-story hotel are $15 double and $12 single. This basic hotel is located next to Los Inmortales Restaurant.

Rock-Bottom

Only those hearty souls determined to live on a starvation level need seek out the **Ocean,** Maipu 907 (tel. 31-4496), up a flight of stairs. A double with private bath (a primitive shower only) is $9; a single with double bed and bath, $7. Rooms without baths are about $4 per person.

NEAR PLAZA SAN MARTÍN: This area—in the northern section of downtown Buenos Aires—is the best location for travelers who have a passion for spectator sports, such as soccer and horse racing. The commuter railway, Bartolomé Mitre, begins its run from the Plaza San Martín (Retiro Station) and will carry you in less than 30 minutes to the 120,000-seat River Plate soccer stadium or to the two major racetracks just outside the city (see "Buenos Aires by Day" for a description of the national craze that South Americans call futbol).

As well, the park-like Plaza San Martín faces some of the city's poshest shops and hotels (the luxurious Hotel Plaza is located here, and the Sheraton is a few blocks away).

Note: An important street in this vicinity is **Marcel T. de Alvear,** which locals prefer to call **Charcas,** its former name. You will hear the Charcas designation used in conversation frequently, but the street signs now say Alvear.

We'll begin our hotel selections with one of the city's best values—the carpeted, ten-story **Hotel Victory,** Maipu 880, near Paraguay (tel. 392-8415), where we recently stayed for $45 double, including tax and service; singles are $36. Our spotless air-conditioned room had a telephone, blue drapes, blue sheets, and a blue-tile bath. The desk clerks, who speak enough English to be understood, provided us with city maps and extremely helpful restaurant and nightlife spots. The Victory is under the same management as our top-rated Carsson Hotel.

On a par with the Victory are two nearby good-value hotels definitely worth checking. The ten-story **Gran Hotel Orly,** at Paraguay 474 (tel. 312-5244), is a fairly new 170-room building that has clean doubles with bath from $25 (front rooms) down to $23 (back rooms). Singles are $17. The Orly also offers a novel option—medicare. For an extra 10¢ a day you'll be covered for all medical expenses incurred while a guest of that hotel! (The management, of course, is not implying that an Orly guest might need medical care.)

The 90-room **Waldorf,** next door at Paraguay 450 (tel. 312-2071), charges $24 for doubles with bath and $20 for singles. Each room is attractively decorated and equipped with all modern conveniences. An American bar is located in the lobby. Both the Orly and the Waldorf are highly recommended.

A fine hotel that would be higher in price if more centrally located is the near-first-class **Promenade,** a 70-room, ten-story place at Avenida de Alvear (Charcas) 444 (tel. 312-5681), between San Martín and Reconquista. Situated a block from Plaza San Martín, the Promenade offers airy, comfortable, twin-bedded doubles for $28 and singles for $19, all with private tile bath and continental breakfast. Highly recommended.

On Tres Sargentos—a short, two-block street that connects San Martín and 25 de Mayo (between Paraguay and Cordoba)—is the outstanding **Hotel Tres Sargentos,** at no. 345 (tel. 312-6081). The 60-room Tres Sargentos, just off Reconquista, is a spotless, modern selection with superior service. Doubles with bath are $16, and singles are $11. Look for the three soldier figures on the marquee. This one, by the way, is a favorite with visiting athletic teams.

A fine choice located in a quiet area is the cheerful **San Antonio,** at Paraguay 371 (tel. 312-5381). All rooms are heated when necessary and have radio and private bath. Manager Luís Laurent speaks five languages. We have stayed here and found nothing lacking. Doubles are $25 and singles run $20.

Yet another good-value hotel is the **Hotel Diplomat,** at San Martín 918, near the Hotel Orly (tel. 311-2708). This 50-room selection has an old Spanish motif. Doubles are $28 and singles run $22. Two elevators service this basic place, which was converted to a hotel in 1969.

Another good pick would be the **Embajador Hotel,** at Carlos Pellegrini 1185, between Avenida Santa Fe and Arenales (tel. 393-9139). Here the 100 rooms rent for $45 double, $35 single. A bonus is the filling breakfast included in the rate.

On San Martín at no. 1021 is the **Hotel Central Cordoba** (tel. 311-1175), where doubles rent for $14 and singles cost $12. This is a small hotel with an authentic stone façade and overhanging balconies. All rooms have private bath (shower only), and, although small, are neat.

The Big Splurge

An aristocrat among our Buenos Aires selections is the **Gran Hotel Dora,** Maipu 963, near Paraguay (tel. 312-7391), which rivals big-splurge hotels that we have seen in Europe. Sumptuous doubles, with bath, air conditioning, and in many cases TV, range from $50 and up, tax and service included. Singles are out of our range at $45. This magnificent 100-room hostelry, over our budget limit, is understandably always crowded. So you should make reservations in advance. Highly recommended.

Far more modern than the Dora is the superb **Gran Hotel Buenos Aires,** Alvear (Charcas) 767 (tel. 312-3001), opposite the Sheltown Hotel. The 100-room Buenos Aires has huge air-conditioned doubles for a high $70 and singles for $55, tax and service included. From the marble steps to the handsome wood-paneled lobby, you are in luxury.

The 100-room **Sheltown,** Alvear 742 (tel. 312-5070), is a near-luxury choice, where $65 gets you an air-conditioned double, with breakfast and tile bath, of course. Singles at $50 are not nearly as good a value. Modern and comfortable.

Other fine choices in this category are the **Hotel Regidor,** Tucuman 451 (tel. 392-8190), between Reconquista and San Martín, and the **Italia Hotel,** Reconquista 645 (tel. 312-6361), between Viamonte and Tucuman. The Regidor has doubles starting at $50 (singles are $42). Very posh! The Hotel San Antonio is under the same management. The Italia Hotel caters to visiting Italian groups and has doubles for $35, singles for $30, a splurge at bargain rates.

The **Hotel Crillon,** Avenida Santa Fe 796 (tel. 312-8180), near the Plaza San Martín, is an excellent hotel where doubles are $70 and singles run $60. Many rooms overlook the plaza and the location is right in the heart of the luxury shopping area. You will enjoy staying here.

A more recent hotel (August 1974) is the **Hotel Eldorado,** Avenida Cordoba 622 (tel. 392-5731). The 100-room, red-brick hostelry charges $58 for doubles and $49 for singles. Look for the black-and-white canopy.

The **Rochester Hotel,** Esmeralda 542 (tel. 393-9339), offers first-class accommodations for $50 double and $42 single. This 100-room hostelry is next door to the Regis Hotel.

Another choice would be the fine **Hotel Principado,** Paraguay 481 (tel. 393-3022), which opened in late 1978. The 88 rooms are spread over 11 floors and the décor is colonial Spanish. The rates are on a par with the other hotels in this category (doubles at $50, singles at $42).

The **Gran Hotel Colón,** at Carlos Pellegrini 507 (tel. 393-1267), offers 196 rooms spread over 12 floors for $60 double, $45 single, including breakfast and tax.

The **El Conquistador Hotel,** at Suipacha 948 (tel. 313-3152), is an almost-deluxe hotel, featuring fancy doubles for $66, including breakfast. This is a well-located, highly regarded hostelry.

In this category there is also the **Hotel Libertador,** at Cordoba and Maipu (tel. 322-2095), a tall, modern structure offering the finest service and facilities, with rates in the $70 double range.

NEAR AVENIDA DE MAYO: This last area possesses an unusually large number of budget choices, but is the least desirable location in terms of good restaurants, nightlife, and sightseeing.

Numerous inexpensive hotels lie between the Plaza de Mayo and 9 de Julio —as many as two or three on each block! There are, however, eight top-quality hotels here which you should consider first.

The best of these is the modern, 160-room **Gran Hotel Argentino,** Carlos Pellegrini 37 at Rivadavia (tel. 35-3071). (As previously mentioned, Pellegrini is the east side of Avenida 9 de Julio.) Doubles here are $35 and singles are $28. A large neon sign quickly identifies it. In addition to offering outstanding rooms (some with separate sitting areas), the hotel has top-notch service.

Equally superior but entirely different in décor is the huge, 200-room **Castelar,** at 1152 Avenida de Mayo (tel. 37-5001), on the Cerrito (west) side of 9 de Julio. The Castelar once was an old-world deluxe hotel, with marble lobby and plush leather furnishings. The rooms, all with bath, are large and luxurious. Doubles are $42 and singles run $35. Off the spacious lobby is a popular cafetería that is usually crowded.

A step below the Argentino and Castelar, but still above average, are the **Du Helder,** Rivadavia 857 (tel. 40-3404), and the **Gran Hotel San Carlos,** Suipacha 39 (tel. 40-7021), off Rivadavia. The Du Helder, affiliated with the Nogaro Hotel in Montevideo, charges $38 for doubles with bath, and $28 for singles. Bathless rooms are less. The San Carlos charges $22 for doubles with bath and $17 for singles. We would give higher recommendations to these hotels if they were more centrally located. Still, both are on quiet streets, two blocks from Avenida de Mayo.

Opposite the San Carlos is the **Suipacha Palace,** a small, 50-room, three-story hotel located at Suipacha 18 (tel. 35-5001). Here, doubles with bath are $16, while singles are $9. Bathless accommodations are even less. It's quite an acceptable hotel, considering the price.

The **Hotel Splendid,** at Rivadavia 950 (tel. 37-2804), is another selection here. Doubles are $16 and singles are $10. Ask for a room with bath since many rooms share baths. As you might expect from the price, accommodations are very basic.

A fine hotel a few blocks from Avenida de Mayo, at Cerrito 286, near the obelisk, is the 129-room, nine-floor **Hotel Bristol** (tel. 35-5401). Plush doubles are a high $30; singles cost $21.

Much cheaper is the plainly furnished **Gran Hotel Cortes,** at Cerrito 308, near the Bristol (tel. 35-2413). The 58-room hotel rents doubles for $19. Singles are $12.

Moderately Priced Hotels Along Avenida de Mayo

Most of the hotels here are far too basic to recommend. But we have culled ten fair selections that you might like to consider if price is the major consideration. Our choices start at the west (Cerrito) side of 9 de Julio and proceed east toward the Plaza de Mayo.

Although the **Hotel Chile,** Avenida de Mayo 1297 (tel. 37-7112), is very basic, it does have some light, airy rooms overlooking the street. Doubles with bath are $10; singles run $8. Rooms without bath are much less. Baths have a shower only and many could use a fresh coat of paint. However, they are clean. The hotel has a pleasant reception area with leather chairs.

The **Madrid,** at Avenida de Mayo 1137 (tel. 38-3016), offers clean doubles with bath for $15 and singles for $10, breakfast included; bathless rooms are less. The smaller **Ritz,** at no. 1111 (tel. 37-9001), charges from $15 (without bath) to $17 (with) for doubles, and $10 to $12 for singles. Lights in the large public bathrooms turn on automatically as the door is closed. Rooms are large and plainly furnished.

The rather basic 120-room **Gran Hotel de la Paix,** at Rivadavia 1155 (tel. 37-7140), half a block from 9 de Julio, has doubles with bath for $28, continental breakfast, tax, and service included; bathless doubles run $22. Singles range from $20 with bath, and $16 without.

For additional hotel choices, stay on Avenida de Mayo, cross 9 de Julio, and head toward the Plaza de Mayo. In this stretch you'll find six acceptable budget selections.

Check out the 40-room **Astoria Hotel,** at Avenida de Mayo 916 (tel. 37-9061), which has doubles ranging downward from $15 (with bath) and singles from $10.

Nearby at Mayo 1120 on the Cerrito side of 9 de Julio, across from the Ritz, is the **Hotel Reina** (tel. 38-2496). Head up one flight to the reception area of this 52-room hotel, where doubles range from $12 to $14; singles are $10.

Then there's the 80-room **Novel,** Avenida de Mayo 915 (tel. 37-5532), very simple, with doubles at $13 and singles at $10. The owner is a retired merchant seaman who speaks English and loves to talk of his adventures in the United States and Europe. Breakfast in bed is a plus here.

Best of the lot is the homey 160-room **Hispaño**, at no. 861 (tel. 34-4431). This is a converted older home with an ample lounge and television area, and an indoor court on each floor. The friendly manager will proudly show you to a spotless room that is spacious and cheerful. Another plus: Private baths that have been fully modernized. Doubles are $16, while singles are $10. A good value for the money!

Located near the Hispaño are the 75-room **Argentina Hotel**, at no. 861, and the 60-room **Tandil**, at no. 890 (tel. 30-2597). Both are similar in price and look. The Tandil has doubles with bath for $19; without, for $16. Singles without bath are about $8.

STARVATION CHOICES: A staple for those who must stick to a $35-a-day budget in a glorious city where prices have soared are the starvation-level hotels along Avenida de Mayo. Head here to save dollars. However, a word of warning: These are so basic that only the young and hardy should attempt them. For $4 a night, you'll get a naked room with bed and chair, and will either share a communal bath or, for a dollar more, use an adjoining private bath—both with primitive shower. A typical hotel in this category is the **Vilesca**, at Avenida de Mayo 776. Enter an imposing building (more like an office building) and look up the floor number on the building directory. There are several similar hotels here—the **Gran Hotel España** at Tacuari 80, and **Carlos Pellegrini**—both offering the same type of very basic accommodations. Take the old-fashioned cage elevator to the hotel of your choice. Rates at the Vilesca are about $6 for a room with bath, $4 without bath.

2. RESTAURANTS IN BEEF COUNTRY

Beef is a major natural resource in Argentina. As a result the locals have developed a gourmet's eye for meat—and food in general. A mediocre restaurant in Buenos Aires has as much chance of profitable survival as a stale pastry shop in Vienna.

Not surprisingly, therefore, Buenos Aires houses more first-class restaurants than any other city in South America. The world-famous national dish is parrillada, a delectable mixed grill of prime steak bits, chicken sections, small sausages, animal organs, lamb and pork slices—all barbecued on small stoves (parrillas) at your table. When you have dined on parrillada—late (as is the custom) and leisurely—you will appreciate why we consider Buenos Aires a city that rivals Paris in culinary pleasures.

The local mineral water (carbonated) is the best we've ever tasted. Try it once and you'll be ordering it with most meals.

Also, Argentine wines vie with the Chilean as South America's best, and they're quite inexpensive. So ritually order some, since it will enhance your dining without pressuring your budget.

Note: In an attempt to alleviate Argentina's negative balance of payments, the government occasionally imposes "meatless days." On those days restaurants are not allowed to serve meat (beef) dishes. However, lamb, chicken, and pork are unaffected by the restriction. On our last visit, fortunately there were no meatless days. ¡Qué lindo!

There is no need to group restaurants here by expense. There are simply too many good choices well within our budget! Instead we'll subdivide by type of restaurant.

Keep in mind that the Porteños traditionally enjoy a light breakfast, a large lunch between noon and 3 p.m., late-afternoon tea and pastry, and a huge late dinner eaten anywhere from 10 p.m. to midnight. Restaurants usually remain open until 2 a.m.

THE CAFETERÍAS: The cafeterías are surely the least expensive dining sites in Buenos Aires. They are scattered throughout the city, offering excellent meals at only a fraction of the prices charged by fancier dining spots. Stick to the cafeterías for all three meals to stay within a budget.

On or Near the Calle Florida and Avenida de Mayo

At Bernardo Irigoyen and Carlos Pelligrini is by far your best bet here, the **Oriente,** where you can choose self-service, if in a hurry. Pick up a slip and the prices will be stamped, item by item; you pay as you leave. Dishes range from sandwiches and coffee to egg platters, or even pretty good parrillada. There are tables in the rear if you prefer waiter service.

Another reasonably priced restaurant for lunch or breakfast is **Las Brases,** Viamonte 683, across the street from the Carsson Hotel. Eggs are a bargain at $1.10, and for lunch you may choose from a number of delicious "plates of the day" such as lasagne ($2), bife de chorizo ($2.50), or lomo ($3). Local wine or cognac is $1. Tax and service are included.

A good breakfast spot is **Mimo's Bar,** at San Martín 954 between Paraguay and Charcas, in the Galería Larretta. A filling breakfast of juice or fruit, ham and eggs, toast, butter, and coffee is not much over $2.50. Homemade soup is featured for lunch here. By the way, head downstairs via the outer entrance for pool, chess, or checkers.

One of our favorite places for breakfast and lunch is the **Florida Garden,** at the corner of Florida and Paraguay, which shares its premises with Harrod's department store. The Florida serves sweet, buttery croissants (medias lunas) with steaming coffee, and eggs are always done just the way we like them. However, this trip we were unhappy to find that inflation had affected breakfast prices too. "Desayuno Americano" (eggs, bacon, toast, and coffee) costs about $3. Stay with the lower-priced continental breakfast. Do consider the Florida Garden for a late-afternoon cocktail (coctelería or aperitívo). Another budget tip: Order domestic rather than imported liquor, as imported is much more expensive. Local scotch, for example, is 90¢ to $1.50 per drink, whereas imported is a hefty $3.

An excellent grill with relatively inexpensive prices is the **Via Florida,** at Florida 261, a block away from the Chéburger mentioned below. Here you can enjoy ham sandwiches at $1.25 or salami sandwiches at 90¢ (add an additional 25¢ for tomato).

Finally, a few blocks away at Lavalle 999 (at Carlos Pellegrini), is the always-crowded **Café Parisien,** a stand-up cafetería where businessmen pop in for a quick lunch or snack between appointments.

Two sit-down or stand-up restaurants frequented by government workers are the low-priced **Grill Oriente,** at the intersection of Mayo and 9 de Julio, and the **Auto Service Grill,** a block away at Mayo and Suipacha. A third is the usually crowded **Café Maramau,** at Corrientes 777, near Esmeralda. Typical dishes in all three: bife de lomo (sirloin steak) at $2 and mixed parrillada at $5. Fast service, good values.

Finally, you can try the **Café Ouro Fino,** at Avenida de Mayo 795. Again the décor is plain, and you have a choice of counter or table service.

FAST FOOD U.S. STYLE: For a change of pace you might try the North American–style **Chéburger,** on Florida at Sarmiento, a bilevel McDonald's-type eatery where the gran Chéburger (with cheese) is $1.25. Fried fish is popular too,

as is the fried chicken (pollo frito) at $2. Also, you might enjoy stopping at **Pumpernic,** at Florida 532 and on Suipacha between Corrientes and Lavalle, whose menu is identical to Burger King. Hamburgers run $1 and up.

McDonald's has found a niche in Buenos Aires with several outlets. The most convenient is on Lavalle near La Estancia. Another is on Florida near Lavalle. You can't miss the double yellow arches.

A popular ice-cream (excellent) chain is **Freddo,** with outlets downtown, in Recoleta, and on Avenida Santa Fe.

Pizza Hut has a popular hangout next to Roma Pizzería on Lavalle near Suipacha.

For malteds and the like there's **Lecherisima,** a milk bar, found all over town with a convenient outlet at Corrientes 839.

Near Pumpernic on Suipacha is **Tío Carlos,** a five-floor ice-cream parlor where you can reminisce over a banana split, waffles with ice cream, or a sundae. Sandwiches too, but come for the ice cream.

Popular with ice-cream aficionados is **Zanettin,** across 9 de Julio at Cerrito near Bartolomé Mitre. This large ice-cream parlor is usually crowded.

Cookie Man, all over town, features delicious cookies and coffee to eat in or take out. Try the convenient shop at Lavalle, corner of Florida, or at Florida, corner Diagonal Saenz Peña.

A Porteña friend also tipped us off to her favorite coffeeshop, **Expresso,** at Lavalle and Maipu. Try it—you won't be disappointed.

Another popular hamburger hangout is **Di Pappo,** on Corrientes at Carlos Pellegrini. The low prices and fast service are the draws here.

THE EMPANADA (SNACK) SHOPS: These individually owned eateries, found on virtually every busy street, serve varied light snacks (including pizza), but they specialize in a wonderful Argentine delicacy—**empanadas,** which are soft-crusted pies stuffed with either beef, chicken, sausage, tuna, cheese, or sardines, and usually eaten while strolling. For a memorable introduction, try the **Roma Pizzería,** on Lavalle between Suipacha and Esmeralda. The Roma also turns out the best pizza in town.

Another popular snack in Buenos Aires is **churros**—thin, hot, crispy, elongated crullers, sold plain or cream-filled. Either way, they're a must. Try Roma's annex around the corner on Suipacha for these.

Incidentally, Calle Florida has long been known as the "Street of the Churros" (Calle dos Churros), because of the male custom of rolling out the word "chur-r-r-o" through pursed lips while ogling the shop girls who stroll by. The prettier the girl, the longer the R is rolled on the tongue. Viva los chur-r-r-r-os.

THE PRIME ARGENTINIAN DINNER SPOTS: The following quality restaurants are among our favorites in Buenos Aires.

In the Corrientes–Lavalle ("Broadway") Area

Many of our choice restaurant selections are located in the Buenos Aires nightlife district, which swings until 4 or 5 a.m. (We often wonder when the Porteños sleep.)

At the atmospheric **La Estancia,** Lavalle 941 near 9 de Julio, we recently savored—for almost two hours—a magnificent parrillada (beef chunks, chicken sections, sausages, and giblets grilled on an individual charcoal-burning stove at your table), a generous tomato salad garnished with red onion, and half a bottle of domestic red wine, for about $12 for two, including cover and service. The quality of the dishes and fine service have made this a "much sought out" restaurant. Little wonder, therefore, that we waited 30 minutes for a table late one night. We arrived about 11:15 p.m. after seeing *Il Trovatore* at the nearby Teatro Colón (the city's famous opera house) and were not seated until 11:45. When we left at 1 a.m., diners were still arriving! La Estancia is open until 2:30 a.m. Huge, comfortable, and scrupulously clean, it is easy to see why this restaurant is always crowded, and considered one of the first-class dining spots in Buenos Aires.

The most popular dish here is the parrillada, enough for two, which you eat by shifting the meat from the small stove near your table to your plate. Your food is hot no matter when you get it, which is a great inducement to dine leisurely. Steaks are, of course, the house specialty, as is true in all the better restaurants in Buenos Aires, and a succulent bife de lomo will cost you $5. The bife La Estancia, recommended as a first steak choice, is $4. It seems foolish to order chicken at this beef oasis, but if you're so inclined, the grilled medio pollo al spiedo ($2.50) is both superb and virtually enough for two. Vegetables, salads, and beverages are modestly priced, and service (10%) is added to your bill.

Note: Most expensive item on the extensive menu is the parrillada! There are additional rooms next door; head upstairs.

While it is superior, La Estancia is certainly not unique in Buenos Aires. If it were, neither you nor we would be able to get within a mile of the place without a government pass. There are comparable restaurants, and one close to being on a par is the **Sorrento,** on Corrientes near Florida. Slightly higher priced than La Estancia, the Sorrento is noted for its unusual assortment of dishes, both Argentine and Italian. We especially enjoy the chicken Portuguesa, recommended by the maître d', a slightly balding George Sanders type whose English is British-flavored. He will reminisce at the drop of a U.S. accent about his numerous trips to the States. Look for him. He will also explain the many dishes on the menu. The chicken we were recently served deserves a word or two. In appearance the dish resembled sectioned chicken cacciatore; it was cooked in a tomato-pepper-onion sauce enhanced by local spices. Served with either vegetables or potatoes, this proved a superb treat. With wine, ice cream, and coffee, the total bill for two amounted to close to $10, including cover and service. For approximately the same tab you can choose instead a grilled steak or veal cutlet. Highest item on the extensive menu? A mixed seafood dish for about $4.

For us, one sure test of a restaurant is how eagerly we pursue the food when we're not particularly hungry. After all, most restaurants can impress the starving patron to some extent. But when there's minimal hunger, that's a different plate of beef. Our first visit to **Las Deliciosas Papas Fritas,** at Maipu 529, between Lavalle and Tucuman, was early one evening, after we'd had a large late lunch. We ordered indifferently—one platter of chicken and one bife de lomo (small steak). Punchline: We cleaned up those plates as if we hadn't eaten in days. In addition to the chicken and steak plates, we had a delicious tomato-and-onion salad, red wine, mineral water, and coffee. Standard with all platters is an enormous serving of potatoes—the best we've found in town—plus a basket of fresh rolls. Our total bill for two: $11, with tax and service. And this is no dive—tables are decked with spotless white cloths, and the waiters are all white-jacketed. *Note:* The puffed fried potatoes, a house specialty, are light, round, and crisp, and represent a taste experience you'll not forget.

Two other papas fritas (fried potatoes) restaurants, located within a few steps of each other at Lavalle 954 and 735, are both called **El Palacio de la Papa Frita** ("The Palace of the Fried Potato"). Each offers excellent beef and chicken values for under $4. The identical menus feature half a baked chicken (pollito al horno) for $3, a baby beef platter for $4.50, as well as 100 other dishes. The colonial décor is quite handsome. Yes, the potatoes are outstanding.

Nearby, **El Mundo,** at Maipu 550 between Lavalle and Tucuman, serves prime steaks, parrillada, lamb, and chicken dishes. The crowds at this large restaurant attest to the quality of the food. The bife de lomo is the best in Buenos Aires.

Another outstanding dinner selection? The new **La Posta del Gaucho,** at Carlos Pellegrini 625, between Viamonte and Tucuman, features outstanding meat platters and local wines. The food is similar to La Estancia and the décor is that of a gaucho ranch. The service is rather good, considering the usual crowded conditions.

A fine restaurant is **La Nazarenas,** at Reconquista 1126, in front of the Sheraton Hotel. This attractive bilevel eatery resembles La Estancia and offers as a bonus a fine view of this bustling area. By all means try the entrecot or baby bife.

THE INTERNATIONAL RESTAURANTS: We have several additional outstanding restaurants to recommend—Italian, German, and Chinese. Across 9 de Julio, and therefore somewhat out of the way, is the good-value **La Churrasquita,** at Corrientes 1220. Here the specialties are beef and veal dishes. Although the regulars who crowd in night after night seem to favor the Italian menu (all dishes are $3 to $5), we are nevertheless impressed with the good-quality beef. A baby beef steak is a delicious taste bargain at $4. The friendly atmosphere makes you feel right at home. You'll return.

A popular Chinese eatery is the bright **Gran Hong Kong,** Lavalle 750, in an arcade one flight up. Try pescados fritos (sweet-and-sour shrimp) at $3, pollo con nuece (chicken with nuts) at $3.50, or the many chow mein dishes. Get a seat near the window and watch the jumping Lavalle scene.

Still hungry for Chinese food? Try **Chino Central,** at Rivadavia 658, just off Florida. A friend of ours, a resident of Buenos Aires, considers it the best Chinese restaurant in town. There is a daily four-course special for about $4.

We also like **Arturito,** at Corrientes 1124, just across 9 de Julio, where the cazuela de mariscos ($5) and the paella valenciana ($6) will make your mouth water. Hanging wine bottles brighten the rather plain atmosphere.

For authentic Italian food look no further than **Mare D'Argento,** at Lavalle 3101 in the Abasto section. By all means try the suprema pollo napolitana for $3, or the calamerettes fritos (squid) for $4. A strolling accordionist will play your requests. The ten-minute cab ride will cost you all of 75¢. Highly recommended.

A happy, crowded Italian restaurant in the heart of the city is **Trattoria Don Carlos II,** on Lavalle off Esmeralda. Locals dig the vermicelli marinara, for under $5; the pollo a la cazadora (chicken cacciatore), $5.50; and the lasagne rellena de ricotta al tomato, $3.50. An Italian trattoria effect is created by the hanging wine bottles and hams.

Subito, at Paraguay 640, just off Florida, on the second floor, is a modern, slick Italian restaurant in the heart of the city. It specializes in pasta. In fact the noodles are made in front of your eyes in the center of the restaurant, so they're definitely fresh.

Wienerschnitzel fans should stop at **Otto,** at Sarmiento 1679. The veal is juicy and tender and the breading is just right. Other favorites here are the schweinebraten mit sauerkraut and the gefulte tomaten mit thunfish. Inexpensive, this ski-lodge-type eatery is not fancy but boasts an extensive menu.

Another attractive restaurant is **Fridays,** at San Martín 965, between Charcas and Paraguay, a bilevel eatery with a fixed four-course lunch for $8. There are daily specials. The meat dishes are good and the décor has a British flavor.

Fine Italian food is offered at **Paparazzi,** on Cordoba near San Martín, an attractive bilevel restaurant where pizza platters are first-rate at $4 and up. Boned chicken with riccotta and steak platters are personally recommended.

If you like German platters in arty surroundings, try **Zum Edelweis,** two blocks from the Teatro Colón opera house at Libertad 431. A delicious appetizer to start with is the leberwurst with pickles ($3), and follow up with kasseler (smoked pork in sauerkraut) or eisbein (pigs' knuckles), each $5. Other popular non-German dishes are cazuela de pollo and milanesa de pollo with ham and cheese.

THE BEST IN PIZZERÍAS:
Buenos Aires has an enormous Italian population with strict food standards. Therefore it should have been no surprise to us that the pizza at **Los Inmortales** (the Sardi's of Buenos Aires), at Lavalle 746 in the movie district, turned out to be the best we've ever eaten. This near-elegant restaurant is far removed from the pizza joint common to urban North America. Here, the service, décor, and wines are all worthy of first-class continental restaurants. The lengthy menu, which also offers steak and chicken platters, lists 50 different pizza choices, ranging in price from $1 to $4. No matter what we promise ourselves regarding diet, we have trouble staying away from the pizzaiola, a tantalizing blend of spices, tomato, and garlic on a crisp crust for $3 (large size, enough for three) or $2 (for the small pie). The empanadas, another house specialty (75¢), are crustier and larger than those served at the Roma Pizzería, mentioned earlier. Considered one of the city's best eateries, Los Inmortales has a branch at Corrientes 1369 on the other side of 9 de Julio, one at Callao 1165, one at M.T. Alvear 1252, another at Suipacha 425, and yet another in the resort town of Mar del Plata.

The ubiquitous **Pizza Hut** has made its appearance in Buenos Aires at Lavalle between Suipacha and Esmeralda. A pizza or spaghetti with a soft drink and coffee costs $1.50.

LESS EXPENSIVE RESTAURANTS:
Two lower-priced restaurants that you might try, particularly if your budget needs stretching, are—

The **Café La Barra,** on Cordoba, offers outdoor dining as a bonus. It's across from Paparrazi and is open late, even on Sunday.

The other is **Marbella,** at 9 de Julio at Rivadavia, where you can choose between the outdoor and indoor tables. Particularly suggested are the inexpensive sandwiches starting at $1.

Both restaurants are good-size and clean, with good service.

A third choice in this category is **La Pipeta,** at San Martín 498, down a flight of stairs. Upon entering, you will notice the open grill where delicious cuts of meat sizzle right before your eyes and the shelf upon shelf of domestic wines lining walls and ceilings. La Pipeta offers a number of inexpensive Italian specialties as well: ravioli at $2.50, spaghetti at $2, and mouthwatering pizzas with mozzarella cheese and anchovies, at $2 (small) or $3 (large). Try the brochette de pollo (chicken) or lomo (beef), which costs about $3. Grilled sausage is $2, and a T-bone steak is $3.

La Pipeta is jam-packed at lunch with local businessmen, and very busy at dinner too. We returned time and time again to stretch our budget on delicious fare. A good find!

THE BIG SPLURGE:
Even if you must skip a meal or forgo buying one more gift, you owe yourself a visit to a restaurant that Porteños insist is not only South America's best, but the best anywhere. Pressed a bit, the Porteño will back off and admit that **La Cabaña** is probably only the world's best *beef* restaurant. After several visits, we can only say "amen."

Located ten minutes from center city at Entre Ríos 438, corner of Belgrano, four blocks south of the Plaza del Congreso, this beef palace reminds us (in décor) of Antoine's in New Orleans. Both have grown old gracefully. But whereas Antoine's main room is a barn-like expanse, La Cabaña has managed to section off its dining room into several relatively small and intimate alcoves, each with an archway entrance.

Now for the food. We vividly remember our last visit, when we feasted on soup, baby beef steak, tomato-and-onion salad with sardines, ice cream, coffee, a flask of wine, and a bottle of mineral water. The total check (for two), including 20% tax and service, was an unbelievable $15! We failed to finish nearly a quarter of the steak—that's how large it was.

Dining here is superb! A spectacular steak dish—particularly if you like your meat cooked in a tangy wine sauce—is the double T-bone steak ($5), which comes on a steaming hot plate. It could be cut with a fork. Vegetables, salad, and rolls are extra. Most steak platters on the six-page menu are under $5, and some chicken dishes are even cheaper. Exotic soups enrich the menu, and the appetizers stretch over two pages.

Note: Most steaks are served extremely rare, which is the way Argentines insist beef should be eaten. If you prefer it done a bit more, tell the waiter. And don't feel intimidated by the elegant surroundings—they don't up the tab one bit.

Open daily from noon to 3 p.m. and 8 p.m. to 1 a.m., La Cabaña is best reached by cab. Expect a lengthy wait on weekends. Your best bet is lunch, or an early-in-the-week dinner. Look for the mammoth stuffed steer in the entranceway, which looks almost edible.

Clark's ranks as one of our favorite restaurants. Clearly a big-splurge choice, Clark's can hold its own with any first-class restaurant anywhere. The décor is vintage England with wood-paneled walls, stained-glass ceilings, chandeliers, and mirrored walls. The food is continental. We particularly recommend the veal and fish platters, which range from $4 to $6. Chicken platters are less; most others are higher. The service is excellent. Clark's has two restaurants, the more convenient being at Sarmiento 645, between Florida and Maipu. The other is at Junin 1777, in the nearby Recoleta district. Be sure to ask for the souvenir recipe postcards.

Resembling a posh East Side New York restaurant is **Harpers,** at Calle Junin 7763, in the fancy Recoleta section. A glass-enclosed garden and well-dressed clientele add to the décor. Recommended are the lomo champignones ($3.50), entrecot bordalesse ($4), and a fine fish dish, gran parana Harper.

Palermo, an area with a large Italian population, naturally houses Buenos Aires's finest Italian eatery. **Paparazzi** attracts diners from all parts of Buenos Aires with its northern Italian favorites, and most pasta dishes are in the $4 range.

Also in Palermo is **El Corralon,** at Pasaje Bollini 2233, located in a converted stable, with indoor and outdoor seating in a patio. The cuisine is international. Ask your waitress (an oddity in Buenos Aires) to serve the rice Ali Baba, brochette of shrimp, or crêpes 1,001 Nights.

Au Bec Fin, at Vicente Lopez 1827, just off Callao (Recoleta), is an elegant international (French) restaurant in an old house. Here you're out of place without a coat and tie. The house still has the original rooms divided, so there are only three or four tables per room and you feel like you're eating in someone's private home. It serves dishes such as lobster Thermidor, onion soufflé, and trout in champagne.

Try **Catalina,** at Reconquista 875 (tel. 313-0182). This popular French restaurant has an attractive bar and cheerful atmosphere—not chic but somewhat elegant. The seafood is the main lure. We've enjoyed the trout, prepared in several ways to your taste. The location is on a quiet street best known for its nightlife.

For classical British fare, Yorkshire pudding and all, try **London Grill,** nearby at Reconquista 455 (tel. 311-2223). The atmosphere is authentic and the kidney pies, roast beef, and the like will convince you that you're back in London. Open seven days a week, London Grill is very popular.

If you have a craving for German cuisine, wienerschnitzel, and the like, head for **ABC,** at Lavalle 545 (tel. 392-3992). The patois and fare are authentic German, with delicious wurst and daily specials. The wurst comes with sauerkraut if requested. Good place!

El Repecho de San Telmo, Carlos Calvo 242 (San Telmo), is an elegant and charming international restaurant in an old house located in the old San Telmo district. The waiters wear white gloves, and reservations are definitely necessary. Men must also wear coat and tie. Specialties include trout with caviar and orange duck.

Our final big-splurge choice would be **La Veda,** at Florida 1. Steak is king here and some Porteños claim that La Veda steaks rival those at La Cabaña. The restaurant, located near the Diagonal Saenz Peña, is often rated in the five-star category.

DINING IN RECOLETA:

Recoleta is Buenos Aires's trendiest area, ten minutes by cab from downtown. It's where the Porteños go to be seen. It's what Soho is to London and the Upper East Side is to New York, only more so. There are many places to meet over coffee or drinks, excellent restaurants, and lively clubs open until the wee hours. Restaurants abound with outdoor tables in use during the spring, fall, and summer. A great meeting place, where from midnight to 4 a.m. Buenos Aires's elite congregate is **Café de la Paix,** at Dr. Roberto Ortiz and Avenida Pte. Quintana, offering coffee and snacks. Popular, too, are the **Café Victoria, Village,** and the **New Park Lane,** all nearby.

Across from Café de la Paix is another favorite of ours, **La Biela,** at Quintana 598. This is a traditional late-night meeting place for both food and people-watching. The fare includes hot and cold platters, full meals, or snacks. We often stop here late for a cake or pastry nightcap.

For dining, you have several excellent places from which to choose. **Clarks,** at Junin 1777, and **Harpers,** at Junin 7763, are two favorites mentioned above, which resemble New York's Upper East Side eateries.

Ristorante Tommaso, at Junin 1735, is highly recommended for its fine Italian dishes. The upper level is a popular nightspot and the restaurant is down a winding staircase. Tortellini ($5), canneloni ($6), and saltimbocca ($7) are all excellent. This is a popular spot and considered one of the best restaurants in the area.

Next to Clarks, at Junin 1773, **Hippopatamus** is a popular late-night disco which hosts a crowded restaurant evenings and is a place to be seen in. **Restaurant Norte,** at Junin 1767, has a fixed-price, four-course menu for $6, with meat, chicken, and fish dishes.

A fine Spanish restaurant is **Don Juan,** on Dr. Roberto Ortiz, off Guido, where the Spanish décor invites you to some of Buenos Aires's finest arroz valenciana ($5) or paella, enough for two at $12.

Nearby in the Alvear Palace Hotel at Ayacucho 2027 is the popular brasserie **Lipps.** While the likes of baby bife ($6) and brochette de lomo ($5) are available, we suggest that you avail yourself of the lighter fare, like pastry and sandwiches.

SUBURBAN DINING:

After futbol or the track, or if you're touring the suburbs, you should consider dining at either of two first-rate restaurants in the suburb of **Nuñez,** 20 minutes by cab from center city.

The better of the two is the enormous **La Tranquera,** Avenida Fugueroa Alcorta 6464, which can seat almost 1,000 customers. Similar to La Estancia, in some ways plusher, the Tranquera offers an excellent parrillada for $10 and half a chicken for $4. Patrons dine in comfortable wicker chairs. Bus 130 from Avenida de Mayo drops you nearby.

The other is **El Aguila,** near the River Plate Stadium, with a similar menu.

Remember, too, **Los Años Locos, Happening,** and **Look,** on Avenida Costanera, recommended in the "Late-Night Dining by the Sea" section.

CONFITERÍAS: When day is done at 5 p.m., the congregating place for friends will, more often than not, be Viennese-like cafés called confiterías. Found throughout the city, these pleasant places serve magnificent pastries—comparable to those in Vienna, in our opinion—and tiny sandwiches which the Porteños usually devour with a pot of tea. Cocktails are served but are not as popular in the confiterías.

You can, by the way, sit for hours amid the strudel, tarts, and napoleons while reaching for conversational tidbits from nearby tables, where the patois might be German, French, English, Portuguese, or of course, Spanish.

Ask for the pastry and sandwich plates (platos variados) and the waiter will quickly put before you a half dozen or more samples of each. The two plates cost about $4, but the waiter deducts from the bill any pastries or sandwiches that remain.

Our favorite confitería is the **Richmond Tea Room,** on Florida between Lavalle and Corrientes, where even the best intentions to stick to a diet will falter in face of the tempting array of strudels, tarts, napoleons, and small ham-and-cheese sandwiches (with lettuce and tomato), all served with steaming pots of tea. Extremely popular with young executive types and chic matrons, the Richmond is almost elegant in an old-world sense. The waiters are courtly and the atmosphere smacks of pre–World War II Europe. If tea is not your cup thereof, try a cocktail for $1. By the way, head downstairs via the outer entrance for pool.

If you'd like to brush up against an Argentine congressman or two, then you'll definitely enjoy a pastry-and-tea respite at **Confitería del Molino,** at Callao and Rivadavia, near the Plaza del Congreso. Prices are a shade over those of the Richmond but the quality and atmosphere are equivalent. The medias lunas are particularly good.

One of the most famous confiterías is **Queen Bess,** on Avenida Santa Fe near Suipacha. Take your choice between the small tables or the bar. Photos of Queen Elizabeth adorn the establishment. A good snack is the ham-and-tomato sandwich and tea for $3. A popular stop for shoppers.

Does Victor Herbert–type music help your disposition? Try the **Confitería Ideal,** Suipacha 384, just off Corrientes, where a piano, accordion, and singer entertain most afternoons and evenings from 5 to 9 p.m. Somewhat resembling Rio's famous Colombo café, the Ideal is best known for its light sandwiches and pastries. You can hear the music from a main-floor table where the bandstand will remind you of what Vienna must have been like in the 1890s. It's Buenos Aires at its campiest.

The **Confitería El Reloj,** at Lavalle 701 (corner of Maipu), is a good one too—handsome, and marked by two huge outdoor clocks. The tables seem to attract exhausted shoppers eager for tea or pastry.

Here's one that's been popular for over 100 years—the **Gran Café Tortoni,** Avenida de Mayo 829, near Suipacha. Founded in 1858, the huge café resembles an old-fashioned U.S. ice-cream parlor—sans soda jerks.

In addition, the café supports the arts by encouraging talented young groups to perform evenings. We were there on a Thursday night and took in a delightful old Hollywood-style cabaret. Other nights, you might enjoy jazz. Food is reasonable: ham sandwiches are $1; coffee with milk and three croissants, $1.50. If you choose to go during show hours, expect a cover charge.

The **Confitería My House,** at Cordoba 616, has won a place in our hearts by being open as late as we have ever been out. It's attractive, and features fine service, sandwiches, pastry, and drinks until 3 a.m. **Café Petit Colón,** in Libertad, one block from the Teatro Colón, is also excellent.

The **Petit Plaza,** at San Martín 1103, and the **Café Mozart,** at Reconquista 1056, are recommended for their fine assortment of drinks, snacks, and comfortable surroundings. Near the Palermo track, try the wonderful **Tabac** confitería, at Avenida Libertador near Coronel Diaz.

Finally, we cannot omit the **St. James,** at Cordoba and Maipu, which was our favorite stop in Buenos Aires when we first stayed at the nearby Victory Hotel. First-rate.

VEGETARIAN RESTAURANTS: Vegetarian fans should head for lunch to **Granix Restaurant Vegetariano,** opposite the Richmond Tea Room at Calle Florida 461. Located above the Broadway Microfono record shop, it serves a self-service lunch from 11 a.m. to 3:30 p.m. only.

Another convenient choice would be **Yin Yang,** at Paraguay 858. The menu is similar to Granix. The restaurant is open weekdays for lunch and dinner, and for lunch only on Saturday; closed Sunday. Healthy eating.

In this category are the **La Lecherisima** dairy chain outlets where you can feast on yogurt, cereals, and the like. Prices are low. They are scattered all over town, with two convenient locations at Corrientes 839 and Santa Fe 726.

OUTDOOR CAFÉS: During the months from September to May, Porteños enjoy sipping cocktails and nibbling on sandwiches out in the open air. On both sides of 9 de Julio and along Avenida de Mayo, the locals relax and watch the passing scene. One of our favorite places is the **Confitería Obelisco,** on the Carlos Pellegrini side of 9 de Julio at no. 329, near Diagonal Saenz Peña. Cocktails, sandwiches, pastry, and Colombian coffee—all are good. An overhead awning over the sidewalk protects patrons from the sun and rain.

Across 9 de Julio on Cerrito near Sarmiento is **Confitería Jockey Club,** another recommended stop.

Now, for the traveler who takes cocktail hours more seriously, we turn to the. . . .

WHISKERÍAS: Good conversation and free-flowing liquor dominate the numerous informal cocktail lounges called "whiskerías," common to Buenos Aires. Prices are roughly comparable to those at the confiterías. But in the whiskerías food is a decidedly secondary consideration: only sandwiches are available.

One of our favorite whiskerías is **Park Lane,** a combination bar and men's shop on Florida and Viamonte above L'Uomo men's shop. The huge panoramic windows overlook Florida and the antique lampposts are a nice touch. Actually there are three levels here—below is the men's shop; the top, a sitting area; and the middle area, an attractive bar.

Back on the near side of 9 de Julio, try **Exedra,** at Carlos Pellegrini 811. We also enjoy the French décor at **Café Paris,** on Carlos Pellegrini at Rivadavia (next to the Buenos Aires Hotel).

You should also try **La Barra,** a popular meeting place after work at Córdoba

and San Martín. Stop at this indoor and outdoor spot for a drink and meet
Porteños, relaxing before dinner.

3. BUENOS AIRES BY DAY

Buenos Aires is endlessly varied. To touch the city quickly and to appreciate
its variety, plan a leisurely 90-minute stroll your first morning. You will be
charmed and at the same time gain a fast orientation to the restaurants we recommend, the theater district, museums, historical sights, and the shopping areas.

A WALKING TOUR: Begin at the **Plaza de Mayo,** considered the heart of
Buenos Aires, where the important government buildings are located. The **Cabildo,** now a historical museum, is the site of the former town hall; from here
began the movement to gain independence from Spain 300 years ago. Also in the
plaza is the pink-hued **Casa Rosada,** which serves as the president's office. The
San Martín Cathedral nearby is where José San Martín, the famous liberator, is
buried.

Once you have circled the plaza, walk west up Avenida de Mayo six blocks to
Avenida 9 de Julio, said to be the widest avenue in the world. Broader even than
a 100-yard football field, this major thoroughfare has been subdivided into three
streets: 9 de Julio, the central portion; Calle Carlos Pellegrini, the eastern segment; and Calle Cerrito on the western side. In general, however, simply refer to
this 13-block-long expanse as 9 de Julio.

Stroll down the tree-lined street for five blocks until you reach the 220-foot-
high **Obelisk** at the intersection of Corrientes (Plaza de la República). As previously mentioned, the Obelisk, constructed in 1936, marks the 400th anniversary of the founding of Buenos Aires. Instantly identifiable, and the most famous
landmark in Buenos Aires, it makes the spot a good meeting place.

Turn right on Corrientes and in a few minutes you'll find yourself in the
movie and nightlife center of the city. **Corrientes** and the neighboring street,
Lavalle, are the "Broadway" of Buenos Aires. Stroll two blocks, and at Esmeralda
turn left. At the next block, Lavalle, veer right. Here are even more film houses, as
well as some of the best restaurants, nightclubs, and whiskerías. You might start
thinking about the evening ahead. To help you in your planning, look for the
Ocean movie theater on Lavalle, between Esmeralda and Maipu. Opposite the
theater is a small alley, roughly comparable to Shubert Alley in Manhattan, which
is the headquarters for ticket brokers. But more useful than the brokers is the
multiplicity of posters in the alley which list all that week's major film, sport, opera, and variety-show attractions. Make your plans here, and bear in mind that
first-run films are usually on a reserved-seat basis. (See "Buenos Aires After Dark"
for more information.)

To continue your stroll, keep walking down Lavalle for another block and
you'll reach **Calle Florida**—the city's main shopping street. Turn left and admire
the shops on either side of you. One of our favorite sections of Buenos Aires,
Florida is closed to traffic all day, when the pedestrian becomes king. The ten-
block shopper's paradise is described in detail in our shopping section, below.

Five blocks down Florida—past two of our cafetería choices, the Santa
Generosa Grill and Florida Gardens—is the beautiful **Plaza San Martín,** nestled
in a stunningly landscaped park. Two luxury hotels—the Sheraton and the Plaza,
both well beyond our budget—border the park.

Look down Florida beyond the plaza and you'll see a replica of London's
Big Ben. No need to walk there, though.

Tip: If you are pressed for time, you can cut five blocks from your walk by
using the **Saenz Peña** diagonal as you leave the Plaza de Mayo. This will lead you
directly to the Obelisk, bypassing much of 9 de Julio.

It is time now to explore Buenos Aires outside of center city.

NATIONAL CONGRESS: Argentina's legislature is located in the **Plaza del Congreso,** on Avenida de Mayo about a half mile beyond Avenida 9 de Julio. In front of the huge edifice is a monument dedicated to the Congress of 1816, which was instrumental in Argentina's fight for independence. Stop at the nearby park and relax with the Porteños.

If you don't feel like walking here, take the "A" train to the Congreso station. Before heading home, make sure you stop for tea at the nearby Confitería del Molino.

LA BOCA (LITTLE ITALY): The original heart of Buenos Aires was a small area that is now populated by working-class Italians and is called La Boca (the mouth). The section still retains the color and air of a village in southern Italy— but surely it's far livelier.

Late one afternoon, plan a trip to the old city, where the cobblestone streets are clogged with futbol- (soccer-) playing children. The houses, unchanged for perhaps a century, are brightly and colorfully painted; still, they cannot hide the poverty of their inhabitants.

To reach La Boca, head for the back of the Plaza de Mayo, where, at the foot of a steep hill directly behind the Casa Rosada, is Avenida Paseo Colón. From the near side of Paseo Colón, take bus 33 or 64 and tell the driver to drop you at La Boca, a 15-minute ride. On the way you pass the University of Buenos Aires.

The driver will drop you near La Boca's main street—**Necochea**—which is lined with neighborhood bars and restaurants. Late at night these are crowded with area residents and other Porteños who dance and sing until 4 and 5 in the morning.

A daytime sight not to be missed is the view from the **Avellaneda Bridge,** which spans the Riachuelo River. To get there, head for Pedro de Mendoza, the street that runs along the dock. Look for the bridge and enter the building at the near end of the span. There, an escalator will carry you onto the bridge itself for a full view of La Boca and the industrial area surrounding it.

Plan to have dinner in one of our recommended restaurants and then spend the evening nightclub-hopping. You will have the Italian time of your life. For details, see "Buenos Aires After Dark."

And now that you have walked through the downtown city and visited the La Boca residential area, you might be interested in seeing how the middle and upper classes live. A trip to the nearby suburbs is therefore in order.

SUBURBIA: Five fashionable suburbs lie northwest of the Plaza San Martín area of center city. Each is distinctive and each is reached via the same commuter railway system—the **Bartolomé Mitre Railway**—which has its terminus at **Retiro Station,** behind Plaza San Martín. Each morning, throngs of commuters crowd into the station and head for the subways to reach work. In the evening, the equally heavy movement heads out of town.

Wait till you see these suburbs—and how the other half lives! They are in sharp contrast to the sights you'll encounter in La Boca and coming in from the airport.

Buy a round-trip ticket (about 25¢) to the farthest—and largest—suburb: **San Isidro.** This will enable you to stop at the four nearer communities— **Palermo, Belgrano, Nuñez,** and **Olivos.**

Palermo, only ten minutes from Retiro Station, is noted for its huge government-owned racetrack called the **Hipodromo** (see below), high-rent apartments, a large zoo, and a magnificent botanical garden and lovely park.

Now back on the train. In ten minutes you'll be in plush Olivos, located on the Río de la Plata; here many U.S. Embassy employees live. The large (160,000 residents) suburb is a popular summer fishing, swimming, and golfing resort (from December to February).

San Isidro, the next important train stop, is another beautiful suburb, known for the finest racetrack in Argentina—the **Jockey Club** (more on this below)—and for its colonial homes. It is also a summer resort area and very picturesque.

If you should be hungry by this time, try the **Mi Casa,** near the train station.

MUSEUMS: There are dozens of museums in Buenos Aires, but we've found the following three to be most interesting:

First, **Museo de Bellas Artes Nacional** (National Gallery of Art), Avenida San Martín 1473, near Plaza San Martín, which houses works of contemporary native and European artists, as well as 400-year-old paintings that depict Argentine history. Closed Monday; open all other days from 9 a.m. to 12:45 p.m. and 3 to 6:45 p.m.

Then the **Museo Histórico Nacional,** Defensa 1600, which features mementos, trophies, and depictions of famous Argentine historical events. Closed Monday, Tuesday, and Wednesday. Open other days from 3 to 7 p.m.

Finally, a valuable collection of Spanish-American art of the Spanish colonial period (17th and 18th centuries) is part of the works displayed in the **Museo de Arte Hispano-Americano,** located on Suipacha 1422 (tel. 393-5899). Open daily (except Monday) from 2 to 7 p.m.

A final choice is the **Museo de la Farmacía,** on Florida at Saenz Peña, where apothecary antiquities are on display.

THE SPORTING LIFE: In case we haven't gotten the point across—South Americans like sports. "Like" is the wrong word—far too conservative. The Latins are passionate about many things, but there are two areas in which their feelings take on a special frenzy—futbol and horse racing.

Futbol

The supreme national sports craze in Argentina is what we call soccer and South Americans call, more logically, futbol.

Without exaggeration, it's World Series time every weekend in Buenos Aires, which has 18 first-division (major-league) teams, each owned by a different social-athletic club. And each club has its own huge stadium. This is big business, and no respectable Argentinian would be caught with his club membership dues in arrears. There is great prestige in belonging to the "right" club, with the prestigious Jockey Club in San Isidro ranking highest on the status totem pole.

First-division games (which draw up to 120,000 fans for ordinary nonchampionship contests) are played usually on Sunday, beginning at 2 p.m. in the summer.

For complete schedules, check the Sunday *Buenos Aires Herald,* a fine English-language daily. Your hotel clerk will be delighted to display his knowledgeability by rattling off data as to who is playing where and when.

A must is a visit to the beautiful 80,000-seat **River Plate Stadium,** owned (naturally enough) by the River Plate Club. Take the Bartolomé Mitre commuter railway from Retiro Station to Belgrano Station (40¢ for a round-trip ticket). Buses will then take you to the stadium. Or you can stay on the train to Nuñez Station and walk the short distance.

General-admission tickets, available at the stadium or in advance at the club's office in center city, run about $1. The best seats are $5 to $20, and tickets are usually available the day of the contest—except during the national playoffs or for international games, which take place in the summer and fall months (December through April). Minor-league contests are held on Saturday at 2 p.m. at most stadiums.

The Turf

Second only to futbol is the track, which raises huge sums for social-welfare projects.

There are two major tracks in Buenos Aires—the huge government-owned **Hipodromo de Palermo,** a dirt raceway in the suburb of Palermo, whose proceeds go to charity; and the swank grass-turfed **Jockey Club** in San Isidro, owned by the exclusive Jockey Club.

Remember the **Tabac** confitería, at Libertador and Colonel Diaz, if you're hungry in Palermo.

The two tracks are open weekends and holidays most of the year. However, the Hipodromo is closed in the summer. Check the *Buenos Aires Herald* or your hotel clerk to find out which track is operating when you plan to go.

The best seat (padded at that) at the Hipodromo will cost you $6 to $10. But to get a truer feel of the excitement this sport generates among Argentines, why not stand at the rail for 50¢? Between races you can sit on stone bleachers and warm your hands (in winter) over pot-belly stoves. Programs in either location are free, and the inevitable tout sheet, "guaranteeing" at least three winners, sells for a dime.

Minimum bet at the Hipodromo is $2. To reach this track, take the Bartolomé Mitre commuter rail line from Retiro Station one stop to Lisandro de la Torre Station. You will see the track from the train just before arriving at the station. Round-trip fare is 40¢ and trains run every ten minutes.

Boxing

The Madison Square Garden of Buenos Aires is **Luna Park,** a 26,000-seat arena at Corrientes and Bouchard, six long blocks downhill from the intersection of Corrientes and Florida. The "B"-line subway, L.N. Alem Station, drops you at the door. Prices for the Saturday- and Wednesday-evening fights are $2.50 to $9. Ice shows, basketball contests, and the circus usually book the arena too. Check the *Herald* for schedules.

READER'S SIGHTSEEING TIPS: "For sightseeing, if you haven't already done so, you should include the **Recoleta Cemetery** in your 'must see' category. You might also mention the **Craft Market,** at Plaza Italia, on Saturday and Sunday from about 10 a.m. to 5 p.m.; the **Artists Market,** on Caminito in La Boca, also on Saturday and Sunday; and the **Flea/Antique Market,** at Plaza Dorrego in San Telmo, on Sunday (roughly from 10 a.m. to 5 p.m.). Also at Plaza Dorrego is the largest concentration of antique stores, most of which are open on Sunday" (Willis E. Herr, Los Angeles, Calif.).

4. TOURS AND EXCURSIONS

A number of center-city bus tours are available through the many travel agencies in Buenos Aires for about $6. Your hotel clerk will gladly make all arrangements for no extra charge.

A 3½-hour night tour through **La Boca** (the colorful Italian section) will cost you $10, including dinner, transportation, and a show. Arrangements can be made through **Buenos Aires Turs.**

Two excursions outside Buenos Aires should definitely be considered. One is an all-day visit to an Argentine ranch (estancia) for about $36, including meals (see below). The other is an afternoon river cruise on the **Río de la Plata** for $18.

READER'S TOURING SUGGESTION: "Arrangements for an inexpensive excursion to **Tigre** via train and a pleasant afternoon river cruise can be made through Buenos Aires Turs for $16. The train ride is most enjoyable, taking you through the prosperous suburbs of Buenos Aires. When you arrive at Tigre, a most delightful little village cut by canals, the boats will be within sight. You can go all the way to the mouth of the river and back in five hours. Along the way we saw schoolchildren, housewives, and lovers. The weather is beautiful, the air fresh, and it is a beautiful change from the big-city scenes. That afternoon was one of the highlights of our three-week trip" (Joan Chognard, Menlo Park, Calif.).

LIFE ON AN ESTANCIA:

Actually, there are two estancia trips to gaucho country available: one is a short 12-mile bus trip and the other involves a two-hour ride across the pampas. Both feature delicious parrillada cooked over an open fire, gaucho dancing, and superb views of the countryside. We suggest that you go on an organized tour—and you won't hear us recommending such a thing very often! These are arranged by various travel agencies and are operated in conjunction with every hotel. The tours offer you the opportunity to see, firsthand, the life of an Argentine ranch: the cattle, the pampas, and the gaucho himself.

The life of the gaucho is steeped in tradition. Dressed today as he was hundreds of years ago, he wears a broad-brimmed black hat, tight-fitting shirt, bolero jacket, baggy trousers, silver-decorated belt, and leather boots. If it's cold, he also wears a ruana (a poncho). He carries a gourd and bombilla (straw) for sipping mate (a type of strong, bitter tea). And finally, he carries on his saddle his "boleadoras," used to fell stray cattle. These tools of the gaucho are demonstrated and exhibited on the tours. After savoring the urban scene, we're sure you'll be surprised to find this rural excitement so close to Buenos Aires.

MAR DEL PLATA:

You might also consider (during the summer) an excursion to Mar del Plata, Argentina's famous resort town. The sum of $200 per person buys you transportation and three days at a good hotel.

READER'S TOURING SUGGESTIONS: "From Plaza San Martín (central shopping area in Buenos Aires), I took a subway to the Constitución stop. Walking upstairs you're in the railway station, and for about $20 you can buy a ticket to **Mar del Plata,** a delightful seaside city—home of the world's largest casino. I stayed at the **Hotel Luso Argentino,** 2075 Santa Fe (tel. 27184). I had a very simple room with bath (shower, toilet, sink) for $30 per night! The owners are delightful, and it's located right in the center of everything —within walking distance of all the shops, casino, and the beaches. For dinner I ate at the **Hostería del Caballito Blanco,** Rivadavia 2534 (tel. 21825). Pork chops were $9, a quarter of a chicken was $8, and both were delicious" (Thomas P. Donnell, San Diego, Calif.).

SAN CARLOS DE BARILOCHE:

This is a year-round tourist resort offering fantastic skiing (July to September) and trout fishing (December to March). For information and reservations in Bariloche, stop at Calle Florida 502 at ONDA. Often called the "Switzerland of South America," Bariloche is less than two air hours from Buenos Aires. Hotel reservations can be made at Florida 502, on the first floor. The best hotel is El Casco.

VALLE DE LAS LEÑAS:

Opened in 1983, Las Leñas has catapulted into one of Latin America's finest ski resorts, featuring 20 miles of ski runs, magnificent slopes, modern hotels, and apartments. Las Leñas is located approximately 700 miles west of Buenos Aires near Mendoza. The ski areas range from beginner, intermediate, and difficult to expert. Hotel facilities include color TV, a shopping center, and fine restaurants. Remember, the ski season runs from June to

November. For further information and reservations, check the office of Las Leñas at Reconquista 575 (seventh floor), Buenos Aires (tel. 312-9812).

IGUAÇU FALLS: One of the world's great natural wonders is located on the borders of Argentina and Brazil near Paraguay. Travelers from the world over are attracted to the mammoth falls (also spelled Iguazu, or Iguaçu, depending on which border you're standing on), 50 feet higher than Niagara Falls. (See our excursion to Iguaçu in the Rio chapter, since we prefer the hotels on the Brazilian side.)

The most convenient method for visiting the falls from Buenos Aires is by bus. Tickets can be purchased from **Expreso Singer,** at Reconquista 866 (tel. 31-5894), or from **Tigre Iguazu** (tel. 31-6850), for about $75. (Prices change monthly, so call to check.) The bus leaves from the terminal at Plaza Once (Bartolomé Mitre and Ecuador) twice daily at 11:30 a.m. and 3:30 p.m. The bus travels steadily, with rest and lunch stops, and the trip takes approximately 24 hours. This is a long, rugged trip, even though the buses have comfortable reclining seats.

You can also reach the falls by train. The trains depart for **Pasados** from Buenos Aires on Wednesday, Thursday, Friday, and Sunday at 8:15 or 10 a.m., arriving the next day. The 8:15 train on Wednesday and Sunday has pullman coaches with sleeping accommodations. The cost is $100 one way for a private room with twin beds, $80 in the pullman car with sleeping berths. From Pasados you can take a bus to Iguaçu for $20 one way.

READERS' TRAVEL TIPS: "I came back from Paraguay last week. I am sure you will agree that the Paraguayans are the friendliest and most helpful of South Americans. You may be interested in the route I took, since it's a good way to see Asunción and Iguazu Falls while based in Buenos Aires. There's a bus service (La Internacional) between the two capitals which takes 26 hours. From Asunción I went to **Foz do Iguaçu, Brazil,** not the actual falls because there is only one, very expensive hotel. There are plenty of local buses to the falls. From the Brazilian side I crossed to Argentina—from Foz to **Puerto Iguazu**—by bus, boat, and bus, I'd say the Argentine side is a must; the Brazilian not so interesting. It's a terrific feeling to be standing on a narrow footbridge with all the water rushing underneath. From Iguazu, I went overnight by bus to **Posadas** (12 hours). It is a dirt road through jungley country. At Posadas I took a local bus for the one-hour journey to the ruins of the Jesuit monastery at **San Iguacio.** This makes a nice day outing, with a picnic lunch in the cloisters. Then from Posadas by bus back to Buenos Aires (23 hours). The whole trip can be done at a nice pace in ten days—well worthwhile" (J. Bryce, Buenos Aires, Argentina).

"When flying from Buenos Aires to the Falls of Iguaçu, it is substantially less expensive to go by the Argentinian internal airline, landing on the Argentinian side of the falls, even if intending to stay at the Hotel das Cataratas on the Brazilian side. The two sides are linked by taxi and ferry service. The alternative of flying direct to the Brazilian side becomes 'international' air travel, attracting a tax and involving a long journey to the international airport in Buenos Aires as opposed to the local airport near the city center. The cost of the ticket is nearly double" (Geoffrey Dempsy, London, England).

"I decided to visit the falls from Buenos Aires by bus. So I bought my ticket from Expreso Singer, at Reconquista 866, the day before. The bus left from the terminal at Plaza Once (Bartolomé Mitre and Ecuador) at noon. We traveled steadily, with brief stops, and arrived around noon the next day. I checked with the tourist office there at the bus stop at Puerto Iguazu and I have several suggestions for you. I stayed one block straight ahead downhill from the bus station at **Residenciales Segovia** for $10 for a single. (Another good place is **El Tucan,** where singles are $11.) I took my bag to the Segovia and returned to the bus station to buy a ticket to the *cataratas* on the Argentine side. The information office there has the bus schedules of the six times daily it makes the return trip from the falls. I caught the last time (6 p.m.) for the day from the falls to return to the town. I was able to buy my meals right there in the bus station and also have them fix sandwiches to take to the falls the next day. The next morning I just continued walking down the hill to the ferryboat to cross over to the Brazilian side (you must clear Customs on both sides). On the Brazilian side I took a bus into Foz do Iguaçu and there at the bus station I bought a bus ticket from the Hotel das Cataratas to Asunción, leaving at 5 p.m. from the hotel, and then I boarded a bus to the Hotel das Cataratas. The hotel personnel were very accommodating, allowing me to leave my luggage while viewing the falls from the Brazilian side. Both sides were spectacular and can be seen without taxi rides. The bus picked me up at 5 p.m. in front of the Hotel das Cataratas and it arrived in Asunción about midnight" (Sammie Faust, Ventura, Calif.).

5. BUENOS AIRES AFTER DARK

This is a city of night people. The Porteños delight in dining late (after 10 p.m.), and dancing and drinking even later.

"When do they sleep?" is a question that occurs to us every midnight in Buenos Aires, when we start to droop and the residents are still going strong. The pace will most certainly do you in unless you nap between 6 and 8 p.m.—an almost necessary respite for the long evenings ahead in some of the best clubs we've seen anywhere. In fact, Buenos Aires, to our minds, ranks with London and Paris in the abundance and variety of its nightlife, as you'll soon see for yourself.

Tip: Most clubs now charge $5 for cocktails (although the entrance fee, in most places, does include the first drink). If you're traveling on a limited budget, it might be wise to save your nightclubbing for cities where it is not quite so expensive. A pleasant (and much less costly) form of nightly entertainment is to drop into a local restaurant or cafetería, take a window seat, and order a bottle of wine to put you in a mellow mood as you observe the city's active nightlife—especially in the "Broadway" section of town (Avenida Florida and Calle Lavalle).

Note: Before stepping out, check the "On Stage and Screen" section of the *Buenos Aires Herald,* and the magazine *Salimos* (available at newsstands). The *Herald* lists movies, theater, and opera daily.

NIGHTCLUBS: Let's start with some exciting traditional nightspots.

If your senses are quickened by the sight of professionals flawlessly executing the bolero and tango, then the historic **Michelangelo,** at Balcarce 433 (tel. 30-4836), is for you. It's located upstairs in a 250-year-old cloister, and patrons make it a point to visit the various rooms displaying memorabilia. The dancers and live music are a nightly ritual (except Sunday) at 10:30 and 11:45 p.m. Drinks run about $5 and you're expected to have at least two each. The lower floor houses a magnificent international restaurant where a memorable dinner will cost about $10. Definitely drop by at least once for a taste of traditional Argentina. Take a taxi (about $2). Not to be missed.

Not far from Michelangelo, at Balcarce and Independencia, is **El Viejo Almacén** (tel. 362-3702), which packs in 250 cheering patrons at its nightly shows (10:30 p.m. and 1:15 a.m.). There's a two-drink minimum ($10), but you can nurse your two drinks all night. No customer dancing, but sing-alongs often develop. Don't let the first negative impression of the area deter you. To get here, head eight blocks along Paseo Colón from the Casa Rosada to the corner of Calle Independencia. A cab will cost about $2.

A club that attracts a young crowd (couples only) is the **Club Union,** located in the 280-year-old building in the oldest part of Buenos Aires, next to El Viejo Almacén. A pianist entertains with tango favorites. Sit in one of the booths on the sides and revel in the history of the club and the area. Minimum is $8.

At nearby **Taconeando,** Balcarce 725, you can dance between and after the 11 p.m. and 2 a.m. shows. Tango and folkloric music predominate and the patrons are at it until 4 a.m. There is a $12 minimum for the 11 p.m. show, $10 for the 2 a.m. show.

A spectacular two-hour show at 9 and 11 p.m. is the lure at **Casa Blanca,** at Balcarce 668 (tel. 331-4021). Set in an attractive colonial home in historic San Telmo, tango is it here. The shows include scores of dancers and singers, and you'll soon find yourself joining in. On our last visit the artists were forced (by applause) to perform four encores. Good fun.

Still in San Telmo, nearby at Chile 318 is **Casa Rosada** (tel. 361-3633), which competes for patrons with Casa Blanca. The show and beat are similar— but Casa Blanca seems to draw a consistently larger crowd.

While a more subdued atmosphere is maintained at **Tango Opeando,** Balcarce 605, tango frenzy is the norm. Everybody joins in at this piano bar. Minimum is $5.

Buenos Aires has its jet-set club at **Le Club,** Avenida Quintana 111, where the likes of Omar Sharif, Ursula Andress, and Alain Delon hang out when south of the border. Come and watch a local celebrity interview. Drinks are about $6 and you're bound to have fun.

DISCO: Picking up the pace, we enthusiastically recommend five swinging discos (for couples only, unfortunately)—the striking Mau Mau, Bwana, the Paladium, Discover, and the Africa.

The **Mau Mau** is a must, if only to see the most imaginative décor this side of the MGM studios. Housed in its own building at Arroyo 866 (tel. 39-3688), between Esmeralda and Suipacha, the Mau Mau has high, beamed ceilings that overlook individual love seats and barrel-like chairs in the dimly lit main room. This spacious, plushly carpeted club manages to maintain an air of intimacy despite its size (600 patrons squeeze in on weekends). There's North American music, and a bongo band takes the stage four times nightly to pound out a frenetic Brazilian beat. While there is no minimum, drinks are high: $5 to $6 on weekends and $8 on weekdays. Open from 11 p.m. to 4 a.m., the Mau Mau has established itself as the city's leading watering hole for the with-it set. The intricately carved African-style totem poles, a conversation piece, were replaced after a fire gutted the club in early 1966. Not to be missed. Closed Sunday.

Similar to Mau Mau is the ever-popular **Bwana,** Avenida Posadas 1588, behind the Hotel Alvear Palace (tel. 41-4031). Open from 11 p.m., the place jumps with local dancing to live music and discs, or drinking ($5 per) while seated on comfortable couches. Note the famous mural by Uriburu. *Caution:* A cover may be charged for a special show.

Probably the most popular disco (weekends only) is **Paladium,** at Reconquista 945 in an old structure that was home for an electric utility company. This is a huge disco with high ceilings and psychedelic effects that on Friday and Saturday nights draws a with-it young crowd. It's dark, noisy, and fun. If you're lucky enough to be in Buenos Aires on the weekend—drop in.

Another "in" place in Buenos Aires is **Discover,** at Carlos Pelligrini 1083. Enter the shopping arcade and head downstairs. The $13 entrance fee entitles you to your first drink. Drinks are $3 and up. The imaginative décor changes weekly. (On our last visit it was floating "Coma" bodies). Open from 11 p.m. to 4 a.m. (closed Monday), this large club could hold its own with most of New York's top discos. Informal attire only.

The **Africa,** in the Hotel Alvear Palace, Avenida Alvear 1885, rivals the Mau Mau for local patronage. Intimate nooks are the attraction, as are the two orchestras that start playing at 11 p.m. Drinks are $13. A cab ($3) is your best bet to get here. Head downstairs.

Note: You may be wondering, as we once did, about the couples-only policy so prevalent here and elsewhere in South America. Several club owners explain that by barring single men the atmosphere is made a good deal calmer. As one manager put it: "Two men seeking the same girl can only lead to trouble and the police. It's just not worth the extra business." Actually, many clubs permit singles—if the manager knows them. Unescorted women might also be admitted, but in Latin America it is still unusual for ladies to venture out alone late in the evening.

A far quieter club is the **Snob,** one floor down at Ayacucho 2038 (near the plush Alvear Palace Hotel), where Sinatra and Streisand tunes dominate the turntable. Drinks are $6. (*Caution:* There may be a steep entrance fee, as well!) Resembling the interior of a ship, this club is open from 11 p.m. to 4 a.m.

One of the newest discos is **San Francisco Tram,** Araoz 2424 in Palermo. Trolley scenes reminiscent of San Francisco plus flashing lights set the mood for this club which opens at midnight and stays open till dawn. There is a sunken dance floor and the place is usually packed.

Another favorite of ours is **Hippopotamus,** at Junín 1787 in Recoleta. This is a huge club with a mirrored dance floor and flashing ticker-tape lights. Several levels create a romantic effect and the dance floor is usually packed till 4 a.m.

Mambo, at Paraguay 937, in front of the Conquistador Hotel, is most convenient since it's in the very heart of the city. Typical of Buenos Aires, the club does not open till 1 a.m. The dance floor is usually packed with an under-30s crowd.

Another popular discothèque is **New York City,** at Avenida Alvarez Thomas 1391. It's a popular club, although a bit out of the way in Balcarce.

PRIMARILY FOR STUDENTS: The whole area around Reconquista is lined with raunchy bars and street hawkers, promising anything if you will only buy the bar girls a drink. However, within this area are two exciting clubs popular with students and others young at heart.

Most popular is **Barbaro,** on Tres Sargentos off Reconquista, which is actually a noisy student hangout, where the beer and soda flow like wine, and peanut shells are ubiquitous. Resembling more an old-fashioned ice-cream parlor (ice cream is served here) than a club, the place is jammed, particularly on Wednesday nights when a combo usually entertains.

LIVE MUSIC: The 28-and-over crowd seems to congregate at the **Karim,** an attractive rectangular club at Carlos Pellegrini 1143. Three Ed Sullivan–type shows nightly amuse the customers, who gladly fork over $8 to $10 a drink. A bonus here for unattached men are the two dozen sexy hostesses who are available as dance partners. Sedate place with a certain charm. Closed Sunday. Shows at 11:45 p.m., 1:30 a.m., and 3 a.m.

Similar to Karim and even more garish is **Rugantino,** at Charcas 628 near the Hotel Plaza. The club seems right out of the movie, including the bar girls. Nightly shows are at 12:30 a.m., and drinks are a steep $8 to $10. Head downstairs and prepare yourself for a night of loud entertainment. We enjoy viewing from the couchettes on the side.

Our final choice in this category is the attractive **Gong,** at Córdoba 634 between Florida and Maipu, which stays open until 4 a.m. The live show is the backdrop for the attractive gals available at the bar, anxious to share drinks with male patrons who frequent here. Attractive couch alcoves and indirect lighting set the mood. There is a $5 minimum charge.

Café Concerts

Popular with Porteños are concerts held in cafés around town. Check with your newspaper to find the particulars. One such popular meeting place for Porteños is the **Café Petit Colón,** near the opera house at Libertad 505 (across 9 de Julio). This "arty" confitería features music, and attracts singles as well as couples. Opera posters abound. If you don't like the scene, head downstairs.

The **Café Mozart,** on Reconquista, is also recommended.

FOR MEN ONLY: There are three clubs that cater to men, who flock here primarily for the female "entrepreneurs" who congregate there nightly. Each club features live shows. The fanciest of the lot is **Karina,** on Corrientes 636 between Maipu and Florida. The club features tango music and is open from 10 p.m. to 4 a.m. nightly, for a $10 minimum.

The **Maison Dorée,** on Viamonte between Florida and Avenida San Martín, offers similar talent, musical and otherwise.

Finally, you might enjoy the regulars at **Mon Bijou,** at Charcas 965 next to La Cuesta. Here, too, drinks are $7 to $9, and you needn't drink alone.

Also, there are numerous strip joints along Corrientes near Suipucha. Try **Pussycat,** at Corrientes 963, and you've seen them all.

Note, too, the stretch of Reconquista abounding with clubs featuring bar girls galore.

FOR GAYS: Buenos Aires's most popular gay spot is **Contramano,** at Rodriquez Peña 1082, half a block off Sante Fe. Look for the canopy and head downstairs to the dance floor packed with clinging couples. The bar is a popular pickup area.

NIGHTLIFE IN LA BOCA: This jumping, older section of Buenos Aires, known as Little Italy, houses the least inhibited nightspots in the city. A dozen noisy, swinging Italian-style clubs line La Boca's main street, **Avenida Necochea,** which is thronged with Porteños until 5 every morning. Ignore your first impression. The street scene—mostly consisting of young guys ogling passing gals—is a minor part of life here. The real La Boca is inside the clubs.

A recommended first stop is a favorite of ours, **La Cueva de Zingarella,** at Necochea 2384, where the owner, whose name we could not get over the din, tries to see that every guest is "king for a moment." Toward that laudable goal, he encourages patrons to take the microphone and do their bit, whatever it is. Magnificent Neapolitan songs flood the club. If you like to sing, by all means queue up at the microphone. While you're singing, the owner will be reminding his guests that "el vino commune," which translates loosely as "in wine there is brotherhood." We agree. Drink up. By midnight the patrons—most are regulars of 20 years' standing—have pushed aside the tables and chairs and have started a kind of group therapy via the tarantella, the most vigorous of Italian folk dances. A four-piece band picks up the tempo and decibels as the evening wears on. By closing time (5 a.m. on weekends) not a soul is seated and the dance floor is packed. Marvelous fun.

Come about 10 p.m., shortly after La Cueva opens, and savor a five-course Italian dinner (antipasto, ravioli, fish or chicken, salad, dessert, and wine) for about $14.

The same festive atmosphere is found at most other clubs in La Boca. Other choices we specifically recommend are the **Spadavecchia,** Necochea 1178, large and lavish, and the similarly priced **Il Piccolo Navio,** next to Spadavecchia, where the family owners keep the customers happy and full.

Dancers should head for **Rimini,** Necochea 1234, where a skillful use of drums powerfully accentuates the pulsating music. An upbeat club, definitely recommended.

Stop in the jumping **Il Tuberon** too.

Most of the tour buses head for **Castello Vecchio,** at Pedro de Mendoza 1455. While the food and wine are fine, it isn't exactly to our taste.

In general, your wisest move is to visit several clubs for a few minutes each and stick with the one that suits you best.

If you don't want to take a cab, take the "A" train to Plaza de Mayo station. Walk downhill to Avenida Paseo Colón and take bus 33 or 64 on the near side of the street. Ask the driver to let you off near Avenida Necochea.

LATE-NIGHT DINING BY THE SEA: The "fisherman's wharf" area of Buenos Aires, where the seafare is fresh, cheap, and first-rate quality, is **Los Carritos,** located north of center city along the Río de La Plata on the Costanera Norte, next to the Airport Aeroparque. Marked by dozens of inexpensive restaurants, this section is popular with young people who enjoy the informality and bargain prices. In warmer weather outdoor dining is standard, and any afternoon you can see the fishermen coming in with their hauls. Incidentally, most of the eateries are open 24 hours a day. The common denominator is good food.

We particularly like **Los Años Locos,** on the main street, where most of the parrilla platters are about $7 and where you can get a small steak (bife de lomo) for $5. Wines, cocktails, and beer are equally cheap.

Two other places that were definitely "in" on our last visit were **Look** and **Happening.** Look is a bilevel eatery serving excellent food; Happening is next to it and is a little larger and usually packed.

There are many other restaurants in this area, all of which are equally crowded and serve fine food. A taxi will cost you about $4, or you can pick up bus 226 at Retiro Station. And if you're heading to Los Carritos from the suburbs, take bus 407 from Palermo. You need only tell the driver to drop you off at Los Carritos de la Costanera.

Note: Los Carritos (as the area and its restaurants are collectively called) is popular with locals (before or after a night out). Originally the establishments here were rundown "hash houses." But they were all renovated or rebuilt as the area caught on with younger Porteños.

OPERA: Buenos Aires boasts a world-famous opera company and opera house —the **Teatro Colón**—which has been called by Metropolitan Opera soprano Phyllis Curtin "the most exciting opera house in the world," and where internationally famous opera singers regularly appear. We recently saw an excellent performance of *Il Trovatore* at Teatro Colón, which cost us $2 per ticket. The best seat was under $10, with standing room (paradero) available for about $1. Tickets, as you can well imagine, are very much in demand—particularly for Wagnerian operas, traditionally presented at the end of the season in September and October. Italian and French operas predominate until then. The box office, located in the Arturo Toscanini side of the opera house, is open from 10 a.m. to 8 p.m., with tickets going on sale at the box office one day in advance. Due to a strong mail-order and advance subscription sale, the only sure tickets available at curtain time may be standing room on the sixth and highest tier—from which you can see and hear perfectly.

Tip: If you stand, arrive about 8:30 p.m., 30 minutes before curtain time, to get the best position. Drape your program on the iron railing in the standee area. Then wait on nearby benches for the opera to start and your place will be reserved. You can repeat this procedure between acts.

The entrance to the magnificent oval hall, completed in 1908, is red-carpeted, and imposing marble columns support the lobby. On the far side of 9 de Julio at Tucuman, the opera house is open from May to October, and it holds almost 4,000 opera-goers.

Ballets and symphonies are presented on non-opera evenings. No performances on Monday.

THE CINEMA: The Porteños apparently believe that Hollywood movies are better than ever. The city is dotted with attractive film houses featuring the latest U.S. imports. Evening performances, generally reserved, are crowded so it's wise to buy your tickets in advance (the afternoon of the evening you wish to go).

If films are your thing, try the **Multicine,** a five-theater complex, each showing a double feature for about $2. As you might expect, Multicine is in the theater district, on Lavalle under the Hong Kong Restaurant.

The "Radio City" of Buenos Aires is **The Metro,** Cerrito 570, near the opera house. Best seats are $1.50; the price includes (for some performances) a live stage show. Other leading theaters are the **Opera,** Corrientes 860, which usually has an art display on one of its three levels; and the **Atlas,** Lavalle 869. The **Rex,** across from the Opera, often features live shows.

Another popular area for movie theaters is in and around Avenidas Santa Fe and Callao. The **Cine America,** at Callao 1057, is modern and shows the latest flicks without dubbing.

Note: You will see the word "Vermouth" on many theater schedules. This denotes, appropriately, a special cocktail-hour showing at about 5 p.m., in addition to the usual matinee and evening shows. Most of the first-run movie theaters are on Corrientes and Lavalle.

6. SHOPPING

Buenos Aires ranks with Rio as the best bargain shopping city in South America. Its top values are alligator and lizard handbags, belts, and wallets. Other good buys are suede jackets and handbags. Incidentally, suede is known here as "antelope." Sweaters, too, are excellent values.

Whether you choose to browse or to buy, an afternoon stroll through fascinating Buenos Aires stores should be included on your agenda.

For the best shops, head immediately for **Calle Florida,** the main shopping area in the city. This plant-lined street, closed to motor traffic, sports good-value stores and magnificent shopping arcades. Most shops invariably have at least one clerk who speaks English. Bargaining per se is generally out, but "discounts" (descuentos) sometimes are given for traveler's checks, or if some hesitancy is shown over the first price quoted.

There are two new shopping centers that you might want to visit. The **Patio Bullrich** shopping center downtown and the **Unicenter** shopping center in Martinez, a nearby suburb (more later).

Store hours throughout the city are 9 a.m. to 7:30 p.m. Monday through Friday, to 1 p.m. on Saturday.

Note: If you happen to be in Buenos Aires during February, you're in luck. Almost all shops have sales and many prices are reduced 50%. Happy hunting!

LEATHER: For quality wallets, belts, handbags, and other leading items, dash immediately to **Michele's,** Florida 681 (near Viamonte). Michele's son-in-law, Leo, will attend to your purchases without high-pressure tactics. Another Michele branch is at Florida 537, between Tucuman and Lavalle, next to the Galería Jardín. Here, too, the quality is Grade A. Say hello to Michel and Leo for us. They are tops.

For fine ladies' handbags in high-fashion leather, we would recommend the **Le Faune** shop at Santa Fe 925. On a recent trip here, I surprised Harriet with a blue leather bag which left her speechless. Quality and style here are tops.

One of our favorite shops for leather goods is **Lebon,** at Florida 1055, near the Plaza San Martín. On our last five visits, we haven't been able to resist purchasing leather and suede jackets for our personal use and for gifts. You get attentive service, rock-bottom prices, and high quality here.

For excellent leather attachés, briefcases, mens' and ladies' bags, try the **Pullman** branches at Florida 350, Florida 985, and Esmeralda 321.

Another top leather shop is **Celine,** at Florida 977, selling the finest leathers with exclusive French fashions. Owner John Manguel regularly visits Paris and gets the latest designs. **Frenkel's Leather World,** at Florida 1075, has lovely antelope coats, alligator, lizard, ostrich, and unborn-calf handbags. Wallets made from porcupine are also featured.

At **Bernes,** at San Martín 1145, on the side of the Plaza Hotel, facing Plaza San Martín, alligator bags run as low as $100 (and up to $500), while lizard bags range from $125.

Would you like to bring back a penguin-skin wallet or a snake handbag? Simple. Head over to **López,** one of the city's largest and best-known stores, near the Hotel Plaza at Alvear (Charcas) 640. Offering exotic—and expensive—goods. López has wallets of frog skin for $30, doe skin for $20, and penguin for $20. Equally unusual are the sealskin jackets for $30 and up, and the snake bags for $90 and up. Alligator and lizard are, however, higher priced than at the Calle Florida shops. Still, exciting for browsing.

For fine browsing, try **Ciudad del Cuero,** at Florida 940, where a multitude of shops featuring leather are housed under a common roof. Here is a good place to check and compare prices of various leather items in the separate alcoves.

We have also been happy with our purchases at **Pellice,** at Florida 953. On each of our last visits we picked up leather jackets that would have cost triple in the U.S. They have held up well and "mavens" back home have attested to the fine quality of the leather.

Popular with local ladies is **Ague,** at Cerrito 1128, where leather bags and purses are of the highest quality. You will not go wrong here. Prices and quality are high.

SWEATERS: The best sweaters we have ever seen are made in Argentina. Styles are magnificent, and the quality is tops. The best place for sweaters of wool and cashmere is **Los Cuatros Ases** ("The Four Aces"), Florida 519. The shop offers handsome men's and women's wool sweaters for $20 to $30, children's slipovers for $20, and warm wool ski sweaters for $25 and up (a wise purchase if you're heading on to chilly La Paz), alpaca sweaters for $75, and magnificent cashmere sweaters for $68. No bargaining here. We've purchased sweaters here on each trip to Buenos Aires and can't seem to wear them out. Terrific!

Other fine sweaters shops include **Tattersall Sweaters,** at Lavalle 614, near Florida, which features shetland, cashmere, and wool sweaters just above factory prices. **Spiguel Sweaters,** at Maipu 519, near Lavalle is also tops.

Also recommended for sweaters is **Iks,** at Paraguay 472 near the Orly Hotel. We found this place while looking for a saloon called Mae West, which was in an earlier edition. Iks is located on that spot and needless to say, Mae West no longer exists.

DESIGNER BOUTIQUES: Licensed boutiques featuring France's top designers are flourishing in Buenos Aires. Prices are generally high, but the quality and style are Paris at half the price. Examples include the **Yves St. Laurent** at

Florida 925, **Monsieur Pierre Cardin** at Florida 915, **Cacharel** at Florida 849, **Christian Dior** at Florida 832, **Ted Lapidus** at Florida 623, and **Cerruti** and **Calvin Klein** nearby round out this designer group.

An Argentine doctor tipped us off to her favorite boutique, **Dede,** at Maipu and Paraguay, where they sell unique designer items at substantially lower prices than most of the other shops. A personal inspection confirmed her opinion. Highly recommended.

One of our favorite boutiques is **Drugstore,** at Florida 902, corner of Tucuman. They carry a large selection of Cacharel and Gloria Vanderbilt attire. They have several locations, but the others are a bit out of the way.

DEPARTMENT STORES: While most Florida shops are relatively small, there are some large department stores on this busy street. One is **Harrod's,** and another is **ETAM,** with several branches.

TÍPICOS: Woodcarving is an art in Argentina, and some excellent wood figures, particularly of gauchos, can be purchased in shops around town. Check, for instance, **Artesanía Tropical,** at Florida 681 (store no. 23 inside). It sells intricately carved gaucho heads ($15 and up), bolos ($15), ponchos ($50), and mate (tea) sets ($35), the latter consisting of a gourd and a thin tube (called a bombilla) through which gauchos drink a dark, strong, bitter tea made of yerba leaves. You might also check the **Mate y Pampa,** at Alvear (Charcas) 473, where gaucho items are the best buys. The products on display are similar to those sold at Artesanía Tropical.

An excellent shop for artesanías is **Manos de America,** at Paraguay 769 near Esmeralda. You'll find a lovely selection of hammocks and woven fabrics. Novelty items include shrunken heads, masks, and Bolivian musical instruments.

Not far away is **El Altillo de Susana,** at San Martín and Charcas. Of particular interest are the colorful hammocks and costume jewelry, along with the usual artifacts found in this type of shop.

Avenida Paraguay sports our final two choices for fine handicrafts: **La Rueda,** at Paraguay 730, and **Kelly's,** at Paraguay 431. La Rueda, in addition to the usual items, has ponchos, carpets, and some simple jewelry. Kelly's, across from the Waldorf Hotel, is huge and has fine hand-carved wood items that we liked.

FURS: For excellent bargains in fur, many with Yves St. Laurent labels, try **Dennis Furs,** at Florida 989. They have a Paris branch. You can get incredible values in all types of furs, from mink to fox to nutria.

JEWELRY: You should look in at **H. Stern,** at the Sheraton Hotel and on the eighth floor of the Plaza Hotel, for the best in gemstones (aquamarine, topaz, tourmaline, and the like). You can also get your Inca Rose (rhodochrosite), a beautiful red stone mined in Argentina. Prices range from $20 to $300, and these make ideal gifts. By all means check the H. Stern outlets at the International Airport.

MUSIC: Two excellent shops feature the best of Argentinian music, boleros, folklore, and the like. Try **Supermercado del Disco,** at Carlos Pellegrini 481, near Lavalle. This is an enormous shop, featuring records, tapes, and the like, of every type of music. The **Broadway Micrófono,** at Florida 463, is a funky shop, with records, cassettes, sunglasses, and the like.

TOYS: If you're looking for a gift for a youngster back home, try **Juguetería**

Avenida, Rivadavia 846 near Suipacha. You might also look in on **Juguetería Lito,** nearby at Rivadavia and Suipacha. There are many other toy stores along Florida recognizable by their children's displays.

Another shop offering creative and unusual toys is **Un Mundo de Ensueño,** on Florida off Lavalle.

CANDY: For the best in chocolates, try **Corcega,** with shops all over town. A convenient outlet is at Florida and Lavalle. Their boxed candies make excellent gifts.

PRE-COLUMBIAN ART: For the best in pre-Columbian artifacts, try **Kramer,** at Florida 960. Señor Kramer is quite an expert, and while his prices are not cheap, the quality is good.

SHOPPING ARCADES: Calle Florida has an abundance of new shopping malls located in arcades on both sides of the street. They contain several levels of stores and every variety of item. Among our favorites are the **Galería Jardín, Galería Via Florencia,** and the **Galería del Sol.**

SHOPPING CENTERS: A new addition to the Buenos Aires shopping scene is the **Patio Bullrich Shopping Center,** on Avenida Libertador about a half mile from the Sheraton Hotel. The center opened in September 1988 and offers hundreds of shops, restaurants, and cinemas over three floors. Its a good place to get an idea of prices and variety of items available all under one roof. Stop by to browse and perhaps to snack.

Farther out in Martinez, a suburb, is the **Unicenter Shopping Center,** a much larger trilevel center open from 10 a.m. to 10 p.m. seven days a week.

ONCE (un-say): The area of Buenos Aires known for its bargain shops selling just about anything is known as Once (New Yorkers might be tempted to call it "Orchard Street"). If you get hungry, stop for a knish at a nearby snackshop. To get here, take the "B"-line subway to the **Pasteur** stop—ten minutes from downtown.

Actually there are probably as many shops here as on Florida. If you like to browse, look in at **Salome,** Pasteur 366, where quality sweaters are sold. For fine suede, try the arcade shops at Corrientes 2450; or **Selección,** 2300 Corrientes at Pasteur, and note the factory in the rear where the jackets are made. For handbags, stop at **El Jabali** at Azcuenaga 365. There are many shopping galleries, and many new shops are opening.

Finally, if your sweet tooth needs soothing, try **Confectionary Bombonería Abel,** at the corner of Suipacha and Saenz Peña.

7. TRANSPORTATION NOTES AND ASSORTED MISCELLANY

You should have little trouble finding your way around Buenos Aires if you use a map, available free at most hotels. Much of center city is easily accessible on foot, but should you need transportation you will find taxis cheap and plentiful, and subways simple to use. Cab fares are reasonable. Meters start at 25¢. A short "in-city" trip can cost under $1. You enter taxis from the right, and a chart will adjust the meter to the current exchange rate.

THE SUBWAYS: As for subways (*subterraneos*), five uncomplicated lines link center city with the terminus stations of the two suburban railroads. One station, of course, is **Retiro,** near the Plaza San Martín, and the other is **Constitución,** outside center city. There are five subway lines—A, B, C, D, and E. The C line, which connects the Retiro and Constitución stations, intersects the other four lines. Transfers are free. Subway maps are available, and the fare is a modest 10¢. Buy a token (*ficha*) before entering.

Note: To identify a subway, look for the sign that reads "subte"; the same sign will list the line and the station.

THE BUSES: The numerous buses are often individually owned and operated. To attract attention, the owner-drivers decorate their vehicles in brilliant colors and unusual designs. Bear in mind that color is no guide to destination, merely the owner's creative stamp. Fares are usually 10¢. Bus numbers and destinations are listed on the front.

CAR RENTALS: If you must rent a car—we advise against it—try either **Hertz, Rent-A-Car, Turicar,** or **Avis.** A Fiat or Renault will cost you about $30 a day, including insurance, plus 20¢ a kilometer. A deposit of $200 is required (plus a passport and credit card), and you must be 25 years of age and have a valid U.S. license. Your hotel clerk will gladly make all the arrangements.

MISCELLANY: Here are several tips designed to ease your travels:

Telephones: A *ficha* (token) is all that's required. Simply dial your number. Cost: 10¢.

Zoo: To reach the zoo, located in the nearby suburb of Palermo, take the "D"-line subway to **Plaza Italia.** While there you can fill up on hot dogs and enjoy the interesting arrangements of animals (set on islands). Across the road from the zoo are the **Botanical Gardens.**

Touch of Home: Cook's, on Córdoba, is a convenient place to cash your traveler's checks. The **U.S. Embassy** is on Avenida Colombia (tel. 46-3211). **Exprinter** is located on Avenida Sante Fe near Suipacha.

No Traffic: Florida and Lavalle, the Broadway-type streets, are closed to vehicles. The result? Pedestrian traffic jams.

Airport Tax: You will pay $2.50 when flying from Argentina to any foreign country.

Bookshops: At Florida 371 near Corrientes, **Librería Florida** carries a full line of English-language books. Other good shops are **Librería ABC,** Florida 725, and **Librería Atlantida,** Florida 643. Another good place to browse is the bookshop at **Harrod's.**

A fine antiquarian bookstore, **Anticuario Fernando Blanco** is located at Tucuman 712, at Maipu.

English-Language Newspapers: An excellent daily is the *Buenos Aires Herald* (55¢), available at many downtown newsstands.

Shoeshines: Numerous shoeshine "boys" (usually over 50 years of age) will gladly put a sparkle on your shoes. He sits, you stand.

Drugs and Such: Largest drugstore in Buenos Aires—the locals insist it's the largest anywhere—is the **Franco Inglesa,** Florida 323, near Sarmiento, which is stocked with U.S. drugs. Open late.

Post Office: The main post office is on Corrientes near Luna Park Stadium. There is a branch at Avenida Córdoba 543.

Tourist Office: The government office is located at Avenida Santa Fe 883 near the main Eastern Airlines office. It is open Monday through Friday from 10 a.m. to 7:30 p.m. There are also two tourist booths on Florida, which offer free city maps of Buenos Aires.

Aerolineas Argentinas: Office at Calle Perú and Avenida de Mayo (*Note:* Perú is the name Calle Florida changes to at Avenida de Mayo).

Consulates: The U.S. Consulate is located at Colombia 4300 (tel. 774-7611). The Canadian Consulate is at Suipacha 1111, on the 25th floor (tel. 312-9081).

Varig Airlines: A large office is located at Florida 630.

First National City Bank: A branch office is at Florida 744 between Viamente and Cordoba. The **Royal Bank of Canada** is on Florida at Congallo.

Street Signs: These are very helpful in Buenos Aires. Each sign names the block and street numbers, with an arrow indicating which way the numbers run.

Bowling: Enthusiasts head toward **Bola Loca,** on Maipu between Córdoba and Paraguay, a combination restaurant and bowling alley. Open only until midnight. Cost: $3 per game.

Argentine Railroad: The main office of the **Ferrocariles Argentinos** is at Florida 753. You should definitely stop here if you intend to visit the interior of Argentina. The efficient railroad links Buenos Aires with Mendoza, Córdoba, and Mar del Plata, among other interesting places.

ONDA: This travel company is the American Express equivalent in Argentina, offering service within Argentina and internationally to Uruguay. Their main office is at Florida 502 (tel. 392-5011). Definitely stop there for any travel arrangements.

Centro Cultural Las Malvinas: A magnificent museum on Florida 750 has a rotating exhibition of Argentine history, current events, and art. On our last visit the museum's theme was the Malvinas/Falkland War, with exhibits used and connected with the war. Helpful guides will take you to the main points of interest.

Dr. Scholl: An office of this foot-care specialist is located at Esmeralda between Florida and Corrientes.

Cue Magazine: A local version of *Cue* magazine is called *Que Hacemos,* a weekly sold at most newsstands listing the movies, theater, restaurants, and TV. Sorry, in Spanish only.

Eastern Airlines: They are located at Sante Fe 881.

Health Spa: A fine place to keep fit while in Buenos Aires is **Fit Callao,** at Callao 1033, on the ground floor. Available here are aerobic classes, gymnastic equipment, exercise machines, etc., for both guys and gals.

Lincoln Center: A U.S. information library is maintained on the second floor at Florida 935. It is open weekdays (except Wednesday) from 9 a.m. to 7 p.m. You must be 18 years old and have a valid passport.

Lumi: A fine magazine sold at kiosks all over town, listing streets and other useful information, is *Lumi* (70¢).

Airport Tax: You pay $10 when leaving Argentina on an international flight.

Arcade Games: Kids of all ages, from 6 to 60, will enjoy and pack **Fascinación,** an arcade full of video games on Lavalle between Florida and Maipu.

Cambios: These money-exchange places are located all over town and offer fair rates of exchange. But you should be prepared and check rates before changing money.

ON TO MONTEVIDEO: If your next stop is Montevideo, consider heading there by boat or plane. **Aerolineas Argentinas** and **Pluna** have daily flights in Montevideo for $50 (one way). Purchase your ticket a day in advance from their office at Calle Perú and Avenida de Mayo.

For a more scenic trip, check out the ferry, leaving daily at 8 a.m. from Darsena Sud (South Dock), and arriving in Colonia, Uruguay, three hours later.

An ONDA bus connects with the ferry for a three-hour ride into Montevideo, arriving at around 3 p.m. Take a taxi ($5) to the dock and buy your ticket aboard ship an hour or so before departure, or in advance (preferable!) from **Ferrytur,** at Florida 780, or **ONDA,** at Lavalle and Florida. For information, call 392-5011. One-way fare for the combined ferry and bus trip is $31. You can also transport a car on the ferry for an additional charge.

Note: The bus connection from Colonia to Montevideo is somewhat irregular on Sunday. Check the schedule before leaving.

A quicker trip? Try the high-speed hydrofoils run by **Alimar** and **Belt,** Córdoba 780. These depart daily at 8 and 11 a.m. and 4:30 p.m. Monday through Saturday, at 5:30 p.m. on Sunday. The one-hour crossing connects with a bus for the three-hour trip into Montevideo. One way fare: $35. Again, purchase your tickets in advance at ONDA or Alimar's offices at Avenida Córdoba 1801.

The luxurious way to make the trip is via ships operated by **Flota Fluvial** (offices at Corrientes 389). For a few dollars more you will board a ship that accommodates 700 passengers, with pullman seating, a comfortable lounge, and café service. The ships leave twice daily for Colonia, at 8 a.m. and 2 p.m., with bus service from Colonia to Montevideo.

If you are pressed for time, consider taking a prop plane to Colonia (the service is run by **Arco**). The 15-minute flight leaves Buenos Aires's Aéroparque daily at 10 a.m. and 7 p.m., with additional flights at noon and 2 p.m. on Monday and Sunday, and at 4:15 p.m. on Tuesday, Friday, and Sunday. Once again, the plane is met by an ONDA bus for the three-hour journey into Montevideo. Fare, one way, is $35.

GETTING TO THE AIRPORT: The best way to catch your flight is to arrange to have the bus pick you up at your hotel. You must give one day's notice and you will be picked up three hours before your flight. (Call or ask your desk clerk to assist you.) The bus is $7. *(Note:* To slice $5 or $6 off your trip to the airport, take the "A"-line subway to Plaza Miserere instead of a taxi. Cross the plaza to the Once bus terminal where you'll catch the airport bus.)

CHAPTER VI

SANTIAGO, CHILE

□ □ □

How magnificent the moment when first you view the awesome Andes on the two-hour flight between Buenos Aires and Santiago! Not even the Alps compare in beauty to the jagged snow-covered peaks that seem close enough to touch. And if you fly here from Lima, you will see the highest peak in the Western Hemisphere—Aconcagua, rising 23,000 feet.

After landing at the modern **Comodoro Arturo Merino Benítez Airport** in Santiago, you'll be struck by the air of Santiago—cool, clean, crisp, much like a windless Vermont day during ski season. Immediately you'll be aware of—indeed, almost overwhelmed by—the physical beauty of the Santiago area. For whenever you look east, you'll see the Andes, 30 miles away, snow-tipped nine months of the year. And just about wherever you are in Santiago, you'll find yourself in or near park-like plazas, oases in a busy urban center.

Santiago is a city of paradoxes. Although large (with a population of three million), Santiago retains many charming small-town qualities. The pace is leisurely, and the residents appear to be somewhat less worldly than the Porteños of Buenos Aires or the Cariocas of Rio. Yet the city supports 12 legitimate theaters, two symphony orchestras, two ballet companies, and three respected universities. The people are easygoing and unhurried. Yet many are avid skiers, almost all are rabid futbol and racing fans, and national and international politics are a constant conversational topic. Santiago is an invigorating city.

A BIT OF GEOGRAPHY: Where exactly is Chile? Directly west of Argentina over the Andes, south of Peru, and south of almost everywhere else. Santiago is, in fact, one of the world's most southerly capitals. The nation itself, shaped like a long, thin pretzel with several bulges, is 2,700 miles long and has an average width of 110 miles.

The population? It bears a strong northern European resemblance. Unlike Peru and Ecuador, there is virtually no Inca influence apparent in the faces or culture of its residents. There was little intermarriage of the settlers (Europeans) with the Indians.

Contrary to popular North American belief, the name Chile has nothing to do with the climate—which is really quite mild in winter—but rather is an Indian word meaning "end of the earth." In fact Chile is called the country of the "three Ws"—wine, women, and weather. Find out for yourself!

A SANTIAGO ORIENTATION: After clearing Customs at the airport, you might consider heading to the "Información" desk and requesting that the clerk phone for a hotel reservation. Give the names of several of our choices.

Your best budget way to travel the 13 miles to downtown Santiago, where you will probably want to stay, is by bus. The comfortable **Tour Service buses** leave from the airport every hour and head for the corner of Moneda and San Martín, downtown. The $1 fare is an absolute bargain. Tickets are purchased on the bus.

Another bus line—**Flota Lac**—offers service for only 80¢. You can also take the metro to center city for 25¢. The metro stops at 10 p.m.

A **taxi**, which will cost about $6, is the most convenient way to travel. The taxi fare is fixed at $6—per cabful, not per person. So use the buddy system with other travelers. The cab will drop you at your hotel, which probably will not be too distant from the main boulevard in Santiago—the two-mile-long **Avenida Bernardo O'Higgins,** known here as the **Alameda.** This bustling street, which cuts through the heart of the city, is the site of the Biblioteca Nacional (National Library, largest on the continent), the University of Chile, and the Catholic University. A major promenade in Santiago, the Alameda is an unusually beautiful, tree-lined street with pedestrian walks running down its center.

To orient yourself quickly to Santiago, keep in mind that the downtown section—where travelers spend most of their time and money—is shaped like a rectangle. The four avenues and landmarks that shape it include: (1) the important **Plaza de Armas** on the north, near which you will find many of our recommended hotels and restaurants; (2) **Bernardo O'Higgins** (the **Alameda),** the promenade to the south that draws visitors and natives like the Champs-Élysées; (3) the stunning **Cerro Santa Lucia** on the east, a large, elevated park that attracts flocks of photographers to its stone stairways, landscaped terraces, the 230-foot-high summit which overlooks all of the center city; and (4) the **Plaza de la Constitución** on the west, site of the Palacio de la Moneda, the president's former residence.

The Alameda runs into the **Plaza Italia** and then becomes **Avenida Providencia.** Avenida Providencia stretches for miles (the numbers going up as you head away from the center), and on it are several of our recommended restaurants.

At the 2000 block, Avenida Providencia is intersected by the important **Avenida Pedro de Valdivia. Avenida Vitacura** also crosses Providencia, and houses several of our highly recommended nightspots.

Continuing out from center city, Providencia successively changes its name to **Avenida Apoquindo,** then **Avenida Las Condes.** The latter avenues are in the attractive, modern sections of Santiago. The "Providencia" bus heads out here from the Alameda, downtown. Better still is the new subway that runs the length of the Alameda and Avenida Providencia.

North of center city is the **Mapocho River.**

Remember that from virtually any point in downtown Santiago you can walk to any other center-city sector. We strongly urge you to follow our recommended walking tour (appearing later in this chapter) for the quickest orientation.

Note: Santiago has another airport **(Los Cerrillos)**, near the downtown area, which used to be the principal airport. These days, all international flights arrive and depart from the newer Aeropuerto, and Los Cerrillos is currently in military use.

IMPORTANT CURRENCY TIPS: We cannot emphasize too forcibly that the Chilean **peso** is subject to wide fluctuation on the world market, often suddenly and without warning. Adding to the traveler's confusion is the fact that at times there have been enormous variations between the international exchange rate and the "official" ratio fixed by the Chilean government. Therefore we strongly urge that you contact a foreign-currency dealer or international bank to receive up-to-date information and advice *before* you leave. In the event that there is a fixed exchange in Chile below the world rate, you had best purchase your pesos in the U.S. before departure.

There is no legal limit on the amount of pesos you can bring into Chile—and you should be able to estimate the approximate amount you'll need by perusing this chapter.

If you do wait until you get to Chile to change dollars, the parallel market may be your best bet. You will undoubtedly be approached by numerous people, especially in the center of Santiago along Huerfanos, Agustinas, and Ahumada, offering to buy dollars. Don't worry. It's perfectly safe, and even commonplace to change money with these people. Just make sure to shop around for the best rate as there is a great deal of variation. You should expect something between 12% and 15% above the official rate (don't accept anything less). In most cases you won't change money on the street. Instead you'll be taken to an office to do so. Nor will you be charged a commission. But the person who brought you to the office will expect a tip.

Having stated the historical background, we are happy to advise that as of this writing there are approximately 245 Chilean pesos per U.S. dollar, whether purchasing in Chile or internationally. What will the situation be like when you're ready to go? *¿Quién sabe?* Look before you weep.

1. WHERE TO STAY

Santiago, unfortunately, has too few hotels. By our own personal tally, there are fewer than 50 "real" hotels in the entire city, and of course a number of these fail to meet acceptable standards. After careful screening, though, we've come up with a number of recommendations in the moderate price range.

Two preliminary points to remember: Many good budget hotels, including several of our first-rate choices, are on the upper floors of high-rent office buildings; second, government regulations require that hotel rates be posted in every room, and of course all our hotels observe this rule.

Note: Hotels add 20% tax and 10% service charges to your bill. The rates quoted include those costs.

IN THE PLAZA DE ARMAS AREA: The best budget hotels are located near the centrally located Plaza de Armas, the traditional meeting place for Santiago's residents.

Higher-Priced Choices

We'll start with several first-class hotels that are priced above our normal limits. However, each one represents an exceptional value for the price.

Our personal favorite in this price range is the 80-room **Santa Lucia**, Huerfanos 779 (tel. 39-8201), where the keynote is superb service. Doubles, all with bath, run $33; singles are $5 less. This hotel occupies the third and fourth

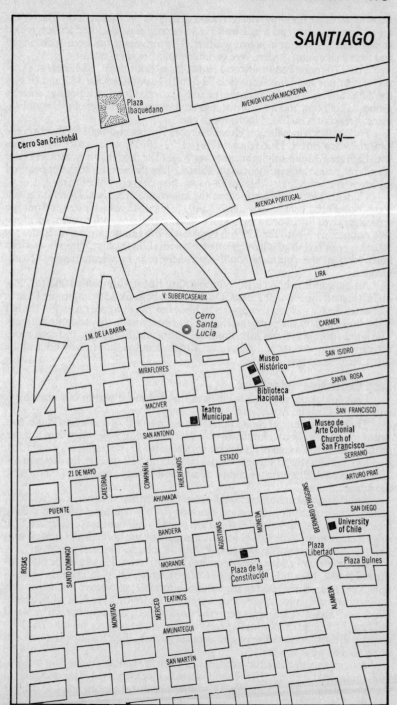

SANTIAGO

N

floors of an office building; the reception desk is on the fourth floor. The rooms are all large and airy, and meals are served in a cozy glass-enclosed terrace, which is particularly fetching in warm weather. The restaurant has been redecorated and faces a charming garden. Free parking is another guest extra.

The 120-room **Panamericano Hotel,** Rosa Rodriques 1314, near the corner of Teatinos and Huerfanos (tel. 72-3060), has doubles for $32 and singles for $24, and is located near the deluxe Carrera Hotel. Carpeting, smartly groomed bellhops, and new furnishings are among the features of this establishment. Breakfast is included in the room rate.

For another top value, on Huerfanos at the intersection of Morande, try the **Grand Palace Hotel,** Huerfanos 1178 (tel. 71-2551), where spacious doubles with bath are $32 and singles are just over $24. (The deluxe Pan American Hotel is under the same management as the Palace.) Take the elevator to the upper-level lobby, on the tenth floor. This is a 74-room, first-class establishment.

Under the same management as the first-class Santa Lucia Hotel is the 63-room **Hotel Ritz,** Estado 248 (tel. 39-3401). The Ritz, which extends from the second to sixth floors of an eight-story elevator building, offers large, comfortable doubles with bath for $29 (no breakfast). You can get attractive singles for $22 (lower-priced singles have private bath with shower only). This is a modern hotel with all the comforts you'll need. Service is excellent. Highly recommended.

An outstanding hotel is the 60-room **City Hotel,** Compañía 1063 (tel. 72-4526), just off the Plaza de Armas. Doubles with bath are $30; singles are $6 less. You enter the City Hotel through an archway leading to a courtyard. On the left is the hotel and on the right the elegant hotel restaurant (beyond our budget). The hotel atmosphere and furnishings are old-world European, and each room contains a large dresser and telephone. Recommended, but heavily booked; be sure to telephone first.

Less Expensive Selections

Let's look now at hotels with rates that fall more within our customary range in the Plaza de Armas area.

The best true budget choice here is the seven-story, 74-room **São Paulo,** San Antonio 359, between Huerfanos and Merced (tel. 39-8031), where a large, neatly furnished, though plain double with bath is $15, tax and service included. Bathless doubles run $14, while singles range from $12 (with bath) down to $9. Ideally situated, this elevator choice offers good service and clean, comfortable accommodations.

Another quality choice is the 48-room **Cervantes,** Morande 631 (tel. 696-5318), which features a charming outdoor patio—complete with Ping-Pong table—for guests. Airy doubles with bath run $16 and bathless doubles are $12; singles range from $10 to $14. Murals throughout the hotel depict scenes from *Don Quixote.* A very good place to stay. Add $3 for a continental breakfast.

At the corner of Morande, opposite the Parliament House, is the 60-room **Hotel España,** Morande 510 (tel. 696-6066), which offers full board as an option. The rooms here are quite large and comfortable; some have full bathrooms while others have sinks only. A double with bath runs just over $15, while a bathless room is about $12. Singles generally run 20% less, and a room with bath and full board (three generous meals) will cost you about $25 per person. The jolly owner will insist on showing you his spotless kitchen. Take him up on it—you'll be pleased by what you see.

You might also check the rather basic **Hotel de France,** Puente 530 (tel. 84-503), managed by a French family and located a block from the Plaza de Armas in the direction of Mapocho Station. This somewhat old, 43-room hotel, which has its reception desk one flight up a winding staircase, offers plain bathless doubles for $14 and singles for $10. There is no central heating, but a pot-bellied stove in the hallway on each floor seems to be adequate enough. Complete dinners are available for $7; continental breakfast is $1.50.

IN THE BERNARDO O'HIGGINS (ALAMEDA) AREA: This area, bustling by day, abruptly quiets down each evening, which makes it particularly inviting for foot-weary travelers who like to retire early. Moreover, the Alameda and the adjoining streets house the greatest number of true budget hotels.

Two of our selections are on or near Avenida Ahumada, between the Alameda and Avenida Moneda.

Two First-Class Selections

Easily the choicest hotel in this vicinity, and the best budget selection here, is the **Hotel Riviera,** Miraflores 106 (tel. 33-1176), a block from the Alameda. The 39-room, eight-story Riviera boasts attractive Spanish-style accommodations for under $25 double and $20 single. Service is excellent. Highly recommended.

The **Libertador Hotel,** at Alameda 853, between Estado and San Antonio (tel. 39-4211), has 11 floors and 110 rooms, which makes it one of the larger lower-priced hotels in town. It has been refurbished (we had removed it from a previous edition because it had run down) and we are pleased to recommend it again. All the rooms are comfortable both in size and décor, with private baths and air conditioners. Doubles are $31 and singles cost $4 less.

NEAR THE IGLESIA DE SAN FRANCISCO: Two additional budget choices are across the Alameda behind the red-spired Iglesia de San Francisco, the oldest church in Santiago.

The best of these is the 30-room **Residencial Londres,** on Londres 54 (tel. 38-2215), which was once a private home and is now primarily a residential hotel. But some transients are accepted, according to the tall, distinguished-looking owner/manager who speaks fluent English; you will frequently find him chatting with his guests before a blazing fireplace in the hotel's sitting room. Unusually large doubles with bath are $20; singles run $12. Telephone first.

A block away on a small street called Calle Paris, corner of Serrano, is the somewhat unusual **Nuevo Hotel Opera,** Paris 888 (tel. 38-2726), which has no identifying sign outside and resembles a private home. The lobby is painted a startling pink and orange—but don't let that frighten you off. Spotless, large doubles without bath rent for $6. Singles pay the full price of a double room. A last-resort choice.

NEAR SANTA LUCIA HILL: A delightful find is the 26-room **Foresta Hotel,** at Victoria Subercaseaux 353 (tel. 39-6262), behind Santa Lucia Hill near Forestal Park. It's well known to commercial cognoscente; tourists are the exception here. Doubles are a good value at $48; singles are $33 (triples, $60). With colonial décor, a panoramic bar and restaurant (seventh floor), and fine service, you can't go wrong here. Look for the green canopy.

HOTELS NEAR AVENIDA PROVIDENCIA: In the heart of Providencia is the **Hotel Orly,** at Avenida Pedro de Valdivia 27, just off Avenida Providencia (tel. 232-8225). The Orly resembles a private house. (Note the carved-wood doorway as you enter.) Doubles rent for $46, and include bath, carpeting, and telephone. Singles are $22. The Alameda is ten minutes away by bus or subway. Highly recommended.

Also in this area is the **Hotel Posada del Salvador,** at Avenida Eleodora Yanez 893 (tel. 49-2072), a block from the subway station. This 27-room hotel offers clean rooms with bath and radio for $20 double, $10 single. Triples are $24, and a filling continental breakfast is included. Several bus lines stop right at the hotel's entrance.

Next door to the Posada del Salvador is another first-class hotel, the **Canciller** (tel. 25-4931). Rooms here, with central heating, private bath, and telephone, are $28 in a double, $15 for singles. A continental breakfast is available for $2.50.

BIG-SPLURGE HOTELS: Due to the inflated prices of most "budget" hotels in Santiago, you might wish to consider these splurge hotels, whose rates are not much higher than some of our previous selections. These hotels are comparable to the deluxe hotels in Santiago, and they ought to be considered.

The elegant **Tupahue Hotel,** at San Antonio 477 (tel. 38-3810), has 209 rooms, all with carpeting, private bath, and TV. The hotel has its own swimming pool and piano bar. Excellent location for business travelers and for exploring downtown. Singles are $55, with doubles running $65.

The new **Hotel Conquistador,** Miguel Cruchaga 920 (tel. 696-5599), offers 350 attractive rooms on its 12 floors. Entered off an alley on Estado (between Alameda and Moneda), the hotel has doubles for $66 and singles for $55. The décor is Spanish and the accommodations are first class.

DELUXE HOTELS: Santiago is home to some of the continent's finest hotels. The **Carrera,** on Calle Teatinos (tel. 82-011), is the classiest hotel in town and the center of its social activities. It is surrounded by government and airline offices. A double here is $110.

The **Sheraton San Cristobal** (tel. 74-5000), a ten-minute cab ride from downtown, is the city's "resort" hotel. It has large, beautifully manicured ground, outdoor pool, sitting area, and tennis courts. Lovely in summer. Doubles here go for $165.

There are two **Holiday Inns** in town. The new 300-room **Cordillera** (tel. 46-5158), on the Alameda at no. 136 (on the edge of Providencia), is very modern both in design and décor. Its pool has a glass dome and it has excellent restaurants and cocktail areas. It is vying for top honors with the San Cristobal. The downtown **Galerías Holiday Inn** (tel. 38-4011) has 160 rooms, a small pool, and several restaurants—a good stop for business travelers. Expect to pay $100 and up for a double room at these special hotels.

2. WHERE TO DINE

While Argentina and Uruguay are steak countries, Chile is decidedly seafood land, although excellent beef is nevertheless served in most restaurants.

Since the Chilean seacoast is almost as long as the U.S. is wide, fishing is a major industry in these parts—and shellfish eating is a major pastime. Highly seasoned oysters, lobsters, clams, crabs, and shrimp, widely served in Santiago, are among the finest seafood we've ever eaten. And what a refreshing and nutritious change!

Typical Chilean dishes include **cazuela de ave** (a chicken soup with onions, corn, potatoes, and spices), **pastel de choclo** (a pie made with corn and meat), **chupe de mariscos** (shellfish), **humitas** (ground corn with seasoning), and **caldillo de congrio** (eel broth).

The world-famous Chilean wines are, of course, consumed in great quantities here, and we recommend that you include them in your dining.

Before listing our favorite dining spots, we should note that Chileans traditionally eat four meals a day—a light breakfast (coffee and rolls); a heavy lunch, served from 1 to 3:30 p.m.; *once* (pronounced "ohn-say"), a sandwich-and-tea snack served from 5 to 7 p.m.; and a late dinner usually eaten after 9 p.m.

Pick up the "once" habit. It's a welcome break, a chance to relax, and will hold you until the late dinner hour.

FOR LIGHT MEALS: For your first morning meal in Santiago, try **La Merced,** conveniently located one block from the Plaza de Armas at the corner of San Antonio and Merced. Breakfast here—eggs, toast, and coffee—should be around $1.25. Also a good choice at lunchtime, the *menu ejecutivo* is under $3. Pizzas start at $1. Other good choices on the same block include **Café Dante,** across the street; **Papa Pollo,** where a complete meal, including a quarter chicken, french fries, bread, dessert, and beverage, is less than $2; and **Centro Pizza.**

Mermoz, Huerfanos 1044 near Ahumada, is a popular eatery. Pizzas, from $2 to $4.25, are filling. Seafood dishes are $3 and up, and most entrees are under $5. The four-course "lunch of the day" for $4 is decidedly popular.

Santiago's version of New York's Zum-Zum, and a favorite of ours for lunch, is **Fritz,** at Huerfanos across from the Teatro Opera. Amid Bavarian scenes you can order fabulous hot dogs (vienesas) for $1. Add a few cents for potato salad and other goodies. A small steak sandwich (lomito) is $2, and beer is 75¢. Counter service only. Look for the large sign outside.

Similar is the **Fuente Alemana,** on the Alameda near the Plaza Italia, known for its excellent, as well as huge, sandwiches. Usually crowded; prices are about the same as at Fritz.

Next to Fritz on Huerfanos is the colorful **Savory,** where you can have a tasty steak (churrasco) sandwich for $2.25. Also recommended is the ham (or chicken) sandwich ($1.50), or the hamburgers ($1). There is a tea room in the rear and you can take the pastries out. Another Savory is at Ahumada 327, between Huerfanos and Compañía.

Another favorite of ours is **La Naranja,** on Teatinos near Huerfanos, next to the Panamericano Hotel. Look for the bright-orange sign and ready yourself for delicious breaded chicken (pollo apanado), burgers, pizzas, or even a roast-beef sandwich, with either table or rapid counter service. Another outlet is on the Alameda near Calle Nueva York.

Naturista, a restaurant serving natural food with a vegetarian menu, is at Moneda 846. It opens for breakfast at 8 a.m. and stays open till 9 p.m. (on Saturday till 4 p.m.); closed Sunday. A breakfast of juice, fruit salad, bread, and beverage is $2.50. Main dishes start at $2.50 and run up to $5.50.

Another vegetarian restaurant, **El Vegetariano** is located at Huerfanos 827 in the Galería Victoria. A three-course lunch here will run slightly over $3. Or stop by late in the afternoon after shopping and sightseeing for an "once" of cookies, ice cream, and coffee for $2.50.

Café do Brasil, on Huerfanos (at Bandera), has an eat-at counter and a few tables. It serves hot dogs, sandwiches, burgers, and ice cream—all inexpensive, good for take-out. Its next-door neighbor, **Bar Nacional,** offers five-course lunches for $3.25. These are listed in the window, so check to see if anything strikes your palate before you enter. Another Bar Nacional is located on Huerfanos, two doors down from the Eastern Airlines office.

El 27 de Nueva York, a small eatery, is open for breakfast, lunch, and "once" only. Nueva York is a tiny street of one block which runs from La Bolsa (the Stock Exchange) to the Alameda. There is a daily three-course lunch, plus sandwiches, pastry, and drinks. Charming.

For a fuller lunch, head to Agustinas and MacIver, two blocks from Santa Lucia Hill, where you'll find the clean **Nuria Quick Lunch,** which is not to be confused with the more expensive Nuria restaurant and nightclub next door. The Quick Lunch has a grocery store in front and offers counter service only. A steak-and-noodle casserole (tallarines con lomito) with fresh-fruit salad and coffee runs about $4.25; more popular with the office workers who crowd the Nuria is a type of hot dog, bien essas, served with a tomato-onion relish, for $1.70. The usual lack of seats attests to the quality of the food.

Burger Inn, a Burger King look-alike, has several branches, with large ones at Estado 326 and Ahumada 167. Hamburgers with all the trimmings are $1.50 and fried chicken is $2. Soft drinks and fries as well. Open for breakfast.

Charlie's, on Agustinas, is an air-conditioned three-level restaurant. Continental breakfast here is only $1.25, and a three-course lunch of a quarter chicken, salad, and drink is only $2.50. Most other entrees are under $3.

Pizza Inn, on Huerfanos at MacIver, is a counter-only stop for lunch on the go.

Another of our personal favorites is **Chez Henry,** located in the arcade area of the Plaza de Armas, at Portal F. Concha 962. Chilean and Italian dishes are featured here. Highly recommended is the pastel de choclo (chicken-and-corn dish) for $4.25; any of the fish or poultry dishes is recommended too. To cut your bill, select from the menu económico, on which you'll find the likes of noodles Italian style, fruit, and beverage for just under $3. While there are three large dining rooms, we always find the middle room most comfortable. Excellent service; highly recommended. Open Sunday.

Elsewhere in town, the **Domus Quick Lunch,** on Bandera between Agustinas and Huerfanos, serves a marvelous bife lomo (steak) with rice or potato for $3.50. There is also a daily plato dirinco, which consists of a hot plate, beverage, and dessert for $4. Sandwiches range from $1.25 to $3. You have your choice of table or counter service.

FOR HEARTIER FARE: After a light breakfast and a moderate lunch, you should be ready to sample some fine dinner restaurants in Santiago. Remember that dinner is eaten quite late.

Downtown Restaurants

A favorite restaurant with just about everybody in Santiago is **El Candil,** Merced 458. One of the smallest and most intimate of all our restaurant selections, El Candil caters to an artistic clientele. It's possible to rub shoulders with a local poet or painter here. The menu is continental and the prices reasonable. Main dishes range in price from $4 to $15 (steak). A fixed-price dinner is available for $10 per person. It consists of an appetizer, main dish, dessert, and wine, plus an additional beverage. Main courses include duck, chicken, steak, and Chinese specialties. Desserts are $1.75 to $4.25. (We've never forgotten the "heavenly pancakes"—*panqueque celestino* in Spanish—filled with jam or meringue. Truly heavenly!) Wines are $2.50 to $10. Eat here at least once. Because of its downtown location, El Candil closes on Sunday. Hours Monday through Saturday are 10 a.m. until midnight.

Another favorite of ours is the **Jacaranda,** at Huerfanos 640 (beyond the Lido Theater through a narrow walkway), which specializes in seafood as well as French and Austrian dishes, all in generous portions. The Yugoslavian proprietor, Ivan Kamberg, speaks seven languages fluently. Ask him to show you the framed autograph of Robert and Ethel Kennedy, who dined here in 1966. You can sit in either of the two neatly maintained rooms. Service is first class. Main dishes run $6 to $8. Try the corvina jacaranda ($6), the coq au vin or cannelloni ($7.50), or El Candelon, which is a seafood crêpe ($7.50). Homemade strüdel is a terrific dessert.

A Swiss restaurant, **Casa Suiza,** recently opened next door to La Jacaranda. The fondue for two ($12) is delicious, as is everything else on the menu. Meat and chicken dishes start at $4; fish, at $3. The interior is charming. Highly recommended!

El Carillon, at Huerfanos 757 (tel. 39-2213), is a budget traveler's dream. It opens at 8:30 a.m. for breakfast and stays open till midnight every day. It has a cafetería for self-service and several levels of tables. There is a grill in one area where meats, fish, and poultry are sizzling, and there are fresh salads. Continental breakfast is $2.50, and an American one is $4. The selection is huge. At night the lights dim and the music starts. Main dishes at night start at $3 and go up to $6. El Carillon is inside an arcade.

Another superior choice is the **Steak House,** at Huerfanos 1052 (tel. 38-0079), near Ahumada. Located downstairs in a shopping arcade (there's a sign on the street), it's huge, with several dining areas. You pick up your main course at the central counter—grilled fish ($4.50), steak ($5.50), or chicken ($2.75). Salads, potatoes, and other side dishes are extra. Open at 11:30 a.m. for lunch and staying open till midnight every day, the Steak House is a perfect budget choice. A branch is at Huerfanos at the corner of MacIver.

Le Due Torri, San Antonio 258, is an elegant restaurant with a strictly Italian motif and décor. The waiters are starchy white and the service first class. Prices are steep and well out of our price range. Dining here should be reserved for a "big-splurge" evening. Most main dishes are $9, with steak running as high as $15. The menu económico runs $19 per person and includes an appetizer, main dish, fruit, and coffee (no real bargain by our standards). Wines run from $7 to $11. Many locals consider this the best Italian restaurant in Santiago. Lasagne ($9), ravioli, and osso buco are house specialties.

Our vote for "best Italian food" would have to go to the festive **San Marco Trattoria,** Huerfanos 612, a block from Santa Lucia Hill, where prices are somewhat lower than those at Le Due Torri. Checkered tablecloths brighten the room and travel posters of Italy adorn the walls. The specialty here is the mixed pasta plate, which combines cannelloni, lasagne, and ravioli. It costs $6.50, but it's enough for two, and with a salad and glass of wine makes a great supper. The veal scaloppine ($8), cannelloni ($4.50), and the flan for dessert ($2) are just fine with us, as is a bottle of excellent domestic white wine ($6). Remo Zoffoli (born in Rimini) takes great pride in his restaurant. He is always available for assistance in your food selection. Very highly recommended.

You can also try **Da Carla,** at MacIver 577, a quaint Italian restaurant recommended to us by an airline employee who lives in Santiago. We tried it one evening and returned the next day for lunch.

For delicious Chinese fare, look no further than the **Canton,** Santa Rosa 83 (tel. 39-4024). Three large rooms accommodate diners. Particular favorites of ours are the chicken with almonds ($4.50), fish with shrimps (corvina con camarones; $4.50), and sweet-and-sour chicken ($3.75). The usual large crowd attests to the quality of the food here too.

Another top Chinese restaurant is **Lung Fung,** at Agustinas 715, on the corner of MacIver (tel. 39-1542), where we recommend to you the pato con pina (duck with pineapple) for $6, or the sweet-and-sour chicken at $3.75. There are five dining rooms to choose from. By the way, we were told Lung Fung means "dragon." A $10, three-course fixed-price dinner is served here, but you can probably do better ordering à la carte.

A French restaurant popular with locals is **Les Assassins,** Merced 297B (tel. 38-4280), near Forestal Park. Les Assassins serves excellent French and continental dishes ranging in price from a low $3.50 to $10. Try the steak au poivre at $6, served with rice, or lenguado stragon (fish) for $5. An inexpensive lunch might be omelette de champignon ($2.50). The bar is always crowded and there is often a wait for tables. Closed Sunday.

Special Mention

For a night of sheer fun, plan to have one meal at **Los Adobes de Argomedo,** Argomedo 411 (tel. 222-2104). This huge restaurant (there are three dining rooms), located in one of the oldest sections of Santiago, resembles a typical Chilean ranch in décor. Waiters are dressed like *huasos* (Chilean cowboys). Prices here are not cheap as they cover nightly entertainment—live shows feature singers, dancers, and stand-up comedians. Try the lemon chicken— delicious!—for $9.50, or the succulent grilled steak at $11. Seafood dishes are less expensive: $6.50 and up. Expect to pay $13 and up for dinner, and to spend the entire evening. Show time is at 10:30 p.m. Closed Sunday.

Restaurants in Providencia and Beyond

Each of the following restaurants is on Avenida Providencia, a short subway or bus ride away. The selections are first by geographic location heading away from downtown. Therefore the initial choices are closest.

If you feel like a steak, hop into a cab or the "Providencia" bus for the short ride to **El Parron,** Providencia 1184 (tel. 22-3982), where Argentine-style parrilladas are featured. You can choose from a large selection of dishes on the bilingual menu. The steaks run from $5.50 to $8.50. Also popular are fish and poultry dishes, and these are somewhat less expensive. A fireplace adds to your enjoyment, as will the service and décor. This establishment was recommended to us by a young New York couple we met in Quito. We weren't disappointed. Head beyond the entrance to the rear.

Lomit's, at Providencia 1980, a German-style eatery with indoor booths and sidewalk tables in summer, is very popular. A half chicken with salad is only $3.50, pork chops are $4.50, and veal dishes are $4.75. A pork loin sandwich is $2.50. Wash it down with a cool Chilean beer.

At Providencia 1979, near Pedro de Valdivia, is the colorful trilevel **La Pizza Nostra,** where photos of famous Cosa Nostra figures adorn the walls. Almost two dozen pizzas vie with the daily specials for customer interest. The lower lunch-bar area is a popular meeting place—no wonder, since its location is in the heart of this area. One-person pies served on wooden planks are $3.50 with a variety of ingredients, while large pies can hit $9. The menu also features pasta dishes and expertly seasoned veal platters for under $6.

Aquí Esta Coco, at Concepción 236A (just a block from Avenida Providencia), is a superior seafood restaurant. Set in a private house decorated with anchors and diving bells, it has several small dining rooms. The ceviche is superb, as is the jardín de mariscos, a cold seafood plate. Its large bilingual menu is confusing to read, but virtually everything is well prepared so you can't go wrong. Appetizers are $3.75 and up, and main courses start at $5.50. **La Concepción,** across the street, is another seafood eatery. Good food and less expensive, but it lacks the pizzazz of Coco.

The **New Orleans,** a colorful restaurant that resembles a card room aboard a Delta paddlewheeler, serves only fish—all kinds! Try sea urchin and let us know what it tastes like. Prices start at $4.50. The New Orleans is on Avenida Suecia at Calle General Holley. Next door is the **Red Pub,** an informal eatery with music.

Just off the 2300 block of Avenida Providencia, at General Holley 2322, is the cozy **Arlequin** (tel. 74-3356), housed in a bilevel home with dining on each level. Prices are high, with fish dishes ranging from $7 to $13. We had a delightful pollo escalope at $7.50 and admired the harlequin paintings on the walls. Closed Sunday.

The suburbs boast one of the best seafood restaurants in Santiago: **Coco Loco,** at Rancagua 554 (tel. 49-1214). Coco Loco offers the perfect combination of fine food served in delightful surroundings. An old colonial home tastefully converted, the restaurant has all of those special touches that make dining a pleasure: soft candlelight, strolling musicians, and courteous service. Elegant atmosphere does not come with an inflated pricetag; most dishes range in price from $5 to $12. A word of caution, however. Since many dishes are à la carte, it is easy to spend $16 per person without batting an eyelash. Forgo the extras! The house wine is excellent ($3 a bottle). Try the chirimoya, a delicate fruit native to Chile. Dining at its best!

Italian dishes prepared in northern Italian style (with delicate sauces) and international specialties are the highlights of the menu at **Montecatini Ltda.,** at Avenida Tobalaba 477 (tel. 232-5999).

Los Buenos Muchachos, Calle Ricardo Cummy 1083 (tel. 698-0112), is a terrific spot to savor typical Chilean foods. Empanadas, pastel del choclo, and all types of seafood are served. Music with dinner nightly.

Rodizio (spit-roasted meats, served Brazilian style) is very popular here. Several new eateries have opened. **Venezia,** at Pio Nono 200 (tel. 37-0900), near San Cristobal hill, is a favorite of the artists who live in the area. Expect to pay about $5 for your dinner. **Rodizio Dominica,** on Bombero Nuñéz, corner of Dominica (tel. 77-9240), is another popular and inexpensive place. Perfectly grilled beef, pork, and lamb are served on the spit and the service doesn't stop until you say "no mas."

Special Dinner Choices

The **Bali Hai,** at Avenida Colón (tel. 228-8273), offers a pleasant typical Polynesian–Easter Island show complete with singer, dancers, and comic. A five-course meal (there are 25 entrees to choose from) will cost about $17.

Another fine restaurant at Avenida Bosque Norte 406 (tel. 215-1090) is **Baltazar,** where seafood is king. A four-course meal will cost about $10. The price and ambience are right.

For a great Spanish meal, **El Club Gran Avenida** is a "must." Located in the southern part of town at José Miquel Carrera 5076 (tel. 551-6563), this Spanish-owned restaurant has been open for over 30 years. And for good reason—the food is excellent. Plus, there's music and dancing every weekend.

Hosteria Las Delícias, Puente San Enrique and El Arrayan (tel. 47-1386), located in a wealthy suburb in the eastern part of Santiago, offers an excellent selection of typical Chilean dishes accompanied by folkloric music. Another good choice!

Two other favorites of ours are in Las Condes, quite a bit out of the central area. While Avenida Providencia is a short ride from Alameda, Las Condes is beyond Avenida Apoquindo (the extension of Providencia). If you find yourself out in Las Condes, by all means try **Los Gordos,** at San Enrique 14880, or **Bric a Brac,** at Avenida Las Condes 9183.

ONCE: The 5 to 7 p.m. period in Santiago is not the cocktail hour as much as it is the tea (or coffee) and sandwich period. The snacktime, called "once" (which literally means "11"), is a relaxing prelude to the late dinner hour, and is a very civilized habit which we North Americans would do well to pick up.

"Once" is a custom that local historians trace back to the time when the man of the house would secretly refer to his favorite 5 p.m. drink (aguardiente)—a potent alcoholic beverage—as "las onces" (the 11-letter drink). In this manner, theoretically, his wife was unaware of his imbibing. We remain skeptical.

Café Paula has virtually cornered the "once" market with five tea rooms.

Danish pastries, strüdel, cookies, and beverages are served at small tables or at stand-up counters. Shoppers should head to the Paula at Ahumada 343, across from the Gobelinos department store, while theater-goers will find the branch at San Antonia 218 opposite the Municipal Theater the most convenient. Two others are in the Pasaje Matte at no. 302 and no. 960, and the last at Moneda 915. Breakfast is served at all of them.

Café Colonia, MacIver 133, is a comfortable spot with good service. Delicious cakes, pastries, and small sandwiches—try the hot chocolate. Ice cream is served too.

One of our favorite stops for "once" is the **Café Santos,** downstairs at Ahumada 312, where the delicious goodies—trays of pastries and sandwiches served with pots of tea, coffee, or chocolate—will tempt you to linger on into the evening hours. Generally, you can have a sandwich, pastry, and beverage for $3, and the pastries are good enough to take home—as many patrons do.

ESPRESSO: Dotting Santiago are small espresso and coffeeshops which open early and close well after midnight. Many are stand-up establishments but some have tables. They are leisurely spots where conversation is endless. You'll find that many of your friendships with Chileans begin in espresso places.

Two of our favorites are the **Haiti** and the **Café de Brasil,** both inexpensive and both always crowded. The stand-up Haiti, a popular businessman's meeting place, is on Ahumada between Agustinas and Moneda. Try the house specialty—leche con fruta, a refreshing fruit milkshake—and the unusual varieties of coffee. The Brasil, conveniently located on Morande, near Huerfanos, has tables, but the service is quite leisurely. At either you can stay as long as you like with only a cup of coffee.

A newer espresso spot, **Café Caribe,** opened next to the Haiti. Lots of stockbrokers in here. We like to stop at an espresso place late in the evening for a nightcap on the way back to the hotel.

Chocolate Stop

For delicious chocolates, cookies, and nuts to eat as you explore the city, drop into the **Confitería Tip Top,** at Huerfanos and MacIver. Two other Tip Tops have opened. Tip Top 2 is at the corner of Morande and the Alameda, and Tip Top 3 is right on the Alameda across from the Museo de Arte Colonial.

3. SANTIAGO BY DAY

Like so many cities, Santiago can be appreciated best by walking its streets for a couple of hours. So here we go again, on—

A WALKING TOUR: The best place to begin is at the most important plaza in the city, the **Plaza de Armas,** which has been considered the heart of Santiago since its origin in 1541. Ringing the square are the main post office, city hall, and the cathedral of Santiago.

Stroll around the handsome shrub-filled plaza and wind up on **Avenida Compañia** on the south side. Facing the plaza, now walk left for two blocks to **Morande,** where you should again make a left. Ambling up Morande, you'll pass Santiago's three main shopping streets, **Huerfanos, Agustinas,** and **Moneda.**

Huerfanos has become a wide shopping mall, closed to traffic till MacIver. Ahumada is also a promenade from the Plaza de Armas to the Alameda.

If you choose to detour for bargains in copperware or ski clothes, check our shopping section, coming up.

Continuing along Morande, you'll come to the **Plaza de la Constitución,** which is between Agustinas and the Avenida Bernardo O'Higgins (the Alameda). Adjoining the plaza is the president's residence, formerly the mint. It is one of the new Spanish-colonial-style structures in Santiago. The Changing of the Guard takes place in the courtyard at 10 a.m. every other day.

Back on Morande, stroll to the **Alameda,** where two plazas—**Libertad** and **Bulnes**—face each other across the wide boulevard. A number of federal buildings are located here, and civil servants throng the area's restaurants. Originally the Alameda was the riverbed of the Mapocho River—until it was diverted. Now it is a wide, two-mile-long promenade lined with trees and statuary that Sunday strollers find irresistible. Turn left on the Alameda and try the center promenade walk. After 1½ blocks, cross to the far side of the street where you will see the **University of Chile** campus (look for the yellow-and-white building, illuminated at night). This, the University of Santiago, and Catholic University are the three universities in Santiago. The strong rivalry among the schools reaches a high pitch during their twice-a-year futbol (soccer) matches.

Two blocks farther down you'll pass the 400-year-old **Church of San Francisco,** with its red colonial-style tower. The meticulously etched sacristy doors date from 1700. Next to the church is the **Museo de Arte Colonial–San Francisco,** which features colonial religious paintings in a cloister setting. Open Tuesday through Sunday from 10 a.m. to 1 p.m.; closed Monday. Admission is 50¢.

Now cross back to the near side of the Alameda and continue on the Alameda for another block until you come to the largest library in South America, the **Biblioteca Nacional,** which houses Chile's national archives. The adjacent structure, around the corner on Miraflores, is the **Museo Histórico,** home of Indian relics, colonial costumes, folk art, and paintings by Chilean artists.

Two blocks ahead is the **Cerro Santa Lucía,** a park on the hill where Santiago was founded by Pedro de Valdivia. The 230-foot summit is reached via numerous paths and stone stairways. Ready your camera for shots of the Andes above and the city below. A popular folk art museum is located at the summit, where there are also a number of quiet nooks in which you might like to partake of a sandwich, so remember to bring one. This is always one of the highlights of Santiago for us.

The final stop on our leisurely stroll is the **Teatro Municipal,** Santiago's major theater, which you reach by heading back to center city along Agustinas until you arrive at San Antonio. The theater is the site of every important musical, theatrical, and dance event in Santiago.

This winds up our brief stroll, which should take you no longer than two hours.

SANTIAGO, SIGHT BY SIGHT: Now we'll take a closer look.

Cerro San Cristobal

A quaint **funicular railway,** which makes an almost-vertical ascent, will carry you to the most striking vantage point in Santiago, the 1,115-foot-high Cerro San Cristobal, located across the Mapocho River a mile from center city.

The railway takes you to the top, stopping en route at the first level, where a zoo—complete with dromedaries—is a must visit. The second level is where a number of passengers disembark—because they live there! (Homes dot the side of this small mountain and to reach them the residents use this elevator-like railroad.) The third and final level is close to the top of San Cristobal—the highest point in Santiago. Trees, shrubbery, and fountains make this one of the most beautiful sights we've ever seen. And above this level is a path leading to the actual summit, where there is a huge statue of the Immaculate Conception—it's partially the work of Bartholdi, the famous sculptor who did the Statue of Liberty. San Cristobal is stunning in the evening when the statue is illuminated and the

Santiago lights are clearly visible. But if you plan a late visit, bring a heavy sweater: temperatures drop sharply at sundown.

The funicular schedule? Every 15 minutes, from 9 a.m. to 8 p.m. Weekend hours extend till 10 p.m. Price: $1.50 up and back. To reach San Cristobal, take a taxi ($3), bus 26 or 29, or the San Ramón microbus. If you like, your taxi can drive you to the top for an extra $1. But you can easily walk to the funicular (our preference, as a matter of fact). Walk along Merced to the end of the street; take the bridge over the Mapocho River and walk along Pio IX (Pio Nono). In a few minutes you'll be at San Cristobal. There are plenty of stores along the way to pick up snacks.

Alternatives to the funicular up to San Cristobal are the open-sided buses affectionately called **"Tortugas"** (turtles). Fare: $1 each way. They are your best bet to take you to the **swimming pools,** open to the public in the summer months ($4). Or for an incomparable panoramic view of the city, enjoy the breathtaking **cable-car ride.** It takes 20 minutes round trip and the fare is $2.

Museo Nacional de Historia Natural and Quinta Normal Park

There's a boy here the likes of whom you have never seen in your life. He is 500 years old—at least—and he is almost perfectly preserved. Needless to say, the **Mummy of Cerro El Plomo,** as the boy is called, is the major attraction of this museum in the Quinta Normal Park. The lad's body was found in 1954 frozen in a mound of snow at the 16,000-foot-high summit of El Plomo Mountain near Lake Titicaca. He has been kept intact since by refrigeration techniques. Anthropologists speculate that the boy was of a pre-Inca civilization, judging from the ceremonial objects found on his person. Apparently he was a sacrificial victim to the sun god, a conclusion drawn from the kneeling, crossed-leg position of the body. The mummy is on the second floor of the museum.

The museum (tel. 90-011) is also well worth touring for the prehistoric dinosaur remains on its main floor; also its collection of mummies. Hours: Tuesday through Saturday from 10 a.m. to 1 p.m. and 2 to 6 p.m., on Sunday from 2 to 5:45 p.m.; closed Monday. Admission is 50¢. Take a cab ($3) or bus 5 marked "Quinta Normal."

Palacio de Bellas Artes

Opposite the U.S. Consulate, three blocks north of the Cerro Santa Lucia near the Mapocho River, is the Parque Forestal, a small park that houses the Palacio de Bellas Artes, home to the **Museo Nacional de Bellas Artes,** the **Museo de Arte Contemporaneo,** and the **Museo de Arte Popular Americano.** Built in 1910, this neoclassical palace is a copy of the Petit Palais in Versailles, France. Art lovers from all over the world come here to see the work of Chilean sculptress Rebecca Matte, a student of Rodin. Hours are 10 a.m. to 1 p.m. and 2 to 6 p.m. Tuesday through Saturday, and 10 a.m. to 1 p.m. on Sunday; closed Monday. Admission is 50¢.

Museo Histórico Nacional

Even if you have no interest in Chilean history, you will enjoy this historical museum located at Plaza de Armas 951. As you enter you pass a military display and approach the rooms dedicated to the colonial and conquistador eras. Collections of flags, cannons, carriages, armor, and furniture are featured. Upstairs the emphasis is on the era of independence. There is a model of Santiago in 1820 as well as the printing press of Camilo Henriquez, who published the famous *Aurora de Chile* in 1812. The model of the Plaza de Armas of 1850 will be of interest in contrast to its present state. Downstairs are relics of the pre-Columbian period. The museum is open Tuesday through Saturday from 9 a.m. to 12:30 p.m. and 3 to 6 p.m., and on Sunday from 3 to 6 p.m.; closed Monday. Admission is 30¢; Sunday free.

Museo de Arte Colonial

Located next to the San Francisco Church, this museum houses an excellent collection of religious paintings, including a valuable collection from the Cuzco School representing the life of Saint Francis of Assisi. Probably the biggest and best-preserved example of 17th-century American art in South America. Also here is the Gold Medal and Pergamin awarded to the Nobel Prize–winning Chilean poetess Gabriela Mistral. Worth a stop. Open Tuesday through Saturday from 10 a.m. to 1 p.m. and 3 to 6:30 p.m., and on Sunday from 10 a.m. to 2:45 p.m. Admission is 25¢.

Museo Precolombino

As the name belies, this fabulous museum features pre-Columbian art and artifacts and is located downtown at Bandera, corner of Compañía, in the building that once housed the royal customshouse (tel. 71-7010). It contains over 2,000 exemplary pieces of artwork from Mexico and Central and South America spanning 4,500 years. The setting is very modern, with subdued lighting, well-placed spotlights, and benches for foot-weary tourists. The entrance fee to this once-private collection is 30¢ and a written description of the artworks in English may be borrowed from the reception desk. Open Tuesday through Saturday from 10 a.m. to 8 p.m., and on Sunday from 10 a.m. to 2 p.m.—a good place to wander during the lunch hours when most other museums are closed.

Mundo Mágico

You can spend a pleasant afternoon while learning about Chile by taking the Metro to the Estación Pajaritos stop. The museum is located in a park near the airport. You can view Chile in miniature, illustrated by region, with emphasis on its historical, economic, and physical aspects. This is a good way to get an idea of the parts of Chile you may wish to visit. Admission is $2. Open Tuesday through Friday from 2 to 6 p.m. and on Saturday and Sunday from 11 a.m. to 9 p.m.

El Palacio Cousiño

Fashioned after Versailles, the Cousiño Palace, Diechiocho 438 (tel. 85-063), is proof of the splendor of Chile's past. This elegant mansion was built in 1871 by the wealthy Cousiño Goyenchea family whose fortune, like most during this period, was made in mining. It was decorated by European artists and craftsmen. The mansion was acquired by the municipality of Santiago in 1941, and has been host to many important dignitaries including Belgian King Balduino, and Presidents Figueiredo, Gregorio Alvarez, de Gaulle, and Prime Minister Golda Meir. Sumptuous chandeliers, exquisitely carved and painted ceilings, lovely artwork and furniture, as well as beautiful parquet floors make this home a showplace. The entrance is free, but the guide (who speaks English) will appreciate a tip. You can visit the palace Tuesday through Sunday from 10 a.m. to 1 p.m. during the winter months, and Tuesday through Friday during the summer.

La Casa Colorada

La Casa Colorada is Santiago's best-preserved example of colonial architecture. Built in 1769, it gets its name from the red color of its stone and stucco exterior. Once the home of Count Don Mateo de Toro y Zambrano, president of the First Junta of the Chilean government in 1810, it now houses the **Museum of Santiago**. This excellent museum chronicles the history and development of

Santiago. Open Tuesday through Saturday from 10 a.m. to 6 p.m. and on Sunday from 10 a.m. to 2 p.m. Admission is 25¢.

FOR CHILDREN: A wonderful amusement park open daily in the afternoon and all day weekends is **Fantasolandia,** located near the Parque O'Higgins station of the Metro. Worth a visit even if you left the little ones behind. While you're here you should take a stroll through **El Pueblito** (the Little Village), in the southern section of El Parque O'Higgins, to get a glimpse of rural life in Chile.

SPORTS: Futbol may be the national sport in Chile, as it is throughout the Latin lands, but the ponies are closing in fast. Chile has its Sunday track widows just as the U.S. has its golf widows. Skiing is the most popular participation sport in Chile—see "Excursions from Santiago," below.

The Track

Santiago has two tracks—the fashionable **Club Hipico,** and the lower-betting-scale **Hipodromo Chile.** The Hipico, open Sunday and holiday afternoons, is situated near the Parque O'Higgins, largest park in the city and site of many parades and festivals. While a taxi (about $2.50) is recommended for reaching the Hipico, you can also get here via bus 55 (marked "Avenida España") which runs along the Alameda, or by microbus 35, which leaves from Agustinas and San Antonio.

The Hipodromo Chile, open Sunday, some Wednesdays, and holiday mornings beginning at 8 a.m., is reached by bus 60 (marked "Ovalle-Negrete"), which you get at the Plaza de Armas; it will drop you at the track in a few minutes.

Note for bettors: The nags run clockwise at the Hipico and counterclockwise (as in the U.S.) at the Hipodromo.

Futbol

Like all large South American cities, Santiago has dozens of soccer teams and eight to ten major matches every weekend. You can see a first-class match every weekend between February and December at the 80,000-seat **Estadio Nacional;** in January, international matches are scheduled. General admission is $2 to $4. Take bus 3 (marked "Irarrazaval"). A taxi ($2.50) is simplest.

Futbol fever is usually highest here in mid-August and early December, when the University of Chile and its traditional rival, Catholic University, play their semiannual matches. The two schools at one time competed as well in lavish pre-game shows, but high costs forced them into a joint presentation, which we urge you to catch.

4. EXCURSIONS FROM SANTIAGO

SKI COUNTRY: Only 3½ hours by bus or five hours by train from Santiago is the most fabulous ski area in South America—**Portillo.** Local skiers argue that Portillo has trails as challenging as any in the Alps. Site of the 1966 World Alpine Ski Championships, Portillo draws thousands of skiers from North and South America between June and October.

Portillo, located 9,400 feet above sea level in the Chilean Andes, is an overnight trip (see "Where to Stay," below) and definitely worth it. Nowhere else but from Portillo can you ski to the **Christ of the Andes** statue, perched atop a 12,000-foot-high peak on the border between Argentina and Chile. There is instruction for beginners as well as twisting expert trails.

Only an hour's drive from Santiago, Chile's newest ski area, **Valle Nevado** promises to become one of the ski capitals of the Southern Hemisphere. It opened in 1988 with eight lifts and 21 trails in operation. More are slated for the future. Its peaks rise to over 16,500 feet above sea level. Two other ski areas, **El Colorado Farellones** and **La Parva** are also nearby.

Getting to the Ski Areas

The most practical way we've found to reach either Farrellones or Portillo is to use a travel service that specializes in ski excursions particularly, like **Tour Service,** on the tenth floor of Teatinos 333. Another good agency is **Grez,** Ahumada 312, between Agustinas and Huerfanos (office 315).

The round-trip bus fare to Portillo is about $20 per person as arranged through Tour Service. A sister travel agency, **Sports Tours,** handles overnight accommodations (see below). Buses leave daily from the Carerra Hotel at 8:30 a.m., returning around 7 p.m. The fare includes a free complimentary cocktail.

Like to head to ski country via car? Make your arrangements through **Nuevo O'Higgins San Martín,** a travel agency at San Francisco 24, across the Alameda and near San Francisco church. The round-trip cost to Farrellones is $25 per person (five to a car), while the Portillo journey is $40 per head. Service is on an irregular basis. A private car runs $90 for up to four people.

Where to Stay

In Portillo, your choice is limited to the magnificent 200-room **Hotel Portillo,** nestled high in the Andes. A share-the-bath bunk in the seven-story main building or at the nearby Inca Lodge annex costs about $50 per person, including four meals and taxes. Private doubles, with bath, range up to $200 per day; singles run as high as $105—again with all four meals included. Inca Lodge guests dine in a self-service dining room.

And when not skiing, you can swim in the heated outdoor pool, skate on a nearby pond, loll in a sauna bath, or relax at a film in the hotel theater. Sports Tours will make your reservation for you.

If you plan an overnight trip to Farrellones, ask Sports Tours to book you in one of the lodges owned by the University of Chile or Catholic University. These budget accommodations are located in La Parva, about three miles from Farrellones.

VIÑA DEL MAR: When Chileans crave ocean swimming, they head 85 miles to Viña del Mar, a year-round community that's crowded from September 15 to March 15. The jet-setters congregate at the famous **casino** here for roulette, blackjack, baccarat, and the nightclub and cocktail lounge. The racetrack is open on Sunday from December to March.

There are more than six beaches (all public) within Viña, and the Pacific beaches extend outside the city for miles in both directions, from Papudo Beach on the north to San Antonio Beach on the south, all with excellent bathing facilities. The water is frigid.

And for those looking for more than sun and fun, the **Naval Museum** (Museo Nava), **Palacio Vergara,** and the **Museo de Bellas Artes** are all worth visiting.

Tourist homes (residencias) are located throughout the city.

Take any of the buses that leave from the Mapocho Station vicinity. The 2½-hour ride will cost you only $3. For variety, return by train, a 3½-hour journey, for 50¢ more.

Organized bus tours including a visit to Valparaíso cost $20. A popular stop is a visit to the sundial made entirely from flowers.

Note: If you go by bus, make sure you take a pullman. Smaller (less comfortable) buses also are available and take an extra half hour.

Recommended hotels in Viña include the **San Martín** (doubles for $37), **Miramar** ($80), and the first-class **O'Higgins** ($60).

A Stop in Valparaíso

On the way to Viña del Mar you may want to stop at Valparaíso, a city built in tiers on the hills rising from the bay adjoining Viña del Mar (your fare to Viña includes this stop). This is Chile's second-largest city, and it bears a striking resemblance to San Francisco—with cobblestone streets and electric cable cars. It is the chief port of the west coast of South America, and a beautiful city for walking. Check the **Palacio Bauriza Art Museum.** The **Lancaster, Salcido,** and **Iberia** hotels are all fine choices. Bring your camera.

TERMAS DE CHILLAN: Farther from Santiago, about 250 miles south in the foothills of the Andes, is the stunning four-season resort, **Chillan.** The area is known for its fabulous skiing facilities and for its mineral baths. The ski facilities and the hotel underwent a costly facelift and are now first-rate. There are five ski lifts in operation, and one is the longest in Latin America. The ski runs vary from expert to novice, but all are covered with a fine powder cover and a few moguls. The ski season here is longer than that at Portillo. The mineral springs and mud baths are relaxing yet invigorating after a day on the slopes. When there's no snow you can play tennis, ride horseback, and hike. Fine restaurants and lively discothèques round out the facilities. Rates vary depending on the season and class of accommodations requested. Write for details and rates: Termas de Chillan, Arauco 600, Chillan, Chile (tel. 23664).

THE CHILEAN LAKE REGION: The Chilean Lake Region is often compared to Switzerland, and the natural features—snow-capped mountains, cold, crystal-clear lakes, clean air, wooded hillsides, and attractive towns peopled by rosy-cheeked, friendly people—are similar. The best months to visit are November through March (summer), although skiing is great in Chile's winter. The food is superb: the trout caught in local lakes and the shellfish caught offshore are fresh and prepared in Chilean fashion. There are many German eateries as well, due to the large German population that emigrated here in mid-19th century.

Temuco, 450 miles from Santiago, is the northernmost city of the region, and Puerto Montt, 200 miles farther south, is the southernmost point. Lan Chile has several flights daily from Santiago, and for those with unlimited time there are excellent rail connections as well.

Temuco has 180,000 people, many of whom are Arancanian Indians, Chile's only indigenous group. They sell their silver jewelry, ponchos, and handcrafts in the market here. **Villaricca,** a small town nearby (50 miles), is one of the area's loveliest lakes, as is **Pucon,** even smaller. Its volcano is used for skiing.

Valdivia, on the coast, and **Osorno** (inland) are the centers of Chile's German community. It is startling to see fair-haired people speaking rapidly in Spanish, although you do hear some German as well. There are hot mineral springs in **Puyehue National Park** near here.

Puerto Montt, a picturesque city of 100,000, is the jumping-off point for treks across the Andes to Bariloche (Argentinian side) and to Patagonia, Chile's southernmost point. Make sure to visit the Angelmo district, where the fishing boats are often left stranded ashore when the tide changes. Excellent handcrafts in the area too.

If you visit in summer (our winter) trout fishing in the lakes is big business, and in winter (our summer) the skiing is first-rate. Contact Lan Chile for flight information and Sports Tours (Box 3300, Santiago) for package tours.

PATAGONIA (MAGALLENES): Punta Arenas is the southernmost city in the world and capital of the province of Magallenes. The temperature is surprisingly mild, with an average of 36°F in winter and 68°F in summer. Days in summer have 20 hours of daylight, which makes it rough in winter when the sun shines only four hours a day. Visitors use this city as a jumping-off point for visits to Paine National Park, South America's largest. The rugged landscape with jagged hills, lakes, and forests look like moonscapes. The herds of animals are interesting to see as well. Contact Sports Tours (Box 3300, Santiago) for more information.

A VISIT TO EASTER ISLAND: Twice a week, on Wednesday and Sunday at 11:30 a.m., a Lan Chile jet lifts off from Benítez Airport, Santiago, and soars off over the South Pacific. Four hours and 50 minutes, and 2,300 miles later, it sets down on a tiny 45-square-mile triangle—Easter Island—the most isolated inhabited island in the world. It has several names: Easter Island, the English translation of the Spanish "Isla de Pascua" was given to it by a Dutch sailor who landed there on Easter Sunday; "Rapa Nui" is the name used by the 1,200 native islanders who use it to refer to their language and themselves—Rapa Nuians. Some 800 Chileans make up the rest of the population, all 2,000 of whom live in the town of **Hanga Roa.**

Most visitors arrive on Rapa Nui on package tours that include transfers, sightseeing, and accommodations. If you've come on your own, stop at the Tourist Office kiosk at the airport. They have a list of the hotels (only two) and pensions available. Most have no phones. And there are no buses, taxis, or even cars on the island. Local tour operators will meet the plane, and while driving you to your accommodation will try to sell you a tour. It's the only way to get around, so listen carefully and compare. **Iorana Tours** (tel. 82) has modern mini-vans and friendly guides. English is a hit-or-miss thing, so you'll need a guidebook (which we'll recommend). Those booked through Sports Tours in Santiago will be guided by Carlos Wilkens, whose English is impeccable and whose knowledge of the island is first-rate as well.

Hanga Roa and Environs

Since you arrive in midafternoon, spend what's left of your day exploring Hanga Roa and the Ahu Tahai, just beyond the town. There are only half a dozen streets in the town, which has small homes, many with tin roofs. The main street has several small grocery stores and shops, and the town's two restaurants. Visit the small church atop the hill overlooking the town. It is here that Father Sebastian, the island's resident historian and most famous citizen, worked and is buried. Continue past the town to the modern cemetery: note the small crosses and the flowers placed lovingly on the graves in Coke cans. Beyond the cemetery are the statues closest to the town. By the way, *ahu* is the Rapa Nuian word for "temple."

The most prominent sight at **Ahu Tahai** is one of the few statues left that has a red topknot in place. The statues, constructed as a form of ancestor worship, were hollow-eyed until they were raised onto their ahus. Then white stones were placed in the sockets. These were lost when the statues were toppled in anger by members of the island's underclass, the short ears. The red topknots were made to resemble the red-headed islanders, who wore their red hair in knots. Every statue on the island was toppled, and none was raised till Thor Heyerdahl arrived here. Nearby are four other statues with the traditional "long ears" (sign of upper class). Try to visit the small museum atop the hill behind this ahu (look for the red roof). It is open from 8:30 a.m. to 12:30 p.m. and 1:30 to 5:15 p.m. every day but Monday, and will give you some background.

Sights Around the Island

You need at least two days to see the major sites. Distances are small, but there are no paved roads so every trip is a major undertaking. You'll be aware immediately of the constant wind that blows across the island. It's often the only sound you hear. The island is barren, with few people and even fewer animals. Only horses seem to thrive and they are everywhere.

Rano Kau is the largest of the three volcanoes from which the island was formed (*rano* means "volcano"). Plants originally sown in its crater have continued to grow wild. They include pineapple, beans, taro, tobacco, coffee, and sugarcane. Others were planted in caves to protect them from the wind. Anyone who wants to climb the steep slopes can harvest the fruit for his own use.

High above Rano Kau is **Orongo**, a ceremonial site where the important annual contest to choose the "Birdman of the Year" was held. Part of the national park now being created, Orongo has an informative pamphlet (in English) to guide you. Get it when you pay the $2 entrance fee. Look for the carved bird petroglyphs on the rocks overlooking the three small islands offshore. Here the island's chiefs and their manservants gathered each September and stood watch. When the first sooty tern laid an egg on the tiny islands offshore, down the cliffs went the servants. Their masters waited nervously as the servants swam cross the shark-infested waters. The first to return with an egg won—however, it was his master who was proclaimed "Birdman of the Year." This was a religious post which included the power to assign the island's virgins in marriage. (The last such contest was held in 1864.) Also at Orongo you will see the curved boat-shaped houses of the Rapa Nuians. Some can be entered.

Rana Raraku, called "la fábrica" (the factory), is indeed that. It was here, and only here, that the more than 600 giant statues that populate this island were carved. And scores of others in various stages are still here. As you climb the volcano walls, you step on the nose of one, the body of another, and all around you there are uncompleted giants—some still attached to the wall and others already lowered for transport. Make sure to climb inside the volcano crater to see the smaller statues there, which are not as perfectly done (it seems that the journeyman carvers learned their art here before moving to the outer wall). Rana Raraku is worth every cent this trip costs you.

Ahu Akivi, in mid-island, is the most photographed site here. A lineup of seven huge stone giants with long ears and tight lips gaze off to the sea, restored to their ahu by a team of archeologists in 1960. These figures are the only ones to face the sea (all the others face inland).

Other interesting sites, if you have the time, are **Vinapu** (site of a huge temple), **Ana Kai Tangata Cave** (with drawings on the walls), and **Ana Kena Beach,** where the first leader (Hotu Matua) landed.

We can't urge you too strongly to consider making this trip in spite of the fact that it will make quite a dent in your budget. It's a once-in-a-lifetime experience. Check with Lan Chile (offices in New York and Miami) for package tours. Some are available only in Chile while others must be purchased here. Sports Tours, Box 3300, Santiago, is another excellent source of package-tour information.

Note: There are several excellent books you should read before taking this trip. *Easter Island, Land of Mysteries* by Peggy Mann (Holt, Rinehart and Winston) is sold on the island. *Aku Aku* by Thor Heyerdahl is easily obtainable at bookstores, and *Island at the Center of the World* by Fr. Sebastian Englert (Charles Scribner's Sons) is full of wonderful photos.

Important Tip: Bring very comfortable shoes, and a flashlight will be useful for night walking.

Food and Lodging

There are only two hotels and a few pensions on the island, and all are well above our budget. The **Hanga Roa,** on Avenida Pont (tel. 99), is the first-class hotel, although it resembles a motel from the outside. The charge is $95 double, with breakfast, and Modified American Plan (two meals) is available. Also on Avenida Pont, the **Hotu Matua** (tel. 42) charges $56 single and $93 double, with all meals included.

All four of our recommended pensions include all meals in the room rate: **Residencia Rosita,** at Te Pito o Te Henua (tel. 50), is run by lovely islanders, where they charge $50 for a single and $80 for a double; **Residencia Manutara,** on Hotu Matua (no phone), charges $45 single and $75 double; **Residencia Terongo,** at Policarpo Toro (no phone), offers singles at $35 and doubles at $60; and **Residencia Pedro Atan,** also at Policarpo Toro (no phone), charges $42 single and $64 double.

Our final two choices are **Residencia Apina Nui,** at Hetere Ky (tel. 92), and **Residencia Orongo Toro Nui,** at Policarpo Toro (tel. 94).

The best restaurant in town is near the church, but most visitors eat in their hotels. After all, in such isolation the camaraderie is part of the fun here.

Lan Chile Schedule

At this writing Lan Chile flies to Easter Island on Wednesday and Sunday at 11:30 a.m., arriving at **Mataveri Airport** at 3 p.m. the same day.

Lan Chile leaves Easter Island for Santiago on Monday and Saturday at 8:30 a.m., arriving at **Merino Benítez Airport** at 3:30 p.m. Round-trip fare is $335.

5. SANTIAGO AFTER DARK

Santiago's nightlife, while not as jumping as that of Buenos Aires or Rio, still has much to offer the late-to-bed, late-to-rise traveler.

THE BEST DISCOS: Young Santiagans gravitate to the suburbs where several discos vie for their patronage. These are exceptional with lovely settings in La Reina Alta section high above the city. We're partial to **Cassamila,** at Alvaro Casanova 298A (tel. 226-0019), located in a large private house where the inside has at least three levels, reached by slides and firepoles as well as stairs. Its round dance floor on the lower level is illuminated by colorful spinning lights, and the music never stops. Tables at all levels overlook the lights of the city. Cassamila is open Thursday through Sunday beginning at 7 p.m., at $8 minimum per couple. Another favorite is **Las Brujas,** on Avenida Príncipe de Gales in La Reina (tel. 227-9812). Reopened after a fire, Las Brujas has constructed a circular disco alongside its restaurant in the most exotic setting on a quiet lagoon complete with swans, surrounded by weeping willows and old gnarled trees. When the moon is out, romance is in the air. Look for the twin witches on their broomsticks at the entrance. There's a two-drink ($8) minimum per couple.

Caledonia, on Avenida Larrain (tel. 226-4438), draws dancers on weekends to its round dance floor. Very dark, with picture windows overlooking the city, it's sedate compared to the other two. Closer to town is the **Amfiteatro Lo**

Castillo, in the Lo Castillo shopping center. The disco and theater are in the basement. **Marrakesh,** on General Holley (off Avenida Providencia), is an elegant disco with an Arabic touch in the décor.

Try **El Organo,** at Avenida Vitacura 2873, where the red love seats are usually occupied by clinching couples. Drinks are $5 to $6. The psychedelic effects are striking. Films and slides are periodically shown. Open until 2 a.m. weekdays, to 4 a.m. on Saturday; closed Sunday. A cab ($1.50) will get you here in 15 minutes.

Another favorite of ours is **Discothèque Eve,** at Vitacura 5480 (tel. 48-6341). Perhaps the most elegant disco, Eve's draws equally from the mod and mink crowds. Open until 5 a.m., this large club has carpeted floors, glass walls, and a fireplace. Drinks are $7; no cover or minimum. A cab ($5) is your best bet to get here. Closed Monday.

Also recommended is **Memphis Jazz,** Avenida El Bosque Norte 0155. This new club has a restaurant, bar, and discothèque. Live music nightly.

CLUBS AND PIANO BARS: Jazz, Santiago style, is the lure at the **Club de Jazz de Santiago,** at Avenida José Alessandre 85, open on Friday and Saturday nights from 9 p.m. Groups alternate so the music rarely stops.

If you don't care about the music but want a comfortable place to have a drink and quiet conversation, stop at **Confetti's Piano Bar,** at Avenida Apoquindo 5002 in Las Condes, or **Gringo Bar and English Pub,** at Pedro de Valdivia 2153. Both draw a mix of locals and tourists.

For comedy, try **Romeo,** in the Barrio Alto on Calle Los Cobres de Vitacura (tel. 212-7117). A few different acts are featured nightly.

FLESH AND FANTASY: If viewing the female form in all its bold honesty is your idea of enjoyment, then you have several clubs to choose from. Each offers a maximum of skin.

Providencia 1100 (that's also the address) is a cabaret with strip and simulated-sex show, and lots of single girls around to help you spend your pesos. First drink is $15. **Crazy Horse de Paris,** on Huerfanos near Estado (tel. 74-8207), has a strip show too. Check for showtimes.

A downtown spot offering a show and privacy is **Night and Day,** at Agustinas 1022. Enter the arcade and head downstairs. Drinks are a steep $13 to $15 and singles are admitted. The show features striptease "artists." The doormen are a source of information for unattached male travelers.

At Bulnes 135 is another club, the **Tap Room.** Drinks here also run $6 to $10 (that's a lot of dough for a little titillation).

You might also check out another downtown club, **Mon Bijou,** at Bulnes 475, adjoining the Plaza de Armas. It has two shows nightly, at 1:45 and 3:45 a.m. All the clubs are similar in décor, so if you've seen one, that's enough.

THE BIG SPLURGE: Scattered throughout the city are dozens of clubs called "boites," which feature live music and late suppers.

The boite that delights us particularly is **El Pollo Dorado** ("The Golden Chicken"), Agustinas 881, corner of Estado—a crowded cellar nightspot bedecked with Chilean flags—which features folk dancing and folk music in addition to fine food. The house specialty—chicken—will run you $11, including an appetizer, salad, dessert, and coffee. For the price of what you eat or drink ($2.50 per cocktail), you'll see a no-holds-barred version of the cueca, Chile's national folk dance, in which the dancers whip around the dance floor with feet vigorously tapping and brightly colored handkerchiefs swirling through the air. At first we were reluctant to try the Pollo Dorado because it's the most heavily publicized club in Chile—we feared it might be a tourist trap. But we were agreeably surprised to find good food, an exciting show, a non-phony atmosphere—and reasonable prices. Shows are on Friday and Saturday only; closed Sunday.

Similar to El Pollo Dorado is **Canta Gallo Restoran,** in the Las Condes district about 20 cab minutes away at Avenida Las Condes 12345.

Newer and more attractive (but more expensive) is **Enoteca,** on San Cristobal Hill. The well-prepared specialties are seafood and Chilean foods, and the service is impeccable. Several dining rooms are available, with typical Chilean folksingers and dancers moving between them. Make sure to visit the fabulous wine cellar here—it's open for tasting and buying. Expect to spend $15 per person for dinner with wine.

Stop in for a drink at **El Giratorio,** a revolving restaurant on Avenida Providencia. It spins once an hour and you see all parts of the city. Their special dinner is worth sampling if it's something you like.

A first-rate folklore show packs them in nightly at **La Ermita,** at Catedral 1143 (in front of the National Congress). Most of the customers take the $15 meal package, which includes a cocktail, appetizer, main course, dessert, a half bottle of wine, and beverage. In a ranch setting, complete with corral walls and arched ceilings, you can view the show, sans dinner. Drinks run $3, and there's a $5 minimum. Between shows the dance floor is usually crowded, while other patrons shop for artesanías in the giftshop. Loud, boisterous, and lots of fun. Don't leave without getting a souvenir ashtray, a gift from the management.

THEATER: Santiago is a city of theaters, all of them open all year round and all of them featuring plays, concerts, and ballet. The major theater is the 100-year-old **Teatro Municipal,** Agustinas and San Antonio, which offers opera in September and October, and ballet and concerts during the other ten months. Seats range from $2.50 to $10 for most events, although a special event might run higher. On our last trip we enjoyed *Faust.* The Philadelphia Orchestra was in town too.

CINEMA IN SANTIAGO: A score of film houses in downtown Santiago present first-run movies, with showings at 3:30 p.m. (matinee), 7 p.m. (vermouth), and 10 p.m. (evening). Seats are reserved, and tickets run about $1.50 to $2.50. To see what's playing, pick up *El Mercurio,* Santiago's best newspaper, or the *Santiago Chronicle,* the English-language weekly.

6. SHOPPING

The major shops in Santiago are located on the streets between the Plaza de Armas and Alameda O'Higgins. The best buys are copper products, woodcuts from Rapa Nui (Easter Island), and ski clothing. Weekdays, store hours are 10 a.m. to 1 p.m. and 3:30 to 7:30 p.m.; on Saturday, from 10 a.m. to 2 p.m.

Huerfanos and Ahumada have become promenades to permit shopping without worrying about traffic. Stroll through them and pass many of our selections as well as the city's newest arcades. **Unicentro,** on Huerfanos at MacIver, is a lovely arcade, with eight floors, glass elevators, and lots of eateries. A new arcade at the Plaza de Armas is also worth a look-in. The **Parque Arauco,** on Avenida Kennedy, is Providencia's nicest mall. It has two department stores and lovely shops.

Your first shop to browse should be at the out-of-the-way **Galería Artesanal de Chile (CEMA),** at Avenida Portugal 35A, several blocks on the far side of the Alameda. Here you will find a complete array of Chilean art filling each of the rooms of this attractive house. On exhibit (and for sale) are mobiles, ashtrays, jewelry, ponchos, tapestries, and a complete assortment of copper products. While we have not purchased many items here, this is a good place to get a feel for prices and variety. Other outlets of CEMA are at Avenida Providencia 1642 and at the airport.

Tea kettles, trays, decorative plates, ashtrays, and candlestick holders are among the best copper buys. Where to get them? We're especially fond of **Chilean Art,** at the San Cristobal Hotel, which has the largest copper-products selection in the city. Ashtrays and tea kettles start at $8; attractive candlestick holders are $15 a pair. Also, you can pick up wood statues imported from Easter Island for $6 to $30, and copper mobiles and ponchos are also sold.

A popular shop featuring most of these items is **Chile Lindo,** on Agustinas near Ahumada. Note the fantastic copper mobiles.

Copperhouse, at Huerfanos 1015, is a small shop stocked full with copper items: tea sets and servers, treasure boxes, cigarette holders, etc.

A cooperative that seeks to promote native Chilean art is Soproart Ltda. An outlet of that organization—**Huimpalay**—is located at Huerfanos 1162 (Local 3), and here you can get hand-woven rugs, woodcarvings, silver, copperware, and pottery. By all means shop here. We purchased a copper mobile which is a much-admired part of our country home.

Another excellent shop is the **Casa Bristal,** in the Plaza de Armas near Chez Henry, at Portal F. Concha, which features high-quality copper items, as well as fine woodcuts from Easter Island. The English-speaking proprietor will be glad to explain how you can distinguish Easter Island woodcuts and local efforts.

Center city has several shopping arcades that house a variety of specialty shops offering exclusive lines at reasonable prices. For good arcade browsing, head for the modern **Galería España,** on Huerfanos between Estado and San Antonio. A favorite shop of ours is located in the rear of the arcade: **Gundert** sells unusual copper and gift items at rock-bottom prices, and has a regular nontourist clientele. While you're there, take a peek inside **Casa Chile,** just a few doors down.

H. Stern has showrooms at the Carrera, San Cristobal, and Cordillera hotels. Not only do they sell Brazilian gemstones all set in 18-karat gold settings, but they feature lovely pieces using two of Chile's natural gems. Deep-blue lapis lazuli, which has become very popular here, and brilliant green malachite are set in rings, pendants, and neckpieces. Set in silver, they are so inexpensive that you can stock up on them for gifts. Stern products come with a one-year international guarantee.

High-quality custom-made stretch slacks or ski pants for men and women can be ordered from **Leo Schanz,** Merced 535 near Miraflores, for $40 and up. Women's orders are delivered within 24 hours. Regular slacks are similar in price.

For all other ski equipment, you might try **Casandina,** on Merced a half block beyond Leo Schanz. Here you can get parkas ($30 to $70), gloves ($9 and up), or hats ($5 and up).

Gucci, the Italian boutique, has found its way to Santiago at Agustinas and Ahumada. Prices and quality are equivalent to New York City.

Each of the four following stores features items you might not find elsewhere in Santiago. They're all first-class, top-quality places—and they're all on the second floor of the Hotel Carrera. **Amancai** sells gorgeous ruanas, ponchos, and sweaters—all wool and most hand-woven. Prices and quality are high. **Kon Tiki** features "artesanías" such as woodcarved figures, leather, and ceramics. **Copper Shop** has a full assortment of copper plus unusual gift items. **H. Stern** is the fourth—see above for details.

Similar are the arcades at the Sheraton San Cristobal and the Cordillera Holiday Inn Hotels, where you can shop in luxurious style at competitive prices.

Another shop with unusual ceramics is **Pablo Zabal,** at Diez de Julio 376.

Along Bellavista there are numerous workshops and showrooms that specialize in jewelry featuring the stunning blue lapis lazuli that is native to Chile, as well as other semiprecious stones including turquoise, malechite, and obsidian. However, there's not much variation from store to store in price or design. A few that merit some attention are: **Chungara,** at Bellavista 0299; **Lapislazuli Cordillera,** at the corner of Bellavista and Salvador Donoso; and **Rofor,** at Bellavista 0284. A noteworthy exception, **Lapislazuli Hector Cespedes,** at Bellavista 0430, features beautiful original pieces, many of which are designed by Hector's lovely wife, Ema Lazcano.

THE WINE COUNTRY: World-famous Chilean wines can be purchased at any liquor store at prices ranging from $1 to $5 a bottle. Try Rhin Undurraga, an outstanding dry white wine, just under $1.50, or the Santa Helena (1954), which will cost you $8—the highest-priced of the lot. Macul red or white wine costs $2, as does the excellent Tarapaca. Try, too, Macul's Don Matias ($2.25), and Casillero del Diablo.

Note: U.S. Customs places wine in the same category as liquor for import purposes. Your limit (without duty) is one bottle per person.

Tip: Check with any travel agency or your hotel clerk for information and details if you are interested in visiting one of Chile's many fine wineries.

Also, you can taste fine wines at the **Restaurant Enoteca,** at the Cerro San Cristobal, where you can also enjoy a panoramic view of Santiago.

7. TRANSPORTATION NOTES AND ASSORTED MISCELLANY

TAXIS: The simplest way to move about in Santiago is by cab, quite cheap and easy to come by. All taxis are black with yellow tops and are metered. The first kilometer will cost you about 90¢, with an additional amount clocked for every 200 meters. The cost comes out to about $1.25 a mile, with an additional 50% charge after 9 p.m. and on Sunday.

METRO: The new **metro** is operating. It has two lines and an extensive network of stops. You can use it to go from the Alameda all the way to Las Condes. There are maps posted in each station. Buy a ticket (*boleto*) for 25¢ and insert it in a machine for entrance. Stations are marked by red signs. The metro does not run all night, stopping service at 10 p.m.

Subway stations are designated with lighted red signs marked "metro." The station in the center of Santiago is **Universidad de Chile.**

BUSES: Fares are about 20¢ to 30¢. You enter from the front and pay the driver. Buses are usually quite crowded and a common sight is passengers hanging out the front or back during the rush hour.

In addition to regular buses, there are also smaller vehicles, called *liebres* (literally "hares"), which cost 25¢ a ride. These do not run as frequently as the large buses and standing room is not permitted. Microbuses run during rush hours only.

Colectivos: Jitney-like taxis holding up to five passengers zip along the Alameda picking up and discharging passengers. Fare: Under $1.

AUTO RENTALS: You will find car rentals quite expensive, but if you feel you must have a car, try either **Hertz Rent-A-Car,** Costanera 1469 (tel. 225-9328); **Budget Rent-A-Car,** Bilbao 2333 (tel. 225-3151); or **Citroarrienda Maneje,**

Santa Maria 0346 (tel. 39-1536). **Avis** has offices at the Holiday Inn Crown Plaza and San Cristobal Hotel. The cheapest car, a Daihatsu Charade, is $16 daily plus 22¢ per kilometer. A Honda Accord or Stanza is $34 daily plus 34¢ per kilometer. There is a $6 additional daily charge for insurance, plus a 20% tax.

If you're planning a motor trip, the **AAA (Affiliated Automobile Club),** Avenida Pedro de Valdivia 195 (tel. 74-9516), will map it out for you and give you helpful hints.

MISCELLANEOUS INFORMATION: Now for an assortment of tidbits:

The Press: Unfortunately, the *South Pacific Mail,* a once-popular English-language weekly, is no longer published. However, the Hotel Carrera publishes its own English-language daily and distributes it free to guests and visitors. You can also purchase *Newsweek, Time,* and *Vogue,* as well as English-language books, at the Carrera Hotel.

Phones: Deposit 5 pesos and dial.

International Calls: The cheapest way to call home is from the **Centro de Llamadas Internacionales Entel-Chile** at Huerfanos 1137—open Monday through Friday from 8:30 a.m. to 10 p.m., on Saturday from 9 a.m. to 2 p.m.

Post Office: The main one is near the Plaza de Armas. Look for the "Correo Central."

The Big Agencies: There is no formal American Express office, but downstairs in the Hotel Carrera is the authorized **American Express agent** in Santiago. **Wagons Lit** is located at Agustinas 1058. **Exprinter** is nearby at Agustinas 1074.

Tourist Office: The Government Tourist Bureau (Dirección de Turismo), whose office is at Catedral 1165 in center city, will provide free maps and advice.

U.S. Consulate: This is at Merced 230 (tel. 71-0133). The U.S. Embassy is next to the Hotel Carrera on Agustinas.

Street Names: Three streets undergo a name change at the Plaza de Armas: Ahumada becomes Puente, Estado turns into 21 de Mayo, and Catedral changes to Monjitas. And most streets change as they cross the Alameda. To avoid confusion, check your map carefully.

Bookstore: The **Librería Studio,** at Huerfanos 1178, has a large selection of books in English. There is also a branch at Andres de Fuenzalida 36 (the Los Leones Underground Station).

Emergencies: Day and night medical and dental service is available through the **Laboratorio Clinico,** Alameda O'Higgins 1616 (tel. 81-921). Your hotel clerk will call for you if necessary.

Drugs: U.S.-manufactured drugs are widely available at pharmacies. Two well-stocked, clean establishments are **Farmacía Petrizzio,** at Estado 93 near Moneda (tel. 38-1096); and **Farmacía-Franco-Inglesa,** Plaza de Armas at Merced and Estado.

24-Hour Pharmacy: The **Farmacía Ahurunda,** at Avenida da Portugal 155, and **Farmacía Reunidas,** Providencia 2012 (tel. 21-0831), are at your disposal —day and night.

Danger: U.S. appliances need a converter to be operated on the 220-volt Chilean current.

Smokes: U.S.-made cigarettes are hard to come across. However, Lucky Strike and Viceroy are produced here under license and sold under those brand names. Many local brands are sold, of course.

Chinchilla: To identify with the wealthy for a time, skip over to **La Super Furs,** MacIver 238, near Huerfanos, where you can gaze at $1,000 chinchilla stoles at your leisure. The owner, Jacobo Zlachevsky, who speaks English and comes from a long line of European furriers, will be glad to explain why chinchilla is more expensive than mink.

Climate: Santiago summers (December to February) are much like those of New England, while the fall and spring are much like southern California— warm. Winters (June to September) are cool and brisk, but temperatures never dip below freezing. Snow is a rarity.

Cowboys: The Chilean equivalent of the Argentine gaucho is called a "huaso." He dominates the rural scene, living on his "fundos" (ranches).

Candy: The huge **Confitería Serrano,** near the Conquistador Hotel, sells delicious candy (loose or in boxes).

Airport Tax: You pay $12.50 in dollars or pesos when you fly to a foreign destination.

Fruit Vendors: Be sure to sample Chile's famous fruits, which are sold in fruit shops and sidewalk stalls. Our favorites are the peaches, mandarin oranges, and of course, delicious grapes. They are perfectly safe to eat. Cost: A dozen peaches for $1.

Duty-Free Shops: While there are no major duty-free shops, you can purchase fine típicos and Chilean wines at bargain prices.

Panorama: Check the fine view of Santiago's downtown area from the 17th floor of the Carrera Hotel, and also from the top of the Sheraton San Cristobal. The snow-covered mountains are gorgeous in the winter.

National Dance: The cueca, so commonly performed in Chile, simulates the courtship of a rooster and a hen.

Fantasyland: A small amusement park in the Quinta Normal with rides and games. It's a pretty park and nice if you're traveling with kids.

Tennis: If you'd like to play tennis, stop at the **Club de Tenis Jaime Fillol,** at Camino de Asis 630, San Fransisco de Las Condes (tel. 224-1147), which has fine facilities and is owned by Chile's most famous tennis player. You can rent equipment and they'll try to set up a game for you. Also, the Sheraton San Cristobal has some courts, but they're only for guests.

CHAPTER VII

LA PAZ, BOLIVIA

□ □ □

La Paz is up so high in the Andes that until recently there was no fire department, the explanation being that fires simply don't have much luck in the city's thin, low-oxygen atmosphere. But the City Fathers decided a few years ago that a city without a fire department really couldn't consider itself part of the 20th century. And so fire equipment was purchased. It doesn't get much of a workout.

We use this story to illustrate the point that change is coming to La Paz, but—fortunately—it is coming slowly. There are lovely new hotels and several surprisingly good restaurants, but La Paz is a city where an ancient Indian civilization still exists—and that's precisely why you should come here. The clothing of the Indians, their markets, and their traditions are not put on for your benefit. They exist here every day, and as a visitor, you can be a part of it. Fascinating!

THE FIRST IMPRESSIONS: El Alto Airport—at 13,300 feet, the highest commercial landing field anywhere—is 1,000 feet above La Paz, itself the highest capital city in the world. After your plane lands and you start toward the city, you will peer down into the bowl-shaped valley that lies below. At the very bottom is La Paz, which at night looks like a bowl of stars. Ever present is the snow-capped Illimani Mountain—an awesome and breathtaking backdrop to the city.

During your flight into El Alto Airport you'll pass over Lake Titicaca, the world's highest navigable lake. It's an incredible and memorable sight. The deep-blue texture of the water blends with the snow-covered mountains to create an almost mystic effect.

You will be standing about 2½ miles above sea level—1½ miles higher than Denver and a mile higher than Mexico City. Fortunately, your body adjusts to the thin air rapidly, certainly within one day.

For us, however, the most intriguing aspect of La Paz is not its altitude, but its Indian population, which represents about half of the almost 1,000,000 residents (called Paceños, pronounced "Pa-*say*-nyos"). Many of the Indians trace their lineage back to the proud and wealthy Incas of the 15th and 16th centuries; today the Indian quarter, located in the highest reaches of La Paz, is the poorest section of the city. Unlike the upper-income groups of many other cities, the wealthy of La Paz live in the lower-altitude areas. The poorer a family is, the higher up in the hills and mountains they live. And the reason for this is that the climate is more moderate in the lower areas, requiring less effort in getting about.

As you wind your way down into La Paz from the airport, you'll be surrounded on three sides by Indian houses clinging to the mountainsides. Made of sun-dried mud brick, the houses have metal roofs, sometimes held in place by large rocks. Few have heat or plumbing. Many Indians are dressed in tatters by our standards, yet the women, no matter how poor, wear several brightly colored skirts (polleras) with a knitted shawl or blanket over the shoulder. And Indian women top off their ensemble with hard brown or black bowler hats. Their jet-black hair is always braided.

A common street sight is an Indian mother breast-feeding one child while her other tots play on the rock-strewn roadside. Often you will see women carrying babies on their backs in a sling made of blankets.

The physical beauty of La Paz is staggering, the Indian culture is staggering —but what never ceases to amaze us most is that within four hours (by bus) you can be in the midst of tropical jungle. Again and again we look forward to witnessing the startling contrast between La Paz and its jungle areas nearby.

ORIENTATION: Until just recently, the best—and virtually only—way to reach La Paz from El Alto Airport was by taxi. Fortunately, **Cotranstur** now offers minibus service to and from the airport. The fare is $1, and buses operate every five minutes from 7 a.m. to 9 p.m. You can be dropped off anywhere along the route, which goes from El Alto, passes through Perez Velasco, the Plaza San Francisco, Avenida Camacho, El Prado, past the university, to the Plaza Isabel La Católica—a very convenient service.

Ask the driver to drop you at the **Dirección Nacional de Turismo,** which has just moved to a new office in a small corner building, La Esquina Cultural Pacena, located right at the end of the **Prado,** La Paz's main boulevard which is also known as Avenida 16 de Julio. Go up to the information booth on the third floor and give the clerk several of our hotel recommendations. He'll call them for you at no charge, while you sip a mate de coca and get adjusted to the altitude. If the office is closed when you arrive, then stroll along the Prado and get your bearings. Most of our hotels are on or near the Prado. This wide double roadway, separated by a grass promenade, is smack in the center of the city and at one of the lower points.

The streets that intersect the Prado run at sharp angles up the hillside, which makes for fatiguing uphill walking when you veer off the main boulevard. Remember that the thin air can cause discomfort when you exert yourself. So move slowly and breathe deeply to absorb the maximum amount of oxygen. This should make the going easier.

La Paz, being the world's highest capital, has one major drawback: its altitude. At almost 13,000 feet, the air is rarified and you will undoubtedly feel lightheaded and headachy. Don't worry. *Soroche* is a normal condition for visitors unaccustomed to the altitude. It will pass within a day. A popular local remedy is cocoa de mate (tea with coca leaf), which is available and really helps. Don't worry—it's legal and safe. Another medical recommendation is taking iron some days before going up to this altitude.

In many South American cities you'll often be surprised to find that the street you are strolling on changes its name two and even three times—often without apparent reason. The Prado is a good example of this. The street is called at various times Avenida Villazon, 6 de Agosto, then 16 de Julio, and finally Santa Cruz. Residents explain that the City Fathers have more key historical dates and names they wish to immortalize than they have key streets to name after them. So the main avenue has been pressed into multiduty service. To simplify things, the entire street is called the Prado.

The most important stretch of the Prado is **16 de Julio,** which runs six blocks from Bolívar's statue at **Plaza Venezuela** to the **Plaza Franz Tamayo** (better known as the **Plaza del Estudiante,** because of its proximity to the University of La Paz).

From the Plaza Venezuela to the Plaza San Francisco the Prado is known as **Santa Cruz** (uphill from 16 de Julio). From the Plaza Roma, downhill toward the university it is called **Avenida Villazon** and then **6 de Agosto.**

Another orientation point is the **Plaza Murillo,** a square located three blocks above the Prado from the obelisk on Camacho. This large square contains the president's palace and an enormous cathedral. Many of our hotels are located nearby.

Sharply contrasting with bustling downtown La Paz is the higher-in-altitude **Indian quarter,** which extends from the **Plaza San Francisco** about four blocks from the obelisk up a fairly steep hillside, or more accurately, a small mountainside. This quarter embraces about two-thirds of the land area in La Paz. A typical Indian street, leading up from the Plaza San Francisco, is the cobblestoned **Calle Sagarnaga,** lined with Indian-owned shops. We'll have more to say about this street later on.

Other Indian centers are **Avenida Manco Kapac** (named after the legendary first Inca) and the tumultuous **Calle Buenos Aires,** a teeming shopping area high in the Indian quarter that's a must during your stay here.

THE CLIMATE OF LA PAZ: Before beginning our hotel discussion we should refer to the climate, which can change rather suddenly, particularly when the sun disappears behind a cloud.

At an altitude of more than 12,000 feet the atmosphere is so thin that the effects of the sun are quickly felt. Therefore when the sun is out it is surprisingly mild, even during the winter (June to September). You will sunburn easily if you're fair-skinned. But when the clouds mask the sun, or in late afternoon, temperatures can and do drop ten or more degrees within the space of minutes.

On your first day here you may experience some light-headedness due to the altitude, but all will be well within a day or less. Visiting soccer teams arrive here a week early to acclimate themselves to the altitude. But it doesn't help much. Visitors seldom win. The sport is too punishing and the air too thin for a team to be ready to play here that quickly. Your exertion, we expect, will be considerably less and therefore your adjustment considerably easier.

While the temperatures do drop quickly, they seldom dip below freezing. The mercury averages about 50° most of the year. Snow is rare in La Paz. Summer (December to February) is the rainy season.

Important: No matter how warm the day seems in the morning, carry a heavy sweater with you. When the sun dips behind a cloud you will immediately appreciate this bit of advice.

GETTING AROUND TOWN: Cabs are so cheap—under 75¢ and up for two passengers to most parts of the city—that we strongly recommend them. But hardcore budgeteers can do even better. There are taxis called **trufis** which operate as jitneys along fixed routes on main streets such as the Prado. Fares are only 50¢ to 60¢. And even cheaper are small modern buses called **micros** (pronounced "meekros") which charge only 25¢ within the downtown area, 50¢ for distances farther out. There are also large buses called **colectivos** which charge 20¢, but these are very crowded.

La Paz has a taxi call service called **Taxiphone:** you can call 3-41-668 and a taxi will get to you soon after. The fare is $3 for the metropolitan area, $5 to residential sections, and $8 to the airport, plus $1 for each piece of luggage.

A WORD ABOUT MONEY: Since a democratically elected government is now establishing new economic measures to stop inflation, the money situation has become more stable. New bolivianos have been introduced. One **new boliviano** equals 1,000,000 "old bolivianos." Now 1 boliviano is equal to 1,000,000 pesos. However, there are still old boliviano bills in circulation, so check your currency carefully. Chances are that if you have a bill for 10,000,000 bolivianos, they are the old ones, and it's actually worth 10 "new bolivianos."

As of summer 1988, $1 U.S. is worth 2.40 bolivianos. This rate is just about the same in the exchange houses, the Central Bank, the hotels, and on the parallel market, where it is perfectly legal to change. We usually change at the **Casa de Cambios Caceres,** in the Hotel Gloria on Calle Potosí (tel. 3-41-457); **Casa de Cambios Sudanier,** at Calle Colón 256 (tel. 3-27-341); and **Casa de Cambios America,** on Avenida Camacho in the Edificio Krsul (tel. 3-40-920).

1. WHERE TO STAY

As elsewhere in booming South America, prices have been increasing in La Paz. And naturally this has been reflected in hotel costs. For example, a double room in the top-rated Hotel Sucre has jumped from $12 to $35 since 1970. To a lesser degree this is true elsewhere in the city.

Still, we have found a number of good-value hotels and pensions. Remember, all prices include a hefty 27% tax and service bite. Before we cite specific choices, we should offer one generalization. For some reason, many hotels here seem to be seriously in need of brightening up, starting with a good paint job.

BEST-VALUE HOTELS ON THE PRADO: The most convenient area for travelers to bed down is in the vicinity of La Paz's main street—Avenida 16 de Julio (the center portion of the Prado), which is as central as you can get to the city. So we start our hotel search here with the **Hostería Claudia,** at Avenida Villazon 1965 (tel. 3-75-950), a basic choice where clean, carpeted rooms with drapes and bare furnishings are a bargain at $17 double and $10 single. Bathless doubles are only $10. Avenida Villazon is the extension of the main Avenida 16 de Julio.

A few blocks away, but still on the Prado, where the street becomes Avenida 6 de Agosto (five blocks downhill from the City Hotel), you'll find the 27-room **Hotel España,** at no. 2074 (tel. 3-54-643), near the University of La Paz. While the management is extremely gracious and helpful, and rates are modest, still the strongest argument for staying at the two-story España is its central location. It is really only a cut above starvation level. Rooms are small and some are a bit on the drab side. But there is a pleasant sitting room where students congregate. Doubles with private bath run $16; singles with bath are $12. Bathless doubles are $10; singles run $8. Prices include breakfast. The hotel is set in an attractive garden. Enter via a stone stairway to the lobby. If you get a room in front, you will be able to see Mount Illimani. Recommended for students only.

Farther down Avenida 6 de Agosto, at no. 2548, is the modest two-story

Residencial 6 de Agosto (tel. 3-55-122). Here you will find comfortable, although basic accommodations, at $10 for singles, $16 for doubles, $21 for triples—all with private bath. There are several bathless singles which run less. The rooms are carpetless and the furniture old, but they are clean.

NEAR THE PLAZA MURILLO: Paceños consider the Plaza Murillo the true heart of the city. This grassy square, whose benches are usually occupied by office workers, housewives, and couples, is about the highest-altitude non-Indian area of La Paz. Perched three steep blocks above the Prado (Santa Cruz portion), the plaza area houses the Presidential Palace and the huge cathedral. A number of shops and movie theaters are located here as well.

Best-Value Selections

A top budget choice is the 20-room **Hotel Austria,** Yanacocha 531 (tel. 3-28-915), a block from Plaza Murillo on a steep street. Recently refurbished, and surprisingly colorful, the Austria offers solid value even if you select the higher-priced front rooms. All the rooms are bathless, but a heater is included in the higher-rate accommodations. Front-windowed doubles, comfortable and sunny, run a cheap $10, and the best singles are $6, tax and service included. The management provides bulky blankets for heatless rooms—and you'll have to remember there is hot water in the morning and evenings only. Highlights: The Austria is gaily painted in yellow, and Austrian travel posters deck the lobby. It resembles a chalet from the outside, and at this altitude it should.

Across from the Austria is the **Hostal Yanacocha,** at Yanacocha 340 (tel. 3-69-835), a small 16-room hotel where rooms with bath are $13 double, $7 single. Head upstairs to the lobby of this basic hotel where rooms have bare floors, a bureau, and not much else. Basic—but not bad.

Another good choice in this price range is the newer **Hotel Calacoto,** Calle 13, no. 8009 (tel. 7-92-524). The Calacoto has rooms in all categories. Singles with bath will run $15, while bathless singles run $8. Doubles are $15 with bath and only $11 without. The hotel has its own restaurant which serves all meals—breakfast at $1.25 and lunch and dinner for about $5.

Another excellent budget selection only two blocks from the Plaza Murillo is the newer, 30-room **Hotel Latino,** Junín 857, at the corner of Sucre (tel. 3-70-947). The rooms all have carpeting and many have private baths. Doubles with bath go for $11 and singles run $9. Prices are more reasonable when you are sharing a bath: $9 for doubles, $6 for singles. There is a cafetería on the premises, and laundry service. Recommended.

Also, you might consider the 49-room **Hotel Avenida,** Montes 690 (tel. 3-76-017), near Calle Boso on the outer fringe of the Indian quarter. Popular with students, the Avenida is an aging four-story walk-up that has been refurbished just enough to make it a good value. An intercom system that connects all rooms with the front desk assures you of getting towels and messages promptly. We recommend staying in a front double for $16 (with bath); you will find it well lit and casually livable, with twin beds, a desk, a bureau, and a sink. Front singles are $12.50. Rear bathless doubles (far gloomier) range from $5 to $9; singles, from $5 to $8. There is no elevator, so try to get a lower-floor room. And be sure to ask for a heater if your room lacks one. Keep in mind that Avenida Montes, a continuation of 16 de Julio (the Prado), is in the city's higher, and poorer, reaches.

The 21-room **Hotel Neumann,** Loayza 442, near Comercio (tel. 3-25-445), offers roomy clean doubles with baths for $8.50, bathless doubles for $6.50. Singles are $5. All rooms are off an inner courtyard and most are on the second floor. Located two blocks from the Plaza, the Neumann has a good budget restaurant on the premises.

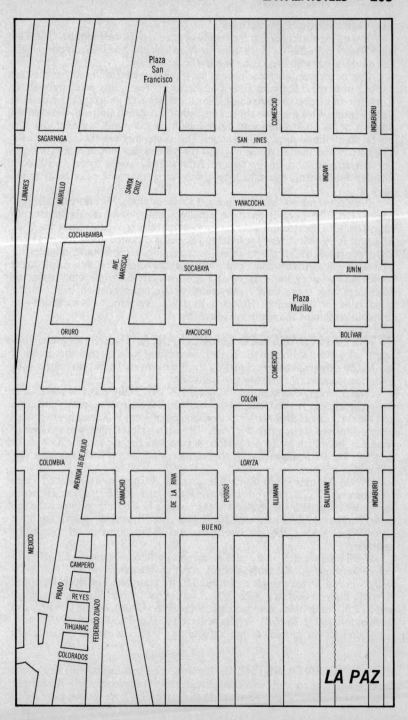

Starvation-Budget Selections

You might also check out the very basic ten-room **Hotel Bulgaro,** Calle Colón 570 (tel. 3-54-298), a block from the Plaza Murillo. The Bulgaro offers bathless doubles, but with breakfast, for a low $6 per person.

Our next three budget selections are somewhat out of the way as they are located near the Miraflores futbol stadium. To reach this area, walk along Comercio until it becomes Avenida Illimani, some seven long blocks beyond the Plaza Murillo. Our first two choices are right on Avenida Illimani. **Residencial Baviera,** at no. 1630, offers very modest, bathless accommodations at low, low prices: $6.75 for doubles, $4 for singles. The rooms are clean though very basic. The Baviera tries hard to please and has a pleasant coffeeroom, as well as offering guests transportation to the airport. At no. 1817 you'll find the 30-room **Residencial Illimani,** where bathless rooms carry the same pricetag as at the Baviera.

Harder to find, and higher in price, is the **Residencial Miraflores,** Calle Managua 1 (tel. 3-58-272). To reach the Miraflores, walk along Avenida Illimani until you come to the stadium and bear to your right along Avenida Saavedra. Calle Managua is the first street to your left off Saavedra. Located at the top of a steep flight of steps, the Miraflores offers bathless singles for $9 and doubles for $10.50. We think it's worth the extra dollars, as the Miraflores offers comfortable rooms in a two-story home that boasts a reasonably fresh coat of paint. In fact the Miraflores rates more than a starvation-level recommendation, representing good value for the money. However, its major disadvantage is location—far from our restaurant and nightclub selections.

IN THE SAN FRANCISCO CHURCH AREA: The following establishments are a short walk from the 16 de Julio area and right on the outer fringe of the Indian quarter. Many backpackers stay here purposely, but no matter your intention, these are for the young in spirit only.

The 60-room **Grand Hotel,** Ev. Valle 127 (tel. 3-23-732), has no elevator for its three floors, no heat, and no sign outside. But the rooms are airy and clean and overlook the Indian market below. Photos of John F. Kennedy are prominently displayed throughout the hotel. The Grand Hotel offers you a choice of rooms without bath for $6 per person. Rooms with private bath are $10.50 for doubles, $8.50 for singles. While roomy, accommodations have only basic furnishings.

Where Montes meets Santa Cruz, you'll discover a street called Perez Velasco; at no. 785 is the acceptable **Hotel Plaza** (tel. 3-22-157), whose 20 rooms are spread over the first two floors—the owner's large family occupies the top floor. Bathless doubles here are $10, singles cost $6, and the rooms are quite clean. While sinkless, they do have basins, and all the rooms are off an open-air courtyard.

We'll briefly touch on three more choices in the San Francisco Church area before we move on: the **Hotel Bolivia,** Avenida Manco Kapac 287 (tel. 3-75-030), will run $8 for a single room and $11 for a double. The **Hotel Oriental,** Avenida Illampu 868 (tel. 3-72-110), is somewhat higher: $10.50 for a single and $12.50 for doubles. And last there is the **Hotel Oruro,** on the Plaza Alonso de Mendoza (tel. 3-25-893). Singles here are $4.50 and doubles are $9.

Don't let the gloomy hallways discourage you. The rooms are large and airy.

IN THE INDIAN QUARTER: The Indian section in the mountain area, above the city center, offers some selections that are truly "last resort" only. All are centered near Avenida Manco Kapac and offer starvation-level rooms, catering to students and backpackers primarily. Accommodations in this area are very basic, with little more than a bed and bureau. Hallways are gloomy, bathrooms dark. Still, if you're adventurous the area does offer an opportunity to experience a fascinating culture.

There is, in fact, one superb budget buy, the three-story, 84-room **Hotel Tumusla,** Avenida Tumusla 580 (tel. 3-41-106). The small rooms are spotless and the prices are startling—only $11 per person for a room with private bath and $7 per guest for share-the-bath accommodations.

A good value is the **Hotel Panamericano,** Avenida Manco Kapac 454 (tel. 3-40-810), which has moved up a notch in both comfort and price since private baths were installed. Doubles are $18 and singles are $15—prices which include hot water at all times, piped-in music, telephone, and wall-to-wall carpeting. There's a cafetería on the premises too.

One that you might consider is the **Hotel Andes,** Manco Kapac 364 (tel. 3-23-461), a six-floor, 50-room walk-up that has bathless rooms for $4 to $10 per person. Obviously, you'll want to choose a lower floor, as walking up six flights in this thin atmosphere can be extremely fatiguing. The Andes is for the younger traveler.

Another selection here is the 33-room **Hotel Italia,** across the street from the Andes at Manco Kapac 303 (tel. 3-25-101), another walk-up. Bathless doubles are a cheap $7 and singles go for $4.50. There are a few rooms with bath for the same price. The large rooms come with sink, bare floors, and sparse furnishings. The pink-hued Italia has the look of a fading Italian castle. An advantage is the good view of La Paz. For the hardy only, though.

A fine hotel which opened in 1980 in the Indian quarter is the **Hotel Sagarnaga,** Sagarnaga 326 (tel. 3-50-252), on the hilly street next to the Indian market. There are 32 rooms spread over three floors. Bonuses are color TV, laundry service, and a restaurant. For all this, doubles are only $15; singles, $12. All rooms have private bath and shower (no tubs).

Near the Hotel Sagarnaga at Sagarnaga 334, is the **Hotel Alem** (tel. 3-67-400), where the 42 rooms rent for $10 double with bath, 20% less without. Opened in 1982, the Alem is a touch below the Hotel Sagarnaga, but is still a fine choice in a great location.

Near the Mercado Rodriquez is the **Hotel Milton,** on Illampu at the corner of Calderon (tel. 3-68-003), where 60 rooms on five floors cost $20 double with bath, $16 single. Laundry service, piped-in music, and TV are bonuses.

Finally, you can consider the **Residencial Rosario,** Illampu 704 (tel. 3-25-348), a colonial-style home with patio, color TV, library, cafetería, and laundry service. Doubles are $10 with bath, $7 without, and singles, a dollar less.

. . . AND THE BIG SPLURGE:

Among the city's newer hotels is the 14-story, 70-room **Hotel Libertador,** Avenida Obispo Cárdenas 1421, which has rates roughly comparable to the Hotel La Paz—air-conditioned doubles with private bath upward to an expensive $30, singles at $26. Good location, three blocks from the Plaza Murillo. The Libertador has a lovely dining room and skyroom, where you can look out at the tile roofs of La Paz's older colonial homes and churches.

For excellent location, you can't beat the **Residencial La Hostería,** Calle Bueno 138 (tel. 3-22-925), just 50 yards from the National Tourist Office. The hotel was once an office building and has only recently been converted. Singles are $25 and doubles cost $29. La Hostería also has a restaurant where guests can have a full American breakfast for $3.50 and international dishes for $6.

In the same price category is the **Hotel Emperador,** Plaza del Estadium (tel. 3-40-013). The Emperador is quite attractive and all rooms have curtains and wall-to-wall carpeting. Rates for rooms with private bath are $24.50 for singles, $28.50 for doubles. An extra bed in the room costs $10.

The **Hotel Gloria,** at the corner of Potosí and Jenaro Sanjines (tel. 3-55-080), offers the luxury of a modern, first-class hotel, along with the small, friendly touches that make a pleasant stay. Owned by the Caceres family, both father and son are on hand to make sure that service is the best. A few short blocks from the Plazas San Francisco and Murillo, the Gloria has cozy singles for $26 and doubles for $32. All rooms are nicely furnished and have private baths. The hotel also has an excellent, moderately priced restaurant.

The **Copacabana Hotel,** at Avenida 16 de Julio 1802 (tel. 3-52-225), is popular with travelers due to its central location and its charming outdoor Parisian-style café where you can leisurely sip a drink and watch the action on the Prado. But prices are high. Many of the singles, at $28, are small with only basic furnishings and no carpeting. Doubles, at $33, are much roomier.

A block from the Copacabana, at Avenida 16 de Julio 1636, is the 100-room **Sucre Palace Hotel** (tel. 3-55-080). Rooms are tastefully furnished and all come with heaters and private baths. Doubles are $35 and singles run $27.50, including tax and service. An additional bed in the room is $8. A light-gray building, the six-story Sucre offers a fine dining room and snackshop.

Farther down the Prado where it becomes Avenida Villazon you'll find the **Hotel Eldorado** (tel. 3-26-952). A few steps away from the Plaza del Estudiante and the National Tourist Center, this hotel offers carpeted, curtained singles with bath for $29 and doubles for $35. Opened in February of 1977, the Eldorado also has a restaurant, coffeeshop, and skyroom.

At one time the 75-room **Hotel Crillon,** near the Plaza Isabel La Católica (tel. 3-52-122), was the city's premier hostelry. The hotel, happily, is on its way to reclaiming that distinction with its recent refurbishment. New carpeting and furniture were recently installed, and the hotel is much brighter thanks to fresh coats of paint. Spacious doubles are a high $42, and singles run $32. An extra bed in your room costs $11.50. Prices include continental breakfast. A restaurant, barbershop, and beauty salon add to the amenities.

TOP-OF-THE-HILL CHOICES: La Paz has two deluxe hotel choices that reflect the growth of the city.

In 1977 the owners of the Crillon opened the beautiful 384-room, 14-story La Paz Sheraton, on Avenida Arce (tel. 3-56-966). It is now run by the government and has changed its name to the **La Paz Hotel.** But it is still everything a big-splurge hotel should be: the lobby is impressive, the service excellent, and there are numerous giftshops, an antique and florist shop, a beauty and barbershop, babysitting services, a travel and Lloyd's airline bureau—in short, all the "extras" right at your fingertips. The rooms are fully carpeted and air-conditioned, and come with large, luxurious private baths. Many have breathtaking views of the city and Illimani Mountain. The hotel has a first-class supper club, a disco, a bar, and rooftop dining. The hotel is installing a pool and sauna. Luxury carries a high pricetag: doubles range from $95 to $105, taxes included. Singles are $75.

The other is the **Plaza,** located on El Prado (tel. 3-78-300), across from the Hotel Crillon. Large, with over 300 guest rooms, the Plaza has modern furnishings with native touches that make it very attractive. The hotel's restaurants, El Arcon de Oro and La Fontana, serve international food and are highly regarded. There is also a coffeeshop. Single rooms run $80 and doubles are $90.

2. RESTAURANTS OF LA PAZ

If you want to dine like the Paceños, then don't leave La Paz without trying two national dishes: **picantes,** chicken or shrimp served in a tangy red sauce; and **chuno,** frozen potatoes mixed with meat, fish, or eggs. They're excellent.

In general, most restaurants—budget or otherwise—are to be found on or near Avenida 16 de Julio. We've placed our selections in two categories: breakfast and lunch choices, then dinner places. Remember that the locals seldom dine much before 8 p.m. Keep in mind, too, to add 22% for tax and service to all prices. The better restaurants accept credit cards.

FOR BREAKFAST AND LUNCH: Possibly the best moderately priced restaurant in the city for any meal, but especially for breakfast, is the **Ely,** 16 de Julio 1497, corner of Bueno, which has speedy service, and offers a Spanish-English menu, on which a U.S.–style breakfast—juice, eggs with ham or bacon, and coffee—runs about $4. While not cheap, the sheer massiveness of this meal is enough to hold you well through lunch. A continental breakfast—of coffee, toast, butter, and jelly—is $2, including tax and service. We also like the french toast ($1.50), served with coffee and jam. And a lunch or dinner specialty at the Ely is a chicken picante dish called sajta de pollo ($4); other meat dishes include a hamburger plate ($2) and a T-bone steak ($2.50). Potatoes, noodles, or rice and a mixed salad come with all plates. The Ely also offers a complete assortment of German-American pastries, the likes of apple cake and cherry pie, as well as complete fountain service. Popular with North Americans. Open seven days from 8 a.m. to 10:30 p.m.

Another well-located restaurant with good food and quick service is the **Verona,** on the ground floor of the Litoral Building, at Avenida Mariscal Santa Cruz and Colón (tel. 3-28-793). Spacious and modern, the Verona is pleasantly decorated with eye-catching ceramic figures. Try the $3.75 special lunch. Open from 8:30 a.m. to 11:30 p.m.

And for the best hamburgers and milkshakes this side of the Andes, pop in at the **Snack Shop,** at 6 de Agosto 2038, operated by a rangy Californian by the name of Bob Feierbach. A minor institution here since 1963, the Snack Shop serves delicious beefburgers with onions, tomato, relish, and french fries, all for $1.75. Ditto for hot dogs. Thick milkshakes (choice of eight flavors) are 90¢; tea, coffee, and soft drinks are 60¢. Donuts and ice cream are available to take out. Open from 11 a.m. to 11 p.m.; closed Sunday.

Ice cream? A block off 6 de Agosto near the university is **Max Bieber's,** 20 de Octubre 2080, which resembles an old-fashioned ice-cream parlor of the 1920s. With three dining rooms, a take-out ice-cream counter, and reasonable prices, you can be sure this place is always crowded with students, who also order from among the two dozen hot plates on the large menu, ranging in price from $1.75 to $2. For $2.50 you can get an excellent small steak served with salad and french-fried potatoes. Excellent ice-cream cones. Closed Tuesday.

Gene's, a hamburger eatery on Avenida 16 de Julio, is a Burger King lookalike. "Whoppers" with lettuce and tomatoes and a tangy sauce run under $2 and taste good. Fried chicken and potatoes in the basket are a good buy as well. Across from the Hotel Sucre Palace, Gene's gets a lot of college students for lunch.

A very large restaurant and a good lunch or dinner choice is **Marilyn's,** on Calle Potosí. Lunch fare includes tasty burgers and hot dogs plus sandwiches and light platters. Dinner includes steaks and fish platters served with potatoes and corn. Dinner should run about $7; lunch is about half that figure.

A Danish veterinarian tipped us off to **Julio's,** near the Eldorado Hotel at Villazon 1936, a small, basic restaurant with ice-cream-parlor-type chairs. Prices are rock-bottom and it reminds us of Ely's. Try the pollo dorado, sandwiches, and desserts here. Hours are 11 a.m. to 10:30 p.m.

You should also try **Naira Crêperie,** on Sagarnaga, a simple, bare-floored place overlooking San Francisco Church, where sandwiches are $1 to $1.50, pizzas run $1 to $2, and excellent crêpes with fruit and marmalade are available. It's a small restaurant with a capacity of 22 places.

Another fast-food eatery is **Gargantua,** near the Plaza Hotel on the Prado, where we recommend the hamburgers, pancakes, and chicken in the basket. There are wood tables and chairs, with posters on the walls, and not much more.

RESTAURANTS FOR DINNER: It takes some determination to savor the **Monaco Restaurant,** up a flight of stairs at Avenida Villazon 1958 (tel. 3-65-014). It looks awful ascending the staircase to the Monaco, but around the bend is a lovely, carpeted, wood-paneled restaurant offering a fine view of Villazon (the extension of 16 de Julio). A fine dish is the mixed grill at $5 or the spaghetti al pesto at $3. The numerous trout dishes are excellent.

An attractive downtown restaurant is **Giorggisimo,** on Loayza at the corner of Comacho, open from noon to 3 p.m. and 6 to 10:30 p.m. You dine in red-leather booths with photos of regulars on the wall. You can choose from omelets, sandwiches, lasagne, and ravioli. Head downstairs to this cellar-like restaurant.

Probably your best bet for Chinese food is **Chifa Emy,** at Calle Cordero 257, a private house with several dining rooms, hanging lanterns, and a bilingual menu. Recommended are wonton frito, deep-fried spiced chicken, and roast duck Peking style. The fried noodles with beef is also good.

There's music in the air, as well as excellent cuisine, at our next three selections, which offer live entertainment while you dine. If your taste leans to organ music and Eastern European ambience, the **Restaurant Zlato,** located at Avenida 20 de Octubre 1824 (tel. 3-25-258), will be just right for you. You will enjoy both musical and vocal selections as you sample the house specialties—bife de chorizo ($4.50) and a delicious meat-and-cheese dish called "scalopa cao" ($3.50). "Zlato" in Yugoslavian means "gold crown," and in keeping with its name, the restaurant is decorated in red and gold colors.

If you like rousing music with your dinner, drop in at **La Escudos,** Avenida Mariscal Santa Cruz, not far from the La Paz Hotel. Rock music blasts out most evenings, and on Friday and Saturday there are live shows with a Bolivian beat starting at 9:30 p.m. Los Escudos calls itself a rathskeller—in its location a flight down from street level, and in its rambling design, it does indeed resemble a German beerhall. Heavy wooden tables and beamed ceilings dominate the look. But the food is strictly Latin, as is the entertainment. Try the parrillada Los Escudos ($6) or any of the beef dishes ($5.50). Locals lean to the pacumtu, a long roll of chicken, ham, beef, and pork, served with potato ($4.50). Check the coats-of-arms that line the walls.

The talented organist Oscar Grajeda is on hand weekdays to entertain dinner guests at the restaurant **El Internacional,** Ayacucho 206 (tel. 3-42-942), not far from the La Paz Hotel. Saturday night's offering is a colorful "Bolivian Spectacle"—folksinging, music, and dance—which goes on at 9:30 p.m. The menu is international; the house specialty is called "El International," a filet flambeado ($5.25). Drinks are $2 and up.

The churrasquería **La Carreta,** near the Prado at Calle Batillón Colorados 32 (tel. 3-55-891), is a fine place to eat dinner. It's open from noon to 11 p.m.

Another of our discoveries is the **Peña Andina,** at Avenida 16 de Julio 1473 (tel. 3-22-108). The atmosphere is pure Bolivian with native musical instruments decorating the walls. Folklorico shows are presented on Friday and Saturday nights. The Andina specializes in "típico" dishes, many of which are priced at a low $2.75.

For Chinese food, try the small and cozy **Hong Kong,** Plaza Franz Tamayo 1920, several blocks down the Prado from the Sucre Palace Hotel. The Kwan family opened the Hong Kong in 1967, four years after their arrival in the city. (La Paz is now home to some 100 people of Chinese descent—that's a lot for La Paz.) Grace Kwan, the beautiful manager, recommends no. 15 on the menu, chicharrón de pollo (fried chicken pieces), for $2.75; no. 38, shredded beef and peppers at $2; and no. 58, the sweet-and-sour pork, $2.50. You might also try the **Restaurant Chifa Casa Lin,** Avenida 6 de Agosto 2420, or the **Chifa el Junco,** Plaza Avaroa (Sopocachi).

Like Italian food? Slip over to the **Círculo Italiano,** 6 de Agosto 2563, where you can have any number of spaghetti and lasagne dishes for about $4.25. Large yet homey, the Italiano is owned by Dusan Lauric, a Yugoslav, who prides himself on hospitality. Enjoy a drink in the garden before lunch or dinner. Open noon to midnight; closed Monday.

Resembling an Argentine parrillada restaurant is the **Churrasquería El Tropero,** Capitan Ravelo 2050, where all courses are served on wooden boards. Succulent cuts of beef, sausage, or chicken are available at a low $4. And best of all, seconds are on the house as the policy is "all you can eat."

The **Club Alemán,** Calle Carlo Bravo, near Colegio Don Bosco, is a private club that opens its dining room to the public from noon to 3 p.m. and 6 p.m. to 1 a.m. Good values are the chicken dishes, at $4.50 and up. The two-level dining room, with only 25 tables in all, is gemütlich and inviting. There's music and típico dancing on Friday, Saturday, and Sunday evenings beginning about 7 p.m.

Typical Bolivian food is served at **Naira,** an unusual eatery (adjoining a peña) on Calle Sagarnaga in the heart of the Indian quarter. You sit at long wooden tables much like the ones Oliver Twist sat at in the orphanage and eat family style. Most of your fellow diners will be Paceños. The dishes used appear to be handmade and each is unique. The food is tasty and this is the place to sample a picante dish or the local soup-stew made of chicken called escabeche. Avoid salads and anything uncooked. After dinner, walk into the adjacent peña (in the basement) and enjoy the typical show, which includes folk music and dancing. You are expected to buy a bottle of Bolivian wine and popcorn plus the $1 admittance fee. (See "Peña Clubs.")

Our favorite French restaurant, **Domenique,** at Capitan Rovelo 2123 (tel. 3-77-173), has changed owners and is now **Diego's.** Diego's only accepts reservations for banquets of ten and more. However, we do have two interesting new selections. . . .

The first is **Pronto Ristorante,** just two steps from the 6 de Agosto Cinema on Calle Jauregui 2248 (tel. 3-55-869). Your first choice here should be pasta. Pronto makes its own, and most dishes cost around $5. The antipasto is also recommended. And don't forget to order wine with dinner. The wine list features a wide variety of fine wines.

La Suisse at Avenida Arce 2164 (tel. 3-53-150), across from the La Paz Hotel, is actually two restaurants in one. Elegant European cuisine is served in the cozy Swiss-style dining room on the first floor, a favorite meeting place for foreigners living in La Paz. The fondue is excellent, and so is the veal. In the hi-tech surroundings of the second floor you can enjoy a great selection of meats—beef, pork, sausage, liver—served grilled or cold, to which you add condiments to your liking, choosing from a great variety of onions, cheeses, sauces, and whatever else they may have to offer. You can also order Argentinian churrasco, Swiss raclette, or trout.

Previously listed in our "After Dark" section as a video pub, **Mocambo,** at Avenida Arce 2796 (tel. 3-61-788), is now a restaurant club specializing in Spanish foods such as paellas. The average cost of an entree is $10.

Dining in the Countryside

For a real dining treat we suggest that you take a mini-excursion into the tropical countryside where we discovered a marvelous little place called **Los Lobos Balneario Restaurant,** Aranjuez zone, Calle Tupac-Katari 15, just 15 minutes from La Paz by taxi ($4). The restaurant blends in nicely with its lush surroundings as it is constructed of the natural materials of the innermost tropics: pachihubas, canahueca, and balsa. The décor reflects the indigenous folk art of Bolivia—hand-designed and -painted fabrics, tropical birds, leather, leopard, and boa skins—all creating a colorful jungle-like aura.

The menu is international and includes a very good medallones a la Provençal at $5. Our favorites are the parrillada mixta at $6 and the picante surtido at $4.50. Don't forget that there will be a hefty 22% surcharge for taxes. You can make a day of it by combining this restaurant with trips to nearby sights—Cactus Park, Aniceto Arce, and the Valley of the Moon. (See our description under "Miscellany," Section 7.)

The Big Splurge

Head over to the luxurious La Paz Hotel for deluxe dining at their rooftop restaurant, the **Alaya,** an Indian name meaning "the best of the best." And you will get the best at the Alaya, but at prices that are definitely "big splurge." The La Paz Hotel also offers a luncheon buffet seven days a week at their **Tiwanaha Restaurant.** It's all you can eat for $8, including dessert and beverage. Fill up at lunch and then dine lightly at night.

Also, we suggest the **Sucre Palace Hotel Restaurant,** located on the second floor of the hotel, and well furnished with crystal chandeliers and all. A seat near the large glass windows gives a good view of the Prado and the mountains in the distance. The five-course lunch special is $8. Dinner is à la carte, but you can eat here within big-splurge limits by selecting carefully from the varied menu.

Other choices here are the restaurants located in the **Hotel Plaza:** La Fontana, El Arcon de Oro, and Utama are the three international restaurants worth eating in if you want to splurge a bit. We personally prefer the **Utama,** where you can have an open salad bar and excellent consommé along with excellent entrées. The entrecôte au vert (steak), truite Bonne Femme with wine, parrilladas (mixed grill), and sajat de pollo are all delicious and range from $5 to $9. The panoramic windows offer great views of La Paz. By the way, *Utama* in Indian means "Tu Casa" (Your House).

CONFITERÍAS: La Paz has several tea rooms, called confiterías, where you can enjoy a light lunch or a late-afternoon bite. Our favorite is the **Confitería Tokio,** 16 de Julio 1832, near the Plaza del Estudiante, which is owned, logically enough, by a Japanese family; the owner's son will probably serve you. The aroma of freshly baked pastries fills the small but cheerful room. The coconut pie, a house specialty, is the best we've eaten anywhere. The cost? $1.75. It's made with strips of coconut and orange rather than custard. Equally tasty are the ham sandwiches ($1.50) or cheese sandwiches ($1). Coffee, tea, and cocoa run 50¢. Open until 9 p.m.

Across from Crillon Tours on Avenida Camacho in the building belonging to the Club de La Paz you will find another very popular confitería, **Confitería Club de La Paz.** Open bright and early at 7 a.m. for coffee, milk, and pastry, the Club de La Paz is one of the few confiterías where you can amble in and order tea without purchasing anything else.

You might also try the **Confitería Rayito del Luna,** Comercio 1072, near Plaza Murillo, which makes its own bread and pastries. The sweetrolls (65¢) are superb.

La Paz also has several confitería/restaurants that offer meals at low, low prices. Confitería/restaurants are open for both tea and dinner. An excellent one is located just a few blocks from the Rayito del Luna at Comercio 1266. **Confitería La Florida** features native and international dishes with prices ranging from $2 to $6 for most plates.

Not far from the Plaza Venezuela at Colombia 153 is the confitería/restaurant **Monte Carlo,** a good stop for typical Bolivian food. Try the chicharrón (fried pork), picante (chicken with hot sauce), or fricasse (pork)—$2.25 each. Very informal.

Next door to the Eldorado Hotel is the elegant **Monaco** restaurant/confitería. Prices here are on the high side.

PUBS: A new phenomenon in the city is the pub. They are scattered along Avenida 16 de Julio and near the larger hotels. Drinks run $1 and up, with beer the least expensive.

3. LA PAZ BY DAY

This is an exciting city for sightseeing—particularly in the hilly Indian section where 350,000 residents (half the city's population) live, carrying on traditions unchanged by centuries.

THE INDIAN QUARTER: Part of the fascination is watching the past and the present meet and sometimes collide. For example, the Indians are devout Catholics. Yet Inca and Aymara religious symbols and rituals are basic to their religious observance. On the secular front, the men farm the rugged terrain as they have for centuries, while the women either tend their many children or operate stalls in the Indian markets in La Paz.

Most of the markets are outdoors and the Indian women customarily spread their goods on the ground on straw mats. Typically, you'll see huge manons (melons), bananas, oranges, grain, rice, fish, beef, and pastries. Indoor markets usually feature home-fashioned utensils, noodles, and canned foods.

The Best Markets

The markets operate daily, but the largest and liveliest are open weekends only.

The **Mercado Camacho,** the closest outdoor market to our center-city hotel selections, begins on Camacho and Bueno and on weekdays extends for only one block. But on weekends this market puts on a new face and mushrooms out for a half a mile along Camacho, which becomes Liberator Simón Bolívar. It also assumes a new name: **Fería Franca.**

Early Saturday morning, hundreds—it seems like thousands—of Indian women pour from their hillside homes with vegetables and fruit bundled in sacks that they carry on their strong backs. Others stream in from the small farms on the plains surrounding La Paz. More often than not an infant is tucked into a second sack, also carried on the back.

You'll be fascinated when you see an Indian mother maneuver her blankets and, with one or two skillful flips, swing her infant and goods from her back onto the ground or vice versa. The women wear their standard cement-hard bowler hats and they are multiskirted.

As you thread your way through the maze of stalls, you will be accosted by the stall operators who will insist that they have the freshest fruits at the lowest prices. Although most are actually speaking in their native Aymara tongue (not Spanish), you are well aware of what they are saying.

The **Mercado de las Brujas** (Witches Market), on Calle Linares, uphill from Calle Santa Cruz, is probably the most interesting market in town. For sale are herbs, spirits, elixirs of love, and other items used by witch doctors in special circumstances. Do you have a problem that seems unsolvable to you? Here's the place to come. They might prescribe crushed lizard cream to cure an aching back. There's a figurine of an embracing couple that will assure a spouse in no time; or if that doesn't work, there's an amulet to wear that's infallible. If you're building a new house, a llama fetus should be mixed into the foundation. If you want a child, a must is a fertility stone (a carving of a mother and child).

There are vendor Indians sitting against the wall. Occasionally a witch doctor will appear to purchase items for the Saumerio ceremony he will perform to put the spirits to work for ailing clients.

Continuing beyond the Witches Market you come to **Galería Artesanal las Brujas,** a gallery of shops selling sweaters, ponchos, carpets, and the like. You are now near Sagarnaga. Fine shops in the gallery include Inca Wasi, Winay Inti, and Kory Inti.

Near the San Francisco Church, up the hill on Calle Figueroa, is an open-air market, the **Mercado Artesanal.** There are lines of booths, each owned by a different family, selling all sorts of items—jewelry, silver, handcrafts, dolls, sweaters. Bargaining is a must. Items like hats, food, and artesanal items are available. Health buffs should try quinua, a local cereal grain that only grows on in the Altiplano. It's used in soup and cereals.

Mercado Lanza, also on Figueroa (you can enter from Montes), is another street full of vendors. It's sort of a black market: whisky, cosmetics, perfumes, gloves, shoes—cheap. Try api, a drink made from corn for breakfast. Rows and rows of beautiful flowers are for sale, and there are shoeshine boys galore, plus fruits, breads, chicken, and meat too. It's on a narrow winding street. If you're hungry, try the **Mercado Popular Restaurant.** Here api is 15¢ (purple), coffee is 15¢, and you can also get pastry, tea, or cocoa. Lunch is $1 and typically includes steak with rice and salad. You sit on benches around tables. Even if you decide not to eat here, head upstairs to take a look at a most unusual restaurant, Indian style.

Calle Buenos Aires

High in the Indian quarter is the most frenzied street you will come across in South America. And this is Calle Buenos Aires, which you can reach by cab for just $1. A cacophony of traffic noise, howling women vendors, and yelping children and dogs greets you, along with odors so exotic it will take some time and effort to forget them.

Stroll through it and see the Indians furiously bartering and trading their goods.

Traffic moves through the streets at a snail's pace. Open trucks crammed with Indians crawl by. Wares are arrayed on rugs, blankets, straw mats, or right on the cobblestones, and you'll have to weave your way through the crowds. It is interesting that there are no scales in the market. You buy by the heaping basketful and the baskets come in several sizes. Your purchase is slapped into a newspaper or brown paper if you're lucky. Most Paceños come prepared with their own large straw baskets. Don't miss this street.

Marriage, Indian Style

Every Sunday, thousands of Indians parade from their homes down into the city to the **Church of San Francisco,** Plaza San Francisco, for mass. It is a solemn time.

But occasionally a day earlier—on Saturday—the church is quite festive, since that is the traditional day of baptism or marriage. Then the parades gaily weave their way from inside the church outside and back up to the hills. These wedding processions, called "The March of the Virgin," which follow every marriage in the Church of San Francisco, are a must for you to see.

For a good view, be at the church about 11 a.m. But wait outside near the gate. You will know a ceremony is going on because on the gate will be a wool blanket bedecked with such symbols as a fish (for fertility), a doll (for a baby), a figurine of the red-nosed Indian god of good luck, Ekeko, and a multitude of miniature household goods. The latter symbolize the hope for a happy household. If you want to see the ceremony itself, better get there before 10 a.m. The church itself is usually quite crowded and you may have trouble getting in, so choose a good vantage-point.

Shortly after 11 a.m. the procession will start leaving the church. First out will be the bride and groom. She will be wearing several multicolored skirts (the more skirts, the wealthier the family), a white shawl, and the inevitable brown bowler hat. He will be in a business suit and carrying a banner.

The respective families follow next, and friends and neighbors after that. Bringing up the rear is a blaring ten-piece band. The procession then marches a mile or more up the hill to the bride's home amid a storm of confetti. Many of the onlookers march along and follow the procession on the long trek. Go along if you can manage the pace. A week-long celebration precedes the wedding.

Indian Shops

Want to buy an Indian relic or curio? Head to **Calle Sagarnaga,** a narrow winding cobblestone street lined with Indian shops, which begin at the Church of San Francisco and continue uphill from there. These shops cater to the needs of the Indians in the city. Here they can buy their skirts and shawls and hats.

Two blocks up Sagarnaga from the church is a primary school, at no. 228, on the right side of the street. Enter the courtyard and you'll be permitted to look into the classrooms and see the students in their white jackets at work. The rooms are dark and the furniture old, but the teachers have decorated them attractively and everyone is hard at work. This is an interesting sidelight, especially for teachers.

You should head back down the hill at this point, because the street becomes quite steep beyond here.

MONTICULO PARK: A beautiful park with an exciting view of the city and Illimani Mountain is Monticulo Park, in the residential district of Sopocachi, which is a mile downhill from center city. Take a cab ($1) and bring your camera. Your taxi ride here will introduce you to some of the better residential sections of the city. The contrast between these modern dwellings and lovely streets and the Indian quarters is astonishing. The park itself is small but is scenically set with the city below it and the magnificent mountains rising in the distance. Established in 1776.

MONOLITHS—INDOORS AND OUT: If you haven't the time to visit Tiahuanaco near Lake Titicaca, you will greatly enjoy a visit to the **Open-Air Museum** in front of Miraflores Stadium. Many pre-Inca statues and heads, some weighing 100 tons or more, have been brought to La Paz from the Aymaran ruins near the great lake. These are surprisingly well preserved and you'll be impressed by the artistry of "primitive" Indians who lived 1,000 years ago. Most interesting are the huge monoliths that guarded the entrance to the Temple of the Sun.

You can easily walk to this square. From Plaza Murillo, follow Comercio, which later becomes Illimani, for about ten blocks, all downhill. Take a cab back.

There is also an excellent **National Museum,** with many artifacts from Tiahuanaco, including pottery and textiles. It's located two blocks east of the Prado on Avenida Tihuanac.

A must for culture buffs is the **Museo de Oro,** located on Calle Jaen, a typical colonial street, within walking distance of the San Francisco Church. It's just opened recently and features beautifully displayed jewelry from the Tiawanacu culture as well as some pottery.

MUSEO NACIONAL DE ETNOGRAFÍA Y FOLKLORE: This museum, at Calle Ingavi 916, near the Plaza Murillo, is dedicated to portraying 15th- and 16th-century jungle life in the Altiplano. On display are photos, headdresses, tools, weapons, pottery, musical instruments, etc. There are ritual tables used by the witch doctors—not to be missed.

VALLEY OF THE MOON: To view incredible natural clay formations caused by erosion, which form row after row of praying white figures across a red mountain panorama, head for the Valley of the Moon, three miles by the no. 11 bus and 20 minutes by cab from San Francisco Church. The trip here is half the fun. You see La Paz nestled in the mountains and Chacaltaya's snow-covered peaks as a backdrop.

When you arrive in the Valley of the Moon it's like being amid millions of sand castles with an incredibly gorgeous red mountain backdrop called "Devil's Tooth" (Muela del Diablo). The world's highest golf course is nearby, as is a lovely park about one block beyond the valley. The winding road leading to the valley is a bit scary, but the drivers are all expert in its navigation.

ONLY ON SUNDAY: A lovely way to spend a Sunday is at **Cerro Laicoata,** a park on the side of a small mountain between the Prado and Miraflores. On Sunday local Indians in typical attire meet to socialize (look for husbands and wives). You can picnic here with great views of the city below and observe another society in action. There are six banks of steps to the top and places to have yourself photographed. There are swings and a playground for children. Naturally, the view is the same Monday through Saturday, but if you do go, try to make it on Sunday.

SKIING: About an hour drive from La Paz, you arrive at a ski resort in the middle of the Andes called **Chacaltaya,** at a height of 17,000 feet—1½ miles higher than any U.S. peak and half a mile above the highest European peak. The resort offers skiing on weekends from August to March, and there are cabins that serve snacks, sandwiches, and beverages. Even just the views of La Paz are fantastic. Many tourist agencies will take you, or a cab will take you and wait ($25). You can rent skis from **Club Andino** in Chacaltaya for about $10—a great bargain. *Warning:* Skiing is only for advanced skiers. Don't be a hero—just watch.

CASA DE LA CULTURA: This government-sponsored arts center, located a few steps from the Church of San Francisco, Plaza San Francisco, features a theater, a library, and a room where painters may work.

The **Casa Costumbrista, Casa de Murillo,** and **Museo del Pacífico,** three interesting restored homes, are all located on a very old street, Calle Jaen, located near Plaza San Francisco.

TEATRO AL AIRE LIBRE:

TEATRO AL AIRE LIBRE: If typical music and dance folklore turns you on, then you should spend your Sunday afternoons (from 2 to 6 p.m.) at this open-air theater directly behind the university on Avenida del Ejercito. More than 1,000 devotees throng the open-air theater every Sunday to see a continuous succession of bands, dance groups, and singers, all dressed in colorful Bolivian folk costumes. The aficionados, many Indian, sit on stone bleachers, and when the seats are all gone, hundreds more stand in back. The involvement of the audience is contagious and you'll be applauding along. Cash prizes are awarded to the best groups, which perform in teams of 20 to 30 dancers and musicians. The music blasts out via tubas, trumpets, drums, cymbals, and the human voice. Our favorite dance is the cueca, which you will recognize by the handkerchiefs held at shoulder level. Admission is 80¢.

FUTBOL IN LA PAZ: Here, as it is throughout South America, futbol is the major sport craze. Every weekend at 2 p.m., at **Olympico Stadium** in Miraflores, there is a big game, and for good seats you'll need to reserve well in advance. Reserved seats (tribuna) are $3.50. A middle category called "preferencia" runs $2. General admission is about $1.50. Seating capacity at the Olympico is 50,000.

As we mentioned before, visiting teams have a hard time adjusting to the low-oxygen atmosphere and generally lose. Bet the home team.

To reach the stadium, walk via Avendia Illimani from the Plaza Murillo or take any yellow bus. A taxi will cost you about 50¢.

A new stadium has been built in Tembladerani by the Club Bolivia, an old and popular sporting organization. The club didn't stint on its home grounds: the new **Stadium Club Bolivia** seats 20,000 and is equipped with lights for night games. You can catch the "M" or "B" micros to get there, and you'll pay on a sliding scale: $1.50 for local games, $2 for national, and $3 for international.

READERS' SIGHTSEEING TIPS: "For anyone visiting South America, this is where life is really very different—native ladies in bowler hats, thriving markets, and strange goods for sale, such as llama fetuses. For those wanting to see the ruins, a couple of points. Even if there are no tickets for sale, check with the bus driver just near the station. Told there were no buses till 11, we got one at 8:15. Be prepared for a long, bumpy, 35-mile ride. On the way back, get a bus to 'La Paz Altura,' see the city view, then take another bus down to the city" (Rod and Kay Sims, Newport, Australia).

4. EXCURSIONS FROM LA PAZ

TIAHUANACO: The center of the impressive pre-Inca Aymara civilization—which flourished between A.D. 600 and A.D. 900—is in Tiahuanaco, not far from Lake Titicaca. This civilization, the ruins of which were found by the Incas about A.D. 1200, is believed to be the oldest in the Western Hemisphere. See the remains of huge aqueducts, temples, sun gates.

Located on the Bolivian Altiplano at 13,000 feet, this find ranks among the world's great archeological sites. Little is known of the people who built the impressive monuments and monoliths, which were rebuilt on several occasions following destructions. But the remains bear witness to an advanced civilization.

The least expensive way to reach Tiahuanaco is by bus, a two-hour journey that will cost you all of $3 each way. Morning buses leave on the hour at 6, 7, 8, and 9 a.m. from in front of the Estación Central (Central Station) near the Plaza Kennedy. Afternoon buses depart from the intersection of Avenida Buenos Aires and Tumulsa at noon and 1, 2, 3, and 4 p.m. Most buses continue on past the ruins to the town of **Guaqui** on Lake Titicaca. Return buses depart every hour. Expect to share your bus with Indian families returning to their homes for a visit.

Balsa Tours goes to Tiahuanaco by bus at 8 a.m. every morning. The round-trip price per person is $20. Reservations for these guided tours must be made in advance.

Private cars, which carry up to four passengers, can be hired with a bilingual guide and chauffeur for $35 each if two people are going. If the car is filled (four people) then the rates descend to $21.50 per person. These can be obtained from **Crillon Tours,** near the Eastern Airlines Office and the La Paz Hotel.

COPACABANA: Copacabana, the famous Indian shrine on Lake Titicaca, is a must excursion if you have the time. In fact, if you're heading to Cuzco from La Paz, you can conveniently detour. **Crillon Tours** has an unusual package arrangement that you might investigate. The first leg is a motorcoach trip from La Paz to **Huatajata,** a village on the southern tip of Lake Titicaca. From there you pick up a 22-seat hydrofoil boat which deposits you at Copacabana after a stop at the sacred **Sun Island,** legendary home of the first Inca, Manco Kapac, who is said to have been born from the waters of Lake Titicaca 1,000 years ago. You continue by hydrofoil to Juli on the Peruvian side of the border and from there by car to Puno. After an overnight stop in Puno, you pick up the regular train by Cuzco. The total cost, including hotel, train, taxes, and insurance, is $144 per person on a double-room basis. If you prefer, you can do the La Paz–Copacabana portion as a round trip for $90. **Exprinter** offers comparable tours.

An alternative is to take a bus to Guaqui (see above) and then pick up another bus to Copacabana. But schedules are erratic from Guaqui, so check at the bus station in La Paz first.

According to legend the Inca Empire began on these islands when a golden rod was brought to earth by Manco Kapac and Mama Ocllo and buried there. Supporting this legend are the remains of a large temple, an Inca fortress, and the Inca Water Spring, a course of eternal life.

An Aymara name known throughout the world, Copacabana is an important religious shrine some 30 miles past the straits of Tiquina. It attracts many pilgrims, who make the trip, often from great distances, on foot to visit the famous cathedral and "Virgen Morena." The town is located on gorgeous Titicaca Bay which, combined with exciting local color, provides a lovely panorama.

A TRIP TO HUATAJATA: If you don't plan to go all the way to Copacabana, we recommend a one-day trip to Huatajata and nearby Suriqui Island. This trip enables you to view Lake Titicaca and the Indian life of the Altiplano. On the way you pass Huayma Potosí and Condoriri Mountains, and a checkpoint leading to the El Alto section. Here is an area near the airport of La Paz that is flat and where many Indians own private land. The homes are rustic and rudimentary and you see people working, building the reed boats (*totora*) that sail Lake Titicaca.

You may want to see the **Hotel Titikaka,** a 22-room hotel with a basic but excellent restaurant where we suggest you stop for lunch. At Huatajata, a small town on the lake, you can glimpse and get a feeling for life on the lake. Tours to **Suriqui Island** leave from Huayma on cabin cruisers operated by Crillon Tours, or you can rent a private boat and a sailor to take you there. On Suriqui Island you will see Indians building reed boats by the same methods employed centuries ago. There is a reproduction of Thor Heyerdahl's *Ra II.*

THE JUNGLE BELOW: One of the greatest paradoxes of cool La Paz is that within three hours, by car, you can be sweltering in the Bolivian jungles (*yungas*). They're found 60 miles below the capital, via steep winding roads.

In the north jungle zone, 80 miles from La Paz, is a small town called **Chulumani.** A trip to this jungle village is a not-to-be-missed experience. You will be overwhelmed at the beauty and green lushness of the jungle flora, coming as it does just a short time after a ride through high mountain ranges.

For the first leg of the trip you'll be on a circular road ascending 16,500 feet. You will be surrounded by the snow-capped Cordillera Mountains, and have a marvelous view of the majestic peaks. There is a chill in the air at this altitude which will change as you descend the mountain—coming upon verdant plantations ripe with bananas and coffee beans and thick forest growth—to become a balmy 75° when you reach Chulumani at a level of 2,700 feet above sea level.

Stop overnight or plan to spend a weekend at the **Motel San Bartolomé,** a pretty motel which offers all the comforts of home in the midst of the tropics. The Motel San Bartolomé's small native huts come equipped with modern conveniences, including a telephone. You can enjoy the silence of a tropical night in cozy privacy in your own little hut, or you can play billiards and Ping-Pong in the recreation hall. There is an international bar on the premises, an excellent restaurant, and for daytime activities, a mini-golf course and a swimming pool. Inquire about the special bus that leaves on Friday at 9 a.m., returning to La Paz on Sunday afternoon. Price of a bungalow for two is $18 a day; for six, $40 a day. The restaurant offers a fixed-price menu for $3; $4.50 to $8 à la carte. Reservations can be made by calling AFIABOL (tel. 3-58-386).

Crillon offers a two-day tour to Chulumani by private car for $95 per person for two, including lodging and meals.

Or you can take a tour of the south jungle to the town of **Coroico**—at the very heart of the southern jungle. Make your arrangements through any tour agency, and choose between a day trip (about $90 for two for a guided tour in a private car) or an overnight trip, which will mean a stay at the government-owned **Hotel Perfectural** for $15 per person per day, including meals. If you'd like to make the trip in a private taxi, it will cost $28.50 for each person.

READER'S TOURING SUGGESTION: "**La Flota bus line** runs buses twice daily over the mountains between **Cochabamba** and La Paz for $6. The seven-hour trip lets you see the backcountry stripped of any glamour. In the main plaza at Cochabamba, the only restaurant serves a delicious chicken dinner for less than a dollar" (Robert Leslie, Toronto, Canada). [*Authors' Note:* **Lloyd's Airline** has morning flights at 8 a.m. to Cochabamba for $40.]

5. LA PAZ AFTER DARK

Most travel guides emphasize that La Paz is not much of a night town, and that because of the altitude and chilly evenings, an early-to-bed routine is best. Not true. This city happens to have some of the darkest—and loudest—nightclubs in Latin America. More than this, La Paz is home to **Peña Folklorica,** a far-out showbiz phenomenon that blends music, dance, audience involvement, and history in one frenetic blast. By all means go to bed early—but only for an hour or two, so that you'll be refreshed for the late-evening action ahead.

Tip: The effect of alcohol can be potent here, because of the altitude. Reduce your intake by 50%.

PEÑA FOLKLORICA: The talk of La Paz night people these evenings is a mixed-media entertainment that has burst onto the midnight scene, now a weekend must for the with-it locals. Labeled Peña Folklorica (literally "place of folklore"), this entertainment brings together Indian dancers, singers, and musicians, who perform around and among spectators sprawled on floors and benches in matchbox-size nightclubs. The audience usually joins in the tribal dancing and singing, which continues at an ear-splitting pitch until the 20 or so performers and the patrons are virtually limp. The material, representing authentic Indian folklore, is performed with such intensity that every visitor, South and North American alike, is caught up in the Folklorica fever. The performers, garbed in native dress, weave through the audience to the accompaniment of charangos (guitars made of armadillo skins). Spectators clap or sing in unison, pausing occasionally to reach out to touch a dancer skipping past. Not to be missed. Singles admitted.

Specific Clubs

There are several Peña Folklorica clubs in La Paz; almost all are in dilapidated quarters—usually in a converted apartment or basement cellar in the city's poorer sections—and most adhere to a standard $1 admission policy, with the understanding that you will buy a flask of Bolivian wine (quite good) or a soft drink for another $1.50. Nothing else is served except popcorn, which is free. Fun and games start at 10 p.m. and end at about 5 a.m.—Friday and Saturday evenings only. Last time we were in La Paz, there was talk of extending the days of operation, so check with your hotel clerk.

Easily one of the best—and largest—is the **Club Kori-Thika,** Juan de la Riva 1435, near Calle Loayza, which is invariably packed with 150 suddenly intimate guests who mind neither the decibels nor the crush. The hip young crowd of La Paz makes this its stamping ground—and stamping is just what it's all about. The stone floor, wood tables and benches, and bamboo-covered walls reverberate to the folk beat. We're partial to the devil dance, which is just what you'd imagine, with Lucifer-like costumes that would be smashing at your next spook party. A touching change of pace is the cueca, the handkerchief dance that you see not only in Bolivia but in Peru and Paraguay as well. One performer eerily creates the voice of Yma Sumac via manipulation of an ordinary crosscut saw.

The Plaza Hotel, one of La Paz's finest hotels, has its own peña on the top floor, the very elegant **Peña 5 Estrellas.** Here you can enjoy some of the best local music and dance performances La Paz has to offer. Drinks are not expensive, and there's ample space for dancing.

The older **Club Naira,** Calle Sagarnaga, near the San Francisco Church, has been slipping in recent years, but it still has its coterie of followers. If you can't get into the Kori-Thika, come on over here. Again, the quarters are in a converted cellar.

Also on Calle Sagarnaga is the **Peña Nueva Viara,** open Thursday through Sunday evenings only. Admission, which includes popcorn and one drink, is $5. Seats must be reserved. There is a small, cozy restaurant located in the same building.

Another club worth checking is the **Palacio del Folklore,** located on Santa Cruz.

THE BOÎTES: Pub-crawlers in La Paz must come alive in the dark. Why else would they jam into clubs where the brightest illumination comes from their eyeballs? The locals love the intimacy of darkness—but watch yourself when strolling from table to dance floor.

Note: Most clubs admit couples only, and the music starts late—usually after 10 p.m. Minimum drinking age is 20.

The best place in La Paz for dancing is **Baccara,** an action-packed disco at Avenida 20 Octubre 1824 (tel. 3-50-500). The owner takes pride in the club's continental décor, and the fact that the club has 120 albums which spin nonstop from 8:30 p.m. to 4 a.m. seven days a week. Disco dancing, rock, and jazz is frenzied. To cool down, try the house drinks—"El David" or "La Sixtina"—at $2.50.

Young well-heeled couples currently are gravitating toward the **Club Jankanou,** Calle México 1783 (tel. 3-26-229), a block off the Prado. Drinks are $2.50 and there is a two-drink minimum. Shows are at 1 a.m. on Wednesday and Sunday. Music is Brazilian and Latin. Capacity is only 60, so the ambience is intimate considering the absence of light. Open from 7 p.m. to 5 a.m.

A popular club in this same area is the exclusive **Discothèque Candilejas,** Capitan Castrillo 458. The dance floor, which can accommodate 200 people, is always packed and the tempo is lively. Drinks include wine, champagne, vodka combinations, pisco sours, and an exotic specialty of the house served in pineapple shell and garnished with sparkler. Prices for drinks range from $2.50 to $3.50. Open from 8 p.m. to 3 a.m. every evening except Monday.

On Avenida 20 de Octubre is another jumping nightspot—the **Señorial Discothèque,** where you can dance to the music of the Bee Gees or other popular American groups until 3 in the morning every night of the week. Single women are not allowed, unfortunately; and to gain admission through their very private door, a reservation should be made at the club door during the evening. The Señorial Discothèque features a large dance floor, light show, and comfortable bar. A second dance floor can be found upstairs, and there is additional seating in the balcony. There is no admission fee or minimum. Drinks are $3.50.

One of our old favorites, the Divina Comedia, has changed owners and is now called **La Esquina del Jazz,** 20 de Octubre 1820, (tel. 3-21-938). However, the décor is still the same as before with antique enameled copper tables being one of the highlights. Occasional shows and weekend jazz are the offerings here. It's a great place to have a drink or dine while enjoying live piano music or a Barbra Streisand tape.

Pacha, at Azpazu 100 (tel. 3-69-107), open from 10 p.m. to 5 a.m., is an excellent private club. Video cassettes on screen near the dance floor and dark flashing lights add to the décor. There are private couches along the side.

Alhambra Disco, Loayza 115, is open until 6 a.m. Head downstairs. The décor is of the Alhambra, with old Spanish-Moorish arches and wrought-iron lanterns. It's like being inside the Alhambra.

A fine bar is **Matheus Piano Bar,** at Calle F. Guachalla, corner of Rinconcito Peruano. Dark wood adds to the British pub look. The bar has hanging glasses and a booth effect is created by leather seats around tables. The jazz is hot.

An attractive bilevel disco is **Baccara,** at 20 de Octubre 1822 (tel. 3-24-039), with its black-and-white dance floor, wool-lined walls, and attractive leather bar. It's next to La Esquina del Jazz and lots of fun.

Ganimedes, a music club bar at Presbitero Medina 2526 (tel. 3-54-465), is the latest addition to the club scene. The décor and music, mostly jazz and Brazilian, are both excellent. They also feature a video, and live music on Thursday and Friday. Live groups are often brought exclusively to Ganimedes from Brazil.

Two discothèques offering great views are **Penthouse,** in the Plaza Hotel, and the **Salon Illimani,** on the 15th floor of the La Paz Hotel. The Illimani is open on Friday and Saturday only. To reach the Penthouse, press the PH button in the elevator. Here is a good spot to try bock, a strong local beer.

On weekends the Hotel Gloria's dining room becomes the lively **Club**

Naranja (tel. 3-55-080), where a folklorica show gets under way at 10:30 p.m. and continues well past midnight. When we were there the place was packed and the crowd enthusiastically clapping and cheering along with the performers. A lovely dark-haired señorita was the favorite of the evening, winning over the audience with her romantic Brazilian love songs. As the club is quite popular, reservations must be made in advance.

FOR MEN ONLY: A strip joint with a bar filled with attractive eager ladies is **La Miel**, at Avenida 20 de Octubre 1820 (tel. 3-40-184). Head upstairs to the club with red couches, red hassocks, and a red motif. The stage features rotating strippers who then join their co-workers at the bar.

TEATRO MUNICIPAL: Located at Plaza Wenceslao Monroy, not far from the Plaza Murillo, is this attractive white building constructed in the 1850s. It is the home of the ballet company and symphony orchestra of La Paz. Prices for most performances range from 80¢ to $3.50. Tickets are, of course, higher for special events, or for internationally known performers or companies. While seats for ordinary performances are not hard to get, they should be bought in advance at the box office.

FESTIVAL: If you are going to be in La Paz during the month of June, you'll be in for a rare treat: the traditional **Festival of Señor del Gran Poder.** Thousands of Bolivians flock to La Paz for this, one of the most important of the country's celebrations. The festivities begin with colorful pageantry. The statue of the saint, arrayed with flowers and religious adornments, is carried through the streets, followed by a procession of dignitaries from all over the country, including the president of the republic and the mayor of La Paz. A Folklore Queen reigns over the day's activities, which include performances by 50 folk-singing groups and dancers galore—some 9,000 participants in all!—who dance and sing from sun-up to sundown in the streets of La Paz. The performers are drawn from different parts of the city and nearby countryside, and their dances reflect the cultural heritage of their region. If you are going to be in La Paz during this month, it's well worth checking on the date of the festival (the exact date is not fixed) and making arrangements to catch this colorful fête.

6. SHOPPING

ARTESANÍAS TITICACA: La Paz has a unique shopping institution and an appropriately special woman to operate it. Artesanías Titicaca Ltd. at first blush resembles a típico shop, although it's located in what was once a private home, at Avenida Sanchez Lima 2320, corner of Rosendo Gutierrez. It is within walking distance of the La Paz and Crillon hotels, only three blocks away.

What distinguishes this showroom for Bolivian alpaca fur rugs, hand-knitted alpaca sweaters and other apparel, crafts, and high-fashion fur coats is that it sells at wholesale prices. But let Mrs. Daisy de Wende, who founded the shop in 1962, explain it: "Our objective is to raise the Bolivian standard of living by making as many families as possible self-sufficient. We organize small family enterprises and family cooperatives in the rural areas of the country around the production of all kinds of crafts that we ourselves design. Over 5,000 families have so far been benefited by our dedicated program, and many artisans have become independent exporters and entrepreneurs. Most of all, we make our people proud of their work ability, capacity, and identity. We are permanently in search of export markets so we can help move the local products. Bolivia's main markets for alpaca knitwear are in the United States and Europe. By wholesaling locally, we try to reach more buyers. By exporting and through the fine quality of our goods, we hope to improve Bolivia's image."

Mrs. de Wende, educated in design at both the University of Michigan and Western Michigan University, not only administers the self-help program that she set up, but she also creates the clothing and rug designs, supervises quality control, and acts as a goodwill ambassador for Bolivia to fashion and trade shows in North America and Europe. Oh, yes, Daisy also helps furnish capital for the participating families so that they can purchase sewing machines, tools, raw materials, and dyes. Understandably, the program has the blessing of the government.

What does all this mean for the tourist seeking shopping bargains? Just this: You can pick up first-class gifts at about 25% of the price asked in the U.S. and far less than in Europe.

By the way, the de Wendes's son, Kenny, is the proprietor of another fine artesan shop, **Alpaca Titicaca Shop,** at Sagarnaga 274, offering a wide selection of high-quality items—alpaca knits in traditional or contemporary designs, a truly unique collection of authentic Bolivian fashions (prices range from $15 to $40), and also weavings, local art, ceramics, jewelry. There is a resident medicine man (*callawaya*) who, for a small fee, will both cure you of your ills and tell your future. Locals swear by it—let us hear from you about your experiences. Kenny de Wende, by the way, is a graduate of a U.S. university, speaks fluent English, and is a great source of information. His wife, Margo, is a lovely lady who hails from Canada.

Best Buys at Artesanías Titicaca

The two-level showroom and shop, which has opened a special section to exhibit and sell textiles from highland Bolivia, offers high-quality alpaca fur rugs and bedspreads starting at $50; sheepskin area rugs starting at $20; a beautiful line of typical, modern, and fashionable alpaca sweaters from $20 to $35; vests at $15, gloves at $4, caps, scarves, etc., all in an assortment of natural pure alpaca; fur sleepers from $8 to $20; and hand-knitted alpaca sweaters, vests, and ponchos for children, from $7 to $14.

Silver jewelry is much in demand—earrings, medallions, and bracelets begin at $6. Pewter ornaments start at $8. The hand-woven wall hangings ($13) and pillow coverings ($5) with appliqué designs make excellent gifts.

On a lower scale, we're partial to the intricately etched wood flutes called pinkillos ($1 and up), and a larger version known as a tarka. Four flutes joined together, called a zampona, is an unusual gift item too. Ceramics, pottery, ashtrays, and such start at $3; straw toys, at $1.

For children there are delicate llamas, knitted dolls, and a seven-inch-tall god of good luck called Ekeko, made of stucco and dressed in típico apparel ($5 and up).

Moving up in price once more, there is a marvelous native instrument called the charango, a stringed instrument resembling a mandolin but covered with tough armadillo skin ($75, and worth it). Be sure to check out the boutique for the couture collection. Last time we were there a white alpaca jacket transfixed us. The price: $350. In addition, there's a full line of fashions in alpaca, including shirts for $18; vests, $15 to $80. A colorful collection of dresses, tunics, and long skirts in cotton will also catch your eye. Other high-fashion coats and evening gowns, all designed by Mrs. de Wende and all with Bolivian themes, start at $100.

Shop hours are 9:30 a.m. to noon and 2 to 6:30 p.m. weekdays, 9 a.m. to 1 p.m. on Saturday. However, Mrs. de Wende will open on Sunday by appointment. Phone her at the showroom (tel. 3-24-811) or at home (tel. 7-92-426).

She is eager to spread her gospel that Bolivian goods are among the world's best values. Ask for a catalog that you can show your friends. Mail orders are accepted—but this can get expensive. Minimum air freight for 22 pounds is $55.

READER'S SHOPPING SELECTION: "When we visited **Artesanías Titicaca** we were offered coffee and treated like guests. A tour group was visiting at the same time and they had booked a showing of an outstanding Bolivian Cultural Show in the fourth-floor theater. We asked if we could join them and they allowed us to. For $5 per person we saw an hour show of dances from all parts of Bolivia, as well as Bolivian fashions. Very entertaining. Soft drinks were served" (Mrs. Helen Adamson, Chicago, Ill.).

OTHER FINE SHOPS: For magnificent monoliths, head for **King's,** in the Sucre Palace Hotel. We purchased a 24-inch-high, seven-pound replica of the monolith that guarded the temple in Tiahuanaco for $40. The crown is removable and we've converted it to a lamp that is the showpiece of our apartment. King's has good prices on authentic silver and pewter items. They also sell silver figurines of the Inca good-luck god, Ekeko, who is an Indian Santa Claus bringing prosperity and good fortune wherever he is: tiny pots and pans hang from his back. These sell for about $3 and go up according to size.

For good buys in gold and silver jewelry, don't skip a visit to the **Joyería Schohaus,** Colón 260 (tel. 2-62-410). Here you will find 18-karat gold nuggets set in earrings, pendants, bracelets, and rings at prices ranging from $150 to $2,500, depending on weight and size. According to Mrs. Schohaus, who is extremely knowledgeable and helpful, the natural shape of the nugget is untouched or altered in any way. A nugget weighing 14 grams costs $250; 28 grams, $500; 18-karat gold rings run $700 to $800. An assortment of silver rings is available at $10, $15, and $18.

The Joyería Schohaus also has an excellent selection of pewter housewares: goblets, flower pots, picture frames, tea and coffee sets.

Mrs. Schohaus fashions rings and pendants with Brazilian stones—these are exclusive designs. And if that's not enough, the Joyería Schohaus has a factory address for quantity purchases: Jacinto Benavente 2230 (tel. 3-24-666).

There are numerous small **tourist shops** in La Paz, but one that we liked is at Loayza 263. Here you will find a good selection of gold and silver bracelets and native woodcarvings that are moderately priced. Also check out the shops at Casilla 2885, and in the La Paz Hotel.

Remember Calle Sagarnaga in the Indian quarter if you want a bowler hat or pollera souvenir, or just if you feel like browsing. Stop in at **Casa de Flora** here for Indian crafts and other handmade gifts. Many shops for handcrafts have opened all along the street. Almost every doorstep is now a handcraft store, and many people sell from the sidewalks.

There is a **Galería de las Brujas** (close to Calle Linares) established in an old house where many handcraft shops have opened, offering a variety of typical products such as alpaca knitwear, fur rugs, silver jewelry, and many other local products.

Also on Sagarnaga are some fine shops and an attractive patio of shops. The **Castillo de Cuero,** at Sagarnaga 270, has fine items in leather at rock-bottom prices. Across the street is **Art Bol,** where we recommend the rugs, carpets, and handcrafts. Nearby is the **Galería Artesanal Chuguiago,** a bilevel gallery off a patio with fountains. **Chaskanawi** is a fine handcrafts shop. Other shops offer high-quality furs and ski clothing.

Two fine shops are located in the Plaza Hotel. **Crisan** has gorgeous handcrafts, pewter, and ceramics, as well as leather and carpet items. Fine alpaca and textiles are for sale at **Milma.** Both shops are elegant and will ship your purchases home upon request.

Another fine shop featuring native handcrafts is **Huayna,** on Calle Colón (tel. 3-22-144). Check it out.

7. SOME FINAL MISCELLANY AND DEPARTURE INFORMATION

MISCELLANY: We couldn't leave La Paz without offering you some useful (or otherwise) tidbits. First—

Tours: A large tour service is **Crillon Tours,** Avenida Camacho 1223. Darius Morgan, the urbane English-speaking manager, plans in-city, jungle, and Lake Titicaca tours, complete with late-model car, driver, and English-speaking guide. A half-day city tour for two, with Moon Valley included, is $20, while a one-day jungle trip will cost a couple $150. Equally good is **Balsa Tours,** in the Sucre Palace Hotel, which charges $20 per person for a city tour. Consider, too, **Exprinter, Travelline,** and **Magri Tours.** Be sure to shop for the best prices.

Postage: An airmail letter to the U.S. costs the equivalent of 75¢. Purchase stamps at any major hotel or at the main post office, on Calle Ayacucho near the Plaza Murillo. Hours: 8 a.m. to 7 p.m. *Tip:* Upon request, and at twice the normal rate, the post office will immediately deliver outgoing mail to the airport to make a flight.

Private Driver: For about $5 an hour, you can hire a taxi and English-speaking driver. One reliable driver is **Gerhard Arnsdorff** (tel. 3-27-078), who also speaks German.

Telephones: Most pay phones are in stores or hotels. Give the owner or desk clerk about 5¢ and dial your number.

Men Only: At the best barbershops you can get an excellent haircut, shampoo, or shave for about $6. Other barbershops are less expensive.

Music: Free band concerts are held on the Prado in front of the Sucre Hotel and in Plaza Murillo at noon every Sunday.

Skiers Only: Good skiing in **Chacaltaya,** 29 miles from La Paz, where peaks reach heights of 17,318 feet. To rent equipment and arrange for bus tours, go to **Club Andino Boliviano,** Avenida México 1638. (Ski season: September to May.)

U.S. Consulate: This is located on Calle Potosí in the Tobias Building.

Cinema: The best movie houses in town are on the Prado and favor U.S. films. Admission is $1.50. Usually jammed on weekends.

No! No! No!: Avoid buses called "Interurbano Transportation." They are more like trucks and are jam-packed with people who stand in the rear part of the truck.

Drugs: Pharmacies are plentiful here and most are stocked with U.S.–made goods.

Airport Tax: You pay $8 when leaving the country.

Capital Fact: The technical capital of Bolivia is Sucre, but the de facto capital is La Paz. Most of the major firms have offices here, and this is for all practical purposes *the city* of Bolivia.

Moon Valley: Near La Paz is a farming zone called **Río Abajo,** where the Indians cultivate their land as they did 1,000 years ago. On the way there you will see odd formations of volcanic stone that resemble moon craters. Most tours include this area.

Language: The official language is Spanish, but the Indians speak their Aymara or Quechua, derivations of Inca and pre-Inca tongues.

Modern La Paz: Three posh residential districts are **Obrajes, Calacoto,** and **La Florida,** all located 2,000 feet below center city. Fashionable homes and exclusive clubs dominate these sections.

DEPARTURE INFORMATION: Two delightful choices now confront you

as you prepare to leave La Paz. You can either go to the Inca world in Cuzco, Peru, via train-boat-train or bus, or you can fly first to Lima, then to Cuzco. (Expect to pay an $8 exit tax at the airport.) Either way, an exciting glimpse into history will result.

Getting to Cuzco

The most interesting way to get to Cuzco is via the buses operated by **Transturan,** which offers service Monday, Wednesday, and Friday. Breakfast and lunch are included in the cost of approximately $45 (one way). Please note our discussion of this trip in the Cuzco chapter. However, you can cross to Peru via Lake Titicaca, a highly recommended trip, the only drawback being that it is only operated (at this writing) one day a week (Friday). See our discussion below concerning that trip.

Crossing to Peru by Train-Boat-Train

The most fascinating journey we've taken in South America is the 28-hour ride from La Paz to Cuzco via **Lake Titicaca.** At 12,500 feet, Titicaca is the highest navigable lake in the world and certainly among the most beautiful. On its blue waters live a tribe of Indians, the Uru, who rarely ever set foot on land. Along the shores, fishermen in their reed boats spend their days casting for trout.

The trip also gives you the opportunity to observe the unusual rural life of the Indians of Bolivia and Peru. The trains pass through farm country and between huge mountain ranges. They are local trains and make stops in small, isolated villages where the Indians come to sell their wares to the passengers. One-car trains leave La Paz once a week, on Friday at 2 p.m. from the Ferrocarril Guaquai (train station), Avenida Montes near Plaza de Antafagosta, arriving at the port of **Guaquai** on Lake Titicaca in five hours. The train connects with a steamer which takes you across the lake in an overnight trip that deposits you at the Peruvian port of Puno at 6 a.m. the next day. First-class passengers (we recommend this) get a comfortable stateroom and an excellent four-course dinner and breakfast. Second-class passengers, for one-third less, sleep in the hold area and purchase food in the commissary. An early rising is a must to see the activity on the lake. Dress warmly. (Women may wear slacks.)

At Puno the boat connects with a regular passenger train that gets you to Cuzco by 7 p.m. that evening. This part of the trip is most interesting, as you will see the Indians on their farms and villages. The important stops are **Juliaca,** where Indians board the train to sell candy and knitted goods, and **Ayaviri,** where women sell food promptly gobbled up by the Peruvian and Bolivian passengers. (We suggest you bring your own.) At **Pucara** you can get off the train to buy the black pottery pieces distinctive in this town. Cost: 50¢. At other stops you can buy alpaca goods and rugs. Meals are served on the train to first-class passengers for $4. Sandwiches can also be purchased, for 75¢.

Cost from La Paz to Cuzco, first class, is about $60, including both trains and ship. Try to get a reserved seat in the comfortable buffet car for an additional $3. There are other first-class cars, but the seats aren't reserved. Second class is extremely crowded and uncomfortable. Avoid it even though the price is low.

You can also take this trip from Cuzco to La Paz, if you prefer it that way. The trains leave Cuzco on Wednesday at 7 a.m. and arrive at Puno at 7 p.m. The steamer leaves at 8 p.m. and arrives at Guaquai at 6 a.m., with arrival in La Paz about noon.

To Cuzco by Air

You can also make the trip from La Paz to Cuzco by air. **Lloyd Aereo Boliviano,** the Bolivian carrier, makes this trip several times a week. Since flight schedules are irregular, check with them before making definite plans.

READERS' TRAVEL TIP: "This overland trip is good value and an excellent way to see the country. The Transturin bus leaves La Paz at 7:30 a.m. on Monday, Wednesday, and Friday. The fare to Puno, at 'parallel-market' rates, is about $20. The bus travels along Lake Titicaca, past reed boats, llamas, and panoramic views. And let's not forget the innumerable Customs and police checks. Lunch is provided at Copacabana and the bus then continues to Puno, arriving at 7 p.m. It is possible to continue overnight to Cuzco, but who wants to travel at night, slowly, over very bumpy roads? At Puno, the **Hotel Ferrocarril** provides double rooms, with heater, for $13 and will change traveler's checks. Across the road is the station and the train to Cuzco. Tickets were hard to come by and we had to settle for pullman class, about $16. It was well worth it, bargaining with vendors through train windows (alpaca slippers for $3) and watching the beautiful countryside. We arrived at Cuzco about 7 p.m. A great trip—highly recommended" (Rod and Kay Sims, Newport, Australia).

Going to Chile

An interesting way to make the trip between La Paz and Santiago is via the train from the Estación Central (Plaza Kennedy) to Arica, Chile. From there you can catch an L.A.N. Chile flight to Santiago.

A modern high-speed train called a "Coche Motor" leaves La Paz every Wednesday morning at 8:40 a.m. and drops you in Arica nine hours later. The fare is $35, first class only.

Slower, overnight trains leave on Monday and Friday morning from the station ($15 for first class, $10 for second class), arriving in Arica the next morning.

There is a direct flight to Santiago from La Paz every Sunday departing at 10:15 a.m. and arriving in Santiago about 2½ hours later. Lufthansa also flies to Santiago on Wednesday and Saturday.

By Train to Buenos Aires

The adventurous with mucho time to kill might like to train it to Buenos Aires from La Paz. The train is direct only to Tucuman, where you must change for another train to Rosario, and then on to Buenos Aires. The three-day journey over the Andes costs $92 to Tucuman (first class)—but there's no heat or hot water. Rugged trip.

CHAPTER VIII

LIMA, PERU

□ □ □

Peru and Lima are largely what they are today because of a 62-year-old conquistador who, four centuries ago, slaughtered thousands of Indians to conquer this territory for Spain.

Most of us continue to think of Peru only in its historical context, and are therefore quite surprised to discover that Lima is the most cosmopolitan of western South American cities. The thriving downtown area, dotted with skyscrapers, gives way in the south to well-planned suburbs that in some respects resemble Westchester communities north of New York City. Eight miles to the west is Lima's seaport city of **Callao** and the modern **Jorge Chavez International Airport.**

Still, to fully appreciate this metropolis, a knowledge of its historic founding is vitally important.

A CAPSULE HISTORY: Francisco Pizarro, now revered as a hero in Peru, landed there in 1532 with under 200 men. His goal: gold. He had heard that there was an advanced Indian civilization living in the mountains, led by their king (Inca) who had access to enormous gold and silver wealth.

The Inca Empire (the name Inca had been applied only to the ruler, but has since been used to refer to the entire population) extended from the mountains of Colombia south through Ecuador and Peru and parts of Bolivia, Chile, and even Argentina.

Five years earlier, as late as 1527, this vast territory had been united as one entity under the rule of the Inca, Huayna Capac. Upon his death he divided the empire between his two sons. Huascar ruled the southern kingdom from Cuzco, and his half-brother Atahualpa (the son of Huayna's favorite concubine) ruled the northern kingdom from Quitu (now Quito, Ecuador). Shortly thereafter a civil war erupted, with each brother determined to survive as the sole ruler of the united empire.

Fortunately for Pizarro, this war was in progress when he arrived in 1532. He and his men worked their way up the steep mountain toward Cajamarca in Peru. Atahualpa, given advance warning of Pizarro's arrival, was convinced that the Sun God had sent a White God to aid him in his struggle with his half-brother.

When Atahualpa and Pizarro met, the Inca was in awe of the white-skinned Spaniards and their horses, which were unknown in his world. When the king told his troops to lay down their arms, a massacre followed in which thousands of Indians were slaughtered and the king imprisoned. But he was promised his freedom if the Indians would fill one room with gold and two others with silver. After this was done, Pizarro ordered Atahualpa—believed to be the son of the Sun God by his followers—strangled to death.

Inasmuch as Huascar had already been killed in battle, the Indians were now leaderless, and for all practical purposes, defeated. Pizarro pushed on to Cuzco, sacked it, and then realized that if this territory were to become an important Spanish colony, a seaport was essential.

Thus Pizarro marched back to the sea and in 1535 founded Lima and its sister city, the port of Callao. He established Lima inland so that Callao could act as a buffer in case of foreign attack.

Pizarro named Lima the "City of Kings" and set about to create a true Spanish capital. He deliberately excluded all Inca influences, and therefore today, unlike Cuzco and Quito, there are no Inca temples or ruins in Lima. Instead the city's older quarter is rich in Spanish colonial architecture.

However, short excursions we'll recommend will take you to Indian ruins nearby. And, of course, the true magnificence of the Inca world still reveals itself in Cuzco and Machú Picchú, described in our next chapter.

LIMA TODAY: The six million residents of Lima (called Limeños) are divided between Indians and the predominant mixed Spanish-Indian group called mestizos. The mestizos and most of the Indians dress in North American–style clothing.

After several years of uncertainty, Lima is on the move again, and the action is all taking place in the suburbs. New hotels, restaurants, modern shopping centers, and homes are being constructed. Downtown, still the city's commercial center, is no longer the center of tourist activity. More than ever we urge you to stay in one of the nearby suburbs and come into the downtown area to sightsee and shop.

A MONETARY NOTE: Peru's currency has historically undergone dramatic change, as severe as in any Latin American nation. Since the first edition of this book, the sol soared from 15 to the dollar to over 15,000. Fluctuating exchange rates confuse the price situation here. Inevitably, prices fluctuate in line with any revaluation so that the dollar's purchasing power rarely shifts markedly. When the sol reached 5,000 per $1 U.S., the government introduced the **inti,** worth 1,000 soles.

Peru is currently suffering one of the most severe economic crises in all of South America. Inflation is running rampant, estimated at 25% in August 1988 alone. One day during our last visit, the U.S. dollar jumped from 330 to 460 intis in the morning, only to settle at around 420 by the end of the day. The economy is so unstable that prices change from one day to the next—always rising, never falling. Thus it is impossible to gauge how much the prices listed here will change, or if the changes in the exchange rate will cancel out price increases.

One final word of caution: In Lima you will undoubtably be bombarded by people trying to change money in the street. Don't! You'll do just as well at the many travel agencies and exchange offices scattered throughout the center of the city.

WARNING: Due to the economic situation in Peru, street crime is on the rise. It's a good idea to leave all valuables and jewelry in the hotel safe. If you must carry a bag, keep it in sight at all times as it's commonplace among thieves to slit camera bags, shoulderbags, and knapsacks when they are carried on someone's back. Be on the alert for pickpockets. Above all, exercise good judgment and caution, just as you would in any large city.

GEOGRAPHY: Peru, with a population of 18 million, has three zones: the west coastal region, where Lima and Arequipa are the main cities; the east coast, in the hot jungle, where Iquitos lies; and the central region, the Andes Mountains, with Cuzco the principal city.

A BRIEF ORIENTATION: Chances are you will arrive at the sleek new **Jorge Chavez Airport,** ten miles from downtown Lima. A cambio, stores, and an upstairs quick-service bar are available. From the moment you step past Immigration, you will be beset by hucksters representing center-city hotels. Check the proffered brochures and rate cards to determine exact hotel prices, which, as we've stressed, can change suddenly.

If you need help finding a place to stay, **Atlas Tours** has a booth right in the airport, not to mention some good connections with the hotels in Lima. They may be able to get you a hotel at a discount price.

If you plan to stay at one of our recommended center-city hotels rather than at one of our preferred suburban pensions, you have three choices of transportation downtown. A **taxi** ($10) is most convenient. Be sure to establish the fare in advance as drivers try to charge a higher price and will expect you to negotiate.

To save a few dollars, use the convenient **"Trans Hotel" jitneys,** which pull up right in front of the airport terminal and provide regular service to downtown hotels for $6. The day before leaving Lima, call "Trans Hotel" for door-to-door service from your hotel to the airport (tel. 46-9872 or 27-5697).

By far the cheapest way to reach your downtown hotel is via a **colectivo** (75¢ per person plus 20¢ for each bag). It will drop you near the centrally located Plaza San Martín. The colectivo, actually a four-door sedan, is preferable in that there are no stops. However, if you are luggage-heavy, you may have a wait since drivers give preference to people without bags. Each piece of luggage, in effect, is a "passenger," in that it may occupy a seat.

Note: Colectivos leave from Avenida Faucett, the main thoroughfare that runs in front of the airport itself. You must walk out of the terminal and cross the parking lot to Avenida Faucett. If in doubt, simply ask anyone, "Colectivo hasta Plaza San Martín, por favor?"

To reach our suburban pensions directly from the airport, take either a taxi ($11 to $13) or the "Trans Hotel" bus marked "Miraflores" ($6). The Miraflores bus will drop you at a hotel in any one of the suburban areas. The alternative is to take the colectivo to Plaza San Martín and then pick up a suburban colectivo (very involved!). Again, luggage could present a problem.

Center City

There are two important plazas in Lima: the above-mentioned **Plaza San Martín,** and the **Plaza de Armas.**

The Plaza de Armas, in the older quarter of the city, was where Pizarro founded Lima in 1535 and where he laid a cornerstone for the huge cathedral of Lima. The remains of Pizarro are preserved in a glass coffin in the cathedral.

Plaza San Martín, in the modern section, is located on the important main street, the **Colmena,** which cuts through the heart of the city and houses plush hotels and restaurants and many of the major airline offices and skyscrapers.

The two plazas are five blocks apart and are connected by a key shopping street, **Jirón de la Unión.** The word *jirón* describes a series of streets—in this case, a series of blocks on Union Street—and the use of that word is a result, again, of an action by Pizarro. Originally he decided that every individual block in Lima would have its own name, that of one of the conquistadores. But as the city grew, it became too complicated to remember the names of the many blocks. And so groups of streets were given a name prefaced by the "jirón," or series. Yet the original names were retained. Thus along Jirón de la Unión the colonial name of each street is noted on street signs below the Jirón de la Unión designation. Ignore the colonial names. Nobody uses them anymore.

Two final important streets are **Tacna-Wilson Diagonal,** and Avenida Abancay. While locals use the convenient Tacna-Wilson designation, actually the bustling thoroughfare embraces two connecting streets: Avenida Wilson, which runs from the suburbs to the Colmena; and Avenida Tacna, which stretches from the Colmena to its terminus at the Rimac River.

Four blocks from the Plaza San Martín (away from Tacna-Wilson) is the traffic-clogged **Avenida Abancay.** Heavily commercial, Abancay houses several of our "starvation" hotels and restaurants.

In summary, then, if you familiarize yourself with the Plaza San Martín and the Plaza de Armas, the Colmena, and the Jirón de la Unión, you should have no trouble finding your way around downtown.

The Suburbs

Handsome private homes, swank modern shopping centers, drive-in restaurants, movie theaters, and fashionable schools mark three suburban areas outside Lima.

In each of the suburbs are a number of pensions (offering room and all meals at modest prices) and small hotels (called hostals) that we heartily recommend in our hotel discussion below. But whether you stay here or not, you should visit these areas. You will be astonished by the modern, well-ordered look of all the communities.

Reaching the suburbs is painless. Take either a colectivo (a taxi that operates as a jitney) or bus 2. Both depart from near the Plaza San Martín and journey along the four-lane highway called **Arequipa,** the main route between the near suburbs and center city.

The nearest suburb to downtown is busy **Lince,** starting to resemble center city as Lima pushes out from its congested center. Next is **San Isidro,** a fashionable residential area with modern shopping centers, good restaurants, and upbeat nightclubs. Finally comes **Miraflores,** farthest from the plaza but still only 15 to 20 minutes away, depending on traffic. You should consider spending most of your time in Miraflores, where the best restaurants, hotels, and nightspots are located. The principal avenues with which you should familiarize yourself in Miraflores are **Avenida José Pardo** and its extension, **Avenida Ricardo Palma,** which mark the beginning of Miraflores. Avenida Arequipa runs perpendicular and ends at those avenues. Two important streets that form a diagonal are **Oscar Benavides** and **Avenida José Larco,** which cut across Miraflores.

Beyond Miraflores are the summer beach areas of **Costa Verde, Barranco, Chorrillos,** and **La Herradura.** The colectivo fare is 25¢ maximum. And you can't beat it for quick, comfortable, cheap transportation.

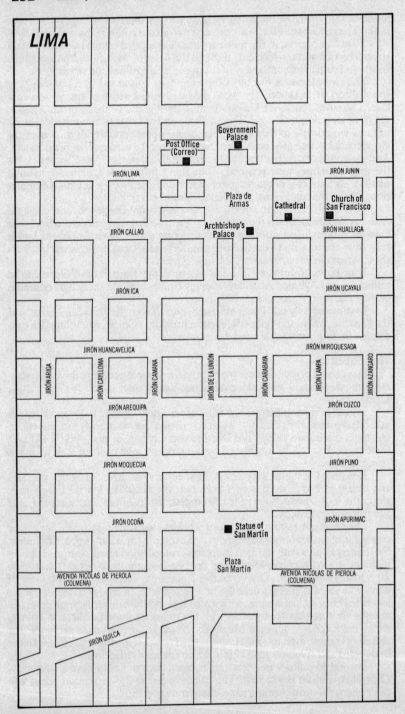

LIMA

Post Office
(Correo)

Government
Palace

JIRÓN LIMA

JIRÓN JUNIN

Plaza de
Armas

Cathedral

Church of
San Francisco

Archbishop's
Palace

JIRÓN CALLAO

JIRÓN HUALLAGA

JIRÓN ICA

JIRÓN UCAYALI

JIRÓN HUANCAVELICA

JIRÓN MIROQUESADA

JIRÓN ARIGA

JIRÓN CAYLLOMA

JIRÓN CAMANA

JIRÓN DE LA UNION

JIRÓN CARABAYA

JIRÓN LAMPA

JIRÓN AZANGARO

JIRÓN AREQUIPA

JIRÓN CUZCO

JIRÓN MOQUECUA

JIRÓN PUNO

JIRÓN OCOÑA

Statue of
San Martín

JIRÓN APURIMAC

Plaza
San Martín

AVENIDA NICOLAS DE PIEROLA
(COLMENA)

AVENIDA NICOLAS DE PIEROLA
(COLMENA)

JIRÓN QUILCA

Callao

This port city of 280,000, founded by Pizarro on the Pacific eight miles west of Lima, served as a first line of defense for the Spaniards against the English. The **Real Felipe Fortress** still stands there as testimony to war games of yesterday. Callao is the main port of Peru. The main avenue, **Avenida Saenz Peña,** leads to the Real Felipe Fort. Avenida Guardia Chalaca and Avenida Argentina head to the docks. Nearby **La Punta** is a popular summer beach area.

Note: Callao is pronounced "cay-ow."

CLIMATE OF LIMA: Twelve degrees south of the equator, Lima is nevertheless mild. The mercury seldom soars above 80° or dips below 50°. Rain is rare. The city is at sea level.

But there is one peculiar weather phenomenon that occurs in the city almost every morning during the winter (June to September), a foggy mist known here as "garua." It sometimes lasts all day.

The fog emanates from the cold Peruvian Humboldt Current that cools the air above as it moves toward Lima. The cool air meets the customary warm air over the city and causes a heavy damp fog that is sometimes dissipated by the afternoon sun.

Oddly, due to rain currents, the garua is limited to Lima proper. Within 30 minutes by train or auto is a delightfully warm sun, suitable for swimming all year round. In **Chosica,** 40 minutes from Lima, winter swimming is common (see our excursions discussion).

CAVEAT: In 1986 there was a **curfew** (*toque de queda*), which started at 1 a.m. and lasted four hours. The effects of the curfew were that clubs and restaurants started to close no later than midnight and during the four-hour interval no people or cars were on the streets. Special dispensation was made for passengers arriving during those hours and taxis bore a white banner on their antennae. Although not in effect during our last visit in late 1988, you should check when you arrive to see if the curfew has been reinstated.

THE SAFETY FACTOR: Many readers have written to us about the safety factor when visiting Peru. For years a group called the Shining Path had confined its terrorist acts to the area around Ayacucho. However, in June 1986 a bomb was placed on the tourist train to Machú Picchú and several people were injured. This has resulted in increased security in tourist areas of the country, and armed police and soldiers are visible. Keep in mind that unlike European terrorist groups the Shining Path does not usually attack tourists, confining its attacks to disrupting the democratic process in the country. Stick to major tourist areas, use the same common sense that you'd use at home, and you should have no problem.

1. WHERE TO STAY

The best budget accommodations in Lima are, without doubt, the pensions located in modern private homes in the suburbs. In these, a couple can get a sparkling-clean room in a U.S.–style split-level home, with breakfast included in the price of the room, for about $15 per person per day.

But while the pensions are the best values we've found, many travelers will still prefer to stay at a convenient downtown hotel and sample a variety of restaurants. Therefore we will begin with our selection of hotels in this area.

Note: Hotel rooms are at a premium in July and October—Peru's busiest vacation months. So write well ahead for reservations.

HOTELS IN CENTER CITY: Because of galloping inflation, there are few truly acceptable budget hotels in downtown Lima. As a result we are including (1) the best-value semiluxury stops, and (2) the best semibasic and basic hotels available. Unfortunately, there's nothing in between. Remember, our prices include the 15% hotel tax.

Higher-Priced Hotels

The 224-room **Hotel Savoy,** Cailloma 224 (tel. 28-3520), is understated and inviting. It would be hard to find a more comfortable hotel. Only the luxury Crillon, Bolívar, and Sheraton are superior—but at higher prices. We think the Savoy offers the better value. Air-conditioned doubles start at $44; singles run $38 and up. The hotel has a bar and restaurant on the roof which is open during the summer months—a delightful spot for a leisurely lunch with a terrific view of the city. Folklorico shows are also held "under the stars" during temperate weather. Other pluses are the hotel's two restaurants and convenient transportation to the Jorge Chavez Airport for $2.50.

Another good hotel, trying hard to be thought of as first class, is the **Hotel Riviera,** Avenida Inca Garcilaso de la Vega 981 (tel. 28-9460). The décor, from lobby to all 180 rooms, is above average, but we feel that the rates are definitely on the high side, approaching "big-splurge" status: $52 for doubles, $40 for singles.

A comparative newcomer in downtown Lima, **Hostal San Martín,** Avenida Nicolas de Pierola 882 (tel. 281-5337), on the second floor, overlooks the plaza. It is heated and has air conditioning, and all rooms have private bath. The 14 rooms are paneled and carpeted and the décor is modern. Rooms have minibars. Doubles are $32, and singles, $26. Very good choice. Breakfast is included.

For modern comfort in the convenient downtown area, be sure to check out the 56-room **El Plaza Hotel,** Nicolas de Pierola (Colmena) 850 (tel. 28-6270), right across the street from the well-known Bolívar Hotel. Prices are high: $50 for doubles, $36 for singles. The rooms are just what you would expect them to be in a newer hotel: fully carpeted, clean, bright, and comfortable. The restaurant is open for all three meals—à la carte only.

Stepping down in price, we come to the **Continental,** Jirón Puno 196 (tel. 27-5890), where doubles run $30 and up; singles cost $20 and up. With 193 carpeted rooms spread over 11 floors, the Continental offers comfort and a top-floor restaurant where you can have a continental breakfast for under $2.50. All in all, it's a cheerful surprise in Lima, where many older hotels are in need of paint.

A less expensive, older establishment is the 60-room **Claridge Hotel,** Jirón Cailloma 437 (tel. 28-3680). An eight-floor, elevator-equipped hotel, the Claridge was once the choice hotel in Lima. But over the years, as newer hotels were built in the city's other sections, and as the suburbs boomed, both the Claridge and the Plaza de Armas area lost their glitter. Yet, still today the Claridge offers good value. The large rooms, traditionally furnished, all come with bath (shower only) and ample sitting alcoves. Home to many visiting North Americans, the Claridge also houses an inexpensive restaurant on the eighth floor which is open Monday through Saturday for breakfast and lunch. Doubles start at $15, while triples are $20 and singles run $12, with tax and service. On our last inspection the hotel needed a good painting—so ask to see your room before you check in.

Across from the Plaza San Francisco is another newer hotel, the **Hostal San Francisco,** Jirón Ancash 340 (tel. 28-3643). Contemporary in décor and quite comfortable, the hotel has 46 rooms with private bath. Doubles are $25 and singles pay $19, with continental breakfast included. A filling American breakfast, lunch, and dinner are also available at the hotel's cafetería.

Budget Hotels

One of our most comfortable downtown choices is the **Hostal Renacimiento,** an elegant Italian-style mansion with beautiful gardens just a ten-minute walk from downtown at Parque Hernan Velarde 52–54 (tel. 31-8461). The rooms are clean and comfortable, all with private bath. The management is very hospitable. A double with breakfast included is $20, and a single is $12.

You should check out the good-value **Hotel Damasco,** Ucayali 199 (tel. 27-6028). Up one flight in a former office building, the 26-room Damasco has bathless doubles for $10 and singles for $8. Add $3 for private bath. Rooms are plainly furnished though quite clean. Try to get a rear room if street noises bother you.

A budget choice that provides free airport transportation for guests is the 75-room **Hotel Wilson,** Jirón Chancay 633 (tel. 28-9670), a short, five-block walk from the Plaza San Martín, between Moquecua and Emancipación. With a bar and restaurant off the lobby, and an elevator, the six-story Wilson is a cut above most low-priced Lima hotels. However, rooms are small and there have been some reader grumblings regarding cleanliness. Examine your accommodations before checking in. All rooms come with bath. Doubles range from $15 to $17, depending on interior or exterior location; singles are $11 to $13.

A reader tipped us off to the 47-room **Hotel La Casona,** Jirón Moquecua 289 (tel. 27-6273), just around the corner from the Claridge Hotel. After checking it out, we were left with mixed feelings. We felt that the hotel, as a whole, could be cleaner. However, the rooms are large and airy, and are clustered around an open courtyard where you can also have meals. The hotel has a small restaurant as well, and a sitting room with television (also somewhat shabby). Doubles with shower are $20, and singles are $12. Bathless rooms are $2 less. Prices include a continental breakfast.

Stepping down quite a bit, we come to the basically furnished **Hotel Colmena,** Nicolas de Pierola 1177 (tel. 28-7720), located diagonally opposite University Park, home of San Marcos University. A 70-room hotel, the five-story Colmena is popular with students because of its location. Situated on a heavily trafficked street between Lampa and Azangaro, this hotel suffers some from casual management, a long, gloomy entrance corridor, and rooms with well-used furnishings; nevertheless, it is adequate for the right sort of traveler. However, we recommend paying the extra money for a private bath, since the public showers are outdoor stalls. Both doubles and singles with bath are $9. Head one flight up for the reception area.

Across the street is a similar hotel, the **Atahualpa,** which you might try if the Wilson is full.

A Special Choice

For the young in spirit, we can recommend the recently opened **Alberque Juvenil Karina,** at Jirón Charcay 617 (tel. 32-3562). The rooms are dormitory style with bunk beds, but the 70 guests spread over three floors get clean surroundings and attentive care for $5 per day. The fourth floor houses the cafetería overlooking the downtown area. Say hello to manager Rosa Martens Zapata.

Pensions in Center City

There are four barely acceptable pensions in center city, and although they are inferior to suburban pensions, still they do offer downtown convenience. One block from Plaza San Martín on a tiny street off Jirón de la Unión is the popular **Hostal Belen,** Belen 1049 (tel. 28-0180), opposite the Wony Restaurant, one of our recommendations. The 20-room Belen, up one flight of stairs, has hosted many of our readers and offers clean, adequately furnished, bathless rooms for less than $10 per person. And much to the budget traveler's delight, the Belen throws in a toast-and-coffee breakfast for an additional 75¢. The owner, the charming and matronly Nella Poletti, takes a personal interest in her guests, offering helpful sightseeing tips. You will find the Belen homey and comfortable—and crowded.

Another pension worth checking is a block over on Carabaya at no. 1033, the 20-room **Casa Vasca** (tel. 28-0459). The Vasca charges only $6.50 per person for a bathless room (small and plainly furnished). *Very* basic!

The **Hostal Roma,** Jirón Ica 326 (tel. 27-7576), is another basic hotel with a good location near the plazas. Its 28 rooms are dark and have little in the way of furnishings, but they do have private baths with hot-water showers, and they are clean. Doubles with bath are $10 and doubles without are $8. Singles must share baths but rates are only $5.

A final pension you might consider is the 13-room **Hostal Machú Picchú,** Jirón Cailloma 231 (tel. 27-9849), opposite the Savoy Hotel. Walk up one flight and look for the "bienvenidos" (welcome) sign. For $5 per person you get a basic room with no meals. Period.

Starvation-Budget Choices

Lima has a large number of starvation-level hotels, but we've selected only those that meet our minimum standards.

The best of these we've found is the 73-room **Gran Hotel,** Abancay 546, between Cuzco and Quesada (tel. 27-1611). Doubles, most with bath, range upward to $11; singles are $5. Furnishings are old and well used, but a central skylight does brighten the lobby and rooms are off an open courtyard. The late owner-manager, a well-bred gentleman, once shook his head while showing us around and sadly murmured, "Not a first-class hotel." No, it's not, but it retains a certain dignity. However, the neighborhood is not the safest.

Another basic hotel is the **Europa,** Jirón Ancash 376, near the Abancay, not far from the Plaza San Francisco (tel. 27-3351), which offers clean but rather cheerless doubles for under $6.50. Singles are $4.50. Some rooms are windowless and the only ventilation is from the transom above the glass door.

And for the even younger in spirit and lighter in pocketbook, there is the **Richmond Hostal,** Jirón de la Unión 706 (tel. 27-9270). Rates there, without bath, of course, are $4.25 for doubles and $3 for singles. Get one of the upper rooms—less dingy.

READER'S PENSION SELECTION: "In Lima, Peru, I stayed at **Hostal San Sebastian,** at Jirón Iça 712 (tel. 23-2740), for $4 single per night. Shared bath and showers. Public transport close by. Señora Vianni speaks English and was very helpful with directions for getting around the city. Trans-Hotel jitney to airport was $3. Call 46-9872 the day before" (Mary Ellen Johnson, Costa Rica).

Big Splurges

The "Big Three" of luxury hotels in downtown Lima are the well-established **Hotel Bolívar,** Jirón de la Unión 958, on the Plaza San Martín (tel. 27-6400) and **Hotel Crillon,** La Colmena 589 (tel. 28-3290) plus the newer **Sheraton,** Avenida de la República 117, near the Plaza San Martín (tel. 32-9050). The Sheraton offers truly modern conveniences and comfort in North American style. Rates are an extravagant $110 for doubles, $105 for singles (tax included). Rates are a little less at the Bolívar and Crillon. All three are outstanding hotels, catering heavily to North Americans as well as to Europeans and Latin Americans.

IN THE SUBURBS: The suburbs of Lima are booming! New hotels, shopping centers, and restaurants seem to sprout up almost overnight. San Isidro, for example, has the largest shopping complex in Lima—El Centro Commercial Camino Real—with dozens of shops, restaurants, movie theaters, and a skating rink.

With all of this feverish construction it's little wonder that some of the most desirable accommodations in Lima can be found in the suburbs. And some of the best values. As mentioned earlier (but the point bears repeating), easily the nicest accommodations for the money are the pensions located in modern private homes. These are easily reached in 15 minutes by colectivos (actual autos) that run along tree-lined Avenida Arequipa. These jitneys, which charge only 25¢ to our most remote recommendations, continually pick up and discharge passengers along the six-mile route between the Plaza San Martín and the principal suburbs of Lince, San Isidro, and Miraflores, which lie south of the plaza; the taxi-like vehicles carry only five passengers when full and are quickly identifiable by the number "81" on their windows. They run every few minutes from the stand diagonally opposite Eastern and Faucett Airlines. Their efficiency is astonishing as they zip up and down Arequipa. We often yearn for them in New York when we futilely try to hail a cab or board a jammed bus on traffic-choked Fifth Avenue.

Since the most distant of our choices is only 15 minutes from the Plaza San Martín, distance should not be a factor in your decision on whether to stay in center city or in the suburbs.

Another inexpensive way to head out to the suburbs is via bus 2 (which you can get in front of the Tauro movie theater, three blocks from the Plaza San Martín), which leans out along Avenida Arequipa for the same 25¢ fare.

We should, by the way, describe Arequipa (the boulevard by which you'll reach the pensions). The four-lane roadway is divided in the center by a lengthy stretch of immaculately kept trees and shrubbery; solid, expensive homes are on either side as you head out from center city, and occasionally you will see an attractive service station. Numbers on blocks increase in units of 100 as you head away from the city.

There are some excellent hostals out this way, which we will discuss shortly. First—

The Suburban Pensions

Our pensions, not listed in any other guide, have really suffered because of the inflation here. They were not permitted to raise their fees and were taxed at the same rate as hostals. Many of them have been forced to close their doors. It's a shame, for they were the best budget buys in the city. Because their ranks have fallen to such a small number, it's best for you to write ahead for reservations. Include a return envelope with an international postal response coupon (obtainable at your local post office). If you fail to make advance arrangements, telephone from the airport and perhaps you'll be lucky.

The **Hostal Astoria,** 29 blocks out on Avenida Arequipa at Camino Real 157 (tel. 22-4797), our home in Lima for 20 years, closed in 1983. However, its lively and knowledgeable owner, Maria Barreto, retained the apartment house next door, where she rents four comfortable and tastefully furnished apartments. Each apartment has a large bedroom with twin beds, a sitting room with daybeds that can sleep two others, a TV, and a fully equipped kitchen so you can cook in. Rates are very low—$15 for one and $25 for two people. Maria is always around to lend a helpful hand. Good choice.

Farther out Arequipa, at no. 4704, at Tarapaca, is the homey and comfortable 15-room **Pension Alemana** (tel. 45-3092). Here you get well-furnished rooms with bath costing $30 for doubles, $25 for singles. Smaller, bathless rooms can be had for $12. The only meal included in the rates is breakfast. Lunch and dinner ($7 each) must be ordered in the morning. The large dining room overlooks a garden, and attractive alpaca rugs cover many of the walls. The owners have acquired another house across the street which they were in the process of fixing up at the time of our visit. The Alemana has no outdoor sign to guide you, so ask the colectivo driver to let you off at block no. 4600 and look for the white house on the corner of Tarapaca.

A good find in the heart of Miraflores is the **Residencial 28 de Julio,** 28 de Julio 531 (tel. 47-3891), a cheerful, bright pension. Formerly a private home, the sunny yellow house is set back off the street. Enter through a gate to the well-kept front yard which sports a lawn table with umbrella. The two-story residencial has rooms opening on a garden patio. Prices are on the high side—doubles with private bath for $28; singles cost $13. The management aims to please (English is spoken) and we think you'll feel right at home at this delightful pension, only a quick 15-minute taxi ride from center city.

The **Residencial Huaychulo** is a three-story, white house located in the attractive Miraflores section, Avenida Dos de Mayo 494 (tel. 45-1195). It is modern and well furnished, with carpeting and a private bath in each of its 20 rooms. Doubles are $30 and singles run $25, without meals.

One block farther out, at Arequipa 3090, is the comfortable **Ella Friedrich Guest House,** corner of Tradiciones (tel. 22-7041). This cheerful eight-room pension has carpeting in all rooms and paintings on most walls. A relaxing spot is the second-floor couch and TV area where guests congregate for evening conversation. A double without bath (there are three large guest bathrooms) and with breakfast is a bargain $10 per person. No lunch or dinner served.

The 22-room **Beech Pension,** at Libertadores 165, at the 3300 block of Arequipa (tel. 40-5595), which was presided over for many years by the delightful Audrey Beech, has changed hands again, but remains on our "best value" list. All rooms, each with bath, are immaculate and attractively furnished. You pay about $25 for a double, $16 for a single with breakfast. While Mrs. Beech no longer pours afternoon tea with scones, you can still enjoy an afternoon respite in the rear garden and have your laundry done for a small extra charge. To reach the Beech, take either bus 1, which drops you on Camino Real near Libertadores, or hop the colectivo and ask to be dropped in the 3300 block of Arequipa near the Petroperu Service Station. Walk to your right for four short blocks, and that is Libertadores. The Beech house is off to your left. Highly recommended.

Another fine choice is the **Hostal Francia,** Samuel Velardi 185, in San Isidro (tel. 61-754), where for $30 you get a comfortable double ($27 for a single), including breakfast and taxes. Señora Dora Salas is a gracious lady and your hostess, who will attend to all your needs. There's a pool and a bar on the premises.

Suburban Hostals/Hotels

Suburban hotels are brighter and newer than those downtown, most having been built in the last 15 years. They are small, and the personal touches of their owners make them a cross between a hotel and pension. They come in a variety of price ranges, but because they are new and located in high-priced sections of the city there are few basic choices.

A lovely choice, the **Hostal La Castellana,** at Grimaldo del Solar 222, Miraflores (tel. 47-3530), is a low Spanish-style building with a flower-filled garden in the rear lobby. There are double beds, carpets, and phone, plus very tasteful furnishings. Breakfast can be served in your room. The sitting room, with comfortable couches and tables, is off the lobby. Doubles with bath are $26, while singles are $22. Highly recommended.

Hostal Sans Souci, Avenida Arequipa 2670, San Isidro (tel. 22-6035), has 24 spotlessly clean rooms, all with carpeted floors, telephones, and private baths. The whitewashed building with wrought-iron lamps has tiled floors in the lobby and a salon with easy chairs and TV. There is a small garden in the rear. Rooms are of good size, and comfortable with desks and lamps. The Sans Souci is well run by very friendly people. Doubles are a high $40 and singles run $35. There is a restaurant on the premises that serves all three meals.

A deluxe hostal, only eight years old, is the **Hostal Exclusive,** at San Martín 550, Miraflores (tel. 44-1919), only one block from the main street of Miraflores, Avenida Largo. The Exclusive has six floors and an elevator. The 35 rooms are richly furnished in modern style and have tile baths. There is a lovely restaurant and bar in the basement. Suites have small kitchens. Considering the quality of the accommodations, the price of $58 for a double and $46 for a single is not out of line.

Hostal, Avenida Javier Prado 250, San Isidro (tel. 22-4274), is a small, 15-room choice in a very good location. Near colectivos and good restaurants, it is only 15 minutes from downtown. The rooms are small but adequate, and there is a pool and sundeck in the garden. A discothèque and electronic game room are in the basement. The small sitting area off the postage-stamp lobby has a working fireplace. Rates are $28 for doubles and $22 for singles, but there is a discount for a week's stay. Breakfast is included.

There's also the **Hotel Limatambo,** in San Isidro at Avenida A. Aramburu 1025. For $30 you get a carpeted room for two with private bath in a five-story building. Bonuses here are living rooms with TV on each floor, a cafetería and bar on the first floor, and individual safes in each room. There are 31 rooms in all in the Hotel Limatambo, which opened in 1984. We have received nice letters from guests who have stayed here. Highly recommended.

Hostal Residencial Firenze, Sebastian Tellería 203 (at the 3000 block of Arequipa), San Isidro (tel. 42-1780), has 19 rooms, clean and simply furnished with built-in desk and closets. Doubles with bath are $20 (without, $15), while singles are $16 with and $11 without.

In Miraflores at Avenida Petit Thouars 5444 is the **Hostal Miraflores** (tel. 45-8745), a clean, modern four-story structure with 40 rooms. Each room is nicely carpeted, with draped windows and a private bath. There are four rooms with double beds which go for $30, tax included, and 36 rooms with twin beds for $22. There are no meals included in the rates, but there is a coffeeshop/snackbar on the premises.

A good find is the comfortable, attractive **Colonial Inn,** at Comandante Espinar 310, at the intersection of Espinar and Enrique Palacios (tel. 46-6666) in Miraflores. The 14-room Colonial has rooms with private bath and telephone that go for $19 in a single, $26 in a double. Décor is Spanish modern with beamed ceilings and tile floors—quite pleasing! Continental breakfast is an additional $1.75, while an all-out American-style breakfast is just over $2. A plus is the dining room, which serves fine food and is open till 11 p.m.

The **Ariosto,** at La Paz 769, Miraflores (tel. 44-1414), will delight you with its authentic Spanish ambience, complete with tile floors, stucco walls, and a delightful restaurant and bar situated around an open courtyard that is reminiscent of a Peruvian coastal farm in décor. The Ariosto tries hard to please and succeeds. The management is friendly and helpful. Services include laundry, medical assistance, but to the airport, plane and tour information—all the nice touches of a first-class hotel. Prices are surprisingly moderate for this attention to detail. The 74 rooms, all with telephone and private bath, run $32 for singles, $38 for doubles, $45 for suites with a parlor area, tax included. Several rooms have balconies overlooking the courtyard. We expect that prices will rise as the hotel catches on. Very nice!

Modern and comfortable, the **Residencial Collacocha,** Manuel Fuentes, corner of Andres 100, San Isidro (tel. 40-5825), opened in 1976. A large, colonial structure, the Collacocha has carpeting, drapes, and a bath with shower in each of its 30 rooms. There are balconies and large Spanish windows on each of its three stories. Altogether, the Residencial Collacocha is a good choice. The rates are $26.50 for doubles and $19 for singles. The rates do not include meals, although breakfast can be purchased.

A good choice on Arequipa, at no. 1421, is the colonial-style, 45-room **Columbus Hotel** (tel. 71-0129), where doubles with bath and carpeting are $29 and up. Singles start at $17.

Also in the same range in Miraflores is the **Hostal Catalina,** on Calle Toribio Polo (tel. 41-0192), where the 16 rooms rent for about $20 double. The hotel is new and the rooms are clean and bright.

Hotel El Dorado, at Avenida José Pardo 486 in Miraflores (tel. 47-6305), opened in 1983 and offers first-class doubles for $37 ($32 for singles) in carpeted rooms with kitchenette, refrigerator, laundry service, and a pool. There are 37 rooms spread over five floors, and it's a great value.

An even better value in Miraflores is the **Hostal Terreblanco,** at Avenida José Pardo 1453 (tel. 47-9988), a recently opened establishment where doubles with bath are a bargain at $22, with breakfast. Singles run about $16.

The **Hostal Alameda,** at Avenida José Pardo 931 (tel. 46-7226), in Miraflores, is another fine value where $25 gets you a carpeted double room, breakfast, and private bath in a colonial setting.

Also recommended in Miraflores is the **Hostal Palace,** Avenida Miraflores 1088 (tel. 45-6040), where doubles are about $30; singles, $23. There are 35 rooms, a restaurant, laundry, and cafetería and the rooms are all carpeted.

Finally, in San Isidro, you should consider the **Hostal Petirojos,** Avenida Petirojos 230 (tel. 41-6044), where the six rooms with bath rent for $15 double, $10 single. While far from fancy, the rooms are perfect for student types.

The Big Splurge

The Miraflores residential area now boasts several luxury hotels. The Miraflores Cesar is the most prominent, the El Condado Miraflores is tucked away in the El Suche Shopping Center, and the city's newest hotel, the Maria Angola, is nearby.

Only 30 minutes by taxi from Jorge Chavez Airport, the five-star **Cesar** is well situated in the heart of Miraflores at Avenida La Paz and Diez Canseco, not far from El Suche Shopping Arcade (tel. 44-1212). It's an area that is abundant in artesanías, boutiques, and restaurants. Opened in 1978, the Cesar offers all the amenities of a truly luxury, first-class hotel at prices that can only be classified as "big splurge." Doubles are a staggering $95 (which is on a par with the high-priced Sheraton), and singles run $70, taxes included. Breakfast is extra and can be enjoyed in your room or at the hotel's European-style café, La Vereda.

If you plan a special "big night out," sample the hotel's rooftop restaurant, La Azotea, where you can enjoy a spectacular view of the city. Dinner, if you go easy on the extras, can run about $12. Or head over to the Sunset Bar, where you can sit and nurse a drink for $2.50 while watching the sun set over Lima. The bar is open from 11 a.m. until 1 a.m. every day except Sunday.

The lobby of the Cesar is worth a leisurely stroll to check out the original paintings and artifacts from the colonial period. The Cesar also has a pool with poolside bar service.

The **Condado Miraflores,** Alconfores 465, Miraflores (tel. 44-1890), in the Suche Shopping Center, is a Spanish-style hotel. Its 46 rooms are large and taste-fully furnished with lots of plants and bright accessories. Doubles are $90 and singles are $79. The hotel has several restaurants and a discothèque. If we were going to splurge on our stay in Lima, we'd head here.

The **Maria Angola,** Avenida La Paz 610 (tel. 44-1280), is midway between the other deluxe choices. It is very modern with a computerized system through-out the hotel. Your room key is a card which you insert outside the door. Don't even think about what would happen if the computer has a problem. Rooms are thickly carpeted, and furnishings are in the rich Spanish mode. There is a pool and sauna on the roof. Single rooms are $70 and doubles run $82. By the way, this is a good stop for business travelers since it has a Telex system.

If you insist on traveling first class (and can afford it), head out to our next suburban "big-splurge" selection—the rustic **Country Club,** Calle Los Eucalyptos, San Isidro (tel. 40-4060), where you will find yourself in a Spanish-colonial country setting, complete with two swimming pools and tennis, basket-ball, and volleyball courts. A golf course is across the road. Situated amid palm trees and manicured lawns on some 30 acres in a secluded suburban setting, this hotel—once a private club—rents out some 65 rooms to guests, most with sit-ting alcoves, at rates that are high but appropriate: $70 for doubles and $42 for singles. Several restaurants are on the premises, including an outdoor snackbar at poolside. The pools, including a kiddie pool, are open to club members, who give the grounds a resort ambience on hot days.

Note: Consider the Country Club only in summer (December to March). It can be chilly and dreary in the winter (June to September).

Another deluxe hotel in Miraflores is the ten-year-old **El Pardo Hotel,** Avenida José Pardo 420 (tel. 47-0283). Modern and first class, the ten-story Pardo has piped-in music, air conditioning, wall-to-wall carpeting, and phones in each of its 100 rooms. Large doubles (many have small terraces and two double beds) run $90. Smaller doubles are $80, and singles go for $77, taxes included. All rooms have a full private bath with tiled shower and tub and bidet. Other "big luxury hotel" touches are a pool and roof garden, cocktail lounge, restaurant, and snackbar. A gymnasium and sauna are also offered. A popular fast-food oper-ation is also part of the hotel complex. Dining in the hotel's restaurant is low-key and elegant. Prices are high.

The final deluxe choice is the **Hotel Garden,** at Avenida Rivera Navarrete 450 in San Isidro (tel. 42-1771). Modern, nicely furnished, with a helpful staff and good location. Rates are on a par with the El Pardo, about $60 double.

Youth Hostel

New in Lima is a youth hostel. The **Alberque Juvenil Internacional,** at Avenida Largo 247 (tel. 47-5374), Miraflores, puts up the young at heart for $3 a night.

2. MEALS IN LIMA

Lima can be an expensive city in which to dine; many of the attractive restau-rants in the center of town and in the suburbs are priced way beyond our budget limits. So you have to select carefully.

Nevertheless, we have found a number of restaurants within our budget.

First, you should know something about dining habits and customs in Lima. Typically, breakfast is light, perhaps coffee and rolls with butter or marma-lade. Lunch, served from 1 to 2:30 p.m., is moderately heavy. The 5 o'clock tea hour turns out to be coffee, when it isn't something stronger, such as the popular pisco sour (a grape brandy with the customary sour mix). Dinner is late, after 9 p.m.

Food specialties that you should try include **ceviche de corvina,** an appetizer made of whitefish in a lemon sauce with onions, chile, and sweet potato; **anticuchos de corazones,** another appetizer, of grilled hearts served on a skewer; **chicharrones de pollo,** chopped grilled chicken; and **picantes de camarones** (shrimp) or **pollo** (chicken), pieces cooked in a sharp chili sauce.

If you have the chance, you should also try **pachamanca,** a typical dish of the sierra. It's a delicious stew of meats and vegetables cooked together over heated stones in pots that are dug into the ground. Also try **picarrones,** deep-fried sweet-potato batter served with molasses.

Don't be surprised to find a great many Chinese dishes on menus here. There is a large Asian population in Lima.

The ubiquitous Pepsi-Cola and Coca-Cola are here, of course, along with an even more popular tasty local soft drink, Inca Kola.

A helpful point is that menus are frequently posted in the window of the restaurant. This allows you to look before you enter. A 18% tax is added to all bills.

RESTAURANTS IN CENTER CITY: We'll deal with these according to the meals in which they specialize.

Breakfast and Lunch

Several readers tipped us to an eatery on the Colmena near the Hotel Crillon. The **Lucky Star** is indeed an excellent choice for breakfast and lunch, and even a light quick dinner. It's spotlessly clean, bright, and cheerful. Service is quick at the counter or at the booths. Sandwiches run $1 to $1.50, as do large steaming bowls of soup. Served with bread and butter, they are a meal. Fish platters are $3.25 and steak dishes run $4. Wine and cocktails are served.

Our favorite breakfast stop is the rather plain **Café Galería,** located in the busy Boza's arcade that runs between Jirón de la Unión and Carabaya, half a block from the Plaza San Martín. Here you can get a hearty breakfast of two eggs, toast, and coffee for $1.75. Inexpensive sandwiches and hot plates are available for lunch. A three-course lunch runs just under $3. The eight tables outside the café in the arcade serve as a magnet for streams of persistent shoeshine boys who won't take anything but yes for an answer. If your shoes are in no need of servicing, sit in a booth inside. Incidentally, the arcade has several shops and bookstalls that are worth browsing in.

A virtually identical restaurant with slightly less charm is the **Gran Via,** across Jirón de la Unión in the arcade with the same name.

Cafetería Nuevo Centro, on Jirón de la Unión, and its sister restaurant across the walk, are excellent choices for both breakfast and lunch. They have large counter areas as well as tables, and the larger restaurant has upstairs tables as well. They serve a four-course lunch for $1.25 that can't be beat. Hamburgers, sandwiches, ice cream, and a large variety of cold salad plates. Look for the bright awning.

You can get just about anything you want at a reasonable price at **Don Alejandros,** a large, clean, cafetería-style restaurant next door to the Hostal San Martín on Colmena.

Mr. Koala, at Camana 565, is another clean, attractive breakfast and lunch choice. Shoppers and office workers drop in for the soup (75¢), pasta dishes ($1.50 to $2.50), and the chicken and rice ($1.50). There are daily specials too.

El Arriero, at Colmena 830, is a good lunch choice. Head to the rear dining room and enjoy the barbecued chicken and potatoes. A whole chicken is $3.50, while a quarter will run you under $1.

Lunch and Dinner Choices

A restaurant that we look forward to returning to time and again is the charming though small **Chalet Suisse,** Colmena 560, opposite the Crillon Hotel. By ordering carefully you can dine in a pleasant atmosphere for just a shade above budget prices. For example, pasta dishes range from $4.50, osso buco, $7.50. The Spanish-English menu features a variety of Swiss and Peruvian dishes ranging from $3.50 and up. A good value for the money is the pepper steak with salad and dessert for $8, tax included. But the dish to order here is cheese fondue, a real treat and moderately priced. Service from the smartly jacketed waiters is as good as you'll find in Lima. The Chalet Suisse proves that a restaurant need not be a big splurge to be a fine dining choice. Recommended. Open from 9:30 a.m. to 4 p.m. and 6 to 11 p.m. daily.

Perhaps the largest meal portions in Lima can be found at the **Restaurant Raimondi,** Jirón A. Quesada 110, near La Merced Church, between Calle Carabaya and Unión, four blocks from Plaza San Martín. A cabbie tipped us to this one, and we're glad he did. The churrasco (steak) with french fries is delicious and filling at $5.25, including tax and service. An even better value is the corvina (whitefish) for $3.75, or the quarter chicken (pollo) for the same price. Both come with salad, potato, or rice. Enter into a small stand-up area (where you can have a sandwich) and then veer left into the first of two dining rooms which seat in all about 100 patrons. Informal and filled with regulars who never seem to tire of Raimondi. Friendly hosts too. Open from 8 a.m. to 11 p.m. daily.

Domino Restaurant and Bar, in the Boza's arcade between Jirón de la Unión and Carabaya, is a new find for dinner and lunch. There are tables in the arcade, but to avoid the ubiquitous shoeshine boys, head for a table or booth inside the small chalet. A Swiss-German restaurant, it serves goulash for $4.25, veal cutlets for $4, and wurst platters for $3.50. Dietetic choices include boiled or roast chicken with vegetables or salad for $3.75. A three-plate special is $3.75.

Halfway down Jirón de la Unión as you walk toward the Plaza de Armas (Jirón de la Unión 835), you will spot on your right the modern Via Veneto shopping arcade. Here you will find one of our favorite stops for lunch or snacks —the popular and busy **Jamboree Snack.** Located at the end of the arcade, the Jamboree has a tempting assortment of sandwiches and hot plates at low prices. You can fill up at the Jamboree late in the day on chicken and rice ($3.25), beef steak with fried potatoes ($4), a cold-cuts platter ($2.25), and easily skip a heavy, costly dinner by substituting light sandwiches and coffee later in the evening (a great idea if you're counting your pennies!). The most expensive dishes on the menu—lemon chicken and a tender beef filet—will still run you under $6, tax included. Filling sandwiches are $1 to $2.

Several blocks down, just off the Plaza de Armas, close to the Presidential Palace, is the **Haiti,** a busy breakfast, lunch, and late-evening spot that resembles a Greenwich Village coffeehouse or a Left Bank café, and serves about the best coffee in downtown Lima. Part of a chain owned by the Haiti Coffee Corp., a large coffee-growing company, this eatery overlooks the plaza, which at night is beautifully illuminated. The outside tables make snacking quite pleasant. Ham and eggs with toast will run you about $2.50; two eggs, about $1.25; continental breakfast with one egg, about $2.25. Try the quarter chicken with salad and potato for $2.75. Sandwiches are $1. Best value is the fixed-price lunch, which may include chicken and rice, dessert, and coffee for $2.25. Open Monday through Saturday from 9 a.m. to 10 p.m. and on Sunday from 9:30 a.m. to 10 p.m. There's a Haiti branch in Miraflores.

On the other side of the plaza is the colorful **Atlantic,** recommended both for lunch and snacks. Sit at the counter for quick service or at one of the small tables. A ham-and-egg sandwich runs about $1.50; a hamburger, about $1.75; and two eggs and toast, $1.50. A tasty cheese omelet is $1.75. The Atlantic also serves a five-course meal for about $2.50. Featured the day we visited was a heavy fish soup, a rice-and-meat dish, spaghetti with hot dog, banana with syrup, and beverage—quite a combination, and definitely filling! Meat and chicken dishes cost $3.75 to $4.50, which seems high to us. The glass-enclosed sidewalk café is lovely in the evening.

Pizza American, Colmena 514, is a favorite with the students who attend the university nearby. Comfortable straw chairs and glass-topped tables are always crowded for lunch. Pizzas start at 75¢ (tomato and cheese for one) and $2.75 will buy a large eight-slice pie. Add 75¢ for each additional topping. Ravioli ($1.75) and spaghetti dishes are also served, as are hamburgers.

The **San Martín Parrillada,** on the Colmena and San Martín Plaza, is an attractive bilevel Argentinian-style restaurant. Prices are a little on the high side, but if you are selective you can keep costs at acceptable levels. The meat and salads are excellent.

Popular and crowded for lunch is the **Chifa Lung Wha,** Jirón Huancavelica 218 (at the corner of Camana). Tables and booths are scattered through one dining room. Wontons, in soup or fried, are 75¢ and there are shrimp and chicken dishes for $2. Peking duck is only $2.50. Informal and good food.

In the mood for French food? Drop in at the **Café de Paris,** Colmena 722 (tel. 23-7453), where the onion soup ($3) and the veal cutlet in sherry sauce ($6) are especially in demand. Wooden beams, Parisian posters, and the marvelous cooking odors help create a fine ambience. Peruvian dishes too.

An informal choice for a hearty meal is the quiet **Gran Restaurant Wony,** Jirón de la Unión 1046, near the Teatro Colón at the Plaza San Martín, which offers a four-course, fixed-price lunch (menu familiar) for $2. Typically, you can get salad, soup, fish (or meat, depending on the day of the week), and fruit salad. Chinese dishes, a house specialty, are somewhat more expensive, starting at $2.25. Daily specials (platos del día) are usually just under $1.50, and might include a delicious fish in shrimp sauce (corvina en salsa de camarones) at $1.10. Steak dishes start at $1.75, as does the stuffed chicken and rice. If you don't see the *menu familiar* listed, ask for it. Convenient to the Plaza San Martín area, the unpretentious Wony is popular during the late-afternoon tea hour. Say hello to owner Juan Ysen for us. Open daily from 11 a.m. to 11 p.m. Modest décor.

A good Spanish restaurant near the Crillon Hotel is the **Casa Vasca,** Colmena 734 (tel. 23-6690). Here you should order the tortilla Española ($3) or the langostinas al ajillo (crayfish) for $5.25, or the corvina (whitefish) for $4. Small booths and tables; an informal place.

Small and Inexpensive

If you have a yen for pizza, there is a fine little restaurant near the Colmena —**Giannino's**—which specializes in both Peruvian and Italian cookery. Located on the Calle Rufino Torrico, this charming restaurant serves a tasty pizza as well as good pasta, both priced at $1.50 to $2.50. Fish is $3 to $4, while the complete lunch (three courses and coffee) costs just $3.25. You get a good meal in a cozy bistro-style atmosphere. Open Monday through Friday from 8 to 11 p.m. and on Saturday from 3 to 7 p.m.; closed Sunday.

The food is good and plentiful at **Papa Fritas,** Colmena 732, right next to the Casa Vascas restaurant. The menu is extensive, with ten soup, fish, meat, and chicken dishes. There is a daily feature of a five-course lunch or dinner for $3.75. Open 24 hours daily except Sunday. You can't go wrong here!

A cozy stop with a piano bar is the dimly lit **L'Apéritif 33,** Avenida Inca Garcilaso de la Vega 949, near the Riviera Hotel, where regulars throng the place for both drinks and the good fare. Try the ceviche de corvina ($4) or the steaks ($6.25). Sandwiches start at $2. A good choice for breakfast too. You might also wander into the **San Tropez,** next door, for breakfast or a light lunch.

Time for a Coffee Break

The delightful **Café D'Onofrio,** located in an arcade near the Plaza de Armas, is ideal for a late-afternoon coffee (or tea) and pastry respite. Catering to well-to-do shoppers for the most part, this café offers wonderful service, bright-pink tablecloths in one room, and comfortable booths in the rear room. Piped-in music helps things considerably. Prices can run high—$1.25 for an ice-cream soda—but quality does too.

Drop into the **Pastelería Kudan,** on the Colmena (next to Silvania Prints), for a cup of tea and delicious pastry. Small sandwiches too. **Don Pepos,** on the Plaza San Martín, is also an inviting stop for pastries.

For an ice-cream break, head to **Galería El Centro,** on Avenida Belen (see "Shopping") near Plaza San Martín.

A Special Big Splurge

To call the **Tambo de Oro** ("Inn of Gold") simply a restaurant is the equivalent of labeling Machú Picchú a historic mountain village. This magnificent converted hacienda in the heart of Lima, at Calle Belen 1066, a continuation of Unión on the other side of the Plaza San Martín (tel. 31-0046), is at one stroke a brilliant architectural restoration of a 350-year-old home; a series of glittering shops displaying Peruvian fashions and contemporary art, including sculptures by Victor Delfin; a fascinating showcase for the native arts of half a dozen Latin American nations (for display only and not for sale); a garden promenade for leisurely strolling; a bookshop; and a restaurant with no fewer than three dining rooms, two bars, private lounges, and a kitchen that would rate four stars with Michelin. It's an event, not a place.

Since 1969 when the massive, perfectly restored mahogany doors of Tambo de Oro first swung open, it has become the conversation piece not only of Peru but of Ecuador and Brazil as well, where we heard it talked about. The owners have done justice to Peru's heritage. The paneling, tapestries, chandeliers, and floor designs all tastefully reflect the Spanish colonial era. A "tambo" in Inca times was a way station for travelers. And that's what the Tambo de Oro is today.

After a cocktail in the Colonial Bar, step into the Mirror Room, where antique mirrors line the walls, for your lunch (or dinner). Or you might prefer the adjoining Bull Room, where the famous Puno bull figurines dominate the décor. The menu, which opens from the center to the left and right, features on the front a photograph of the massive entrance doors. Open the menu to an array of à la carte dishes that should overwhelm any palate. If you're hungry, start with the scallops parmesana ($6—prices are not cheap) or the asparagus cream soup ($2.25) before moving on to the main reason for coming here: the duckling à l'orange ($9) or the corvina charrillana ($6.50), which is bass cooked in an onion, chili, and tomato sauce, served on white rice. Recommended, too, are the "shrimp flamed colonial" ($7.50) and any of the chicken dishes. Rabbit, squab, and partridge dishes are yours for the asking.

For dessert, there are crème suchard, an ice-cream confection, and mangos with ice in a cherry liqueur ($3). Superb crêpes Suzette are $3.50. Prices include the hefty tax, but there is an additional $1 cover charge. Prepare to spend $20 minimum per person, assuming one cocktail and careful food ordering.

Reservations are a must: open from noon to 3:30 p.m. and 7 to 11 p.m.;

closed Sunday. Sorry to say that local organizations often take over the entire premises for special occasions. But even if you can't get a reservation, you are permitted to stroll around. You owe it to yourself to do so—even if you have to fast for two days to afford it!

. . . and Another

For a treat you will long recall, have one meal (preferably dinner) at **Las Trece Monedas** ("The Thirteen Coins"). This renowned restaurant is located at Jirón Ancash 536 (tel. 27-6547), half a block off Avenida Abancay, near the Court of the Inquisition and the National Congress. Specialties here are the tempting French (Swiss) and Créole dishes. Equally important to you as a visitor to Peru is the 250-year-old colonial mansion in which the restaurant is situated. This home, built in the colonial period, still retains its original ceilings and panels. It is almost like eating in a museum, since all about are examples of Spanish life: goblets (300 to 400 years old), antique paintings, wooden floors, and a carriage (in the garden entrance) fit for a marquis. If you're in a French mood, try the canard à l'orange. Typical criolla dishes include ceviche de corvina ($5) and anticuchos mixto al gusto ($4.25). Try crêpes Suzette ($3.50) for dessert. There is no sign to guide you here. Enter through a heavy wooden door. Twelve dishes are priced at $7, and many fish platters at $5, plus tax and service.

DINING IN THE SUBURBS: Now we head slightly out of town where there's equally good eating.

For Light Meals

Faison Restaurant, Avenida Diez Canseco 119, Miraflores, is the best budget restaurant in this exciting area. Very clean, its dozen tables are filled by students, trim matrons, and families. The menu changes daily, but for $3.50 you can have a three-course meal that is tasty and varied. The appetizers include soup or stuffed avocados and the entrees are a fowl, pork, or beef dish, and a vegetarian plate. Desserts vary, of course. There is an à la carte menu too. Highly recommended.

Faison is so popular that a second Faison recently opened nearby at Calle Bellavista 258.

In the mood for a hamburger or sandwich for lunch? Cross the street from Faison to find **Churrería Manolo,** an informal eatery with delicious burgers and ice-cream concoctions. This is a good spot to sample churros—long, thin, fried cakes, often stuffed with chocolate and covered with powdered sugar. Great with coffee.

An inexpensive Chinese restaurant in Miraflores is **Chifa Miraflores,** Ricardo Palma 322. Chinese lanterns provide a bit of color, but the décor is rather drab. The food is well prepared and quite inexpensive. Soups run 60¢ and main dishes start at $1.75.

Boom, on Diez Canseco, is a colorful ice cream-burger eatery seemingly decorated by Martians. Oversize booths and counters and swaths of color on the walls make it bright and cheery, and it's a great hangout for young Limeños. Two three-course fixed-price meals are served daily from noon till 11 p.m. They are excellent values, running $3.50 and $4.50 with an apéritif or wine included. You get a choice of appetizer as well as main course plus dessert. You can't beat those prices anywhere.

Weary? Get off your feet and relax over a coffee or snack at the **Haiti,** a modern coffeeshop in Miraflores half a block off the 5700 block of Arequipa on Avenida Diagonal. Head for an outdoor table and watch the colorful stream of shoppers in the busy Miraflores commercial area. Sandwiches can be had for $1 to $2, hamburgers for $1.15, and hot dogs for 75¢. Hungrier? Try the "plates of the day," ranging in price from $3 to $4, tax included—a good bargain, and filling!

A block down from the Haiti is a popular Italian restaurant, **La Pizzería,** Avenida Oscar Benavides, which is invariably jammed on weekends with young couples out on a date. Chicken and pasta dishes start at $5. Pizzas are about $3.25, spaghetti goes for $3, and there are sandwiches too. Service is fast.

A lunch spot that reminds us of a McDonald's in the U.S. is **MacTambo,** with locations in Lince, San Isidro, and Miraflores. Some have curb service while others have inside counters and tables. Sandwiches ($1.50) are delicious, and the Super dogs ($1.15) and burgers come with all the extras. Mac Pollo (the chicken plate) and Mac Plato (the breakfast special) are both under $2. **Kentucky Fried Chicken** has several branches here, with one on Avenida Arequipa in San Isidro and another on Avenida Schell in Miraflores. And there's a **Pizza Hut** on Comandante Espinar in Miraflores.

Stop into **Marcelino's Pizzería,** in the Camino Real Shopping Center in San Isidro, after shopping or a movie. This attractive place is an Italian restaurant and pizza is only one of the specialties. Music at night. Inexpensive.

The **Bavaria** (right near the Haiti) is a smaller restaurant with the same menu. Most platters are German.

Café Strauss, on Avenida Diagonal, sounds and looks German but serves a continental menu with pastas, meats, and chicken dishes, all in the $2 to $3 price range.

Finally, a late-night snackery you should know about is the **Fuente de Soda Del Pilar,** across the street from the lavish Los Condes de San Isidro restaurant (123 Pancho Fuerro). We've been known to head to this basic little snackshop for a chicken sandwich at all hours. This is a typical fast-food operation and fried chicken is king. Local residents consume it eagerly, ordering seconds and thirds unashamedly. Chicken with french fries is $1.50; sandwiches are $1.25 to $2.75. You can't beat the prices, and the chicken is "finger lickin' good."

Coffee Break

If you're out shopping or walking in Miraflores, a lovely interlude would be an afternoon stop at the homey **La Tiendecita Blanca,** a café situated across the wide Avenida Larco opposite the Haiti. In warm weather there are outside tables where you can enjoy a respite amid well-dressed matrons and local businessmen. It seems that every other patron speaks English. Savor a strawberry tart ($1.50) while gazing at the chic men and women.

For a taste of Paris in Peru, you can visit the **Vivaldi.** Its cheerful orange-and-blue canopy over a cluster of outdoor tables is most inviting. Indoors, you will find mirrored walls and glass-topped tables—an elegant setting in which to relax with your afternoon tea, cappuccino, ice cream, pastry, or apéritif. Cocktails are also served. The Vivaldi is located at Ricardo Palma 260, Miraflores. Open till 2 a.m.

Next door to Vivaldi is **Liverpool,** at Alameda Ricardo Palma 250, a pub-style restaurant with indoor and outdoor tables. Although not as crowded as Vivaldi, Liverpool attracts a regular following for late-afternoon tea and sandwiches and dinner. It has the best salad bar in town and is open from noon to 4 p.m. for lunch. A sandwich, salad, dessert, and beverage cost $2. At night for dinner you can fill your plate with salad and order a main course (beef, fish, or fowl) for under $6. Beatle music for background.

Another fine place for afternoon tea, cookies, or a sandwich is **Cherry,** at

Avenida José Larco 835, in Miraflores. Decorated in bright red and white, you can choose between comfortable indoor or outdoor dining. Look for the red-and-white awning over the street.

For a delicious, cool ice cream, stop into the **Donofrio's** shop on Avenida Diez Canseco, near Miraflores Park. The ice cream is very much like Häagen-Dazs in the States. Eat-in or take-out.

Cocktail Break

Drop in for a cocktail in the late afternoon or early evening at the **Orient Express Bar** in El Suche Shopping Center. You'll spot it by the train platform in the entrance. Another romantic choice is **Le Bistro,** nearby.

For Full Meals

Head "back to the ranch" for some of the most succulent baby beef in town, a specialty at **La Tranquera,** Avenida José Pardo 285, Miraflores. Set back from the street and surrounded by a rail fence, this Argentinian-style restaurant, with its beamed ceilings and cowhide rugs, is reminiscent of the Old West, South American style. Its mainstay is the famous Argentinian mixed grill—parrillada—cooked right at your table on the parrilla. A parrillada for two is $16; baby beef, $10; half a chicken is $6.50. The large windows let in plenty of light, making dining a pleasure.

The top hat and cane logo across from La Tranquera is your cue to **Chevalier,** at Avenida José Pardo 300, an attractive restaurant in old Paris décor. The restaurant is a flight up from the piano bar, with rattan couches below. The spiral staircase leads to the elegant restaurant with tables adorned with embroidered place settings and red roses. We enjoyed the pollo ala cerveza ($7) and the lomo ala pimienta (pepper steak) for $8. For lunch there is a daily four-course menu turistico for $8. Nearer Arequipa on Avenida José Pardo is the restaurant **Firenze,** which has good Italian food for $6 and up. Closed Tuesday.

An international restaurant we're fond of in the Centro Commercial Suche (El Suche Shopping Center) is the intimate **Restaurant Carlin,** Avenida La Paz 646, Miraflores, between Calle Shell and Avenida Benavides. While only eight main dishes are offered, each is superior. Whether you order the fettuccine with orange, the corvina, the pollo Cordon Bleu, the delicious rice with olives and scallops (arroz olivar), or any of the four other main dishes, you'll find each superior. Platters run $8 and up. Start with a tangy pisco sour ($2 for a giant drink). Salads here are crisp and clean. You serve yourself from an elaborate salad bar that includes the works: bean sprouts, beets, carrots, radishes, etc. Salads are $2. Prices include tax, but there is a 75¢-per-person service charge added to your bill. By the way, the Carlin is part of a charming gallery of shops set in an authentic Spanish-colonial-style street. Ideal for browsing before or after dinner.

In the mood for cheese and wine? Then head over to the El Alamo Shopping Center, Avenida La Paz, 500 block, where you will find the **Cheese & Wine Restaurant** tucked away upstairs in this interesting shopping arcade. The atmosphere is delightful, reminiscent of an old wine cellar. There are mock vats of wine along the walls, wooden tables, chairs with cushions covered in red plaid, and matching Scots-plaid curtains. Candles and hanging plants enhance the warm wood. The Cheese & Wine Restaurant serves six different kinds of local cheeses along with a carafe of excellent red or white Peruvian wine. Cheese boards range in price from $5 to $9. Portions are small so don't go with a man-size appetite. The Cheese & Wine Restaurant would be an excellent dinner choice after a day that included a hearty lunch. Try the fondue ($10). Nice atmosphere!

Las Tejas, adjoining the El Alamo Shopping Center at Diez Canseco 340, is a criolla restaurant that is very inexpensive and therefore usually busy. Try for one of the outdoor tables since the dining rooms are crowded. Anticuchos are only $1.50, as are the shish kebabs. Ceviche of corvina is $3.50, and humitas, tamales, and choclo are only 50¢ each. Very attractive for dinner when the terrace is lit.

For an excellent continental dinner in comfortable surroundings, try **Bullfish,** at Tarata 299 in Miraflores, a private house on the corner of Avenida José Larco. The arroz con mariscos and the corvina (scallop) dishes are recommended. As you might have guessed, shellfish is king here.

Perhaps the best criollo restaurant in Lima is **Nautilus,** across from Vivaldi, specializing in mariscos (shellfish). Look for the blue-and-white sign and the yellow-and-blue awning. It's not fancy, but the food is good and inexpensive.

For Chinese-food fans there is **Chifa Pacífico,** above Haiti on Avenida Oscar Benavides, one flight up (look for the Cine Pacífico). The food is typical Chinese, quite good, and the bonus is excellent viewing of the bustling Miraflores street scene.

La Pizza Nostra, down a few steps on Avenida Oscar Benavides, Miraflores, is a happy combination of criolla and Italian. Antipasto, pizzas, and a variety of specials are served, as well as frijoles, anticuchos, cabrito, and other local favorites. There are daily specials of the criolla food.

An old French country chalet with polished brass, copper pots and pans, and antiques is home to **La Crêperie,** Avenida La Paz, Miraflores. The menu is limited to soups and 32 varieties of crêpes. These come stuffed with cheese and bacon ($5), anchovies and shrimp, and asparagus (each $4), and cannelloni ($3). Dessert crêpes are $2.50. A delightful way to eat a late supper.

A good Argentine restaurant in Lima is **El Cortijo,** Avenida Panamericana 675. Resembling an Argentine parrillada restaurant, complete with large grill, the Cortijo specializes in steak and chicken at prices that can run your check up if you're not careful in your selections. We emphasize strongly that this is one restaurant where you should order chicken, and only chicken, if you are at all budget conscious. A good value is the medio pollo (half chicken), served with french fries for $4. The chicken is crisply grilled and marvelously seasoned. Steaks start at $7 and, while okay, are really more than you need spend. Open from noon to midnight.

Calle San Román—the Street of Pizzas

This three-block diagonal street, leading from Miraflores Park, is where you should head if you want some good pizza or hearty Italian food. There are at least six restaurants on the block that specialize in those foods, and several others in the immediate vicinity. **Don Corleone** has a counter and sells by the slice. The others are all attractive, tables-only restaurants. **Parking Pizza** has a branch on either side of the street. Pizzas are sold by the quarter, half, or whole. A quarter portion of cheese pie is $1, while the whole pie is $4. With additional ingredients it can run up to $6. Ravioli, lasagne, and fettuccine are also served. **La Glorietta, El Piaaton, Las Pizzas Bar,** and **Al Capone's** have virtually identical menus and prices. Check them out and try the one that appeals to you.

Other Dinner Choices

If "Chinese super-modern" is to your taste, hike out to the huge (1,000 capacity) **Restaurant Lung Fung,** Avenida Limatambo 3165, ten blocks from Arequipa, in San Isidro, where a stream flows between two of the dining rooms and lush vegetation has been landscaped into the décor. While the food is only mediocre in our view, still it's worth coming out here to see what has to be a minor design masterpiece. Stroll from left to right, passing through two dining rooms, the bar, another large dining room, finally reaching a series of small private dining areas all in brilliant colors. Apparently it is considered déclassé to eat in the large dining room: the last time we were here there was a one-hour wait for the private dining areas while the main room remained half empty. Prices are high, so stick to the fowl dishes of pollo, gallina, or pato (duck), each starting at $8, including tax and service. Peking duck is $8; a Chinese antipasto called Lung Fung ping pung (no joke) is also $8. Waiters speak only Spanish and the menus have nary an English word on them. Lung Fung is convenient for a night on the town as it's right in the heart of the nightclub district. Open from noon to 3 p.m. and 7 to 11 p.m. seven days.

Another fine restaurant, much closer to downtown, is the **Restaurant El Dorado,** perched on the 18th (top) floor of a modern office building at Arequipa 2450, in Lince. Besides the plush surroundings and views of Miraflores, Monterrico, and downtown Lima, the restaurant offers surprisingly reasonably priced food. Pasta dishes (that's right, pasta) start at $6, and duck (recommended) is $8. Chicken dishes (gallina) range upward from $7. One minor inconvenience is the speed of the two elevators: an octogenarian could climb the 18 floors faster. Open from 11:30 a.m. to 3 p.m. and 6 p.m. to midnight daily.

A Chinese restaurant where squab, of all things, is a house specialty is **Chifa Mandarin,** Juan de Arona 887 in San Isidro, opposite the Todos Shopping Center. Have a drink in the lower-level rear bar and garden, and then proceed upstairs for the pichon (squab) con champignon ($4 to $8, depending on portion size) or pato con jenjibre, a delicious duck delicacy ($4.25 to $7). Popular, too, are the camarón (shrimp) dishes. Oh yes, you have a dozen soups to choose from too. Private booths offer complete privacy for your party. Open seven days a week till 11:30 p.m. Nice indeed!

Lima's most talked-about seafood restaurant is **Todo Fresco,** a must for anyone who considers food more than just a means of satisfying hunger. Located in San Isidro at 116 Miguel Dasso, seven blocks to the right of the 3700 block of Arequipa, Todo Fresco is surprisingly unpretentious in appearance, with Formica-topped tables (no cloths) and rather unremarkable décor. But the food . . . that's something else again. Gourmets—quasi, pseudo, or actual—should point their forks directly at the lobster thermidor, which is a high $22 but sweetly succulent. Other not-to-be-missed dishes are oysters (picantes de mariscos) for $6 and any of several shrimp platters. For a better deal, stick to the daily special, which usually runs from $8. A Buenos Aires businessman we know would never think of coming to Lima without eating at Todo Fresco at least once. Another Todo Fresco is at Avenida Petit Thouars 32.

Three restaurants well worth a visit are on Camino Real in the Centro Commercial shopping arcade, San Isidro, near the Hostal Astoria. Our favorite is **Restaurante La Calesa,** M. Banon 255 (tel. 40-5568), popular with local businessmen during the lunch hour. We can understand why. The restaurant is restful and intimate with wooden tables, some bench seating, and bright-orange tablecloths. The food is excellent. Prices range from an economical $2.50 for fettuccine, $3.75 for fish dishes, to $4.50 and up for tender, juicy beef (taxes included). On evenings when we haven't been particularly hungry, we've stopped by the Calesa for a bowl of their delicious creamed vegetable soup, served with a mini-loaf of bread ($1). Smooth and filling.

For excellent seafood, head next door to **Don Adolfo,** where lobster, crab, and oysters are their specialty. A complete dinner will cost you $5, including tax. Corvina—very fresh—is $3; sopa de camarones, $3.70.

Nearby is a charming pizzería—the **Beverly Inn**—offering 22 varieties at prices starting at $3.25. Indoor and outdoor seating.

DINING BY THE SEA: Picture yourself dining outdoors by candlelight, watching the moon rise over the Pacific. Then just hop a cab to either of our next three selections for a superb dining experience. (Taxi travel cost is $2 from the center of Lima, 75¢ from Miraflores.) The **Rincón Gaucho** (tel. 47-4778), nestled on the beach, is the closest to the city. The view is incomparable and so is the parrillada, grilled Argentinian style at your table and served with green and red sauces. Parrillada for two is $16; medio pollo is $4; baby beef is $8. Closed Monday.

A little farther out, in the Costa Verde section, you'll find an indoor-outdoor restaurant where you can watch the fishermen haul in the day's catch. The **Costa Verde Restaurant** serves mainly seafood: the ceviche pulpo (marinated cold octopus) is interesting, or you can sample the ceviche corvina or the tortuga (turtle). A treat for the adventuresome palate, as well as a happy seaside dining experience. Open from 12:30 p.m. until midnight.

Nearby **La Rosa Náutica** (tel. 47-6765) is the newest and most attractive restaurant in town. Built on a pier over the water, Rosa Náutica serves fresh seafood, nonthreatening salads, and beef Peruvian style. Of course, it does cost more to get here and to eat here. Expect to spend $16 a person.

Not to be Missed!

To recapture the romance and beauty of colonial Lima, be sure to spend one evening at the elegant **Los Condes de San Isidoro** restaurant, Paz Soldan 290 (tel. 22-2557). This magnificent colonial home is every bit as memorable as the Tambo de Oro and Trece Monedas. Built in 1777 and filled with priceless antiques, Los Condes de San Isidoro retains the grace and elegance of this important historical period while offering top-notch service and excellent cuisine.

The name translated means "Counts of San Isidro," and indeed you can picture the handsome counts and their ladies strolling arm-in-arm on the veranda, where you can dine in the warm summer months—an unforgettable experience as you look out over the lovely garden and savor the fragrance of exotic flowers.

Inside, you will find gilded mirrors, richly carved doors, antique locker chests, massive breakfronts, crystal chandeliers, and Louis XIV–style furniture. Costumes from the period are carefully preserved in glass-front window cases as you enter the restaurant. The management has kept all the elegant touches of the past, with fresh-cut bouquets of flowers and strolling musicians adding to the pleasure. The descendants of the counts still use the old chapel for family baptisms and weddings.

For all this, the food is surprisingly moderate in price. We enjoyed the mixed grill of tender cuts of beef, veal, pork, and kidneys for $10, and a juicy filet mignon for $9.50, including tax and service. Open till 11 p.m. daily.

3. LIMA BY DAY

Put on your comfortable shoes, because we're going to start off with a—

WALKING TOUR: It is fitting that you start your foot pilgrimage through Lima where Pizarro started his—at the **Plaza de Armas.** It was here that in 1535 Pizarro founded the city which he called the "City of Kings." The Indians later renamed it Lima, their name for the Rimac River that flows through the town. Today this is the heart of the capital's older section, a haven for sightseers.

Floodlit at night, this plaza is quite handsome and in our opinion ranks with the Plaza de la Independencia in Quito as the most beautiful in South America. The buildings surrounding the plaza are blessed with superb wooden balconies that are intricately carved. The massive **cathedral** here, which houses the remains of Pizarro in a glass coffin on public view, has been rebuilt several times. The altars are coated with pure silver and the mosaics on the walls bear his coat-of-arms.

Next to the cathedral is the **Archbishop's Palace,** and not far from there in the plaza is the **Government Palace,** which is the presidential residence. Precisely at 12:45 p.m. every day is the Changing of the Guard at the palace, a ritual that involves blaring trumpets and clanking swords. The red-uniformed guards, trained originally by Prussian officers, goosestep in perfect timing.

The bronze fountain in the plaza's center has been there for over 300 years.

If you sit down on one of the benches, expect to be surrounded by shoeshine boys who won't give up easily. The kids will ask you endless questions, and if you know any Spanish at all, you'll have a lot of fun while learning firsthand about life in Peru.

When you are through strolling about the plaza, follow **Jirón de la Unión** out of it toward the Plaza San Martín. You will now be on the main shopping street, which is closed to traffic part of each day to give pedestrians freedom of the way. If you feel like bargain hunting, check our recommended best buys in the shopping section below.

When you reach the **Plaza San Martín,** after a five-block walk, you will be entering the modern part of Lima. The plaza is surrounded by lavish hotels, such as the Bolívar, and several theaters. Opposite the Bolívar is where you catch the colectivos to the suburbs. As you wander around the plaza, note the equestrian **Statue of San Martín** (San Martín helped liberate Peru from Spain in 1821).

The main thoroughfare, **Nicolas de Pierola** (the **Colmena**), leads into the plaza, but don't turn onto it. Instead pick up Jirón de la Unión again on the other side of the plaza and continue for two more blocks, passing Tambo de Oro restaurant on your right, until you come to the **Paseo de la República,** a wide tree-lined promenade that houses the **Palace of Justice.** To your right is the Sheraton Hotel and the civic center. Good spot for browsing in the shops. Benches line the center and there are numerous sculptured llamas, the national animal, made of marble and bronze. Occasionally you will see Indian families sprawled out on the grass enjoying the midday sun. On your right is the **Museum of Italian Art,** which houses copies of famous Italian paintings.

When you reach the end of República after several blocks, you will find yourself at the **Plaza Grau.** Turn right here on **Paseo Colón** (also called 9 de Diciembre), a mile-long street that is the home of Peru's **Museum of Art.** Nearby is the **Parque Neptuno,** where you might like to rest. Three blocks farther along is the **Plaza Bolognesi,** a circular plaza housing a good deal of statuary. Many streets branch out from the plaza. Turn left now onto **Avenida Guzmán Blanco** for three blocks to the **Statue of Jorge Chavez,** famous Peruvian aviator for whom the airport was named. Across the street is the attractive **Campo de Marte,** a popular children-filled park that is the site of frequent parades and celebrations. Pause here a minute and relax as the locals do. You'll enjoy watching the children play soccer.

Now we suggest a visit to Lima's poorer section, which will give you a better-rounded view of the city. To reach that quarter from here, walk along **28 de Julio** away from the park (the street numbers will get higher). Nine blocks up you will reach **Manco Capac Plaza,** distinguished only by the statue of the legendary first Inca. Stroll along any of the side streets in this vicinity and you will see firsthand how the poor live here. This area, despite the poverty, or maybe because of it, is the scene of the gayest, liveliest street fairs in Lima, usually held on holidays.

Back on 28 de Julio, look toward the distant mountains, clearly visible. On the mountainside you will see the Peruvian equivalent of the Brazilian favelas, called **barriadas** here—a vast slum area. North Americans rarely glimpse this area of Lima, but we feel that it adds to our understanding of the nation and its people.

To return to Plaza San Martín, either walk back along 28 de Julio or hop any bus heading that way. They all go to the plaza—the most centrally located section of the city.

LIMA, SIGHT BY SIGHT: Now that you have a feeling for the city, let's take a closer look at some of its treasures.

Torre Tagle Palace

Peru's Foreign Office Building, at Jirón Ucayali 363, off Avenida San Pedro near the Plaza de Armas, was at one time the palace of the Marquis of Torre Tagle, who built this handsome structure in 1735. An outstanding example of Spanish architecture, many of its rooms are closed to visitors during the week as they are used as offices. However, on weekends it is possible to see the entire palace. Note the intricately carved balconies made of mahogany and the massive carved doors. You enter through an open courtyard. There is no formal admission charge, but it is customary to tip the guard.

Court of the Inquisition

In the Plaza Bolívar, at Avenida Abancay, are two other buildings you should definitely visit. The larger one is the **National Congress** and the other, to the right of Bolívar's statue, is the infamous **Court of the Inquisition,** where heretics were tried during the dark period between 1570 and 1820.

As you enter the court's main hall, you will see up front the seven red-felt chairs of the judges behind a mahogany table. To the right is the witness box. Thick, ornately carved wooden beams criss-cross just beneath the high ceiling.

It is usually eerily quiet here, and it doesn't require too much imagination virtually to hear the heretic asking forgiveness for his sins. Open Monday through Saturday from 10 a.m. to 5 p.m.; closed Sunday. Quite an experience.

Church of San Francisco

Probably the most beautiful church in Lima is the baroque Church of San Francisco, on Jirón Lampa, two blocks from the Plaza de Armas. Completed in 1674, the structure has strong Arabic influences in its design. When inside, look closely at the gold monstrance that was made in Cuzco almost 300 years ago. The jewels you will see are quite real. There are also a number of famous paintings in the church. The adjoining monastery, which admits men visitors only, is famous for its tilework and paneled ceiling. Open every day from 10 a.m. to 1 p.m. and 2 to 5 p.m.

Museum of Anthropology and Archeology

This museum (tel. 62-3282), dedicated to the study of the aborigines of Peru, is located in the small Plaza Bolívar in the suburb of Pueblo Libre. Don't confuse this plaza with the much larger plaza of the same name near the Plaza de Armas.

On display here are ancient woven capes, shawls, and ceramic objects that predate the Incas. But there are Inca relics here, as well as artifacts from the Paracas, Chavin, and Pachacamac cultures. The oldest, the Paracas, date back to 500 B.C., which would make them contemporaries of the ancient Greeks about the time of their Golden Age. In the Inca room is a fine scale model of Machú Picchú, the famous "Lost City" of the Incas that was not discovered until 1911. This museum is a must as preparation for your upcoming trip to the Inca country of Cuzco and Machú Picchú. But even if you have been there already, the museum will help you better appreciate what you witnessed. Hours are 10 a.m. to 6 p.m. every day except Sunday, when the museum is open from 9 a.m. to 1 p.m. Admission is $1, plus 65¢ more for permission to take photos. To get here, take the Pueblo Libre colectivo from Plaza San Martín. You will be dropped at Avenida Brasil, three blocks from the museum. Or you can hop a slower omnibus at the Plaza San Martín and ask to be dropped at the museum. Cabs are $1 each way.

Dining Note: For a fine lunch or snack break during your museum hopping, stop at the modern, multilevel **Restaurant Piselli,** Calle La Mar 215, corner of Avenida Brasil, one block from where the colectivo drops you. Through clever use of plants and water, an outdoor feel has been created. Sit at a mezzanine table overlooking the lower-level dining area and order the corvina ($3.25), whitefish in an asparagus sauce; or the cordero ($4.35), lamb in a wine sauce. Steaks (churrasco) are good values at $4.50 per platter. If you're snacking, try the tortas (tarts) for $1.50. Say hello to owner Alberto Piselli. Open from 11 a.m. to midnight Monday through Saturday, on Sunday to 4 p.m.

Museo Arqueologico Rafael Larco Herrera

Ten minutes by colectivo from the Museum of Anthropology and Archeology is the famous privately owned Herrera Museum, at Avenida Bolívar 1515 (tel. 61-1312)—noted for its erotica (artistic, of course). But for us, the room on the main level directly ahead of the entrance is what makes the museum well worth a visit. Twelve 2,000-year-old mummies, some shockingly "alive," are in glass cases, most with their faces exposed. Incredibly, parts of some faces are perfectly preserved, while others are hideous skulls. Most are dressed in ceremonial garb. One appears to have had a fatal chest wound, perhaps from a spear. Several child mummies too.

Aside from the mummies, there are invaluable gold and silver jewelry pieces from Indian civilizations in an adjoining room that is sealed by a massive metal door. You enter into what appears to be a vault—and that's what it is. Check out the huge colorless pearl on the left. Another room (the one on your left from the courtyard) has a fine collection of rocks, minerals, and ceramic pieces.

And now (sound of trumpets in the distance), time for the erotica. After exploring the three rooms on the main level, head back outside and follow the wide brick pathway down to the lower level where a matron understanding your needs is on duty; upon request she will unlock the magic doorway to the X-ratings of the past. At last you are in the midst of hundreds of rather small ceramic pieces, most showing Indian figures in various stages—and contortions—of coupling (animals, apparently, were much favored).

You enter the museum grounds from Avenida Bolívar and wind your way up the brick pathway to the entrance. The charge is a steep $4.50, but remember that it's privately owned. Hours are 9 a.m. to 1 p.m. and 3 to 6 p.m.; closed Sunday.

Getting to the Herrera Museum: Take the green-and-white microbus 37 which runs along the Avenida Emancipación. It will be marked "Clement." Ask to be dropped at the Museo Rafael Larco Herrera, a three-mile trip. From the Museum of Anthropology and Archeology (ten minutes away), take the Avenida Bolívar colectivo at the Plaza Bolívar, checking first to make sure it goes past the Herrera Museum. If you're heading to the Museum of Anthropology and Archeology from the Herrera Museum, take any colectivo heading to your right as you leave the grounds. Exit at the Plaza Bolívar.

Museo del Oro del Perú

The Spanish colonial era is re-created magnificently in this gold museum where perfectly restored armor, cannon, pistols, swords, and other armaments are handsomely displayed.

The lower level is devoted to the artifacts of Inca and Indian civilizations, with spears and shields and marvelously crafted gold and jewelry pieces imaginatively mounted. Some of the pieces go back 3,000 years.

It is a showplace of a museum (tel. 35-2917). Highly recommended. Hours are 3 to 7 p.m. Monday through Friday, 9 a.m. to 1 p.m. and 3 to 7 p.m. on Saturday; closed Sunday. Admission is $4.

Getting to the Museo del Oro: Located on Alonso de Molina in the suburb of Monterico, near Miraflores, it is a two-colectivo trip here. First, take a colectivo from the Plaza San Martín to the center of Miraflores. Ask to be dropped where you can get the colectivo to Monterico. Tell the driver of the second colectivo "Museo del Oro, por favor," and he will leave you a block or so from the museum. Total cost: About 50¢ each way. You can also take bus 2 to Miraflores in front of the Cine Colón (near Plaza San Martín). Get off in Miraflores at the intersection of Arequipa and Angamos. On Angamos, catch microbus 72 to Monterico and ask to get off at the Museo del Oro (50¢ round trip). A cab from Miraflores will run you about $5 and take 15 minutes. The trip by public transportation is about one hour.

National Museum of Art

The magnificent art of ancient Peru, which dates from the Paracas civilization of 2,500 years ago, is on display at the National Museum, located on the Paseo Colón near the Plaza Grau. The building was the official palace of the International Exhibition held here in 1868. Instead of having the structure leveled, the government made it a repository of the country's artistic treasures. You will find silver goblets, ceramics, tapestries, and Spanish-colonial furniture, as well as delicately worked jewelry and ivory fans. The exhibits include artwork from every period in Peru's history—right up to the excellent collection of contemporary art.

Open from 9 a.m. to 6 p.m. every day but Monday, when it's closed; open on Friday until 8 p.m. Admission is $1.75.

READER'S MUSEUM SUGGESTION: "If you find large museums overwhelming, check out the **Museo Amano**. This small archeological museum in Miraflores houses a fine collection of Inca and pre-Inca artifacts in two rooms. There are woven shawls, tapestries, ceramics, and Inca jewelry. It's an excellent orientation before visiting the larger museums or going on to Machú Picchú. The collection can be seen Monday through Friday by appointment only. There are hourly tours (tel. 41-2909)" (Leigh Infield, New York, N.Y.).

SPORTS IN LIMA: Lima is one of the few cities south of Mexico where you can take in a **bullfight** on a regularly scheduled basis. Some cities in South America permit an occasional bullfight event, but Lima schedules one every Sunday and holiday afternoon in October and November at the **Plaza Acho** bullring, located in the older Rimac section just across the Rimac River. The toreadors, imported from Spain, pack the stadium for every event and, predictably, are absolute heroes in Peru. Posters all over the city will remind you of the coming attraction.

Despite their high price ($7 to $13), tickets are much in demand, and are available at most hotels. Be sure to ask for seats in the shade. To reach the ring, take a taxi ($1.25), or walk via Abancay across the Rimac River Bridge. The stadium is visible from the span, which links center-city Lima with a poorer section of the city.

Cockfighting

If you have a strong tolerance for blood, you might like to look in on a cockfight, which attracts high-stakes gamblers to the matches. A popular ring is the **Coliseo de Gallos Sandia,** Sandia 150, near University Park. The specially trained birds have razor-sharp curved blades strapped to one foot and they fight to the death. The crowds shriek as they do in the U.S. at bloody prizefights. Admission is $1.50 to $2. The blood-letting starts at 8:30 p.m. on weekends (Friday, Saturday, and Sunday).

If the sight of blood makes you queasy, the action is much tamer at the **Gallo de Oro** ring, Avenidas Tayacaja and Guillermo Dansey, not far from the Plaza 2 de Mayo. Here the cocks fight with just their beaks. Check the newspaper *El Commercio* for the schedule.

The Track

Easily one of the finest tracks in the world is the **Hipodromo de Monterico,** located 30 minutes outside of Lima. Owned by the fashionable Jockey Club, the track holds races all year round on Saturday, Sunday, and holidays starting at 1:30 p.m., and Tuesday and Thursday nights at 6 p.m. Admission is 50¢ to $1 and the minimum bet is 50¢.

Take a colectivo from the Plaza San Martín (50¢) or a cab ($2.25). On race days a special bus, marked "Hipodromo," departs from the plaza too.

Futbol

In Peru, as elsewhere south of the border, soccer is the national sport, and every weekend throughout the year 45,000 frantic fans jam the **Estadio Nacional,** which offers seats for $1.50 and up, $3 and up for better seats.

Take the suburban colectivo from Plaza San Martín, which passes the stadium. You can easily walk here from any point downtown, though.

A PERSONAL COMMENT. On August 31, 1969, we had the pleasure of being in Lima on the Sunday Peru beat Argentina in Buenos Aires to qualify for the World Cup in Mexico. Never have we witnessed such unrestrained and spontaneous celebrations. It seemed that everyone piled into cars (some with as many as a dozen passengers), honked horns, screamed, and waved Peruvian flags in a communal spirit of national pride. This kept up all day and all night.

Folklorico

For a dip into Peruvian folklore via music and dance, catch a folklorico show on Monday evenings at the **Teatro Municipal,** Jirón Ica 323; on Tuesday evenings at **La Cabaña** theater. We're partial to the marinera, a mating dance marked by a handkerchief in the hand. The cheapest seats at the Teatro Municipal are up near the rafters ($2.35). Seats downstairs run $3 to $3.75. Locally popular is the delightful folkloric show that goes up Wednesday, Friday, and Saturday evenings at 9 p.m. at a small restaurant called **Wifala.** The $3 admission includes a beer.

READERS' SIGHTSEEING TIP: "Don't miss the Folklorico Show in the **Crillon's Skyroom.** Make reservations. Cover charge is $6.25 for the continuous 3½-hour show starting at 9 p.m. every night except Monday. If you don't want a meal ($13 each, approximately), you can sit in the lounge and nurse a pisco sour ($3.25). Arrive at 8 p.m. to ensure good seats" (Norm and Heather Rath, Ontario, Canada).

4. EXCURSIONS AND TOURS

PORT OF CALLAO: Peru's largest port is Callao, eight miles to the west of Lima, and the most interesting attraction here is the famous **Real Felipe Fortress,** which at one time protected this city and Lima from British raids. Sir Francis Drake sacked Callao in the 16th century, but failed to get past the fortress on the road to Lima. This was also where the Spanish royalists made their last stand —which lasted two years—against Bolívar and his liberators in 1824–1826.

There is a small museum in the fortress called the **Museo Histórico Militar.** It is usually open on Tuesday, Wednesday, and Friday from 9 a.m. until noon and 3 to 5 p.m.; and on Saturday and Sunday from 2 to 5:30 p.m.; closed Monday and Thursday. The hours of admission frequently change, so call first to get the latest schedule (tel. 29-1505). Admission free.

Callao is easily reached by microbus 71 in 30 minutes from Nicolas de Pierola in front of the Bolívar Hotel. The bus marked "Lima–La Punta," which charges 30¢ each way, stops at a sign reading: "Lima–Callao–La Punta–Linea 56." An alternative is to travel via colectivo (Lima–Callao) for 30¢. Pick it up near the Bolívar.

At the southern tip of Callao is **La Punta** ("The Point"), a popular summer (December to February) resort, noted for its many fine summer homes and ocean swimming.

AN EXCURSION TO THE PACHACAMAC RUINS AND MUSEUM:

These stunning ruins, 20 miles south of Lima in the Lurin Valley, were once pyramids built by pre-Inca Indian tribes to satisfy an omnipotent god. Upon the same structures the Incas later constructed their own temples and pyramids dedicated to the sun god and to the moon, which they filled with silver and gold objects. Sadly, the conquistadores, led by Francisco Pizarro's brother, Gonzalo, killed the Inca priests, destroyed the religious idols, and looted the temples.

Much, however, of the era's history has now been pieced together by archeological discoveries in this century. Indeed, so many relics and artifacts were uncovered that a museum was erected on the site to house them. Mummies, pottery, original woven textiles, and many silver objects can be seen here. Hours are 10 a.m. to 5 p.m. daily, and admission is $1.

CBS Tours, Miguel Dasso 274 in San Isidro (tel. 70-4090), operates daily tours leaving at 9:30 a.m. to the area for $18 per person, which includes a private auto tour to both the museum and the ruins. Other services offering a similar tour for the same price include **Lima Tours** at Jirón de la Unión 1040; **Travelex,** Colmena 757; **Receptour,** at Rufino Tourico 889; and **Condor Travel,** at Colmena 677 (second floor).

To save money, you can go on your own. Buses leave from Plaza Santa Catalina every half hour, and the one-way cost is about $1.50. Get off at kilometer 31 of the Southern Panamerican Hwy. There is an admission of $2. The trip takes around an hour.

EL PUEBLO HYATT HOTEL (LA GRANJA AZUL):

This smashing restaurant resort complex (tel. 35-0777) has long been a favorite of ours. La Granja Azul, as many natives still call it, is located on the road to Chosica in Santa Clara and is well worth the ten-mile trip. Once simply a restaurant specializing in exotic cocktails and chicken-only dishes, it has evolved into a planned Peruvian village-cum-resort, embracing a 250-room Spanish-colonial inn complete with tennis courts, swimming pools, horseback riding, and a full health club with sauna, gymnasium, and bowling alley. A golf course is open to guests. A funicular railway carries guests from the restaurant area to secluded cottages with private swimming pools.

This newly created village features a multitude of shops (Silvania Prints and Artesanía have outlets here), discos, a movie house, piano bar, three restaurants, museum, conference hall, and even a chapel. Plus marvelous vistas of the Andes —and all of this in brilliant sunshine most of the year (no garua here).

If you can't stay overnight, plan a Sunday day trip to see the folklore show! The grounds surely are worth it and you can dine in one of six dining rooms in the restaurant, where you can order unlimited barbecued chicken (excellent indeed) for $7.50. Chicken is actually what La Granja Azul built its reputation on, and some 30 years later it is still barbecued the same way—on hickory logs. It's the best chicken we've eaten anywhere. No limit on salad—nice bonus. If you like, you can drink your day away; huge potent drinks are served in coconut husks, among other exotic containers. But prices are steep—up to $3 for cocktails. All breads and pastries are baked on the premises and are first rate.

Staying Overnight

Doubles at El Pueblo run $100 (tax included). Singles are $85. All rooms come with private bath. Bungalows are $100 for two people, $110 for four people. For full American Plan (all three meals), add an additional $25 to the room rate. Modified American Plan (breakfast and dinner) is an additional $15. A continental breakfast will cost $4; American breakfast, $5.

On Friday and Saturday evenings, the nightlife pulses frenetically when the under-30 set moves in.

Getting There

There is now a free shuttle-bus service to and from El Pueblo, with pickup at many of our recommended hotels (cost: $1 each way). Check your hotel for the schedule. Another inexpensive way to reach this resort complex is via bus 202V marked "Santa Clara," which leaves from the Parque Universitario, not far from the Plaza San Martín. It costs $1 round trip. It will drop you in Santa Clara, a short walk from the village. A taxi at $7 each way is high, but five passengers can share the cost.

NASCA: More and more tourists are drawn each year to the magical lines of Nasca—the site where an ancient civilization carved, with absolute precision, huge animals, birds, human figures, and geometric lines into a rock plateau that extends for miles. Visible only from the air, these amazing drawings and lines (known as von Däniken's runways) suggests that a highly developed knowledge of hydraulic engineering and astronomy existed in pre-Inca times.

We have taken this excursion and can only share our absolute awe in viewing this amazing work of art. We promise you that the experience will haunt you long after your trip is over. Were the lines actually an airstrip? Did a knowledge of aeronautics exist in pre-Inca times? If so, can we draw the conclusion that a civilization as sophisticated technologically as our own, or more so, existed so many thousands of years ago?

Getting There

Numerous tours are now available to the area. **Lima Tours** offers a three-day package that includes viewing the lines and sightseeing in Ica and Paracas, the nearest villages, at a cost of $325 per person.

The budget traveler can put together a do-it-yourself excursion by taking a colectivo from offices in the side streets of Avenida Abancay (around no. 1000). They leave for both Ica and Nasca at 4 and 8 a.m., and 2 p.m. Cost to Ica: $12; to

Nasca, $18. It's possible to do the trip all in one day by leaving at 4 a.m., but it's a very long day indeed. Driving time to Nasca is seven hours alone, and there can be delays in waiting for the colectivos to fill (they prefer to leave with six people, although you can offer to pay the extra fare if you're only one person short). Call Comité 4, Leticia 591 (tel. 28-8608).

You can also bus it to Nasca. The Roggero, Ormeño, and Morales Moralitos bus lines have regular service. Check with the company for current schedules and be sure to pick up your ticket a day in advance. **Ruggero,** not our first choice, is located at Avenida Grau 711 (tel. 28-9624), **Morales Moralitos** at Avenida Grau 141 (tel. 27-6310), and **Carlos** at Zavala 145 (tel. 28-2099). Minimum fare to Nasca is $7.50; the trip is seven hours one way.

Staying Over

For big-splurge living, check into the new **Las Dunas** resort, just three hours by car from Lima on the Panamerican Hwy. in Ica. A lush oasis among sand dunes, Las Dunas serves as a center for those wishing to spend a few days in the area to view the lines, sample local wines (Ica is known for the manufacture of red, rosé, and white wines), and check out the important archeological sights and museums in both Ica and Paracas. Best of all, the resort has direct flights over the Nasca lines from their own airstrip. Other pluses: Swimming pools, tennis courts, and horseback riding. A sparkling white Spanish structure, Las Dunas has ultramodern doubles at $75 and singles at $60. For reservations and current price changes, write: P.O. Box 4410, Lima, Peru (tel. 42-4180 or 42-3090), or call American Express in the U.S. (tel. toll free 800/327-7737).

The **Montecarlo Motel** has clean modern rooms, a swimming pool, and a restaurant for $33 double. They also offer flight service over Nasca. Three companies offer these flights. They are Montecarlo, Condor, and Troica. The rate is $50 per person, but in the off-season you can bargain a bit.

JUNGLE VISITS:

Visits to Peru's jungle outposts have become increasingly more popular in the last few years. Iquitos is the number one destination, with Pucallpa second.

Iquitos

Iquitos, 1,000 miles from Lima, sits on the Amazon River 2,300 miles upriver from the Atlantic Ocean. Iquitos is reached by flying one of **Faucett's** nonstop flights from Miami (three days a week) or from Lima (two flights daily). The city has existed since the mid-18th century and has had a roller-coaster existence much like its sister city, Manaus, on the Brazilian Amazon. At its height, during the rubber boom, huge steamers loaded at its docks and the city had magnificent hotels and an opera house. When it became cheaper to buy rubber in Malaysia, the boom died and with it the glory of Iquitos. The city is certainly worth strolling through (bring lots of insect repellent), especially the Plaza de Armas and the market. The **Turista Hotel** (government owned) is tops in town and its bar a real hangout. A **Holiday Inn** is outside of town. Most visitors head out of Iquitos to **Explorama Lodge,** 50 miles downriver. It offers clean and comfortable accommodations and surprisingly good food. Tours from Explorama to visit the jungle and its inhabitants (animal and tribal) are first-rate. Write for information to **Exploraciones Amazonicas,** Box 446, Iquitos, Perú. Leave yourself lots of time because mail is slow.

Another popular spot to stay is the new, modern **Amazon Lodge,** a village of thatch-roofed huts on the Momon River, a tributary of the Amazon. Amazon Lodge is only a 90-minute ride downriver from Iquitos. Trips from here are also well organized and well run. For more information, write: Lima Tours, Box

4340, Lima, Perú; or Amazon Village, 5805 N.W. Blue Lagoon Dr., Miami, FL 33126 (tel. 305/261-3024). Faucett Airlines offers package tours from Miami and others from Lima. You should contact them at Suite 450, 1150 N.W. 72nd Ave., Miami, FL 33126.

Pucallpa

Pucallpa, on the River Ucayali, is Peru's second most popular jungle destination and in the center of its oil-exploration activities. Use the city as a jumping-off point for trips along the nearby lake which was once part of the river. Close by is a village lived in by the Shipibos tribe. Their huts are made of open-sided wood and palm leaf, and are raised from the ground to avoid snakes. Barter for one of their unusual glazed pots or an eight-foot blowgun. Other tribes live nearby. Although a frontier town in the midst of the jungle, Pucallpa is only a one-hour flight from Lima. Contact Faucett for more information.

There are several lodgings in Pucallpa, including a government tourist hotel at Jr. San Martín 552. The best restaurant is in the **Hostal Inambu.**

HUANCAYO: A three-day excursion, well worth the time if you have it, is the 192-mile trip to Huancayo, a typical mountain village 10,000 feet up in the Andes, that has the most famous market in Peru. At the first sign of dawn on Sunday, the Indians come in from the countryside laden with alpaca rugs, hats and slippers, food, pottery, woven baskets, gourds, and jewelry. The goods are spread on the ground in the town square and then the bargaining—serious, low key, persistent—begins. You will hear little of the shrill wrangling common to the Rome and Paris flea markets. Instead, voices are kept low and conversation is limited to numbers representing soles. The price is given, the customer counters, the dealer drops his price, and the deal is consummated.

Getting to Huancayo is much of the excitement. The train in its nine-hour journey from Lima winds its way through the highest reaches of the Peruvian Andes and at one point rolls along at a height of 15,800 feet. Some airplanes cruise at that altitude, so little wonder that the railway brags that its tracks are the "highest in the world."

You will cross over no fewer than 59 bridges and through 66 tunnels to reach Huancayo.

Entur, at Portal del Zela in Lima, will make reservations for you to stay at the **Turista Hotel.** Rates were $28 for doubles and $20 for singles the last time we investigated, but check for recent changes.

We recommend that you leave on Saturday and return on Monday. A train leaves Desamparados Station at 7:40 a.m. every morning (except Sunday) for Huancayo in the winter (on Tuesday, Thursday, and Saturday in the summertime). Return service is just as frequent. Schedules change frequently, so check with the station prior to your trip. Desamparados Station is located behind the Presidential Palace, near the Plaza de Armas. Round-trip fare is approximately $10 for first class and $6 for second class. Try to get Buffet-Coach for $2 extra; the comfort is worth it. Get your ticket a day before your trip at the station.

If you prefer, any travel agency will make arrangements for you. If you cannot make it to Huancayo and yet are interested in seeing an Indian mountain village, make sure you include the market in **Pisac,** near Cuzco (see the next chapter).

THE BEACHES: The best nearby swimming resort is **La Herradura,** a short distance from the suburb of Miraflores, on the Pacific. Between October and May there is swimming virtually every day, and even in the winter (June to September) there are days warm enough for an ocean dip. While not a major resort, it nevertheless has a good deal of physical beauty, mainly stemming from the mountains that close in from east and south. From Miraflores, hop a taxi ($3.50) and you will be at Herradura in less than 20 minutes. A bus (30¢) marked "Playa" leaves regularly from the Plaza San Martín (summer only, January to March). But avoid weekends, when roads and beaches are jam-packed. Other closer beaches are **Costa Verde, Barranco,** and **Chorrillos.** But Herradura is probably the best.

Avid swimmers should head to **Chosica,** 25 miles east of Lima in the Rimac Valley, where there is swimming all year round. Many wealthy Peruvians have vacation homes here and it's a popular weekend retreat. And it is a good way to escape the garua (June through August) mist in Lima.

Chosica can be reached by colectivo (catch one on Nicolas de Pierola) or by bus 200A which leaves from the 1500 block on Nicolas de Pierola. You can also hop the train to Huancayo, which leaves from Desamparados Station daily except Sunday at 7:40 a.m. and stops at Chosica. You pick up the return train at 3:30 p.m. One-way fare is about $1. Lima Tours, as well as a number of other travel agencies, offers bus tours to Chosica and to the nearby Cajamarquilla Indian ruins, except from December to March, when the summer temperatures make the trip uncomfortable.

READER'S TOURING SUGGESTION: "The trip to **Chosica** is worthwhile even in winter (July and August), but it helps to know where to go after getting off the train, because there is no place to swim or sunbathe close to the station. There is a **Parque Sol y Aire** some distance outside of town, where there is a soccer field, a food concession, a swimming pool, and plenty of open space, both sunny and shady, to enjoy a picnic or a stroll or just to enjoy nature. Admission is about $1 and to get there you cross the bridge across the river from the railroad station, go uphill to the next main road, and get on a colectivo (car or small bus) in the same direction as the train was going. Fare is about 50¢" (George Condoyannis, New York, N.Y.).

TOUR SERVICES: Lima Tours and **Receptour** are the recommended services. Both operate half-day tours of modern and colonial Lima (about $11), and excursions to Pachacamac ($18), Chosica ($15), and to mountain villages across to Peru's Central Hwy. ($35 per person in groups of four or more).

5. LIMA AFTER DARK

For a quick orientation to Lima's nightlife, check the Sunday edition of *El Comercio,* Lima's large Spanish-language daily, which lists cultural and sporting events for the upcoming week. The English-language newspaper, *Lima Times,* does not have as comprehensive a listing of cultural events as *El Comercio.*

TEATRO MUNICIPAL: For fine concerts and ballet, head to the Municipal Theater, Jirón Ica 323, near Cailloma, three blocks from the Plaza de Armas. Prices range from $4 to $10. A good balcony seat runs $6.

A second hall for concerts is the **Teatro Segura,** Plazuela del Teatro, two blocks from the Teatro Municipal. Check *El Comercio* for programs.

AMAUTA ARENA: This indoor arena on Avenida Venezuela in Chacra Ríos seats 9,000 and has diverse bookings ranging from the Moscow Ballet to the circus and Peruvian festivals. Check the Sunday edition of *El Comercio* for programs.

ENGLISH-LANGUAGE FILMS: First-run U.S. films in English are shown in about 12 downtown theaters. Prices range from $1 (balcony) to $1.75 (best orchestra seat). Seats are reserved. Most of the better movie houses are now located in Miraflores. They are very crowded, so go early. There are also English-language films on TV.

WHERE THE MUSIC IS: Lima has a number of late-evening clubs where the dancers and bands are equally uninhibited. The suburban clubs swing the most, but there are two downtown spots that are well worth checking out—the **Skyroom** in the Hotel Crillon, and the beautiful Bar 1900. Spend one evening at the Skyroom, where three rotating bands keep the dance floor crowded until 1 a.m. When you're tired of dancing, look out over the skyline of Lima through the panoramic windows on three sides.

A Budget Tip: When you get off the elevator on the 20th floor, stroll casually straight ahead toward the couches, where you can lounge comfortably much of the evening for the price of a single drink (about $3.50 plus tax). If you sit at a table, you will be expected to drink more.

A Special Treat

Not to be missed is the new **Bar 1900,** Galería el Centro Belen 1030 (near Jirón de la Unión and the Plaza San Martín). An evening here will be long remembered. The bar is the ambitious project of two outgoing young men, Raphael and Ricardo, who have faithfully restored one of Lima's most impressive examples of early Republican architecture—the Mansion Barreda—turning it into an elegant concert salon, bar, and restaurant. From the moment you step off busy Avenida Belen and enter through the giant oak doors, you will be transported into another world. Built in 1915, the mansion, which has been declared an official historical sight, will captivate you. The impressive open courtyard has been converted into a special dining area. The owners have shopped Lima's antique shops for Viennese chairs and tables to complement the old-world elegance of this richly tiled patio area.

Numerous rooms open off the courtyard, now housing artesanías shops which are open to the public daily until 9:30 p.m. The bar is off to the right (note the art deco chairs as you enter). Settle into a cushy sofa and take in the ornate framed mirrors, stained-glass windows, and oak paneling. Order a pisco sour (one of the best bargains around, as they are only $1.50 per drink) and get in the mood to hear authentic Peruvian music, performed by Lima's most celebrated groups. Relax and let the music flow over you. It's like listening to a concert in your own private dining room. The bar is open from 1 to 10 p.m. daily. The concert, for which there is a $1 cover charge, starts promptly at 7:30 p.m. Longer hours are anticipated during the peak tourist months, so call to check the schedule (tel. 23-3590). Say hello to Raphael and Ricardo, who deserve "kudos" for bringing this delightful entertainment experience to downtown Lima.

The Créole Clubs

Lima really comes alive for us in the Créole clubs, where the rhythms, dancers, décor, and cuisine all come together in one cacophonous wonder. These clubs get going late—usually after 9 p.m.—and wind up near dawn. The food is typically Peruvian, particularly the anticuchos de corazones (skewered hearts), corvina (whitefish), and various churrasco (steak) and pollo (chicken) dishes.

Let's start with **La Casa de Edith,** on Avenida del Ejercito (cuadra 6), Miraflores. Edith offers a 2½-hour show nightly at 10:30 p.m. that has the audience cheering for more. Cynics might call it vaudeville with a Latin accent, but the way the audience is drawn into the festivities makes it distinctive.

In one dance called the alcatraz, two black couples in típico garb chase around after each other trying to ignite a cloth tailpiece with a lighted candle. But the climax comes when a member of the audience is invited to grab a candle and start chasing. Larry Hulack of our team did that one night and he hasn't been quite the same since. Also, there are the inevitable comics, singers, and folk dancers, all appropriately tireless.

Invariably jammed on Friday and Saturday evenings, Edith is best and less expensive during the week (it is closed Sunday). Come around 10 p.m. There's a special $16 package price that includes the steep cover charge ($6.50 per person on weekends, $5.50 during the week), one drink, and a full-course meal (three dishes, dessert, and coffee). Can't beat that! If you plan to dine elsewhere, you can get one drink and the show for $10. Drinks are high: beer is $1.75, pisco sours run $2.25, and whisky costs $3. It is possible to order dinner à la carte; however, there is little savings when the cover charge and price of drinks are added to your tab. Edith is not cheap, but worth every inti. There's dancing too, in the dim, wood-paneled room. If the weather's warm, leave your jacket and tie home. Informality reigns.

Besides Edith, you should consider two other clubs nearby offering the same style of entertainment. **La Palizada,** at Avenida del Ejercito 800 (tel. 41-0552), and **Sachun,** at Avenida del Ejercito 657 (tel. 410-123), where dancing, handclapping, and merriment accompany the escabiche and mariscos. Both have Créole shows with $10 minimums. Another good choice is **El Otro Sítio** in Barranco.

A final Créole club—one preferred by many Peruvians—is **El Palmero,** in the San Felipé Shopping Center in San Felipé, just outside San Isidro. Smaller and half the price of Edith, Palmero attracts a large singles crowd. The music beats with the same uninhibited power. Marvelous fun. Take the San Felipé colectivo from Plaza San Martín and ask to be dropped at the Palmero. A cab will cost $2.

For folkloric music, head to **Hatuchay,** just across the river on Trujillo. Admission is $2 and drinks run about $1.50. Although it caters to tour groups, the music is great and represents not only Peru but all of South America. There's plenty of room for dancing, so don't be shy.

LIMA AFTER MIDNIGHT: The fast-moving and fast-spending young set gravitates to a number of suburban clubs, largely in San Isidro and Miraflores. The settings in most follow a rigid formula: dark, crowded, and echoing with the high decibels of hard rock, with an occasional Sinatra-type record thrown in. The pulsebeat picks up around midnight, and little wonder, since most of the clubs reverberate till dawn. Couples-only in many clubs.

Arizona Colt, a western-motif bar and discothèque in the Edificio El Pacífico, Miraflores, is a small, intimate saloon. Its small dance floor is bathed by strobe lights. Good music. Drinks start at $2.50. No minimum.

An interesting combination is the soda fountain and discothèque at **La Miel,** at Avenida José Pardo 120, downstairs in the shopping arcade. There are two rooms, the first of which houses the ice-cream parlor and is dimly lighted. There is a counter and booths. Milkshakes ($2) and sundaes ($3.50) are served side by side with piña coladas and hard drinks. The back room is darker and more intimate. Both have dance floors.

A more traditional choice is **La Monella,** Diez Canseco 148, Miraflores. As you descend into the discothèque you find yourself at the circular mirrored bar. You have your choice of dance floors: the left side of the disco is larger and holds more people, and the right is more intimate. Couples only. Drinks start at $3.

Another dark choice is the small **El Tunel,** near El Suche Shopping Center. The red lights guide you along the tunnel and downstairs to the postage-stamp dance floor, which is surrounded by booths. Curtains keep out every ray of light. There are no strobe lights either. Dark!

El Escarabajo, Avenida Nicholas Arriola 270, Santa Catalina, sets the tempo for the youth set nightly, rising to a crescendo well after midnight. Gazing down on the circular bar is a rather benevolent-looking beetle (el escarabajo himself). The dance area is dark indeed, and bodies could hardly be pressed more tightly. Prices are steep—$3.50 for a drink, plus a $6-per-person minimum on weekends. Look for the beetle (more like a ladybug, really) outside.

On Avenida Canabal in Corpac is another high-velocity club, **Peppermint,** where the meet-'em game is the only game. Hard-rock music of course, and mucho singles. Drinks are a high $3, but who's to prevent you from nursing it along? Nearby is **Le Popol,** almost a twin—dark and loud.

Heading back toward Arequipa, near the Todos Shopping Center in an arcade is the **Club Ebony,** Las Magnolias, with a downstairs club and an upstairs restaurant. Enjoy elegant dining to soft piano music upstairs where the specialty of the house is lomo Oscar (beef served with artichoke stuffed with lobster, $7) and French cuisine. The restaurant is paneled in rich wood, with plush brown velvet chairs in the lounge area. Nurse a drink at the bar and enjoy the music. Then head downstairs for the action.

To reach the Todos Shopping Center, grab a colectivo at the Plaza San Martín and exit at the Petroperu gas station (3300 block of Arequipa). Walk left four blocks.

In San Isidro is the **Club Las Rocas,** at Rivera Navarete 821 (tel. 42-0960). Here the décor is strictly jungle, with waterfalls and primitive masks. Head downstairs, pass over the bridge and waterfall, and enter the intimate romantic club. The photos of nude nymphets remind you that this place has the same owner as Ebony. There are stained-glass windows with tropical-bird designs.

Another youthful nightspot is **Jubilee,** at Miguel Dasso 143 (tel. 40-8221) in San Isidro, near the Todo Fresco restaurant. Formerly the popular Manzana Club, Jubilee is packed on weekends with a college-age clientele. Enter beyond a long walkway from the street.

The most action-packed nightspot in the suburbs is neither a disco nor cocktail lounge. It's a pizzería! A pizzería with nightly musical shows, that is. **Mediterraneo,** at Camino Real 111 in San Isidro (next door to the Astoria Hotel in the same Centro Comercial Shopping Center that houses three of our suburban restaurant choices), packs them in on weekends and draws an attractive crowd weekdays as well. This is the place to see and be seen. Each night there is a different musical offering. At the time of our visit you could sample Criolla music on Monday night; Mexican on Tuesday; international and jazz, Wednesday through Saturday; Latin sounds on Sunday. Shows start at 10 p.m.; however, it is advisable to come earlier to get a table (the restaurant opens at 7 p.m.). The bar is always crowded and the action goes on into the wee hours with customers testing their vocal cords on their favorite ballads. There is no cover charge for all this merriment. The menu advertises the Mediterraneo's fare as "pizzas, pastas, and pop." The pizza is undistinguished by our standards, but then no one seems to pay too much attention to the food. We had a decent-size mozzarella pizza that filled three people nicely for $7.50. A small pie is $4, as is lasagne. A pisco sour costs $2.50, and whisky, $3. Lots of fun!

A TOUCH OF JAZZ: One of our favorite nightspots in Lima is **Satchmo,** at Calle La Paz 538 (tel. 44-1753), a jazz club in Miraflores, set in a private house in typical New Orlean French Quarter décor. Bourbon Street signs and photos of famous jazz figures adorn the club. There's a bar and restaurant, and a bandstand for shows. Louis Armstrong played here, as did the likes of Lionel Hampton, Dave Brubeck, Dizzy Gillespie, and Benny Goodman. The bar is open from 6 p.m.; the shows start at 10:30 p.m.

CAFÉ TEATRO: A popular form of entertainment in Lima these days is café teatro. Similar to our own small café theaters, the café teatro serves up comedy sketches, short dramas, and musical revues while you sip a drink or a cup of coffee and nibble sandwiches or pastries. The price of admission is about $5. Much of the humor might escape you as the sketches are usually in Spanish; however, you can't help but enjoy the enthusiasm of the performers and audience. The night we visited, we caught a comedy team and acting troupe from Spain. The refreshments served at a café teatro are often native to the country of the performer. For example, we enjoyed Spanish meat pies for 40¢. Small round tables are clustered around a tiny stage, and the performers use piano accompaniment. There are several good café teatros in Miraflores: **Barrabas,** on Avenida Larca; **Roller Room,** at Cantuarias 175; and **La Tapada** and **Chiribiris.** A delightful way to spend an evening.

FOR MEN ONLY: Perhaps Lima's best-known club boasting attractive ladies of the evening is **Four Stars,** at Avenida República de Panamá 3560, in San Isidro. There is a bar area packed with hostesses eager to attend to you.

6. FOR SHOPPERS ONLY

Your best bargain bets in Lima are pottery, woodcarvings, native artwork, silver jewelry, trays, candlesticks, specialty flatware—and best of all, alpaca rugs, slippers, and hats. The designs, as you might expect, are largely of Inca influence. Remember that if an item is made of pure silver, the number 925 must appear on the back. Discounts of 10% or more are available. How? Read on.

Note: Store hours are 10 a.m. to 1 p.m. and 3 to 7 p.m. Monday through Saturday. Many souvenir shops are open later.

BARGAIN TOWN: Without question, the best shopping values in Lima are to be found at the **Centro Artesanal de Pueblo Libre,** a kind of shopping center run by Indian families in Pueblo Libre. There are 28 independent, semi-enclosed stalls that in all offer an enormous variety of gold, copper, and silver jewelry, alpaca rugs, leather goods, wall plaques, handcrafts, ponchos, and miscellany that should warm any bargain-hungry tourist's heart. Many items are handmade. Bring your Spanish dictionary: English is not spoken here. And service is sometimes downright indifferent. Be patient. It's worth it.

Several Tips

First, before buying item one, browse through the 28 stalls to get a feel for price and quality. Start on your left at Stall 1, called **Tumi** (most stalls have no names, only numbers), and then slowly wind your way around the horseshoe-shaped oval. Then return to those stalls that impressed you and start bargaining furiously. Which leads to. . . .

Tip 2: Getting a 10% discount is infant's work. Getting a 15% discount is worthy of an adult. And gaining 20% off will require the experience of an Orchard Street veteran. The Indian vendors—sometimes children of 8 or 9, since it is a family affair—are remarkably uncommunicative considering they're trying to make a sale. They might stare impassively at you saying nothing, so offer a counter price. Or perhaps you might hear a faint "no" and nothing more. Patience is the key to winning this game.

Tip 3: Be sure that alpaca rugs and garments are 100% alpaca and not mixed with wool. You can tell by feel and by price differentials (wool mixtures are at least 25% cheaper).

Tip 4: Since nothing is shipped from here, be sure to buy only what you can comfortably carry with you back to your hotel and aboard your flight home.

Tip 5: If the weather is foul, remember that you will be outdoors. Dress accordingly.

Finally, keep in mind that some stalls accept intis only and your traveler's checks might be useless. Fortunately, some of the vendors are smart enough to pocket any and all traveler's checks heading their way.

Prices, Hours, Etc.

What about prices? We knew you'd ask. You can pick up handcrafts for $2, and you can buy copper, gold, and silver jewelry for up to $900. A hand-sewn wool tie was reduced after bargaining from $4 to $3. We saw lovely copper earrings for $5, shoulder purses (alpaca and wool) for $6, hardwood bookends for $20, silver pendants for $5, leather coasters for 45¢ each (fine gifts), copper-framed mirrors for $15, block leather-covered footstools for $13, ponchos for $20, alpaca rugs from $80, alpaca sweaters from $15, and 18-karat gold bracelets for $150 on up.

The most professional booth is Tumi's (no. 1), but his prices are a shade high on some items. Be sure to comparison-shop. Luís Quísre at no. 22 speaks English "un poco."

Open seven days, from 6 a.m. to 10 p.m. To get there, hop the San Felipé bus from Plaza San Martín heading toward the airport (the shopping center is actually midway between San Isidro and the airport). Ask the driver to drop you at the center, which is on the main road, Avenida Marina, 1000 block. (Tell the driver "Cuadra Diez," pronounced "Kwadra Dee-ez.") A cab will run you about $3. It looks ramshackle and it is, what with goods sprawled about and sometimes blocking the walkways. But the trip here is recommended. It's a kick even if you buy zero.

Note: There's a similar but smaller shopping center about a half block nearer town. Stick to the one just mentioned. It's the third one as you head away from the city.

IN THE SUBURBS: **Artesanías Peruanas,** with four locations in Lima, is your best stop for handcrafts. Our favorite shop is located in a private home at Avenida Orrantia 610, San Isidro. Only the finest-quality, authentic Peruvian crafts are on display and for sale here. The atmosphere is rather like an art gallery, with beautifully hung exhibits of silverwork, enamel, rugs, knitted goods, and lovely ceramic pieces displayed in the garden. Prices are as good if not better than those downtown, and there's less high pressure too. Other branches are found at Avenidas Perez Aranibar 749 and José Pardos 450 in Miraflores and the market adjoining the Hotel Sheraton downtown. Credit cards accepted.

Nearby in a private home at Orrantia 1235, San Isidro, is **Exportadores del Inca.** They have an excellent selection of unusual handcrafts in ceramic, straw, and wool. Christmas decorations are lovely gifts, and they're for sale most of the year. Check out the unusual giraffe-head vases and the ceramic band of musicians. Unique items from the jungles of Peru. Open Monday through Friday from 8 a.m. to 4:30 p.m.

For fine pottery, woodcarvings, alpaca wool sweaters, and leather, try **Urpi,** at Avenida La Paz 592 in Miraflores, near Cesar's Hotel. It's a small shop brimming with Peruvian handcrafts of top quality.

For reproductions and authentic antique works of art, try **Arte Antiguo Peruano,** at Avenida La Paz 588 in Miraflores. There are many works from the Cuzco school of art available, including candelabras, mirrors, and frames.

A SHOPPING CENTER: A fine shopping center is **El Suche,** near the Condado Hotel. There are many shops and restaurants.

DOWNTOWN: There are several handcraft shops and many silver/jewelry shops on Jirón de la Unión between Plaza San Martín and Plaza de Armas. Many fancy silver shops looking as though they were on Fifth Avenue have opened here. Avoid them like the plague, as their wares also carry Tiffany-like pricetags. It's best to browse several shops because although the items look almost identical, there are nuances that might strike your fancy. And don't forget to bargain.

Inca Products, at Jirón de la Unión 838, seems like a good place to start your browsing, since they have a large selection of crafts. Alpaca rugs, which have gone way up in price and are not as well made as they once were, start at $75. Hand-knit sweaters with Peruvian motifs seem a good buy at $25. The **Old Cuzco** shop nearby at no. 823 had an excellent collection of silver. Candlesticks ($40), plates ($20), and a variety of bells, ashtrays, and the like make good gifts.

We've always had good luck with the values at the large **Casa Mas,** Jirón de la Unión 814, where you can get a wide variety of silver pins in striking Inca designs ranging in price from $17 to $40. There is another branch at Colmena 779. Recommended.

One of our favorite silver shops downtown is **Vicky's Artesanía,** at Colmena 783. Besides a wide variety of silver items, there are crystal displays worth your attention. Casa Mas is next door.

The latest addition along the Jirón de la Unión is **"La Gran Via"** shopping arcade—a fine browsing spot. We especially liked **Mabex,** a small boutique which features a fine assortment of alpaca sweaters in every style—V-necks, pullovers, and vests. With all the new arcades which are added each year, Lima is fast becoming a shopper's paradise.

The **Galería El Centro,** Avenida Belen near the Plaza San Martín, has 24 handcraft shops. They are all small and most are run by the artisans themselves. Knitted sweaters, scarves, and ponchos are good buys, as are gilt mirrors and gaily painted ones starting at $8. This gallery houses the Restaurant 1900 as well as an ice-cream parlor.

Two shops that especially caught our eye were on the other side of the Colmena. The **Art Nusta,** Jirón de la Unión 1045, is a long, narrow shop which carries all types of handcrafted items, including Inca-motif ties ($3), alpaca rugs from $25, ornately carved book racks, and woolen ponchos ($15 to $30). Puno bulls are $3, $5, and $8, depending on size. English is spoken here.

Next door is **Artesanías Huamanqaqa,** a shop which is spread over several floors and which has many handcrafted decorative items from all over Peru. These include Sulca wall hangings, Paucar weavings, and Quinua and Shipibo ceramics. The Krikor mirrors and attractive light fixtures are especially good buys.

FOR ANTIQUE-LOVERS: The large **Casa Paracas,** at Jirón de la Unión 713, houses many antiques (*antiguedades*), such as pottery and artifacts. Some items are claimed to be over 5,000 years old. There are wares in all price ranges. Come in and browse, but be careful about your purchases.

THE COLMENA: The best alpaca buys we have found in Lima are at the **Casa**

Inca, Colmena 727. Magnificent throw rugs are $10 and up; slippers, mittens, and caps start at $5. Good values, too, are the alpaca, silver, gourds, and handbags available here. Say hello to owner Blanca Fajardo de Cisneros.

High-quality cotton and linen yard goods in Inca and pre-Inca designs can be purchased at **Silvania Prints,** Colmena 714. Its owner, Silvia Lawson, who was educated in the U.S., also sells ready-made blouses, dresses, scarves, and bikinis, as well as tablecloths, placemats, and cloth bags. And she hasn't neglected men: ties, sport shirts, and swim trunks are fast-moving items. Prices are reasonable, considering the high quality. Blouses, for example, that might sell for $40 to $50 in the U.S. are $35 here. The designs are copies from the textile and ceramic artifacts found in Peru, and each is more exciting than the last. Ideal gifts are the print purses ($7.75), bright-colored scarves ($15.50), and ponchos ($25).

Two outlets of Silvania Prints are at the Cesar Hotel in Miraflores and at Avenida Conquistadores 905 in San Isidro.

Another highly recommended shop is the **Cuzco Palace,** across from the Hotel Crillon. Owned by the Cisnero family, it specializes in alpaca items and handsome leather-topped furniture. Good quality. Readers of this guide are promised a 10% discount. Remember, if you're shipping goods, get estimates on freight charges. Duty and freight can add considerably to your cost. Credit cards accepted.

And for the best in gemstones, such as aquamarine, topaz, and tourmaline, visit the **H. Stern** shop in the Bolívar Hotel (enter from Jirón Ocona). Also available are inexpensive tie pins (and other jewelry) in Inca designs. Other Stern shops are located in the Sheraton and Miraflores Cesar's hotels, and at the airport. H. Stern also sells replicas in silver and gold of museum figures, such as ceremonial masks and *collar de tumis* (necklaces).

Our final recommendation in this area is **Artesanía del Cuzco,** at Colmena 791 (with a branch at Jirón de la Unión 847). Here you can pick up items in gold or silver, alpaca and llama clothing, leather goods, and wood handcrafts.

READER'S SHOPPING SELECTION: "We would like to recommend the **Inca Wasi,** Colmena 522, across the street and to the right of the Crillon. We were served by the daughters of the proprietor. Both of them spoke fluent English and their manner was both pleasant and soft-sell. They explained the various qualities of the merchandise and spontaneously quoted the discounts available on different items. When we completed our purchases, the final price was exceptionally fair" (Alice Herb).

7. TRANSPORTATION NOTES AND HANDY DATA

COLECTIVOS: As we've mentioned before, those jitney-like taxis called colectivos are the best inexpensive way to move around Lima. They hold up to five passengers and have regular stops. When seats are available, the driver holds up one or more fingers to indicate how many passengers he can take on. Fares average about 50¢. The most important colectivo routes for our purposes are those that head from the Plaza San Martín out on Arequipa to the suburbs of Lince, Isidro, and Miraflores.

TAXIS: Most cabs lack meters here. Establish the price with the driver in advance, based on distance to be traveled. Don't be afraid to try bargaining for a better rate. It sometimes helps. The city has been divided into zones and rates are based on these. From one downtown area to another will usually cost under $3. To hail a cab, wave your arms and hiss loudly. It works. Evening rates are higher, as are those charged by taxis stationed in front of hotels.

BUSES: These are cheap (about 35¢), but terribly crowded most of the time. You will get accustomed to seeing passengers hanging on to the outside back railing at precarious angles. They do this not to avoid paying a fare, which is what does result, but rather because it is the only way to get aboard. Exceptions are the modern Volvo buses that run from Plaza San Martín along the Arequipa, particularly the S.M.–Arequipa no. 2 line. Bus stops are designated **Paradero de Omnibus.**

AUTO RENTALS: As in most South American cities, car rentals are relatively expensive. A two-year-old VW or Hillman will cost you $28 a day plus 20¢ a kilometer. Weekly rates are about $100 plus 15¢ a kilometer. Shop around and compare prices. Rental agencies include: **Turamerica,** Jirón Ocona 164 (tel. 27-6415); **Hertz Rent-A-Car,** Jirón Ocona 262 (tel. 28-8478); **U Drive Autos,** Los Mogaburu 179 (tel. 24-3764); and **Avis,** Avenida Petit Thouars 901 (tel. 32-1990).

HANDY DATA: Last, some miscellany you may find useful:
  Telephone: To make a phone call, purchase tokens called *ring.* Each ring allows three minutes of talking. One inti will buy three rings.
  Newspapers: The weekly English-language *Lima Times* (50¢) is available at most newsstands. The stands in the Bolívar, Sheraton, and Crillon hotels sell the *New York Times* (New York edition), the *Wall Street Journal,* and the *Miami Herald* for $4. *Time* and *Newsweek* are available anywhere.
  Post Office: The main post office is past the Haiti Restaurant, two blocks from the Plaza de Armas on Conde de Superunda.
  Cook's: The famous travel company has its Lima office on Ocona. **Exprinter** is at Colmena 805.
  Siesta Time: Many stores, offices, museums, and government offices close from 1 to 2:30 p.m.
  Tourist Office: Free tourist information and assistance is available from the Peruvian Official Tourism Bureau (government operated), Belen 1066 (tel. 32-3559), through the Tambo de Oro restaurant. Hours of tourist assistance are weekdays from 9 a.m. to 7 p.m. and on Saturday from 9 a.m. to 1 p.m.
  U.S. Bank: First National City Bank has a branch here at Colmena 1062, just off Plaza San Martín (tel. 27-3930), opposite the Sheraton Hotel.
  U.S. Consulate: Located at Grimaldo del Solar 346, in Miraflores (tel. 44-3621).
  Drugstores: U.S.-manufactured drugs are plentiful in Lima. A good pharmacy is **Botica Inglesa,** Cailloma 336, where English is spoken.
  Electricity: Current is 220 volts, A.C.
  Clapping Permitted: When signaling a waiter, it is perfectly acceptable to clap.
  Women's Gym and Spa: Women can pamper themselves at **Gymnasio Helena Rubinstein,** Shell 411, in Miraflores (tel. 45-1547), open daily from 8 a.m. to 8 p.m., featuring aerobics, Turkish bath, exercise machines, and the like. The instruction equipment and surroundings are first class and it's an interesting way to meet local, upscale Limeñas.
  Instant Lightning: Pisco, a grape brandy that is virtually the national drink, is available at $5 a bottle (compared with $9 in the U.S., if you can find it).
  Airport Tax: The $15 tax is paid in dollars upon departure.
  Government Tourist Hotels: These are operated by **Entur Perú,** Portal de Zela 965, near Plaza San Martín. You can make reservations through any travel agent.

Reading Matter: A good outlet for U.S. books and periodicals is **ABC Librería,** in the Todos Shopping Center, San Isidro.

Five & Dime: Tía's, a Woolworth-type variety store, is located on Jirón de la Unión near Puno.

Getting to the Airport: In addition to going by cab, you can reach the airport by colectivo. Colectivos (five-passenger cabs) leave from the Galería Internacional, Avenida Nicolas de Pierola 733 ($1.50, plus 50¢ for each bag). The colectivos leave regularly during the hours between 6 a.m. and 9 p.m.

Duty-Free Store: The duty-free store at the airport sells liquor, perfume, jewelry, and tobacco at bargain prices.

Guide: An incredibly knowledgeable guide who speaks English is Mariella Samame Marcazzolo, who works for **El Dorado Travel Agency,** at Jirón de la Unión 1015 (tel. 52-0143). Say hello to Mariella for us.

ON TO CUZCO: And now you should be ready for a leap back into Inca history as you fly up to Cuzco in the Andes. Two domestic airlines—**Faucett** and **Aeroperú**—fly to Cuzco from Lima. Round-trip air fare is $185. Flying time is one hour.

The larger and more popular is Aeroperú, with offices in the Plaza San Martín, while Faucett has offices in the Hotel Bolívar. Each has two daily early-morning flights into Cuzco leaving at approximately 7 a.m. Neither airline accepts traveler's checks, but they do accept credit cards. Make sure to check on the rate in intis before you pay.

By the way, you may hear in Lima that it's necessary to book your Cuzco hotels in advance because they are invariably full. The hotels referred to are usually the top two or three. There are many more hotels available and you should be able to book yourself upon arrival. However, you may have problems during holidays and possibly in July. It might be wise to book ahead for those times. For reservations, call Limatour or Receptour. For reservations at the government-owned Turista Hotel, stop by at Entur Perú, Portal de Zela 965.

NOTE: In early 1987, because of the political situation, Lima, Callao, and surrounding areas were put under a 1 to 5 a.m. curfew. In April the U.S. State Department advised visitors to Machú Picchú, Cuzco, the Inca Trail, and other sights to use caution while traveling. For current information at the time of your trip, call the U.S. State Department (tel. 202/647-5225) before you leave or the consular officer at the American Embassy in Lima when you arrive (tel. 44-3621).

CUZCO AND MACHÚ PICCHÚ

□ □ □

Cuzco, a magic name among the Indians who lived in the Andes 500 years ago, and Machú Picchú, the incredible Lost City of the Incas, are still magic names today. The two Peruvian cities, one occupied by Indians living as they did centuries ago, the other a magnificently preserved testament to the genius of the Incas, represent South America at its peak of traveler fascination and excitement. In personal terms, nowhere else—Athens, Budapest, Rome, Tangiers included—have we ever been so completely captivated as in Cuzco and Machú Picchú; when we first gazed upon the latter site, the sheer beauty of it left us in wonderment.

Cuzco was the fabled gold-laden capital of the Inca world 500 years ago, when that world extended from what is now Chile and Argentina north through Bolivia, Peru, Ecuador, and Colombia. In some respects, the city—located 350 miles southeast of Lima—has changed hardly at all since it was razed and rebuilt by Pizarro's conquistadores beginning in 1533.

Machú Picchú, which most historians believed is the legendary lost Inca city where a small band of Incas fled during the Spanish occupation of Cuzco, was not found until 1911. After years of labor it was unearthed—and instantly became the most famous sight in Peru. It deserves to be listed among the great sights of the world. Situated 75 miles north of Cuzco, this wondrous place where the sun hardly ceases to shine retains all its glory for the visitor. We cannot urge you too strongly to make this and Cuzco absolute musts in your South American trip.

Now, let's get settled into Cuzco.

CUZCO—A SLICE OF LIVING HISTORY: When the Spanish arrived here, Cuzco was the largest and most important city in the Western Hemisphere. Its population today is 140,000—99% Indian and 1% mestizo (a mixture of Indian and Spanish).

The conquistadores sought gold and there was more of it here than even their most wild-eyed dreamers foresaw. Pizarro found temples filled with gold, and monuments and ritual baths made of the yellow metal. After looting the city, the Spanish leveled it, sparing only a few buildings and the city walls. On the ruins the conquerors built a settlement of churches, residences, and military buildings, all of colonial design. A Spanish city was thus transplanted to the New World; one culture was destroyed and another superimposed on the rubble. The identical transformation took place in Quito, another Inca center to the north, a year or so later.

Today this city—more than two miles in elevation—is an unusual combination of Spanish colonial in its architecture and old Indian in its culture. You will find that the Indians here have not altered their dress, methods of farming, or traditions for over four centuries! And yet many of them are in almost daily contact with the so-called civilized world of Lima, Rio, Buenos Aires, and Chicago, via the stream of visitors that flock here. Tradition does not die easily in Cuzco.

The color brown seems to dominate the city. The surrounding mountains, the earth, the homes, the cobblestone streets, the women's skirts, the men's hats, and the complexion of the people all seem to blend into a single reddish-brown hue. It is as if, over the centuries, varying shades of brown have blended and reblended until now there is only the single shade. And it is as if, finally, the city and its people have become one.

The ever-present sun is of course the catalyst, and after a day or two you will find—if you are fair—that your complexion has started to turn a reddish brown.

The smell of history is stronger here for us than it has ever been at the Colosseum in Rome or the Parthenon in Athens. And for good reason. Rome and Athens today are modern Western capitals, and the historical remains of their stunning pasts are anachronisms in their present-day settings.

In Cuzco the past and present are inseparable. They confront each other in the streets, in the homes, in the traditions. The only anachronisms are the tourists and the planes that wing into Cuzco airport. Even the newer hotels blend into the whole.

Moreover, the meaning of Cuzco has greater impact when you remember that the Inca civilization was abruptly strangled in a single year—at its zenith— while the Roman and Greek cultures died more leisurely after long, full lives.

No one knows what heights the Incas might have scaled in world history. And this question will pass through your mind as you stroll past the Inca walls, the stonework, and the intricate, centuries-old terracing on their farms that enables the soil to retain precious moisture for many months. And then look hard at the shoeless Indian women in their high stovepipe hats as they tote enormous loads on their sturdy backs.

A CAPSULE HISTORY: The Incas, who began stirring from their home in Cuzco in about the year 1000, quickly conquered Indian tribes south to what is now Chile and north to what is today Colombia. The empire flourished for over 500 years, during which time the Incas imposed their own social order on the conquered people. They worshipped the sun, source of all light and warmth, and encouraged but did not force their subjects to worship similarly. The sun god's representative on earth was the Sapa Inca. Originally the term *Inca* applied only to the ruler. The Spaniards extended it to the nobles and priests, and it has since come to mean the entire race.

Subject peoples were assigned land to work and assorted tasks, such as weav-

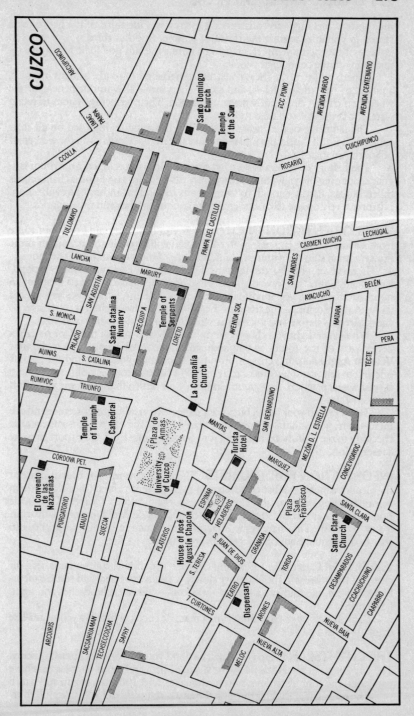

ing, pottery making, and constructing fortresses. One-third of the harvest was stored in granaries against the threat of famine. Another third was devoted to upkeep of the sacred temples, erected to honor the sun god. The final third remained with the conquered people.

Superb builders, the Incas constructed networks of roads, bridges, tunnels, aqueducts, irrigation ditches, and stone stairways—all without benefit of the wheel, which they apparently never developed. Their terracing system to retain water for farming is still used today.

The language of the Incas was the Quechua tongue, imposed on all their subjects. It is still the dominant language of five million Indians on the west coast of South America.

The history of the era is sketchy, since the Incas developed no written language, not even hieroglyphics. Meager records were kept on knotted llama cords called quipas, hardly enough to form a basis for understanding the civilization. Historians rely on the accounts left by the conquistadores and missionaries.

YOUR ORIENTATION IN CUZCO: If you take the train-boat-train route from La Paz (see the end of Chapter VII), you will arrive in the afternoon at the **Puno** railroad station, within walking distance of most of our hotel selections.

If, however, you fly from Lima, you will probably take one of the two popular Faucett flights that leave each morning. You will arrive in Cuzco in about an hour. Alternatively, you might take the Aeroperú flight, which also leaves Lima daily, in the morning. The times of these flights are always subject to change, so check carefully before you go. At this writing the round-trip fare is $150.

Whichever flight you choose, sit on the left-hand side of the plane to gain a better view of the Andes as you approach Cuzco. After you land at the new **Velasco Asete Airport,** crowds of Indian tradesmen will surround the aircraft offering to sell you souvenirs or rugs or even a package tour. A polite but firm no is your wisest reaction. *Important:* Confirm your return flight to Lima when you arrive in Cuzco.

Take a taxi to your hotel, but arrange the price in advance as there are no cab meters here. You should pay no more than $2. Ask the cab to wait while you're checking to see if the hotel has room for you. Or phone from the airport to make a reservation.

INFORMATION FOR TOURISTS: There is a government tourist office at the airport which has a list of hotels and their current prices. Check with them before heading into town. Their office in the Lourdes Chapel (Capilla de Lourdes) adjacent to La Compañía Church in Plaza de Armas is open daily from 8 a.m. to 7 p.m. They have some literature (not much in English), but they can answer questions about train schedules and the like.

WARNING: Cuzco, like La Paz and Quito, is a high-in-the-mountains, thin-air city, and therefore you should move slowly your first day here and rest frequently. Otherwise, the tourist's ailment—soroche—will cause headaches and light-headedness.

Some hotels offer a soothing cup of mate de cocoa, which is a yellow tea-like drink. It helps a bit.

THE CITY ITSELF: Cuzco is a small city and you will orient yourself quickly. The city center is the **Plaza de Armas,** site of Inca walls and temples that have withstood the conquistadores, two earthquakes, and 400 years of sun and wind.

The main street leading through the city is **Avenida del Sol,** an uphill thoroughfare that runs from the airport to the Plaza de Armas. Most of our hotels and restaurants are on or near Avenida del Sol, not far from the plaza. The Puno railroad station is at the bottom of Avenida del Sol.

Follow **Calle Loreto,** a narrow street lined with Inca walls, out of the plaza to visit the remains of the massive Inca **Temple of the Sun,** a must sight. It's two blocks downhill from the plaza between Avenida del Sol and Pampa del Castillo.

Follow **Avenida Santa Clara** uphill out of the plaza. Three blocks away is the **Plaza San Francisco,** which marks the start of the Indian quarter of Cuzco. It may sound strange to mention an Indian quarter in a city that is 99% Indian; however, the differences in garb and the quality of life, and especially the customs, are immediately obvious as you pass through the arch. Three blocks into the area is the sprawling Indian market which is adjacent to the railroad station from which you'll get your train to Machú Picchú.

Note: Sad to say, the market has become a favorite haunt of skilled pickpockets. We've received letters detailing slashed purses and camera snatchings. Leave valuables and cash in your hotel.

CLIMATE OF CUZCO: It's similar to that of La Paz, but warmer. The sun shines brilliantly much of the year, and afternoon temperatures hover in the 60s. Evening lows are in the 40s, and winds are constant but not strong. Bring a raincoat in November and May to June. Most important, though, heed our warning on the thin air, which can cause you to become fatigued easily. Indeed, our best suggestion for you is to dine lightly and rest often the first day. However, if you've come here from La Paz or Quito, you should experience no discomfort. You should carry a sweater with you no matter how warm it may seem, since the temperature shifts rapidly.

1. HOTELS OF CUZCO

Cuzco is a small city, but it has a large number of hotels. In the last 15 years, a dozen new hotels have opened—several in the deluxe category but many in the budget category as well. Many of the older hotels have remodeled to stay in business.

THE BEST MODERATELY PRICED HOTELS: For a hard-to-beat combination of comfort, friendliness, and good location, head for the four-story **Hostal Wiraqocha,** where many rooms command an excellent view of the Plaza de Armas. Located at the corner of the Plaza de Armas at Mantas (tel. 221283), the Wiraqocha is a family-run affair. Owner Arturo Samanex and his wife take great pride in their hostal and couldn't be kindlier and more helpful to guests. The 28 rooms have comfortable beds—you'll sleep well here—rugs, writing tables, and heaters. Doubles are $30 and singles run $22, all with bath. An extra bed in the room is $8. One flight down is a restaurant, and there's a soda fountain on the main floor for snacks. The large, public sitting room is a homey spot—perfect for letter writing or resting your feet after a day of sightseeing. Here you can spend hours taking in the scene on the Plaza de Armas or warm up on chill evenings in front of a big open fireplace. Television is also available. Don't skip heading to the roof where you can sunbathe and enjoy a breathtaking view of the city's cupolas silhouetted against the clearly visible Andes. Other pluses: Laundry service and elevator. An excellent choice!

Just a few steps from the Plaza de Armas, at Santa Catalina Angosta 149, is the 28-room **Hotel Conquistador,** opened in 1973 (tel. 22446). The rooms are small but well-furnished, with wall-to-wall carpeting, floor-to-ceiling drapes, and electric heaters. Doubles are $30 and singles cost $21. There are no elevators, so foot-weary travelers should avoid the third floor. For those who don't mind the climb, the third floor is cheerful and sunny as it's covered with a skylight. The hotel has a bar, restaurant, and comfortable sitting area.

Without question the most historically intriguing hotel here is the fantastic 16-room **Hotel Los Marqueses,** Calle Garcilaso 256 (tel. 232512), two blocks from the Plaza de Armas. A converted 300-year-old hacienda, the Marqueses has been lovingly restored, and much of the original mahogany and other woodwork can be seen in doors, paneling, and bannisters. In fact the massive, intricately etched doors to each room, as well as the colonial floor chests and closets, make a visit here mandatory whether you're a guest or not. All rooms are off a common courtyard, and all have been redone in exquisite taste. Rooms are large and each has its own floor chest and hot-water heater. However, the Marqueses may not be to everyone's taste. For one thing, many of the rooms are windowless and the baths could be upgraded. It is still basically an old structure and is not in any sense modern. But the hotel captivated us. Doubles with bath are $20, singles run $15, and triples cost $22.

And now we come to the Plaza San Francisco, and an old colonial-style hotel with its own special charm—the 18-room, two-story **Hotel El Solar** (tel. 232451). Here you will find spacious rooms, many with balconies overlooking the plaza, opening onto a pleasant courtyard. All are carpeted, with nicely draped windows, and have electric heaters. Doubles are $30, singles are $25, and triples run $32, with bath. The hotel management is very friendly and you'll get lots of good advice and assistance. Note that several of the rooms have no windows. We're sure you'll want a view of the plaza, so check your room first!

Turning to more conventional hotels, a good value is the 37-room **Hostal Ollanta,** Avenida del Sol 346 (tel. 232473), which was renovated in 1971, complete with new elevator. The four-story Ollanta, located three long blocks downhill from the Plaza de Armas, offers doubles with bath, bidet, and phone for $18 and singles for $13; triples are $26. The Hostal Ollanta's restaurant serves a hearty full-course meal for $6. Good service, including hand laundry.

A hotel with one of the city's best restaurants is the 27-room **Hotel Garcilaso,** Calle Garcilaso 233 (tel. 233031). Modern, carpeted, twin-bedded rooms with sitting area and private bath run $28, while singles are $20 and triples go for $30. While high for the budget traveler, still the Garcilaso offers solid value. Dine at one of the three outdoor patio tables. Opened in 1971, the hotel is home to many tour groups from Lima.

Another hotel that seems to cater to tour groups is the four-story **Hotel Espinar,** Portal Espinar 142 (tel. 233091), just a block from the Plaza de Armas. The 40-room Espinar offers doubles with a tiled bath for $31; singles are $22. The rooms are very clean, with carpeting and drapes. There is a restaurant, bar, elevator, and another extra: piped-in music.

For ideal location, it would be hard to top the **Hotel Virrey,** situated smack in the Plaza de Armas at Portal Comercial 165 (tel. 221771). If you like lots of room to move about, the Virrey is for you—the carpeted rooms are very spacious, and even the bathrooms are large. The décor in this three-story hotel is comfortable, and the management friendly and helpful. The rooms, clean and cheerful with gay red-and-white bedspreads, cost $20 for a double, $13 for a single, and $28 for a triple. Try to get an upper room for a full view of the Plaza de Armas. Continental breakfast can be had for $1.50.

A hotel in the neighborhood of the Plaza San Francisco is the **Hotel Inti,** at Matara 260 (tel. 228401), which opened its doors in 1976. An attractive modern building, the Inti offers clean, sunny singles for $25 and doubles for $33—all fully carpeted and with private baths. Enter the lobby and check out the shop to the left featuring native handcrafts. The Inti has an attractive dining room with a cozy brick fireplace where the specialties of the house are trout, chicken, and beef (special, too, is the complete dinner for $7, including tax). All rooms have bright-green bedspreads and matching drapes. One of the nicest places we've seen for the price.

Farther from the Plaza de Armas at Ayacucho 233 is the sparkling white, red-tile-roofed **Hotel Tambo** (tel. 223221). Doubles with private bath are $30, and singles are $22. Add $8 for an extra bed. Opened in 1973, the modern 43-room, two-story Tambo is very inviting. There's a large, colorful lobby with carpeted staircase, wrought-iron grillwork, and graceful arches. Try the restaurant on the premises and enjoy 24-hour room service. A pretty place!

Less convenient to the Plaza de Armas yet closer to the airport (great if you're catching an early flight) is the **Hostal Malaga,** Avenida Infancia 535 (tel. 233031). We first heard about the Malaga from a tour guide who spoke highly of its services. We visited and were impressed by the clean, modern rooms, all with private bath, heaters, and telephones, at prices that seemed just right for this type of contemporary hotel. Singles are $20 and doubles are $28, taxes included. To offset the distance from the downtown sights, the hotel offers free transportation to the Plaza de Armas every hour from 8 a.m. to 11 p.m. The restaurant is open from 5 a.m. (for early risers catching the train to Machú Picchú) to 11 p.m. Another extra: Bus service to the airport is $1. Present yourself in the lobby 15 minutes before departure time.

"Better than basic" is what you'll find at the **Hostal Mantas,** Calle Mantas 165 (tel. 231431), less than a block from the Plaza de Armas. The 20-room Mantas has doubles at $16.50 with private bath; singles are a particularly good buy at $10. All rooms are carpeted and have heaters. There is a restaurant on the main floor, and a bar. Head up one flight.

You might also check out the 18-room **Hotel Residencial K'Ancharina,** Calle Tres Cruces de Oro 555 (tel. 233351). The rooms here are sadly in need of a coat of paint; however, the staff tries hard to please and will make your stay pleasant. Say hello to Arturo Medina Salas, a young desk clerk who speaks excellent English and knocks himself out to arrange tours to local sights and pick up tickets to Machú Picchú. Doubles are large and run $18, tax included. Singles are $11 and triples cost $23. All rooms have a private bath. There is one single room without a bath that is negotiable at around $5. The bar is quite attractive. Unwind over a pisco sour at the end of the day. Prices for breakfast are very low— around 75¢ for toast and coffee, $2 for heartier fare.

Two blocks from the railroad station to Machú Picchú you'll find a small, comfortable hotel. The three-story **Hostal Tambo Real,** Calle Belen 588 (tel. 221621), offers a private bath in each of its 18 rooms, along with telephone, carpeting, and nicely draped windows—all at $20 for doubles, $12 for singles, and $26 for triples. A cut above basic and a very good value.

Hotel El Sol, at San Andres 338A (tel. 226421), is a fairly new hotel. All rooms have private bath and heating. There is laundry service as well as a bar and restaurant on the premises. Single rooms are $13, while doubles will run you $19.

The same owners run the quiet 14-room **Santa Catalina Hotel,** up a steep flight of stairs at Calle Santa Catalina 366 (tel. 228471). Doubles with bath across the hall are only $12, and $8 is the charge for a single. Check the mattresses; some have a valley look, which may cause a protest from your spine. Well maintained, however!

SPECIAL MENTION: You will be transported into the past at the tiny, nine-room **Hostal Loreto,** Calle Loreto 115 (tel. 226352), built against the ancient Inca wall that wends its way down this old street. The hostal has four interior rooms, each of which retains an original Inca wall, spotlighted so that you can fully observe the historic craftsmanship. This piece of fascinating Inca past runs $25 in a double room and $17 in a single, including private bath. All rooms are carpeted and are reached by walking through a charming open courtyard. The five exterior rooms have windows but they are very basic. The hostal is also conveniently located just off the Plaza de Armas. The thrill at the Loreto is in observing Inca history, right in your own room. Be sure to ask for the interior rooms.

BEST-BUY PENSIONS: Business is booming at **Leonard's Lodgings,** Avenida Pardo 820 (tel. 232831), and we think this charming hostal deserves every bit of the attention it is getting. Californian Bill Leonard and his Peruvian wife, Luisa, have created an inviting home away from home at their pension, which is located just beyond the post office on Avenida Sol. For $12 a person, including a North American breakfast, you get a cozy, comfortable room in the Leonard home (share a bath). Bill and Luisa have the facility of making a guest feel instantly like a family member, and that, for us, beats a hotel anytime. The Leonards have added more guest rooms in addition to the nine spotless and simply furnished rooms available when we were there. A bonus is that Luisa (who speaks English) is a folklore scholar and fluent in several Indian tongues. Also, she is an inveterate shopper and will guide you unerringly to where (and what) to buy and how much to pay. She's unfailingly accurate. When writing, address the Leonards at Apartado 559, Cuzco.

Not far from Leonard's on Avenida Pardo 954 is the **Hostal Raymi** (tel. 225141), an attractive, two-story green house that contains 15 rooms, each with its own bath. The Raymi's rooms have wall-to-wall carpeting, and most baths contain a full tub with vanity sink. Doubles are $18 and singles cost $12 with breakfast. There's a dining room, coffeeshop, and bar. We've run into several people who've sampled the meals at the Raymi and given them high marks.

Another pension—for men only, unfortunately—is in the YMCA-like **Seminario San Antonio Abad,** Avenida de la Cultura, which offers 20 small, spartan rooms for $10 per person per day, including all three meals. And the food is good besides. In fact, guests are given a box lunch at no extra cost to take with them on the Machú Picchú trip. If you should miss a meal, you get a deduction—beat that! Without food, the rate is an incredible $5 per day. As befits a seminary, you're expected to be quiet, to bed down early, and rise just as early. Write well ahead for reservations to the Oficina de la Administradora.

LOW-BUDGET HOTELS: A block and a half up Avenida del Sol toward the plaza is the 18-room **Residencia Monte Carlo,** Avenida del Sol 138 (tel. 224751), which charges $8 for a double without bath and $5 for a single. All rooms are on the second floor, up a steep stairway. Rooms are small but adequate. There is no central heat, so check to see if heaters are available when you stop here. The young people who run the Monte Carlo are eager to please, and guests, especially North Americans, are given instant service. Very basic.

One of the best low-budget buys is the **Hostal Residencial Machupicchu,** Quera 282 (tel. 231111). A cut above starvation level, the Machupicchu offers clean rooms, without bath, for $5 per person. The motherly proprietress does her best to make guests feel welcome. On our last visit she pointed out that each room had beds with comfy mattresses—no valleys in the mattresses at her hotel! Popular with students, the Machupicchu is entered through a pleasant courtyard.

A good selection in this price range is the 40-room **Hotel Imperio,** Chaparro 121 (tel. 228981), located near the Santa Ana railroad station, where trains depart for Machú Picchú; this is in the Indian quarter. Here the small but clean rooms, all upstairs, overlook a garden on the grounds. You enter through a courtyard and off to the right is the office, called "administración." An excellent value, the Imperio offers doubles without bath for a low $4.50 per person. Doubles with bath are $6.50 per person. The rooms with bath have no separation between the bath and sleeping facilities. Don't be startled if the desk clerk has a parrot on his shoulder—he's a bird fancier. A cut above starvation level.

Very basic but ideally situated is the **Hotel La Casona,** right in the Plaza de Armas at Portal de Panes. If you must stick to rock-bottom lodgings, try the Casona as its convenient location may make up for the lack of comfort. Rooms are sparsely furnished, yet clean. Mattresses have valleys. Many of the rooms face the busy square and have small balconies. These are much lighter and less gloomy than those off the courtyard. Singles sans bath are $6; doubles run $8. The entrance to the hotel is through a courtyard on Procuradores 315. For the hearty only!

Nearby are two starvation choices, and we do mean starvation! Try them only if you are out of cash or desperate for a place to stay. The better of the two is the **Hostal Caceres,** Plateros 368, a three-story white house with a blue balcony located about a block from the Plaza de Armas near the Archeological Museum. The rooms, clustered around a courtyard, are $6.50 for a double, $5 for a single. The **Hostal Plateros,** Plateros 340 (tel. 227251), has doubles for $4. Period.

The **Residencial Posada del Corregidor,** in the Portal de Panes, Plaza de Armas, is a basic choice. With only seven rooms (five with private bath) it is very small and its rooms reflect this. They are off a tiny courtyard and there is no lobby to speak of. Doubles all have private bath and will run $11 a night, while singles with bath are $8 (only $4 without bath). Very basic.

Easily the cheapest buy in town is the basic **Hotel Palermo,** San Agustín 287 (tel. 226481), which has bathless doubles for $3 and singles for $1.50. San Agustín is a narrow street lined with Inca walls and is a good area for local sightseeing. Rooms are small, furnishings minimal, and electric heaters can be rented. You enter from the street into an open courtyard. In the rear is a garden and patio. The owner of the Palermo seemed surprised that his hotel is listed in a guidebook for North Americans. His clientele is almost exclusively Peruvian. Starvation level.

If you are really stuck, two other basic choices on the same block of San Agustín are the **Pan Americano,** at no. 312 (tel. 231312), and the **Central,** at no. 249 (tel. 231941). We are talking desperation here!

BIG-SPLURGE HOTELS:
We are pleased to say that the deluxe hotels are all colonial in style and add to the character of the city rather than detract from it.

For truly big-splurge living, check into the classy **Libertador,** San Agustín 400 (tel. 231961), the pride of Cuzco and rightly so. We must hand it to the Marriott chain for having constructed a first-class hotel totally in keeping with the colonial feeling of the city. The hotel is actually two establishments in one: the older Casa de Los Cuatro Bustos, a Spanish-colonial home built over original Inca walls; and the newer Marriott, next door, which retains an old-world feeling in its décor. Peru's conqueror, Francisco Pizarro, is said to be the original owner of the Casa de Los Cuatro Bustos, which has 18 large suites all opening onto a cobblestone courtyard. We spent a delightful afternoon just sitting in the courtyard catching the late-afternoon sun and admiring the big earthware pots filled with cactus and the small fountain. In the newer part of the hotel you will find handcrafted furniture and artifacts in wood and leather that are part of the Spanish-colonial influence. There are, of course, a cocktail lounge, coffeeshop, and gourmet restaurant, the Inti Raymi. Singles are $61 and doubles run $73.

On the site of the old El Dorado is the spiffy, newer **El Dorado Inn,** Avenida del Sol 395 (tel. 233112). This white, three-story hotel boasts a sauna, wading pool, beauty shop, boutique, and a small solarium on every floor. It has a modern elevator smack in the middle of the lobby. Order a pisco sour (just under $1) from the bar and leisurely sip it in front of the open fireplace. Strolling musicians set a romantic mood. The El Dorado's restaurant serves first-class meals. Single rooms with bath are $61; doubles, about $73.

One of the loveliest colonial-style hotels in Cuzco was the Hostal Alhambra on a quiet street off the Plaza de Aruyas. However, at this writing, it is closed and no work is going on. Its sister hotel, **Alhambra II,** at Avenida del Sol 594 (tel. 224076), is in the same Spanish-colonial style. A comfortable lobby with plush couches around the sparkling fireplace give the Alhambra a cozy, friendly feeling. Rooms are spacious and immaculate. Singles are $40, while doubles run $57. Continental breakfast is an additional $3 and an American one will set you back $4.50.

The delightful 70-room **Hotel Marques de Picoaga,** Santa Teresa 344 (tel. 227691), opened in late 1977. An older colonial hacienda converted into a luxury hotel, the Picoaga offers modern singles with bath for $47 and doubles for $60. The hotel, just two blocks west of the Plaza de Armas, is set back off the street and is entered through a private courtyard. Cocktails are served around a roaring fire and dining at the restaurant is first rate.

Some veteran travelers head to the **Hotel Savoy,** which is part of the Holiday Inn chain that is downhill from the Plaza de Armas at Avenida del Sol 954 (tel. 224322). Recently renovated, the Savoy's 200 rooms are spread over five floors (yes, there is an elevator). There is a restaurant, but the food is just fair. The Savoy's discothèque is the best in town. Doubles here run $70, while singles are $60.

The renovated **San Agustín,** at Calle Maruri 390 (tel. 231001), has 69 carpeted rooms spread over three floors. It has an elevator, which is rare here. Rooms are whitewashed and have small sitting areas. There's a good restaurant, lovely private bar, and a coffeeshop. Rooms have heaters. Singles are $35 and doubles are $53.

The **Hotel Royal Inka** is a lovely addition to the city. In the Calle Regocijo, the Royal Inka's owner is a Peruvian who owns three restaurants in New York. He has imported everything from pots and pans to stainless steel to make the Royal Inka's kitchen the most modern in Peru. The chef has prepared a variety of dishes to be served in the elegant dining room. There's a small bar off the lobby that has a jukebox. Suites are duplex (there are three) and they run $62.50 (with breakfast). The other 36 rooms (four floors—walk up) run $48 double and $36 single. Stop in for a drink or dinner. You'll like it.

A fairly new arrival on the Cuzco hotel scene is the colonial **Hostal del Mariscal,** at Avenida Tullamayo 465 (tel. 233472). The hotel has two wings, the modern one housing the 25 rooms on its two floors. The facilities are top-notch with three large sitting areas, one with a fireplace, and an attractive restaurant and bar. The restaurant serves a prix-fixe dinner for $9. There is a large garden with stone benches in the rear of the colonial house which houses the lobby. Singles are $30 and doubles are $40. Nice choice.

Our last selection in this category is the aging but still proud **Hotel Cuzco Turista,** at Avenida Heladeros and Marques overlooking the Plaza Regocijo (tel. 222832). Once the only deluxe hotel in town, the Turista is one of 31 government-owned hostelries in Peru. They were built when there were few privately owned hotels for tourists. Large and homey, the Cuzco has a willing staff and is built round a small inner garden. Check out the handsome bar whose rich wood paneling and large windows make it an inviting place for a leisurely drink. A roaring fire in the lobby's main sitting area draws guests every evening. Standard topics (in English, French, German, and Spanish) are Machú Picchú, Inca ruins, the Pisac Market, and soroche. Join in—it will remind you of a ski lodge. A large dining room is off the lobby but not worth a stop. Rates run $48 for a single and $58 double.

READER'S HOTEL SELECTION: "In Cuzco, the **Hotel Samana,** at Nueva Baja 474 (tel. 226327), offers private bathroom, hot water, and electric heat. It is located 1½ blocks from Machú Picchú train station. One receptionist spoke English and was very helpful. Rates are $8 single" (Mary Ellen Johnson, Costa Rica).

2. DINING IN CUZCO

If your hotel has a dining room, chances are you will use it often—both for a quick start in the morning and at the end of a day's sightseeing when your feet "won't take you a step farther." However, Cuzco has many interesting restaurants, offering good food at budget prices, which you'll want to try.

Our favorite stop for lunch, dinner, or late-afternoon coffee is the **Tumi Restaurant,** at Portal Belen 115, right on the Plaza de Armas. Easily the most cheerful and best-value nonhotel restaurant in Cuzco, the Tumi makes us feel right at home with its bright-red tablecloths and ladderback chairs. The prices are right too. Start with an appetizer such as the avocado vinaigrette ($3) or shrimp cocktail ($4.25). Sample a delicious beef steak ($5) or another house specialty, the trout with garlic sauce—a real bargain at $4. In fact the most expensive dish, the chateaubriand, is still a buy at $9.50. Sandwiches and omelets are available for about $1. The Tumi offers up some exotic specialty drink such as the Cuba or Perú libre at low prices: just $1.75. Upstairs dining as well. Highly recommended.

A popular stop for light dining is the **Trattoria Adriano,** Mantas 105, just off the Plaza de Armas and across from the Hotel Wiraqocha. Open from 8 a.m. till midnight, the Trattoria serves up hamburgers, sandwiches, and pasta dishes at low prices. A salami sandwich is just under $2; hamburgers, about $2.75; and beef steaks, under $3.75. At night, stick to the pasta dishes if you're on a tight budget. The Trattoria Adriano is a great place to linger over a cup of coffee and watch the street action.

Walk through the Portal Carrijos to our next selection, the **Restaurant Paititi,** where Spanish-style tables and chairs coexist happily with an old Inca wall hanging and an ancient map. The bilingual menu offers beef dishes starting at $5 and fish at $4. Soups are $1.75 and omelets are $2.50. A hamburger with french fries and beer or soda is only $2.25. We've had many a pleasant dining experience here. The Paititi now serves pizza too.

Smack in the Plaza de Armas at Portal de Panes 105 is the **Roma** restaurant, which offers an extensive menu. As you enter the Roma through the swinging doors, you will hear the hubbub of voices and clattering dishes. You have a choice of dining on the main floor or up in the balcony, which is somewhat quieter and warmer. Either way, you'll be handed a large menu which lists 70 items (we counted), including 20 soups, and a lengthy wine list. The most expensive dish on the huge menu is lomo à la Roma (steak), which runs $6. It is as filling a platter as you're likely to find in Cuzco. The stuffed avocado ($3) is also a treat, with a variety of fish, cheese, and vegetables. And finally, we've enjoyed the bistec à la parrilla (fried beef steak served with potatoes) for $3. The Roma opens at 8 a.m. and closes late. The menu familiar is a best buy for $4: you get a four-course lunch or dinner, including soup, meat or fish, fruit, and coffee.

A few steps from the Roma are two popular snackshops offering light, tasty meals. The **Piccolo Restaurant,** at Portal de Panes in the Plaza de Armas, attracts a cosmopolitan crowd which keeps the oval counter busy. Students meet here to enjoy the "fuente de soda" (light food) and low prices. A good hamburger costs

$1.75; ham and eggs is $2.25. Sandwiches, omelets, spaghetti, soup, and juices round out the menu. Counter service only.

Students from Cuzco University seem to fill the counters and tables at the two **Chef Victor** restaurants, which stand virtually adjacent to one another near the Piccolo. Sandwiches, hamburgers, hot dogs, and drinks are the fastest movers. The Victors also have beef, fish, and chicken dishes, soups, pastas, and eggs. Good stop for breakfast or lunch.

Govinda, the vegetarian restaurant formerly at Procudadores, has moved into larger quarters at Espaderos 136. They still offer a four-course lunch, home-made breads, cheeses, and yogurts. Run by Hare Krishnas, Govinda offers tracts on the sect as a side dish. Very inexpensive.

The **Pura Vida** vegetarian restaurant, in the Hotel Marqueses on Calle Garcilaso, also serves vegetarian food. The fare here runs to fresh fruit, fruit drinks, salads, and vegetables rather than the Indian fare served at Govinda.

A late arrival on the restaurant scene is the **Real Salon,** at Portal Harinas 195 (Plaza de Armas). White cloths on the tables and plush armchairs give the large dining room an elegant look. Open only for dinner at this writing, the show starts at 9 p.m. You can have a pisco sour and ceviche or a whole meal. The bubbly tomato soup served with a dollop of cream is a good starter and the asparagus omelet was excellent. Pastas, Hawaiian chicken, and assorted fish dishes round out the menu.

Another choice is the **Meson El Padrino,** a few steps away at Portal de Panes 163. Italian dishes are features here, with pizza, spaghetti with meat sauce, and chicken cacciatore leading the way. Main dishes run $2 and $2.50. Head upstairs to eat, since the lower level is rather crowded.

La Esquina, in the Plaza Regocijo, serves fried chicken, salad, and french fries in its tiny location behind the Turista Hotel. Half a chicken is $2.50, while a whole one runs $5. Head for one of the indoor tables, because the street traffic makes the outdoor ones unpleasant.

La Barca, at Tullamayo 270, has only ten tables, but they serve some of the best fish dishes in Cuzco—they serve *only* fish. Fish stew at $2.25 is enough for an entire meal. Another stop for fish only is the counter at **Monaco,** on Calle Ayacucho. Ceviche is the thing here. It's fabulous.

Check the daily luncheon specials at **Pollería El Tronquito** and **Los Candeles,** which are half a block from Plaza de Armas on Calle Plateros. Each offers a four-course meal at lunch, which consists of soup or appetizer, a main dish, dessert, and a drink. The price is an unbelievable $2, but these are basic restaurants, so check first.

Chifa Hong Kong, in the basement of the Ollanita Hotel on Avenida del Sol, is Cuzco's best Chinese restaurant. It functions as the hotel's dining room, but you should try the Soup of Seven Flavors ($1.50) or the duck with pineapple or mushrooms at $2.75. Chinese noodle dishes are under $2 and the most expensive dish on the menu is chicken with orange slices and leechee nuts at $3.50.

For low-cost fare and fast counter service, head to **El Sumak,** Mantas 117 near the Plaza de Armas. The Sumak's menu features "light eating" at prices the budget traveler can well appreciate. Open at 9 a.m., it's a good place to grab a quick breakfast. Scrambled eggs are $1; a cheese omelet, $1.25; ham, cheese, and eggs, $2. A beef steak with french fries is a low $3. Don't skip the dessert pancakes with mangos, bananas, or honey—just $1.75. Delicious! Table service as well. Closed Sunday.

An informal restaurant popular with locals is the inexpensive, family-run **Koricancha,** at the corner of Maruru-Pampa del Castillo, two blocks from the Plaza de Armas and one block from the Avenida del Sol—just opposite the Calle

Loreto. Be sure to check out the original Inca walls at the right rear of the restaurant. Specialties are the pollo (chicken) at $3.75 and the bistec chorillana (steak) for $4.75. There are 16 tables in all, including a few upstairs. Filled with regulars. Open from noon to 11 p.m. every day.

For the best in Cusquenian cuisine at unbelievably low prices, head to the **Peña de Don Luís,** Avenida Centenario 904. We found ourselves returning again and again to this cheerful, homey restaurant to sample local delicacies such as the fried guinea pig, trout from the Urubama River Valley, rocoto relleno (a spicy, stuffed pepper), and "lengua a tomatada" (tongue prepared in an aromatic tomato sauce). Start off your meal, as we did, with another specialty; tamales served in their corn husks ($1.25). Tasty! We then moved on to the stuffed peppers with mozzarella cheese ($1.25), and for an entree, chose fried trout (pink and delicate) for $2.50, and a small T-bone steak (succulent and only $3.25). The total bill for two: $8.25, tax included. You can't beat that! The restaurant is not far from Leonard's Lodgings on Avenida Pardo. From Leonard's, walk down Pardo until you come to the first fork in the road. Take the unpaved dirt road to your right. This will be Avenida Centenario. Walk up Centenario toward the Plaza de Armas and the restaurant will be on the left side of the street. Enter a cheerful courtyard and choose either outdoor patio tables or the light, airy dining area to your immediate left. Bright Inca-patterned tablecloths and "typical" music help to make this a special dining experience. The place is packed during lunch hour. Certainly one of the best finds in Cuzco for the budget traveler!

Cuzco's newest steakhouse is the charming **El Meson de Espaderos,** Calle Espaderos 105, upstairs over the Eppa store. The specialty? Parrillada, at reasonable prices. A T-bone here runs $5, a juicy filet is $6, and a beefsteak costs $3.25. There is an excellent wine list featuring local vintages. The room itself is small and intimate. You can watch your steak being prepared over an open fireplace. The restaurant hums with the relaxed conversation of diners. A pleasant way to spend an evening.

Pizza has arrived in Cuzco and there are several restaurants that specialize in it. Our favorite is **La Mamma Pizzería,** in the Plaza Recocijo near the Turista Hotel. It's a bright, cheerful restaurant with checkered cloths, wicker chairs, and hanging planters. Pizza is served by the slice (75¢) or the pie ($4.25 for cheese and tomato sauce). Add 50¢ for any extras you want on it. La Mamma also serves lasagne, spaghetti plates, and empanadas. An alternative is **Maggy's,** at Procudadores 365, which has a similar menu. Maggy's is open for lunch and dinner but is closed in the afternoon, while La Mamma is open all day.

Calle Procudadores deserves special mention. In the last two years it has blossomed into an eating mall, with tiny restaurants and bars lining both sides of the narrow street. Besides Maggy's there's **God's Food,** a vegetarian spot, where you can digest tracts from various mystical religious groups with your yogurt. The food is very tasty and the restaurant is very well maintained. There is a four-course lunch for $2.25 that includes soup, vegetable plate, bread, and dessert. **Kukuli,** at the top of the hill, has only half a dozen tables, which are often crowded with young backpackers and rafters (there are several raft operators on the block as well). Kukuli serves burgers, sandwiches, soup, and spaghetti, and prices are all very low. Other eateries on the block are **La Maximum** and **La Casa Antica.** It's an interesting spot. The owners seem like displaced flower children.

Two small cafés have opened in town. The more interesting of the two is **Varayoc,** in the Plaza Recocijo. A poor man's literary café, it has a number of tattered magazines and newspapers in a variety of languages in a rack on the wall (drop off any printed material you don't feel like carting home). Good for breakfast and sandwich foods, it's open from 8 a.m. to 11 p.m. daily. The other is **Café**

Ayllu, in the Portal de Carnes. It's filled with students from the nearby schools. An electronic game arcade is next door.

3. CUZCO BY DAY

ON YOUR FEET!: Again, our suggestion is that you make a walking tour of the city your first sightseeing activity here. And you should start at the most logical point—the **Plaza de Armas,** the center of the city both now and when it was the Inca capital. Five centuries ago the square was called Huakaypata, which, loosely translated, means "leisure square," an apt description of it today. The major religious temples, all filled with gold and silver, were located here.

Pizarro's sacking of Cuzco in 1533, followed by earthquakes and armed revolts in subsequent years, destroyed most of the Inca and early Spanish structures, but the walls of the old Inca city are still intact near the plaza.

Pause a moment in the plaza—there are benches all around—and observe the Indian families walking through the area. The women are multiskirted, with white stovepipe hats perched atop their jet-black hair. Many carry huge loads on their backs or lead donkeys and llamas laden with enormous burdens of food and wood. At midday you see children trudging through the square with pails of hot food which they are taking to their fathers at work in the fields and stores.

Facing the square is the largest structure in Cuzco, the **cathedral,** which took 94 years to build. The Spanish began the project in 1560 and did not complete it until 1654. The stones in it were culled from the destroyed Inca temple that was on the site.

Adjoining the cathedral to its right is the totally intact **Temple of Triumph,** constructed by Pizarro's three brothers to celebrate the crushing of the 1536 Inca revolt led by Manco Capac. Many historians believe that after this defeat, Capac fled to the mountain retreat now called Machú Picchú—the fabled Lost City of the Incas. Before his defeat, he and his followers laid siege to Cuzco for a year.

On the south side of the plaza is Cuzco's finest church, **La Compañía,** which was built over the ruins of the Inca Temple of the Serpents, where the last great Inca ruler, Huayna Capac, resided. After an earthquake in 1650, it was rebuilt in its present form. Note the intricately etched gold altars and handsome wooden dome. Check the paintings for a view of the dress and architecture of 16th-century Cuzco. One portrait depicts a wedding of an Indian princess and a Spanish nobleman.

Adjacent to the church is the **University of Cuzco,** founded by Bolívar after Peru's liberation in 1821.

At the risk of sounding corny, we continually return to this plaza just to sit and contemplate the historic importance of this place. But on a recent visit we were reminded that historical artifacts are truly fragile things. For many years an Indian statue commanded the central position atop the fountain. No Inca warrior this, but rather a U.S. model, feathers and all. We were told that the statue was that of Chief Powhatan (remember his famous daughter?), and had ended up in Cuzco because of a shipping error. Nonetheless the stately Indian suited his home even if it was the wrong continent, and had become, in its own way, a part of Cuzco's history. Now the warrior is gone—lost during a recent labor dispute —and has been replaced by a very incongruous white flamingo. We were saddened by the loss of the statue, and it made us appreciate even more all that has been saved over the centuries.

Now for a stroll along a true Inca street—**Calle Loreto**—which runs alongside La Compañía. This narrow cobblestone street is lined on both sides with Inca walls, on top of which adobe homes have been built. On your right will be the rear ruins of the **Temple of the Serpents** and on your left the remains of the **Inca House of the Women of the Sun.** This was the residence of the Chosen Women of the Incas, who were reared and trained for marriage to the ruler and certain high-ranking noblemen. The Incas were polygamous.

A block down Loreto the street becomes **Pampa del Castillo,** where a small market is open daily.

Farther on is the **Temple of Corichancha,** renamed the Temple of Santo Domingo by the Spaniards. It is on the site of the sacred Inca Temple of the Sun built in the 12th century, the largest and most important structure in the Inca kingdom. When the Spanish arrived, it housed most of the gold later taken by the conquistadores. Within the temple were five subtemples in honor of the sun, moon, stars, lightning, and rainbow. A sixth room was the residence of the temple keepers.

It wasn't until 1950, when a tremendous earthquake rocked Cuzco, that the walls of the temple were uncovered virtually intact. The Santo Domingo church has been rebuilt around the temple's walls so that visitors have a clear view of the temple remains. Most of the nearby walls and streets are Inca in origin.

Head back to the Plaza de Armas on any street from here. They all converge at the square.

At the plaza, turn left and stroll along **Mantas** beyond the Plaza San Francisco, through the arch of the Old City. On your left you'll see the **Cuzco Indian Market,** a bustling place much of the time, with fruit and household goods trading hands (see below).

All around you here, and on the other streets, are Indian families who have not changed their living patterns for centuries.

TOURIST TICKET: A tourist ticket went into operation in Cuzco in 1982. How long it will continue to operate is anybody's guess. For a $10 fee you can visit the cathedral, temples, and museums of the city, the four major ruins on the outskirts of the city, and the ruins near the town of Pisac. The ticket can be purchased at any of the sites as well as the Tourist Office in the Plaza de Armas. The fees paid at each of the sites would equal that amount easily. If you do not visit most of them, then you are overpaying. However, it's a small enough contribution to the upkeep of these memorable sites. The tourist ticket is available in high season only.

THE CUZCO INDIAN MARKET: One of the busiest spots in Cuzco is the colorful open-air Indian market. The streets are packed with vehicles and with people browsing and buying at the bright-red-roofed stalls. Located in the Indian quarter, the market extends for several blocks along Calle Tupac Amaru—just a short uphill walk from the Plaza San Francisco—and spills over from the street into the railroad station. The street stalls are chock full of interesting items ranging from the banal (cheap trinkets) to the beautiful (fine, handcrafted alpaca rugs). Selling in the Indian quarter is a family affair—everyone from grandpa to toddler gets into the act, and bargaining is a must. Be prepared for down-home earthiness: there are food stalls in abundance and the butchers proudly display whole carcasses—head, blood, and all—hanging from the hooks. The clothing items are of special interest; good-quality wool sweaters—hand-knit and bearing Indian motifs—can be purchased, as well as ponchos, hats, and mittens. There are hand-carved wood and metal pieces too. The items vary in quality and craftsmanship, so it's a good idea to inspect the merchandise carefully. You can do this market by taxi, but to really feel its vibes you should hoof it. *Note:* The market is a favorite haunt of pickpockets. Be alert! Leave all valuables at your hotel.

MUSEUMS AND ARCHITECTURE: Are you a museum bug? The **Museum of Archeology** won't disappoint you. Located two blocks from the Plaza de Armas on Calle Tigre, this small (nine-room) home of antiquity is crammed with Inca and pre-Inca stonework, mummies, and woven textiles. Huge four-foot vases, extracted from the Inca ruins, are on the enclosed porches which overlook an open courtyard. One room is loaded with hand implements used by the Incas to weave textiles and to construct temples. Room 5, devoted to the burial rites of the Incas, has several mummies on view, and Room 4 houses relics of the Paracas Indians, who predated the Incas. Hours are 8 a.m. to noon and 3 to 6 p.m. Monday through Friday, on Saturday from 9 a.m. to noon; closed Sunday. Admission is $1.

Next, for architecture buffs, the blending of Inca and Spanish construction makes a visit mandatory to three sections of Cuzco.

Behind the cathedral on Calle Palacio is **El Convento de las Nazarenas** (Convent of the Nazarenes), which is a fine example of the architectural mixture mentioned above. The stones of this building were taken from the Temple of the Serpents, while the walls above the stonework are adobe. The original conquistador owner had his Inca builders etch two mermaids in the stonework above the doorway.

Other examples of the blending are the **Santa Catalina Nunnery,** and a private home opposite it on Calle Santa Catalina at Arequipa, a block from the Plaza de Armas. The convent's walls were built of stones from the Inca House of the Chosen Women, while the home, **La Casa de Concha,** is a good example of an 18th-century colonial palace. The upper walls are true colonial, with hanging balconies; the lower walls are of Inca stone.

The **House of José Agustín Chacon,** on Heladeros near the Turista Hotel, has an exquisite doorway made of Inca stone. Señor Chacon was executed by the Spanish in 1815 for his underground effort in behalf of the liberation movement.

And a final historical residence you might like to visit is the **House of Garcilaso de la Vega,** on Heladeros across from the Turista, home of the famous Inca historian who was born here in 1539.

READER'S MUSEUM SUGGESTIONS: "In Cuzco there are two museums not mentioned in your book that are of great interest especially to colonial buffs like me with a passion for Cuzco painting. They are the **Museo Histórico Nacional** (formerly the Museo del Virreinato), located in the old colonial mansion of the Casa de los 4 Bustos at Calle San Agustín 400, which features a sizable collection of colonial canvases and also pre-Columbian archeological objects; and the **Museo de Arte Religioso,** once the archbishop's residence, Casa del Marques de Buenavista, on the corner of the Hatunrumiyoc and Herrajes, which houses a collection of colonial ecclesiastical furnishings, woodcarvings, religious vestments, and over 100 canvases of the Cuzco school" (George D. Eager, Los Angeles, Calif.).

4. EXCURSIONS AND TOURS

OUTSIDE TOWN: Just outside the city are four imposing Inca ruins, all on the main highway that leads to Pisac, a small village 20 miles away, best noted for its Sunday and Thursday markets (see below). Seeing all four ruins will take a half day at most and can be nicely combined with a trip to Pisac.

Most impressive of the quartet is also the nearest—**Sacsayhuaman,** one mile from the Plaza de Armas, which was a huge fortress and parade ground for Inca warriors. A remarkable engineering achievement, the 1,000-foot-long structure was built of stone blocks, some weighing 300 tons, which were fitted together so perfectly that today a razor blade cannot be inserted between the sections.

No cement or mortar was used. The stones, cut from a quarry a mile away, were transported by levers, since both the wheel and the pulley were unknown to the Incas. Climb to the top for a stunning view of the city below and the surrounding mountains. (An even better view of the city is from the nearby **Christ Statue**.) Llama and sheep graze in the nearby fields.

Five miles from the city is **Tambo Machay,** used by the Incas as a ritual bath. Cold water gushes down the wall into what was the bathing area. The water source has yet to be found. Again, huge stone blocks were used in the construction.

The last two ruins, located just before Tambo Machay, are the **Puca-Pucara Fortress** and the **Kenko Amphitheater.** From the top of Pucara you again have a wonderful view of the countryside. Kenko, far more interesting, has an underground network of tunnels and cellars. The stone altar here was used for animal sacrifices.

Several local tour operators will provide a guide and include the ruins in a city tour. However, it only lasts 3½ hours, which will not leave you enough time to see the ruins as you should. Take this option only if your time is extremely limited. You can take a tour of the ruins for a half day and see them all well, and combine them with a visit to Pisac. Both tours cost $35 per person.

An interesting alternative is to see the ruins on horseback. Make arrangements through **K'Antu Tours,** Portal Corrizos 258, Plaza de Armas (tel. 23-2021). The four-hour tour costs about $10.

PISAC: On Thursday and Sunday mornings, in the village of Pisac (20 miles from Cuzco), an Indian market takes place that you should make every effort to see. The vendors spread their wares on the ground and all around the town square are colorful arrays of alpaca rugs, hats, and mittens, knitted wool caps, gourds, vases, native jewelry, fruits, vegetables, and metals. Best buys are the alpaca items and the jewelry. But bargain, by all means. We recently purchased an unusually carved gourd for $2.50 and a pair of alpaca slippers for $5.

A highlight each Sunday is the formal procession of the village's 12 mayors through town to the local church. Accompanying them are musicians who blow into a reed-like instrument that resembles a recorder.

The market on Thursday tends to be quieter and more típico.

Another fascinating aspect of Pisac is the Indian dress, quite different from that of Cuzco. The women wear red skirts and flat, round, red hats; the men are garbed in brown trousers and jackets and multicolored knit caps. And everyone is shoeless, with the result that the bottoms of their feet are like smooth stone.

To get a real feel for the town, walk through the narrow, unpaved streets and observe the homes and the shops. The cows there are surely among the thinnest in the world. Donkeys, llamas, and pigs are other wandering animal life you'll see.

Above the city on a mountainside are an Inca fortress and ruins, within walking distance. This is a healthy hike and should take you about an hour.

Lunch Anyone?

The Pisac market is over by midday, and you will probably be hungry by then. Stop for lunch at **Chongo Chico,** a converted hacienda about a half mile from the central square on the road leading to the Inca ruins. The food is superior and the furnishings are largely handmade. Impressive indeed.

Getting There

The best way to reach Pisac is by taxi, which will cost you about $45. Again, five passengers will be accommodated for the one price, so you can work up a party and share the cost. Establish the cab fare in advance; the driver will wait for you, and you needn't be concerned about taking the time to wander through Pisac. But try to return to the cab when the market closes. Your driver will probably speak enough English to describe the sights. To make the most of your day, leave Cuzco by 9 a.m.

The picturesque ride out carries you over a winding road that leads up into the mountains. When you want to snap a picture or two, ask the driver to stop. As we indicated earlier, you can combine this trip with visits to the ruins outside Cuzco. The cab fare should again be the same—about $45.

Organized tours are available to Pisac on Sunday and Thursday. They leave for the market at 9 a.m. with a 12:30 p.m. return. On nonmarket days, you can explore the Pisac ruins. Cost is $25 per person either way. Groups travel by minibus. You can combine your visit to Pisac with a visit to the Sacred Valley of the Incas. You follow the newly paved road to Ollantaytambo about 35 miles away (see below). Cabs will run about $60 for this trip. Tours run $35 per person and leave at 9 a.m., with a 5:30 return. Lunch is included.

Another way to reach Pisac is by bus, which departs two blocks from the Plaza de Armas on Calle Saphi, on Sunday at 6 a.m. and returns in the early afternoon. The cost is only $10 round trip, but these, of course, are ancient vehicles, packed with Indian families.

If you're really hardy, you can take one of the open-air trucks that leave sporadically from the plaza. Passengers are jammed into the rear for the stand-up ride.

READER'S TOURING SUGGESTION: "At the **Chincheros Market,** near the Urubamba River Valley, they still barter and bargain as they used to hundreds of years ago. The market is genuine, and it is a great place to purchase Indian handcrafts. We particularly liked the weavings. Take in the nearby ruins too. It is necessary to go to Chincheros by taxi. Be prepared for poor roads. Round-trip cost is $45" (Leigh Infield, New York, N.Y.).

Organized Tours

There are a number of reliable tour operators in Cuzco. They run modern minibuses and seem well organized. The tour includes an English-speaking guide. Private-car tours are also available if you want to pay the price. Rates seem fixed, although they do vary a bit. You can save money by hiring a car and driver if you speak Spanish.

Lima Tours (American Express), at Avenida del Sol 567 (next door to Faucett Airlines), is the largest tour operator in Peru. They run a half-day tour of Cuzco and the nearby ruins (every day) that leaves at 2 p.m. with a 5:30 p.m. return. It costs $18 per person. Pisac, the Sacred Valley, and Ollantaytambo tours run $35 per person. **Receptur,** in the Hotel Savoy, is another reputable tour operator. Tours to Machú Picchú cost $90 per person and the cost includes the train, minibus to go up the hill, and lunch plus entrance to the ruins.

THE SACRED VALLEY: The Urubamba Valley was the heart of the Inca Empire. Points to visit are **Pisac** (already discussed) and **Ollantaytambo,** with a short stop at the village of **Tarabamba.** Cross the Urubamba here and spend a few minutes at the village of **Pichinjoto.** The cliffs and mountains above this village are thickly encrusted with salt deposits which have created an overhang. The small village is poised right below the overhang—in fact you can't see it at all until you are right there. Someday the mountain will fall and crush the village.

Ollantaytambo, about 35 miles from Pisac, is reached by a paved road. It was from here that the Incas defended Cuzco from attacks by other tribes. Ollantaytambo is a true Inca town and was not rebuilt by the Spanish. The square has several narrow streets leading from it, one of which is called the "Avenue of the 100 Windows." The town was the site of a great battle during the Inca rebellion, and when they lost, Manco led his followers to their last fortress at Vilcabamba. You will want to visit the ruins and the valley nearby, where the "Bath of the Princess" lies. It's a natural spring still running over a rock that was shaped to form a waterfall.

Staying in the Sacred Valley

If you have the time and the interest, you can spend some time in the Sacred Valley. With many more tourists visiting the area, several small, rather basic hotels and dormitories have opened.

Albergue de Chongo Chico, a mile from Pisac on the main road, has a dozen rooms encircling a central courtyard. They have colonial furniture and modern baths. Singles run $25, with food. Dinner features such Indian specialties as suckling pig with maize. Still on the main road, but not as close to Pisac, is **Quinta El Carmen.** The 11 rooms here are also built around a courtyard, but there are no singles (if you're traveling solo, you may have to double up). A bed will cost you $7 and dinner runs about $15. The nicest accommodations in the area are at the **Hotel Alhambra,** at Yucay (a tiny village on the Pisac road). This restored Dominican monastery has a score of rooms and all have balconies that overlook the courtyard. Singles run $40 and doubles are $50. Dinner will cost about $12 and fish is the house specialty. The people you meet here are a cross-section of the world. German professors, Swedish backpackers, French archeologists, and American journalists all gather in the tiny dining room and swap Inca tales and drink pisco. It's fabulous!

In Urubamba, the government-run **Colonia Vacacional Center Turistico** is the most popular stop. It resembles a motel but it has a pool and small bungalows are the accommodations. No privacy here: beds run $8, and there are four or five to each room. Breakfast is $1.50; lunch and dinner are each under $5.

In Ollantaytambo, the **Restaurant Hotel Parador,** in the Plaza de Armas, is owned by a charming Italian gentleman and his Peruvian wife. They offer three large dormitories and each has four beds. Each bed is $8, and you can add $10 for two meals daily. There is no other place to eat. The Italian influence is felt in the kitchen where pizza is the pièce de résistance.

River Rafting and Trekking

You can explore the Sacred Valley by rafting down the Urubamba River and you can trek the Inca trails all the way from Cuzco to Machú Picchu. Treks to Machú Picchu take six days or more. Some treks involve mules. Check with **Expediciones Mayuc,** on Calle Procuradores (tel. 23-2666), for information. **Explorandes,** at Urb. Magisterio 77-17 (tel. 22-6599), and **Rio Bravo Tours,** at Avenida del Sol 900, are well known too.

JUNGLE TOURS: Bill Leonard's (of Leonard's Lodgings) guided tours through the Amazon jungle were extremely popular with visitors here—alas, Bill no longer leads them himself. He has turned the reins over to his nephew, Hugo Pepper, a charming and knowledgeable young man. Hugo, operating his **Naranja Tours** from Procuradores 372, leads tours of various lengths and experiences.

Hugo provides guides who take groups of four to ten people to the beautiful **Madre de Dios** area, some 150 miles north of Cuzco. Traveling by Jeep, and with all supplies provided, you can watch the sun come up from the 12,500-foot Tres Cruces Mountain—the display of colors staggers the imagination. You will also explore the jungle itself—visiting a Franciscan mission deep in its interior, and getting a glimpse of Indian life available nowhere else. You will wind up at the Leonard's jungle outpost on the Madre de Dios River—the comfortable Hacienda Erica, a sprawling ranch adapted for travelers. In this exotic jungle setting, you can enjoy river fishing (the trout are huge) and boating.

These tours operate only April through October. Longer tours to the National Park at Manu are even more exciting. Write to Hugo for the latest information.

Cuzco Tours Amazonico, at Procuradores 48, is another excellent group to deal with. Their Cuzco Amazonico lodge is downriver from Puerto Maldonado.

READERS' TOUR SUGGESTIONS: "One of the main purposes of our trip was to experience the rain forest. We offer the following, which may be of interest to some of your readers. Working through **International Expeditions, Inc.,** Suite 104, 1776 Independence Court, Birmingham, AL 35216, we arranged for a one-week visit to the Amazon jungle in the vicinity of Iquitos. Our visit was prearranged by International Expeditions working with **Explorama Tours,** Box 446, Iquitos, Perú, or Office 1501, Edificio 'el Sol,' Camana 851, Lima 1, Perú. Peter Jenner, owner of Explorama, is an American who has set up four camps in the Amazon, each one farther from Iquitos and each more primitive in accommodations. Jenner's purpose in establishing these camps has been to preserve sizable blocks of rain forest purchased from the Peruvian government as nature preserves and to provide a nature-study experience to interested travelers. He has expertly trained local residents as naturalists. These individuals serve as guides, much like national park rangers in our own national parks. We visited two camps, the Explorama Lodge (four hours from Iquitos by boat) and the Explornapo Camp, on the Napo River, an additional four hours away by boat. Accommodations at both are comfortable but primitive, consisting of thatch-roofed, open-sided buildings connected by covered walkways. There is no electricity (oil lanterns are used), as Jenner doesn't want to disturb the surroundings with the roar of a generator. There are gravity-fed showers, but no other running water. All accommodations are kept spotlessly clean by a sizable staff, who also serve meals, fix drinks, landscape the grounds, paddle the canoes, and entertain at night. The program is flexible and tailored to the interest of the tourist. Jungle hikes, boat rides, canoe rides, visits to local homes and schools and to a local Indian tribe, birdwatching, fishing, and swimming are all available. For birdwatchers, it is paradise: two-thirds of all bird species in the world exist in Peru, and many of those are in the Amazon basin. For fishermen, the piranhas are willing, as are a variety of other tropical fish. For hikers, the jungle is most interesting. Jenner provides a quality experience at a fair price. Expense for a seven-day visit, including air fare from Miami, all accommodations, full-time guide service, all meals, and everything except drinks, was $998 per person. For those interested in an off-the-beaten-track nature experience, we highly recommend this program, which is available for an any-length stay from overnight (at a camp very near Iquitos) to one of many weeks. An extension to Cuzco and Machú Picchú (including the excellent overnight stay) can be readily arranged through International Expeditions, an organization that appears to be sincerely interested in providing interesting nature-oriented tours at reasonable prices" (Bill and Jeanette Maxey Kalamazoo, Mich.).

"I recently had the pleasant surprise of finding an American lady named **Barbara Fearis** with a guide service in the remote jungle town of Puerto Maldonado, Peru. I'm writing because I feel the readers of your guidebook to South America should know about her. Barbara has lived there since 1978, studying birds and photographing the wildlife for one of the jungle hotels. In 1981 she started her own guide service, and we found her the answer to our desire to explore the jungle. She is very knowledgeable and reliable. Her trips are arranged according to what the visitor wishes to see for the length of time desired. She provides all food, equipment, and transportation. We (there were four of us) made three day trips: one to the gold mining area, one to a jungle lagoon, and one to the local Huarayo Indian community, where she has many friends. She charges according to what people can afford to pay, within reason. Barbara also provides lodging, and has an interesting library on Peru and the jungle, which we could use at our leisure. Her house is full of baskets, bows and arrows, jungle craft, and her photography. She saw to it that we sampled all the delicacies of the region—picuru, picarones, pan de arroz, anticuchos, and more. While we were at her house, we met some of the local gold miners, some Mormon missionaries, and an expedition from Cuzco arrived on rafts. All in all, we wouldn't have missed it for the world. As you can see, we liked her very much. The best way to locate Barbara is to inquire at the Hotel Turistas (she lives close by)" (Timothy Anderson, Calif.).

5. CUZCO AFTER DARK

The town generally closes up early. And for good reason. Most tourists are tuckered out after a day of tramping through Inca ruins and retire early. So the evening pastime for most travelers is talk, endless talk, about the Incas. But there are a few options open to night people.

TÍPICO SHOWS: If you have yet to be introduced to Indian music and dance, then definitely plan to see the nightly show at the **Centro Qosqo,** Avenida del Sol (tel. 3708), a new 604-seat theater near the new post office, not far from the Savoy Hotel. All performers are students at the University of Cuzco and their enthusiasm is contagious. We're partial to the cueca dance (look for the handkerchiefs at the shoulder). The 90-minute shows start at 6:40 p.m. sharp. Tickets are about $5, but many hotels have signs posted which offer a package including round-trip transportation. Walk it and save.

COCKTAILS AND DISCO: The newest and classiest disco in town is **Las Quenas,** in front of the Hotel Savoy. Looking like the inside of a spaceship, its green booths enclose tiny tables. The white walls are sculptured and the dance floor is long and centrally located. The music starts at 8 p.m. and goes strong till 3 a.m. nightly. There's a two-drink minimum, with drinks running $2.50 and up.

Muki, just off the Plaza de Armas on Santa Catalina, opposite the Conquistador Hotel, is another lively popular hangout. The white walls and many small coves will make you think that you've stepped into a cozy snow cave. Check out the original Inca walls on the right as you enter. Muki is open at 8 p.m. and the action goes on well into the late-night hours. Drinks are $2 to $3. Couples only.

Somewhat out of the way but very similar in style and atmosphere are two new discothèques—**Camino Real** and **Dancin' Days,** both on Avenida de la Cultura, a five-minute cab ride from downtown. **Grand Prix,** Avenida Antonio Loren 18, also off the beaten track, is acceptable. Couples-only at all the above.

Lovers and such should head to **El Tunel,** Calle Maruri, near the Cine Cuzco, where it's dark enough for anything in the semi-enclosed booths. There's live music Thursday through Saturday, discs the other evenings. Bamboo-covered walls but otherwise fairly uninspiring décor. A pisco sour is $1.50; beer and juice (quite good), $1 each. Couples only. Open from 7 p.m. to 2 a.m. Popular with young locals.

The Three Musketeers would have felt right at home at our next selection: **El Truco,** a bilevel restaurant resembling an old Spanish cave, located at Calle Regocijo across from the Turista Hotel. You'll enjoy the "swashbuckling" atmosphere suggested by the Spanish arches, whitewashed walls, bare wooden floors, high ceilings, and bright-red cloth-covered tables. The food is good and inexpensive: rice with shrimp is $1.75; arroz con pollo, $2; riñones parrilla, $1.75; pancake desserts, $1.32; and a pisco sour, 95¢.

We've included El Truco in our After Dark section as the tavern features live-entertainment shows every night at 8:30 p.m., for which there is a $1.25 cover charge. You'll be transported back in time as you listen to the native instruments: the hena (flute), the changa charango (small guitar), the tambor (drum). You may never want to leave.

You'll enjoy the music and the soft lights at Cuzco's newest disco, **Very**

Nice, which is at Portal Comercial, Plaza de Armas. You can nurse a pisco sour or try the local drink, "biblia," for $1.50.

To find out what Cuzco is like after dark, you must spend an evening at **La Calesa Bar** and **Los Violinas.** Both are jam-packed every night with a lively local crowd that comes to enjoy the dancing, drinks, music, and camaraderie. La Calesa has soft piped-in music, just the right backdrop for intimate conversation.

There's much dancing, clapping, and pure enjoyment at **Qhatuchay,** Portal Confiturías 233, as local couples clear an area around the bar to dance to the native rhythms that are so much a part of their heritage. Qhatuchay is so popular that on weekend nights you'll find people sitting under the bar—every table is taken. The drink to sample is Kaipi, made from pisco, lemon, ice, and cinnamon. Most drinks are $1. Try the coconut liqueur—delightful! It also serves a cold platter for $1. Open from 6:30 p.m. until 2 a.m., and there's a $1 minimum. Lots of fun!

Just as lively is **Ahjawasi,** Plaza del Cabildo and Espaderos. A restaurant that is packed nightly with locals, the Ahjawasi is known for its specialty: the foamy, pleasantly sour chicha (a drink made from grapes and corn) and the sound the drinker makes when taking the first sip (an intake of breath that sounds like "ahja"). Skeptical? Well, we tried it, and sure enough, a quick "ahja" passed from our lips. We've listed the Ahjawasi in our nightlife section, for while the restaurant offers excellent native cuisine at remarkably low prices, people flock here primarily for the dancing, music, and "chicha." You might also try the "poncitada habas," a drink made from lima beans and pisco ($1), or fill up on a hearty soup such as the "chairo" (vegetables, barley, meat, and potatoes) for just under $1—a meal in itself. Chicha, incidentally, grows on you! And you'll find yourself sipping, singing, and dancing into the wee hours.

6. CUZCO SHOPPING AND MISCELLANY

THE SHOPS: Best buys in Cuzco are knitted sweaters, scarves, leg warmers, and knee socks. Alpaca and llama rugs are still available, but the good-quality items have risen in price. Handcrafts and silver pieces are also good values. The best place to shop is the **Indian market** on Santa Clara. Since there is no overhead, the handcrafts are less expensive here than in the shops—but be prepared to bargain. Check the shops first so you have some idea of prices.

Don't miss the Cuzco branch of **Eppa,** the fine handcraft shops that are located throughout Peru. In a large store on Plateros 359 (half a block from the Plaza de Armas), the shop features the widest variety of crafts. Browse here before heading elsewhere. Woven wall tapestries of Indian life are stunning and start at $12. Gilt mirrors for as little as $2 make unusual gifts. Knitted sweaters, scarves, mittens, and leg warmers are brightly colored, and you'll be a hit on the ski slopes in them.

A good first stop is the smart **Bazaar Huasi,** near Parque Espinar and not far from the Turista Cuzco Hotel. Good-quality alpaca rugs range from $125 on up, depending on size. Nice gift items are the alpaca seat mats ($3 each). Handcrafts too, $2 and up.

A great shopping street is **Calle Triunfo,** which leads from the Plaza de Armas. It has an artisan's market called **Yachay Wasi** which has inexpensive knitted goods and alpaca rugs. An excellent store for ceramics is **Cerámica Ruiz Coro,** at Triunfo 387, which has items we didn't see elsewhere. **Ramac Maki** and **Hirca,** both off Triunfo, also have unusual handcraft items.

Inca Wasi, at Plateros 344, has lovely knitted sweaters and scarves. Or if you'd rather knit your own alpaca sweater, stop in at **Alpacas 111,** on Ruinas, to pick up some alpaca yarn. Two nearby antique shops worth browsing are

Artesanía Peruvianas and **Makiwan,** on the second floor of the Portal Confiturías.

Check out the original art at **Mérida,** Portal Espinar 288 at the corner of Espaderos. You'll also find the usual tourist items, rugs, and alpaca.

For the finest sweaters in the city, don't miss the **Bazar Paracas,** at Santa Catalina Angosta 163 (tel. 3535). You can have an alpaca sweater made to order. This store stocks sweaters in all sizes—even extra-large—and if you don't find one to your choosing, the owner will whip one up for you within 24 hours. The shop also features a good selection of silver jewelry, ponchos, pillowcovers, and other Indian handcrafts.

Another shop for silver and pottery is the **Bazar Pisac,** Portal Comercio 189 in the Plaza de Armas. Ponchos and sweaters too, at prices comparable to Paracas.

A small market has opened in the Plaza de Armas adjacent to the Lourdes Church. Its stalls feature knitted goods.

Josefina Olivera's shop, at Santa Clara 501, has some fine weavings, as does **Narciso Vilcahuaman,** in the Plaza Regocijo. **Souvenirs Teqsemayo,** at Teccsecocha 432 near the Archeological Museum, has some things not seen elsewhere.

SOME MISCELLANY: Cabs here have no meters, so establish all fares in advance. Tipping not expected. The trip from the airport is $3. Owners of the newest cabs belong to a group called Comité de Servicio Aeropuerto. Most cabs in the group are late-model four-door U.S. sedans.

There are only a few **telephone** trunk lines into Cuzco. Therefore long-distance calls can be slow. To call Lima will cost you $5 for three minutes. After 7 p.m. the toll drops to $3.50.

Faucett Airways, one of the two airlines that fly into Cuzco, acts as clearing agent for all other airlines. To change a reservation, inform the Faucett clerk on Avenida del Sol, opposite the Ollanta Hotel, who will wire his Lima office. That office will pass your message on to your airline. A confirming message will be sent you c/o the Faucett office here. No charge for the service.

The **post office** is located on the corner of Avenida del Sol and Garcilaso. It costs about 30¢ to send a postcard.

DEPARTURE INFORMATION: We know you're getting itchy to get to Machú Picchú, but first some information necessary for those going next to La Paz. If you can plan to leave on a Wednesday, there is a really pleasurable way to travel to La Paz via train and boat. We have already waxed enthusiastic about this journey—flip back to the end of the La Paz chapter. The train leaves the station at 8:10 a.m. and you will arrive at Puno around 7 p.m. There you can catch the *only steamer,* which leaves at 8 p.m. There are trains other than the Wednesday train, but this is the only day you can match the train with the steamer. The steamer trip will drop you off at Guaqui, Bolivia, at 6 a.m. The 7 a.m. train for La Paz will be waiting and will get you to your destination at about noon. This is a very long and very lovely trip, certainly worth the careful scheduling and extra time.

The most convenient route is by bus. Buses with comfortable seats and bathroom depart on Tuesday, Thursday, and Sunday at 6 p.m. It's an enjoyable direct trip which will have you in Puno at Lake Titicaca for an early (5 a.m.) breakfast. You'll cross the lake by barge and have lunch at the Copacabana at 11 a.m., and finally arrive in La Paz at 5:30 p.m. This congenial trip is made merrier by bar service on the bus.

The buses are operated by **Transturin** (tel. 2317), located at Portal Harinas 191 (second floor) in the Plaza de Armas. The fare is about $45 (one way), and breakfast and lunch are included in the price.

Finally, there is daily train service to Puno, from which you can catch one of the buses run irregularly by the **Morales Bus Co.,** or a taxi to La Paz. Not recommended.

7. MACHÚ PICCHÚ—THE LOST CITY OF THE INCAS

We have been to Europe half a dozen times and have traveled through North Africa, Mexico, the Caribbean, much of the United States and Canada, and of course South America. If we were asked to cite the single most exciting moments of our travels, we would fairly shout (with no hesitation): *Machú Picchú!* No other city, monument, relic, mountain, or valley on this earth will affect you quite the way Machú Picchú does as you first stroll casually around a bend high in the Andes and suddenly come full face upon the glory of this wondrous city.

Our first words were "My God, it can't be!" We're still not sure it can be.

A CAPSULE HISTORY: For centuries historians believed that a small band of Incas established a mountain kingdom not far from Cuzco after an unsuccessful effort to overthrow the Spanish in 1536.

But it wasn't until 1911 that an unheard-of professor from Yale named Hiram Bingham uncovered support for this thesis by discovering a remarkably preserved city high in the mountains 75 miles north of Cuzco. Professor Bingham, later Senator Bingham from Connecticut, promptly named the city Machú Picchú after one of the two mountain peaks nearby, and declared unequivocally that this was the Lost City of the Incas.

Abuse swirled about the scholar's head after the pronouncement, largely from other scholars who disputed his interpretation that this was the site of the lost Inca kingdom. But Professor Bingham insisted he was correct and in subsequent years many other historians rallied to his support. Today there is no serious challenge to his thesis.

In his fascinating study, *The Lost City of the Incas,* Professor Bingham reconstructs the founding of the city in this fashion:

The Spanish, after crushing the Incas in 1533 and razing Cuzco, installed a puppet Inca ruler, Manco Capac, who believed that the Spanish truly meant to reinstate the Inca dynasty as they had promised.

When Manco Capac realized instead that Spanish control was to continue, he and his followers revolted in 1535. After laying siege to Cuzco for a year, the Incas were finally forced to flee before the superior firepower of the conquistadores. They settled in two areas in the mountains 75 miles from Cuzco.

One, the fortress city of Vitcos, was quickly located by the Spanish and destroyed. The other, the Royal City of Vilcapampa, which became the home of Manco Capac, was never located by the Spanish, although try they did. Why they couldn't find it is another part of our story, described below.

Vilcapampa was situated between two mountain peaks—Machú Picchú and Huayna Picchú—on a plateau about 3,000 feet above the Urubamba River Valley. Here the Incas built homes and temples and intricate terracing for farming. In all, about 1,000 Incas lived here until the last Inca ruler died in 1571. After that, for reasons no one has been able to fathom, the city was abandoned.

And not until 340 years later, when Professor Bingham made his discovery, was the city unearthed.

The scholar, as we said, renamed the city Machú Picchú after the nearby mountain peak. And the Peruvian government appropriated funds to reclaim the area from the tremendous overgrowth. But there has been no formal restoration work done beyond the clearing of earth and bush from the structures. Only the roofs of the buildings, which were made of straw, are missing. Otherwise the condition of the buildings is astonishing.

Machú Picchú, said Professor Bingham, was a self-sustaining community which grew its own food and produced its own goods. As far as is known, there was no regular contact with other Incas.

Key to the successful farming methods were the elaborate terraces cut into the sides of the city and into the mountainside above. These were so designed—in a horizontal pattern, each about four feet apart—that rainwater was retained for long periods. So successful was the terrace design—which is also seen today in Cuzco, Pisac, and along the Urubamba Valley—that the retained water over the centuries softened the earth and the city slowly receded into the ground.

Professor Bingham made his discovery by laboriously tracing down every legend, rumor, and document that came to his attention. And his persistence led to one of the great archeological finds of the 20th century, one still largely unfamiliar to many sophisticated travelers of today.

THE GENERAL IMPRESSION: When you come around the bend in the road and see the city stretched out in front of you, you are struck by the incredible vastness of the scene and the absolute quiet.

Your eyes will sweep across row on row of neat gray buildings, and you will look beyond the city to the distant peak of Huayna Picchú, which is regularly climbed by hearty travelers. It is connected to the city. To the left of it is a smaller sister peak.

As you turn slowly, in the brilliant sunlight, you will see behind you the larger peak, Machú Picchú.

Slowly you will thread your way down into the city itself and then work quietly through the buildings. You will catch your breath again when you peer over either side of the plateau to view the Urubamba River and Valley 3,000 feet below.

In the highest area of the city are the temples, among them the sacred **Temple of the Sun** with its famous sundial used by the Incas to "tie down" the sun symbolically at the winter solstice each year. Expert astronomers and mathematicians, the Incas believed that on June 21—the day of the winter solstice in the Southern Hemisphere—the sun was farthest away from the earth. The Incas sought to prevent the sun, which they worshipped, from "escaping" by roping a huge gold disk to the sundial. (They were successful every year.) Inspect the dial. It is in almost perfect condition, a testament to Inca craftsmanship. And be sure to have your photo taken here.

Another structure, in equally good condition, is the circular **Temple of the Chosen Women.** Not far from that is the cemetery, the source of a great unsolved mystery—of the hundreds of skeletons uncovered here, only a few are male and all of these are young boys or old men. The Incas in other areas buried males and females in the same cemeteries and they were all quickly found by archeologists. But not here.

You will wind your way through the city using the 100 or more perfect stairways constructed by the Incas. And as you walk you will realize gradually that you are in a kind of semitrance, as if drugged by the beauty and the enchantment. You will be astonished to find that four hours have passed and it is time to catch the bus for your return trip.

SOLVING THE MYSTERY: We mentioned earlier that the Spanish could not locate this city. Let's clear up that mystery now. The fact is that from below the plateau on which Machú Picchú rests, the city is invisible. And this was by design. The Incas brilliantly arranged the placement of buildings and terraces so they could not be seen from below. And they succeeded very well. Still today the city cannot be seen until you actually come upon it directly.

These days 18 men (and four alpaca) care for the grounds that went untended for so long.

WHAT TO BRING TO MACHÚ PICCHÚ: The city requires nothing from you other than film. Bring as much as you have. We shot six rolls on our first visit and then tried to buy more from other travelers. No one was selling.

As for clothing, a light sweater will do. You will be back in Cuzco by early evening.

You might want to take along a sandwich or two. But you can get a fixed-price lunch at the adjacent **Turista Hotel** for $10.

GETTING TO MACHÚ PICCHÚ: You have two choices: a tour or a do-it-yourself trip.

Many travelers, of course, prefer the convenience of a tour, and this can be arranged through the travel agents of Receptour or Limatour in Cuzco. The cost for a one-day excursion—via train and microbus—is a high $90 to $100. This includes the admission, all fares, a guide, and lunch at the Turista.

However, we strongly urge you to try doing it yourself—you will wind up saving about $25. The only difference will be the absence of a guide and no pre-paid lunch. We suggest that you bring your lunch along.

The train—called the "Tourist Train" since it is the same one the tour people use—leaves from the San Pedro (Santa Ana) Station near the Hotel Imperio at 7 a.m. each day. Since seats are limited, tickets must be purchased a day ahead. These tickets are now sold in a booklet for $65 which also contains your round-trip bus tickets (up and down the mountain) and entrance ticket to the ruins.

The train will drop you about 9:30 a.m. at the base of the mountain, 3,000 feet below Machú Picchú. Look up and see if you can spot it, even after someone points out its approximate location. A microbus will then carry you up the winding road to the city in about 20 minutes. The view on either side is stunning.

You will remain there from about 10 a.m. until 3 p.m., when the buses start to load to catch the 4:20 p.m. train for the return trip. You will be back in Cuzco by 7 p.m., exhilarated as if you had just conquered the highest mountain peak or skied the steepest trail in the Alps.

Early risers may prefer the local train used by the natives, which departs at 6 a.m. Since this train is not an express, it stops at each station, where Indians board to barter and sell their handmade goods. In addition, you will save at least $8 when you take this early train. And best of all, you will arrive in Machú Picchú before the tourist train and therefore will be able to tour the ruins all by yourself before the crowds arrive.

Note: The train passes through a number of Indian villages and farms and through the sacred **Valley of the Incas** in the Urubamba River Valley. At a mid-point stop, Indians sell bananas and other fruit. If you do plan to stay overnight, make reservations for the recently renovated, 31-room **Hotel Turista** through a travel agent. Doubles are $75; singles are $60. If the Turista is full, you might spend the night in one of the three very basic hostals located on the main street in Águas Caliente, a small town about half a mile from the Machú Picchú station. These hostals do have hot water, and rates are $15.

BACKGROUND READING: In addition to Hiram Bingham's *Lost City of the Incas* (which we urge you to read), you might like to dip into Victor Von Hagen's *The Realm of the Incas,* and *The Conquest of the Incas* by John Hemming.

READER'S BOOK SUGGESTION: "Of interest to backpackers is a guidebook, *Journey Through the Clouds,* which describes a four- to eight-day trek along the old Inca highway from Cuzco to Machú Picchú. The scenic wonders make it one of the most desirable hikes in this part of the Andes. Those who have taken it consider it memorable. The book sells here in Cuzco for $3" (William R. Leonard, Cuzco).

READERS' TOURING TIPS: "Concerning Machú Picchú, I believe that you should recommend more strongly that visitors try to obtain reservations to stay at the **Turista Hotel** for at least one night. Contrary to your description of the abundant sunshine, it was the rainy season when we were there, and almost every day (and we understood this would be true for several weeks) it would cloud over by noon, and there would be either showers or steady rain in the afternoon. By staying over, one can get up early in the morning, have sunshine, have better sun angles for taking pictures, and better yet have the time to make unhurried hikes over the entire area without rushing to get back on the afternoon train. For the traveler who is not a member of a tour, a suggestion is that it is easier to obtain reservations for Saturday and Sunday evenings than for other days of the week, for the reason that most of the organized tours take in the market day at Pisac on Sunday, and there is not the tour traffic on those days. This also is an advantage in taking pictures, for one does not have a crowd of people in the pictures.

"Concerning the train trip, it is possible to get reserved seats on some cars, and they can be obtained by going to the railway station the day ahead of departure (I would try to do it two days ahead), and there are local trains in addition which have no reserved seats. Since the Cuzco mercado is just across the street from the station, one should take a camera along because there can be some interesting activities there, and it is one of the Cuzco sites a tourist should see in the first place.

"Perhaps one other suggestion concerning Machú Picchú is in order for those who are not planning to stay overnight. To get the most time at the ruins, waste no time in getting off the train and getting in line for the buses, for it is almost an hour before the last passengers can get the bus accommodations. Also, I suggest taking a lunch along and either eating this on the train just before it arrives at Machú Picchú or eating it while hiking, for if all 300 or more tourists were going to stop for lunch first, at least another hour is taken up, and time for viewing the ruins is short if one is going back on the afternoon train. Have lunch after viewing the ruins. Wear tennis shoes or good hiking shoes, for under any conditions it is easy to turn an ankle, and it can be wet and slippery. Take a light raincoat along. I agree with you completely that Machú Picchú gives one a feeling different from that of any site I have ever visited, and one leaves with a feeling of awe at the majesty of the site and admiration for the building skills of the Incas.

"Just one other recommendation for those going on their own—confirm and reconfirm your airline reservations. They do not have the efficiency of United States offices. I would also do this for Turista Hotel reservations at Machú Picchú, although we personally had no difficulty at the hotel. Also, a recommendation to those who are not on tours—do not be afraid to take the little side trips even though you do not speak Spanish (I could get by with my meager speaking ability) for they can become highlights of a trip and give unexpected rewards" (W. M. Goetzinger, Elbow Lake, Minn.).

"I have to agree with the comments in the edition we have about Machú Picchú. We stayed not just one but two nights, and it is essential to do so. I would have died if I had had to leave again after a quick tour, lunch, and then a bus dash to catch the afternoon train. The peace and majesty of that fantastic site cannot be taken away by anything human, but it is felt at its best when the train leaves and before it comes. We went on a Sunday and had the place almost to ourselves from about 2 p.m. on—there were nine people staying in the hotel that night. We were out in the grounds at 6 the next morning to hike extensively up the Inca Trail before breakfast, and again had the whole wonderful site almost to ourselves until almost noon, when the train and buses came. More people were staying overnight on Monday, but still it was a magical experience to be there for almost three days. The hotel, rebuilt in 1982, is now an absolutely first-class hotel, with prices to match, but it is worth it. We paid $62 for the two of us a night including a fine breakfast. They gave us a room in the front corner so we had a wall of windows looking out into the valley, and we couldn't have been happier. And the hotel is decorated in exquisite taste, simple, using Indian art and pottery. The staff were uniformly pleasant and helpful. For us that was what we pinched pennies everyplace else for" (G. Baird, Canada).

CHAPTER X

QUITO, ECUADOR

□ □ □

If your knowledge of Ecuador is derived from current travel posters, then you may very well think that Quito's sole claim to fame is that it lies on the equator. But after you arrive here, you'll quickly discover that this city deserves its place in the traveler's sun for more reasons than its proximity to that imaginary line.

For one thing, Quito is a physically enchanting city with one of the most ideal climates in this world. Because of its two-mile-high elevation (it's the second-highest capital), temperatures are like May in New England for 12 months of the year. And the breezes are just brisk enough to require a light sweater in the evenings.

Second, Quito's towering beauty—the city is nestled in a valley that is surrounded on all sides by the northern Andes mountains—will make you wonder where nature has done any better. A must sight is the view at sunset from the Plaza de la Independencia of the dormant volcano **Pichincha,** where the Ecuadorian hero General Sucre defeated the Spanish in 1822, gaining Ecuador's independence. Also visible from the plaza is the beautiful statue of the Virgin of Quito atop the **Cerro Panecillo** ("Little Breadloaf Hill"). Sculpted in Spain and modeled after a 16th-century painting by Bernardo de Legarda, the statue was unveiled in 1976. The people of Quito are proud of their Virgin, and rightly so, for it adds both beauty and drama to the Cerro Panecillo.

Another exciting aspect of Quito is that within a few hours by bus or train you can be strolling through a primitive Indian village that hasn't changed for centuries. And that equatorial line, imaginary or not, is 15 miles and 30 minutes away. In the spring and fall, the sun rises promptly at 6 every morning and sets 12 hours later.

Quito is, at 9,400 feet, one of the world's highest capitals and must certainly rank among the loveliest as well. On our flight into Quito to update this guide, the pilot asked the passengers if they were as touched by Quito's physical beauty as he was. He wondered aloud whether the Ecuadorians on the flight were as impressed as he, a North American, was. His query was met by sustained applause.

If this is your first high-altitude stop, you may experience some light-headedness and you may feel your heart pounding. A short stroll will seem like a hike and a small hill like Mount Everest. Don't be overly concerned. Soroche, a mild case of altitude sickness, is common and will usually pass in a day.

Ecuador has a population of seven million. The majority of the population in Quito and the villages of the Andes are Indian, while those on the coast in and near Guayaquil are mestizo. Days in Quito will be warm and sunny while evenings are far cooler. On the coast days are much warmer and the air doesn't cool off at night.

A CAPSULE HISTORY: We probably should devote a few words to the city's history, which really begins for our purposes with its reconstruction in 1534 by the Spanish conquistadores. Originally settled by Indian tribes a thousand years ago, the area was conquered by the Incas during their expansion into the northern Andes in the 13th century and then razed by them when Pizarro's troops approached the city in 1533. After its rebuilding it became the artistic and cultural center of Spanish America.

A CONCISE ORIENTATION: You will arrive during the day (there are few night flights into Quito) and this is a blessing, since the beauty of the city will captivate you from the air as your plane glides through the northern Andes mountain ranges into modern **Mariscal-Sucre Airport.** The airport has a cambio where you can exchange your dollars for sucres, as well as a National Car Rental and an office of **Dituris,** a government tourist service which will be glad to assist you by supplying maps and making arrangements. **Latin Tours** also has an office here, and will gladly make hotel arrangements and provide transportation to your hotel.

After the customary Customs check, which is extremely efficient, you'll want to head into town. Grab a cab ($2) for the 20-minute ride. If you prefer, you can take a bus (15, 21, 26, 1, or 7) for 10¢ and cab it from town. Buses marked "Inaquito Villa Flora," which leave from Avenida de La Prensa, go to downtown Quito for 10¢.

To orient yourself to Quito quickly, remember that there are two important sections: the **Old City,** which centers around the **Plaza de Independencia,** and the **New City,** which extends north from **Ejido Park** to **Avenida Colón** and then into the suburbs. The Old City is bustling with workers by day but very quiet at night. The new city is growing by leaps and bounds. It is hard to keep up with it from one visit to the next. The liveliest street in New City is **Avenida Amazonas,** which is filled with cafés, shops, and restaurants. This is where you'll want to be at night. So we have ferreted out new hotels, restaurants, and nightspots within the oddly shaped rectangle of Ejido Park (south) to Avenida Colón (north), **Avenida 12 de Octubre** (12th of October) on the east and **Avenida 10 de Agosto** (10th of August) on the west.

Note: The terms "Old" and "New" are ours, to make identification simpler for you. We are always struck by the contrast between these two sections—the one overflowing with a Spanish-colonial tradition that seems not to have changed for centuries, and the other brimming over with new private homes, shopping centers, and wide thoroughfares. The two areas are not far apart and you can easily walk from one to the other.

The lovely and tree-dotted Plaza de la Independencia—center of the city—

is particularly beautiful at dusk, when from the Avenida Chile side you can gaze at the nearby mountains that seem to close in on the city. Office buildings and shops surround the plaza; the famous cathedral, which houses many valuable Ecuadorian paintings, is on the south side.

Two key thoroughfares that run alongside the plaza are **Venezuela** and **Guayaquil,** which are the main shopping streets. Guayaquil becomes **10 de Agosto** as the street heads north into the New City.

The oldest section of the Old City lies south of the plaza at **Avenida Morales,** popularly called the **Calle de la Ronda.** Here, all the streets are steep, narrow, and cobblestoned, and the tiny, brightly colored residences are packed solid for block after block.

The New City, in sharp contrast, has large homes built on huge lots. **Ejido Park** is large enough to house a soccer stadium, and it once did. It also is the site of the Legislative Palace. The major street cutting through the New City is 10 de Agosto (an extention of Guayaquil). Many of our recommended hotels are located near 10 de Agosto as far north as Avenida Colón.

The street that probably evokes the most attention from locals and visitors alike is **Calle Vincente Ramón Roca** (not far from Colón), where many houses resemble a castle, a fortress, or a mosque. An architect friend of ours from the U.S. once walked here with us and continually shook his head in disbelief at the designs of the massive structures. He suggested that the street might have come out of feudal Europe. Don't miss it.

THE CURRENCY: The North American budget traveler will find that dollars stretch wonderfully here with virtually all hotels (except deluxe) and restaurants within one's price limits.

Ecuador's currency was a South American rarity—stable. However, it, too, has soared to 500 sucres to the dollar from the 150 it was just two years ago. Quito remains a paradise for the thrifty traveler.

QUITO'S CLIMATE: This enchanting city has one of the world's more perfect climates—sunny, mild days and cool, clear evenings year round. Fortunately, Quito's proximity to the equator is offset by its 9,400-foot elevation (2,000 feet higher than Mexico City). But the altitude can lead to light-headedness, or even a headache, on your first day here; therefore walk slowly, rest frequently, and breathe deeply to absorb maximum oxygen upon your arrival. All should be well after a good night's rest.

1. WHERE TO STAY

Relative to its population of almost a million, Quito probably has more good (moderately priced) hotels than any other city in South America, with the possible exception of Buenos Aires. In general, the Old City offers the best budget hotels, while the New City has the best pension (rooms with three meals) values. Yet we have found good pensions in the older section, and acceptable hotels in the modern area.

Before listing our budget choices, we should mention the luxurious—and expensive—**Hotel Quito.** Government-built, but now an Inter-Continental hotel, the 250-room Quito is a showplace for Ecuador. You should make it a point to stroll across the deep rugs in the lobby and the high-stakes casino. Unfortunately the Quito has dazzled many a travel brochure writer and the impression is sometimes left that there are no other hotels in the capital. That, of course, is not true, as our some two dozen recommendations will attest.

Quito's most modern hotel is the **Hotel Colón,** which some travelers prefer for its North American–style comfort and décor. Prices are about the same as the

Quito and the values are good. Bistros and restaurants abound on the premises. If you're not sure where to stay, why not compare the Colón and the Quito before checking in? Either way, you will be comfortable indeed. See below for full descriptions of both hotels.

Our prices, incidentally, include the 20% tax and service charge.

HOTELS IN NEW CITY:
As noted, we have divided Quito for reader convenience into our own designations of New City and Old City. Generally we're partial to the hotels in New City, although there are good values in the older section as well.

The **Alameda Real,** at Calle Roca 653, at Amazonas (tel. 56-2345), is one of the newer spots in town. Its 150 rooms are modern and elegantly furnished. You'll like the comfortable lobby and bustling casino. Expect rates here of $65 double and $55 single. Other branches of this chain are in Cuernica and around Ecuador.

The **Hostal Los Alpes,** at Tamayo 233 (tel. 56-110), is like a home away from home. Set in a comfortable private house on a quiet street, rooms look lived in and comfortable. Screened porches for sunning and relaxing, a fine restaurant that serves all meals and specializes in Italian food, and very friendly owners make this a special stop. Rates run $35 double and $30 single. Best buy in town.

Special mention has to go to the exquisite **Inca Imperial,** Bogotá 219, near Ejido Park (tel. 52-4800), where the design of all 35 rooms is of Inca inspiration. From the sculptures and friezes in the lobby to the paintings on each floor, to the carpeting, lamps, and furniture design, and even to the carefully crafted stone walls, this four-story hotel is a loving tribute to the Incas. Yet the designers have been wise enough to remember that the Inca Imperial is first a hotel and second a memorial. Therefore the amenities are all a traveler could wish, and include comfortable rooms and modern baths. Rates are a reasonable $12 and up for a double, and $9 and up for a single. It is one block north of 10 de Agosto.

Just beyond Ejido Park we come to the 16-room **Residencia Lutecía,** Avenida Jorge Washington 909, corner of Paez (tel. 23-4024). It resembles a Spanish-colonial home, and is furnished with replicas of colonial furniture. The wooden bannisters are intricately carved, as are the downstairs archways; old Ecuadorian paintings grace the walls, and there is a quiet bar off the sitting room. At $11 per person for doubles, and $9 for singles, the Lutecía represents good value in a homey setting. To get there, take colectivo "Colón–Camal" from Guayaquil and ask to be dropped at Jorge Washington (at the corner of 10 de Agosto). Walk one block to your right to Paez. No food.

A large pension, just four blocks farther out on 10 de Agosto, is the well-recommended **Residencia Santa Clara,** Gustavo D. Teran (tel. 54-1472). The Santa Clara offers singles and doubles with bath and breakfast at $8 per person and bathless accommodations for $6 per person. Several students we've talked to who resided here gave the Santa Clara an "A" grade. Located half a block left (west) of 10 de Agosto.

You might also try the two-story **Residencia Borja,** Santa Maria 740 and 9 de Octubre (tel. 23-1173), another pension in a private home. The Borja has comfortable rooms with private bath that run about $9 per person. Breakfast can be purchased for about $1. The rooms are clean and the management friendly.

On Avenida Carrion are two more attractive homes housing pensions that offer bright, cheerful rooms at good prices. Near Avenida 10 de Agosto at Carrion 1250 is the ten-room **Residencia Carrion** (tel. 23-4620). Set back off the street and entered through a garden, the Carrion has roomy doubles with bath at $14, and singles at $10. Continental breakfast is an additional $1.50. The Chifa China restaurant, one of our recommendations, is right next door.

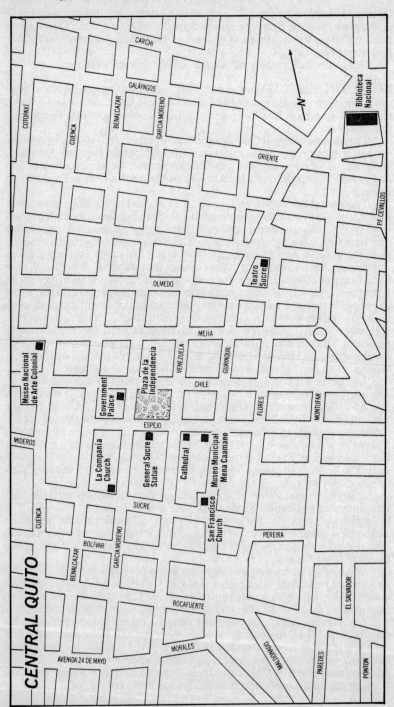

CENTRAL QUITO

At the corner of Carrion and Plaza is the newer **Ejecutiva Pucara,** Carrion 300 (tel. 54-7090), a modernized older home in a quiet residential section. In the two-story Pucara all 12 rooms have private bath and all are fully carpeted. Rates are $11 for singles, including breakfast, $19 for doubles. *Pucara* means "fortress," according to Indian legend. A good value.

Another good budget choice is the **Hotel Majestic,** at Mercadillo 366, corner of Versalles (tel. 54-3182). This spotlessly clean hostelry offers bright, well-furnished rooms at under $15 for doubles. The front rooms face Panecillo and the hotel is near most bus routes and the main Avenida 10 de Agosto, and within walking distance of Avenida Amazonas and its fine boutiques and restaurants.

At Cordero 1495 and 10 de Agosto you will find the lovely, two-story stone house belonging to the 15-room **Hostal Imperio** (tel. 23-4415). Rooms with telephone are $18 for a double, $13 for a single—bath included. The dining area has a large stone fireplace, wood-beamed ceilings, and Spanish-colonial furniture. Other touches are a carpeted staircase and comfortable sitting area. Enter through a delightful garden. Very inviting!

North of the city and quite a bit farther out is the four-story, 25-room **Hotel Zumag,** 10 de Agosto and Mariana de Jesus (tel. 55-2400), where you can get a comfortable, carpeted double with bath for $28 and a single for $16. Opened in 1975, the Zumag is the annex to one of the best hotels in Quito—the Colón. On our last visit the manager advised us that the Zumag would offer a 10% discount on a guest's total bill for a stay of more than two days, and a 20% discount for a stay longer than a week. Check first.

Just one block from the Zumag is the seven-story, 36-room **Hotel Santa Maria,** Calle Ingleterra 933, one block off 10 de Agosto (tel. 52-9945). Prices here are higher than the Zumag's, with doubles commanding a steep $29 and singles getting $19. All rooms are nicely furnished and have private bath and telephone. The Santa Maria boasts a sauna, bar, and restaurant where guests can take all three meals. A 20% discount is offered to guests who opt for full board at the hotel (room and three meals).

Two additional selections in this area are the **Residencial Hilton,** at Cordero 1386 (tel. 23-0645), and the **Hotel Versalles,** at Versalles 1442 (tel. 54-7321). By far the better choice is the Versalles, which features a fine restaurant and doubles for $15, singles for $8. All rooms have bath and music. The 30 rooms are spread over three floors. Enter through the alley. If price is a consideration, the basic Hilton is for you. For $4 per person you get a room without bath—period. The room is clean, but basic.

Another hotel, a bit out of our rectangle, but within easy walking distance, is the **Tambo Real,** across from the American Embassy at 12 de Octubre and Avenida Patria (tel. 52-4260). Rooms here are quite large and furnished nicely with undistinguished furniture. There is a mini-bar in your room and a coffeeshop downstairs that's open 24 hours. There's also a casino. Doubles here are $20, while singles run $19.70. Breakfast is $1 extra.

Hostal Karol-Jennifer, around the corner from Residencia Lutecía, is run-down, but has a good location and is fairly neat. Try it if you're in a pinch. Doubles run $12, and singles, $9.50. Karol-Jennifer is at Valdivia 152, near Washington (tel. 23-2287).

Avenida Colón (Far North Side)

Let's start with the **Hotel Embajador,** Avenida Colón 1046, corner of 9 de Octubre (tel. 56-1777), adjacent to Las Candelabras Restaurant. Resembling an aged, sprawling private home, the 50-room, two-story Embajador charges $15 for a roomy double, with breakfast and bath, and $7 for a single. A bar and restaurant are on the premises; laundry service is available. Rate discounts will be given to groups or guests planning a long stay. Entrance is on 9 de Octubre.

Not far is the 20-room **Residencia Bethania,** at Calle J. León Mera 370 and Avenida Wilson (tel. 23-1267), where the full-board rate, with private bath, is $9 per person. Deduct $1 for bathless accommodations, and slice off $3 for rooms without meals.

The **Hotel República,** at Avenida República, corner of Azuay (tel. 45-0075), is an excellent four-star hotel in the New City. The 40 rooms spread over four floors and rent for about $30 double, $25 single, and they're all carpeted, with color TV and music. There's a restaurant and bar on the premises, as well as a popular disco, Zion. The location is great since Avenida República runs diagonally between Avenida Amazonas and Avenida 10 de Agosto.

Opened in 1983, the **Hotel Royal Inn,** at 6 de Diciembre 2751, corner of República (tel. 23-8260), offers 13 rooms, all on the top (second) floor for under $20 double. The rooms are clean and carpeted, and have all the necessary amenities. A restaurant and piano bar are on the premises. A good, quiet choice.

A captivating hotel-pension is the 12-room **Residencia Americana,** Avenida 6 de Diciembre 2559 (tel. 23-0778), which is popular with U.S. Embassy families. But there is one major drawback: location. This hotel is situated at the corner of Avenida Panagra, opposite a high-priced suburban housing development. If the 20-minute ride to center city by colectivo fails to discourage you, then we can unhesitatingly recommend this find: lovely doubles, with bath, rugs, draperies, and bedspreads, are $30. Singles run $20. Prices include breakfast. Heading out 6 de Diciembre, the Americana is on your left. Look for the sign. A 25-inch TV along with a hi-fi unit marks the modern sitting room, and a nice design touch is the winding stairway to the second-floor rooms.

The Big Splurges

The 250-room **Hotel Quito Inter-Continental,** an Inter-Continental (Pan Am) hotel on Avenida 12 de Octubre 2500 (tel. 23-0300), is an appropriate showpiece for Ecuador and is home to industrialists, diplomats, and wealthy tourists from the world over. As we suggested earlier, some travel agents and writers refuse to recognize the existence of any other acceptable hotel in Quito. Its reputation is justified, what with superb Ecuadorian handcrafts (rugs and woods) enhancing the lobby, the panoramic dining room on the top floor, and the aristocratic casino where South America's wealthiest gather regularly. A stroll through the lobby and gaming room is a must, even if you think that $80 and up might be too much to pay for a double. Singles are a high $70. There are a few singles for $55, but these go quickly. On the premises too: a lovely heated swimming pool and a miniature golf course. A drink at the nightclub will cost you $2. If you want to splurge, this is the place.

Another big-splurge choice is the relatively new 450-room **Hotel Colón Internacional,** on Avenida Amazonas, corner of Patria, a block north of Ejido Park (tel. 52-1300). A starkly modern eight-story hotel that would be at home in Los Angeles, the Colón charges a justified $110 for lavish doubles, $95 and up for singles. Rooms are plush. Pool and casino.

Equally impressive is the exquisite **Hotel Príncipe,** Avenida America 660, next door to the Teatro America (tel. 54-3795). To stay at the Príncipe is to recapture Quito's colonial past. Built 100 years ago, the Príncipe was once a luxurious private mansion. It isn't hard to imagine a gathering of colonial Quito's elite in one of the mansion's many small drawing rooms. Opened in 1977 as a hotel, the Príncipe has retained the special touches that have made it a showplace: a winding staircase, Greek columns, Louis XIV–style furniture, and priceless statues on each of its three floors. The 15 rooms are unnumbered and are named according to their décor—"The Yellow Room," "Blue Room," and so forth.

In converting the mansion into a hotel, some problems did arise. Private baths were installed in each room and these, of necessity, are small enough to be called a closet. Yet this does not detract from the comfort of the rooms, which have lush carpeting and floor-to-ceiling drapes. Doubles are $38 and singles run $23, tax included. An American breakfast in the hotel's small sunny dining nook is $3.50; continental breakfast is $2. The Príncipe has a small cozy bar, ample wine cellar, and a lovely dining room. At the time of this writing, they were planning a small concert salon.

A good hotel (1976) is the **Hotel Dan Internacional,** at Avenida 10 de Agosto, corner of Colón (tel. 23-2083). This 46-room, six-floor choice features TV and carpeted rooms with drapes at reasonable prices. Doubles are $22; singles run $15.

An almost deluxe choice is the **Hotel Chalet Suisse,** at Calama 312, corner of Reina Victoria (tel. 54-8766). Built around a fine restaurant, the 52 rooms (six floors) are plush and the hotel offers a piano bar, casino, beauty shop, and sauna. Highly recommended if you can handle the tab—$45 for a double.

Another recommended selection is the **Hotel Rapa Nui,** at 6 de Diciembre 4454, in front of the Colegio Alemana (tel. 24-1578). The 20 rooms rent for $30 double, $20 single—all with bath and carpeted floors. A highlight is the sauna. One drawback is its slightly out-of-the-way location.

Finally, the **Savoy Inn,** Calle Yasuni (tel. 24-62-63), is another fine hotel in this category, with a major drawback of being near the airport and not convenient.

HOTELS IN THE OLD CITY: Hotels in this colonial part of town are aged and lacking creature comforts. However, there are a few acceptable choices.

If you plan to stay in the Old City, your first choice should be the **Hostal Cumanda,** at Calle Morales 449 (tel. 51-6984), just down the block from the stairs leading to Old Quito. Although it had just opened at the time of this writing, the family-owned Cumanda was always full. And for good reason. The hotel is immaculate, the management friendly, and the rooms very comfortable. All are carpeted and have private baths. Plus the beds are new and very comfortable. The prices are an unbelievable $10 for a double and $5 for a single. They go quickly, so you may want to write ahead for a reservation. The hotel has its own restaurant featuring delicious home-style Ecuadorian meals at super-economical prices. A complete dinner can cost less than $2.

Another good choice is the **Hotel Real Audiencia,** at Bolívar 220, corner of Guayaquil (tel. 51-2711). It's a fine hotel, almost of four-star quality (which it boasts). There's a busy casino downstairs and a scenic restaurant on the fourth floor with great views of bustling Santo Domingo Church and square, filled with busy shoeshine boys (really old men). Sorry, but there's no elevator so you have to hoof it to the restaurant. There are 36 rooms on three floors, and doubles are $25. But check to make sure it's open before going there. At the time of this writing it was closed because of a strike.

Hotel Plaza, Espejo 818, near Avenida Flores (tel. 51-4860), opened in 1972. Blue-and-red-checkered bedspreads are cheery, and it has large bathrooms. Rooms are clean. The reception desk is on the second floor. The dining room on the left draws a good lunch crowd. Doubles are $14, singles cost $12, and triples run $20. Breakfast is included.

The **Hotel Viena,** at Flores 610, corner of Chile (tel. 51-9611), is not to be confused with the dingy Hotel Viena at Flores 562. The no. 610 Viena has small but clean rooms, all with private bath, all leading off a small inner courtyard, and all renting for $5 per person. The one at no. 562 is starvation level.

Stepping down a bit, we come to the family-operated **Hotel inter-americano,** Calle Maldonado 3263. Secluded and quiet, the hotel is showing its age and could use paint and freshening up. Nevertheless, the rates are low —$4.50 per person for a small room with bath in an alcove (no door separates the bedroom and bath). Some rooms are even cheaper.

The **San Agustín,** at Flores 626, near Chile (tel. 21-2847), is another acceptable hotel without much in the way of comfort, but it's clean. You get a cot-like bed and little else. Of course it's only $8 double.

The **Auca Continental,** small and rather modern, is nicely located and clean. Its cafetería is known for its inexpensive filling meals. The Continental is at Calle Venezuela near Sucre (tel. 51-1868). Doubles run $16, and singles, $9.

Hotel Juana de Arco, at Rocafuerte 1311, near Maldonado (tel. 511-417), is the best hotel in this, the oldest section of the city. A cut above basic, the Juana de Arco has hot water and all rooms have a private bath. Doubles run $12 and singles are $7.

Starvation Budget

Five blocks south of the Plaza de la Independencia is the oldest section of Quito, whose center is **Avenida Morales,** popularly known as the **Calle de la Ronda.** The streets here—narrow, steep, and cobblestone—house the oldest and cheapest hotels in the city. We cannot emphasize strongly enough that these selections are quite basic and for the young in heart and low in cash *only*.

Your best choice probably would be the 40-room **Hotel Colonial,** Maldonado 3035 (tel. 51-0338), a block from Morales, whose small rooms are neat and adequately furnished, and have showers; the dining room serves low-priced meals (optional). Rates are $4 per person. You enter through a narrow courtyard which has an outdoor prayer altar carved into one wall. Follow the winding stone courtyard path for almost a block to reach the entrance.

Three blocks down Rocafuerte, past Santo Domingo Church, at Rocafuerte 1009, is the 48-room **Grand Hotel** (tel. 51-9411), once a first-class hotel, now an older four-floor walk-up that offers a large double room with telephone and shower for $4.50 per person, without meals. Avoid the dingy rear rooms ($1 per person).

Less than half a block from the Colonial is the 30-room **Hotel Guayaquil,** Maldonado 3248 (tel. 21-1520), a simple three-floor walk-up where rooms (some with private bath) run $2 per person. The rooms are rather dark and bare in furnishings. Hot water.

Another old hotel catering mainly to international students and backpackers is the four-story **Gran Casino,** Garcia Moreno 330 (tel. 51-6368), where 60 sparsely furnished, bathless rooms go for as little as $2 per person. A large doorway enters onto a foyer and reception room with TV. The main hallway leads to a patio with a scattering of tables. There is a restaurant on the premises serving substantial fare at rock-bottom prices. For the hearty only!

TRAVELING WITH CHILDREN: The **Motel Embassy,** Calle Wilson 441, near 6 de Diciembre (tel. 52-5500), is uniquely set up to handle families. And that's what you find here—particularly U.S. Embassy families. There are 14 two-bedroom suites, complete with kitchen, living room, and fireplace, that run $45 a day. Single rooms are $20. Full restaurant on the premises too. Since the motel is ten blocks from Avenida 10 de Agosto, a car is helpful.

Another fine family choice is the **Hotel La Castellana,** at Calle Ingleterra, corner of Vancouver (tel. 54-8988). Suites come with kitchen, bedroom, dining room, and small oven. One-bedroom apartments go for $35 daily; two-bedroom, $40. Most guests bargain for excellent monthly rates. All apartments are carpeted and are in demand.

2. WHERE TO DINE

The cuisine in Ecuador, while not entirely distinctive, includes several unfamiliar dishes that you should try. The **ceviche de corvina** (whitefish marinated in lemon sauce), for one, is a favorite of ours, and so is **locro** (a potato soup made with cheese and avocados). The locals here are fond of **humitas** (corn tamales) and **llapingachos** (a cheese-and-potato dish served with a fried egg on top). You should try the **naranjilla** fruit, which is a cross between an orange and a peach. But steaks, beef, and chicken are served in almost all restaurants. As for drinks, as in Peru, the **pisco sour** (made from aguardiente and lemon juice) is a national favorite. Remember that it's quite potent, particularly at this altitude.

RESTAURANTS IN THE NEW CITY: Whether you're staying in the Old City or the New City, you will want to sample the newer restaurants in this section of Quito.

Light Snacks and Lunches

Snag a table at one of the sidewalk cafés that line Avenida Amazonas at Robles. You can snack on pizza, hamburgers, beer, or coffee and watch the passing scene. The most popular is **Mario's,** where the house specialty is the cena al maigo; a hamburger or hot dog with french fries and beverage is $1.25. The cena al minuto is chicken, salad, and coffee for just $2.75. Next door is **Manolo,** where the sandwich is king. Next door is **El Chacarero,** a nice place for pastry and coffee. The low prices and fast but hearty fare draw a young crowd, mostly university students. At the corner, the **Hotel Almeda Real Cafetería** also has sidewalk tables.

Still in this area at Roca 736 is a delightful pastelería called **Chantilly.** Walk into the pastelería, order coffee at the counter, and choose your favorite pastry or fresh baked sweet roll. Upstairs is the cafetería, where you can order sandwiches for 75¢ and up, or a full-course meal after 12:30 p.m. The Chantilly has tasty beef steaks, whitefish (corvina), or chicken in wine sauce for $4.50. Dine at attractive tables covered with crisp white cloths, or linger over a drink at the bar. The Chantilly is open for breakfast and lunch Monday through Saturday. **Sandy's** is a delightful cafetería on Avenida Amazonas. It's self-service. Items are fresh salads and fruit bowls, hot soups, and a variety of daily specials with vegetables. Sandy's is closed on Saturday.

Pims, at Calama 413, is a pub. It's quite small, but worth the wait. It serves hamburgers, sandwiches, beer, and ice creams.

Pizza Nostra, on Amazonas and Washington, is a small pizza place with specials that are so inexpensive it's embarrassing. A whole pizza for one and a glass of wine for $1.50 is what we enjoyed one day.

For any meal at rock-bottom prices, we highly recommend **El Americano,** a self-service bar at Avenida 10 de Agosto 674, open from 8 a.m. to midnight seven days a week. The floors are bare and the tables have glass tops, but pick up a tray and get a half chicken dinner for 50¢ or pork chops for 25¢. There are noodle dishes (pasta), yogurt, and salads.

A popular chicken chain is **Pollo Gus,** where you can get a whole chicken for $2 (half a chicken is $1). They have self-service and you sit on wooden benches, but the place is clean. You can watch the chickens roasting. Hamburgers are also available. A good Gus is at 10 de Agosto, corner of José Riofrio, across from El Americano. Incredible value.

The **Café Colón,** in the rear of the Hotel Colón lobby, is open 24 hours a day and offers sandwiches, soups, pizzas, and full-course meals in almost elegant surroundings. The chairs are upholstered and there are attractive murals of old Quito. On the expensive side for Quito, a four-course dinner will run about $6, to give you an idea of prices.

The ubiquitous American-style fast-food eatery is here in Quito too. **King Chicken,** at Avenida 10 de Agosto 2156, offers Kentucky-style fried chicken, plus "dogs and shakes"—just like home. Half a chicken with french fries is $3.50; fried fish, $2.50; hot dogs, 40¢; and milkshakes, 90¢. The complete menu is printed on placemats, and there is a breakfast special of juice, eggs, bread, and coffee for just $1. Adjoining King Chicken is an ice-cream and hot-dog stand.

McDonald's and Kentucky Fried Chicken, or **Pollo Kentucky,** have established themselves in Quito. McDonald's is on Amazonas at the corner of Luís Cordero. Prices are similar to the U.S. (a quarter-pounder is $1.50). Pollo Kentucky is on 6 de Diciembre next to the Alexander Restaurant.

Lunch and Dinner Restaurants

Our favorite in this area for either lunch or dinner is **Las Cuevas de Luís Candelas,** at the corner of Calle Grecia and República (tel. 23-3867), where the "must" dish is the locally celebrated chateaubriand (steak marinated in wine sauce), a fine value for $6, including salad and vegetable. One afternoon we wandered in not particularly hungry and owner-manager Luís Yepez Baca whipped up some scrambled eggs with herbs—marvelously light and tasty ($2.75). The restaurant is located in a Spanish-colonial-style home on a residential street. We've had many enjoyable meals here and recommend it highly.

Luís operates another restaurant of the same name in center city at Benalcazar 709, corner of Calle Chile (tel. 21-7710). Head downstairs from street level onto a simulated bridge and into either of the two small dining rooms. Bullfight (toro) murals, flamenco music, and a fireplace make for an ideal atmosphere.

In addition to the chateaubriand, consider the langostina (shrimp) a la plancha ($6.50) or the tortillas ($2), as well as any of the beef dishes at either location. Luís divides his time between the two places, so ask for him. In both the New City and center-city units, the food, ambience, and prices are right. We give a special nod to the mussels in garlic sauce at $1.75—don't miss this dish!

Columbus, Avenida Colón 1262, is the best budget steakhouse in town. Cooked Argentinian style over a charcoal grill, thick, juicy steaks are prepared to order. They are served with two special hot sauces. Side dishes include fabulous cole slaw and potato salad. A delicious meal will run less than $5.

Where do the locals go for good, inexpensive Italian food? To the **Ristorante Vecchia Roma,** Roca 618 (tel. 56-5669), near the Hotel Alameda. Drop in any hour of the day and enjoy the old-world comfort of the Vecchia Roma's main dining room. You'll swear you're sitting in New York City's Little Italy. The prices are comfortable too. Cannelloni and ravioli dishes are $3; pizzas cost $2 to $4. We particularly enjoyed a delicious chicken cacciatore ($3). During the warm weather, dine outdoors at curbside tables. The Vecchia Roma serves breakfast outdoors from 8 a.m. on, charging just $1 for a hearty American breakfast and under $1.50 for rolls and coffee. The restaurant is open for lunch, and dinner is served from 6 to 10 p.m. The management is friendly and courteous. A pleasant dining experience.

El Ceviche, at Juan León Mera 232 (near Calama), serves the largest and best ceviche in Quito. Raw shrimp, mussels, assorted fish, and a mixture of all of the above are served in a tangy lime juice with garlic and onions and peppers. The juice "cooks" the fish. It's fabulous and tastes great with a margarita.

Rincón Cubano, at 993 Amazonas, has replaced the Bronco Bar, one of our former choices. Cuban food is rather different than most Spanish cuisine, and its staples are black beans, rice, and yucca with a variety of meats. This restaurant is inexpensive and is owned by nice people.

Near the Hotel Carrion is a good Chinese restaurant, **Chifa China,** Carrion 1376, corner of Versalles (tel. 23-9954), a block from 10 de Agosto. Enter through a garden and a gate into a rather large dining area divided into several rooms, each bedecked with hanging lanterns. The lengthy bilingual menu features some 20 soups and a good number of duck (pato) dishes (about $4.50). Squab is favored by the regulars. Dishes we like are the bola de camerón con congrejo (shrimp balls with crabmeat) and the gallina (hen) concoctions. Open daily from noon to 3 p.m. and 6 p.m. to midnight.

Nearby is another similar Chinese restaurant—also very good—the **Chifa Oriental,** at Colón 1169. Look for a white building.

Our favorite place for German food in Quito is, without question, **Taberna Bavaria,** at Juan León Mera 1238, corner of Garcia (tel. 23-3206), set in a large private home with a roaring fireplace. The food is authentic Bavaria with appetizers such as leberwurst (liver pâté) and entrees the likes of gemischte wurstplatte with home-fries and sauerkraut (mixed wurst platter) or huhnerbrustrollchen (breast of chicken rolled with ham and spinach). Of course there's wienerschnitzel. The ceilings are beamed and the menu is in three languages, including English. Opened in 1984, Taberna Bavaria was an instant hit.

Rincón Alemán is a good second choice for authentic German platters. Set in an even larger private house at Avenida 6 de Diciembre 1436, between Carrion and Veintimilla (tel. 23-1667), you will be able to savor the house specialty, chuletas ahumadas au cher crut y salchichas (kasseler with wurstchen and sauerkraut) at $5 for two. There is also bratwurst or bockwurst too. If you like, you can have Italian or French dishes. There are two dining rooms, each with a fireplace. Charming Claudia Schopp is a fine hostess.

An authentic Brazilian rodizio churrascaría is **El Toro Partido,** upstairs on Avenida Amazonas at Veintimilla (tel. 23-6551). They serve 10 types of meat and 18 salads—all you can eat for $3. Strolling musicians add to the fun. Head upstairs and try for a table that overlooks Avenida Amazonas. Another good choice is the **Churrascaría Tropeiro,** at Veintimilla 546 and 6 de Diciembre (tel. 54-8012).

For the best in seafood, try **Las Redes,** on Avenida Amazonas at Veintimilla. The specialty of the house is mariscal. Similar to paella, it's made with shellfish and rice and serves two to three people. Another seafood choice is the lobster casserole dish for two at $15.

Big-Splurge Dining

Would you like to dine on superb food beneath a bamboo-beam ceiling on manila hemp placemats before a roaring fireplace? Consider the large, striking, bilevel restaurant **La Choza,** a handsome showplace in a new building at Avenida 12 de Octubre 1821 (tel. 23-0839), where the typical Ecuadorian dishes would satisfy the most fastidious palate. Open from noon to 3 p.m. and 7 p.m. to 3 a.m., La Choza charges $5 to $7 for most platters, including delicious filet mignon. But go Ecuadorian and try the llapingachos (cheese-and-potato dish) for $3, the empanada de morocho for 75¢, as well as the ceviche camarao (shrimp appetizer) for $2. Go all the way and start with a potent rice cocktail called chicha (80¢), and don't miss trying the rosero, a delightful fruit drink. The elegant beamed ceiling is made of local bamboo called caoba wood. The menu is changed daily. You enter via a 50-foot-long outdoor walkway, covered by a canopy fashioned of branches and straw that's illuminated at night with colored lights. Enchanting.

Rincón La Ronda, at Bello Horizonte 400 and Almagro (tel. 54-0459 or 54-5176), is another excellent choice for typical Ecuadorian cuisine. In a setting reminiscent of colonial Quito, you can dine on national favorites such as llapingachos, locro de cuero, hornado, and fritado, or choose something from the extensive international menu. The whitefish (corvina) with mushrooms (con champiñónes) is excellent. Expect to spend close to $10 per person for a complete meal, including wine and appetizers.

Probably one of the best seafood restaurants in Quito is **Moby Dick's,** on Avenida Amazonas at the corner of Jorge Washington, not far from the Residencia Borja. Walk down two flights of stairs to the small bar and large, pleasant dining room decorated in blue and white. Moby Dick's is worth a visit just to have a taste of the delectable bouillabaisse de mariscos ($6.50)—a real standout. Other specialties include shrimp dishes, breaded with garlic sauce ($7), and delicate sole, either grilled or poached in a sauce, for $3. Moby Dick's varied menu has a price list that ranges from $5 and up, except for that special treat—lobster —which starts at $9.

Bring a big appetite to our next splurge selection, the charming **Casa de Mi Abuela** ("My Grandmother's House"). Located in an old colonial home at Juan León Mera, near Pinta (tel. 23-4383), Casa de Mi Abuela features succulent cuts of meat served in huge proportions. And no wonder! Grandmother Maria reigns over the dining room and sees to the preparation of meals herself. It is her intent that guests eat well and leave the table well satisfied. We ordered a 400-gram filet mignon which covered the plate. Stick to the Italian dishes if you want to shave a few pennies off your bill, or order a generous salad and soup—quite filling! Most dishes run a high $5 or $9, but the atmosphere is well worth it! The personal touches of Señora Maria make a visit to Casa di Mi Abuela a must. As if the careful attention to the preparation of your meal isn't enough, Grandma often will treat a guest to a complimentary glass of wine or an after-dinner apéritif. Now that's hospitality! Be sure to ring the bell. The front door is often locked.

Very popular with the business crowd at lunchtime, **La Costa Vasca,** Avenida 18 de Septiembre 553 and Paez (tel. 56-4940), is probably Quito's best Spanish restaurant. As the name suggests, it specializes in Basque cooking, considered by many to be the best in Spain. Here you should try the parrillada de mariscos accompanied by a Spanish wine, either from the Rioja or Cataluña. Expect to spend around $25 for two people, including wine and coffee.

If there were an award for the restaurant with the best view of Quito, it would surely go to **La Terraza del Tartaro,** located in a penthouse 20 floors above Quito at the corner of Veintimilla and Amazonas (tel. 52-7987). This is one of Quito's finest restaurants, offering not only a breathtaking view, but an international menu specializing in steaks. Dinner for two, including wine and dessert, will cost between $25 and $30.

Perhaps Quito's finest restaurant—and a must—is **Rincón de Fráncia,** at Roca 779, corner of 9 de Octubre (tel. 23-2053). The chef-owner, Gilles Blain, is your host. The guitarist adds to your enjoyment where you can enjoy such favorites as coq au vin, chateaubriand, and tournedos grillé. Expect to spend at least $13 per person. The décor and food are on a par with fine French restaurants worldwide.

On the Calama

The "Restaurant Row" of Quito is a small street—Avenida Calama— tucked in between Amazonas and 6 de Diciembre. On the "strip" are some of the finest "big-splurge" restaurants of Quito—establishments that would be hits in Paris, Rome, New York City, or any other part of the world. Each restaurant is in its own private house. We'll start with those closest to Amazonas and work up the avenue toward 6 de Diciembre.

A particularly delightful choice is the **Juan Sebástian Bar** (tel. 54-6955), known for its excellent variety of marisco dishes ($5 to $8). Try the mussels appetizer ($3) or the tortilla langostinos ($2)—delicious! Head downstairs to the main dining room: there are two large rooms with a wooden bar and pool table. The atmosphere is dark and intimate, much like a disco, and the food is international. The Juan Sebástian Bar is fast becoming one of *the* places to go after dark in Quito.

Excellent, too, is **Le Chalet Suisse,** Avenida Calama at Reina Victoria (tel. 23-0686), where the roaring fireplace, beamed ceiling, and white stone walls make this restaurant inviting indeed. Here the fondues are the thing—either cheese or meat (each is $13 for two). The chef is justifiably proud of his chateaubriand Chalet Suisse ($7). Enjoy soft piano music as you dine. Growing in popularity and size, the Chalet Suisse recently opened a gambling casino that is packed on weekends, and a modern new hotel under the same name and management. Attractive and recommended.

La Crêperie has opened on the Calama; however, we feel that its prices are very high for wafer-thin crêpes ($3 and up). There are 34 different varieties from which to choose, including dessert crêpes. If you can't resist the temptation of a chocolate crêpe with vanilla ice cream, and you don't mind the prices, drop in.

Continuing on restaurant row, we suggest **Excalibur**, at Calama 380 (tel. 54-1272). By all means try the lomo al jerez ($5.50) or the corvina al jerez ($5). This cozy restaurant sports carpeted floors and attractive wood-paneled walls.

For the best in Argentinian-style steaks, stop at **Shorthorn Grill**, Calama 216. This new and attractive restaurant is largely decorated with typical cowhide. There's an open salad bar and all dishes come with a baked potato and sour cream. There are sauces on your table, green and red-hot red. Beamed ceilings are a plus and the menu is in English as well as Spanish. Owner Estéban Díaz is proud of his restaurant and sees to it that all requests are attended to. He is also the owner of Le Club, one of our top nightspot recommendations.

Not as attractive as most other restaurants here, **Sorrento**, at no. 329, serves very inexpensive Italian food. Cannelloni, capelletti, and fettuccine are cooked al gusto.

The steakhouse, **Pinis,** and several ice-cream parlors round out the four-block stretch where you can virtually eat every type of food served in Quito. Calama is the street adjacent to Avenida Colón.

Two final restaurants on Calama Street that you should consider are the **Hereford Grill Steak House,** near Juan Sebástian, and **Dickens,** next door. As you might surmise, Hereford Grill is a steakhouse comparable to the Shorthorn. Head downstairs. Dickens is a typical English pub with a menu that alters between Yorkshire pudding and local fare.

RESTAURANTS IN THE OLD CITY: First the snack and light-lunch places, then the dinner selections.

For Lunch and Snacks

The **Madrillon,** a soda fountain located a block from the Plaza de la Independencia at Chile 1270 and Benalcazar, is a recommended breakfast and light-lunch choice. A long, narrow eatery, with Formica-covered tables and a small, compact menu, it offers such nonheavy items as orange juice, toast and butter, and coffee for 80¢, a ham or cheese sandwich for 75¢, a hot chicken sandwich for 60¢. We suggest the tasty tortilla (omelet) made of lobster, shrimp, or chicken and served with tomatoes and potatoes, 95¢. A plain tortilla costs 45¢, and with ham, tomato, and potato it's 25¢ more. Good for a quick snack.

A popular little "hole in the wall" where you can grab a quick breakfast or light lunch is the busy **Café Niza,** Venezuela 624. The Niza offers an assortment of simple sandwiches—hot or cold—for just 35¢. Coffee with two pieces of bread is also 35¢. A complete breakfast—large orange juice, two eggs, bread, and coffee—is a bargain at $1, tax included. Drop by in the late afternoon and linger over a pastry and coffee. No one will hurry you here!

For perhaps the lowest prices in Quito, drop in at **Tía's,** a Woolworth-type variety store on Guayaquil between Chile and Espejo, which has a stand-up snackbar on the mezzanine. For example, you can get a small chicken platter.

Dinner Places

For leisurely dining, head for the **Chifa Chang,** a cafetería at Chile 927. Half the menu is devoted to Cantonese dishes such as wonton soup (90¢), beef with vegetables ($2), rice and beef ($2.25), and chop suey (95¢). We've sampled several dishes, including the wonton soup, and feel that the Chifa Chang could hold its own in New York's Chinatown. Non-Chinese platters range from 80¢ to $2; omelets go for as little as 75¢ and sandwiches are as low as 40¢. The Chifa Chang is open for breakfast too. Hours are 7:30 to 11:30 a.m. and 2:30 to 6:30 p.m. daily.

A similar place, and equally as good as the Chifa Chang, is the **Manila Restaurant and Cafetería,** at Chile 1050 (tel. 51-2419). The Manila has a large, pleasant dining area upstairs as well as a spacious dining room downstairs. Their extensive menu (printed in both Spanish and English) features typical Ecuadorian dishes and Chinese selections at low, low prices. The Manila also serves cocktails, imported wine, and sangría. Open daily from 7:30 a.m. to 12:30 p.m. and 2:30 to 6:30 p.m.

For a quick snack or a complete meal, try the **Chifa Chang,** at Chile 927, just two blocks below the Plaza de la Independencia. Listed in previous editions as a cafetería specializing in Cantonese cuisine, the Chifa Chang has been remodeled and is now actually a small complex consisting of an ice-cream bar, pastry shop, and cafetería. The cafetería offers a complete menu ranging from pizza and hamburgers to roasted chicken, churrascos, and rice dishes. A complete meal, including soup, should not cost over $2. After lunch or dinner you could stop in the pastry shop for coffee and dessert. Speaking from experience, the pastries are definitely worth a trip!

Quito Viejo, just off the Plaza Bolívar on Guayaquil, is a good choice for breakfast, lunch, or dinner. Practically two restaurants in one, there is an informal, cafeteria-style dining room in the front, good for breakfast or lunch, and a more formal one in the back with cloth tablecloths, napkins, and a piano bar. The prices can't be beat. The American breakfast, juice, eggs, ham, toast, and coffee, is less than $1, while a T-bone steak is only $1.50. A cheeseburger and shake will cost a little over $1. Definitely a good choice.

And there is the center-city branch of **Las Cuevas de Luís Candelas,** Benalcazar 709, corner of Calle Chile (tel. 21-7710), entrance downstairs. Designed to resemble a cave that the owner-manager once visited in Spain, this restaurant serves first-rate beef and shrimp dishes, particularly the chateaubriand (about $5). Say hello to owner Luís Yepez Baca, but not during futbol season. He's an avid fan and rarely misses a local match. A sister unit is in the New City (more above).

The **Wonder Bar,** at Espejo 847, serves delicious Ecuadorian food. Several inexpensive cafeterías have opened on Avenidas Chile, Flores, and Venezuela. Good for lunch.

For Fast Food

Pizza lovers should head to **Pizza Hut,** on Espejo next to the Cine Bolívar. **Kentucky Fried Chicken (Kentucky Pollo)** is located next door to the Luís Candeles restaurant on Benalcazar. At **Kikiriki,** next to the Interamericano Hotel, you can get a whole grilled chicken for 50¢.

3. QUITO BY DAY

Quito is one of the world's most scenic cities, and as a bonus, from here you can visit fascinating Indian markets in nearby Andean villages. But first you should get to know and feel Quito, so get on your walking shoes and let's go.

A WALKING TOUR: Begin at the **Plaza de la Independencia,** in the Old City, one of the loveliest squares in South America. The trees, shrubbery, and monuments contribute to the calm beauty here. Largest structure in the plaza is the city **cathedral,** with its green cupolas. General Sucre is buried here, and Caspicara's famous painting *The Descent from the Cross* hangs inside.

On the northwest side of the plaza is the **Government Palace** and behind it Pichincha Mountain rises in the distance. You can pick up native handcrafts in a main-floor shop in the palace.

Amble along Calle Garcia Moreno to the south to Calle Sucre. At this intersection is **La Compañía Church,** whose altars are gold-plated.

Turn right on Sucre, and two blocks over, along narrow winding streets with adobe houses, is the city's oldest and most famous church—**San Francisco** —built in 1535. The church is rich in works of art.

Now head left on Cuenca to **Avenida 24 de Mayo,** which is the center of Quito's oldest section. Here the streets are steep, cobblestoned, and quite narrow. Many of the whitewashed homes have red-tile roofs and carriage lamps outside. Nearby, on 24 de Mayo, an Indian market (household goods) is held every Tuesday morning.

Make a left and head downhill to **Calle Morales** (popularly known as **Calle de la Ronda),** which is a sightseeing must. The oldest and most picturesque street in Quito, Morales is a cobblestone, alley-like avenue that winds its way downhill into Avenida Guayaquil. Look for the Indian families gathered in front of the buildings and notice the true Spanish-colonial architecture.

To leave this section, turn left on Guayaquil, a bustling shopping street that becomes 10 (Diez) de Agosto in the New City. Guayaquil shop owners pile their goods on the sidewalks, and you may find yourself walking in the roadway. Along the way you'll pass the **Teatro Sucre** (at Manabi) and three blocks later, the **National Library.** Just ahead is **Alameda Park,** which marks the beginning of the New City; the contrast between this area and the Old City is startling.

Surrounding the park are modern office buildings, attractive shops, and private homes, and wide, tree-lined streets. At the entrance to the park is a statue of Bolívar and inside the park is an observatory. There is a well in front of the statue where Indian women fill huge pails.

Three blocks beyond Alameda Park is the huge, six-square-block **Ejido Park;** its neighbor to the right (east) is the **Ejido Sports Stadium.** The U.S. Embassy faces the stadium.

Continuing on 10 de Agosto for four more blocks you come to Jorge Washington. Make a right at Paez (one block) and two blocks left is **Calle Roca,** a wealthy street that might have been designed by a medieval architect. The colors and shapes are astonishing. One house appears to be a green mosque, another resembles a stone fortress, and there is one that is surely the only pink castle in the Western world. All the other houses in this area are like those in suburban communities back home. If you tire, take the Colón–Camal colectivo on 10 de Agosto back to the center of the Old City.

MUSEUMS OF QUITO: Ecuador's best art can be found at the **Museo Nacional de Arte Colonial,** Cuenca and Mejía, which also features examples of Spanish-colonial furniture as part of its permanent exhibition. Enter into a colonial courtyard with fountains and plants. As fascinating as the paintings is the museum building itself, a fine example of colonial architecture. The museum is open Monday through Friday from 9 a.m. to noon and 3 to 6 p.m., on Saturday and Sunday from 9 a.m. to noon. Admission is 60¢.

For an outstanding look at pre-Columbian art, definitely stop in at the **Museo del Banco Central de Ecuador,** located on the fifth and sixth floors of the Central Bank of Ecuador Building, 10 de Agosto, corner of Briceno, opposite the Bolívar monument near Alameda Park. The exhibition includes rare gold and silver coins, regal crowns, and a display of colonial art and furniture. Open Tuesday through Friday from 9 a.m. to 8 p.m., on Saturday and Sunday from 10 a.m. to 5 p.m. Admission is 50¢.

The fifth floor is replete with archeological discoveries and offers fascinating insights into the region's history. Upstairs (sixth floor), colonial art is the thing. Which floor is better? *Try both.*

Anthropology buffs should head to the **Jacinto Jijon y Caamaño Museum,** Avenida 12 de Octubre 1436, near the Catholic University. This museum features an excellent collection of Indian clothing, hunting implements, musical instruments, and assorted religious artifacts gathered in Ecuador and Peru by the museum's founder, Jacinto Jijon y Caamaño. There is also a section devoted to colonial art where paintings and sculptures by 17th- to 19th-century artists of the Quito School are displayed. Open Monday through Friday from 9 a.m. to noon and 3 to 6 p.m. Admission is 10¢.

To see works from Ecuador's earliest colonial period, visit the **Museo Franciscano** (Museo del Convento de San Francisco), located in the San Francisco Church building in the huge Plaza San Francisco (tel. 21-1124). To enter, climb up the flight of steps, heading toward the door on the right of the church façade. Once upstairs, knock on the convent door and a guide will appear to conduct you through the museum, which stresses religious works. Admission is 30¢; the hours are 9 to 11:30 a.m. and 3 to 5:30 p.m. Monday through Saturday; closed Sunday.

And you should stop in at the **Museo Municipal Alberto Mena Caamaño de Arte y Historia,** housed in what was originally a Jesuit monastery until 1747 when Charles III of Spain banished the Jesuit order. During the Wars of Independence from Spain it served as an army headquarters, and became known as "El Cuartel Real de Lima." This museum houses a collection of paintings and sculptures from the era of independence. Open Tuesday through Friday from 9 a.m. to noon and 3 to 5:30 p.m. Admission is 20¢.

The era of independence is also represented at the **Museo Historico Casa de Sucre,** located at the corner of Venezuela and Sucre, in a beautiful colonial home which once belonged to Mariscal Antonio José de Sucre, who liberated Ecuador from Spanish rule in 1882. Directed by the Ministery of National Defense, this museum has a collection of weapons, uniforms, furniture, and documents from the era of independence.

Tip: A good guidebook to local museums is *Quito Colonial,* in English.

If you are fascinated by the heavens, drop by Quito's observatory **(Observatorio Astronómico)** in Alameda Park. Make your appointment during the day for an evening peek at the stars. The winding stairway to the tower seems endless, and watch the low bridge at the top. Free.

CASA GUAYASAMIN: Ecuador's most famous artist is Oswaldo Guayasamin, world renowned for his magnificent paintings depicting the fate and destiny of the Andean Indians. Himself 70% Indian, Guayasamin maintains at this magnificent colonial home in the Bella Vista section of Quito many of his famous paintings. Nearby is the Guayasamin Museum, which you must visit. Any taxi will bring you to his home, which is open to the public from 9 a.m. to 12:30 p.m. and 3 to 6 p.m. daily. We were truly touched by his self-portrait and his painting depicting life in the concentration camp. Members of the family will escort you through the home and museum, and you can purchase prints and inexpensive jewelry designed by Guayasamin.

SPORTS: Futbol is the thing, so we'll start with that:

Futbol in Quito

The main season for soccer is June to November. However, there are games held every Sunday and on holidays throughout the year in various stadiums throughout Quito.

The best stadium for futbol is the **Estadium Atahualpa,** where the admission charge for regular events ranges from a minimum of $1 to a top of $3. Special games will cost you more. Check with your hotel clerk for schedules.

To reach the stadium, take a taxi (up to five passengers) for $2, or a colectivo for 15¢.

"Stoneball"

A game that resembles volleyball but involves a 20-pound bat and a 2½-pound ball is "pelota de guante" (stoneball). Free matches are held on Saturday and Sunday afternoons at Barrio Vicentina near the American Embassy. Check with your hotel clerk.

Mountain Climbing

Both novice and expert should head to the **Nuevos Horizontes Club,** Pasaje Royal and Calle Venezuela, in front of the Iglesia Compañía (tel. 21-5135). The club sponsors day-long and weekend hiking and climbing expeditions. Cost is minimal. Keep in mind that the high elevation fatigues most visitors the first day or two—so don't rush into serious climbing until you have acclimated a bit.

Bullfighting

Offered during December only at the **Plaza Monumental.** Admission ranges from $5 to a high $25. You can easily get to the arena by colectivo for 50¢, or by taxi (up to five passengers) for $5.

4. TOURS AND EXCURSIONS

GUIDED TOURS: Organized tours of Quito are readily available through a number of agencies. Among the best are **Metropolitan Touring,** Avenida Amazonas 239 (tel. 56-0550); **Ecuadorian Tours** (the American Express Agency here), Espejo 935, in the Hotel Humboldt arcade and on Avenida Amazonas (tel. 54-3722); and **Turis Mundial,** Venezuela 736 (tel. 54-6511). A three-hour city tour runs about $11 for up to three people, with larger groups paying $4 per person. A group of ten will pay $5 per head.

During our last visit we discovered a brand-new agency which had just opened in 1988, **Latin Tours,** located next door to the Hostal Cumanda on Yanez Pinzon (tel. 56-8657), with another office at the airport. Run by a very ambitious young woman (it's hard to believe she's only 22) named María Lourdes Jijon, Latin Tours, like the larger agencies listed above, offers city tours at comparable prices. But the groups will always be smaller, with no more than five or six people in each. They also offer tours to the Indian markets and Cotopaxi, but we'll get to that later. If you do go see them—and you should—say hello to María Lourdes, Cristina, José Antonio, and Cristobal for us.

A TRIP TO THE EQUATOR: The most popular excursion in Ecuador is the one that takes visitors 15 miles north of Quito to the monument that officially marks the imaginary line that girdles the globe. The altitude is 7,700 feet, so temperatures are quite moderate. Travelers never tire of being photographed with one foot in the Northern Hemisphere and the other in the Southern Hemisphere. And if you are here on March 21 or September 21, you will find that you cast no shadow, as the sun is directly overhead. A small museum at the site (open on Sunday only) has a display of Inca relics and a solar chronometer in its garden. There is also a fine restaurant at the site, the Equinoccio.

Getting There

Your best bet is via bus (a 30-minute, 20¢ trip each way). No. 22 buses marked "Mitad del Mundo" ("Middle of the World") leave every half hour from the Panecillo (the hill that has a beautiful view of Quito). If you are in the Old City you can take the bus on Bahía de Caraquez and 24 de Mayo, or if you are in the modern part of Quito, on Avenida America, every half hour.

The bus trip is worthwhile in itself—a chance to see the countryside and the surrounding villages (Pomasqui and San Antonio, two sleepy towns through which the bus passes, seem to have stopped in time).

Another way to reach the monument—where the plaque reads "0° 0′ 0″"—is by taxi, $15 for up to four passengers. Tour services charge $5 to $10 per person, depending on the number in the group and the type of transport used (bus or limousine).

There is limousine service available from Ejido Park for about $1.

As of this writing, the construction of new monuments and a tourist center was nearing completion and were scheduled to open in early 1989.

GUAYAQUIL: A bustling prosperous city with a much faster pace than Quito, Guayaquil is Ecuador's largest city, and its most important seaport. The River Guayas is almost always congested with cargo boats bringing coffee, cocoa, pineapples, and above all, bananas from the inland villages and plantations. Of interest here are the beautiful colonial homes on Numa Pompilio Llona, a narrow, twisting, cobblestone street in Las Peñas, a district at the foot of Cerro Santa Ana next to the river.

You should also stop in at the **Museum of the Ecuadorian House of Culture,** at Nueve de Octubre and Marbela. This fine museum is home to the Carlos Zevallos Menendez Hall, Ecuador's most valuable gold museum. There are also sections devoted to archeology and colonial art. Also interesting is the collection of shrunken heads *(tzaotzas)* made by certain tribes in eastern Ecuador, which is displayed at the **Municipal Museum,** on the corner of Sucre and Cabo.

Since it's at sea level, not far from the equator, it is warm. It's best to visit in the dry season (May to November), when the warm, rainless days give way to cool evenings. Locals are justifiably proud of the racetrack **(Hipodromo Santa Cecilia),** as well as the futbol stadium, golf, tennis, and yachting clubs.

Two hours further is Ecuador's most popular resort—**Salinas**—where you can swim all year round, and visit the posh gambling casino. This area is also famous for deep-sea fishing.

Getting There

The most comfortable, inexpensive mode of travel is via the privately owned buses operated by **Trasandina** from its terminal at Terrestre. Buses leave daily on the eight-hour (300-mile) trip, and the fare is only $4 each way. But tickets are in demand due to the relative comfort of the buses, and you must purchase your seats at least one day, preferably two days, in advance. Another bus company with a Quito-to-Guayaquil trip is **Flota Imbabura,** which also operates from the Terrestre Terminal. Again, buy your tickets ahead of time. Don't forget to bring a sandwich or two.

As a last resort, use the public bus that departs from the Panamericana Terminal. Tickets are $3.50 each way for a ten-hour, far-less-comfortable ride in older buses.

Another alternative is to book the 300-mile trip through a travel agency, which, chances are, will arrange a train journey (departing from the Estación Central in Chimbacalle). You may also go by autoferro, a coach with reclining seats that holds up to 40 passengers (12-hour trip). The autoferros have bar and snack service on board, and will stop for picture-taking. You pass small Indian villages, fertile farmland, towering snow-capped volcanoes, desert areas, tropical forests with banana trees, sugarcane, and pineapple. One-way fare is $4. Departures are daily (except Sunday). It's a good idea to use a travel service for reservations.

Also, you might have stopover privileges on your plane ticket. The flight to modern Bolívar Airport takes about an hour.

INDIAN MARKETS: While you can glimpse Ecuadorian Indian life in Quito's old quarter, you must go to the countryside for a fuller view.

Despite the fact that they are descended from the Incas, the Indians of Ecuador have developed entirely different customs, dress, and modes of living from the Indians of Peru and Bolivia.

Your wisest plan is to combine a trip to the countryside with a visit to an Indian market; these are generally held daily (except Sunday). However, a trip to these delightful villages is worthwhile even on Sunday when the outdoor market is not held.

Otavalo

Seventy-five miles north of Quito, in the province of Imbabura, is the village of Otavalo, which has its market day every Saturday from 7:30 a.m. until noon, and where you can pick up magnificently woven wool shawls, ponchos, and fabrics. This is perhaps the quietest Indian market in Ecuador. Bargaining (a must) is done in soft tones; there is no shouting as in other markets. The Indians are garbed quite colorfully, the women in bright skirts and shawls, and the men in equally bright colors and with braided hair.

There are actually two markets in the village, one dealing in wool goods and the other in pottery, baskets, and handmade jewelry.

You should note that only members of the tribe wear traditional costumes. For men this includes a felt hat, a reversible dark-blue or gray poncho, a pair of white, calf-length pants, and sandals. He wears his hair in a long braid. Women are attired in a blue-and-white cotton headcloth, white embroidered blouse with shawl, and long black skirt.

Nearby is the town of **Calderón**, where the bread dolls you see sold all over Quito are made. These dolls are made of dough dyed and shaped in the form of animals and other figures. These dolls are traditional grave decorations.

After the market closes there are cockfighting matches, and in June there is bullfighting.

Buses for Otavalo leave frequently from Calle Manuel Larrea 1211. The one-way fare is $2.50 for the 2½-hour journey. Buy tickets in advance. **Metropolitan Tours** arranges all-expense-paid trips (on Saturday only) for $35 each. Taxis will cost $3 per person for a group of five.

Latin Tours also offers day-long tours to Otavalo ($35 per person, including lunch), not only on Saturday, but during the week as well. They not only go to Otavalo, where you will visit the Indians' workshops, but to other places of interest in Imbaburra, including Cotocachi, a small village famous for its many leathershops (prices here are great), Ibarra, a small colonial-style city and capital of the province, and San Antonio de Ibarra, famous for the carved wooden figures that are made there. Lunch at the Hostería Chorlavi, a lovely colonial-period plantation which has been converted into a hotel (a perfect spot for a weekend retreat), is included in the tour.

Ambato

The largest market in Ecuador (Monday only) is in Ambato, 75 miles from Quito. Called the "Garden City of Ecuador" because of its fine orchards and magnificent summer homes, this village is a center of Panama hat production (that's right, Panama hats come from Ecuador and not Panama). You can also buy handsome wool goods, ponchos, and wooden masks here. Because of its high elevation, many wealthy Ecuadorians have second homes in the area.

Getting there is part of the fascination, since you drive on the modern Pan American Hwy. through the **Valley of the Volcanoes**, where homes have been fashioned of the light-gray lava rock. The market, which begins early and is over by 2 p.m., is spread over the entire town.

Bus is the most scenic—and the cheapest—mode of travel to Ambato. Ten buses ($2.50 each way) leave daily from Terminal Terrestre for the three-hour journey. Get tickets in advance. If Monday is inconvenient, then you might visit the smaller market at **Latacunga** (Saturday and Tuesday), near Ambato.

Saquisili

The noisiest, wildest market in the Quito vicinity is at Saquisili, 45 miles south of the capital, where every Thursday morning the Indians pour into the village to hawk their pottery, tablecloths, and wood etchings. Bargaining is intense and loud. Don't be bashful. Remember, it starts early and is usually over by noon. Buses, which pass the huge **Cotopaxi Volcano**, the world's highest active volcano, leave from Terrestre Terminal. Buses depart daily, charging $1 each way for the 90-minute trip. Tours run $17 per person and up. Better still, take the bus to Latacunga (service is more frequent) and from there take a local bus for the short 20-minute trip to Saquisili. Other buses leave from the southern bus terminal.

Santo Domingo de Los Colorados

An unusual Indian community, the primitive Colorados reside in the jungle 7,000 feet below Quito. Every Sunday (the day you should visit) the tribesmen come to the town of Santo Domingo to buy and sell. The Indian men and women, who wear very little clothing, paint their torsos and hair with a red paste made from the achiote seed to ward off evil spirits. The village, in the midst of banana coffee and cacao plantations, is quite warm and you should dress accordingly.

Note: On our last visit, very few Indians came to town. Those who did came to earn some money for being photographed.

Transportes Occidentales and **Transportes Esmeraldes** operate regular bus trips from Avenida 24 de Mayo ($7 round trip). The journey takes four hours. If you prefer, an organized tour will run $20 to $25 per person. Remember, Sunday only.

Riobamba

The town of Riobamba, four hours from Quito, has a wonderful market on Saturday mornings. It gets under way very early (by 9 a.m. it's going strong), so it's best to go on Friday. You can go by bus, but it's more interesting to take the "autoferro." This is a one-car train, and the trip is scenically stunning. The train ambles through colorful valleys, villages, and towns, and you'll see Cotopaxi, the highest active volcano in the world. In Riobamba, visit the museum of Sacred Art in the Cloister of the Sisters of the Conception. An English- (sort of) speaking guide will escort you. Wake up early and head for the market, which is spread throughout the town's 11 plazas. Each plaza is reserved for a particular type of merchandise—interesting carvings in one, leather goods in another, and ponchos and sweaters in still another. As for accommodations, the **Hotel Galpon** has 20 rooms and a good restaurant. The **Hotel El Troje** is another good choice.

Metropolitan Touring operates overnight tours to Riobamba. You can go by motorcoach or by train, but the best way is to go by train and return by coach. These tours run on Tuesday and Saturday.

Cuenca

This colonial city of 100,000 built on an Inca site is famous for its colonial homes with overhanging balconies, its Panama hat industry, and its Thursday market. Thousands of Indians fill the city on Thursday selling their wares. Bargains galore.

Adding to the charm is the Tomebamba River flowing through Cuenca. On the outskirts of town are Spanish "pueblos" and the Inca fortress ruins of **Ingapirca**.

Hotels are sparse, but a good choice is the **Hotel La Laguna** (doubles about $40) or the **Hotel Paris International** ($25 doubles). Round-trip fare from Quito by air is $40, and the flight takes one hour. **Metropolitan Tours** provides three-hour group tours for under $10. Full-day tours to the fortress ruins cost $15 per person.

READER'S TRAVEL TIPS—IBARRA: "If you're staying in Ibarra, there is a lovely little 'meson' (inn) called the **Shyris.** It's very inexpensive, but tourist accommodating, and has good standards. The price at this time is $6 a night per person, as opposed to the Ajaui (an excellent hotel on the road into Ibarra) for $27 a night. I find the Shyris (although offering less) quite nice and in a better situation (location wise), as well as being cheaper. The Shyris is located on Rocafuerte con Moreño.

"Between Ibarra and Otavalo is the little town of **San Antonio.** Woodcarvings of excellent quality and all shapes and sizes can be had here for low prices. The best places to shop are the humbler-looking shops around the plaza. To look and study styles, etc., the very best place is **Luís Potosí,** a three-story building next to the plaza in San Antonio. The upstairs gallery should be one of the wonders of the world. To get to San Antonio from Ibarra you can take the "San Antonio" bus, at 6¢ per person. It will go right by the plaza and returns to Ibarra by almost the same route, or take the Ibarra bus in Otavalo for 25¢ per person and get off at San Antonio, but you must walk three blocks up the hill to the plaza.

"In Ibarra you can find the buses to San Antonio near the Mercado Amazonas on Sanchez y Cifuentes street. If you get lost, ask one of the Mormon missionaries working there. They wear white shirts and ties all the time, and are very courteous and friendly. They have helped me find things in many cities of South America" (Von Merethand, Canadensis, Pa.).

COTOPAXI VOLCANO:
On a one-day excursion from the capital, you can visit Cotopaxi Volcano National Park. It was recently set aside for an ecological sanctuary to protect the fast-disappearing llama and other animals such as wolves, bears, puma, and deer. Turning off the Pan American Hwy., you can drive through fields of lava boulders right to the base of the volcano.

On the national park outing, and on most of the market tours on the southern route, **Metropolitan Touring** takes groups to lunch at its own working hacienda, Tambo Mulalo.

EXPLORING THE AMAZON:
For those with time and money to spare, a visit to that most mysterious of places—the Amazon jungle—can be the highlight of your stay in Ecuador. Again, planning is necessary since the tour, also offered by Metropolitan, is a leisurely five-day cruise down the Napo River, headwaters of the Amazon, aboard a luxurious, 180-ton floating hotel, called a "flotel." During the day you will venture out via motor canoe to explore the world's deepest rain forest and visit the villages of the Yumbo Indians, the tribe which has lived here for centuries. Metropolitan provides well-trained guides who will help you to discover and understand the flora and fauna of the region and translate for you so that you can barter with the Indians. Current rates include round-trip air fare from Quito, accommodations and meals aboard the flotel, lectures, and tour guides. A two-berth cabin is about $390 per person; a four-berth cabin, $300. A double-berth cabin with single occupancy is $465—for big spenders only! For information and reservations, contact **Metropolitan's Unseen Amazon,** P.O. Box 2542, Quito (tel. 52-4400). In the U.S., contact Adventure Associates, 5925 Maple, Suite 116, Dallas, TX 75235 (tel. toll free 800/527-2500). A $50 deposit is required.

READERS' JUNGLE TOUR SUGGESTIONS: "For tourists who want to visit the jungle without discomfort or the expense of a guided tour, we recommend the trip from Quito to **Puyo,** a city of 6,000 located in the jungle of eastern Ecuador, 140 miles southeast of Quito. Puyo has the appearance of a U.S. frontier town. The recommended hotel here is the **Hostería Turingia,** used by some tour companies. Most of the accommodations are in cottages on cement stilts. They might be compared to summer lake cottages in the U.S. A double room is $11 a day, including tax and service. The food is excellent and reasonable. Although regular bus and microbus service is available, we arranged with the Residencial Florida in Quito (under the same management as the Turingia) to have a taxi from Puyo pick us up in Quito and drive us to Puyo at a charge of $40, one way. The trip takes five hours, depending on how often you stop for snapshots of the magnificent scenery—the stately Andes above and below you, many waterfalls, orchids growing wild, and a river flowing between the mountains, carrying water to the mighty Amazon" (Byron M. Haines, Middletown, Ohio).

"Our jungle excursion on the **Flotel Orellana** (a floating hotel plying the Río Napo) was outstanding. Using the flotel as our base we were able to explore (with a guide) the surrounding jungles, rivers, and lakes using motorized or paddle dugout canoes. At $300 each for three nights' accommodation, all meals, plus air transport from and to Quito, we thought this was money well spent. The food was excellent and the organization (generally) was very good. My one reservation about organization was that because of an unexplained alteration to the itinerary in the brochure (which was probably due to nearby border fighting between Ecuador and Peru) we had to take a long detour by bus to reach the flotel, and again on leaving. On the second occasion there was a great deal of confusion over the supplying of the buses and we all had to crowd into one for part of the journey—in fact eight of us ended up traveling on the roof-rack! Although this added to the fun of the adventure, it was very bad public relations on the part of the company and potentially quite dangerous, although we came to no harm" (K. R. Arnott, Palmerston North, New Zealand).

5. A VISIT TO THE GALÁPAGOS ISLANDS

You may be as unimpressed as we were at your first glimpse of land in the Galápagos Archipelago. The islands look as if they are made of swirls of solidified mud, but it's actually lava, since the islands themselves are the tops of gigantic volcanoes. However, that first fleeting impression will be rapidly dispelled, for a visit to the Galápagos National Park is truly a unique experience. Even if you aren't a bird fancier and you find iguanas repulsive, you'll find yourself fascinated by the animal life on these 13 islands, 600 miles in the Pacific Ocean off the Ecuadorian coast.

Having been formed by eruptions during the past million years (the most recent in 1968), the islands became slowly inhabited by creatures and plants brought by wind and the Humboldt Current. No large land mammals ever reached the islands, so reptiles are the dominant species here, as they were all over the earth long ago. Because of the islands' isolation from the mainland of South America, and even from one another (by deep water and treacherous currents), these creatures developed uniquely. They adapted themselves to conditions on the islands and became different from their ancestors on the continent. No two of the islands have identical flora or fauna, although some of the animals are found on several of the islands. Also, there are creatures here that do not exist anywhere else on earth.

The 22-year-old Charles Darwin came to these islands in 1835 on his scientifically equipped ship *The Beagle*. He stayed for five weeks. What he saw and recorded here provided the basis for much of the information that Darwin published 30 years later in his momentous work *The Origin of Species*. In 1835 the fundamentalist view of the creation of the earth, only 6,000 years before, was prevalent. Species of animals and plants were seen as fixed, unchangeable, immutable organisms in this young world. In spite of mounting geological evidence to the contrary, the fundamentalist views remained the accepted theory because those scientists who felt that the earth was far older and that creatures could adapt to their environment had no unquestionable evidence to support their claims. Darwin and others aboard the *Beagle* set out to collect evidence of evolution. Pressure was so great that Darwin didn't publish his findings for 30 years after his return to England.

It was a species of finches (now known as Darwin's finches) with 13 varieties that provided Darwin with the initial thrust. These finches were all clearly related to one another and to similar finches on the mainland. However, they all had developed independent characteristics. Some ate hard nuts and had developed stocky, powerful beaks to crack open the shells. Others ate soft fruit and their beaks were shaped differently and were longer, while a third variety, known as the woodpecker finch, made itself a tool of cactus which it used to pry insects out of cracks in trees. As Darwin studied the finches, he noted the developmental changes. He also became aware of adaptation by the giant tortoises.

On one island, the vegetation eaten by the tortoise grows quite tall and the tortoise shells had evolved to permit these turtles to lift their heads to eat. Identical creatures on another island, where the vegetation hugs the ground, have shells that do not permit these tortoises to lift their heads. Other species studied by Darwin include land iguanas, marine iguanas, and such birds as the cormorant, which swims in search of food but has lost the ability to fly.

All these creatures, as well as others we haven't mentioned, still exist on the Galápagos Islands today, and because there are no predators on the islands, and since few people come here, the creatures have no fear of one another or of people. The birds land on the iguana's head, while crabs scurry alongside boobies. The extraordinary tameness of the animals (they swim with you, approach you instead of moving away, and even birds allow you to stand beside them) is astonishing.

That a place as peaceful and natural as the Galápagos can still exist in this modern world is a credit to the Ecuadorian government, UNESCO, and the Charles Darwin Foundation. In 1959 they established the Galápagos as a national park and protected all native animals, reptiles, and birds. They established the Charles Darwin Research Station on Santa Cruz Island, which is staffed by scientists and conservationists. They have set out to preserve those species endangered by outside influences. The tortoises, for example, had been captured for centuries by pirates and whalers and used for food. Several islands' tortoise communities were completely decimated. Also feral animals (domesticated animals allowed to run wild), brought to the islands by people trying to settle there and then abandoned when these people moved on, are a serious threat to the indigenous animals. Goats eat the vegetation, pigs and dogs attack the iguanas, while rats eat the eggs of tortoises and birds. These animals are being eradicated in order to preserve the natural environment.

By the way, Galápagos is the Spanish word for "tortoises," and these giant animals can live 160 years. The islands have Spanish and English names which makes for some confusion. Visitors to the islands are limited to 1,000 a month, and may come only with prearranged groups. Tours vary from three to eight days, and what you will see will vary with the tour you've chosen. All groups fly in from Guayaquil and Baltra (Seymour) Island, where a U.S. military base was established during World War II. You board your cruise ship here.

THE ISLANDS: Here's a rundown on some of the islands and a brief note about each. You should definitely do some reading before coming here.

James (Santiago) Island has a fur seal colony living in its black lava rock formations. Sharing this home are sea lions, crabs, pelicans, and marine iguanas. Espumuilla Beach is great for swimming alongside the seals and observing diving birds and flamingoes.

Tower (Genovesa) Island is a bird haven. The frigate bird, with its bright-red throat, red-footed and masked boobies, doves, and gulls populate this island.

Plaza Island is small but heavily overgrown with thick brush and cactus. As you come ashore, you'll be welcomed by sea lions and land iguanas. On the cliffs you'll see blue-footed boobies, gulls, and many other sea birds.

On **Hood (Española) Island** you'll see blue-footed boobies and lava lizards. During mating, the male lizards whistle while the females honk. Watch the albatross as he takes off from the rocks as if he were a jet plane.

Charles (Floreana) Island is one of the few permanently inhabited ones (5,000 nonscientists live on the Galápagos). Check the post office barrel, where mail was traditionally dropped to be picked up by a whaler going in a different direction.

Indefatigable (Santa Cruz) is the location of the Research Center. You can visit it and see firsthand the work being done here. The island is rich in wildlife, with the largest number of finches, gulls, and mockingbirds living in its cactus forest.

Among the reptiles that exist here are the giant land tortoises (galápagos), sea turtles, land iguanas, marine iguanas (the only sea-going lizard in the world), lava lizards, and the nonpoisonous Galápagos snake. Birds can be divided into two categories—sea birds and land birds. The Galápagos albatross, the Galápagos penguin, and the flightless cormorant are found nowhere else on earth. There are three species of boobies (red-footed, blue-footed, and masked), 13 species of finches, frigate birds, gulls, hawks, and mockingbirds. Mammals that are indigenous include sea lions and fur seals. All other animals were brought here later.

GETTING THERE: While a visit here will far exceed your budget, it is certainly worth saving for and we urge you to consider it. It is an unequaled experience and you should definitely take advantage of your proximity to it. You must make your arrangements long in advance, and of course the cost will depend on the length of the tour you select and the cruise ship you are on. A good way to start would be to contact **Metropolitan Touring,** C.P.O. Box 2542, Quito, Ecuador; or call their U.S. representative, Adventure Associates (tel. toll free 800/527-2500). Metropolitan Touring is the largest tour operator in Ecuador and to the Galápagos. They are highly regarded and absolutely reliable. Ask for literature about the cruises and arrangements available when you want to go. A recent arrival (1980) to the Galápagos scene is the M/V *Santa Cruz,* a ship designed especially for the Galápagos. It is comfortable, the food is excellent, the camaraderie infectious, and the multilingual guides well versed and highly knowledgeable.

Another reputable company operates the 90-passenger ship *Buccaneer.* Contact them through **Galápagos, Inc.,** in Miami, Florida (tel. toll free 800/327-9854).

There are several yachts that cruise the Galápagos as well. So get together a group of people and contact the previously mentioned Metropolitan Touring company. You cannot simply fly to the islands on your own. Visitors are limited in number and must be accompanied by a naturalist guide. By the way, there is a $30 fee to enter the Galápagos National Park.

Background Reading: Before you go, you should read *Darwin and the Beagle* by Alan Mooreland and *Galápagos Guide.* Both are available from the Complete Traveller Bookstore, 199 Madison Ave., New York, NY 10016. Mention *South America on $35 a Day* and receive a discount.

6. QUITO AFTER DARK

Quito is not one of South America's swinging night towns, and places go out of business here quickly. As our cab driver replied when we asked him which were the best nightspots in town, "In Quito, when it is night, we sleep." The big hotels are your best bets; there you can gamble away your sucres in slot machines and at blackjack tables. There are casinos at the hotels Colón, Quito, Alameda Real, and Chalet Suisse. Each of these hotels has a cocktail lounge or nightclub. **Rincón Quiteño** in the lower level of the Hotel Quito is a club with live music. You can spend the entire evening and nurse one drink for $2.50. Have another at **El Techo del Mundo,** the Quito Hotel's top-floor restaurant. The view is breathtaking—so are the prices, so stick to a drink.

GAMBLING: If you like to gamble, Quito is for you. You bet as little as 70¢ and play blackjack, roulette, or poker in elegant or near-elegant surroundings. One night we cashed $10 and played blackjack at the Hotel Colón casino for 3½ hours. When we quit (at 3 a.m.), we redeemed $8 in chips. The rules are similar to those in Las Vegas or Atlantic City. There are casinos at the hotels Quito, Colón, Alameda, and others.

LIVE MUSIC CLUBS: Probably the best club in town to see an Ecuadorian show is **Le Club,** at Calama 161 (tel. 54-9799), where for a $3 cover, plus drinks, you can see a show of Ecuadorian artists Wednesday through Saturday. On Monday and Tuesday, when it operates as a disco only, there's no cover. The bar area is lovely and the club has the same ownership as the Shorthorn Grill, a recommended steakhouse.

La Vieja Taverna, downstairs at Avenida Amazonas, corner of Pinto, in the Edificio Varing (tel. 52-3724), advertises itself as a club/piano bar. Actually it's more. While there is a resident pianist, they have occasional shows with special guest performers. Joe Mont, the pianist, writes his own songs. Open from 7:30 p.m. to 2 a.m., there's a sunken dance floor and leather couches, and the music is loud.

One of the nicest clubs in town is **Juan Sebástian Bar,** on Avenida Calama (also in our restaurant section). It draws a well-dressed, attractive crowd. The music goes on all night.

The Hotel Colón boasts the ingratiating **La Licorne** (just beyond the casino downstairs), where the prices are right—$2 and up for drinks. But when there's a show, the tab jumps to $4 to $8 minimum per person, so check first. Good pop music, much of it via U.S. discs. Nice for a late-evening drink. Open nightly from 9 p.m. to 4 a.m.

You can't miss our next club. The sign over the door features a shocking-pink, pipe-smoking pussycat. Located at Calle Juan Rodriquez, the **Pussycat** is a marvelously noisy, psychedelic place. Drinks are $2.25 and you can revel till 4 a.m.

DISCOTHÈQUES: The most popular discothèque in Quito is **Vocú,** a private club at Avenida Brasil, corner of Itaborda (tel. 45-3273), a ten-minute drive beyond the Channel 4 TV satellite station. It's a large place that gets active after midnight when the club members start to arrive. There are couches all about, set on different levels. If you like, there's a poolroom below and beyond the dance floor. You must pay about $3 to enter. Introduce yourself through the "speakeasy" window.

Quickly becoming one of the city's hottest nightspots, Quito's newest disco, **Nucleux,** located at Gaspar Villareal and Los Shyris, is another private club. To get in here, you have to present an ID from either the Hotel Colón or Quito. But don't worry, it isn't necessary to be staying at the hotel to get an ID. Just show your Tourist Card at the front desk, and they'll be happy to give you one.

Another great club, **Piramide,** is set in a lovely private house on Avenida Amazonas. The club, which is always crowded, opens at 11 p.m. with shows starting at midnight. The music here varies from boleros to Latin rock to salsa to musica folklorica.

Gasoline, at the corner of Santa María and Juan Leon Mera, is another popular disco, especially with the younger set. Like Vocú, it's a private club, but much smaller and not as formal. The music here, mostly rock, is very danceable although the dance floor is on the small side.

A pleasant discothèque at Reina Victoria 1138 is the **Ice Palace** (tel. 54-6035). Head downstairs where there's an attractive dance floor with clinging couples surrounded by couches set up to afford privacy.

Amadeus, Coruña 1398 at the corner of Orellana, is one of Quito's most elegant clubs. You could come here for dinner (French cuisine is the specialty), and spend the entire evening. There is a live show nightly, as well as a dance floor with videos and a game room. It draws the same type of crowd as the Juan Sebástian.

For a more subdued atmosphere, try **Cafe 3.30,** at Whimper 3.30. Here you can relax and listen or dance to soft music in very elegant surroundings.

PEÑAS FOLKLORICAS: Quito sports several peñas clubs where live folkloric music with audiences participating is the thing. They are loud, fun, and inexpensive. Our favorite peña club in Quito is **Peña Pacha Mama,** at Jorge Washington 530, which is open from 9 p.m. to 3 a.m. The blazing fireplace adds to the décor, particularly on a cold evening. Another favorite of ours on Calama (remember, this is the famous restaurant strip) is **Peña del Pasillo.** Farther out on 6 de Diciembre is **Peña Jatari Tambo,** which opens about 5 p.m. A third of our favorites is **La Lira Quiteña,** at Orrellana at Amazonas. Also recommended is **El Chucaro,** on Reina Vicloria. These clubs are generally closed on Sunday and Monday.

FOR MEN ONLY: If striptease is your cup of tea, drink it at **Hot Pants,** LaNina and Avenida Amazonas. There is a large bar with attractive "hostesses," and a small dance floor. Suddenly a go-go–type dancer appears on a small round dance floor and girates herself nude. Open from 10 p.m. on.

Most cab drivers with a male passenger will suggest a stop at **Mirador,** an almost-elegant club with resident ladies for hire for on-premises action. The place has been around for years and enjoys a good reputation, considering what it is.

Men on the prowl might also consider **Los Años Locos,** at Amazonas 1324 (tel. 54-2521), where the dancing girls also frequent the large bar area lined with men. The place is open until 3 a.m. weekdays, later on weekends.

CULTURE: Concerts, operas, and plays—often performed by international touring companies—can be seen at the **Teatro Sucre,** Plaza del Teatro, Guayaquil and Flores. However, tickets are high-priced, frequently starting at $5 and sometimes running to $12. Check with your hotel clerk for schedules.

The U.S. community here (including many embassy people) sponsors a theater group called the **Pichincha Playhouse,** which performs plays at various locations. Their production of *South Pacific* was a "smashing" success.

7. A SHOPPER'S GUIDE

The shops here are noted for exquisite handmade rugs done in old Indian designs, intricately designed wooden masks and figurines, and wool goods, straw handbags, silver articles, and Panama hats.

Many stores can be found on Avenida Guayaquil around the Plaza de la Independencia, but the best are in the New City on Avenida Colón.

Shop hours are 9 a.m. to noon and 3 to 6:30 p.m. weekdays, 8:30 to noon on Saturday. Some shops remain open Saturday afternoon.

Among our favorites is the **Folklore–Olga Fisch,** Avenida Colón 260, not far from the Hotel Quito. Olga Fisch is well known in Ecuador as a loving collector of the country's folk art which she is both preserving and popularizing. Among the items for sale are fine hand-knotted rugs of original design for about $32 a square foot. Mrs. Fisch does her own designs, using early Indian motifs. She borrows heavily from pottery and other artifacts that have been uncovered by archeologists. (Five of her rugs and wall hangings are in the United Nations in New York, 14 in the Metropolitan Opera House at Lincoln Center; others hang in museums.) Ready-made rugs range in price from $300, and workmanship and quality are first-rate.

Folklore also sells all the finest in old and modern Ecuadorian folk art in wood, leather, straw, copper, silver, and hand-woven materials. The prices range from $1 for an Indian reed flute to $2,000 for exquisitely polychromed, 17th-century figures. Embroidered dresses are $30 and up. There is an excellent selection of hand-woven and embroidered dresses too. Don't leave without asking to see Mrs. Fisch's Ethnographic Section—El Galpon—where you will find, displayed under a thatched roof, a collection of representative folk art that would be a proud addition to any museum. Many of the pieces here are not for sale.

Take the Colón–Camal colectivo from Santo Domingo Square on Calle Flores. It will drop you at the shop. An Olga Fisch shop can also be found in the Hotel Colón Internacional.

Probably the best handcraft outlet is **Ocepa,** with three shops around Quito. The most convenient is at Calle Jorge Washington, corner of Amazonas, near the Colón Hotel. Weave your way among good-quality ponchos, woodcarvings, ceramics, purses, chess sets, and handmade jewelry, all in a broad range of prices. The other two branches are in New City at Calle Carrion near Versalles, and downtown at Pasaje Espejo y Venezuela.

Highly recommended also is **La Guaragua,** at Jorge Washington 614. Browse amid the antique clocks, carvings, religious hats, and paintings, as well as the more popular native handcrafts. Prices are competitive and the selection is large.

Gold and silver jewelry made in Ecuador—with or without gemstones—is a good value at the local **H. Stern** outlet in the hotels Colón and Quito. Prices vary widely, but the quality is uniform. And for chess lovers, H. Stern carries a unique silver and gold-plated handcrafted set. Other excellent values are in Colombian emeralds which are sold at bargain prices.

The best in gold and silver, handmade and at low prices, can be found at the **Hamilton,** Avenida Amazonas, across from the Colón Hotel. Besides jewelry, tableware, and the like, the Hamilton sells other wares, such as a striking chess set made of Guayacan wood. Prices on all items range from $1 to $100.

For inexpensive ($1 and up) masks, trinkets, and wood gifts, stop in at **Najas,** under the Government Palace (Palacio de Gobierno) in the Plaza de la Independencia. There are a half dozen similar stores here, but this seems the best.

The **Galería Artes,** situated in a pretty town house at 6 de Diciembre on the corner of Veintimilla, features a different selection of handcrafted items every three weeks. You will find paintings and handcrafted jewelry in gold and silver, as well as pottery and antiques. Prices start at $10 and climb to $600. A nice touch is the cheese-and-wine room—stop for a light snack. Very civilized.

For a wide selection of handcrafted items at the best low prices in Quito, **La Bodega,** at Juan León Mera 614 (tel. 23-2844), comes highly recommended.

If you can't get to San Antonio de Ibarra, you can still see the woodcarvings the village is famous for at the **Galería de Arte Ruben Potosí,** in the Centro Comercial El Espiral on the corner of Amazonas and Jorge Washington. All the pieces are for sale, including some original works by Potosí himself.

The **Thimara Folklore,** Avenida Amazonas 430, is worth a visit. Polished ivory figures, dolls, Panama hats, ponchos, pillow cases, and beetle jewelry are nicely displayed in a bright atmosphere.

Artesanías Yanzar, Amazonas 515 at the corner of Roca, is a "must see" if you're looking for alpaca rugs, and nothing but alpaca rugs. That's all they carry —alpaca in all different sizes, shapes, and colors.

For authentic pre-Columbian figures, sweaters, and jewelry, try **Quipus,** Amazonas 634. **Ecuafolklore,** at Robles 620 and Juan León Mera, is also a good choice.

One of our favorite shops is **La Llama,** at Amazonas in front of the Hotel Colón. Here you can get all types of handcrafts in wood, ceramics, or textile. It's a good place to buy your Panama hats at prices from $20 to $60. Look for the llama logo on the sign.

Next door is **Tenería Cotacachi,** a terrific leather shop with items in antelope, suede, and regular leather—handbags, wallets, travel bags, etc. They export and will ship your purchase on request.

During our last visit to Quito, we were walking down Guayaquil, just beyond Sucre, toward the theater and the New City, when we were approached by two young Indians selling ponchos. After much pleading, they convinced us to go with them to their shop, "just to look" ("para mirar, no mas"). The shop itself, located in a courtyard off Guayaquil, was lined with shelves overflowing with sweaters, tapestries, bags, ponchos—everything imaginable. Needless to say, we did some of the best bargaining of our lives there; and left with a lovely woolen poncho (for less than $10), and a few assorted odds and ends.

HOW ABOUT THAT: The world-famous Panama hats, once the rage in the U.S., are actually made in Montecristi, Ecuador, and always have been. You can buy them at **Donat's,** Chile 1062, near Avenida Venezuela, for $20 and up.

THE COLÓN SHOPPING ARCADE: Without doubt, the most elegant shops in Quito are centered in the rear of the lobby of the Colón Hotel. Expect to find no inexpensive items, but what you get will be good-value high-quality (and high-priced) items. The **Bazaar** has elegant gift items. **Paipaco** has popular art. There's an antique shop, a bookshop, and an H. Stern jewelry shop. Excellent for browsing.

READER'S SHOPPING TIP: "An excellent place for shopping is **Products Andino,** on Avenida 9 de Octubre at Avenida Robles" (Emerson Tjart, Pa.).

8. TRANSPORTATION NOTES AND OTHER TIDBITS

CABS: Cabs are reasonably priced, but be sure to establish the cost in advance when you call for a cab since they have no meters. Cruising cabs do have meters, however. Within the city, the price for a 15-minute ride should run about $1.50. To New City from the Plaza de la Independencia, the tab could run $2.50. The airport fare is about $2.50 (up to five passengers). The base fare starts at 80¢.

A NOTE ABOUT BUSES: Buses in Quito are called *colectivos*. These are small, fast, and most convenient with seats for about 20. The names on the front indicate the first and last stops. The most important line is the Colón–Camal, which leaves every five minutes from Avenida Guayaquil, one block from the Plaza de la Independencia, and heads to almost all our recommendations in the New City for 5¢.

Buses 1 and 7 will take you to the airport. Three other major bus terminals are at the Plaza T. Cumandá and El Recreo, 45 minutes out of town.

Double-decker buses run on major streets in the New City. They have been imported from England. The fare is 10¢.

AUTO RENTALS: Rates for an aging Volkswagen are high—$16 a day plus 14¢ a kilometer. A $200 deposit is required too. The usual weekly rental rate is $93 plus 14¢ per kilometer. The monthly rate is $374.50 (14¢ per kilometer). Gasoline is included in the rates. The **Hertz** agency is at 10 de Agosto 6102; **Natcar** is at 10 de Agosto 343, at Jorge Washington (tel. 54-1380); **Avis** is located at 10 de Agosto 3155; and **Dollar** is at the Hotel Colón. If you want wheels for just a few hours, rent a cab—the per-hour rate is about $3.75.

THOSE OTHER TIDBITS: Here are a few last odds and ends:

Phones: To make a call, deposit 1 sucre and dial.

Letters: Airmail postage to the U.S. is about 40¢.

Post Office: Open until 8 p.m., it is located at Benalcazar 688, between Chile and Espejo, a block from the Plaza de la Independencia, near the Cueva Restaurant. There is also one in C.C. InaQuito near the airport.

U.S. Embassy: You can find the embassy at Avenida 12 de Octubre and Patria (tel. 54-800), near Ejido Stadium.

Tourist Office: A new government office is located at Reina Victoria 514 and Roca, directly behind the Soviet Embassy (tel. 23-9044).

A Bit of History: The Tenth of August is Ecuador's independence day, and thus a street is so named. The street called 6 de Diciembre marks modern Quito's founding in 1534 by Benalcazar.

Trains: The central railroad station, from which trains depart for Guayaquil and elsewhere, is in the section of Quito called Chimbacalle, south of the Old City. Both standard trains and autoferros (small coaches with reclining seats) operate from here. The ticket office is at Calle Bolívar 443.

Airport Tax: Quito has a good duty-free shop for departing passengers at the airport, featuring perfume and other items. However, when departing there is a $25 tax.

International Airport Shops: On departure you can spend all your leftover sucres on duty-free liquors, handcrafts, and jewelry.

CHAPTER XI

BOGOTÁ, COLOMBIA

□ □ □

From the instant you land at the sleek new **El Dorado International Airport,** you feel a privileged guest in this warm, receptive city which has much to offer beyond Juan Valdez and his superb Colombian coffee.

While the people here are more imbued with the conservative traditions of old Spain than in any other South American capital, nevertheless Bogotá is totally modern in its approach to tourism. The better hotels are on a par with good hotels in Lima and Santiago, and we have been able to locate fine budget choices in many parts of the city.

An example of Bogotá's accommodating approach to visitors is the treatment you receive upon arrival at the airport. A **hotel reservation service** on the second floor is at your disposal. There is also an office of the **Corporación Nacional de Turismo** nearby.

In common with much of South America, Bogotá is a city in transition. The greatest building boom in Bogotá's history is permanently altering this old, proud city which is slowly adjusting to a wave of high-rise luxury apartment houses and office structures. The skyline is unrecognizable to visitors absent for five or more years. The pope's visit to Bogotá in 1968 accelerated the boom, with miles of new street paving and many new hotels.

While the largely mestizo population (Spanish and Indian mixture) is deeply traditional in religion, dress, and customs, there are indications that attitudes are changing among the young. Women still rarely venture out alone in the evenings, and men are rarely seen without a tie and jacket.

FIRST IMPRESSIONS: A colorful custom—quite a surprise at first look—is the handsome wool poncho called a "ruana" worn by both men and women. The custom, apparently of Indian origin, has survived the Spanish invasion and conquest of the 1530s and is today a rather charming anachronism. And quite useful for chilly evenings.

You will find most Bogotanos reserved, not only toward strangers but even toward each other. The people here tend to be somewhat formal, but be patient and you will find, as we have with each visit, that courtesy and good manners go a long way toward relaxing relationships. Most locals also tend to be home oriented, and if they have money, private club oriented.

Emeralds and coffee are, of course, constant topics of conversation—and why not? Colombia mines 90% of the world's emeralds, and many experts insist its coffee is the world's best.

A QUICK ORIENTATION: To get yourself situated with the least effort, make the hotel reservations office on the second floor of the El Dorado Airport your first stop. As explained above, the representatives of the government tourist office there will book you at a hotel.

Tip: Review our hotel choices carefully for guidance as to where you want to stay and how much you will have to spend.

A 20-minute cab ride (the only practical transportation to the city) puts you in downtown Bogotá for about $5. There are also minibuses which cost under $1 and will take you downtown. Once there, you will find the city's sensible planning a great help in learning how to find your way about. A few basic points to remember: The city is divided into north and south at Calle 1 (you will spend all your time in the north, since the other half is exclusively residential).

Streets here have three designations: **carreras**—the main, wide streets that run north-south (the main carrera is no. 7, where you will find outstanding shops, restaurants, and theaters); **calles**—the east-west streets; and **avenidas**—the diagonal streets.

Finding Your Way Around

Getting lost in Bogotá is virtually an impossibility. Street addresses are so ingeniously clear, once you understand the system, that you can locate any number instantly in your mind. We're so impressed, we're thinking of starting a movement to get all cities to adopt this system.

Let's illustrate. The address of Colombia's most famous hotel, the Tequendama, is Carrera 10, no. 26–32. This immediately tells you that the hotel is on the 10th carrera, between Calles 26 and 27, at building no. 32. If an address is Calle 12, no. 4–35, this indicates that the address is on Calle 12, between Carreras 4 and 5, building no. 35.

Avenidas are exempt from the system.

A further aid: Remember that on calles, even numbers are on the north; and on carreras, even numbers are on the east.

The heart of Bogotá for visitors is a rectangle bounded on the south by the **Plaza de Bolívar** at Calle 10; on the north by the city's social hub, the Hotel Tequendama at **Calle 26;** on the west by the thoroughfare **Carrera 14** (also called **Caracas**); and on the east by **Carrera 4.**

The huge, pigeon-filled **Plaza de Bolívar,** a major tourist attraction located between Carreras 7 and 8, is the bustling site of most political rallies (the oratory is a lot more restrained than in London's Hyde Park) and is home to the royal-like Cardinal's Palace, the imposing National Cathedral, and the stately Capitol Building and City Hall.

Carrera 7, a lively thoroughfare crammed with shops and restaurants, as well as banks, airline offices, and churches, is a must on your first day in Bogotá.

A key cross street, intersecting with Carrera 7, is **Avenida Jimenez de Quesada** (called Avenida Jimenez here) which becomes **Calle 15** in the downtown area. Here you will find the Hotel Continental, one of our choice recommendations, as well as Colombia's most important bank, the Bank of the Republic (Banco de la República). The bank building, by the way, formerly housed the famous Gold Museum—now located a block away and definitely worth a visit. Nowhere else will you see incredibly beautiful gold artifacts that date back 500 years to the Chibcha Indians.

For a stunning view of Bogotá, follow Avenida Jimenez to **Monserrate Mountain.** This is particularly lovely at twilight. Incidentally, the mountain is a famous religious shrine where pilgrims from all over Colombia journey during important festivals.

Modern Bogotá

Carreras 7 and 13 and Avenida Caracas are the major thoroughfares heading out from central Bogotá toward **Chapinero,** which begins at about Calle 50. This newer section is replete with lovely homes, shops, clubs, cinemas, and restaurants.

Beyond Chapinero, at Calle 90, you enter **Chico,** which in our opinion is the city's most modern and attractive residential district.

Beyond Chico is **Unicentro,** an enormous shopping complex housing shops, restaurants, nightspots, and cinemas. Parking and babysitting services are available.

Heading farther from Center City, we come to **Santa Barbara,** another wealthy residential area and the site of several lively discos and clubs.

A WORD ABOUT CLIMATE: The local weatherman has an easy task. To be accurate day after day, he need only remember to predict: "Cloudy and mild with a chance of brief afternoon showers." That in a nutshell is Bogotá's weather most of the year. Since Bogotá is just north of the equator, there are no distinct seasons. Yet temperatures are refreshingly moderate due to the city's elevation (8,600 feet above sea level). Afternoon temperatures range in the mid to upper 60s all year round—ideal for sightseeing sans fatigue—while evening lows usually hover in the mid-40s.

Clothing Tip: No matter how clear the morning, always carry a light raincoat. Afternoon sprinkles can come up rather suddenly. If you plan to remain out into the evening, bring along a heavy sweater and lined raincoat.

THE LOCAL CURRENCY: The basic currency here is the **peso,** and it has fallen in value from 210 to the dollar in our previous edition to 310 at press time. Prices for accommodations and food have fallen dramatically from those in the previous edition. Prices in this edition are based on 200 pesos to the dollar because the drop in prices cannot be allowed to continue. So it seems obvious that they will gravitate upward in the next two years. *You should use our listed price as a ballpark figure, and add at least 10% in 1990.*

Note: The $ sign is used here to indicate pesos (5 pesos is written $5). There are 100 centavos to a peso, and coins come in denominations of 5, 10, 20, and 50 centavos. Pesos are issued in $.50, $1, $2, and $5 coins, and $10, $20, $50, $100, $200, $500, $1,000, $2,000, and $5,000 bills.

Important Note: Keep all receipts for dollars you have converted to pesos. You cannot change pesos to dollars without them.

A LANGUAGE NOTE: Spanish is, of course, the national tongue; nonetheless a surprising number of Bogotanos speak English and speak it well.

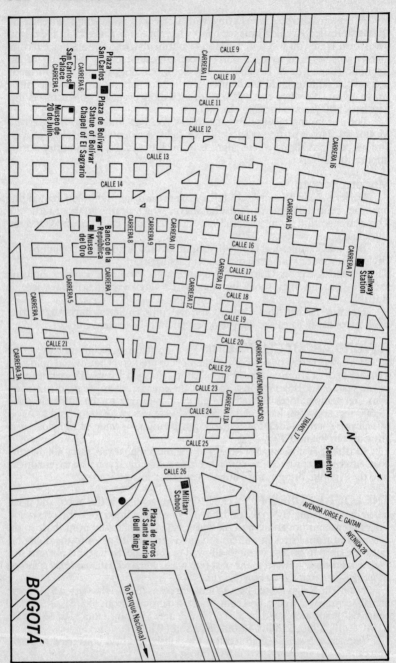

CALLE 9
CALLE 10
CALLE 11
CALLE 12
CALLE 13
CALLE 14
CALLE 15
CALLE 16
CALLE 17
CALLE 18
CALLE 19
CALLE 20
CALLE 21
CALLE 22
CALLE 23
CALLE 24
CALLE 25
CALLE 26

CARRERA 11
CARRERA 5
CARRERA 6
Plaza San Carlos
San Carlos Palace
Plaza de Bolívar
Statue of Bolívar
Chapel of El Sagrario
Museo de 20 de Julio
CARRERA 8
CARRERA 9
CARRERA 10
Banco de la República
Museo del Oro
CARRERA 7
CARRERA 5
CARRERA 4
CARRERA 3A
CARRERA 12
CARRERA 13
CARRERA 13A
CARRERA 14 (AVENIDA CARACAS)
CARRERA 15
CARRERA 16
CARRERA 17
Railway Station
TRANS. 17
Cemetery
N
AVENIDA JORGE E. GAITAN
AVENIDA 28
Military School
Plaza de Toros de Santa María (Bull Ring)
To Parque Nacional

BOGOTÁ

CALLING ALL SOCIOLOGISTS: Colombia's crime problem has received a good deal of North American press attention. And while we've personally seen no evidence in our visits here of the well-publicized "bandidos," still we have in our files innumerable letters sadly detailing incidents of stolen property and physical beatings, many in broad daylight, even on main streets. Therefore we feel we should remind you to stick to main streets when wandering about at night and take taxis to unfamiliar areas, just as you would in New York or Chicago. The most popular attractions for the bandidos are watches, cameras, and jewelry. We suggest keeping your camera under wraps and your watch and other jewelry as inconspicuous as possible. Pickpockets ply their trade in crowded areas, particularly in elevators and buses.

A businessman acquaintance of ours who resides here suggests, half in jest, that we cultivate Swedish accents to confound the bandidos. Apparently, Swedes are thought to be more impoverished than Norte Americanos.

Along these lines, read the following readers' comments:

READERS' WARNINGS ON CRIME: "Your treatment of this very serious problem, nationwide (with the exception of Nariño state in the extreme south, where the tiptoff that things are different is that local women are once again wearing earrings on the public buses), is far too light considering its magnitude and seriousness. I strongly recommend a straight-forward warning of how the thieves and pickpockets operate and what they expect.

"The pickpockets operate in groups of two or three. They are willing to board your bus and put a gentle squeeze on you in the aisle, either as you enter or leave, cleaning out your pockets in the process. Bags held between your legs on the bus may be pulled out backward by thieves sitting behind you. When waiting in a bus station or sitting in a city park, *always have a hand on all baggage or handbags at all times.* Peace Corps volunteers gave me this excellent advice. They didn't know a single volunteer in the country who hadn't had something stolen, often when guard slipped for only a matter of seconds. They also said, however, that the ordinary pickpocket does not want a direct confrontation, and therefore plies his trade as stealthily as possible—you won't notice anything missing until sometime later.

"The teleférico in Bogotá, and the area around the lower station, are notoriously bad. Not only do the thieves get on the teleférico with you (often assured of a crowded situation), but even a well-dressed middle-class-appearing man and woman tried to get their fingers into the camera bag of my Colombian friend while we were waiting in line in the upper station for the trip down. Tourists should *not* use the teleférico on Sunday, however tempting, when it's jammed with the locals. (Even my Colombian friend, very wise to the ways of his city, said it was ridiculous to go up on Sunday.) The local tourist office publication in Bogotá strongly advises tourists to avoid the road to Monserrate *at all times.*

"The political instability in Bogotá is at a crisis level, and the place really isn't safe for tourists these days. (The Peace Corps even pulled out.) The police action I saw on Plaza de Bolívar two hours after arriving in the city left me trembling. Some British tourists witnessed a runing gun battle with the police from their hotel on Carrera 5. Peace Corps volunteers said it was inadvisable for gringos to wander around downtown Bogotá after 7 or 8 p.m. All of this is very sad, because there is so much that is worth seeing in Bogotá, and in Colombia as a whole. But as the Peace Corps volunteers I met said (and having been one in Iran, I know they generally know what they are talking about when it comes to local customs, happenings, and procedure), 'All the horror stories you have heard about thieves in Colombia are absolutely true.'

"In Popayan, one potential thief entered the family hotel we were checking out and asked for a room directly opposite the one we had looked at, just in case our guard might not always be up. The proprietor well knew what he was dealing with and offered the fellow a room elsewhere, which he declined.

"As to your comment on Swedish accents, a Danish businessman, who had been robbed of $500 as he went from the airport in Cali to the bus terminal there, just snorted when he read it. All white-skinned tourists are treated equally in Colombia. They are the scapegoat victims of much of the hostility and aggression that the 'Robin Hoods' would rather be directing to their own oppressors—who live in those magnificent homes, magnificently guarded by private *and* public guards, in northern Bogotá. (I said white-skinned because that's what the Chinese-American Peace Corps volunteer I was speaking with said. He felt his racial features were a distinct asset for him in Colombia—he 'blended in' much easier and was not so easily identified as a scapegoat.)

"Tourists in Colombia should remove *all* watches, rings, and other jewelry *before* entering the country. Even a 200-peso bill is a considerable amount of money and can cause heads to turn, and pickpockets to move in. Don't even use a camera in the large cities, although it's all right in smaller towns like San Agustín. (Heed the hotel warnings about traveling alone by horseback there, though!)

"My biggest liability ended up being my gold wire-frame glasses. Swiss friends said that's exactly why they got contacts before they went to Central and South America. We have to be careful in large American cities too, but the ordinary pickpockets here don't operate in well-organized groups the way they do in many parts of Colombia—at least not yet! I have traveled in many parts of the world and have never had to be on my guard the way it was necessary in Colombia" (Emerson Tjart, Pa.).

"Police vigilence of the road to the teleférico has been greatly intensified. Saturdays are a very good day to go, for it's not too deserted or too busy. I want to add this: While there is a lot of violence in Colombia resulting from police–guerrilla activity and police–narcotics traffic activity, I personally experienced no problem in regard to safety of myself or my property. Nor did I in my travels throughout the country see or hear of any robbery of a tourist. Other books' repeated warnings frankly almost caused me not to go to Colombia. In fairness to Colombians, whom I found to be extremely nice people, I would like you to mention this" (Roberta Finke, New York, N.Y.).

[Authors' Note: Increased police vigilence is highly visible at tourist sites and government buildings throughout the country. Since the bloody event at the Government Palace in 1985, armed police have a high profile, particularly so at night. Again, we repeat that although we have been in Colombia at least a dozen times, we have never experienced any problem whatsoever. Be cautious, dress accordingly, and exhibit the same good common sense you would at home.]

WARNING: The Colombian government does not tolerate the illicit possession of, or traffic in, drugs. Dealers, pushers, and mules are given long prison terms. The mere possession of drugs is a serious crime. Under *no* circumstances should you have any drug in your possession for which you do not have a medical prescription.

1. WHERE TO STAY

Until recently Bogotá never had too many tourists, so understandably it never had too many hotels. This was the major problem when the pope made his first Latin American visit in August 1968, even though several new hotels had been constructed for the visit. We have therefore included most acceptable hotels in the city regardless of price. The only decent hotels not mentioned are those too inaccessible for you to consider.

Notes: All our selections include bath, but no breakfast, unless otherwise noted. You must add the 5% tourist tax to all rates. As for heat, the deluxe Tequendama and Hilton hotels are currently the only ones with central heating. But keep in mind that cold weather is a rare phenomenon.

HIGHER-PRICED CHOICES: One of our great favorites in Bogotá, ideally located for nightlife, is the charming 150-room **Hotel El Presidente,** Calle 23, no. 9–45, between Carreras 9 and 10 (tel. 284-1100). Within walking distance of the Tequendama Hotel on Carrera 10, as well as the city's best nightspots, the Presidente offers clean, roomy doubles from $27, singles from $19, triples at $36, all with bath. Floors are carpeted and in many instances furnished with upholstered couches. Breakfast is $3 continental style, $4 with eggs. Guests have use of the garage on the premises; there is a bar, and the restaurant is located on the upper level. One of our recommended nightspots is located here. Highly recommended.

Another superb choice—beyond our budget limits, but worth every extra peso—is the almost-luxurious 200-room **Hotel Continental,** Avenida Jimenez no. 4-16, near Carrera 5 (tel. 282-1100), which ranks just behind the magnificent Tequendama and Hilton as the best hotel in Bogotá. Large front doubles are $38; singles are $30.

This nine-story oasis offers spotless rooms with carpets that are scrupulously vacuumed daily. We stayed in a $23 rear double during a recent visit and were delighted to find each evening that the maid had turned down our beds, scrubbed down the shower stall, and left us with fresh soap. The room had colorful draperies, a modern bureau, two end tables, and a most comfortable double bed. The Continental also houses one of our recommended restaurants (the arroz con pollo is outstanding), a clean, quick-service coffeeshop, and a relaxing cocktail lounge and bar that we recommend to you. Added fillips are the beauty parlor and the uniformed doorman. We consider the Continental the equal of European hotels we've inspected that charge almost twice the rate. Highly recommended.

Nearby is one of Bogotá's newest hotels, the **Nueva Granada,** at Avenida Jimenez no. 4-81 (tel. 282-3697). Opened in the fall of 1982, the Nueva Granada is a luxury stop in the heart of the downtown area offering large modern rooms with private baths and TVs. Singles are $32 and doubles run $44.

Hotel María Isabel Bogotá, Carrera 33, no. 15-05 (tel. 245-9262), is a spiffy hotel in an out-of-the-way location. Its furnishings are modern and the service is superior. Many rooms have kitchenettes. Thickly carpeted and with double beds and large bathrooms, the rooms are light and airy. Singles run $27, while doubles go for $39.

Another top-rated choice is the 120-room **Hotel Cordillera,** Carrera 8, no. 16-85, between Calles 16 and 17 (tel. 284-7200), only a few blocks from the Continental. A startling bonus in the eight-story Cordillera is the size of the rooms, which could comfortably sleep six in most instances. A double, with bath, telephone, and carpeting is $32; singles are $25. Convenience is the keynote here. Elevators are self-service and the very good restaurant on the second floor remains open until 10 p.m. The reasonably priced cafetería on the lobby level serves until 9 p.m. every night. Excellent value.

A relatively new hotel is the centrally located **Hotel Dann International,** at Avenida 19, no. 5-72 (tel. 284-0100). This 150-room, 13-floor luxury stop offers guests a restaurant, beauty parlor, barbershop, laundry, bar, and convention room. Rooms are carpeted and have drapes and modern furniture (most come with TV). Doubles range from $45 up; singles are $33.

Its sister hotel, **Dann Colonial,** at Calle 14, no. 4-21 (tel. 241-1683), is in the heart of Bogotá's colonial quarter, La Candelaría. It is within easy walking distance of the Capital, Plaza de Bolívar, and Gold Museum. The streets around it are narrow and the buildings are red-roofed. The hotel itself is modern and very luxurious. Singles are $21 and doubles are $30, not that high for a first-class hotel.

The **Hotel Monserrate,** Calle 17, no. 7-71 (tel. 242-3574), starts on the second floor where there is a small lobby and restaurant. The rooms are also small and well maintained, although some mattresses seemed to sag a bit. The location is excellent. All rooms have private bath. Singles are $18 and doubles run $25.

Its neighbor, the **Hotel Cristal,** Calle 17, no. 7-92 (tel. 243-0030), has a small ground-floor lobby and then an elevator will whisk you up to your room. The 28 rooms are spread over ten floors. All rooms are large and airy, with twin beds, couches, and sitting area. The restaurant and bar on the second floor are worth trying. Singles run $17, while doubles go for $25, with private bath.

Across from the El Presidente Hotel is the **Hotel Del Duc,** at Calle 23, no. 9–38 (tel. 234-0080). Open since 1966, the hotel offers 57 rooms on eight floors; all rooms are carpeted and have small sitting areas. Doubles are a very reasonable $24; singles, $18. A bar and restaurant are on the premises, and laundry service is available. Excellent value.

A cozy find that we like for its *gemütlich* qualities is the tall, narrow **Hotel Regina,** Carrera 5, no. 15–16, between Calles 15 and 16 (tel. 234-5135), where the friendly owners offer guests a choice of twin or double beds at no difference in cost. The Regina's 31 rooms, spread over eight floors, all come with bath and are spotless. A restaurant and cafetería, as well as a bar, are on the elevator-equipped premises. Located near the Continental, the hotel charges $23 for doubles, and $15 for singles. Comfortable and recommended.

Another good choice is the **Hotel Tundama,** Calle 21, no. 8–81 (tel. 284-5900). Doubles are under $15; singles are $12. This eight-story hotel has 70 rooms and offers a TV room, an intimate restaurant, and a good bar.

A newish near-luxury choice is the 277-room **Hotel Bacata,** Calle 19, no. 5–20 (tel. 283-8300), near the Hotel Dann. Everything here is first class, but the prices are rather high; doubles are $45 and singles run $35. Guests have private parking facilities. A good bar and restaurant are on the premises. Worth it if you're willing to spend the money. Note the automatic entrance door.

For a change of pace you might want to consider the small **Fontana Hotel,** Calle 17, no. 7–92, at Carrera 8 (tel. 243-0030), eight blocks from the Presidente. We were tipped off to this clean, 18-room hotel by a U.S.–born Peruvian who stays here on business trips. "The location is perfect for business and pleasure, and you can't improve on the service," our friend insists, and we have to agree. A seven-story, red-brick structure, just around the corner from the Cordillera, the Fontana offers neat doubles for $30 and singles for $20, all with bath. A U.S.–style bar is off the lobby, as is a TV room. A large yellow neon sign alerts you to the Fontana. Nights can be noisy here. Don't confuse this hotel with the five-star La Fontana.

Another small hotel is **Los Cerros,** at Calle 19, no. 9–18, three blocks from Carrera 7 (tel. 283-8458). The four-floor Cerros has 19 rooms that make up for in comfort what they lack in size. The rooms are carpeted and all come with private bath. Doubles are $19, while singles pay $15. The hotel has a small restaurant serving all three meals, and a bar. Good location.

Or consider the **Hotel San Diego,** at Carrera 13, no. 24–82 (tel. 284-2100), where a comfortable double is only $25 and singles are $18. Service here is first class; there are a bar and restaurant on the premises.

LOWER-BUDGET CHOICES: Thus far we've surveyed the better hotels in Bogotá, most of which have been at the top of our budget limit or have exceeded it. Now it's time for a look at true budget choices that meet our standards of cleanliness and comfort.

The **Hotel de Lujo,** Carrera 13, no. 22–46 (tel. 241-3318), tries hard and has done the most with what they have. Freshly painted and carpeted, with attractive posters and planters around, the hotel is constantly being cleaned. But the rooms are small—in some cases the bed is virtually all of it. To compensate, there are sitting areas on each floor. Doubles are $13 and singles are $9. Good value.

Another favorite is the 33-room **Residencias Dorantes,** Calle 13, no. 5–07, between Carreras 5 and 6 (tel. 234-6640), which offers fine doubles for $12 and singles for $7, with bath and bidet. Bathless doubles, a rarity in Bogotá, are $6 and singles are $4.50. The owners seem to delight in polishing the furniture daily, and as a result there often is a faint but pleasant odor of polish in the bright, airy rooms.

Like to swim? The **Hotel Alexia,** at Carrera 9, no. 16–35 (tel. 243-0222), has two indoor pools, one for each sex. The 36 rooms, all with bath, are apartment-like, with anterooms. Doubles are $18 and singles pay $9.

Another good budget choice is the 19-room **Manila Hotel,** Calle 17, no. 8–23, between Carreras 8 and 9 (tel. 243-9010), just around the corner from the Cordillera Hotel. Clean, though rather plain, doubles are $15, while singles are $10, all with bath. This nine-story, elevator-equipped hotel, while basic, is well maintained.

Fading fast, but still a good value is the white-and-yellow, colonial-style **Hotel Residencia Santa Fe,** Calle 14, no. 4–48 (tel. 242-0560), where three meals are included in the modest rate. Furnished in an old Spanish motif, the hotel's 44 rooms all come with bath and telephone. Clean and airy, most rooms have awnings and window shutters. The per-person charge is $15, including meals. Apartments are also available. Doubles without food are $13; singles are $9.

The 21-room **Hotel Ejecutivo de la 19,** Calle 19, no. 5–98 (tel. 245-0501), is a basic selection that offers small doubles for $14, singles for $10, all with bath. A green awning and red sign help identify the Hotel Avenida, which, while plain, offers good value. The hotels Dann and Bacata are nearby.

Equally basic is the larger **Hotel Miami,** Carrera 7, no. 23–56 (tel. 282-4378). The 20 public rest rooms—six to seven per floor—are more than ample for the 78 guest rooms. The rates? Doubles are $12 and singles are $8. Expect the furniture to be well used and the service less than first class.

An unusually low-priced find is the 18-room **Hotel Menendez,** Calle 20, no. 5–85 (tel. 241-3542), which offers guests a comfortable lobby sitting room, complete with fireplace and TV, and rooms that are plainly furnished but clean and acceptable. All rates include three exceptionally generous meals. Doubles, with shower, tub, and meals, are only $15, while singles are $9. Look for a gray building set back from the street and a small sign. Fine budget value.

The **Hotel Carlos V,** at Carrera 7, no. 30–28 (tel. 232-2540), is a 42-room hotel with basic rooms, bare floors, but good value. Doubles without bath are $12; singles are $6.75. Rooms with bath are also available at $6 for doubles and $4 for singles.

Several readers recommended the older, five-story home belonging to the **Hotel Virgen del Camino,** Calle 18A, no. 14–33, off Avenida Caracas (tel. 282-4450). We can report that the hotel offers clean, cozy rooms at moderate prices. Singles with private bath run $9, while doubles are $13. If you opt for a bathless room, you'll save around $1.50 to $2. There are no elevators here, so ask for a room on one of the lower floors if you wish to avoid a climb.

Continuing in this category, you can choose the **Residencia Zaratoga,** conveniently located at Avenida Jimenez no. 4–56 (tel. 242-8041), near the Continental. Rates and services are rock-bottom: $5 for a single, $7 for a double. Don't expect anything fancy here.

Also, you might try the 50-room, three-story **Hotel Panamericano,** Calle 15, no. 12–70 (tel. 281-2957). Doubles are a high $10; singles run $8.25—the accommodations are basic. Head to the second floor for the reception desk.

FAMILY CHOICES: Traveling with your family? An outstanding budget pension is the three-story **Pension Alemana,** Caracas, no. 25–15, on Carrera 14 (tel.

241-7590), which differs from most pensions in that it includes only breakfast in the rate. Enter on Caracas and ascend one flight, where you register. The large, bright rooms, all immaculate, with full-length mirrors, are an excellent value at $15; triples are $20. Lower weekly rates can be negotiated. Five public bathrooms, each with a shower and bidet, are more than adequate for the 17 guests. Breakfast, by the way, includes juice, toast, eggs, and coffee. Hostess Julia de Pinilla takes good care of her guests.

A similarly priced choice is the **Hotel Cardenal,** at Avenida Jimenez no. 4–38 (tel. 242-4217), next to the Hotel Continental. The 39 rooms are like small apartments, with anterooms, bedrooms, and a refrigerator. Doubles, all with bath, are $15, and singles go for $9. A bar and restaurant are on the premises of the five-floor hotel.

Another stop for you to consider is a pension called the **Hotel Île de France,** Calle 18, no. 14–56, between Carreras 14 and 15 (tel. 242-0680), which is operated by a hospitable Spaniard, José Lopez. A family of four can get a two-bedroom flat, with living room, kitchenette, and private bath, for $24 a day. Doubles are $19 and singles are $13. The three-story, 45-room pension is not impressive in appearance, but it is well maintained by the owners, who of course live on the premises. Note the French scenes in the spacious dining hall. Recommended especially for families on a tight budget.

Our final choice in this category is the **Hotel Monaco,** at Calle 23, no. 7–49 (tel. 234-2994), which shares a lobby with the highly recommended Alpino Refugio Restaurant. The 40 rooms, spread over nine floors, are actually small suites, each with a sitting room, refrigerator, oven, and dining room. While the facilities are well worn, the value is there. Doubles run $15; triples are a bargain at $19. Remember, if you are so inclined, you can eat in and thereby substantially cut down on your food costs.

THE BIG SPLURGE: Bogotá's **Hilton,** at Carrera 7, no. 32–16 (tel. 232-7520), has proven to be so popular that they have built a second tower, which has double the size of the 200-room stop. It boasts a heated swimming pool and health club, several excellent restaurants, and Telex services for business travelers. Doubles run about $75 for large, well-furnished rooms, and singles run about $60.

The **Tequendama Hotel,** Carrera 10, no. 26–32 (tel. 282-9066), part of the Inter-Continental chain, along with the Hilton, is the best hotel in Bogotá and among the best in South America. The Tequendama is to Bogotá socially what the Waldorf-Astoria is to New York City. It is in reality a small city unto itself with some of the best restaurants, bars, nightclubs, and shops right on the premises. This is the meeting place for all the important people. Many an important business deal has been closed here. Even for budget travelers, this is a good place to meet for tea or a nightcap. The 800-room hotel is constantly being enlarged. Doubles start at $75; singles are $60 and up.

IN THE SUBURBS: As the city expands northward, progress follows. Modern shopping centers, beautiful private homes, restaurants, and boutiques have sprung up in the area beyond Calle 90, called **Chico.** This lovely sector of Bogotá is well known for its highly regarded eye clinic, which draws patients from all over the world. They stay in the modern new hotels and pensions that have opened to meet the demand. For those who don't mind the 20-minute bus or taxi ride into downtown (longer at peak hours), a stay in the suburbs is an interesting way to experience a different side of this city, while enjoying moderately priced lodgings in an attractive, private home.

Big-Splurge Hotels

Before taking a look at the area's pensions, we'll quickly cover Chico's two ultramodern, big-splurge hotels: the **Bogotá Plaza** and **Hotel El Belvedere**. The Plaza, at Calle 100, no. 18A–30 (tel. 256-0975), has 20 rooms with wall-to-wall carpeting, air conditioning, large private baths, television, and phone. You pay handsomely for these extras: $66 for doubles, $60 for singles. Prices for similar rooms at the Belvedere, Carrera 18, no. 100–16 (tel. 257-7700), are somewhat lower than the Plaza, with singles starting at $45, and doubles at $60. Both hotels have restaurants and bars.

Cosmos 100, Calle 100, no. 21A–41 (tel. 257-9200), is a 128-room hotel located near Unicentro. The hotel has several restaurants, bars, and a sauna. Rooms have TVs and mini-bars. Rates run $50 for singles and $60 for doubles.

Pensions

By far the best buys in the suburbs are the pensions. Here, the price of your rooms will often include three meals. And you will be made to feel like a member of the family as the atmosphere tends to be more informal and relaxed.

Señorita Mariette Delolme, the personable manager of the **Don Jorge Residencias,** Avenida 15, no. 105–16 (tel. 256-4695), goes "all out" to make your visit a pleasant one. She has no qualms about your using the kitchen to cook up something special, or running a washer full of laundry. She also has numerous helpful shopping and sightseeing suggestions. But it is babies that receive Mariette's special attention. She'll proudly show you a desk covered with photographs of these little guests. At first we didn't quite understand. Then we learned that many couples come to Bogotá to adopt babies and stay in a private hotel during their first few weeks as new parents. If you don't mind the occasional babble of a baby, we think you'll be happy at the Don Jorge Residencias. The 28 rooms, many with private bath, are $25 per person with all three meals included. If you wish to have only one meal at the pension, your room rate will drop to $20.

Next, we come to the ranch-style home of **Chico Norte Residencias,** Carrera 22, no. 101–39 (tel. 236-5099). Enter a spacious living room where guests often congregate around a small, modern fireplace. Rooms, located off the living room, are large, clean, and contemporary in décor. Most rooms have a private bath or a bath close by. Rates are $20 per person with three meals included, slightly less if you eat only one meal at the hotel. Well recommended.

If these two pensions are full, check out the **Halifax,** at Calle 93, no. 15–93 (tel. 256-6143). Prices are somewhat higher than at our previous two selections for rooms that are similar in size and furnishings. However, the Halifax is popular. Make reservations at least two weeks in advance. Three meals are included in the rates of $29 per person.

RENT AN APARTMENT: Mario Romero informs us that he has a two-bedroom apartment in Unicentro for rent by the week or by the month. If you are here for a long stay you might enjoy having your own kitchen, living room, etc. Write for details to Mario Romero at Carrera 13, no. 101–96, Bogotá, Colombia. Rates are very flexible.

2. WHERE TO DINE

Bogotanos dine relatively early for South America—as early as 8 p.m. Most restaurants are closed by midnight. But early or not, Colombians eat with gusto and prefer their evening meal to be generous in portion and rich in spices. Other meals are light. Meat and chicken dishes, highly seasoned and served with heaping cooked vegetables, are menu staples in most restaurants.

A superb national specialty—a recommended must in your dining—is a marvelously tangy beef stew called **puchero** that brims with fresh vegetables, sausage, and chunks of chicken. Another must here is the **arroz con pollo**—best we've ever eaten—which is a long dinner-table jump from the chicken-and-rice dishes served us elsewhere in South America or even in Madrid. The chicken, carefully boned and sharply seasoned, is mixed with four or five vegetables and rice and is usually served in a large bowl. You should also try the **ajiaco,** a deliciously filling soup made with three different types of potatoes, and served with cream, hard-boiled egg, corn, and avocado. Very traditional in Bogotá, it is served in most restaurants, and you can always ask for seconds. Another specialty is **empanadas** (potato pies), eaten as a snack. The national beverage is **tinto,** a demitasse made with rich Colombian coffee (which we consider the world's best). U.S.–style coffee is called **café,** coffee served with cream. But black is best.

Beer drinkers should rejoice here, for the Club Colombia brand is as good as the best coming out of U.S. breweries, and is now sold in the U.S.

In general, the better hotels have good restaurants, and most also operate inexpensive coffeeshops or cafeterías.

Tip: Most restaurants close on Sunday and your dining is limited generally to hotel restaurants on that day. Keep this in mind when planning your Sunday activities. Also, service is not included in the bill.

BREAKFAST AND LUNCH: Located across from the Teatro Jorge Eliecer Gaitan on Carrera 7, **Punto Rojo** is clearly one of Bogotá's best budget choices. A complete meal here is less than $3, and you won't go away hungry. This large self-service restaurant offers a wide selection of chicken, fish, meat, and rice dishes, as well as tempting desserts, salads, and sandwiches (empareados). Check for the daily specials, which include such national favorites as sancocho con pollo, piquete mixto, and ajiaco bogetano. With locations along the highways, Punto Rojo is a favorite pitstop among travelers.

El Torito, in the Tequendama arcade, is a good choice for breakfast. A complete breakfast of ham, eggs, home-fries, and coffee is less than $2.

You might also consider **Ramses,** on Carrera 7 near Calle 19, where a continental breakfast will cost about $1.75. The leather booths are comfortable and the atmosphere is cheerful. Good for an inexpensive lunch too.

For a hefty lunch at a not-so-hefty price, try the executive lunch (*almuerzo ejecutivo*) at **La Plazuela,** on the Plaza Jimenez. A complete meal with soup, salad, main course, and dessert is just over $1. Always crowded at lunchtime, a good sign, the restaurant itself is fairly small and sparsely decorated, the food simple yet filling. You definitely won't find anything better for the price. You can also order à la carte, but it will cost a little more.

A charming Italian spot for filling lunches—or early dinner—is the **Romana Cafetería,** Jimenez at Calle 15, which is not a cafeteria as we know it, since there is table service. Wood-paneled walls make the décor worthy of a far more expensive restaurant. A particular bargain is the daily special, which includes an Italian-style meat or chicken dish, with vegetable, bread and butter, and beverage for $5. Open from 8 a.m. to 8 p.m., the Romana serves breakfast too, but these seem high-priced to us.

Across the plaza is the **Sorrento Cafetería,** similar to Romana, which is another good breakfast stop.

Drop in for a quick pizza fix at **Domo Taberna and Pizza,** Carrera 7, no. 21–52. Pizza by the slice is 75¢ and up, depending on the toppings.

If the daily lunch special suits your palate, stop for lunch at **La Taberna de Sancho,** at Carrera 7, no. 18–20. A four-course lunch is a very low $1.50. Another inexpensive lunch stop is **La Brasa Roja,** Calle 17, no. 8–76, where booths line the walls and whole chickens rotate over glowing coals. Chicken and french fries are $2.50. Yet another quick lunch stop is **PPC** (Pollo, Pizza, and Carne), Calle 22, no. 8–42. Pick up your whole pizza ($2.50), whole grilled chicken ($4.50), or sizzling steak ($3.50) and head to an upstairs table.

Lechonería Tolimense, Carrera 7, no. 22–01, has a stand-up area as well as booths. Specialty: A variety of ice creams with exotic toppings. A newer, more modern **Lechonería Tolimense** has just opened on the next block in a small shopping arcade.

Want to meet younger Bogotanos and down an authentic U.S.–style hamburger at the same time? Then race over to the **Crem Helado** (literally "ice cream"), Avenida Caracas no. 31–49, near Calle 31, the closest reproduction of a Howard Johnson's available in South America. Located near the Tequendama Hotel, this modern beef haven features succulent burgers (with french fries, fried onions, and tomato) for $3.25. The slow service doesn't seem to deter the hundreds of young Bogotanos who flock here on evenings and weekends, particularly on Sunday, when it is one of the few places open. A nice touch is the phone in each booth that you use to call your order in. A fine value is the chicken-in-the-basket at $4, and the fried shrimp, served with french fries and tomato, for $7.50. The chile con carne ($3.25) and tasty steak sandwiches (also $3.25) are other good values. Don't leave without sampling the oversize pineapple pie à la mode ($1.50). Open from 11 a.m. to midnight.

Fine inexpensive hamburgers and other fast foods are **Wimpy's** specialty. For as little as $1 you can have a hamburger, and for $1.75, a bacon and eggs burger. Add 30¢ for the quarter-pounder (Wimpy-Maxi). There are several Wimpy's around town, the most convenient on Carrera 7 between Calles 23 and 24.

Broaster, at Carrera 13, no. 27–08, is another inexpensive breakfast, lunch, or dinner choice. Eggs run a bargain 80¢; with ham, $1.25. Sandwiches start at $1.25, and a chicken-and-rice platter is only $3.75. Hamburgers are delicious at $1.25. Another location is at Carrera 13 at Avenida 39.

The **Koko Rico** chain, rather like Kentucky Fried Chicken, has several branches around town with one on Carrera 7 at no. 23 and another on Carrera 10 at no. 24. Fried and roast chicken pieces, burgers, and hot-dog platters are all inexpensive. Eat-in or take-out. **Del Oeste Hamburgers,** at Carrera 10, is another inexpensive fast-food establishment, serving spaghetti, fried chicken, and sandwiches.

Vegetarian fans should head over to **El Vegetariano,** at Calle 18, no. 5–74, where yogurt and dairy dishes are king. If you like you can take advantage of the take-out service run by this nonprofit organization. Other branches are at Carrera 8, no. 21–39; and Calle 22, no. 8–89 (third floor).

Pecos Taberna, Carrera 9, no. 19, is a fun place to stop for lunch. Look for the plaid curtains in the window—they're the only Pecos touch as the food is strictly Colombian. All main courses are served with potato and vegetable. These include grilled meats and fish, and pastas. Entrees start at $3.

Two unostentatious lunch places you might like to try if you're in the vicinity are the **San Martín,** Calle 18, no. 6–35; and the **Restaurante Delphi,** Carrera 7 at Calle 22, opposite the Cinema Colombia. The San Martín, spread over two floors, offers roomy booths on the upper level which are fairly comfortable. Stick to the daily special (about $1.50) which frequently includes clams, one of the better dishes here. The Delphi, open from 8 a.m. to midnight, is rather plain but it features a filling six-course meal for $2.75.

Ley's is a national Woolworth-type variety store chain (35 stores in 17 cities) that has a clean lunch counter in each outlet. We've enjoyed delicious empanadas (15¢) with a spicy sauce at the branch at Carrera 7 between Calles 22 and 23. Sandwiches are extremely low-priced (50¢ for ham and cheese); you might want to try the grilled-meat plate for 60¢.

Tía's, a similar-type chain with comparable prices, is a cut below in food quality. A good one is at Carrera 7 and Calle 17.

Hours for both Ley's and Tía's are 9 a.m. to 7 p.m. Monday through Saturday and 10 a.m. to 12:30 p.m. on Sunday and holidays.

READER'S LUNCH SELECTION: "**Bretaña, Delicias del Tropico,** on Avenida Jimenez, is another good, inexpensive place for breakfast and lunch. It has a circular glass front that allows a lot of light to enter. Scrambled eggs with onions and tomatoes, a large glass of orange juice, bread, and tinto costs only $1. Friendly, efficient service and very clean" (Roberta Finke, New York, N.Y.).

TEA TIME: A late-afternoon culinary custom in Bogotá is tea and pastries—Bogotanos seem to devour enormous quantities of baked goods. An ideal spot for relaxing after a day of sidewalk-pounding is the charming **La Suiza** ("The Swiss"), Calle 25, no. 9–41, diagonally across from the Hotel Tequendama, which manages to invoke a *gemütlich* atmosphere by skillful use of bright table-cloths and 19th-century-style red-leather chairs. It will cost you all of 70¢ for a cream-filled pastry and tea or café. Closed Monday.

The **Chesa Restaurant,** at Calle 23, no. 17–39, is an attractive large restaurant with German management, serving take-out pastry in front and at the tables, plus sandwiches ($1 and up) and empanadas (50¢), and light foods.

If you're a coffee lover, don't miss **Oma,** a café-restaurant at Carrera 10, no. 27–91, in the modern Bavaria Building. Drop by in the late afternoon and linger over a cup of Colombia's finest, which can also be purchased by the pound and ground to your specifications.

There are a number of small cafés scattered around the Plaza Jimenez. All are very popular with the Bogotanos, and crowded at tea time. Or as a healthy alternative to pastries, stop in at the **Frutería Las Catorce,** also on the Plaza Jimenez, for a refreshing fruit salad or shake (crema de fruta). You'll be glad you did. In our estimation, Colombia's fruits are just as noteworthy as her coffee.

DINNER ON A BUDGET: The **Pizzería Napolitanas,** in Chapinero (Carrera 7, no. 59–10) or Chico (Calle 84, no. 16–38), are attractive Italian restaurants in the suburbs of Bogotá. The décor and cuisine are flawless. The manager of the Chico branch is from Parma, north of Rome, home of Parmesan cheese and opera aficionados. You can have a huge chicken cacciatore platter for $5 and up, depending on what you order with it. Veal and beef platters, served with fresh vegetables and pasta side dishes, are $5 to $7.50. And if you like pizza, try it here. A favorite among regulars is pizza con mariscos (shellfish). A huge pie is $6.50. Well recommended.

Green House and **Jenos Pizza** stand side by side at Calle 19, no. 5–40. They serve pizza and Italian specialties as well as a general menu, including soups, sandwiches, and hot platters. Another branch is located in the Unicentro shopping center. There is music at night.

A boon for a casual dinner is the intimate and clean **Chalet Suizo,** Carrera 7 at Calle 21, where the grilled chicken (medio pollo a la brasa) is a fine value at $5.75, especially since it includes french-fried potatoes, salad, and vegetable. A small, tender baby beef is $5.75. A popular Swiss dish is the fondue at $6.75. You will find the wooden booths and unusual black-and-white horsechair chairs most comfortable. Service is outstanding. Recommended. Open from 1 to 10 p.m. on Sunday, 2 to 11 p.m. all other days.

An attractive restaurant near the Continental Hotel is **La Guayacana,** on Avenida Jimenez between Carreras 3 and 4. There are several intimate dining alcoves in this fine restaurant. Beamed ceilings and antique mirrors create a fine Spanish atmosphere. Recommended are the chicken dishes which run about $6. Charcoal-broiled steaks are $7.25. Specialties feature typical South American dishes.

La Gran Parrilla Santa Fe, at Avenida Jimenez, no. 5–65, is an attractive small restaurant. Its dozen tables are crowded at lunchtime with government workers who are lured by the homemade soups ($1.50), salads, and grilled meats. Steaks are $5 and pork chops are $5.75. Arroz con pollo is only $3.50. The food is very good.

The **Café Parrilla Cardenal Churrasco,** next door to the Hotel Continental on Avenida Jimenez, is an excellent choice, especially if you're on a tight budget. Definitely worth trying here is the churrasco Argentino ($3.50). The grill (or parrilla) is right in the dining room, so you can make sure your steak is just the way you like it. On our last visit we ordered the menu of the day, ajiaco criollo, fruit cocktail, and spaghetti with chicken—all for a mere $3.50.

An excellent choice for all meals is the **Salerno Cafetería,** Carrera 7, no. 19–48. Very large, with an upstairs dining terrace, the Salerno is very clean and well run. There is an English menu. The à la carte menu is extensive, but the daily specials are the best buys. These may include spaghetti ($2.50; with seafood sauce, $6), chicken curry ($4.50), or lasagne ($4). Pizzas are $2.50 and up. You'll enjoy eating here.

A fine lunch or dinner choice, **La Fonda Antioqueños,** at Calle 19, no. 5–43, is a restaurant typical of Colombia's "cowboy" region. Its tables are tree trunks and the director's chairs are covered with cowhide. The foods are typical as well. Try sancocho with beef or chicken—it's a soup-stew with lots of vegetables and avocado. Enough for an entire meal, it costs only $3.75. Roast chicken, pork, and steak à la caballo (with eggs) are the most popular choices. Main courses run $3 to $4.50.

We have received many letters praising our inclusion of the **El Fogonaza Restaurant** in our prior editions. The carne al Fogonaza at $5.75 is a fine buy, as are the churrasco Argentino ($5) and arroz con pollo ($3.50). This is a bilevel restaurant with glass-topped tables and booths that doubles as a tea room in the late afternoon. It has a stand-up section too. Located next to Chalet Suizo at Carrera 7 at Calle 21, El Fogonaza also serves pizza.

For a wonderful budget-priced meal, hop over to the **Pasapoga Restaurante,** near Calle 12 off an alley leading from Carrera 7, where beef steak à caballo (fried egg on top) is only $4. And delicious. There are daily menu specials from $1.75 to $4.25. The tables are covered with white tablecloths. Of the two dining rooms, the upstairs is a bit more cheerful. Both levels are usually jammed with working-class Bogotanos, so expect a short wait. Exceptionally good values here. If you're on foot, approach the Pasapoga from Carrera 7 and you'll come upon the small courtyard the restaurant faces. A sister restaurant with the same name, at Calle 15, no. 9–35, offers an excellent Sunday brunch.

In the same area is **Campanela's,** at Carrera 9, no. 16–83 (tel. 242-1001). This one specializes in fine Italian dishes. Sit in one of the wooden booths and savor the lasagne romana ($3.75) or the cannelloni ($3). Excellent minestrone ($1.75). Closed Sunday, when this area is deserted.

A delightful Chinese eatery is **Restaurante Hong Kong** at Calle 23, no. 5–98, where, amid red Oriental designs, you can savor chop suey dishes ($3 and up), egg fu yung ($4.75), arroz oriental ($5.25), as well as wonton soup. Our favorite is the arroz oriental—fried rice with lobster, chicken, pork, and shrimp. Recommended. Open from noon to midnight seven days a week.

A large house with separate dining rooms is **El Zaguan de Las Aguas,** at Calle 19, no. 5–62, where Colombian dishes are the thing. Try the sancocho gallina ($4.75), puchero ($5), or the arroz bogotano ($3). There is music nightly from 8 p.m. to midnight, on Sunday from noon. Service and food are first class.

A tavern-like effect is created at **Fundador,** located at Carrera 8, no. 19–46, where the waitresses garbed in Swiss outfits add charm to this bilevel eatery. By all means, dine on the upper level and enjoy the piped-in music with any of the meat dishes ($5), chicken ($3), and fish (from $4). Good choice.

A similar restaurant can be found in the Tequendama arcade across from the telegraph office. At the **Resi Berlin,** the Bavarian theme is carried out in the waiters' garb. Traditional sausage dishes are priced at $3 to $5. Each day there is a delicious specialty of the house for $2.50. The Resi Berlin is open from noon to 11 p.m. for both lunch and dinner.

Finally, on the fourth floor of the Hotel Hilton is the **Hacienda Restaurant,** in elegant surroundings which include strolling musicians and singers who entertain at each of the tables. Surprisingly, rates are not astronomical. Pasta and omelet dishes are under $5, but most steak and chicken platters run about $7 each.

When a North American and a Bogotano have a dinner date, they seem to wind up at the Hotel Tequendama's elegant—this too is misnamed—**Cafetería El Virrey,** on the main floor. While certainly not a cafetería, the Virrey nevertheless offers some surprisingly reasonable values. For example, we've savored a fine fish filet (filete de robalo), served with a delicate mushroom sauce, for $5.50. A superb treat is the sirloin in pepper sauce, or the filet mignon—about $7. You can order hamburgers for $3. After dinner, stroll through the Tequendama's lobby to see why this hotel is considered one of South America's finest.

For fine pizzas in a ranch setting, try **El Rancho de la Pizza,** Carrera 9, no. 23–14, where the aroma of pizza wafts from the open stoves. Prices start at $3. Ravioli and spaghetti dishes too (under $3).

To end this section, we now announce that we found a marvelous restaurant at incredible prices. We ate there twice and still can't believe it: daily specials consisting of juice, a very large bowl of soup, and a choice of three different main courses (chicken, fish, etc.) with potatoes, rice, a cooked vegetable, and a nice salad—all for under $3. The name is the **Colonial Restaurant,** Carrera 13, no. 56–42, a 90¢ taxi ride from the Tequendama Hotel in Chapinero. And the food is delicious.

HIGHER-PRICED RESTAURANTS: When a Bogotano boasts about the "bests" in his city, he will cite the Tequendama or Hilton in hotels and the **Pollo Dorado** in restaurants. Located at Carrera 9, no. 17–38, near Calle 17, the Spanish-colonial-style Dorado is a roomy, red-carpeted quasi-palace where guests sit in soft armchairs at large red tables or in leather-backed booths. Fresh flowers adorn every table and the high walls are covered by imposing paintings depicting the conquistadores, or by reproductions of old Colombian maps. The food is appropriate to the surroundings: we have gorged ourselves on wonderful butterfly shrimp ($7.50) and succulent filet mignon ($5.25). Many Bogotanos insist that the shrimp here $6) is the best to be found in Colombia. Delicious, too, is the curry de pollo ($5.75). You may eat in either of two dining rooms, but we find the downstairs décor less formal and more to our liking.

Bonus: Seconds of curry are free, and your waiter will remind you to reorder in the unlikely event you forget. However, platters are filling enough so that seconds are unnecessary. You can spend an entire evening here.

A restaurant which serves superb food in a Swiss-lodge-type setting is

Refugio Alpino, Calle 23, no. 7–49, between Carreras 7 and 8 (tel. 284-6515). Ski scenes and hanging wine bottles make this small hideaway one of our favorite stops. Steak dishes we enjoy are entrecôte St. Moritz ($5.75) and lomito alpino ($4.50). Fish platters are $4. Arroz con pollo, well prepared, is a bargain at $4. Piped-in music adds to the ambience, and the dozen or so tables are usually occupied by locals enjoying a casual night out.

"Rodizios," restaurants serving grilled meats in Brazilian fashion (on long skewers carried by waiters in a rotation of beef, chicken, lamb, and chorizo until you beg for mercy), are the newest culinary rage in Bogotá. Several new rodizios have opened, but most of them are in the outer areas of the city. We found a terrific one that you can easily walk to from center city, the very attractive **Cozineiro,** at Calle 38, no. 13–28. A plus is that there's a good discothèque on the corner which you might head to after dinner. Going upstairs (the bar is on the main floor) as you walk to your table you can eye the huge circular salad bar. You can also order the meat à la carte. Expect to pay under $10 (without beverage).

Located right in front of the bullring, **La Giralda,** Calle 24, no. 6–92, is decorated accordingly with bullfighting posters and memorabilia. This small Spanish restaurant, reminiscent of a Spanish *meson,* offers a variety of Spanish and Colombian specialties. Try the arroz con pollo ($4) or the robalo con champiñones (halibut with mushrooms). The paella and the cazuela de mariscos (seafood casserole), although slightly more expensive, are both excellent choices as well. One order is enough for two people.

Taberna del Toro, Carrera 8, no. 23–58, is an attractive restaurant with gleaming wooden tables and a small bar. Flowers brighten the large room. Grilled meats start at $4.50 and come with vegetables and salad.

For the best in seafood, head for the elegant **La Fragata,** at Carrera 13, no. 27–98, on the second floor of the Edificio Bavaria. The place is decorated like a 19th-century ship (the bartender resembles Captain Bligh), complete with portholes and captains' couches. Most platters are about $7. Try the trucha salmonada (trout), lenguado (sole), or robalo (haddock). Open from noon to midnight; the organ music adds to the fun. Or try the **Fragata,** at Calle 15, no. 9–30, farther downtown.

Housed in what was once the old San Diego cloister, the lovely **Casa Vieja** restaurant, Carrera 10, no. 26–50 (tel. 284-7359), across from the Hotel Tequendama, is an excellent choice if you want to sample native cuisine. The cloister's walkways, once quietly trodden by monks, have been converted into a picturesque dining area that looks out onto a pretty courtyard. We enjoyed the puchero (a hearty stew brimming over with sausage, beef, bananas, and vegetables) for $6.75. Served with soup, this dish was so filling we wondered if we need eat again for a week. The menu also features steak with grilled potatoes or Créole steak for $7.25, roast pork with apple sauce at $7.75, jumbo Créole prawns at $10, and chicken with capers at $4.75. A strolling musician sets a romantic mood while you dine. Another Casa Vieja is located at Avenida Jimenez no. 3–73, near the Continental Hotel.

SUBURBAN CHOICES: Many of Bogotá's best dining spots, although most will stretch your budget, are located in the suburbs. Although there are many others, here are a few of our favorites:

Feel like some tangy barbecued ribs? Bogotá has two terrific rib eateries. **Tony Romas** is a familiar name, for it's part of a U.S.–based chain. The ribs are delicious and are served with the traditional onion loaf and potatoes. Tony Romas, at Calle 93, no. 13–85, is open nightly till midnight. More attractive is **Mister Ribs,** Avenida 82, no. 9–52, with a colonial atmosphere, brick walls, and a long bar that has high wooden armchairs for serious imbibers. Prices are similar and both serve barbecued chicken and beef dishes as well.

O Sole Mío, at Calle 90, no. 17–48, has the best pizza in town. It's crusty and covered with globs of thick cheese and any topping that strikes your fancy. They serve pasta too, but stick to the pizza. It's very similar to pan pizza.

But if you're in the mood for pasta, try the slightly more formal **Restaurante Piccolo Caffè,** at Carrera 15, no. 96–55.

The Place, at Calle 94, no. 15–45, is an informal eatery best known for its enormous hero sandwiches. Also fine burgers and Tex-Mex finger foods. Open till midnight daily, it's frequently crowded with young Bogotanos.

One of the most romantic restaurants, and one of our favorites anywhere, is **La Bella Epoca,** at Carrera 11, no. 89–08 (tel. 236-3421), in Chico. This colonial house with beamed ceilings and piano music creates a mood that's perfect for intimate dining. Add delicious food and you can't miss. The smoked trout (trucha ahumada) is magnificent (although a steep $8) and the steak pimienta delicious ($8.75). There are excellent seafood dishes to please any palate. Popular, too, with locals is the Sunday brunch and daily 5 p.m. tea time. Highly recommended.

For great fondue, go to **El Fondue,** Carrera 13, no. 82–52. They serve traditional cheese fondues as well as some more Colombian-style varieties with meat, chicken, or even lobster. There is also an Argentinian-style parrilla.

Nouvelle cuisine has made its way to Bogotá, and can be found at **Bourgogne,** Carrera 18, no. 93–55 (tel. 257-9261). This elegant French restaurant doubles as an art gallery, displaying a collection of fine antiques as well as works by some of Colombia's best modern artists. Definitely not one of our budget selections, dinner for two here could run over $30, but would be well worth it. Another good choice for French food, and not quite as costly, is **Le Petit Bistrot,** Calle 76, no. 10–28.

Many of Bogotá's finest restaurants have opened locations in the north as well. **El Zaguan de las Aguas** is at Calle 100, no. 20–52; **La Fragata,** Calle 77, no. 15–32; and a fourth branch of Casa Vieja, called **Casa Vieja del Norte,** has opened at Carrera 11, no. 89–08.

If you tire of Colombian cooking, and want something a little more adventurous, why not opt for sushi at Bogotá's finest Japanese restaurant, **Nihonkan,** Calle 90, no. 11–31. Or order a Japanese steak prepared right at your table. Specialties here include sushi, sashimi, teppanyaki, and shabu shabu.

Or if you'd rather go Chinese, **Gran China,** at Calle 77A, no. 11–72 (tel. 249-5938), is a good choice. The menu offers a wide selection of Beijing and Szechuan dishes.

It's a favorite among Bogotanos, so you may want to make reservations ahead of time.

And finally, a favorite dining-out spot in Chico, Bogotá's exclusive suburb, is **Cactus,** Carrera 15, no. 94–78 (tel. 257-3032), a wonderfully modern restaurant that has a salad bar featuring 15 different kinds of vegetables. Owned by a delightful young couple, the Cactus's waiters are all students and the atmosphere is informal and friendly. Hanging plants, a skylight, chrome-and-leather chairs, and a raised wooden platform, creating two separate dining areas in the back, make this an attractive restaurant indeed. Order a three-quarter-pound steak ($6) and accompany it with a bottle of chilled wine ($8.75—cheap by Colombian standards). Barbecued chicken, another Cactus specialty, is $7.50. Hamburgers are $2.75. Nice atmosphere.

THE BIG SPLURGE: Bogotá's most spectacular restaurant is, without a doubt,

Tramonti, located about a mile above the city on Via a la Calera. Named for a village in the mountains of northern Italy, Tramonti is indeed, as the name suggests, "among mountains." And the view of the city is breathtaking, especially at dusk. As our friend Najda Cajiao remarked on our last visit, you have Bogotá right "at your feet." So be sure to request a table with a view, which, incidentally, shouldn't be too hard to come by as there are windows all around.

Besides the view, the restaurant itself is, as owner Humberto Aguirre Orozco was proud to point out, a showcase. There are five dining rooms, all on different levels, in this chalet-type structure which has been built right into the side of the mountain. In fact, one of Tramonti's two bars, appropriately named Las Rocas, has the actual rock of the side of the mountain as its back wall! Don Umberto's future plans include the construction of a discothèque with two dance floors right inside the mountain.

The menu and wine list are as extensive as the restaurant is big. But don't worry—fires glowing in the fireplaces, the candles on the tables, and just the overall ambience of the restaurant, plus the excellent service, will make you feel as if you're in a much smaller and very intimate place. There's something here to please every palate, from a simple T-bone steak ($5) to lobster thermidor ($10), with a highly recommended ajíaco Santafereño ($4) and pasta dishes ($4) in between. Tramonti is a definite must-see. If dinner is out of your budget, why not go up at tea time from 3 to 6:30 p.m. Monday through Friday. It's also popular for drinks in the evening. Don't miss this chance to have Bogotá "at your feet."

Another good choice for a "big splurge" is the **Gran Vatel,** Carrera 7, no. 70–40. Few restaurants in the world can claim a more attractive setting—in a mansion that once was the home of former Colombian President Alfonso Lopez. You enter through a garden to dine in any of several elegant rooms, each with a different décor. Madam Goerres, the owner, is a gourmet's gourmet. The food is superb, and prices, surprisingly, are not astronomical. Specialties are French and Belgian platters. Most individual dishes are under $10. Try the hors d'oeuvres variados platter for $7 (for two people), which includes meatloaf, salami, ham, pickles, and smoked trout. Then the demi-poulet Gran Vatel, a chicken dish with sauce for $7, or the filet pargo cardinal for $7.50. Ismael, the headwaiter, will attend to your every need—he's been here for over 25 years. Not to be missed.

3. BOGOTÁ BY DAY

As in all our cities, we recommend a leisurely stroll through Bogotá on your first day here.

BOGOTÁ ON FOOT: Our recommended walking tour, which can be wrapped up in under one hour if you trot just a bit, starts at the imposing **Plaza de Bolívar,** Carrera 7 between Calles 10 and 11. Here you roam about benches and statuary and resting Bogotanos. Look around at the magnificent Athenian-style **Capitol** building, where Congress convenes, and the 400-year old **National Cathedral** (built in 1572 but renovated several times since), graced with jewel-encrusted monstrances and the famous **Chapel of El Sagrario.** Dominating the plaza is an enormous statue of Simón Bolívar. (Paradoxically, Colombians fervently hail Bolívar for freeing them from Spain. Yet this country clings to more of old Spain's traditions than any other Latin nation.)

Leading away from the plaza are the steep, narrow streets of the famous **Barrio de la Candelaria,** the nucleus of the city during colonial days. Here you'll get a glimpse into early Bogotá, for this area has hardly changed in 200 years. Typically, the buildings here are one- or two-story brown adobes with barred windows, massive wooden doors, and red-tile roofs. Inner cobblestone courtyards seem to be standard in many homes. Look carefully at the street signs. The faded colonial designations over the modern street names are still visible.

Stroll up Calle 10 and after half a block you'll find yourself in the lovely palm-tree studded **Plaza San Carlos,** surrounded on three sides by historic structures dating back to the 1600s. Owned and preserved by the University of America Foundation, the buildings include the house of Bolívar's mistress, Doña Manuela Saenz, and the printing shop where the famous *Rights of Man* was printed just prior to Colombia's revolution in 1810. A bigger-than-life reproduction of the text covers the far wall of the plaza. Be sure to take a peek inside the **Church of San Ignacio,** opposite the plaza.

Another block up, beyond Carrera 6, is the striking **San Carlos Palace,** home of Colombia's president, where handsomely uniformed guards parade in precise routines that never seem to vary. We saw one U.S. tourist—we recognized him by his Polaroid camera—attempt to interrupt the routine long enough for a quick photo, but the guard did a quick-step to avoid the cameraman. The palace, which houses much of Colombia's prized art, is open to the public. A few steps down from the main entrance to the palace is the window through which Bolívar fled to avoid being assassinated. Visiting hours are Monday through Friday from 9 a.m. to 5 p.m. Free admission.

Across the street is the **Teatro Colón,** Bogotá's cultural center, which houses in one structure the city's ballet, opera, and theater companies. See "Bogotá After Dark," below, for specifics.

Turn right on Carrera 6, and just beyond Calle 11 you'll find a small jewel— the nine-room **Museo de 20 de Julio** (see below), a perfect example of Spanish-colonial architecture. Just beyond the museum is Bogotá's main shopping thoroughfare, bustling **Carrera 7,** normally jammed with pedestrians and cars. Don't let the din startle you. Head right on Carrera 7; four blocks down is a main intersection, at Avenida Jimenez. Off to the right is the sleekly modern **Banco de la República,** and behind it at Carrera 6 and Calle 16 is the remarkable **Museo del Oro** (Gold Museum). Stop in and buy an emerald. On your left is the venerable **San Francisco Church.** Now four centuries old, it is a magnificent example of Latin American baroque architecture.

You have the choice now of continuing along Carrera 7 to the Tequendama Hotel and the pink bullring just beyond it; or you might amble along Avenida Jimenez to either Carrera 10 or 14. Both these streets wind up at the Tequendama as well. If you prefer browsing in shops, stick to Carrera 7.

Modern Bogotá

To see the other side of Bogotá—new, fresh, and modern—set aside one afternoon and head out to Carrera 15 and Calle 76. Start at the **Centro Comercial El Lago,** a shopping center with fine boutiques and a La Fragata restaurant branch. After browsing, head back to Carrera 15 and head out toward the higher numbers. You will pass modern boutiques, tea shops, restaurants, private homes, and clubs. Plan to walk to Calle 95. At Calle 90 you enter Chico, Bogotá's chic-est area. If you're hungry, plan to eat at the Pollo Kentucky at Calle 87.

Unicentro, one of the largest and most modern shopping centers in South America, is located on Calle 127 and Carrera 15. The bilevel center is a complex of department stores, boutiques, restaurants, movie theaters, and nightspots. You can nosh on pizza at Pizza Nostra or Little John's, or a knockwurst at Taberna Baur or the Plaza Café. Edelweiss is a rather nice German restaurant and Uni-club is the deluxe eatery here. Bus (30¢) or a taxi ($3) will take you there from downtown.

MUSEUMS: You should definitely set aside time to visit Bogotá's museums, which are among the continent's finest. The Museo del Oro (Gold Museum) is an *absolute must;* then select the others according to your interests.

Each museum has a nominal entrance fee, which ranges from 30¢ to $1.

Museo del Oro

Bogotá's most famous museum, and justly so, is the **Gold Museum,** housed in a relatively new four-story structure at Carrera 6 and Calle 16, no. 5–41 (tel. 281-3065). The magnificent collection of emeralds and 8,000 gold pieces includes exquisite arm bracelets, nose rings, crowns, bowls, whistles, and even gold and copper weapons. The English-speaking guide explains the historical significance of the treasures. Inexpensive copies of the collection's eye-catching gold masks are sold throughout the city. The collection traces its beginnings back to two early Indian tribes—the Quimbay and the Chibcha, who laboriously fashioned each piece for festivals. The conquistadores in the mid-16th century sent many of the finest pieces to Spain where presumably they were melted down for gold bullion. An outer room features antique pottery (mostly funeral artifacts) from the same era—roughly 800 to 1,000 years ago.

Make sure you ask the guard on the third floor to open the vault. You will enter a dark room, and gradually, as the room is slowly illuminated, you will realize you are completely surrounded by gold. The effect is overwhelming.

Don't leave without viewing the world's four largest emeralds—the largest is 1,795 carats—on display here.

The Museo del Oro is open Tuesday through Saturday from 9 a.m. to 4 p.m.; Sunday and holiday hours are 9 a.m. to noon. Admission is 75¢; children under 7, half price. Films in English are shown at 10 a.m. and 2:30 p.m. (on Sunday at 11 a.m.).

Museo de Arte Colonial

This museum, specializing in Spanish-colonial art (1650–1800), is located near the San Carlos Palace at Carrera 6, no. 9–77 (tel. 241-6017), between Calles 9 and 10. Erected behind mammoth 17th-century-style stone walls, it is marked by massive wooden doors and Moorish-style archways that lead into eight rooms, each housing paintings, sculpture, silver, or furniture. Hours: Tuesday through Friday from 10 a.m. to 5:30 p.m. and on Saturday and Sunday from 11 a.m. to 5 p.m. Admission: 25¢.

Museo de Artes y Tradiciones Populares

This enchanting museum displays the handcrafts produced throughout Colombia. Located in an old monastery near Plaza Bolívar, the museum is closed on Monday and open from 9 a.m. to 5:30 p.m. Tuesday through Friday. A small shop in the monastery sells many of the handmade items on display in the museum at very good prices. Colorful woven baskets, rugs, woodcarvings, and ceramics make great accessories in your home. Stop in **Claustro de San Agustín** for a cool drink or a sandwich. The shop and restaurant are open every day.

Museo Nacional

The best historical museum, well worth a visit, is the Museo Nacional, Carrera 7, no. 28–66 (tel. 243-2639), between Calles 28 and 29, which was once a prison—and looks it. The formidable gray stone walls could use sandblasting, or just blasting, to make the building resemble what it has been since 1948—a repository for historical documents relating to the Colombian revolution and a home for archeological finds as well. Hours: Tuesday through Saturday from 10 a.m. to 6:30 p.m. and on Sunday from 10 a.m. to 5 p.m. Admission: 15¢ (on Thursday, free); children under 5 not admitted.

Museo de 20 de Julio

If you'd like to see the famous press that was used to print Colombia's *Rights of Man* petition during the revolution, drop in at the charming Museo de 20 de Julio, Calle 11, no. 6–94 (tel. 234-4150), near Carrera 7, which houses other remembrances of Colombia's bolt for freedom in the early 19th century. Often called **La Casa del Florero ("House of the Flower Vase")**, the museum was named after an incident on July 20, 1810, that helped trigger the revolution. It seems that the owner of the house then located on the site was severely lashed after refusing to lend a handsome flower vase to the Spaniards for use at a reception. The house and the vase thus became a symbol against tyranny. Hours: Tuesday through Saturday from 9:30 a.m. to 6:30 p.m., on Sunday from 10 a.m. to 5 p.m. The museum is housed in an authentic early-19th-century structure and presents a vivid example of the architecture of the period. Admission: 25¢ for adults, 10¢ for children. Closed Monday.

Quinta de Bolívar

A quarter mile from the funicular at Monserrate Mountain is the widely visited **home of Simón Bolívar,** Avenida Jimenez Carrera 2a Este (tel. 284-8619), now a mansion-like museum of the colonial era. Built in 1800, the structure was given to Bolívar after the revolution, and he lived there from 1826 to 1828. The cannons are relics of the war of independence. In 1966 a summit meeting of the presidents of Chile, Venezuela, and Colombia was held here. Open from 10 a.m. to 6 p.m.; closed Monday. Admission: 35¢ for adults, 10¢ for children.

Museo de Arte Religioso

The **Museum of Religious Art,** at Calle 12, no. 4–31 (tel. 281-0556), is open Monday through Friday from 9 a.m. to 12:30 p.m. and 2 to 5:30 p.m. The museum does not have a permanent collection of its own but exhibits works borrowed from monasteries and churches throughout Colombia.

Museo Arqueológico

The **Archeological Museum,** at Carrera 6, no. 7–43 (tel. 282-0940), is closed Monday and open from 9:30 a.m. to 5 p.m. every other day except Sunday, when it closes at 1 p.m. It is located in the House of the Marquis of St. George (Marques de San Jorge), one of the most beautiful buildings in the city. Recently remodeled, the original dates from the 17th century and houses one of the best pre-Columbian pottery collections in the world. Each whitewashed room in the house is built around an inner patio, with gushing fountains and lush plants. An inexpensive restaurant for lunch only.

Cano Gallery (Private Museum)

Located at Carrera 13, no. 27–98, the museum (tel. 242-8851) is open Monday through Saturday from 10 a.m. to 7 p.m. It contains the private collection of artifacts gathered by the Cano family over the last 50 years. Gold, jewelry, ceramics, tombs, and semiprecious stones are on exhibit. Demonstrations of different methods used by the ancient artist are given as are slide shows.

THE SPORTING LIFE: Bogotanos are sports enthusiasts, with bullfighting and futbol vying at the gate virtually every Sunday all year round.

Toreador!

First-class bullfighting can be seen between December and February at the **Plaza de Toros de Santa María,** near the Hotel Tequendama at Carrera 6 and Calle 26, every Saturday and Sunday beginning at 3 p.m. The best seat (barrera) can cost you as much as $25, but you can get a bleacher ticket (sol) for $6.35. Novices take over from March to November, and you can see a fair match for the $5 general-admission charge. Top tickets, off-season, are only $10.

Futbol

On most Sunday afternoons starting at 3 p.m., local sports fans who are not at the bullring are certainly at **El Campin Stadium,** Avenida 57, near Carrera 28, where 40,000 soccer devotees are packed into the 30,000-seat park. The best seat is $6.25, with general admission at 75¢. Take a cab ($1).

The Track

Another Sunday (and Thursday) afternoon event that draws the sports-minded is racing at the **Hipodromo Techo,** located on the Avenida de las Americas (a cab costs under $1 and is recommended). A day at the races will run you under $10 allowing for the admission, the minimum bet (apuesto) per race, and transportation. Races are on Thursday and Sunday, and the festivities get under way at 10 a.m. A new racetrack, **Los Andes,** has opened north of the city. Admission is $1.50 (tel. 272-3243 for information).

Tejo

A popular Indian game that loosely resembles horseshoes, tejo is played by farm workers in the rear of small rural taverns and restaurants. If you take an excursion, you'll see the game being played in the countryside. Some games are played near the bullring.

Swimming

Although there is no outdoor swimming in Bogotá, you can take an excursion to the warmer climes, particularly **Giradot** ($10 round trip for a three-hour bus ride), where you can swim in a hotel pool. Even closer is **Melgar,** 1½ hours away.

THE VIEW FROM MONSERRATE:

Tourists from all over Colombia stream into Bogotá on Sunday for the trek to the top of 2,500-foot **Mount Monserrate.** Not only is there a magnificent view of the capital, but the hillside takes on a festival air every Sunday. Vendors hawking candy, food, and trinkets wend their way through laughing, picnicking families sprawled on the grass, drinking in the clean, crisp air. The Sabana plain, on which Bogotá rests, is visible for miles and miles beyond the city limits. Bogotá itself is fully visible, down to the red-tile roofs in the old section. Visible, too, is **Mount Guadalupe,** accessible only by car, which is marked by a huge statue at the top. (*Warning:* Do not drive to Mount Guadalupe unless you're part of an organized group tour. It's a lonely road with many reported crimes.)

You can enjoy a sandwich and soft drink at the mountaintop **Panorama** restaurant while viewing the countryside through glass windows. Little wonder that families often travel up to eight hours to spend half that time here. There are many artesanía shops to browse in, so don't forget your traveler's checks.

A sobering note is the world-famous church and shrine located here, which draws hundreds of cripples each week to the **Lord of Monserrate,** a statue in a glass case elevated on an altar. Many kiss the glass in penance and then pray in the neighboring chapel for escape from their affliction.

Getting to the Top

You have two choices in your ascent—either a seven-minute ($2.75) funicular ride (100 passengers) that carries you through a 750-foot-long tunnel excavated out of the mountainside; or via a cable car called a teleférico, holding 40, that puts you at topside in three minutes for the same $2.75. The one-car teleférico is not only more comfortable but far more scenic, since it makes an outside ascent. Incidentally, the 80° slope near the peak on the funicular is literally breathtaking. You can hike to the top if you're so inclined; many of the poor, who cannot afford to do otherwise, hoof it regularly—but we do not recommend hiking.

Note: The teleférico runs regularly—normally every half hour—from 8 a.m. to 4 p.m. Monday through Wednesday, to 6 p.m. Thursday through Sunday. The funicular runs only on Sunday.

The foot of Monserrate is a longish stroll from the Hotel Continental (not a walk to take at night), or at most a ten-minute ($1.50) cab ride from any part of center city.

Before leaving, stroll the streets, a replica of Bogotá circa 1830. Browse in the shops, and if you're hungry there's a snackshop and two scenic restaurants.

4. EXCURSIONS AND TOURS

ZIPAQUIRA: How about a visit to an underground cathedral located in a salt mine half a mile below ground? One of the wonders of Latin America is the huge **Zipaquira Cathedral,** which draws thousands of worshippers and tourists each week to this town (pop. 30,000), 35 miles from Bogotá. The region, which has vast salt resources, is noted, too, for the finest beef cattle in Colombia. The country's better restaurants and private clubs serve Zipaquira beef, exclusively. But salt was the major economic bulwark for many years, and as a tribute to the blessings it brought to the community, a cathedral was erected in a salt mine. Today it is a major tourist attraction; visitors flock here from throughout the continent to worship at an altar carved out of salt rock within walls made of salt. Roads have been built into the mine and cars drive right to the cathedral. We're told there's enough salt in the mine to supply the world for 100 years. Open from 10 a.m. to 1 p.m. weekdays, on Sunday and holidays to 4 p.m.

Getting There

The least expensive way is by bus ($2.50 each way), which takes 1½ hours from downtown Bogotá and passes through the lovely northern residential section and into the countryside, where Indians and donkeys are a common sight. From anywhere along Avenida Caracas (Carrera 14), take a bus marked "Zipa" that will be heading north toward the higher numbered streets. The fare is collected en route and you exit at the town square.

The walk from the village to the cathedral is uphill and it will take you less than half an hour to walk it. If you prefer, an inexpensive cab ride will take you right into the mine for $2. You can easily walk back to the center of town.

If you prefer a package tour, any travel agency will handle it for you ($16 per person). Ask your desk clerk.

READERS' SIGHTSEEING TIPS: "We only spent a short time in Bogotá, but we were not assailed by armed groups, as we had been warned. The only excursion we made was to the salt mines and cathedral at Zipaquira, about one hour from the city. The cost was $10 a person and we saw some beautiful countryside, the mines, the cathedral carved from solid salt with a gigantic altar and an incredibly good alcove—acoustically amazing. The bus also stopped at some small shops which were quite cheap. I bought a beautiful hammock for only $17" (Rod and Kay Sims, Newport, Australia).

TEQUENDAMA WATERFALL: Nineteen miles south of Bogotá over the southern highway is the 450-foot **Bogotá River Falls,** which for years was a major tourist attraction. Sadly, they opened a hydroelectric plant up the river from the falls in 1975. Since then the falls have literally been turned off. It is still worth a trip as the area is very beautiful. You'll also enjoy seeing the old, turn-of-the-century hotel which sits on a precipice. It is closed to the public for that reason, but for those with a romantic nature, it's fun to gaze at the hotel and imagine what it was like in its heyday when it served as a honeymoon spot for wealthy newlyweds.

Make the 40-minute trip to the falls on a modern bus operated by **Flota Macarena** ($2.50 round trip). The buses leave every half hour, starting at 4:30 a.m. from the new bus terminal that has been built south of the city—Terminal de Transportes Terrestres, at Calle 33B, no. 69–35. It's quite impressive, with shops and restaurants. To reach the terminal, look for the special bus stop at Calle 13, no. 15.

MONOLITHS IN SAN AGUSTÍN: Some 300 miles southeast of Bogotá lies Colombia's archeological equivalent of Peru's Machú Picchú—the monolith-strewn ruins of San Agustín, which archeologists trace back to the time of the Golden Age of Greece (500 B.C.). This incredible site has yielded thousands of sculptures, ranging in height from a foot or so up to ten feet and more, as well as temples and shrines and tombs. First written about in the mid-18th century, it wasn't until 1913 that serious digging began (Machú Picchú was uncovered by Hiram Bingham in 1911). In 1935 the Colombian government wisely purchased the sites containing the principal ruins.

The Ruins

Hundreds of stone statues, most of which were originally buried (many in tombs), have been uncovered. The ruins are scattered over a large area. Your first day should be set aside for a visit to **Parque Arqueológico de San Agustín,** where the principal monuments are located, the most famous of which is the huge **Fuente de Lavapatas** (foot-washing fountain), a ceremonial fountain carved by natives in the bare rock. A brook winds its way through the carved human and animal figures (monkeys, serpents, lizards, etc.). Many anthropologists speculate that the site was probably used for sacrificial ceremonies. A great deal has been learned of the lifestyle of the original inhabitants from these numerous sculptures.

The archeological park, about two miles from San Agustín, also has a museum (with stone and ceramic objects) and the **Forest of Statues** (approximately 35 in all) located along the path amid the forest. These statues typically are excavated funereal art.

Before leaving this area, make sure to visit the **Doble Yo** ("Double I") sculpture on the Alto de Lavapatas, one of the many samples of a statue containing a second face (sometimes that of an animal). There are many efforts psychologically to explain this art as representing man's alter ego. Your guess is as good as any.

Your next visit should be to **El Alto de Los Ídolos,** near San José, 18 miles from the park. Here you will find huge statues and colorfully decorated tombs. Most of the finds here were uncovered after 1970.

Time permitting, you should then consider heading for **Alto de Las Pie-**

dras, which is located beyond Alto de Los Idolos on the road that passes San José de Isnos to Pitalito. This "hill of stones" contains some marvelous statues. Note **La Gordita,** literally a fat woman, but actually a symbol of fertility, as well as the **Doble Yo statue.**

There are more sites to see, and the Government Tourist Office in San Agustín will offer all the assistance you will need.

The best way to tour the park is to rent a Jeep in San Agustín or Nieva and drive along the tree-lined paths that meander through the park crossing small streams. The statues pop up all along the road. Other exploring options include horseback and foot power. Don't forget to buy a map and guidebook (sort of in English) at the entrance or at the tourist office in town.

Getting There

Many travelers head to San Agustín via organized tours. Any travel agent would be glad to make these arrangements for you. Check with your hotel clerk.

Do-it-yourselfers should note that there is air service from Bogotá to Neiva. Schedules vary. A good airline is **Aires,** at Carrera 5, no. 18–85, in Bogotá. From Neiva you can rent a car or Jeep for the trip to San Agustín.

The road from Neiva passes through **Garzon** (halfway between Neiva and San Agustín) and Pitalito (one hour—20 miles—from San Agustín). Neiva is approximately 180 miles from San Agustín and six hours away by auto. Roads are fair. (Public buses take some eight hours and cost about $8 to San Agustín.)

Another way is to go via bus or special taxi directly from Bogotá. **Coomotor,** at Carrera 25, no. 15–36, operates buses which leave on the hour from 4 a.m. to 10 a.m. The trip takes 12 hours and the one-way fare is $18. Your hotel clerk will give you the information you need about the "taxis verdes," which offer service to San Agustín from Bogotá via Neiva.

Where to Stay

You have your choice of staying in San Agustín itself or in Neiva, Garzon, or Pitalito, nearby. In San Agustín, you can choose to stay at the 27-room **Hotel Yalconia** (tel. 7-3013), where doubles run $22 and singles are $17. This state-run hostelry has a swimming pool and is right near the park. Many budget travelers prefer the more rustic **Hotel Osoguaico,** which is about half a mile from the park. Boasting a restaurant, sauna, and campsites, the Osoguaico charges $10 double for its 29 rooms. The **Hotel Central,** at Calle 3, no. 10–44, offers 25 clean, well-maintained rooms with private bath for $6 single and $10 double.

In Pitalito, your first choice should be the **Hotel Calamo,** located in the heart of town at Carrera 5, no. 5–41 (tel. 6-0600), which offers air-conditioned rooms, a swimming pool, and a restaurant in a modern setting. Each of the 24 double rooms cost $20. The **Pigoanza,** nearby at Calle 6, no. 4–42 (tel. 6-0430), has bathless rooms at $7 double. It's rather basic. The **Timanco,** at 1 Sur Via a San Agustín (tel. 6-0666), has 22 rooms all with private bath at $15.

In Neiva, the three best stops are the 97-room **Hotel Plaza,** at Calle 7, no. 4–62 (tel. 2-3980), which has a pool and a disco. Rooms are air-conditioned and run $15 double. The nearby **Hotel Arayaco,** at Calle 8, no. 3–26 (tel. 2-6695), has 50 air-conditioned rooms. Doubles here are $19, and singles are $5 less. Finally, the **Americano,** at Salida del Sur no. 5 (tel. 2-7778), is a three-star hotel with a pool and steambath. Most rooms are air-conditioned. Doubles run $20, and singles, $15.

READER'S HOTEL SELECTION: "New in Neiva is the **Hotel Pacarcle,** which has a pool, good restaurant, and bar. Singles are $20, and doubles, $27" (Sam Stein, New York, N.Y.).

Notes

Bring comfortable shoes for walking and climbing, and if you are sensitive to the sun, make sure to bring a hat. Don't forget to bring your camera and lots of film.

The **Government Tourist office** is located at Calle 9, no. 3–63, in Neiva.

Climate: Temperatures average in the 60s. Heavy rain can be expected in June and July. December to February is the dry season.

READERS' TOURING SUGGESTIONS: "About San Agustín in Colombia, we recommend the following way to go and visit this very interesting archeological park. Fly from Bogotá to Neiva by Aires airlines for $22, round trip, and take a bus from Neiva to San Agustín, $2 and eight hours. There you might try the quite simple but clean and quiet **Hotel Ullumbe** ($3.25 for a four-person room). The day you arrive in San Agustín, rent horses for the next day, to go to the Alto de los Idolos in the morning. It will cost you $2.50 each, plus $2.50 for the guide horse. The adventurous and very scenic ride lasts two hours each way, and you have one hour on the spot to see the statues. During the rest of the day you may walk through the archeological park and museum. You may go back to Bogotá the same way you came or cross the Andes from Neiva to Popayan (11-hour bus ride for $3)" (Phillippe and Dominique Rinaudo, Enghien, France).

LETICIA:

LETICIA: Colombia's major port in the Amazon Basin is Leticia. This region in Colombia's southeastern sector borders both Brazil (the town of Marcos is just over the border) and Peru. The area is filled with dense jungle inhabited by huge snakes, colorful birds, and an astonishing range of animal life. Surprisingly, Leticia is quite modern and has about 20,000 inhabitants. The surrounding areas are peopled by primitive Indian tribes. The villages of the Ticunas, Yaguas, and Chamas can be visited and the villagers often come to Leticia to sell their bark masks, arrows, and necklaces. The most feasible way of visiting Leticia is to arrive by air. At this writing the round-trip fare from Bogotá is $150.

Don't even think of visiting here if creature comforts are important to you or if you're squeamish about snakes, mosquitos, or high humidity. You will have all three no matter what time of year you visit (July and August are the most popular months). The town itself is of little interest and the major reason for visiting here is to explore the Amazon and the nearby jungle. Two well-respected tour operators are found here, **Amatours,** in the Hotel Anaconda, and **Turamazonas,** in the Parador Ticuna. How good a job they do will really depend on the guide you are assigned. We met people who had great experiences with both groups and others who were disappointed. If you are unhappy about your guide, speak up! Trips include photo and hunting safaris, visits to local Indian villages, and a trip upriver to **Monkey Island.** The island is very natural and the monkeys and birds are wild. The lodge on the island was closed when we were there but should reopen soon. Check on it at the Parador Ticuna (same ownership). You can also engage a local guide—there are many offering their services in front of the hotels and at the dock. If you take this route, check on the boat being used and pin down the itinerary carefully. Make sure the price is agreed on in advance.

Tourism which had risen dramatically here in recent years has hit a valley of late. It would appear that Leticia is one of the transfer points in the narcotics operation of Colombia—there are often raids on the boats carrying the narcotics. Another problem is the dearth of adequate electricity and thus hot water. Hotels here are often without lights and hot water, and in fact turn off both from 11 p.m. to 6 a.m. While the lack of hot water is not a major problem (it's very hot here), it's not a plus to have lights out at 11 p.m.

There are not a lot of acceptable hotels here so don't show up without a reservation. The **Parador Ticuna,** on Avenida Libertador, has 30 rooms and both hot (sometimes) and cold water. Nearby, the **Hotel Anaconda,** at Carrera 11, no. 7, has 33 rooms and only cold water. The **Hotel Colonial** has 16 rooms and they are fan-cooled. There's even a swimming pool, but it didn't look inviting. As noted previously, the lodge on Monkey Island was under repair, but check on it.

Swimming in the Amazon River is not highly recommended, but if you simply can't resist, make sure that you have no open wound that might bleed and attract hungry piranhas.

READERS' TRAVEL TIPS: "Anyone going from Bogotá to San Agustín and on to Ecuador can also do the trip by bus. The journey up to San Agustín takes about 12 hours; the bus leaves Bogotá promptly at 9 a.m. Allow yourself two days in the city which claims to be the "Machú Picchú of Colombia"; its monoliths are among the world's finest. At 6 a.m. a bus leaves San Agustín (no reservations needed) for Popayan, and arrives in this bustling city at about 7 p.m. the same day. A connecting bus leaves Popayan for the border town of Ipalis at about 9:30 p.m., and arrives at about 11 a.m. the next morning. It is then necessary to take a por puesto to the actual border, where you walk across the bridge into Tulcan, Ecuador. Then there's a brief cab ride to the bus terminal where vans (which seat 12) leave approximately every 90 minutes for the Ecuadorian capital. Arrival in Quito is between 3:30 and 4 p.m. the same day. Total cost from Bogotá to San Agustín to Quito is about $32" (Michael Romano, New York, N.Y.).

"**Train between Bogotá and Santa Marta**—you didn't mention this. I tried it, but would only recommend it to the very hearty. It cost $18 one way, and took 24 hours, with dinner on board—fairly interesting. Trains leave on Monday, Wednesday, and Friday at 8 a.m. from Bogotá. Rough ride. An experience I will never forget, but *very* tiresome" (Kent Higman, Kansas City, Mo.).

5. BOGOTÁ AFTER DARK

TEATRO COLÓN: This old but elegant theater on Calle 10 near Carrera 6 houses every important opera, ballet, concert, and play presented in Bogotá. We saw a performance of *Carmen* here that certainly was worth seeing. During our last visit we were fortunate enough to catch the Venezuelan National Ballet, which was superb. We paid $4 for a good orchestra seat; balcony tickets run as low as $1. The custom here is for two performances per evening, at 6:30 and 9:30 p.m. Check your hotel clerk for the current attraction and pick up your tickets at the box office.

Another fine theater is the **Teatro Municipal,** at Carrera 7 between Calles 22 and 23 (box office in front of the theater). For the latest information, check with your hotel clerk.

CINEMA: Colombians cannot seem to get enough of English-language films; consequently almost every downtown theater seems to feature one U.S. or British flick. Stick to Carrera 7 for the best movie houses. Admission is about $1. For schedules, check the cinema section of *El Tiempo,* the local daily here. Clint Eastwood, in any language, still comes out Clint Eastwood.

THE BEST CLUBS AND DISCOS: Bogotá's newest and nicest clubs are located in the modern urban area of Chico, Chapinero, and Santa Barbara. Many of the clubs in center city have closed down. Since the younger, more affluent Bogotanos who frequent these spots live in these areas, the nightspots have gravitated there.

If you like to dance, make your first stop **Michelangelo,** at Calle 90, no. 11, one of Bogotá's most popular night spots, which draws an attractive, well-dressed clientele. Drinks run $2.75, and unless there is a special show there's no cover charge. If the action at Michelangelo isn't to your taste, walk over to **Keops Club,** at Calle 96, no. 10, which is rather similar.

Stefanos, on Carrera 7 at Calle 135, is Bogotá's newest club. It attracts the same type of crowd as Michelangelo and Keops, and is quickly becoming one of the city's most popular clubs, offering not only a dance floor, but a casino as well. Very elegant.

Saturno, atop the Hotel Cosmos, is the disco with the best view in town. Open every night from 8 p.m. to 1 a.m., Saturno occasionally has live music. If so, there's a cover charge. Lots of flashing lights and noise here.

Bar La Rockola, Carrera 11, no. 84–20, is a great place to go if all you want to do is dance. They play great dance music here, and they play it loud. For the young.

MARIACHI CLUBS: In Chapinero, next to each other are three mariachi
clubs, each basically the same, where the nightly crowds attest to the good food, camaraderie, and fun. **El Gran Garibaldi,** at Carrera 7, no. 59–56 (street level), is probably the most popular of the three. Next door is **La Ronda,** at no. 59–34. Upstairs is **Rafael,** at no. 59–30. Each club has a two-drink minimum per person, and drinks run about $2.50 to $3. The orchestra starts at 9 p.m. Each club has beamed ceilings and a Mexican décor.

A mariachi club downtown that serves up authentic Mexican food and lively music is **Guadalajara,** at Carrera 7, no. 30–04. Customers here sing along with the strolling musicians who wear sombreros and serapes. Occasionally on a Saturday night there will be a cockfight.

If you like flamenco music, try the **Club Cacique** at the Hotel El Presidente. You can enjoy your cocktails for $2 to $3 while seated in a black-leather chair in this intimate club (no cover or minimum). A three-piece flamenco group entertains you. Carpeted floors and dim lights.

STRIPTEASE SHOWS: Le Palace, Carrera 15, no. 98–78, chico, is the most
exclusive strip joint in town. Open nightly from 7 p.m., there are two shows each night (three on weekends). Phone 257-9292 for the latest information. Lots of gals around to talk to. Other less pretentious clubs are the **Teatro Lucky Strip,** at Calle 58, no. 10–23, with its bunnies attired in red bathing suits and matching ears; and **Jolly's,** at Calle 28, no. 6–83, which looks like a storefront except for the two bouncers in front. These clubs all have a minimum, naturally.

CLUBS WITH A VIEW: For one of the best views of Bogotá, head to the 41st
floor of the Hilton and turn left to **Le Toit,** a piano bar offering a fantastic panorama. Surprisingly, drinks are not expensive. A daiquiri or Cuba libre is $3; scotch, $2. Another fine view is yours from the rooftop **Guadalupe Bar** at the Hotel Tequendama. Prices are equivalent to those at the Le Toit.

To escape civilization, yet keep the lights of Bogotá in view at the same time, jump in a cab and go on safari at **Club Massei,** located in the wilds above Bogotá on Via a la Calera. But don't expect to find solitude here. Massei is one of Bogotá's hottest new clubs, attracting a mixed crowd of young professionals (yuppies) and students.

Using the wide-open plains of Africa as his theme, owner Rafael Alba really took advantage of the excellent location when he built Massei. The club is wideopen and spacious, with tables set up on various levels surrounding the dance floor in the center. Windows covering the entire side of the club facing Bogotá give it an even more open feeling, not to mention a magnificent view of the city. The African theme is even carried over to the cocktails. One that sticks in our minds, "La Jirafa" (The Giraffe) is a potent mixture of rum, vodka, crème de café, and tropical juices. Most drinks are $2.50, but you'll pay more for the exotic ones.

GAMBLING: Gambling has become discreetly popular in Bogotá. No big casinos or Vegas-type shows, but lots of small clubs have opened for roulette, blackjack, and other games (no slot machines). Our favorites are **C R Casino,** in fashionable Chico at Carrera 14, no. 90–23; and **Galería Club 21,** at Carrera 10, no. 27 in Tequendama arcade. **Caesars Palace Club** in Centro Comercial Los Héroes, Transversal 18, no. 79–35, draws the high rollers.

COCKTAIL LOUNGES: For that late-afternoon cocktail, by all means meet at the **Bar Inglés** on the main level of the Hilton Hotel. In a plush English country setting you can order from the comfortable leather chairs or couches. Hanging flags add to the décor. Drinks run about $3.50.

More reserved is the intimate **Bar Chispas,** on the main floor of the Tequendama Hotel, where you can have a quiet cocktail until 2 a.m. (3 a.m. on weekends). While drinks are about $3 each, there is no cover or minimum. Recorded music provides pleasant background in a lovely, relaxed atmosphere. No dancing.

The Den, Carrera 14, no. 85–24, is a good choice if you're looking for a place to relax and have a drink after a long day of sightseeing. Its homey interior and friendly atmosphere make it a favorite after-work meeting place. **Lloyd's Pub,** on Calle 94 at Carrera 14, is also a favorite watering hole among Bogotanos. There's often live music.

DINNER WITH MUSIC: Civilized Bogotanos consider dinner without music in much the way that Frenchmen view dining without wine—it just isn't done. If you share the viewpoint, and even if you don't, by all means spend one evening at the charming and exotic **Balalaika,** Carrera 15, no. 32–83, a Russian-style restaurant that has as fine a shish kebab ($4.50) as we've tasted anywhere. Housed in what resembles a huge shrubbery-surrounded private home, this lovely suburban find features a guitar-accordion-piano trio that ripples out old Russian melodies while you're feasting on superb beef Stroganoff ($5.75), borscht, or shashlik. Of the two dining rooms, we prefer the larger, rear room where a roaring fire nicely silhouettes the Cossack-garbed waiters, who somehow manage to look busy while being leisurely. Appropriately, Cossack scenes adorn the walls. Apparently showing no ideological favoritism, the Balalaika also features Chinese food ($5 and up for dinner) on the right side of the menu. A cab ($2.50) is your best bet for transportation. Hours: 6 p.m. to 1 a.m. Victor Roland is a fine host. Lunch is served from noon to 2:30 p.m. Monday through Friday.

The flamenco beat floods the atmosphere at the candlelit **As de Copas,** located farther out from center city in Chapinero at Carrera 13 and Calle 59 (tel. 249-0710), where the food is as Spanish as the music. Situated off a small street, the Copas is marked by a large sign that highlights a guitar, the dominant instrument in the 9:15 p.m. nightly music. Try the langostino (shrimp) for $6 or the arroz con pollo for $5. Drinks are a high $3.50, but there is dancing. Closing time is 3 a.m. Open for lunch. A show kicks off nightly at midnight.

To catch a colorful folklorico show while dining on native fare, check out our next two recommendations. The **Tierra Colombia,** Carrera 10, no. 27–27 (tel. 234-9525), offers an excellent selection of "típico" and international dishes. And the show here is first-rate. However, a word of caution is necessary. Prices are high! The Tierra Colombia must be planned as "big night out" only. Reservations are a must. **Las Ramblas,** at Avenida 13, no. 79–90, in Centro

Comercial Los Héroes, is known for its enormous delicious paellas. These, made with lobster chunks, chicken, and sausage, or a variety of shellfish are a perfect dinner, especially with a bottle of good Chilean wine. The show, which starts at 9 p.m., often features folkdancers and singers. It's lively and fun, especially if you join in.

Hosteria Los Sauces, Carrera 16A, no. 76–38, is a lively spot that features Colombian foods and folk shows. It's now in a lovely colonial building with a rose-filled open patio.

Cocos, at Calle 73, no. 10–70, is a restaurant by day and a tavern/dance hall by night. There is a live orchestra starting at 5 p.m., and you can dance till dawn. The kitchen is open till 11 p.m. Stick to basic stuff like sandwiches and burgers. No minimum.

Previously mentioned in dining choices is **El Zaguan de Las Aguas,** at Calle 19, no. 5–62.

6. BARGAIN SHOPPING

Emeralds are the thing here—we'll go into some detail about judging them and buying them in a few paragraphs.

Other fine buys in Bogotá are wood handcrafts, ceramics, brass and copper pieces, and Indian masks.

Most stores are open from 9 a.m. to noon and 2 to 6 p.m. daily (9 a.m. to noon and 2 to 7 p.m. on Saturday; however, Saturday hours vary from store to store, so check ahead of time). Unicentro shops are open from 10 a.m. to 7 p.m.

By the way, Colombia is considered a developing country and jewelry items purchased here are not subject to duty when you return home. That includes emerald jewelry too.

EMERALDS (ESMERALDAS): Colombia is the world's greatest source of emeralds, that brilliant-green gem that ranks above diamonds in the jewelry hierarchy. The finest varieties come from the mines of Muzo, Cosquez, Gachala, and Chivor. If you're in the market, here are some things you ought to know:

The most important attribute of an emerald is its color. It varies from light to very dark green; the most desirable and rarest shade is an intensive dark green without noticeable blue or yellow tint. Emeralds are not free from imperfections. In fact the ever-present crystallization marks (called "jardín" by connoisseurs) produce the velvet effect of the true emerald that makes it, for us, the most beautiful of gems; and irregular light reflections through the crystallization cause the special glimmer, found only in emeralds, often called "green fire."

In the evaluation of emeralds, size is also of great importance, as the larger gems, which are translucent and of good color, are very rare. All factors considered, unset emeralds can range from as little as $50 up to $10,000 and more *per carat.*

Best Buys in Emeralds—and Jewelry in General

In general, unset polished stones offer the best values. As emeralds are difficult to evaluate, a guarantee is offered only by reliable jewelers up-to-date on gem research. So shop carefully.

For the best orientation, your first stop should be the **Jewelry Center** stores, Calle 12 between Carreras 6 and 7, which feature extensive selections in all price ranges. Definitely browse here from store to store to get a feel for prices and design. Then try browsing in the shops on and around Carrera 10, between Calles 26 and 30.

When you've "done" the jewelry centers, your next stop should be **H. Stern,** at the Hotel Tequendama. This international jewelry concern features the highest-quality emeralds and offers an emerald guarantee accepted worldwide.

You'll find items from $100 up to $5,000 and higher. And 18-karat gold rings with small emeralds start at $150. Popular men's items are the 18-karat gold tie tacks with top-quality small emeralds. Browse all you want—no sales pressure here. If you make a purchase, you get an incredible one-year money-back guarantee. (The New York branch, at 645 Fifth Ave., will refund your money.) Other H. Stern outlets are in the Hilton Hotel and at Eldorado Airport.

Another good-value jewelry shop is **Joyería El Lago,** at Carrera 7, no. 16–46, in the Edificio Avianca. Here you can pick up interesting replicas in gold of items from the Gold Museum. Earrings, rings, and tie pins are big sellers. El Lago also has an outlet in the Edificio Bavaria at Carrera 10, no. 27–63.

Good, too, is **Willis F. Bronkie,** in the Edificio Bavaria, Carrera 10, no. 28–49, Room 2001, where there is a large selection of choice unpolished and polished stones, women's rings, earrings, and bracelets, and a varied men's selection as well. Ask to see the film about emerald mining and production. For convenience you might try the branch in the Hotel Tequendama in the lobby near El Virrey.

Outstanding buys include rings with rough emeralds from $50, bracelet charms with rough emeralds for $25, and earrings from $30 and up. Other good buys are gold-finished emerald tie pins and tie tacks. Even if you're not buying, you can experience the thrill of looking.

Finally, the **Sociedad de Metales Preciosos,** Calle 24, no. 20–72, has a large selection of gold and emerald jewelry. No fancy front here—just good values.

NATIVE HANDCRAFTS:
For the best in handmade leather, wool, straw, or ceramics, try the nonprofit **Artesanías de Colombia,** at the Iglesia de Las Aguas on Calle 19, near Carrera 3. The outlet is worth browsing around, for the large variety of attractive items from all over Colombia. Prices are rock-bottom. A more convenient outlet is on Carrera 10, across from the Hotel Tequendama. Another branch is located in the San Felipé fortress in Cartagena. Open from 10 a.m. to 7 p.m. weekdays, from 9 a.m. to 2 p.m. on Saturday.

You must also visit the **Associación Colombiana de Promoción Artesanal,** at Carrera 8, no. 7–21, beyond the Plaza Bolívar. Actually a museum of artesanías, the setting is in a magnificent Spanish-colonial house, set around a patio. Choose from the matted rugs, wicker items, colonial art, baskets, dolls, pottery, wood, and much more. Prices start at as little as $1.

You can also consider purchasing brass and copper artesanías at the **Museo del Cobre** (Copper Museum), Avenida Jimenez, no. 14–40, which, true to its name, is more of a museum than a shop. Spread over three floors, the copper and brass items range from souvenirs to large pitchers, pots, plates, and candlesticks. Good fun.

Casa Grison, at Carrera 10, no. 26, has an unusual assortment of copper mobiles, gaily painted ceramic salt and pepper shakers, and beautiful brass urns. Across the street on Carrera near the Eastern Airlines office, the **Centro Comercial Turisto,** an open-air handcraft center, recently opened. It has several stores selling straw products, leather goods, and ceramics. Prices seem a shade lower here but the unique aspects of the merchandise are nil.

PRE-COLUMBIAN ART:
Bogotá is the place for collectors of ceramics dating back 2,000 years or so. The ceramics are primarily funeral objects that have been retrieved from tombs. The Indians believed in life after death and many of the possessions of the deceased were buried with him in the belief that they would be necessary in the afterlife. How can these objects survive centuries of

burial? The answer is simple—they were buried as deep as 30 feet in order to be preserved against dampness. Many shops selling these items are scattered throughout the city. But your first stop should definitely be at the exposition of Chilean-born **Jaime Errazuriz,** in the Hotel Tequendama on the ramp in the main entrance. While prices are not low, the quality is there, and you need not worry about misrepresentations. Say hello to Jaime for us—he speaks perfect English. By the way, you can buy small figures for as little as $15. Mr. Errazuriz is one of Colombia's great authorities on pre-Columbian art. He is a lecturer on the subject and is writing a book on the Tumaco culture. Incidentally, you'll receive a certificate identifying and authenticating your purchase. Recommended without reservation!

Also worth exploring is the **Precolombianos San Diego** shop in the Tequendama Center (not the jewelry store in the hotel). This large shop has a wide selection of ceramic pieces, jewelry, and stones. The **Galería Cano** shop nearby is another excellent source for ceramics but is especially proud of their gold reproductions of jewelry. Very special!

THE TEQUENDAMA ARCADE:

The International Arcade, built on a terrace behind the Tequendama Hotel, has the city's finest shops. The prices are high but competitive with quality shops elsewhere in the city. The arcade is a lovely place to browse, window-shop, and eat as well. Besides shops, there are gourmet food stores, airline offices, art galleries, fast-food eateries, restaurants, movie theaters, and a gambling casino (see "Bogotá After Dark").

Many shops feature leather goods, and these range from inexpensive to very costly. Leather goods are one of the best buys in Colombia. The leather is soft and worked much like higher-priced Italian leather. **Boots 'n Bags** and **Colombian Bags** are two of the better shops. Suede bags start at $35 and leather ones are $50 and up. Suede and leather jackets are lovely.

Handcraft shops abound in the arcade and there are three that we especially like. Try **Quimbaya** for the best ruanas in town, made of wool and very warm. **Tropicana,** nearby, has unusual and unique items which we haven't seen elsewhere. Their ceramics are gaily painted and make nice gifts for children and adults. **El Zaque** also carries ruanas and you may find a style here that you prefer. Note the cheerful appliqués which look wonderful framed on the wall.

When you tire of browsing, stop for a quick lunch at **El Torrito,** a fast-food emporium with emphasis on tacos and other Mexican specialties. We prefer to eat outside at a small table set up by **Sanduchon and Dulcinea,** which makes overstuffed sandwiches or subs and has delicious pastries. Sandwiches start at $1. If it's dinnertime, try **El Spaghetti,** where pasta is the order of the day (other items too expensive). An inexpensive restaurant in the arcade, **Parador Suizo,** serves chicken, fried fish, and burgers. There are two very elegant restaurants in the arcade as well, but they're way over our budget limits.

OTHER SHOPPING BUYS:

Bogotá is home to a great many leather shops whose prices range from fairly inexpensive to expensive. Some good choices are **Cuerorama,** on Calle 19, no. 4–90; **Cuerolandia,** nearby on Calle 19, no. 4–90; and **Confecciones Orhid,** at Carrera 16, no. 51–46.

A newer store with offbeat items is the **Artesanías–El Lago,** Carrera 7, no. 16–81, opposite the Avianca office. Particularly popular are the ceramic copies of Chibcha Indian god figurines ($15 and up). You will find odd bottle openers, bookends, placemat sets, and brass candlesticks, as well as a large choice of ceramic copies of Indian artwork.

For antique items in pottery—some as old as 2,000 years—try **Joyería**

Clasica, at Avenida Jimenez, no. 5–06. Prices range from $6 to $100. Also on display are silver and gold jewelry items, coins, and ruanas.

In Chapinero, at Calle 59, no. 13–62, try **Típicos 59.** Here you can find just about any item from raunas to brass planters. A good store for browsing.

An interesting boutique for men and women is **Lulieth,** at Avenida 19 in the Hotel Dann. The men's shop is upstairs on the left; women should try the down-stairs shop. Excellent values in macramé shawls and ruanas.

For antiques, stop at **Antiquedades,** at Carrera 7, no. 10–66, opposite the Plaza Bolívar, where both originals and reproductions are available. Although the outlet is small, the values and quality are high.

For those who enjoy a host of top-quality establishments in one area, head over to **La Plazuela,** a shopping arcade at the Bogotá Hilton, to the rear of the lobby floor. You can pick up fine pre-Columbian pieces in one shop **(Cano),** hand-woven ruanas in another **(Aglaya),** fine emeralds at H. Stern, and handcrafts too. If you're tired, relax in the comfortable sitting area and sip Co-lombian coffee or a cocktail.

Note: These shops have no connection with the Hilton, and prices are com-petitive. We like browsing here particularly because at times we've found items not available elsewhere.

And then there's **Sears** (Colombian goods, largely), on Carrera 7 near Calle 14. **Tía's** and **Ley's** are two variety stores useful for notions, toothpaste, and such.

READERS' SHOPPING SELECTIONS: "As for shopping, I recommend **Chapinero,** on Carrera 13, between Calles 66 and 50. It's a large district which has many shops. I prefer this section to El Centro. I also recommend that the ladies buy some stockings in Colom-bia. I bought pantyhose for $1.50 a pair and I went through the whole summer wearing stockings every day with only two pair" (Mary Jane Hunter, Cheektowaga, N.Y.). . . . "A good place to shop for Colombian ponchos (ruanas), blankets, and kerchiefs in Bogotá at reasonable prices is **Distribuidora Colombia,** Carrera 9A, no. 13–27. I bought several ruanas there. This store was recommended to me by my Colombian friends when I visited Bogotá" (Paul A. Murphy, Fort Lee, N.J.).

"The favorite shop for myself and my fellow students from Cincinnati was **El Balay,** on Carrera 15, no. 74–43, on the outskirts of the Chico shopping and residential area. The entrance is not terribly impressive, but once you worm past the assembled baskets, you wind back into several rooms with all types of souvenir items. When I mentioned that I had paid more for an embroidered shirt (nearly 250 pesos) in another store, a clerk told me that they weren't worth more than 190. Her honesty endeared me to the shop and I went back several times. They also include little souvenir baskets gratis with your purchase. A nice inexpensive store that you might like to recommend to future readers. Any Chico 15 bus goes directly there—get off as the bus turns onto Carrera 15 and it's half a block away" (John Marshall, New Richmond, Ohio).

7. TRANSPORTATION NOTES AND ASSORTED MISCELLANY

BUSES, COLECTIVOS, AND TAXIS: Buses are plentiful and cheap—15¢ until 8 p.m. In the residential sections, the best way to travel is via colectivo, small Volkswagen buses that carry up to five passengers and charge 60¢. Cabs are rea-sonable and at night should be used exclusively. The rate is about 1¢ for each 100 yards plus 60¢ at the flagdrop. A slight extra charge at night.

AUTO RENTALS: Hertz has branch offices at the airport and in the Tequendama Hotel arcade, Carrera 10 near Calle 26 (tel. 234-7961). Rates typi-cally are high—$25 a day plus 14¢ a kilometer for a Ford Falcon, and $20 a day plus 9¢ a kilometer for a VW. Weekly rates are $70 a day and 14¢ a kilometer for a Ford, and $48 a day and 9¢ a kilometer for a VW. **Avis** has a branch at Calle 99, no. 11–26, and at the Hotel Bogotá Plaza.

MISCELLANY: Here are some helpful odds and ends of Bogotá life:

Airport Tax: As elsewhere in Latin America, Colombia charges foreign visitors an airport tax—$15—which you pay upon leaving the country. Domestic flights are taxed $6.

Banks: Open from 9 a.m. to 3 p.m. weekdays, until 3:30 p.m. on Friday.

Domestic Flights: When you buy a ticket to fly within Colombia, be sure to pay in pesos. There is one rate for credit cards and another for pesos, and the difference here is not mere pennies.

Tax-Free Shopping: Good values in liquor, perfume, cigarettes, and coffee are available at the airport, second floor, international departure area.

Telephones: Listen for the dial tone and then deposit a 10-peso coin (under 10¢).

Newspapers: While no major English-language newspapers are published here, you can get the *Miami Herald* ($1.25 a copy), as well as the *New York Times,* at the Tequendama and Hilton hotels. *Time* magazine's Latin American edition is available here. Best of the Spanish-language dailies is *El Tiempo*.

Post Office: The main branch is at Carrera 7 near Calle 17 (Edificio Avianca). Avianca at the Tequendama Hotel receives mail.

Street Vendors: You can buy virtually anything—from cigarettes to lottery tickets to fake or stolen Omega watches—from vendors, who are unusually persistent. Stick to store purchases.

Bank International of Colombia: Some of the Bogotá branches: Avenida Jimenez, no. 8–89; at the Hotel Tequendama; and at Carrera 7, Calle 19.

Cigarettes: U.S. brands are relatively cheap—($1) for Philip Morris. Piel Roja (Red Skin), the local brand, is 50¢.

Exprinter: Exprinter is at Avenida Jimenez and Carrera 6.

U.S. Embassy: This is located at Carrera 10, no. 38–49 (tel. 285-1300).

Government Tourist Office: Corporación Nacional de Turismo is at Calle 28, no. 13A–15, first floor.

Aguardiente: This popular (and inexpensive) liquor is taken straight with a slice of fresh lemon or orange for a chaser.

Planetarium: This is located next to the bullring. Open Tuesday through Sunday. Shows are held on weekends at 11:30 a.m. and 3:15, 4:30, and 6:15 p.m. Tuesday through Friday shows are at 11 a.m., 4 p.m., and 6:15 p.m. Admission is 25¢. The **Museum of Natural History** is in the same building.

Records: For the best selection of records and tapes, stop in at any of the **Bambuco** branches along Carrera 7.

Credit Cards: VISA, AMEX, Diners Club, and MasterCard are accepted virtually everywhere.

Photocopies: A photocopy center is at Carrera 13, no. 27.

The World's Best Coffee: We are fond of coffee, and we don't argue when our Colombian friends insist their brew is the best anywhere. We've never tasted any better, that we know. The National Federation of Coffee Growers of Colombia (Federacafé, for short) spends a great deal of money promoting that viewpoint through Juan Valdez, and for good reason. More than 80% of the foreign exchange pouring into Colombia derives from overseas coffee sales. Federacafé represents 200,000 coffee growers, most of whom have coffee plantations of under eight acres. Four out of five coffee farms are owner-operated. The federation bolsters the coffee industry by curtailing foreign sales during high-supply periods when ruinous price wars could develop. Moreover, the organization supports local prices by buying the farmers' coffee when prices fall below a certain level. The purchased coffee is stored until world demand picks up, when it is sold at better prices.

As an indication of the size of this country's coffee market, keep in mind that the United States buys about $250 million worth of Colombian coffee annually. That's an awful lot of coffee.

Airline Offices: Avianca's office is in the Hotel Tequendama, while Eastern Airlines is across the street at Carrera 7, no. 26–20.

CHAPTER XII

WHERE COLOMBIANS PLAY

□ □ □

1. CARTAGENA
2. SANTA MARTA
3. SAN ANDRES ISLAND

At the top of Colombia on the Caribbean are two resort cities, Cartagena and Santa Marta—only one hour from Bogotá by air—where Colombians throng for holidays and long weekends.

A third Latin playground is San Andres Island, perched in the Caribbean off the coast of Nicaragua some 480 miles northwest of the Colombian mainland. North Americans are discovering all three for different reasons: Cartagena, for its Spanish-colonial ambience amid walled fortifications; Santa Marta, for its splendid beaches; and San Andres, for its primitive remoteness and marvelous fishing and snorkeling. All are warm the year round.

If rates in these towns seem high compared to those in Bogotá, keep in mind that these are resort areas and cater to tourists year round. Rates are high, especially for food, but not when compared to comparable resort areas in the Caribbean.

GETTING THERE: Avianca, the Colombian airline, has one flight a week from New York to Cartagena. It takes five hours. At other times, or to go to Santa Marta, fly to the northern coastal city of **Baranquilla.** Then hop a 15-minute shuttle flight east to Santa Marta or west to Cartagena. From Baranquilla, it takes one hour to fly to San Andres.

ORIENTATION NOTE: Keep in mind that both Cartagena and Santa Marta use the Carrera and Calle street system of Bogotá. For example, if a restaurant is at Carrera 4, no. 8–10, this tells you the place is on the fourth Carrera, between Calles 8 and 9 at building no. 10. If the address is Calle 6, no. 4–20, then you know that your destination is on the sixth Calle, between Carreras 4 and 5 at building no. 20. Avenidas are exempt from the system. In Cartagena's Old City, however, many streets retain their colonial names.

1. CARTAGENA

Much larger than its coastal neighbor Santa Marta, the walled city of Cartagena is a Caribbean city of 400,000, where the people (called Costeños, "people of the coast") are much darker than Bogotanos. Which is not surprising, since the sun beats down ceaselessly, as it does throughout the Caribbean. Afternoon temperatures hover in the upper 80s and 90s most of the year, while evenings cool down pleasantly. By the way, there are no real seasons as such. The December to March period is considered summer, but it simply is the dry season. It is more humid June to September.

The fascinating aspects of Cartagena are the fortress-like walls, which surround the city (originally built as protection against pirates) and the faithfully preserved streets and houses of the inner city. Carefully restored, the walls today are much as they were 300 years ago, as is the city itself. We will recommend a walking tour which should be a must for you. Also, there are good beaches with flat, dark sand. The nice balance between history and the beaches gives Cartagena a certain tourist magnetism for us. See if you agree.

GETTING TO CARTAGENA: Chances are you will fly here from Bogotá, in which case you will fly directly to Cartagena in just under one hour. A desk at the airport will call a hotel for you. When you buy your ticket at Avianca in Bogotá, check the price in pesos before paying with a credit card. There is often a big difference in price and the difference is not in your favor. A round-trip ticket was $110 at the time of this writing.

CAUTIONARY NOTE: We have received several letters regarding purse snatchings and pickpockets in the walled city. Virtually every one of these crimes occurred after dark. Crime is serious business no matter what time of day it occurs. However, with a little common sense many of these unpleasant incidents could be avoided. Don't wander around the walled city after dark—it is not well lighted. If you go into the city for dinner, have the restaurant call a cab for you. Don't wear expensive jewelry downtown, and leave valuables in your hotel.

A QUICK ORIENTATION: Hop a cab from Cartagena's modern international airport. The $3.50 ride is a good opportunity to get a feel for the city. First you pass through new suburban areas with neat small homes and manicured lawns, then skirt the barrios where the poor have only a rickety shack between themselves and the pounding sun, and finally you pass the center of Old Cartagena, where there was once an inner wall designed to separate the wealthy from everyone else. Note, too, the dock area and outdoor markets.

Eventually your cab will slide onto the peninsula of **Bocagrande,** where most of our recommended hotels, restaurants, and beaches are located. But sightseeing will be in the **Old City,** thereby balancing your trip here nicely.

To orient yourself quickly, keep in mind that Cartagena has a large outer wall encircling the Old City, designed originally to keep out marauding visitors such as Henry Morgan and Captain Kidd. Each block in the Old City is known by its colonial name, noted on a corner plaque.

Main Streets in the Old City

Key avenues to familiarize yourself with are **Avenida Venezuela,** which cuts through the Old City from the **Tower of the Clock** northeast to **Cabrero Lake.** Southwest of the tower the street is called **Avenida Blas de Lezo,** which leads to Bocagrande, where most of our recommended hotels are. Following are some important landmarks.

Tower of the Clock: Actually a gate with a clock on top of it, this spot once served as the entranceway for residents to pass through the old inner wall which in colonial times separated well-to-do homes from the poorer working-class sections. Now the inner wall has been leveled, except for the area around the clock, and there is free access between all parts of the Old City. *Tip:* The Tower of the Clock is a natural meeting place.

Plaza de la Independencia: Located near the dock area, near the Tower of the Clock, this plaza is actually a small park. Note the outdoor markets nearby.

Plaza de Los Coches: Just beyond the Tower of the Clock in the original inner city, this area has some interesting shops and arcades.

Plaza Bolívar: Inside the inner city, this small park houses the **Palace of the Inquisition,** which today serves as the **Tourist Office.**

Plaza Bovedas: Here is where you get a fine view of Cartagena Bay from atop the outside wall.

Calle Larga: This street leads from the dock area.

Bocagrande

Avenida San Martín is the major street here. Most hotels and restaurants are on it, and the bus runs along it too. San Martín is Carrera 2. The beach street is Carrera 1. The calles are numbered with the lowest numbers at the Hotel del Caribe and the higher near the Old City. The bayfront thoroughfare is Avenida Chile.

El Laguito is a small peninsula off the tip of Bocagrande behind the Caribe Hotel. Produced by a vigorous landfill project that took several years, it now has private homes, restaurants, shopping centers, and the Hilton and Las Velas hotels.

WHERE TO STAY IN CARTAGENA:

You should definitely stay on Bocagrande. The nicer hotels, better restaurants, and nightspots are there, and it's cooler and has far less commercial traffic. It is safe to walk on Bocagrande at night. There are always lots of people at the sidewalk cafés.

Seasonal Rates: We are quoting rates for Cartagena's high seasons— December 15 to April 30 and June 15 to August 31. At other times you can expect to pay about 25% less.

Extra Charges: Hotels in Cartagena add several unusual charges to your bill without informing you when you check in. We have seen "security tax," "telephone tax," and a variety of others. Several readers have written us about extra charges for singles who were placed in a double room without being informed of the extra charges. Check your rates very carefully and ask about these extras.

Hotels in Bocagrande

The 199-room **Hotel Caribe** Carrera 1, No. 2-87 (tel. 50-155 or 50-813), which was closed for renovation and refurbishing, has reopened and it looks almost like its old self. Once the center of social activity in Cartagena, the Caribe retains its colonial section, lovely gardens, huge pool and sundeck, and good restaurant at poolside. Accommodations in the smaller, more modern buildings are more than the colonial main building. Expect to pay $60 for a double in the colonial section and $70 in the newer ones. Singles run about $7 less.

Three recently built moderately priced hotels have opened on Bocagrande. **Hotel El Dorado,** Avenida San Martín, no. 4–41 (tel. 50-830), is the largest of the three, opened in 1976 and quite attractive. It has 110 rooms—all air-conditioned, with modern private bathrooms—a good restaurant (serving international-style foods), and although located on the beach, a small pool.

Rooms are decorated in colonial style and are sunny, large, and attractive. Singles are $27; doubles are $39. Good value.

The smaller **Royal Park,** on Avenida 3, Calle 7, no. 171 (tel. 47-507), has 30 rooms on four floors. Located a few blocks from the beach, the Royal Park is decorated in modern plastic-bright colors and towering plants. It has a snackbar and restaurant, and the coldest lobby in Cartagena. Single rooms are $23, and doubles run $30—all with air conditioning.

The **Hotel Turipana,** Avenida San Martín, no. 11–67 (tel. 48-061), has bright rooms, all clean and newly painted, and furnished with air conditioning and private bath. The Turipana is located ten blocks from the Hotel del Caribe and several blocks from a good beach. These are the only disadvantages as it is a good choice. Doubles are $23, while suites go for $30.

An old favorite is the **Hotel Bahía** (tel. 50-316), within a block of the Del Caribe. The Bahía has only 66 rooms, comfortable lobby, round pool, backyard, and innocuous furnishings. Nice people run it. Doubles are $27 with air conditioning, and singles are $20.

Other excellent moderately priced choices which we've listed for years are the 86-room, four-story **Hotel Playa,** Avenida San Martín (tel. 50-552), a block from the Del Caribe, where you can bed down in a plainly furnished but clean double with bath for $23, in a single for $16. Air conditioning is included. Nice bar with terrace on the second floor.

The white-hued **Flamingo,** Avenida San Martín (tel. 50-301), offers a private beach and an attractive outdoor restaurant facing the water. The 32 rooms spread over two floors; small yet comfortable, they represent a good value at $17 for a double with bath, $12 for a single with air conditioning (less without air conditioning). They also own the Hotel Bahía (see above).

Still on Avenida San Martín, there is the three-star, 38-room **Residencia Bocagrande** (tel. 54-435), which offers cozy, spotless doubles with bath for $21, singles for $16. Enter through the door on Calle 8.

Behind the Hotel Bahía is the small 30-room **Hotel Quinta Avenida,** Calle 5 and Carrera 5 (tel. 41-932), owned and operated by a charming Greek family eager to satisfy. While there is no beach, the Quinta does have a small pond and the hotel is surrounded by towering palm trees. Attractive setting. Doubles are a good value at $12, all with bath. Air conditioning is $2 extra.

A new hotel has opened on Avenida San Martín at no. 6–40. The **Hotel Paris** (tel. 52-888) is a modest establishment with minimal charm. But it does have a good location (near the beach and restaurants) and it is clean and adequately furnished. Doubles start at $22, with singles $6 less, all rooms with baths.

With less location and even less charm, but with air conditioning and bath, is the **Tajamar Hotel** (tel. 53-121), on Carrera 3A, no. 5. Rooms are small and the hotel looks as if it needs a paint job, although it's been open for only two years. Doubles cost $20 with air conditioning and $16.50 without it. Take it!

A final choice is the good-value **Costa Caribe,** at Carrera 3, no. 5–66 (tel. 51-546), only one block from Avenida San Martín. Doubles here are $16, and singles run $11.50. A quiet residential block.

Newer "Residencias"

The newer residencias that have opened in Bocagrande are located in private houses a few blocks from the beach. They are uniformly small; most have a few tables for breakfast, a TV in the lobby, and a porch to rock on. Your room will be small and basically furnished, but almost all have private bath and most have air conditioning. You will feel comfortable, especially if you speak a little Spanish.

Residencias El Retiro, Avenida 3, Calle 7, no. 2–50 (tel. 45-796), is the most attractive one we found. The 13 rooms spread over two floors are clean and sunny, and all have air conditioning and private baths. The lobby has comfy furniture and Spanish-colonial décor. A double is $17 and a single is $10. You have the option to take it with meals for $20 for one person (only $30 for two)—but we think you'd have more fun eating out. For a reservation, write Ramiro Ruíz, Apartado Aereo 2596, Cartagena.

A close second is **Residencias Astoria,** a block away on Avenida 3, Calle 8–96 (tel. 52-237), another two-story house with 13 rooms—all air-conditioned with private bath. The décor here is more modern than colonial—again, not luxurious but comfortable. Cost? Only $12 single and $20 double. A restaurant is on the second floor for meals if you desire.

Another acceptable choice is the **India Catalina,** Avenida San Martín, no. 7–115 (tel. 55-392), set back off the street in a passageway. The Catalina is right on the beach and rooms have a view of the ocean and the Old City. The restaurant here is well regarded, and while the rooms have all the furnishings, they could use a little sprucing up. Comfortable, clean doubles are $28 and singles run $19.

Residencia Internacional, at Avenida San Martín, no. 4 (tel. 80-675), is a recently opened pension here. Rooms are small, each furnished with a bed, nightstand, and table. The staff is friendly and helpful. A single room will run $15, and a double, $22, all with private bath. Most rooms have ceiling fans.

Leonela, at Carrera 3, no. 7–142 (tel. 54-761), is rather in the same vein and has a well-regarded restaurant and bar in front. It is slightly less expensive because it's a block farther away from the beach. Expect to pay $12 for a single and $16 for a double. If you want a twin-bedded room, the cost is $20.

Basic Residencias

The following places are for those of you who spend little time in your rooms and are not particular about furnishings and surroundings. They have bare floors, beds, a chair or two, a dresser, and that's it.

Residencias Rosandy, Avenida San Martín, no. 9–42, has ten rooms with bath and friendly owners, but no one who speaks English. A garden in front and clean rooms. Rates are $15 double, $13 single. **La Giralda,** Avenida 3, Calle 7 (tel. 44-507), and **Jenny,** at Carrera 3, Calle 8, are in the same category.

Other possibilities in this section are **El Caribe,** at Carrera 3, no. 5–93, and **Residencias Mary,** at Carrera 3, no. 6–27. Built around a courtyard inevitably decorated with drying laundry, these are only for the hardy. Rates are $10 single and $15 double.

Higher-Priced Hotels

The stunning 287-room **Cartagena Hilton International** (tel. 50-660) on Laguito (the top of Bocagrande) is a five-star hotel, and it deserves every one of them. A great place for a honeymoon, a winter sojourn, or a family vacation, the Hilton is modern and elegant. Rooms have small terraces overlooking the ocean or bay and large, comfortable beds. There is a pool and the hotel sits right at the edge of the beach as well. The Las Chivas coffeeshop serves all three meals at indoor or outdoor tables. The elegant Tinajero de Doña Rosa restaurant specializes in continental cuisine. There are barbecues and poolside parties several nights a week. Singles run $78 and doubles are $90 off-season, about $15 a night more in high season. You can't beat those rates on any Caribbean island.

The **Las Velas Hotel** (tel. 50-000) is a favorite among the more reasonable deluxe choices. Also on Laguito, across the street from a lovely shopping arcade and gambling casino, Las Velas is small enough to be called intimate. The lovely pool is set in a quiet inner courtyard and the slide is fun for young and old. The hotel is on a secluded part of the beach too. There's a good restaurant (serving kosher food) in the hotel, and most rooms have an ocean view or a view of the walled city. Doubles are $46; singles are $9 less.

The larger **Capilla del Mar** (no relation to the restaurant of the same name) is on Avenida 1 at Calle 8 (tel. 51-140). Its 190 rooms are spread over 21 floors, and although it sits on the beach, it has a small pool and sundeck on the roof. There's a good restaurant and a health club on the premises. The service here is only fair, which is disappointing considering the prices. Rooms have stocked refrigerators. Doubles are $54 and singles are $39 in high season. Watch out for extra charges.

Three other deluxe hotels, but with slightly lower rates, are apartment hotels. These are the Cartagena Real, the Hotel Don Blas, and the Hotel Barlovento. The modern, 80-room **Hotel Cartagena Real** is located at Avenida Malecón, no. 1–150 (tel. 55-555). The rooms and service are truly first class and $90 gets you a suite for four. The larger 250-room **De Cameroon,** at Calle 10, Carrera 1 (tel. 54-400), has doubles for $40. The small, 48-room **Hotel Barlovento,** at Carrera 3, no. 6–25 (tel. 53-965), is our final recommendation. Doubles are about $47 and offer excellent value. Write ahead for reservations.

Note: There are a few hotels located near the Old City—one in the Plaza Bolívar itself. We do not, however, recommend that you stay downtown or on Marbella beach. We have received some letters from readers about purse, watch, and camera snatchings downtown *at night*. While this can and does happen in any city, we feel that walking to and from your hotel is something you should be able to feel unconcerned about. 'Nuf said!

THE BEST RESTAURANTS: Since Cartagena is a coastal city, seafood is the thing here. Highly recommended is the red snapper (pargo), prepared in a variety of ways. As the city has developed into an international tourist center, a wide variety of restaurants has opened, and you can find French, Italian, Arabian, Spanish, Colombian, and good old steakhouses all within the boundaries of Bocagrande. We think you will enjoy eating in Cartagena.

But there are four restaurants that deserve special attention, and two are in Bocagrande. You should definitely dine in these restaurants during your stay.

Cartagena's most famous restaurant, and one that would stand out anywhere is **Capilla del Mar,** now in a lovely house overlooking the bay three blocks from San Martín on Avenida Chile, near Calle 8 (tel. 55-001). The restaurant has a porch and several dining rooms cooled by ceiling fans and bay breezes. Michelle and Pierre Daguet, a brother-and-sister team, owned this restaurant for 25 years. The fare is seafood and, while international, it leans a little toward French since the Daguets were French-born. After Pierre's death, Michelle ran the restaurant alone for a number of years, until her death just recently. Now the restaurant is owned and run by the staff, as had been arranged before the Daguets passed away. We highly recommend the cazuela de mariscos (seafood casserole) for $7 and the arroz con mariscos (rice with seafood) for $9. The cazuela was the best we've had anywhere. Be sure to try a rum sour before dinner. And save room for dessert. The coconut pie and baba au rum are both excellent choices. Service is slow, making dinner here a great way to spend a relaxed evening. Open from 12:30 to 3:30 p.m. and 7 to 11 p.m. Phone ahead for reservations. Closed Monday.

A change of location, but not of quality, leads to the **Club de Pesca,** located in the historic Fort San Sebastian on the nearby island of La Manga. You can reach it in a 15-minute walk from the downtown dock area or a $2 cab ride from Bocagrande. A fun way to go is to rent a horse and buggy (bargain over the price —figure $5 to $6, but you get a long, picturesque ride). The view of the bay is relaxing, and you eat outdoors under the shade of a huge old caucho tree which has probably been there longer than the restaurant, with the guard towers and gun embankments of the fortress around you. All this combined with the candle on the table will make this an evening you'll never forget. Any of the fish dishes are recommended and start as low as $8. Lobster dishes are a high $15, but the shrimp is less and they're large and delicious. Open from 11 a.m. to 11 p.m. daily, it's a nice place for lunch or dinner.

The third special choice is the **Bodegon de la Candelaría,** located in a romantic 16th-century house in the walled city. Legend has it that it was in this house that the Virgen of the Candelaría appeared to Fray Alonso of the Cross, and instructed him to build the Monastery of the Popa. Located on Calle de las Damas, Bodegon is administered by the Cartagena Hilton Hotel and furnished with colonial antiques and early wine-making equipment. Its menu is virtually all fish and shellfish. Half an avocado comes stuffed with shrimp, squid, snails, and claws, accompanied by a delicate-pink sauce. Hot lobster is served with a mustard sauce and cold lobster with a sherry sauce, and both are fabulous. Try the fried shrimp with grated coconut. Of course, Bodegon is far more expensive than the other two restaurants, so save it for a big night out. Expect to spend $23 per person here without drink or wine. Open till midnight.

Doris herself will be there to greet you and make you feel at home at the **Restaurante de Doris** (tel. 53-808). And if she doesn't charm you, which is most unlikely, the restaurant itself will. It's located in a spacious house overlooking the bay in Bocagrande. Here you have the choice of dining indoors or outside on the balcony (we prefer the balcony). Once you're settled, Doris will be at your table to take your order. El langosto de la casa (lobster served in a pink sauce with rice, vegetables, almonds, and pine nuts) and lobster minarete (served with three sauces) are both excellent choices. If you're really hungry, try the Fiesta Marinera, an incredible seafood platter. Reservations are suggested.

Dining in Bocagrande

Bocagrande has an international restaurant strip which includes gourmet restaurants and small informal eateries serving a wide variety of food. Basically, all the restaurants serve continental food, but each adds a few dishes to give the restaurant its ethnic character. You need not confine your eating to your hotel, although several have good restaurants.

La Olla Cartagenera, at Avenida San Martín, no. 5–100, is one of the loveliest eateries here. Walk through the unimpressive storefront to the beautiful garden covered with a tin roof. A spraying fountain stands in the courtyard surrounded by tables and flowering plants. Grilled meats, fish, and shellfish dishes dominate the menu, and prices here are the same as at less impressive restaurants. Highly recommended.

One of the best restaurants in town is **La Fonda Antioqueña,** Avenida San Martín, no. 7–52. A typical restaurant from Colombia's "west," it has cowhide chairs and tables hewn from tree trunks. Steaks and other grilled meats are served with typical sauces made from hot peppers and avocados. You can eat inside the fan-cooled dining room or head out back to the garden. Chorizos (sausages) are very tasty with drinks, and you should sample a sancocho (soup-stew) of chicken or beef with a lot of vegetables. Grilled pork chops are excellent. Most main courses are under $7. Beer, wine, and drinks are served. Excellent choice.

For a lovely, romantic evening under the stars, and for delicious food prepared in Colombian style, spend one evening at the **Costa Brava** in Laguito. With a lovely setting on the harbor's edge, it is built in Spanish style around an inner courtyard and garden. Try for a table on the water. Arroz con pollo is $6;

with shrimp it's $7, and with assorted shellfish (paella) it's $9.50. Fried chicken is under $6, as are several other entrees.

Aficionados of Italian food have the widest choice of all. There are several good Italian restaurants, and several pizza places as well. **O Sole Mío,** at San Martín and Calle 5, is owned by a husband-and-wife team. O Sole Mío specializes in pizzas in four sizes and with a variety of ingredients. The pizza is much like New York, with a slightly thick, chewy crust, and costs range from $2.50 to $6, depending on size and type. Booths, checkered cloths, and posters provide the décor. Other Italian foods are served as well. Most main dishes will run under $6.

Giardino Restaurant and Pub, at San Martín, no. 5–122, has been redecorated. The outdoor tables are on a patio, but you should head indoors to the air-conditioned section. It is dimly lit and attractively decorated. Pizza for one is $3 and a large pie (eight slices) is $7. For extra toppings, such as peppers or sausages, add $1. Spaghetti dishes are $6, while ravioli and cannelloni are a bit less.

Restaurant Jeno's Pizza, at San Martín, no. 7–54, offers a selection of 20 different pies. Toppings range from anchovies to—ugh!—pineapple. Pie for one is $2.50, while an eight-slice pie is $9. Tables on a covered porch are cooler than those inside.

Piccola Italia, at Avenida San Martín, no. 7–58, is an oldtimer. Italian flags decorate the inner dining room, and the rear garden is cool and pleasant in the evening. There's a sidewalk café in front too. The sauces here are the tomato-garlic type, and they're delicious. Spaghetti dishes start at $3.75, while pizzas start at $4.50 (large pie). Cannelloni, lasagne, and ravioli are all tasty entrees. The food is always good and the Italia is a lively spot.

An attractive pizzería on San Martín near Calle 7 is **Vino Pizza,** with tables on an outdoor patio and wooden booths indoors as well. Multicolored lights and colorful tablecloths make it a festive place to have your pizza or spaghetti dish.

Our last Italian food eatery is **Da Teresa,** Avenida 4, at Calle 8, a little off the beaten path and set in a private house. All the food is cooked to order, and Teresa is quite a cook! It's like eating at home. Prices for most items are less than on the main drag.

Chef Julian, at Avenida San Martín, no. 9, is an attractive restaurant in a private house marked with an old-fashioned lamppost outside and a colonial-style dining room. Julian also has an outdoor garden. The specialties are three lobster halves, each with a different sauce, and the best paella in Cartagena. Main dishes are $5 to $8, but lobster starts at $13.

A large restaurant at Avenida San Martín, no. 8, is **Los Quijotes,** set in a private house. You can dine inside or on the covered, fan-cooled terrace. Continental cuisine is featured. Main dishes (beef, fish, and pork) are $5 and up, while chicken is less expensive.

Crêpes n' Waffles, in La Pierino Gallo Shopping Center, has stuffed crêpes (with shrimp, chicken curry, and ham-and-cheese) for $3.50. Waffles and ice cream make a cool afternoon pick-me-up at $1.50.

El Patio de la Atarrava, Carrera 1, no. 4, is a thatch-roofed rectangular terrace that sits right on the beach. From its white straw chairs you can see the tide rise, and at night you can hear the waves roll in. El Patio specializes in seafood. Fish soup is $2.50, cazuela is $6, while fried fish costs only $3.50. Nice choice.

Los Pinos, at Avenida San Martín, no. 8–164, is quite large and has a huge menu. There are indoor tables, but the sidewalk café is nicer. Pastas are only $2, steak Cartagena style is $4.50, and barbecued meat is $4, while arroz con pollo costs $2.50. This is a great budget restaurant.

Nautilus, at Avenida San Martín, no. 10–26, was built to look like a ship with portholes, fish nets, and ballast on the walls and diving gear on the floor. Each table has a nautical map and comfortable chairs. Organ music sets the mood while you dine on ceviche ($4.50), fried pargo ($5), and calamari ($4). Bend as you enter—the door is very low, as we found out the hard way.

If you're in the mood for Chinese-Créole dishes, try **Mee Wah,** on San Martín at Calle 8, where you have a choice of five dining rooms. Specialties include vuc kai (chicken Cantonese) at $3, or vag tiac ja (shrimp and ham in an oniony sauce) at $5.

Another recommended dining place is the **Arabe,** where the Syrian family that owns and operates the place is justly proud of its chicken breasts with nuts and rice, shish kebab, and grape leaves on a bed of rice. The Arabe is located in a private home with a large patio in front on Avenida 3 near Calle 8.

An inexpensive choice with drab décor is **Terraza Alameda,** on Avenida 3 at Calle 5. You can smell the meats grilling on the open hearth. Baby beef is $6 (the most expensive item on the menu), while roast chicken is only $3.75. Cazuela de mariscos (a mélange of shellfish in a tangy sauce) is $5.50.

Dining in the Old City

Generally, restaurants downtown are not on a par with those in Bocagrande, but we have found a few exceptions. **El Pargo Rojo,** near Avenida Venezuela, and the **Nautilus,** at the traffic circle outside the walled city (look for the statue of the Indian princess) both specialize in fish. **Baru,** located nearby in the Seguros Bolívar building, offers diners the option of outdoor dining overlooking the sea or comfortable air-conditioned indoor tables. Try the filet de Pargo Norwegian style ($6).

For French cuisine and ambience in the middle of the walled city, try **Marcel,** on Calle de la Inquisición in the recently restored Casa Skandia. Be warned that Marcel is significantly more expensive than our other choices. **La Crêperie,** on Plaza Bolívar, is more within our budget.

Also recommended, but a little more expensive, is **La Casa del Almirante Vernon,** located in the upstairs portion of a restored colonial house opposite the Church of San Pedro Claver. Try the filet of snapper au gratin on spinach.

Snacks, Light Lunch, and Breakfast

There's a **Kiko Riko Chicken House** on Avenida San Martín at Calle 8, and a **Presto** (like McDonald's) across the street. They both have tables and take-out service for picnic lunches. **Whopper King,** a few blocks away, is on a par with the first two. They all serve burgers, fried chicken, hot dogs, and drinks.

Pizzería Bodegón Margarita is a small eatery serving only pizza. Located on the water's edge on Laguito near Las Velas, Bodegón puts all kinds of ingredients onto its thin crisp dough base. A pizza for one starts at $3 and goes up to $6 with many toppings. Order a tall, cool beer, and enjoy a tasty light lunch. A branch is on Carrera 1 and Calle 5.

Small sandwich and soft-drink places abound through Bocagrande. They serve heros, some other sandwiches, ice-cold beer, and soda. Try **Cubanos** for breakfast, lunch, or a snack.

Pío Kiko and **La Piragua,** next door on Avenida San Martín, take over the entire sidewalk with their bridge tables and chairs, serving rotisseried chicken, sandwiches, and drinks. Nice places to sit at night when a live combo plays on the bandstand into the wee hours.

Try **Pipos,** on Laguito and at Avenida San Martín at Calle 8, for ice cream. **Palacio de las Frutos** is a good stop for a drink of freshly squeezed orange or pineapple juice. Mango and coconut drinks are popular too. **Delicioso**

Internacional, a round green-and-white take-out seafood stand in front of the Hotel del Caribe, offers oysters, clams, shrimp, and snails in a variety of sauces. Another stand is located at Carrera 1 and Calle 8. **Heladería Arabe,** on Avenida San Martín at Calle 7, is a good breakfast stop. Tea and sweet pastry are delicious.

Robin Hood serves very good ice cream. Last, we always drop in at **La Cassata** for our final Coke before retiring. It's open late, is air-conditioned, and has some young people who often speak English. They serve a continental breakfast for about 85¢.

CARTAGENA BY DAY: We recommend at least two visits to the Old City during your stay here. Accordingly, we've outlined two walking tours that will give you a good feel for the city. Streets generally are crowded with peddlers, cars, and pedestrians. It's a good idea to try to make one visit on a weekday and the other during the weekend.

Walking Tour 1: The Inner City

As noted earlier, the inner city was originally the area located within the outer protective walls. An inner wall, now leveled for the most part, segregated the wealthy from the poor sections of the inner city.

Start your stroll at the city's main gate called **La Boca del Puente,** marked by three gates, and the famous **Tower of the Clock.** This is the **Plaza de Los Coches,** which is filled with vendors selling mostly homemade candy. Turn left at the gate; a short distance up is the **Plaza de la Aduana** (where stands the old Customs House). Look for the statue of Columbus there. Continue along the wall area to the **Church of San Pedro Claver,** which honors a great priest who devoted his life to ministering to the needs of the African slaves imported by the Spanish to Cartagena. Streets here are extremely narrow—wide enough in some places for only one person. **Santa Teresa** and **Calle de Boloco** are typical.

Nearby is the **Parque Bolívar,** a large plaza in the El Centro section, once the wealthiest section of the city. Notice that the houses are two stories high and have ornate carvings and overhanging terraces. The **Palace of the Inquisition**—dating from 1706—still stands in the west end of the plaza. Its doors are massive and ornately etched. Look for the Inquisition's coat-of-arms over the door. Across the street is the **Casa Skandia,** named after the Swiss insurance company that restored it. Feel free to step inside the courtyard for a glimpse of 18th-century Cartagena. On the other end of the plaza is the pink-hued **basilica,** which resembles a mosque. If you look up at the outer wall here you will see a sunclock dating back some 300 years.

Continue along **Calle Santo Domingo** one block to the **Santo Domingo Church and Convent,** which date back to the 16th century. Note the oddly shaped steeple. Inside, the statue of the Virgin Mary has a gold-and-emerald crown. At this point the street becomes **Calle Factoría,** which leads to the outer walls and also the **Plaza de La Merced,** site of an old church now used as a theater. Climb up the outer wall nearby and take in the breathtaking view of the bay. Follow the promenade to the **Plaza Bovedas,** where 22 cells were used as prisons in colonial times, and now are used as shops for souvenirs and handcrafts. Continue following the wall and shortly you will find yourself back on Avenida Venezuela, not far from Boca del Puente, where you began.

READER'S SIGHTSEEING SUGGESTION: "Tucked away on the second floor of the Jesuit convent adjacent to the Basilica of St. Peter Claver in Cartagena is the **museum of religious colonial art,** which includes lovely sculptures from Santa Fe de Bogotá, the

Quiteno School; several paintings, including a charming angel in 17th-century viceregal garb, from the Cuzco area; and a sundry collection of ecclesiastical furnishings and liturgical implements. Sister Carolina Le Mactre is a charming attendant" (George D. Eagar, Los Angeles, Calif.).

Walking Tour 2: The Outer Walled City

This tour carries you through parts of the outer walled city. It was once called the Getsemani Barrio, and here the working classes lived in one-story houses called "casas bajas." It remains a working-class area.

Start your tour again at the **Tower of the Clock (La Boca de Reloj)** near the dock area, and stop at the nearby **Parque Centenario,** where you will see a series of busts called the **Camellon de Los Martires,** commemorating the city's heroes in the fight for independence from Spain. Here, too, is an outdoor flea market. Just beyond the dock is the wide **Calle Larga,** the major street of the barrio, which leads to the yellow **Puente Roman** (Roman Bridge) leading to the island of **Manga,** formerly a fort, now a well-to-do suburb. From the bridge you get a good view of **San Felipe Fortress** and **La Popa Hill.** Walk along Calle Larga to the bridge, but instead of crossing it, follow the outer wall (which you will find yourself on) to the left along Calle Lomba until you reach another old bridge, called **Paseo Heredia.** At this point there is a grassy knoll housing a touching monument called **Los Zapatos Viejos** ("old shoes"), a loving tribute to Colombia's great poet, Luís Lopez de Mesa. The poet once compared Cartagena to a pair of comfortable old shoes. The poem and a symbolic pair of shoes are here. Cross the bridge to San Felipe Fortress (see below), which stands some 135 feet above sea level. It was the highest of the many forts built here and thus was strategic in the area's defense.

At this point you can bus it back to the Tower of the Clock along Avenida Venezuela. The same bus usually continues past the tower to Bocagrande.

La Manga

Or if you still have time, catch a taxi and ask the driver to take you across to La Manga, and drive along the **Calle Real de la Manga.** The private homes along here are beautiful examples of Cartagena's splendor at the turn of the century. One of the most beautiful is the home of the Romana family. Teresita Romana, author of the best selling cookbook *Cartagena en la Olla,* and one of the family's few surviving members, will be more than happy to show you around. There is a beautiful tile fountain in the front garden, and the huge patio in the back stretches all the way to the next street.

San Felipe Fortress

This massive fort commands a magnificent view of the approaches to Cartagena, sitting as it does 135 feet above sea level. Completed in 1657, it took 18 years to construct. Be sure to explore the background tunnels. A **Sound and Light Show** re-creates the era Saturday evenings at 8 (in Spanish only). Admission is $1. A very good handcraft store is located here, Artesanías de Colombia; part of a government-operated chain, it has another shop in Plaza Bolívar.

San Fernando Castle

Well preserved despite its construction some 200 years ago, this fort protected Bocachica when a sandbar closed the Bocagrande entrance to the Bay of Cartagena. Check out the vaults and dungeons. The castle features two main bulwarks connected by a circular rampart.

Fort San José

Recently restored, this fine 18th-century fort in Bocachica consists of a battery of 21 cannon as well as a powderhouse. Note the ingenious system of valves, designed to control the force of waves and tides.

Fort San Sebastian

Completed in 1743, this battlement complemented San Felipe Fortress. Home today to the Cartagena Fishing Club, the fort houses a restaurant open to the public.

The Dungeons (Bovedas)

As part of the city's outer walls, a system of 22 shell-proof cells was constructed in the late 18th century. Although built for defense purposes, these cells were also used as prisons. Complete restoration was carried out by the Colombian Government Tourist Office. The cells are now filled with small boutiques.

La Popa Monastery

A lovely cloister with stone columns and brick archways, this church and convent is located on a hill overlooking the entire city. Founded in 1607 by the Agustín Fathers, it is still used as chapel and monastery. The view from the hill is stirring. By the way, if you're ever here on February 2, Feast Day, be sure to see the candlelight procession. Admission is 75¢. Take any bus marked "Popa" from the Old City and hike up the hill, or have a cab take you all of the way up for $3 round trip.

Other Daytime Tips

Rent a bicycle: $2 an hour; near the Hotel Del Caribe.
Rent a kayak: $3 an hour at **Acuatur** on Bocagrande Beach, at Calle 5.
Paddleboat: $2.50 an hour; Bocagrande Beach.

CARTAGENA AFTER DARK: This is hardly a jumping town, but with its growing popularity and new hotels, you need not be bored when the sun goes down. For gamesters there's—

Gambling

One of Latin America's best casinos is located in Cartagena, the **Casino del Caribe,** in the Pierino Gallo Shopping Center beyond the Del Caribe Hotel. It's red carpeted and comfortably air-conditioned. Buy your chips (*fichas*) and "buena suerte." Open from 4 p.m. until 4 a.m.

Clubs and Discos

La Escollera, just off Avenida San Martín in Bocagrande, across the street from the beach, is the hottest spot in town. It was even recommended to us by someone in Panama. Cartagenians and tourists alike come here to dance until dawn.

In our previous edition, El Templo de Cleopatra, Avenida San Martín no. 9–96, was the hottest spot in town. It has since closed and a new club has opened at the same address, **Nautilus Video Bar Disco.** It is very popular with the younger crowd, who as the name suggests, come here to catch their favorite videos. The overflow from the Escollera usually winds up here.

The **Portobello Club,** in the Pierino Gallo Shopping Center in Laguito, is a more sedate club, drawing an older, well-dressed, more sophisticated crowd. The music varies from disco to Latin and back. Drinks are $3.

For a supper club, head to **La Gruta Grill and Disco,** at San Martín and Calle 11. The music is lower in decibel and the atmosphere is like that of a nightclub. Lots of food but nothing to write home about.

Moulin Rouge, on Calle 3, is saner, and small and intimate. Same price on drinks. Discs about the same.

If you like a view with your drink and dancing, the **El Tormentin,** on the top floor of the Hotel Velas, is a good spot. It has a view of the harbor and the walled city, and occasionally live music. One hitch—it has a $5 minimum. But you can stay till the 2 a.m. closing.

Minerva, the disco in the basement of the Hotel Capilla del Mar, is a lively spot, or climb up to the revolving bar on the top floor of the hotel.

Our last two choices are inside the walled city. Why not choose one and go there by horse and buggy? **Pacos Restaurant and Tavern,** on the Plaza Santo Domingo, is a great place to relax over a cold beer after a long day of sightseeing. And if you're hungry, try the tapas. The grilled shrimp and the squid are both delicious. Live music is provided every night by Los Veteranos del Ritmo (the Rhythm Veterans), a delightful group of men ranging in age from 57 to 72 years. Nick, Paco's English proprietor, who came to Cartagena years ago on an engineering contract and never made it back home, is always around to make you feel at home and to fill you in on all the local happenings.

There's live jazz every night at the **Taberna La Quemada,** Calle de la Amargura no. 6–45, just off the Plaza de la Aduana. A replica of the English taverns of the early 19th century, it was built for the filming of *Burnt,* directed by Gillo Pontecorvo and starring Marlon Brando, Evaristo Marquez and Renato Salvatori. The walls are covered with photographs of scenes from the movie.

Other Evening Ideas

Grab a folding chair at **La Piragua,** San Martín and Calle 8, and listen to the music while sipping a cool beer or soft drink. Very pleasant.

Rent a **buggy** and ride around Bocagrande and the walled city. Bargain over the price.

El Laguito, on San Martín and Calle 5, is a store filled with pinball machines and other electronic games. Games are 10¢.

BEST SHOPPING BUYS: If you are going to be in Bogotá, you are probably best off shopping there. The selection is larger and the prices are a bit lower. Most shops in Cartagena are branches of well-known Bogotá firms. The one exception is handcrafts, since these are locally produced.

Make your first stop the **Artesanías de Colombia** shop in the Plaza Bolívar, part of a nonprofit chain located in different parts of the country. The big things here are the large wall hangings ($12 to $15), some in tree shapes. (The same items were triple the price in Bloomingdale's in New York.) You can also find a good selection of straw mats, handbags, belts, ceramic pieces, and ruanas. Soft leather duffel bags and cases are good buys. Another branch is on Avenida San Martín and Calle 5.

Artexpo, a very small shop across the plaza in the Inquisition Palace, has a wide selection of handcrafts and costume jewelry. It is run by a Peace Corpsman. A fun buy here is a "Colombia" T-shirt in blazing color for $4.

The **Colombian Tourist** shop, at Calle Roman no. 5, has stuffed alligators for $3, a great gift for the boy in your life. This is a place for souvenir-type buys.

Tropicana, Avenida San Martín, near Calle 5, is a large store adjoining Bronkie jewelers. Nice buys here are colorful hammocks and placemat sets. They carry a large selection of the soft leather bags and suitcases made in Colombia. Also wooden masks.

La Tienda, across the street, has reproductions of antique mirrors and pre-Columbian artifacts.

Galería Cano, in the Pierino Gallo Shopping Center, is an attractive store with pre-Columbian artifacts and reproductions, and outstanding jewelry in Indian motifs. Another branch is located in the Hilton.

Genuine pre-Columbian artifacts are for sale at **Valdivia,** Calle Santo Domingo no. 33–94. Archeologist-owner Michel Brenon, a specialist in the pre-Columbian cultures of Ecuador, will fill you in on the background of any piece you may be interested in. Prices start at $10, and all pieces come with a certificate of authenticity.

Land leather goods are considered Colombia's finest. Very soft and worked in the same manner as those leathers from Italy, they are fashioned into handbags, luggage, briefcases, and less expensive accessories. There are two Land outlets here, one on San Martín at Calle 7 and the other in the Pierino Center (second floor).

Three shopping centers are now located in Bocagrande. **Pierino Gallo** on Laguito is a modern two-story center with chic shops and airline offices. Coffee and refreshments are served in the patio. Two fine jewelry stores are here: **H. Stern,** famous for its Brazilian gemstones in a variety of colors, as well as emeralds; and **Willis F. Bronkie,** known for emeralds. Another Stern shop is in the Hilton Hotel. Típico clothing and handcrafts can be purchased at the Tropicano Típicos. The center also houses the Bank of Colombia, the Casino del Caribe, and the Royal Night Club, plus other fashionable shops.

El Pueblito, the smallest of the three, is of least interest to the tourist. On San Martín at Calle 6, it has toy and record shops, and service stores. The bar and disco complex behind it on the beach is a good spot to head to at night.

The newest center in Bocagrande is the large and modern **Centro Comercial Bocagrande,** on San Martín at Calle 8. It has several levels, fashionable shops, and best of all, movie theaters that sometimes have English flicks. **Ventatom Artesanía,** located on the street level of this center, is one of the best handcraft shops in Cartagena. Start your browsing here.

EXCURSIONS: Consider a day trip to the **Rosario Islands,** 2½ hours away over the open sea. The unspoiled islands, site of vacation homes and villas, have sandy beaches and an intact coral reef populated by colorful tropical fish. The $30 fee includes the boat ride (five hours) and lunch. Bring your own snorkel gear or rent equipment for an additional fee. The boat leaves at 8 a.m. and returns at 5 p.m. Bring lots of suntan lotion. Buy your ticket the day before at **Yates Alcatraz,** Avenida San Martín no. 8–19.

Boquilla: A small fishing town called Boquilla is a 15-minute ride by cab. The fishermen here live much the way their grandparents used to.

Boat Ride to Bocachica: An hour's ride will take you to the island in the bay. The *Alcatraz* leaves from the dock in front of the clock tower—$5 round trip. Smaller boats leaving from the same site cost $3 round trip. You can buy your tickets for any of the boats at the dock, or make arrangements with Acuatur in front of the Del Caribe. Boats leave between 9:30 and 10:30 a.m. Waterskiing can also be arranged here.

MISCELLANY: Some helpful odds and ends:

Avianca: There's an office in the Pierino Shopping Center, Laguito, and you should reconfirm your flights there. *Note:* It's imperative for flights within Colombia.

Post Office: Located on Avenida Urdaneta, near Avianca.

Cambio: Other than those at the major hotels, a good one is the **Banco de la**

República, near the Plaza Bolívar in the walled city. **Citibank** is another, near the plaza.

Pharmacy: The **Droguería Nueva York** has two well-stocked branches on Avenida San Martín and another on Calle Román downtown. The large one on San Martín is open 24 hours, and there's another one near Pierino Gallo.

Supermarket: For picnic lunches or sightseeing excursions, buy your fixings at the market in the Edificio Seguro Bolívar.

Tourist Office: The government office is in the Plaza Bolívar. Maps and brochures (some in English) available.

Transportation: Buses (10¢) and cabs (inexpensive) are joined by horse-drawn carriages (get one in front of the Del Caribe—$4 an hour).

2. SANTA MARTA

Developed around a graceful bay with calm blue waters, Santa Marta is blessed with natural beaches that would be the envy of any resort city. Ten minutes away on inviting Rodadero Beach are good hotels and restaurants. The towering Andes, complete with snow-tipped peaks, are a magnificent backdrop for the city.

Founded in 1525, the city once was the Spanish center in the battle against Simón Bolívar and the revolutionaries, who finally liberated the city in 1821. And it was here that Bolívar came when his federation plan for South America collapsed. He died in Santa Marta in 1830. Today it is a thriving city of over 230,000 that draws a heavy tourist flow all year.

CAPSULE ORIENTATION: Rodadero Beach is the resort area of Santa Marta. Located 15 minutes from Simón Bolívar Airport by cab, it's the place to stay when coming to Santa Marta. The newer hotels, better restaurants, and nightspots are here, and we think you should be too.

Guide to Rodadero

Carrera 1 is the avenue that runs along the beach. It is closed to traffic and part of it is a promenade.

Carrera 2 is the major thoroughfare of the community. It is residential and commercial. The calles (streets) are numbered, with the higher numbers at the Hotel Tamaca end of the beach.

The area is small, having only a dozen streets and even fewer avenues.

Guide to Downtown Santa Marta

The downtown area is ten minutes by auto beyond Rodadero Beach. **Carrera 1** runs along the beach and has benches and trees. Be there one evening at sunset—lovely.

Quinta Avenida (Fifth Avenue), four blocks away, is the major shopping street, and banks and airline offices are here as well.

Paseo Bastides, which is named for the city's founder, is a lovely promenade extending from Calle 15 and Carrera 1 along the beach to the dock area.

The calles (streets) are colonial and often only wide enough to walk single file.

A Word About Climate

As befits a Caribbean city, the weather is warm and "swimmable" the year round. Humidity rises June through September.

WHERE TO STAY: Hotels in Santa Marta are comfortable and moderate in cost. There are several good budget choices on Rodadero Beach, some low-budget and basic choices in downtown Santa Marta, and three first-class choices on the road from the airport to the city.

Hotels in Rodadero Beach

A fine choice here is the 72-room, five-story **Hotel Tamaca,** Apartado Aereo 5032N (tel. 27-202), located smack on the beachfront. Try to get a room facing the bay—lovely at dusk. The Tamaca is at the end of the beach near the native-style rancho restaurants, a natural sand slide into the sea, and the newest modern apartment houses of Rodadero. Attractive doubles, furnished in Spanish-colonial style, are $27 with bath and air conditioning. Singles are $19. Restaurants, bar, and beauty shop, and for evening fun, a gambling casino.

Another fine choice is the smaller, 53-room **Hotel Lilliam,** Apartado Aereo 816 (tel. 27-166). Located on Carrera 2, and so a one-block walk to the beach, it has been a popular stop with our readers. No frills, but very clean, comfortable rooms with air conditioning and bath, and a very friendly and helpful staff. The restaurant in the lobby is open for all three meals and the food is good. Doubles are $20 and singles run $15. With three meals, doubles are $26 and singles are $21. A good buy.

The **Hotel La Sierra** (tel. 37-770) is located on Carrera 1, right on the promenade. A brightly lit lobby with a busy restaurant and coffeeshop make this an "up" place to stay. Always busy, the Sierra has 74 air-conditioned rooms spread over ten floors. The rooms are comfortably furnished, and many face the bay. Doubles are $36 and singles run $27.

Next door, **El Parador del Mestre** (tel. 27-000) has 51 rooms that are all rather plainly decorated. They do have a good location and air conditioning. The rate is $12 single, $16 double.

Hotel La Riviera, on Carrera 2, no. 5–42 (tel. 27-666), is a hotel built in 1973 on a quiet street with but a two-block walk to the beach promenade. It has 48 rooms, all with bath and many with terraces. Doubles are $19 and singles cost $13, but you can take off $1.50 if you don't want air conditioning. If you write for a reservation, specify with or without air conditioning.

Hotel El Rodadero, on Carrera 1 (tel. 27-262), has only 45 rooms, but the hotel looks much larger. The halls go off in all directions from the desk. Doubles are $22 and singles run $15. Furnishings are adequate but not very attractive, yet they all have baths and most have air conditioners.

Hotel Canaveral, Carrera 2, no. 11–65 (tel. 27-002), is an even more attractive choice. A five-story, 60-room, white building, the Canaveral has modern, attractive furnishings and an elevator. All rooms come with bath and air conditioning. Doubles are $18 and singles are $12.

Hotel Betoma, Calle 8, near Carrera 1 (tel. 27-112), is a six-floor hotel with 47 rooms. All the rooms have baths, but only 40 have air conditioning. Doubles run $23 and singles go for $16. The Betoma has a large, comfortable lobby and a downstairs restaurant.

The **Hotel Valladolid,** on Carrera 2, no. 5–67 (tel. 27-464), is another small hotel with 28 rooms. All have bath, none is air-conditioned, and all are basic. Doubles are $13.75; singles cost $10.

Big-Splurge Choices

Our favorite big-splurge stop is the **Hotel Irotama,** Km14, Vía Ciénaga 598 (tel. 33-591), located five minutes from the airport on its own beach. The original hotel has 36 small bungalows built in an arc away from the main house along the beach. It also has 28 rooms. The bungalows have sitting areas, bedrooms, and bath (shower), with air conditioning. Doubles run $40 to $58; triples are $10 more. The Irotama has an indoor air-conditioned restaurant and an outdoor restaurant on the porch of the main house. Lunch is served on a patio at the beach. The brilliant-blue swimmable waters have proved so popular that another section has been added. Known as Irotama II, this section has 48 apartment-type rooms, each with a refrigerator. They are moderately decorated and are air-conditioned —good for families. This area has a pool. Cost: About $53 per day and up.

One of the city's newest hotels is the **SantaMar** (tel. 27-317), five minutes farther from the airport on the way to Santa Marta. Built in much the same way as the Irotama, the SantaMar has 32 cabins and 36 rooms, all air-conditioned, with colonial furniture and garden areas. They have outdoor hammocks for lounging, and a pool, tennis, and a golf course of sorts nearby. Don't bring your clubs yet. Single rooms are $35; doubles and cabins go for $48 to $60.

A very attractive hotel, but located near the airport, is **Puerto Galeon,** on a private beach strip. It has its own pool and restaurant, and is attractive but expensive—the least expensive rooms are $64 (and up) for one to four people. It is 25 minutes to town. Casino.

Hotels in Center City

If you prefer staying in center city, you should consider the **Hotel Marlindo,** right on the beach at Carrera 1, no. 23–84 (tel. 32-167). The street is quiet and residential, and the three-story building has 29 rooms. Doubles at $17 and singles at $12 make this a best buy.

The nearby **Hotel Castillo,** Carrera 1, no. 22–26 (tel. 33-576), is a smaller hotel with only 13 rooms. All have bath, but only fans for cooling. The large white house has a restaurant and bar. Furnishings are basic, but it's well cared for and has an excellent location. Doubles are $10 and singles run $8.

Another inexpensive choice is the 31-room **Residencia Miramar,** Carrera 1, no. 18 (tel. 33-351), where doubles are $9.50 and singles only $7.50. Add $1.50 for air conditioning.

The **Gran Hotel,** Calle 17, near Carrera 3 (tel. 35-760), is a hotel you might consider. It has 45 rooms in a white, four-story building. Try to get an air-conditioned room. Doubles are $20 and singles pay $15. The rooms are large but plainly furnished. Three blocks from the beach.

Hotel Andrea Doria, Calle 18, no. 1C (tel. 35-323), has 12 rooms, all with bath. Doubles run $9.75; singles, $6.50.

Hotel Yarimar, Calle 29 at Carrera 1, and the hotels **Park** and **Zulia,** on Carrera 1, Calles 20 and 18, are other basic choices, with prices for doubles ranging from $10 to $12; singles run $9 or $10. We recommend them only for the most hardy among you.

The **Tayrona Hotel,** which was once the loveliest hotel downtown, was shut down for a while and is partly reopened. There are only 12 rooms available, and they are not air-conditioned. Rates run $7 single and $10 double. The Tayrona, on Carrera 1A, no. 11–41 (tel. 32-408), has a terrific view of the beach as the sun sets.

THE BEST RESTAURANTS: Many visitors to Santa Marta seem to eat at their hotels. It's too bad, since Santa Marta has some very good restaurants. We suggest having breakfast in your hotel, a light lunch on the beach or at a "rancho," and dinner at one of our suggested restaurants. All are informal.

Restaurants at Rodadero Beach

The Italian touch is supplied by the **Portofino,** Carrera 1 at Calle 7. Owned by a Neapolitan family, the Portofino was originally located downtown. It has an indoor air-conditioned restaurant, but on cool evenings we like the covered terrace—dimly lit and very relaxing. We invariably eat some pasta ($3.75) or carne pizzaiola (slightly higher). They have some exotic octopus dishes as well. Not everything on the menu is Italian.

We're partial, too, to **Los Cumbieros,** Carrera 2 near Calle 3. One of the most attractively decorated restaurants here, the Cumbieros is French style with white wrought-iron touches. Colorful and with an interesting menu we think you'll like. The salade niçoise, steak pimienta, and pollo normandie are outstanding.

Restaurant Los Delfines, Carrera 2 at Calle 9, is a seafood restaurant featuring arroz langostinos (large shrimp with rice) and cazuela de mariscos. The Delfines has both indoor and patio dining.

El Conquistador, in the Hotel Tamaca, is a classy restaurant open for dinner from 7 to 10 p.m., with modern décor and air conditioning. Here you can dine on trout, pargo, or seafood brochette, or any number of meat and poultry dishes.

Restaurante Capri, on Carrera 1 (at the other end of the beach), is another attractive choice. It has a bar and an outdoor patio, as well as a wood-paneled, air-conditioned dining room. Seafood and Colombian dishes (arroz con pollo at $4.50) are featured.

Karey, at Calle 9A, no. 1–19, is a small eatery with a cozy atmosphere. The menu is eclectic, but has something to suit everyone's taste. Prices start at $5 for pasta dishes and run higher for meats.

La Rodadita, Carrera 2 at Calle 7, specializes in seafood, and since many fishing villages are in the area, the catch is always fresh.

La Brasa, nearby, is known for the area's best arroz con pollo and other Colombian specialties.

Lunch and Snack Restaurants

Montreal, Carrera 2 at Calle 8, is a small counter-only restaurant serving hot dogs, hamburgers, and spaghetti plates—very inexpensive. Cold beer and soft drinks.

El Caracol, at Carrera 2 near Calle 3, is a snail-shaped restaurant of white stucco with bright-orange plastic tables and chairs. With a breakfast of juice, eggs, toast, and coffee for $1.25, and light lunches for $2.25, you can't beat the Caracol. Arroz con pollo ($2.50) or bistec a la criolla ($3) are typical dinner choices.

Mi Ranchito, on the beach near the Hotel Tamaca, is one of the thatch-roofed native restaurants where you can get fine criolla food at prices ranging from $1.75 and up per platter. Look for toucans and parrots on the premises.

By the way, all along the beach street are small snackshops ideal for breakfast or a light lunch. They serve hot dogs, fried chicken and fish, sandwiches, and soft drinks.

Center-City Restaurants

Panamerican, at Calle 18, no. 1C–10 (tel. 32-900), is the best restaurant downtown. The menu is continental, with steaks, pork, and chicken dishes starting at $6. Desserts are delicious pastries and fruits. Lovely view of the bay.

An attractive restaurant in center city is **El Turista,** Carrera 1 and Calle 22, opposite the city's main hospital. The dining room is semi-outdoors—with a roof but no sides! Ocean breezes keep things cool. Set in a white colonial house, the Turista specializes in fried snapper ($3.75 per platter) as well as arroz con pollo ($4.50). The half chicken is a good buy at $3.25, and there are various meat dishes starting at $2.50.

La Brasa Restaurant, Carrera 1, no. 17–05, has three separate dining areas —an indoor dining area, some outdoor tables under a covered roof, and a patio area in the center. The specialty is seafood, and most dishes are $3.

Fonda de las Colonias, Carrera 1 at Calle 18, is a long, narrow restaurant with overhead fans and ice-cream-parlor booths along the thatched walls. A variety of dishes is on the menu, with criolla foods in the lead. Quite inexpensive, a typical dish is $2.50.

Sorrento Pizzería and **Fuente de Soda** are on Carrera 1, and the tables on the sidewalks in front are big hangouts for locals and young tourists. Sandwiches, pizza, and ice cream are served.

El Molino Restaurant, at Carrera 1, no. 15–29, is a narrow restaurant serving typical foods. Very inexpensive—most dishes are under $3.75.

Finally, we have **La Real Parrilla y Pizzería,** a white-stucco restaurant on Calle 22 at Carrera 2, which is very popular with locals. It is crowded on weekends. The meats are grilled Argentine style.

WHAT TO SEE IN SANTA MARTA:
About three miles outside the city is the **San Pedro Alejandrino Estate,** where Simón Bolívar died in 1830. The house has been rebuilt in colonial style and today contains many relics of Bolívar's life, including his bed, chair, desk, and clock (stopped at 1:03, the time he died). A statue of Bolívar at age 28 is here too. On the grounds is a memorial building, reminiscent in some ways of the Lincoln Memorial in Washington, D.C. To get here, take a bus from Fifth Avenue (Avenida Quinta) that says "Mamatoco" (25¢). It goes through much of the city as well. Open from 9 a.m. to 5:30 p.m. daily.

Punta Betin is a peninsula that juts out into the bay. Nice views of the city from here. The area houses a small aquarium and several seafood restaurants (good red snapper). To get here, take a cab ($1.25). The aquarium is open from 8:30 a.m. to noon and 2 to 6 p.m. daily; 50¢ admission.

THE BEACHES:
The best beach is **Rodadero Beach,** ten minutes from center city. Beaches are free and the waters calm. Ideal for year-round swimming and boating. You can swim at **Center City Beach** too. It extends virtually the entire length of the city. This area is more crowded on weekends.

SANTA MARTA AFTER DARK:
The most popular evening pastime is gambling, and the place to catch the action is at **Casino Tamaca,** on the main floor of the hotel. It is air-conditioned, and informality in dress is the key. Open from 9 p.m. to 2 a.m. every night. There are 10¢ slot machines, blackjack tables, roulette, and dice tables. The minimum bet is 50¢.

Drop in at **Roberto of the Tropics,** at Calle 9 near Carrera 1, and say hello to Robert Selnick of New York, who owns it. With wicker chairs and tables, and a gleaming dance floor, Roberto's is the most attractive bar in Rodadero. With your drink ($2.75) comes a spicy guacamole dip. Ask Roberto about the discos, since they seem to close quickly here.

At this writing, the three most popular are **El Pulpo,** in Edificio Los Corales; **El Molino,** on Carrera 2 at Calle 7; and **Puppy,** in the Edificio Irora.

Guigo's Piano Bar offers dim lighting and oldtime tunes as well as the latest in American music. Nice place for a quiet drink.

THE BEST SHOPS:
Santa Marta does not have many good shops, and if you are traveling in Colombia you can do better elsewhere.

Artesanía, on Carrera 2 at Calle 7 in Rodadero, is the nicest store we found.

Some carved masks, woven wall hangings, and leather goods. The **Del Caribe** in the Plaza Bolívar is the best store in downtown Santa Marta. Souvenir-type articles.

MISCELLANY: Here are some odds and ends before we go to San Andres Island.

Buses: These are plentiful, clean, cheap, and recommended. Price: 25¢ from downtown, Carrera 1 and Calle 11 (stops all along Carrera 1) to the Hotel Tamaca. Buses leave when full.

"Train": An electric train travels up Carrera 3 and down Carrera 2, and you can get on and off at different points. Cost: 50¢. Called "Rodatren," its schedule is irregular, but it stops at 11 p.m.

Banks: The largest bank here is **Banco de la República,** Carrera 5 and Calle 17.

Festival of the Sea: In July the city celebrates the Festival of the Sea. A queen is crowned; there are fireworks and dancing in the parks and just about everywhere else. Waterskiers from all over Latin America come to compete. It lasts four days.

Pharmacy: The **Droguería Neuva York,** on Calle 10 and Carrera 2 in Rodadero and in Plaza Bolívar downtown, is convenient.

Tours: An agency, **Tayrona Tur,** in Plaza Bolívar downtown, is your best bet.

Ley: This chain has a 5¢ and 10¢ store on Carrera 5 downtown.

Golf: The **Gaira Golf Course** allows tourists to play its nine-hole course.

Rentals: Bicycles can be rented at Rodadero, $2.75 per hour. Paddleboats and waterskis are rented on the beach near the Hotel Tamaca: per hour, boats are $2.50; skis run $7 to $14.

Outdoor Stalls: Small outdoor stalls selling fresh fruit, cooked food, and sundries are located on Carrera 3 near Calle 7.

3. SAN ANDRES ISLAND

Travel brochures talk a great deal about unspoiled beaches. Rarely do the facts fit the prose. But at tiny San Andres Island—in the Caribbean just under 500 miles from Colombia and 150 miles east of Nicaragua—the beaches are truly virginal—and the population is only 25,000.

English is widely spoken here, a leftover, presumably, from the days of pirate Henry Morgan, who used the island as his base for striking out at Panama and other Spanish settlements. Also, gambling is legal here, and there are two fine casinos as well as several nightclubs.

The island—only 7½ miles wide at its widest point—is shaped like a seahorse. Coral reefs surround it, as well as the neighboring islands of **Providencia** and **Santa Catalina.** Waters are perfect for snorkeling and scuba-diving. There are only two towns—**San Andres** and **San Luís.** Essentially underdeveloped, the island depends heavily on tourism. Temperatures are virtually perfect—afternoons in the upper 80s and low 90s, and evenings pleasantly in the 70s.

Little wonder that Colombians flock to San Andres the year round.

QUICKIE ORIENTATION: Your flight lands at a jetport only five minutes or so by cab ($2.75) from town. It's actually near enough to walk if you're light of luggage.

The main street is **Avenida de la Playa,** which parallels the beaches. Most hotels are located here, as are the better restaurants. Key shopping streets are **Avenida Las Americas, Avenida 20 de Julio,** and **Avenida Costa Rica.**

HOTELS IN SAN ANDRES: The newest hotel on the island is **Aquarium,** Avenida Colombia 1–19 (tel. 3117), which sits right on Punta Hasa at the edge of the bay. It's actually a series of connected circular three-story buildings, all with dome roofs, built along the shore and in the bay itself. The restaurant, bar, pool, and shops are in these unique buildings as well. Lovely but expensive. Doubles start at $55 and go up, while singles are $43.

Two of the newer and better hotels in San Andres are located right on the beach. The **Casablanca,** Avenida Colombia, no. 3–59 (tel. 6315), offers roomy doubles with air conditioning and a small refrigerator for $47. Suites accommodating up to four people are available for $120. The hotel has a small pool and dining room.

Only a block away is the 100-room **Abacoa,** Apartado Aereo 16 (tel. 6313), which is fully air-conditioned and has a casino. Rooms here run $44 for doubles.

The **Isleño,** Avenida de la Playa, no. 5–117 (tel. 6590), is still one of the best hotels in this area. Located right on the beach, the Isleño offers two meals a day as part of your room rate. Doubles are $37 and singles cost $29.

Another recently built hotel on the opposite side of the island is the **El Cove,** Avenida El Cove (tel. 6064), which has been open since 1978. This deluxe establishment is on a rise overlooking the Caribbean, and although there is no beach on that side of the island, El Cove compensates with an Olympic-size swimming pool. The hotel is five miles from town, but provides transportation for guests who wish to make the trip. A first-class dining room is located on the premises. Room rentals start at $35.

Two other acceptable choices are the **Gran Hotel Internacional,** on Avenida Colón (tel. 6818), with doubles with air conditioning for $32, and the **Palace Hotel,** nearby ($26.50 doubles). Not located on the beach but only a few blocks away near the shopping area.

Coming down in price, there are a number of hotels that cater to budget tourists, particularly those from Colombia and Nicaragua. Two blocks from the beach is the 47-room **Hotel Morgan** (tel. 6475), which boasts a barbershop and beauty parlor. The entrance resembles a movie theater lobby. Doubles with air conditioning are $19 and singles run $14. Deduct $1.50 if you don't care about air conditioning. But do request a balcony.

The beachfront **Hotel Tiuna,** Avenida Colombia no. 3–59 (tel. 3235), is a lovely three-star hotel. Doubles are $25 and singles cost $17. Request a room with a terrace facing the beach. Next door is the **Hotel Monaco,** run by the same management. Doubles here are $10 and singles are $7.75.

A newer hotel, the **Tropicana,** located near the Casablanca (tel. 3256), has 41 rooms and comfortable doubles for $12, singles for $10. There is a pool on the top (eighth) floor. Good value.

RESTAURANTS OF SAN ANDRES: An Argentine owns **El Oasis,** Avenida Colombia, but the cuisine is strictly nautical—and superb. Sea breezes make dining here refreshing. Fish nets, diving bells, and wicker chairs shape the atmosphere. The potent rum-based cocktails put you in the right frame of mind to sample the house specialty, lobster in coconut sauce ($8), and quite good. Meat dishes are excellent—try the chateaubriand—as are the fish platters.

Another fine choice for seafood is **Restaurant La Bahía,** also on Avenida Colombia. All manner of seafood, in comfortable surroundings.

For a wider variety of menu, with meat and poultry dishes leading the way, try **La Carreta,** on Avenida Colombia. The steaks are charcoal-broiled and quite good. Another international-type eatery is the **Restaurant El Romano,** on Avenida Las Americas.

La Fonda Antioqueña, on Avenida de la Playa, is a charming Colombian restaurant, with no entree priced over $10 (lobster dishes command the highest prices). Although the menu is somewhat limited, food and service are quite good. A large restaurant extending out over the water, La Fonda is quite popular and is also an excellent breakfast choice. A continental breakfast costs 90¢, while a full American breakfast with two eggs and arepa (corn cakes) costs just 30¢ more. Your second cup of coffee here is free, and the usual 10% service charge is not added to the check.

For tasty seafood, head to **La Tortuga** ("The Turtle"), on Avenida Colombia (tel. 6310), where shellfish is king. Prices are reasonable.

For pizza fans, there's **Pizzería de Giovanni** (tel. 6073), in front of Cañon de Morgan.

SIGHTSEEING: Most of the island is uninhabited. The eye sees little more than tall palms, thick bush and grass, and of course the brilliantly blue ocean. Nicest homes on the island are in the **Sarie Bay** section near the airport. To see the island, consider renting a bicycle for about $3 a day. A taxi runs about $3.50 per hour.

Morgan's Cave, where Henry the pirate was said to have stored his treasures, is near Sarie Bay. Water fills the cave periodically, but you can climb down to it from the roadway. It's 50¢ to enter.

At the tip of the island is a **Blow Hole,** where water rushes in at such force that it shoots 30 feet into the air.

San Luís, the island's other village, houses many of the local residents, who depend on fishing for their living. There's a beach here but not much else for tourists. Stop for lunch at the Sound Bay Beach Restaurant—excellent fish.

Johnny Cay

It's ten minutes by motor launch to this small coral island where the swimming and snorkeling are as perfect as we've seen anywhere in Latin America. Sand is thick and multicolored due to the coral. You can walk around the tiny reef in ten minutes. A snackbar sells soft drinks, but you should bring a picnic lunch. Pick up the launch at the dock near the Tiuna Hotel ($1.25, round trip). By the way, you can rent snorkeling equipment and a boat at the **Hansa Club** for $10 an hour.

Acuario

Not far from Johnny Cay is a natural aquarium where snorkelers endlessly explore the marine life and coral. A motorboat from Tiuna Hotel takes you there in under 15 minutes ($3, round trip).

SAN ANDRES AFTER DARK: There are two casinos worth exploring, both in hotels. The **Casino Hotel Abacoa,** open from 9 p.m. to 3 a.m. (closed Monday), requires neither jacket nor tie. The **El Dorado Hotel** houses the other casino, with much the same rules. You have a choice of roulette, blackjack, or a high-rolling game called punta y banca. The roulette tables accept 50¢ bets.

For music with a dance beat, there are a few discos scattered throughout town. Tame by big-city standards are **Cinco Estrellas,** on Avenida Colombia, and the **Alegro Club,** on Avenida Las Americas. The **Hotel El Dorado** has a beer hall and a good grill serving international food.

Las Palmas, in the Hotel Tiuna, is a "with-it" disco that is usually crowded; and finally, **Estudio 54,** on Avenida 20 de Julio, is worth a try.

MISCELLANY: Here are some useful tidbits to wrap it up:

Auto Rentals: A Spanish-made Fiat (called a Seat) now rents for $12 for four hours with gasoline included and unlimited mileage. See **Alis,** Avenida Nicaragua.

Avianca: Located in an office building a block and a half from the ocean on Avenida Duarte Blum.

Post Office: Right next door to Avianca.

Bicycles: A charming double bike, with canopy, is yours for $1.50 an hour. Conventional two-wheelers are 90¢ per hour at the stand across from the Hotel Casablanca.

Tennis: There are four courts for rent located near the Hotel Isleño on the beach.

Water Sports Equipment: Can be rented at the **Hansa Club Villas** or at the **Sea Horse Inn.**

Charters: Snorkeling, scuba-diving, and deep-sea fishing are available through the larger hotels and **Bahía Marina.** The cost is $15 per hour.

Tourist Office: Avenida de la Playa (tel. 6433).

CHAPTER XIII

PANAMA CITY, PANAMA

□ □ □

Panama City, anyone? This immediately conjures up in most people a vision of hacking through a dense subtropical jungle to glimpse a view of a 50-mile "ditch." This, we suspect, derives from the hazy Hollywood view that comes through via old James Cagney–Pat O'Brien films on TV.

If the canal and the "jungle" image come to mind first (complete with U.S. expatriate losers trying to find a way home), forget it. It is inaccurate and it may deter you from making this intriguing stopover at no additional transportation cost.

What can you expect in this city of over 450,000 located on the Pacific and yet only 90 minutes by auto from the Atlantic? Well, for one thing, it's a night town, with plush gambling casinos and swinging nightclubs that don't really get moving until well after 11 p.m.

For another, Panama City is truly an international city, with North and South Americans, Asians, and Europeans mingling on busy, congested downtown streets along with Hindu shopkeepers and Panama's large black population. Surprised?

And you certainly will not want to leave this beehive of a city without scooping up some of the Western world's great bargains in linen, silk, or china. Japanese imports, particularly transistor radios, cameras, and tape recorders, are extremely good values here.

Then of course there is that tribute to early-20th-century engineering skill —the Panama Canal, 15 minutes by bus from downtown Panamá. The Canal Area (formerly the Canal Zone), which embraces many separate communities, links the Atlantic and the Pacific across 50 miles of what was once jungle. Visitors still marvel at the fantastic feat of flooding the giant locks to raise huge ocean liners so they can sail across the above-sea-level isthmus. A trip here is a must, and we shall take it.

Panamá is rightly called the "Gateway City to South America," bordering as it does on Colombia. Flights depart from Panamá to virtually every major South American destination. Eastern, Pan American, and Air Panamá have daily service from Miami to Panamá with connecting flights to New York.

You can stop here either at the beginning of your trip or on your way home. We prefer an end-of-trip stop so we don't have to tote our bargains with us and because we can usually count on good weather. Even in the rainy season (May to November) you can count on sunshine each morning. Panamanian lore has it that only on 14 days in the last 16 years was there no sunshine at all.

LANGUAGE, CLIMATE, CURRENCY: While Spanish is the official tongue, many residents speak English, and you will not have the problem of asking questions and understanding no answers. We are constantly surprised to hear bus drivers respond to questions in flawless British-accented English.

The city's international character, deriving from the former Canal Zone influence, explains the English-language emphasis.

Note: Panamanians refer to this city as Panamá and never as Panama City. Don't let this confuse you when asking directions.

Again contrary to Hollywood notions, the climate, while warm, seldom is hot and the evenings are surprisingly cool. Although humidity can be high and somewhat uncomfortable from June to September, midday temperatures are equivalent to Miami Beach's summer readings—in the 80° to 85° range—and are perfect year round for swimming. There is little climate variation here between the dry season (December to May) and the rainy season (June to November).

As for currency, there is virtually no difference between Panama and the U.S., since the basic money unit here is the U.S. dollar, called a **balboa**. Five dollars is written B/5, meaning 5 balboas, and the paper currency is the U.S. $5 bill. There are local coins in 1¢, 5¢, 10¢, 25¢, and 50¢ denominations, although U.S. coins circulate freely.

Tip: Local silver dollars are collectors' items and as such are worth considerably more than $1. So if you come across one, hold onto it.

CAUTIONARY NOTE: Panama is currently suffering a severe economic crisis. As a result street crime is on the rise. However, as long as you exercise good judgment, there is no need to be alarmed. Jewelry and all valuables should be locked in the hotel safe. Stick to the main streets, and keep cameras out of view when walking around the city. Ladies, unless it's absolutely necessary to carry a purse, don't. Also, it's advisable to travel by taxi when going out in the evening.

As of this writing, President Norriega is still in office. Common sense dictates that travelers remain aware of the current political situation. Anti-American feeling is not directed at tourists, only American government institutions.

FIRST IMPRESSIONS: You will be surprised at the hubbub of noise and activity that permeates this city, with office employees, shoppers, government officials, and visitors threading their way at a no-nonsense pace through traffic-clogged downtown streets. This is no sleepy city. While most downtown buildings are old, a vast government rebuilding project is dramatically altering the face of the city.

You will no doubt be impressed, as we were, by the building boom and the endless parade of horn-blowing, gaily decorated privately owned buses which swarm the streets everywhere. We would wager that you will see more buses here than anywhere else in the world. We don't recommend driving in the downtown area.

AIRPORT ARRIVAL: After landing at modern **Omar Torrijos International Airport,** 30 minutes from center city, head to the government-operated tourist office there, which is open daily from 8 a.m. to midnight. Any of the polite clerks will gladly call a hotel for you to make a reservation at no charge. The only practical way into center city is via taxi, which will cost you $16 to $20 for up to three persons to the same destination. To save money, join a group of four or five, and take one of the cabs operating as a colectivo. Fare is $10 each this way.

READER'S TRANSPORTATION TIP: "About 200 yards from Torrijos Airport along the main highway, you'll see a small booth. A **local bus,** 'Tocumen/Chorillo,' stops here every 20 minutes or so. These are rickety buses and below the average American's standard of comfort, but for the starvation traveler you can't beat the price—35¢. The bus will get very crowded as you approach the city so watch your bags carefully. It took one hour to get downtown. I caught the same bus going back" (Oliver Van Der Berghe, Seattle, Wash.).

A QUICK ORIENTATION: Ten minutes before your cab reaches the downtown area you will pass through the fashionable suburbs of **Campo Alegre** and **El Cangrejo,** which house two luxurious hotels—El Continental on your left and the Hotel Panamá on your right, both on the main street of **Via España.** Keep in mind that Via España—called **Avenida Central** in center city—is a key thoroughfare for orientation purposes, since many of our hotel selections are on or near this busy street. On most maps Via España and Avenida Central are designated jointly as **Avenida 7a** (Seventh Avenue). This important street divides the city east and west.

Two other fashionable hotels in this area are the Hotel Granada (El Cangrejo) and the Hotel Ejecutivo (Campo Alegre).

As your cab continues south on Via España you will pass through the residential section of **Bella Vista.** Then ready yourself for a view of **Calidonia,** one of the capital's poorest neighborhoods. Situated between the **Plaza 5 de Mayo** (site of the Internacional Hotel) and the more modern sections of Panama City, Calidonia is noted for its children, children, and more children. Autos—clogged in the narrow, winding streets—outdoor vendors, and shouting lottery salesmen add to the cacophony that is so peculiarly Calidonia. Slowly being rebuilt, this area offers the visitor a sometimes startling, always fascinating alternative view of 20th-century Latin America.

Beyond Calidonia is bustling **Santa Ana Plaza,** a popular midday gathering place for office workers and shoeshine boys in the heart of downtown. An oddity here is the profusion of rather good Chinese restaurants—Panama City has a sizable Chinese population—that dot this area. Busy shops, outdoor stalls, and office buildings circle the plaza—which also attracts amateur politicos and the resultant speechmaking. Santa Ana also seems to be a bus depot—the supply is endless.

An important street that parallels the Bay of Panama, five blocks east of Avenida Central, is **Avenida Balboa.** Most prominent landmark here is the **Statue of Balboa** (the first European to see the Pacific).

Between Avenida Central and the bay street of Avenida Balboa are these major avenues, heading down from Central: **Avenida Perú, Avenida Cuba, Avenida Justo Arosemena,** and **Avenida México,** the last a block from the bay.

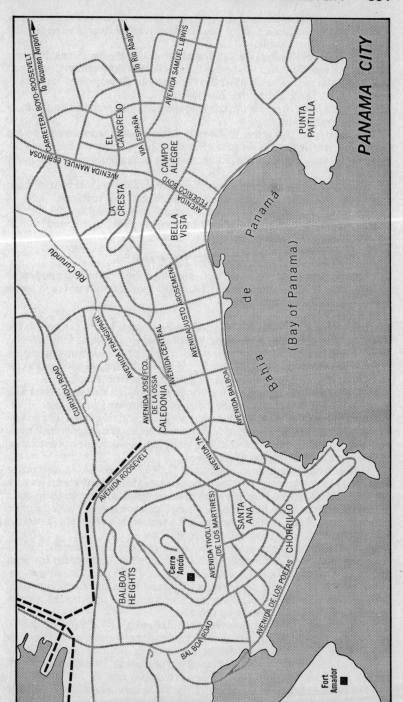

Nearby is **Paitilla,** the local airport from which small aircraft will wing you to Contadora in the Pacific and the San Blas Islands in the Atlantic. The Holiday Inn hotel is on Punta Paitilla.

East of Punta Paitilla is the **San Francisco** area on the bay. Scenic Panamar Restaurant is here. This area also houses the new **Atlapa Convention Center** and **Marriott Hotel** on Via Israel. **IPAT, the Panamanian Government Tourist Office,** is in the Atlapa building (tel. 26-7000).

North of El Congrejo is the **Los Angeles** section, home of Lung Fung, a fine Chinese restaurant.

Another important street is **Avenida Tivoli,** also called **Avenida de los Martires,** formerly **Cuatro de Julio** (Fourth of July), which is adjacent to the Canal Area. Many fine shops and airline offices are here, along with some popular G.I. bars.

The Panama Canal visitors' area at Miraflores Locks is a short bus ride from downtown, and we have more to say about this "must" side trip later.

The better budget hotels and restaurants are scattered throughout the city, unlike in most other Latin American cities where they are concentrated in a single section or two. Time now for our hotel choices.

1. WHERE TO STAY

Panamá is a small city, but one with quite an unusual number of good-value hotels in all price ranges. Remember to add 10% tourist tax. Most hotels have a late (2 to 3 p.m.) checkout time.

HIGHER-PRICED HOTELS: One of the best hotels in this category is the 150-room **Hotel Caribe,** a ten-floor, air-conditioned choice at Calle 28 and Avenida Perú (tel. 25-0404). A bonus is the location, one block from a huge public pool. The rooms are small but comfortable. Doubles are $44 and singles cost $40 and up. A coffeeshop and bar are on the premises. Fine choice.

Another good selection is the **Hotel Internacional,** located at the Plaza 5 de Mayo (tel. 62-1000). Here, in the heart of downtown Panamá are 70 air-conditioned remodeled rooms, all with private bath and telephone. The service is first class and the new amenities include a rooftop restaurant (popular for parties), cocktail lounge, and brasserie. The lobby has an alcove for slot machines. Doubles here are $57 while singles run $51.

El Ejecutivo, Calle A. de la Guardia and Calle 52 (tel. 64-3333), is set up for business travelers who don't have big expense accounts but need a hotel for conducting business. Rooms here have work desks complete with swivel chairs and a bed that doubles as a couch. Direct-dial phones keep you in touch with the office when necessary. There's a pool and sundeck when work is done, plus a cocktail lounge. Doubles are $70, while singles are $65.

Within easy walking distance of the Via España (one block) and the posh El Panamá Hilton and Continental hotels is a deluxe hotel, somewhat lower in price, the **Granada,** Calle Eusebio Morales (tel. 64-4900). Its 175 rooms are attractively and comfortably decorated, with private baths and air conditioners. The Granada has a pool, coffeeshop, and its own casino and cocktail lounge. Doubles here run $82, while singles run $72.

A fine choice is the **Hotel Premier,** Avenida Central 18–105 (tel. 62-2655), in downtown Panamá. This 56-room, seven-story hotel offers rooms with air conditioning, bath (shower), and sometimes terraces. Doubles start at $32 and singles are $28. The lobby is located up a flight of stairs, and a good restaurant is on the lobby floor. The only drawback here is the noisy area.

The **Hotel El Doral,** downtown on Calle Monteserin near Calle Estudiante (tel. 62-5144), has 128 rooms, all with air conditioning and bath. A restaurant, bar, and coffeeshop are also on the premises. Doubles run $35 and singles are $5 less. A drawback here is the street noise, since the hotel is right off the major shopping street.

Opposite the well-known Bella Vista Cinema is the **Hotel Bella Vista,** Via España 31 (tel. 64-4029). This 40-room hotel was converted from a pension which we'd been recommending for years. Now we recommend the hotel. Doubles with air conditioning and bath are $26 and singles start at $24. Look for the red sign outside and climb one flight to the registration desk. An outside porch is for guest use. Next door is the popular Gran Muralla (Chinese) Restaurant.

The **Europa Hotel,** at Via España 33 in front of the Bella Vista Theater (tel. 63-6911), is another good choice. Doubles are $45, singles run $40, and the 100 rooms are in demand. The pool and bar are popular, as is the cafetería.

Another hotel deserving your consideration is the recently renovated **Hotel Roma,** on Avenida Justo Arosemana at Calle 33. The Roma boasts 150 beautifully furnished air-conditioned rooms, all with private bath, color television, and direct-dial phones. A cafetería, two restaurants, a pool with its own bar, and a piano bar with live entertainment are all on the premises. Singles are $44, and doubles, $49.50. Mauricio, the hotel representative from the InterClub Travel Service, is a great source of information, and will be glad to recommend restaurants or nightclubs, as well as make any travel arrangements you need. He can also arrange a three-hour guided tour of the Old City, Panamá Viejo, and the canal. The cost of the tour is $17 per person for two people, or $30 to $35 if you're alone.

The **Hotel Centroamericano,** on Avenida Ecuador near Avenida Justo Arosemena (near the Pension America), offers 32 comfortable, air-conditioned doubles for $29. Singles are $5 less. A bonus here is the fine self-service cafetería directly across the street. Good value.

A newer hotel you may like is the **Hotel Veracruz,** Avenida Perú and Calle 30 (tel. 27-3022). Its 64 rooms are air-conditioned and have color TVs. The rooms are not large but they have all the requisites and are clean. The hotel's coffeeshop is open 24 hours. Singles are $30 and doubles run $38.

BUDGET CHOICES: The best budget selections are scattered on and near the main street of Avenida Central. We also have located several good-value pensions (no meals) in private homes.

Let's start with what we consider to be a value buy in Panamá—the four-story **Hotel Ideal,** Calle 17 Oeste, no. 15–55 (tel. 62-2400), located several blocks off Avenida Central and not far from the Canal Area. The 170-room Ideal offers guests the option of paying more for private bath and air conditioning—up to you. A double with bath, but without air conditioning (you get a fan), is $22 per night; singles are $17. Add $2 for the cooling system. Deduct a dollar if you'd like to economize in a bathless, fanless room, with sink. Triples range from $25. An annex with less desirable rooms has lower rates. The management offers a 5% discount for a one-week stay and a 10% reduction for a month's visit. Now to the rooms themselves, which contain worn leather chairs (couches in some cases) in each room along with a dressing table and comfortable beds. Free guest parking is available in a garage beneath the hotel. A TV in the lobby is a guest bonus. A self-service restaurant, a boite, a dining room, pool, barbershop, beauty parlor, and laundry—all are on the premises. The hotel is popular with economy-minded Central Americans. For the young in spirit only.

Nearby, but closer to Avenida Central, is the smaller, 46-room **Hotel Riazor,** Calle 16 Oeste, no. 15–105 (tel. 28-0777), a clean, comfortable, colonial-style lodging with roomy doubles for $25, triples for $30, and singles about $18, bath and air conditioning included. Deduct a dollar for rooms without air conditioning. Some bathless rooms with double beds instead of twin beds are cheaper still. The large rooms have dressers, chairs, stall shower, and telephone. The lobby, one floor above street level, is partially covered with a skylight, which adds some brightness. The Riazor is a mini version of the Ideal, and contains the same very basic standards. A restaurant and bar are on the premises.

A hotel that seems to have a new name each time we check it out is the **Residencial Sevilla,** formerly the Tivoli, Lincoln, and Montreal. (Honest Abe's photo still adorns the lobby.) Located at Avenida Justo Arosemena no. 46–40, at Calle 46, one block off Via España and not far from the Riviera Residencial (tel. 27-2436). Here for $16 you get a double room with air conditioning, bath, and quiet neighborhood surroundings. Singles are $13. The 30 rooms are large but have bare floors. A cut above the basic.

Nearer to Santa Ana Park, one block off Avenida Central, is the colonial-style, 45-room **Hotel El Colón,** Transveral 1, no. 7–55, corner of Calle B and 12 Oeste (tel. 22-0770), which is somewhat higher priced. Airy rooms with shutters, bath and shower, telephone, air conditioning, and balconies (in some cases), are $22 double and $19 single. Triples are an excellent value at $26. Doubles without air conditioning are $18, while triples are $24 and singles cost $14. This four-story, elevator-equipped hotel has blue mosaic tile on the lobby walls and offers a small rooftop patio overlooking the Pacific. On a clear day the canal is visible. A Dairy Queen cafeteria is next door. If you plan a stay of a week or longer, by all means negotiate for a better rate. *Note:* Checkout time is 2 p.m. daily. One drawback is the noisy, crowded area.

Hotels in Colonial Panamá

In the older section of Panamá is the large, once-first-class, 145-room **Hotel Central,** in the Plaza Catedral (tel. 22-6080), which could have been the setting for an old Hollywood film, complete with ceiling fan. This old, fading three-story palace, once the city's leading hotel, now somewhat renovated, offers extremely large rooms, all with balconies and wicker chairs, for $18 double (with bath), $12 single. Bathless doubles are $13 and singles run $9. No rooms have air conditioning, but the Central does have an elevator (if that compensates). Location is good, directly in the important Plaza Catedral in the heart of the old section, which houses the Presidential Palace. Checkout time is 3 p.m.

An interesting old hotel in the colonial part of town is the **Colonial** (tel. 22-9311), in the Plaza Bolívar. It has all the amenities of a deluxe stop; however, they have not all aged well. It even has a small pool, restaurant, and bar. Doubles run $11 and singles cost $8.

READER'S HOTEL SELECTION: "In Panama City, I was delighted to find the **Hotel Acapulco,** Calle 30 Este, between Avenida Cuba and Avenida Perú across from Hotel Soloy. It's air-conditioned, clean, and accessible, with good transportation nearby, and the staff is extremely friendly and helpful. One night for a single is $20; checkout time is 3 p.m. the next day. Get there early as the rooms fill up by early afternoon" (Ms. Yoshimoro).

Pensions

Many of our Panamanian friends insist—and we're inclined to agree—that the best budget lodging values in Panamá are to be found in private homes that rent rooms to tourists. These homes are called pensions here, but unlike those in Europe and in some Latin American cities, these do not serve food to guests.

We regret to inform our readers that our favorite pension, and an institution in Panamá, Pension México, closed at the end of 1986. Its owner, Harold Maduro, died and his widow, after running this friendly stop for over 40 years, decided to retire. She sends her thanks to all of you who stayed at her "home" for 22 years. Good luck, Mrs. Maduro!

The pension is going the way of the dinosaur in Panamá, for several other popular stops have closed recently. But the **Pension America,** Avenida Justo Arosemena no. 33–54, near Calle 34 (tel. 25-1140), is still in operation and in fact has expanded. This large pink house, located on a quiet residential street two blocks from Avenida Balboa, has many plants and trees on the grounds and offers bathless doubles for $14 to $16 and singles for $11 to $13—without food, of course. Add $3 for rooms with bath. The rooms are modestly furnished but clean. Three public bathrooms are reserved for guests. Higher rates for rooms with air conditioning.

The **Residencial Santa Fe,** Avenida Nacional (tel. 27-2587), is a relative newcomer on the pension scene, having opened in 1984. Its 36 rooms vary in price from $12 for a single, fan-cooled and without bath, to $18 for an air-conditioned room with bath. There is a small dining room. Not as conveniently located as our other choice, the Santa Fe is near the Canal Area and the Ancon Railroad station.

RESIDENTIAL HOTELS:
If you enjoy living in an apartment with the services of a hotel, you might consider one of Panamá's several fine apartment-hotels. In these establishments you get an apartment with a kitchen, stove, refrigerator, sitting area, and bedroom. Maid service is included in the rate. You can save your food dollars by shopping in the supermarkets and eating in. A fine idea for families.

A good first choice would be the **Hotel Residencial Las Vegas,** in El Cangrejo near the El Continental Hotel (tel. 64-2424), at Calle 55. Daily rates are about $25; weekly and monthly rates are available and run less. For reservations write: Sonia Stec, Apartado 7186. Fine location.

We particularly like the **Aparthotel Plaza,** nearby at Avenida Manuel Espinoza Batista no. 40–6 (tel. 64-5033) in El Cangrejo. There are 53 apartments in all. Rates are $32 on a daily basis, $25 to $28 daily if you're staying at least a week, and $20 to $23 daily for stays of a month or more. A bonus here is the roof garden complete with pool. Write Apartado 1387, Zone 1, Panama City.

Two other fine choices are **Apartamientos Caracol,** at Via Brasil (Obarrio Section), and **Apartotel El Presidente,** near the local airport on Punta Paitilla. The Presidente has a pool. Both are slightly out of the way and that is their only drawback. Rates are similar to the Las Vegas and Plaza.

Finally, we recommend the **Suites Alvear** (tel. 69-4055), which offers 34 large suites for $60. For reservations, write to the hotel, Apartado 4598, Panamá 6.

HOTELS ON TABOGA:
A stunning island one hour by ferry from Panamá is Taboga, which is one of our highly recommended excursions (see below). There are only two hotels on the island. In the event you plan to stay overnight, you can choose between the romantic 32-room **Hotel Taboga,** which charges $38 for an air-conditioned double; and the economical 30-room **Hotel Chu,** where you can bed down for $21 double and $16 single. More about these when we get there.

DELUXE HOTELS:
Many business travelers come to Panamá. For those on unlimited expense accounts (or with unlimited cash) or for those visiting Panamá for a winter vacation rather than a Caribbean island, there are four deluxe hotels here as fine as any on the continent.

The **Hotel El Continental** is conveniently located on Via España (tel. 64-6066), in the commercial and banking sector. While not quite in the same class as the other deluxe choices, the Continental has a terrific seafood restaurant, a swinging disco, casino, and coffeeshop. The pool and sundeck are small. There is another Continental located by the airport.

The **Marriott Caesar Park** (tel. 26-4077), adjoining the Atlapa Convention Center, is a wonderful choice. Located on Via Israel just outside the city, this 18-story, 400-room hotel offers superior accommodations and all the extras that make a hotel special. Fine restaurants, tennis courts, a large pool, and a posh casino are but a few. One drawback is that the hotel is often crowded with conventioneers.

The **Holiday Inn,** located on Avenida Balboa in the Punta Paitilla section (tel. 69-1122), is the only hotel in town with an ocean view—actually it's the bay. Its 260 rooms are located in a 20-story round tower which also houses a pool, tennis courts, and discothèque. The Belvedere Restaurant is one of Panamá's best.

The **Gran Hotel Soloy** (tel. 27-1133), a 20-story, 200-room choice, is located in downtown Panamá, but not in a heavy traffic area. On its roof is the pool and you can see the city and the Panama Canal. The Soloy has a fine restaurant and casino.

You must figure on rates of $70 and up for singles and $80 and up for doubles at these hostelries—far less than comparable choices on Barbados or St. Croix.

2. DINING IN PANAMÁ

Panamá's restaurants come in all categories and are scattered throughout the city. While there are a sufficient number of good eateries in our price range, Panamá's finer restaurants are rather more expensive. Since you will want to sample them, save money on breakfast and lunch by eating in our recommended cafeterías and small restaurants. The least expensive choices are the fast-food places that have proliferated here. Restaurants charge no tax, and tips are not included in your bill: a tip is customary. Dining hours follow U.S. patterns. Keep in mind that many restaurants in town close on Sunday or Monday, so it's a good idea to call before setting out.

Italian foods are very popular here, with pasta dishes and pizza the best-sellers. New Chinese restaurants seem to pop up each time we revisit Panamá, and to our eye at least, seem to be half of all the moderately priced eateries in town. In the last two years restaurants serving a variety of foods have opened throughout the city, but most are a cut above budget levels. You can enjoy Spanish, Colombian, Peruvian, Japanese, and Korean specialties if you are prudent when ordering. The seafood here is outstanding, both in the variety of dishes served and the high quality of the preparation. Panamá means "abundance of fish," and this is not a misnomer.

Note: Panamá is not the place to wander idly into a restaurant in search of some exotic fare. Stick to the well-known places where you can't go wrong.

Now for some of our favorite Panamanian dishes. **Sancocho** is a popular soup-stew, almost a meal in itself—an excellent lunch. **Ropa vieja** is a blend of shredded beef and vegetables, served with rice and plátano (plantain). **Ceviche** is marinated raw fish in a delicious sauce.

FOR BREAKFAST AND LUNCH: Your best bet for a scenic breakfast or lunch is the popular **El Boulevard,** Calle 31 on Avenida Balboa, facing the Bay of Panamá. We look forward to breakfast here of ham and eggs, toast, and coffee for $2.50. A continental breakfast is only $1.25. For lunch, the sandwiches are popular ($2 to $3.50). For heavier fare, try the pepper steak ($3.25) or chicken in the basket ($2.50). Cocktails are an inexpensive $1 to $2.25.

A good-priced breakfast is served starting at 7 a.m. at **Café Manolo,** on Via España. Another good breakfast (in fact, all three meals) stop is the **Alfa Restaurante,** above the Ben Btesh store on Via España, next to the Plaza Regency. It has an air-conditioned dining room as well as an outdoor terrace.

Niko's Cafetería, which stays open 24 hours a day, is a budget traveler's delight, serving a wide variety of fare at low prices. Many Panamanians eat lunch here. Look for the Supermarket El Rey on Via España.

A fine breakfast spot is **Delirys,** located under the Charlot Pub on Avenida M. Ycaza near the Continental Hotel. Head downstairs to the cafetería-style restaurant, pour your own juice, and make your selections from the food counter. If you are like us, you will dine al fresco. Others choose to eat at the indoor tables.

El Vegetariano Mireya, on Calle Ricardo Aria, is open seven days a week and serves fresh-fruit salads and drinks, delicious sandwiches on home-baked wheat bread, yogurts, and vegetable hot plates. It's a small restaurant and the specials change daily. Good choice.

Romanaccio Cafetería and Pizzería, in the Plaza Regency Shopping Center (Via España), is a great lunch or dinner choice. The food is well prepared, spicy, and hot. Thronged with shoppers and workers from the nearby banks at lunchtime, Romanaccio quiets down at dinner. Italian specialties are the biggest draws, but there are beef and fish dishes as well as hero sandwiches and desserts.

Romanaccio is so popular it has opened a second eatery in the Marbella section of town near Felipe Motta's building. Open for all three meals, it's quieter and dining is more leisurely.

For breakfast or hamburgers, look no further than **McDonald's,** with six branches scattered all over town. Most popular is the outlet on Via España across from the Continental Hotel. Another one is on Calle 3 de Noviembre near the Hotel International. A quarter-pounder (cuarto de libra) is $1.10 (add 15¢ for cheese). A Big Mac is $1.25. Fried chicken is available here too. Look for the familiar yellow sign. Other fast-food stops include **Burger King,** on Via España; **Popeye's,** for fried chicken, on Via España; and **Mr. Pollo** and **Big Mama's,** on Calle R. J. Alfaro.

The late Colonel Sander's **Kentucky Fried Chicken (Pollo Kentucky)** is equally well represented around town. The most convenient location is on Via España in the Obarrio section. Prices and selection are similar to those in the U.S.

Panamá has several **Dairy Queens,** somewhat different from their U.S. counterparts in that they have outdoor tables and serve sandwiches as well as milkshakes. Some of the nicer branches are near Paitilla Airport, on Avenida Central at Calle 17, and on Via España. Besides ice-cream dishes, hamburgers, fried chicken, and such are available.

Dunkin' Donuts, next to Kentucky Fried Chicken on Via España (at Galerías Obarrio), is open daily from 8 a.m. to 11 p.m. A wide variety of doughnuts are sold for take-out, but you can enjoy them at one of the shop's counters with coffee or tea.

Remember also that many of Panamá's larger hotels have 24-hour cafeterías.

DINNER RESTAURANTS: Panamá's dinner hour generally ends by 10 p.m., although many places close earlier. So if you are planning a very late meal, call first.

Budget Choices

The **Hotel Ideal Cafetería,** Calle 17 Este (near Avenida Central), is one of the city's most inexpensive eateries. Open from early in the morning to the wee hours, it's perfect for all meals as well as late-night snacks. Well known for its exceptional desserts, it is more of a restaurant than a cafetería as we know it. Whole dinners start at $7, which is very inexpensive for Panamá. Clean but drab and uninspired décor.

Two similar inexpensive restaurants with outdoor and indoor tables as well as counter service (good choices for all three meals) are the **Costa Azul,** at Calle Ricardo Arias 11, and **El Mesón,** at the end of the same block. The outdoor tables on roof-covered decks are jammed with locals enjoying the daily specials, which range in price from $1.75 to $7, and include omelets and chicken dishes as well as steaks. Sandwiches and soups are available too. Good value.

You'll like the **Cafetería del Prado,** on Via Argentina and 1B Norte (a block off Via España). Delicious sandwiches start at $1, while a western omelet will run you $2. Hot plates are well within our budget. Popular with patrons is the delicious ice cream and the variety of desserts and coffees served at the outdoor tables, which are surrounded by tall rubber plants.

Always crowded and lively is the **Cafetería Manolo,** with one branch on Via Argentina and the other on Via España across from the Hotel Continental. Fresh vegetables, steaming beef and fish dishes, and for dessert, churros (powdered doughnuts)—almost as good as those in Buenos Aires and only 60¢.

A bit out of the way, but worth it, is **El Pote,** on Via España near Via Brasil in Galerías Obarrio. Try the delicious breakfast platters starting at $2.75. Luncheon favorites are the sandwiches and corvina platters ($4.50). Ice cream, beer, and churros are our favorites here.

Panamanian friends of ours directed us to the **Pizzamigo** outlet on Avenida Balboa at Calle 28. You can dine indoors (air-conditioned) or at the outdoor tables. Pizza for two is under $7, and the sandwiches are reasonably priced. A glass of wine is $1. A festive atmosphere is enhanced by the bright tablecloths.

A fine self-service cafetería is the **Restaurante Libertador** in the Hotel Centroamericano. Luncheon and dinner specials are under $5 and you will find the cafetería usually jam-packed for breakfast.

A typical Panamanian restaurant—with bilingual menus to ease your language problems—is the modern and clean **Restaurant of the Americas,** off Via España at Calle 70 (Calle San Miguel) in the suburb of Obarrio, near the Teatro Opera. Look for the circular red neon sign that blazes away from the 11 a.m. opening hour to the 10 p.m. closing. In this spacious, brightly lit dining spot you have a choice of indoor or outdoor dining. Stick with the executive menu, which offers splendid five-course dinners at reasonable prices ($6.25 to $12). For example, you can have a crisp antipasto, seafood chowder, pepper steak with rice and peas, flan (pudding), and a marvelous coffee for $9. We're convinced this is as good a dinner value as you will find in Panamá. An à la carte menu is also available.

Don't skip the opportunity to dine at **La Cascada,** on Avenida Balboa (between Calles 25 and 26). An unusual open-air restaurant with life-size figures of animals peering out of verdant, abundant greenery and water cascading down a high rock wall, it draws a happy-go-lucky crowd of both adults and children. Portions are very large and the food at dinner (served from 4 to 11 p.m.) is very tasty. Meat dishes and fish platters are very popular.

The restaurant at the **American Legion** has as its lure a fantastic view of the Panama Canal. You can look out one of the large glass windows which front the Bridge of the Americas and watch the ships passing into the canal or into the ocean. A large bar, too, so you can stop in just for a drink. You'll need a cab to get here.

A good Italian eatery is the bustling **Napoli,** Calle Estudiante and Calle 1, near the Instituto Nacional in the center of town, which seems filled with students every time we stop by. Open until 1 a.m. the indoor-outdoor Napoli is proud of its clams parmigiana ($2.75) and its chicken cazadore (cacciatore, that is) for $6.50. Lower down on the price scale are pizzas ($1 to $3) and sandwiches ($1 to $3.50). Here again, the menu is bilingual and offers a wide variety of low-priced fare. A good breakfast will cost you about $1.75.

Want to sample Chinese food? Try the air-conditioned **Mandarin,** Avenida Cuba and Calle 33, behind the Tribunal Electoral in a quiet residential area. Most attractive in décor, the Mandarin features wood paneling, red-leather booths, and spotless tablecloths. Specializing in northern Chinese food, this charming restaurant offers a choice of four family dinners ranging in price from $6 to $11 per person, depending on your party's size. Beef consommé, chow mein, shrimp in a tomato sauce, egg foo yung, and hot-and-spicy chicken dishes are all worth sampling.

Two pizza spots we enjoy are **Sorrento** and **Tambal,** which are neighbors on Via Porras. Both serve delicious pizzas and other Italian fare as well. Many of our Panamanian friends insist that the only "real" Italian food in Panamá is served at **El Hostal de Bella Vista,** on Calle 42—delicious and spicy.

Higher-Priced Restaurants

Las Rejas, on Via España near Galerías Obarrio, a delightful eatery featuring international foods with a dose of Peruvian specialties, is open daily for lunch and dinner. Live music at night. This is the spot to sample ceviche and sancocho. And if seafood is your thing, be sure to order the house specialty, "El Piqueo de Mariscos."

El Pavo Real, at Calle 51 in Campo Alegre, is an informal eatery with a Soho atmosphere. The owners, Sarah and Derrise, are very friendly and will be more than happy to recommend something from their menu, which includes a delicious selection of homemade pâtés, quiches, and stuffed crêpes. There is also a help-yourself salad bar. A good spot for a light dinner or lunch. Or drop by their pub for a game of darts and an English beer. Tournaments are held on Tuesday and Thursday. Open from noon to midnight; closed Sunday.

La Fonda Antioqueña, a tavern typical of the cattle-raising areas of Colombia, has been reproduced here amid the ruins of Old Panamá. Spend the afternoon exploring the area, then stop for dinner. Grilled meats are the specialties, but we prefer the grilled fish. Bistec a caballo (steak with eggs on top) is very popular. Try a chorizo (typical sausage) with a cocktail. The restaurant is a popular nightspot and the jukebox is kept busy all evening.

Le Bistrot is Panamá's first pub, and it's delightful. At Calle 53 in the Centro Comercial La Florida, Le Bistrot has French rather than British overtones. Serving light salads, quiches, fish and meat platters in tasteful fashion, this is a highly recommended eatery. Enjoy it every night but Sunday.

Or travel back to the beginning of the century to **Lesseps,** on Via España in La Cresta, where exquisite French cuisine is served in an art nouveau setting. You are sure to enjoy the special bar atmosphere, even more so if you try the Brigitte Bardot or Panamá cocktail.

For a seaside setting and excellent seafood, try the **Club Panamar,** Calle 50 Final in San Francisco de la Caleta (take a cab, $1). Seafood (shrimp and lobster) dishes are superb. Shrimp Créole is $10; baby red snapper, $6.75; filet corvina alemendrine, $6.75; and lobster thermidor, $12. Whisky is $2.75. You have a choice of eating in the air-conditioned salon or the outdoor garden. Ask manager Victor Sierra to show you the huge refrigerators filled with fresh fish.

Another good choice for seafood is **La Corvina,** located in the basement of the Marriot Hotel. Try to go there on a Friday night to take advantage of their incredible buffet "Seafood Fantasy." Sunday brunch, served from 11 a.m. to 3 p.m., is also recommended.

Another restaurant choice in this category is the **Restaurant Pana-China,** Via España near the El Continental Hotel, second floor. This Chinese eatery is decorated with red lanterns and offers excellent Chinese dishes in air-conditioned rooms with piped-in music. Family dinners (six items) are reasonable if you have a group: $16 for two, but only $42 for a group of six. À la carte dishes start at $4.25. Cocktails are $2. Try to get a table near the window over-looking Via España.

Los Latinos, at Calle 52, one block off the Via España, is a large restaurant with an eclectic menu. Steaks, chicken dishes, fish, and salads are attractively served. There's a lot of food.

For a delicious Panamanian dinner plus a folklore show, make reservations for dinner at **Tinajas,** Calle 51 in Bella Vista. The restaurant is located in a private house, the décor is ranch-style Spanish, and the seafood stew, tamales, and Panamanian-style shrimp are excellent. There is a $5 cover charge for the show, which goes on at 9:30 p.m. on Thursday. A small shop sells handcrafts, but you probably can do better elsewhere.

Tasty Panamanian food is served at the small but popular **El Trapiche,** on Via Argentina near the Café Manolo. The restaurant itself, which specializes in the cuisine of the central provinces, is modeled after a trapiche, an old-world sugar mill which is still used in some parts of the country to squeeze the juice (*guarepo*) from the sugarcane. Be sure to try the en hojaldra (flour fritters filled with chicken or meat), mondogo (seasoned tripe), and the gallo pinto (a rice-and-bean casserole). A sidewalk terrace is popular with Panamanians, but we prefer to eat inside to avoid the fumes of the passing traffic.

For a typical native Panamanian restaurant in an earthy setting, hop a cab to **La Tablita** on the Transisthmian Hwy. The thatch-roofed restaurant offers such treats as pollo ahumado (smoked chicken), $4.50; churrasco (steak), $6.25; and ceviche de corvina (marinated fish), $3. The menu is on the wall. Note the grill in front preparing the steaks.

A former private home, facing the Bay of Panama, is **Marbella,** on Avenida Balboa at Calle 39, a small restaurant where you can dine on paella ($9), arroz marinera ($6), and tortillas ($5). Informal. The sidewalk terrace is popular on cool evenings and the large windows offer excellent views of the bay.

Another excellent choice for Spanish cuisine is the newly opened **Meson de la Paella,** at Calle 50 and Calle 48.

And if you're in the mood for ribs, why not try **Tony Romas,** "el lugar de las costillas"? This well-known chain came to Panamá in 1987 offering the delicious barbecued meats and (of course) ribs for which it is famous. There is even a happy hour Monday through Friday from 4 to 8 p.m. It's on Boulevard El Dorado, in the Condominio Dorasol.

The Big Splurge

Le Sauvage, located in the most exclusive sector of Panamá, Punta Paitilla, across from the Holiday Inn (tel. 23-7645), is undoubtably one of Panamá's most elegant restaurants. Here you can sit back and enjoy exquisite French cuisine in an elegantly European atmosphere. The chef, a Panamanian, graduated Cordon Bleu from the Paris Culinary Academy. Need we say more? Open from noon, Monday through Saturday.

Can you think of a better location for a French restaurant than the Plaza de Francia, with the Bovedas and the French Embassy nearby? **Casco Viejo** not only takes advantage of this very fitting location, but named itself after the colonial section of Panamá, El Casco Viejo ("ancient compound"). This fine French restaurant is definitely worthy of both its name and its location. The food is excellent and so is the view of the bay and the entrance to the canal.

Sarti's is a small, expensive Italian restaurant serving some of the best Italian dishes in Panamá and located on Calle Ricardo Arias 5, just beyond the Continental Hotel. Here we suggest that you stick to the pasta and pizza platters to keep down your costs. Ravioli and lasagne are about $8, while a ham-and-pepperoni pizza is $5.75. Most other platters start at $7.

Umberto Lazo, a Peruvian who arrived in Panamá from Lima in 1976, was the moving force behind one of our favorite restaurants here, El Pez de Oro, in Plaza Einstein. We were very disappointed to find it had closed, but we are happy to report that Umberto has opened another restaurant, **Ebony,** in the Marbella section, and that the same high-quality food and first-rate service apply here. Ebony is a Peruvian-style seafood eatery, where ceviche (Peruvian style), anticuchos, and corvina are prepared in a variety of sauces. Expect to pay $15 per person for dinner. The name **Pez de Oro** ("The Golden Fish") has been taken by a new eatery in the Bal Harbour Shopping Center on Punta Paitilla. A bit pricy, it is nevertheless a possibility for lunch if you're in the area.

El Cortijo is another of Panamá's finest restaurants. Set in a beautiful white-washed building that would be at home in Seville (in Spain, a *cortijo* is a ranch), Spanish dishes are the specialties here, with seafood used in many of them. Try a delicious paella. Expect to spend around $18 per person. The restaurant is on Calle Morales across from the Hotel Granada.

Panamá's largest and most attractive Chinese restaurant is **Lung Fung,** in the Los Angeles section ($1.25 by cab). This enormous oasis of fine food can feed almost 1,000 starving customers in its three huge main dining rooms. Try the po-po platter, $10 for three. Most six-course dinners are about $6 to $10. Fantastic Chinese atmosphere in almost-elegant surroundings (unusual for Chinese restaurants).

Japanese restaurants have become very popular here, and three very good choices are recommended. **Ginza Teppanyaki,** near the Granada Hotel, is a Japanese steak-house. Two ferocious stone dragons guard the entrance to the Chinese-lantern-bedecked house. Join other diners at a long rectangular table, where your dinner will be cooked on a hot tray built into the table. Steak, chicken, shrimp, and other shellfish are popular selections. Dinners include soup and dessert. Prices start at $9.75.

Another option is the **Restaurant Matsuei,** at Avenida Euschio Morales A12, a home away from home for Japanese businessmen. Here you can savor the traditional favorites—sukiyaki, tempura, sushi, and the like. Prices start at $8.

Another excellent Japanese restaurant is **Fuji,** on Via Brasil. The large restaurant has areas separated by dividers. Try the sukiyaki cooked at your table or the shabu shabu, each $9.25. Beef curry with rice is $6. Fish fans should order the tempura, $4. The menu is in English and Spanish. Fine choice.

Le Trianon, in the Marriott, and the **Belvedere,** at the Holiday Inn, are considered the best "continental" restaurants in town. Music while you dine, soft lights, elegant surroundings, and well-prepared food starting at $15 per person. Big splurge!

3. PANAMÁ BY DAY

As we recommend in all cities in *South America on $35 a Day,* you should start familiarizing yourself with Panamá by foot. Inveterate walkers that we are, we first experienced the diversities that Panamá offers via a two-hour stroll early one morning during our initial trip. We'll repeat it with you now.

A WALKING TOUR: An ideal starting point for a foot tour is **Santa Ana Plaza**—where the shoeshine boys won't take no for an answer. By all means treat yourself to a shine (it will cost you all of 25¢). The boy—sometimes rather middle-aged—will spot you as a Gringo instantly and might offer a colorful broken-English, arm-waving description of the busy shops and office buildings that surround the plaza. He might even offer to act as your guide.

Stroll around the plaza and its church and then wander leisurely down **Calle 13,** the city's busiest street. Shops, outdoor stalls, grocery stores, and Chinese restaurants vie for your attention. Poke around the stalls—you may be able to find a good-quality piece of embroidery or native pottery. However, the best shopping bargains are to be found on Avenida Central and Avenida 4 de Julio.

Four blocks down in the bustling dock area there is a huge public market that sells fresh fish. Incidentally, the stretch between Santa Ana Plaza and the dock area is jokingly referred to by residents as "Sal si puedes," which means loosely "get out if you can." The name derives from the ease with which one can get lost in this hectic section.

At the dock area, pick up **Avenida Alfaro** and stroll to your right (south). You will pass old but well-maintained Spanish-style homes with ornate balconies and courtyards modeled after 16th-century colonial Spain. Just beyond Calle 5 is the stunning white **Presidential Palace,** called the Palace of the Herons, because five of these graceful birds (actually small flamingos) have free run of the grounds. Normally the white creatures congregate around a large fountain in the center of the marble lobby. Visitors are permitted.

Continue along Avenida Alfaro to Calle 4 and turn right into the **Plaza Bolívar,** a lovely, peaceful square dominated by a statue of Simón Bolívar. All Latin American countries took part in the dedication of this statue.

A few steps from the plaza on Calle 3a are three older but important structures, the **National Palace,** which houses government offices, the famous **San Francisco Church,** and the famous **Teatro Nacional** (National Theater), a restored jewel. Be sure to take a few minutes to step inside and admire the interior of this Renaissance-style theater. Completed in 1909, El Teatro Nacional was designed by the same architect who designed La Scala in Milan, the world-famous Ruggieri. It is in fact a scaled-down version of La Scala, with only three balconies to La Scala's five. The fresco on the ceiling is *El Nacimiento de la República* ("The Birth of the Republic") by Roberto Luís, a Panamanian educated in Paris.

Continue left on the short block back to Avenida Central to the **Paseo de Las Bóvedas** ("Promenade of the Dungeons"). Built on the ruins of an old sea wall, which once protected the city from pirates, this historic walkway houses some private homes. At the end of the street is the **Plaza Francia** (French Plaza), which sits at the city's most southerly tip. Here are the **Palace of Justice,** old dungeons for pirates, and a variety of monuments and statuary erected to honor the French, who were the first to attempt to build the Panama Canal. The French Embassy is located here. Relax on one of the many benches nearby for a few minutes amid the well-kept trees and shrubbery, where you can observe children avidly playing futbol.

Return along Avenida 8a and at Calle 3a is an old stone-and-brick arch between two walls that served to show U.S. engineers that the area is earthquake-free and therefore that the canal could be built through Panama. The flat arch still stands as originally built. Also here is the **Museum of Colonial Religious Art.**

Retrace your steps along Avenida Central to **Plaza Catedral,** also called Plaza de la Independencia, which houses the city's major cathedral as well as numerous busts of the city's founders.

Pick up Calle 7a (not to be confused with Avenida 7, which is Avenida Central) and you will stroll by the walls of the city's old church. At Calle 8, the next block, is the famous **Church of San José,** which was rebuilt here after Henry Morgan's pirates sacked and burned much of Panamá Viejo (Old Panamá) in 1671. The church's famous gold altar, which had been painted to disguise its value from the pirates, was undamaged by the flames, and it was transferred to the new church in present-day Panamá. If the front door is locked, stroll around to the side entrance (to your right) and ring the bell. A priest will admit you.

Stroll back to Avenida Central and you will find yourself a few blocks from Santa Ana Plaza.

PANAMÁ VIEJO (OLD PANAMÁ): Four miles from the present site of Panama City, right on the Pacific, is Panamá Viejo, where the city was originally settled in 1519 as an embarkation point for the numerous expeditions to South America. The city was an important storage point for gold and other treasures from Peru, which were transported across Panama via the historic **Las Cruces** trail (Camino Real) to the Atlantic and then onto Madrid.

Panamá Viejo was easy prey for pirates, and there were never-ending raids. In 1671 Henry Morgan sacked the city, and it was moved four miles inland to its present location behind protective walls.

Today Panamá Viejo is a ruin, standing mutely on the Pacific, a monument to a majestic past. Many of the famous landmarks are standing though, and have been identified from a map drawn by an engineer in 1609. The four main buildings are grouped together near the **cathedral** (the tallest structure). Down the road is the **Convent of San José,** which housed the famous golden altar that was saved from the pirates and later moved to its present location. Many of the ruins are unidentified since they were built subsequent to 1609.

At the far end (a ten-minute walk) is the 350-year-old **Puenta del Rey** (King's Bridge), the stone span that linked the city to the Las Cruces trail. The Panamanian Tourist Bureau publishes an excellent pamphlet (with annotated maps) about the ruin. They are sold at hotel newsstands.

Getting There

A visit here is a must and the most comfortable mode of transportation is by cab. The charge is $8 an hour (the ride each way is only ten minutes), but four people can be accommodated, so if you can round up a carload, the per-person charge is kept to a minimum. You can also get near the ruin by local bus. Take any bus marked "PMA Viejo" (yellow-and-blue bus). The fare: 75¢. The bus driver will point you in the right direction.

ANTHROPOLOGICAL MUSEUM REINA TORRES DE ARAUZ: This eclectic museum is one of Latin America's finest and most interesting to visit, located near the Plaza 5 de Mayo in an impressive building with stone pillars. You can view here pre-Columbian ceramics, tools, pottery, monoliths, and much more. On the first floor we enjoyed viewing the monolith from Barriles, near Volcan, of the priest on the shoulders of a nude man bearing a necklace— stunning. There are six rooms spread over three floors. Don't miss the Gold Room on the mezzanine, which is a small version of Bogotá's famous Gold Museum. Interesting, too, are the funereal remains on display. There are collections of Hindu, African, and even Sephardic Jewish artifacts. Inaugurated in December 1976, the museum is open Tuesday through Saturday from 10 a.m. to 3:30 p.m., and on Sunday from 3 to 5:30 p.m.; closed Monday. Admission is 50¢ for adults and 25¢ for children.

TWO OTHER MUSEUMS: The **Museo del Arte Religioso,** downtown at

Calle 3, Avenida A (near the flat arch), features historic religious art that is interesting from both its artistic and historical perspective. Hours are Tuesday through Saturday from 10 a.m. to 4 p.m., on Sunday from 3 to 6 p.m.

Finally, history buffs will enjoy the **Museo de Historia,** in the Plaza Catedral in the Municipal Palace. The hours are the same as the above museums.

BALBOA MONUMENT: When you stroll along the Promenade, Avenida Balboa, your eye is caught by a startling testimonial to the discoverer of the Pacific in 1513. The explorer is standing on a globe, held up by four men who symbolizes the races of man.

THE SPORTING LIFE: Panamanians, like most Latin Americans, enjoy athletics, but whereas in most southern climes futbol (soccer) is the favored sport, here it is the track that captures the heart and mind.

Horse Racing

If the ponies hold the slightest attraction for you—and even if they don't—a must in Panamá is a weekend visit to the **Hipodromo Presidente Remon,** the city's major track, located in the suburb of Río Abajo near the airport. Admission to the grandstand is a paltry 75¢ (occasionally, when business is slow, tourists are admitted free—show your Tourist Card); the minimum bet is $2. All bets are to win or place. Thursday, Saturday, Sunday, and holidays only; the action starts at 1 p.m. By the way, four of the world's most famous jockeys, past and present—Gustines, Baeza, Pincay, and Velásquez—are Panamanians; also, local horses are widely sought for stud purposes. To reach the track, take the Río Abajo bus (50¢) along Via España. Remember, you will be heading toward the airport. A small taxi will run about $2 per person.

Cockfighting (Pelea de Gallo)

A sport for the strong in stomach is the battle to the death between two razor-blade-equipped roosters. Yet this bloody contest has its fascination just as boxing does, and if this is your cup of gore, hop the same Río Abajo bus to the indoor **Club Gallistico de Panamá** (tel. 24-6337). Admission is $1, but the betting among spectators sometimes gets fierce. Sunday and Monday afternoons only. Check with your local clerk for exact times, which vary.

Baseball

Practically a national sport here between December and February, baseball demonstrates the historic influence of the U.S. via the former Canal Zone. Panamanians are fiercely partisan to their teams, which play a brand of ball roughly equivalent to a top minor-league team in North America. Players here seem somewhat smaller and less powerful, but certainly faster than their U.S. counterparts. Admission to the **Estadio Justo de Arosemena,** near Balboa, the major stadium here, is $1 to $2. Check with your hotel clerk for home-team schedules and the bus to take you there.

Boxing

A weekend draw here are local prize fights at the **Gimnasio Nuevo Panamá.** Top price is $8 to $10, and your hotel clerk should know the nightly card. By the way, Roberto Duran is a Panamanian, and several other Panamanian boxers have held world championships as well.

LOTERÍA NACIONAL: A national craze in Panama is the national lottery, which benefits hospitals and other charities. Cash prizes can run up to a healthy $1,000 for a mere 55¢ investment on a four-digit number. There are 10,000 separate four-digit numbers, but 100 tickets on each combination are sold. A smaller two-digit drawing with a $12 top prize is available for 35¢. The odds are much better but the take is smaller.

A major event here every Sunday morning is the noon drawing for the four-digit lottery winners, held on an outdoor stage at Lottery Plaza, between Avenidas Cuba and Perú. Television cameras zero in on the festive proceedings which are hosted by local dignitaries. The poor throng the area with that constant hope that lightning will strike and presto! riches. The smaller lottery drawings are conducted at noon Wednesday at the same place. But as you might expect, far fewer Panamanians attend this ritual. If you're interested in buying a chance, just look for the street vendors throughout the city, who will be only too pleased to take your money. Winnings are tax exempt.

4. THE CANAL AREA AND THE PANAMA CANAL

THE CANAL ZONE: The Canal Area, formerly the Canal Zone, a 50-mile-long, 10-mile-wide strip of territory surrounding the Panama Canal, was from 1914 to 1979 a chunk of North America in Panama. When the canal was constructed, a treaty was signed granting the U.S. jurisdiction over the zone, in order to operate the canal, till the year 2000. The Canal Zone was as typical of middle America as Columbus, Ohio—maybe more so. Teenagers in fashion jeans on ten-speed bicycles and slim, tanned matrons hitting drop shots amid magnificently manicured green lawns and smart modern homes are the pictures of the zone that stand out in my mind. These were the families of U.S. engineers and administrators of the Panama Canal Company which operates the canal. Most had lived here all their lives and for several generations. The Canal Zone was the only home they had ever known. However, building and maintaining a bit of the U.S.A. in the midst of Panamá created a great deal of unrest and was a constant source of friction between the two nations. The anger was exacerbated by the history of the signing of the original treaty and by the striking difference in the standard of living between Zonians and many Panamanians.

The dividing line at **Avenida de los Martires** (formerly Tivoli, and before that, Fourth of July) made the differences immediately and painfully obvious. This, a poor section of the city, with buildings crowded together, badly in need of paint and repair, was directly across the street from an immaculate, green oasis.

After years of negotiation, a revised treaty was signed in 1979 by President Jimmy Carter and Gen. Omar Torrijos. The treaty abolished the former Canal organization, which had included the Panama Canal Company and the Canal Zone. In its place a Panama Canal Commission was established. This, a U.S.–government agency, is responsible for the overall management of the canal until the year 2000, when the treaty expires and the entire operation is turned over to Panama. More Panamanians have become involved in the canal's operation.

Of course, Zonians were saddened by the treaty, which meant the loss of their special way of life. Many families have returned to the mainland. An era had passed. The Canal Zone, now called the Canal Area, is very different but is still a fascinating place to visit.

THE PANAMA CANAL: Engineering friends of ours assure us that no one today could build the Panama Canal any better than it was built in the early part of this century. Construction men the world over still come here to marvel at the brilliance and skill of the U.S. Army Corps of Engineers in building this remarkable "ditch," which took ten years (1904–1914) and cost $525 million. The cost today would run into the billions. Over 300,000 visitors view the canal each year.

A Bit of Background

To appreciate the engineering genius behind the canal's creation, remember that most of it was constructed above sea level. The hard rock base of the isthmus would have made it far too expensive to lower the land surface to the level of the Atlantic and Pacific Oceans. Therefore it was decided by George Washington Goethals and his engineers to build the canal above sea level via an ingenious use of locks. These locks would raise (or lower) the canal's water level to allow ships to enter, and later leave, the 23½-mile-long **Lake Gatún,** in the center of the isthmus. Lake Gatún, among the world's largest freshwater lakes, is 85 feet above sea level, which means that the canal had to be designed to enable ships to reach that height.

Today a typical ship might require eight hours to make the 40-mile canal journey plus the 10 extra miles covering the approach and the exit. Moreover, the Panama Canal today is the world's only multilock canal that can handle two-way traffic. The Suez Canal, in contrast, whose opening predated the Panama Canal, has no locks since it is at sea level. Yet the Suez Canal can only process one-way traffic.

Many engineers declared the Panama project sheer lunacy, and they said so loud and often. So much for the experts.

A Ship's Journey

Let's trace a typical ship along its eight-hour journey across the 40-mile-long canal plus the 10 miles of approach and exit.

Assuming the vessel enters on the Pacific side—where there are three separate sets of locks—the first "stop" will be the locks in Miraflores, a Canal Area community quite close to Panama City. (Below we describe the best way to reach and tour Miraflores Locks.) A special ship's captain, employed by the Panama Canal Commission, takes over the helm and guides the craft through the locks. A fascinating sight in Miraflores is seeing the ship rise as water rushes into the locks. At first only the stacks are visible, and then the top deck, lower decks, and finally the hull glides into view. It never fails to impress us.

At Miraflores, all vessels are raised precisely 54 feet above sea level—in two equal lifts of 27 feet. Proceeding past Miraflores, the ship is raised the remaining distance of 31 feet in the Canal Area community of **Pedro Miguel.** Our escalating vessel has now reached Lake Gatún, and a few hours later is ready for its 85-foot descent to sea level, which takes place in three equal stages in a trio of locks in Gatún on the Atlantic side. Total time elapsed: About eight hours. The cost is measured per ton—it's a bargain, considering the cost and time required for the alternative route around Cape Horn. Incidentally, you can observe the entire canal via a Panama City–Colón train ride, which we recommend below.

The 52 thousand gallons of water used per ship is all fresh water, which accounts for the locks' durability over the last half century. Stored in reservoirs and flowing by the force of gravity only, the water passes as needed from and into Lake Gatún.

Oddity: The canal runs north-south, not east-west as is commonly believed.

Touring Miraflores Locks

If you're touring Panamá, the best site for a look at the canal is from Miraflores, a short bus ride away. Getting here is no problem. Simply hop the Balboa bus from any major Via España intersection. Ask to be dropped at the post office in

Balboa (a 15-minute ride). You change here (near the post office) for another bus (a brightly colored North American model)—marked either "Pedro Miguel," "Gamboa," or "Paraíso"—(each is a Canal Area community). You pay 60¢ as you enter this bus. Be sure to *avoid* the "Clayton" bus. Ask to be dropped at Miraflores Locks, a ten-minute ride, and then you have a pleasant 15-minute stroll to the tourist area. The driver will point the way. Plan to arrive after noon, when traffic is greatest.

A taxi from downtown Panamá will run you $8 an hour, and the cabby will wait for the return trip. There are no Canal Area cabs, so don't plan on hopping a taxi from the Balboa post office. Admission is free to the visitors' area, which is open daily from 9 a.m. to 5 p.m., including Sunday. Once past the imposing gates, follow the white arrows up to the Observation Tower, where there are grandstand seats overlooking the canal. It is a stunning sight. On the arm of each chair is a map detailing the entire canal—including each of the locks and Lake Gatún. Well-informed bilingual guides deliver a recitation of the canal's history and operation. And here is where you can glimpse the striking elevation of a vessel as it enters the lock.

Tip for Camera Bugs: A great photo is the before-and-after shot of a vessel entering and then leaving the Miraflores Locks.

Unfortunately, the canal is too busy to permit ferry rides through it, but **Argo Tours** (tel. 23-7279) runs a launch tour through the canal on Saturday during the dry season (November to May). The launch *Fantasía del Mar* is comfortable and drinks and light fare are available. Expect to pay about $20.

If you aren't able to cruise the canal, the next best way to see the canal is a scenic, 90-minute **train ride** across the isthmus (see the excursion to Colón). The train transverses the 10-mile-wide, 50-mile-long area. The Canal Area now has a population of 40,000 and most are involved in the operation of the canal. Major towns on the Pacific (Panama City) side are Ancón, Balboa, and Gamboa, while on the Colón (Atlantic) side Cristóbal and Gatún are the largest towns.

You will also enjoy a visit to the **Panama Canal Commission Administration Building,** a high, domed edifice atop a hill in Balboa Heights, open from 7:15 a.m. to 4:15 p.m. daily, free entrance. The murals vividly depict the construction of the canal.

For an interesting and concise historical background, you should pick up a copy of *The Path Between the Seas* by David McCullough.

5. PANAMÁ BY NIGHT

Panamanians like to step out at night, and the evening action here centers around the government-supervised gambling casinos and the many nightclubs. For a more sedate evening, there are theater performances and concerts of quite good quality. Let's start with the casinos.

LET THE CHIPS FALL . . . : It's one thing to gamble away your money in a rundown casino such as in Nice. It is quite a different experience to lighten your checkbook in elegant surroundings such as Monte Carlo or in the three swankest hotels here—the **Marriott, Holiday Inn,** and **Gran Hotel Soloy.** All three plush hostelries offer action equal to what we've seen in Las Vegas in tempo, style, and hard cash. Glance across the green-felt tables in either casino and be awed by the exquisite Latin women, often in evening dress, and their cool, suave, white-jacketed escorts. However, informal attire is okay, so don't feel obligated to wear a jacket or tie. We never do.

The best part of this highly recommended evening is that admission is free, so it need cost you nothing. If you care to bet, you must buy at least $5 worth of chips. Minimum table bets are $1; however, the omnipresent one-armed bandits accept coins and will methodically relieve you of your money in smaller doses.

While the three casinos are roughly comparable—they feature roulette (ruleta), blackjack (21), dice (dado), and the slot machines (tranganiquel)—the Marriott's is plushest and seems to draw a better-heeled crowd. Yet some friends of ours seem to prefer the more informal atmosphere of El Panamá's casino. Look in on all of them. The roulette wheel starts rolling as early as 5 p.m. every evening and doesn't stop till 3 a.m. The slot machines open in midafternoon.

Other casinos are located at these hotels: **Continental, Granada,** and **Continental Airport Inn.** In Colón, the **Hotel Washington** has a casino.

THE CLUBS: Panamanian nightclubs really swing, but you must be selective. You can really get stung badly here if you wander about, casually dropping in on clubs indiscriminately. Clip joints, complete with ladies who will promise you anything for a price, abound. Avoid them if you value your wallet, and stick to our recommendations.

The Best Discos

A large whitewashed private house at Calle A. de La Guardia 5 is home to the hottest disco in Panamá. The **Bus Palladium** opens at 8 p.m. and stays open till the last dancer drags out. It draws a young, spirited crowd of Panamanians and tourists.

Another spot popular with Panamá's yuppies and students is gleaming **Magic,** in a large private building on Calle 50. Psychedelic lighting creates a with-it atmosphere, and the well-dressed crowd rocks and drinks till the wee hours. Drinks are $4.

Stelaris Disco, in the Marriott Caesar Park Hotel, is one of the city's most popular night haunts. The crowd, a mix of trendy Panamanians and hotel guests, swings from 9 p.m. till the action winds down at 2 a.m. One drawback is the stiff cover charge of $7.50 for men; only $3.50 gets a member of the fairer sex entrance.

An older crowd gravitates to **Bacchus,** on Via España at Calle 52, which is like a cocktail lounge with a dance floor. Bacchus boasts a Karaoke room, which they imported from Japan. It permits guests to entertain, using the machine as background music. If you go, write and explain it to us.

Also popular is **My Place,** a pub located in the Galería Shopping Center on Via Veneto. Rock music and the latest videos attract a younger crowd.

Live-Music Clubs

Charlot Pub is a bar and restaurant on Avenida M. Ycaza (near the Hotel Continental), which has live jazz groups on Thursday, Friday, and Saturday evenings, starting at 8:30 p.m.

El Sotano ("The Basement"), located in the Hotel El Continental, is a club that sways to the sounds of the large Wurlitzer organ that plays nightly for dancing as well as listening. It's not church music. No cover and drinks run $3.

The swinging doors lead to **La Huaca,** a thoroughly relaxing lounge decorated in ranch style. Located next door to Sarti on Calle Ricardo Arias, La Huaca is open till 2 a.m. and is a fine place to stop for a nightcap or some quiet conversation. There is piped-in music, comfortable seating, and an interesting décor.

Don't forget the hotel lounge areas, which frequently feature "happy hours" (5:50 to 8 p.m.), live music, and small dance floors. Most popular are the **Inna Nega,** in the Holiday Inn, the **Mai Tai** in the Gran Hotel Soloy, and **Mi Rincón** in the Marriott.

For Men Only

Panamá has its places for men seeking a female for a drink or more. You can choose from B-girl bars, strip joints, or legal bordellos. Any cab driver will be happy to escort you to any of the several bordellos around town.

Let's start our raunchy rounds on and around Calle J, just off Avenida de los Martires (formerly Avenida Tivoli). Check out the **Bar Ovalo Inn,** the **Paris,** and **Five Stars.**

Nearby, the **Ancón Inn,** the self-proclaimed "Paradise of Single Men," also offers to cash G.I. checks—wonder why? Drinks are $1 to $2, and there is lots of feminine talent.

Bar Relax and **Taberna Don Quixote,** both on Via España, feature strippers, brassy bands, and B-girls. Drinks in all three start at $3.

TYPICAL SHOWS: Several hotels have Panamanian buffets and folk shows. These are very enjoyable—the dancing and the costumes are lovely, and you should certainly see one. One of the most notable is at the **Holiday Inn** on Wednesday nights. "Miercoles Típicos" feature typical Panamanian food, live folkloric music and dances, and even a cockfight. **Tinajas,** already mentioned above under higher-priced restaurants, offers a show on Thursday nights at 9:30 p.m.

CINEMA: Panamanians are film buffs, and 20 or so theaters scattered about the city offer first-run North American and European features. Admission ranges from 50¢ to $3. Among the best downtown film houses are the **Presidente, Lux, Metro, Opera, Central, Bella Vista, Majestic, Plaza Galerías Obarrio, Aries 1 & 2, Cinema Arte, Plaza, Multicines America.**

6. EXCURSIONS FROM PANAMA CITY

There are three exciting excursions which we think you should consider. Each is different, so if you have limited time, read this section carefully and choose the one that appeals to you.

A DAY TRIP TO TABOGA: This "island of flowers," a mere one-hour launch ride from Balboa in the Canal Area, is one of the few vacation places anywhere where the government travel literature does full justice to its joys. Nestled in the Pacific 12 miles from the mainland, Taboga gave us one of our loveliest days in all our travels to Latin America and Europe. As expected, the beaches are endless, the sun is ceaseless, and the tropical vegetation provides glorious color. But beyond this, there is a serenity here and a well-ordered beauty that seems to seduce visitors into a gentle state of relaxed joy. You will be reluctant to leave. We cannot too strongly recommend a side trip here for a day or even two, if you can spare the time. Evenings are delightfully cool (and quiet) while the afternoons are a sun-worshipper's delight. And there are no automobiles here.

Where to Stay

On our first trip here we missed the last boat back—partly by design—and we stayed at the charming and unspoiled **Hotel Taboga,** one of two hotels on the island, owned by the Panama Institute of Tourism. The 28-room, two-story Taboga, located near the dock, charges a healthy $45 for a double, but this is well worth it. Keep in mind that only the second-floor rooms are air-conditioned, but most evenings are cool enough for comfortable sleeping with the help of an open window only. The grounds are superbly landscaped with flowers, shrubbery, and trees. Our room was rustic, with twin beds, a bureau, and a private bath.

If the Taboga's prices seem too high, try the island's only other choice, the 30-room **Hotel Chu** (named for the Chinese family who own and run the establishment), located a quarter of a mile to the left of where your boat docks. Somewhat basic bathless doubles are $26 without meals, while singles are $21. Doubles with bath are $33. Meals are served on the terrace.

Time Out for a Snack and a Swim

The Hotel Taboga's outdoor restaurant, which overlooks the sea, offers a variety of sandwiches as well as heartier fare at reasonable prices. For $1 the Taboga will rent you a locker and shower.

Getting There

The launch, which charges $2 each way per adult and $1 for children, leaves from Pier 18 in the Canal Area community of Balboa. Take the Balboa bus to the post office. It's only a short walk from there (directly ahead). Look for the sign "Taboga – Launch Landing." The pier is on the left. Monday through Friday the ferry leaves at 8:30 a.m. and 5 p.m. On weekends and holidays an additional ferry leaves at 11:30 a.m. Try to avoid a weekend visit for the ferries and facilities are overcrowded. Call **Argo Tours** (tel. 23-7279) for more information.

PORTOBELO: One of the first Spanish settlements on the isthmus was Nombre de Dios, on the Atlantic side. Panamá Viejo became a transfer site for the shipment of gold from Peru to Spain. From Panamá Viejo the gold was shipped overland to Nombre de Dios, then on to Spain. In 1572 Drake destroyed Nombre de Dios. Thereafter the Spanish built a fortress city in a more protected area which they named Portobelo. Five separate fortresses were built.

Modern Portobelo houses 300 families. But tourists flock here to view the fortresses, the historic relics, and the church. Musts are **Fort San Gerónimo, Fort San Fernando,** the **Customhouse,** and the **Black Christ Statue**—in the town's church. Also, take a launch to **Isla Grande** and explore the beaches there. If you'd like to stay overnight, arrange for accommodations at **Cabanas Jackson** (tel. 47-9128).

If you don't rent an auto, take the Panama Railroad to **Colón** and from there take the bus that passes nearby. Portobelo is about 25 miles northeast of Colón.

COLÓN: A trip to Panama's second city, Colón, is well worth it, if only to get a better idea and view of the workings of the Panama Canal. The city lies 50 miles north of Panamá on the Atlantic coast.

Colón's **Front Street** is famous for its many stores which specialize in perfumes, china, and ivory products, as well as electronic equipment. But don't go there only to shop. Go there also to view the canal, the Canal Area, and the magnificent lakes in between. Where else on earth can you travel from one ocean to another in about an hour and a half?

Getting There

The trip is more than half the fun. Best way to go is by the Panama Railroad, which has five daily departures (only three on weekends). Schedules are usually available at the post office in Balboa or in most of the big hotels. Trains depart from Balboa (a five-minute walk from the post office); sit on the left side of the train while going to Colón to get your best view of the canal. The seats are like the old trolleys in the U.S. If you have a party of four, they can be reversed to face each other. The trip takes 1½ hours and costs $2.50 round trip. You can buy your tickets on the train if the booth at the station is closed. There are second-class compartments (hardback seats) at cheaper prices. Express buses, which leave from center city (near the Internacional Hotel), cost only $2 round trip, but we recommend going by train.

Arrival at Colón

The maritime importance of Colón will strike you in the form of the numerous steamship offices you will observe near the station. The Canal Area portion of Colón is called **Cristóbal.**

Colón houses one of the most luxurious (and historic) hotels of Panamá, the **Washington Conquistador,** at Calle Segunda.

The **Free Zone,** located in the eastern part of Colón, has given the city an enormous economic importance, due to its tax-free status. If you have the time, tour the zone, open until 3:30 p.m.—but keep in mind that this is an area of wholesale distributors and many do not sell retail.

Gambling casinos are in the Washington Conquistador Hotel and Hotel Sotelo.

On Front Street there are several fine shops you might wish to browse. Famous is the **Bazar Frances,** for porcelain, including Hummel figures, as well as Lalique mirrors. Nearby are **Aldao,** for Monte Cristi (Panama hats); **Bazar Gandhi** (a wide assortment of items); and **Benny** (specializes in Japanese watches).

If you want to have lunch in Colón, try the **Café Nacional** on 11th Street between Amador Guerrero and Herrera, or La Fortuna nearby. **La Fortuna** offers tasty Chinese food as well as international dishes. **Pizzería Siciliana,** on Front Street, makes the best in town. More formal dining is in the **Hotel Washington** dining room.

Note: While walking through Colón's streets, you will observe many nightclubs and bars. These establishments cater primarily to the seamen who pass through.

Three recommended hotels in Colón are the **Sotelo** (doubles at $25), **García** (doubles for $15), and the **Carlton** (doubles at $40).

SAN BLAS ISLANDS (KUNA INDIANS): Twenty-five minutes by air from Panama City are the San Blas Islands, an archipelago of some 365 islands stretching for 200 miles off Panama's Caribbean coastline.

As you might suspect, many of the islands are barely visible from the air, so tiny they house only a few palm trees and a patch of sand. Others, somewhat larger, do have homes with families, while still others are small villages, with a general store, a school, and possibly even an athletic field.

The bronze-hued short-in-stature Kuna (Cuna) Indians have lived here for centuries, with little change in customs, traditions, or lifestyles. Except in one way. Since many Kuna men work on the mainland, they and their sons have adopted Western-style clothing. The male Kunas speak Spanish, some English, and of course their native Kuna tongue. Females speak only Kuna.

The Kunas have adopted a form of communal sharing which has served them quite well. The land on all the islands is owned communally. However, the palm trees are privately held and this is vital since the coconut is the accepted currency. A coconut has a value of about 25¢. Trees, therefore, are so valuable that families hire caretakers to watch over their trees on a particular island. Normally one family owns all the trees on a small island.

"Molas" and Kuna Women

As a result of the new interest in "mola" designs (reverse appliqué embroidery), Kuna women have achieved a certain fame in fashion circles. The designs, used to make throw pillows, bedspreads, and curtains, are sold in many better U.S. department stores. Most molas are on red cloth, and black and green are used frequently to accent the design. Unusual and imaginative, molas represent individual expression of Kuna women. Quality varies with the sewer's skill.

Kuna women are their own best advertisements. They wear their own molas as blouses and then add wrap-around ankle-length skirts. Accenting the threads are bracelets and anklets. A lovely ring is worn through the nose and the feet are shoeless. Wealthier women wear heavy gold necklaces as well. Finally, add a scarf to cover the close-cropped hair and a black-painted stripe down the bridge of the nose and you have a picture of a well-dressed Kuna woman. Fascinating and authentic (no tourist show here).

Visiting the Islands

Regular day trips are available to several of the San Blas Islands. You can fly into Porvenir Airport and rent a canoe or flat-bottomed boat to make your visit. Make sure to pick up a mola while here. If you want to stay over, your options are quite limited. The American-run hotel on Pidertupo Island is gone, as is the Hotel El Porvenir. Try for the **Posada Anai,** on Wichub Walla Island. The ten-room, two-story hotel has a small pool and electric lights. A few rooms even have baths. Rates are a whopping $110 double. Your only other option is the **Hotel San Blas,** on Nalunega Island, where your accommodation is a candlelit thatched hut, open-air showers, and it's a hike to the bathroom. The hotel charges $20 per person and will take you fishing, snorkeling, and island-hopping. Obviously, food is included in both. Primitive, but lots of fun. There are other accommodations on Ustupo and Aligandi Islands.

CONTADORA ISLAND: In the Bay of Panamá in the Pacific Ocean sits this pearl of an island, part of the 100 **Las Perlas Islands.** You can stay overnight at the **Hotel Contadora,** a complete resort. Tours are available. Check with your hotel clerk for current information.

Head here for a delightful day of swimming. Two-engine flights depart from Paitilla Airport. There are several flights daily. You can get a locker at the Contadora Hotel (about $15—good for four people).

In addition to swimming, sports fans come here for the snorkeling, scuba-diving, and sailing. The luxurious 210-room Contadora Hotel has a popular casino which draws the jet set. Rates at the Contadora are about $120. The Shah of Iran spent some of his time in exile on this island.

Aero Perlas operates regular flights to Contadora from 8 a.m. to 5 p.m. daily. Call 69-4555 for reservations.

PANAMÁ'S BEACHES: Considering Panamá's delightful climate, you might wish to swim at a nearby beach. Apart from Taboga Island, the only other beach in the area, is on **Naos Island** at the end of the causeway from Fort Amador, a 15-minute drive from Plaza de Mayo. Enjoy swimming on the small beach and watch the ships moving through the canal. Admission is $1 and there are changing facilities. You can rent a beach chair, and a small cafetería serves the usual beach foods.

If you rent a car, you can explore some of the country's lovely beaches stretching along the Pacific coast. **Gorgona Beach,** 46 miles away, is closest, and is followed by **Coronado, San Carlos, Río Mar,** and **Corona.** All have tourist facilities. At Gorgona you can rent a cabin complete with kitchen at **Cabanas Gorgona.** Stay at the **Playa Río Mar Hotel** at Río Mar. Doubles with private bath are $39 during the weekend (50% discount the second night) and $20 during the week. Coronado is the most developed, with restaurants, villas for rent, and an 18-hole golf course. To get to the beaches, just cross the Bridge of the Americas onto the Pan American Hwy. It's an easy road to drive.

PIÑAS BAY: Piñas Bay in Darien Province is the home of the **Tropic Star Lodge.** This resort was carved out of the Darien jungle 150 miles southeast of Panama City. Well-to-do marlin anglers from all over the world find their way here. The cost is high. While we cannot recommend the Tropic Star Lodge because of its rates (a week here will cost over $1,000), it is worth knowing about if you are an angler.

EL VALLE: About 75 miles from Panama is **El Valle de Anton,** or simply El Valle, a quiet mountain retreat. Originally the crater of a huge volcanoe, El Valle is now one of Panama's most popular summer resort areas. Tourists and Panamanians alike come here to enjoy the fresh mountain air and take advantage of the medicinal value of its spas.

An area of great natural beauty, El Valle has often been compared with the Spanish Pyrenees, and is famous for two rarities—trees with square trunks, and brightly colored fluorescent frogs. Here is your chance to escape Panama's heat.

If you decide to spend a day or two, you can stay at either the **Hotel Greco** ($25 for a double) or the **Turistico** ($50 for a double).

7. BARGAIN SHOPPING

Due to extremely low import duties, you can purchase goods from Hong Kong, Japan, Europe, and even the United States at bargain levels in Panamá. You will find, for example, that Japanese transistor radios are priced well below what you might pay in a large U.S. discount store.

Caution: Before citing the best buys here, a word of caution: *Bargaining is a must,* particularly in the Hindu-owned shops, where price negotiations are taken as much for granted as they are in the flea markets of Paris and Rome. Therefore, never accept the first or even the second price offered—unless you are splurging in a first-class shop where prices are marked and fixed. We watched a determined Brazilian bargain for an ivory chess set until the price came down to a good buy at $85—from $150. As a gift, we purchased a British pipe for $12 that was originally at $35.

Many shops, as an inducement to tourists, advertise boldly that their goods are "duty free." This is not true; although duties are low, there are still duties. Panama's taxes are also quite low, which is another consumer bonus. Some stores are licensed to sell duty free and your purchases will be delivered to the airport. Check with the owner. This usually applies to high-priced electronic goods and not to handcrafts, linens, etc.

Avenida Central from Plaza 5 de Mayo to Santa Ana Plaza has many good shops, and others can be found on **Calle J.** New shopping centers have sprung up all along Avenida España and near major hotels. These shops are worth checking out.

In general, your best buys in Panamá are in linens, cameras, tape recorders, portable radios, antiques, silks, Oriental ivory figurines, and French perfume. In addition, Panamanian handcrafts make particularly inexpensive and often original gifts, especially the molas.

LINENS: The best linen shop we found in Panamá is called **Casa de los Manteles** (Linen House), Avenida de los Martires, no. 21–60, which was highly recommended to us by Panamanian friends. However, there is no bargaining here—they charge one price and one price only for their quality goods, many of them hand-embroidered and appliquéed. We purchased a lovely linen tablecloth—a 108-inch oval—plus 12 napkins for $70. Prices here start as low as $20 for cloths made of linen or fine cotton. Don't pass up the finely crafted sheets, luncheon sets, napkins, and beaded handbags. In general, prices here are about half of what you would pay in New York.

FROM CAMERAS TO PERFUMES: When shopping for cameras, tape recorders, or radios, bargaining is an absolute must. Prices vary tremendously, so you should as a first step do some comparison-shopping to get a feel for prices and quality.

A good place to start is the **Audio Foto Internacional** shop at Avenida Central 151, or the branch in the Plaza Regency building on Plaza España. You can buy a Japanese transistor radio for as little as $15, but of course prices rise as the quality rises. Shortwave radios and "boxes" start at $35.

Camera prices vary, so shop carefully and avoid hasty buys. Near Foto Internacional are any number of Hindu-owned shops that sell similar lines.

Another good-quality store is **Toby's**, at Avenida Central 122, where Mr. Cohen, the proprietor, claims to sell novelties "from the universe." Recommended are the radios and tape recorders. Good buys are also available in Japanese watches and electronic goods. All Sony products too. A branch is in El Panamá Hotel.

A high-quality Hindu-owned shop is **P. Jhangimal,** Avenida de los Martires near Plaza 5 de Mayo, where Japanese pearls run as low as $12. Lovely ivory jewelry boxes are priced at $15, while French perfumes, Swiss watches, and transistor radios are priced as low as $13.

If you are partial to woodcarvings, head for the **Sol de la India,** Avenida Central 123, where you can pick up rosewood figurines for $7, carving sets for $5, ivory Buddhas for $12, and superb ivory chess sets for $14 and up, way up. A nice gift is a set of hand-woven cocktail napkins, 12 for $3.25. Remember to bargain here, although the shop advertises itself as a one-price store.

For silks, your best buys are at **Casa Salih,** Avenida Central 125, where lovely bed jackets or kimonos are only $15. Other good buys are in silk blouses, perfumes, alligator bags, incense, wooden boxes, and ivory pieces. Since goods are displayed without pricetags, this is your invitation to bargain—so don't be shy about it.

Salomon's stores, with two branches on Avenida Central and a third in the Hotel Continental, offer a wide range of Oriental goods, brass and rosewood furniture, as well as perfumes and linens.

Two other Oriental shops you should check out are **Casa Tokyo,** nearby on Avenida Central, and **Casa Hong Kong,** around the corner on Calle J. No bargaining here.

One of the most popular Panamá stores is **Marcos,** at Avenida Central 129 at Calle J. You can get just about anything here that is sold in Panamá at competitive prices, whether it is sweaters, silks, perfumes, appliances, or pipes. This is a good place to browse.

HI-FIS, RADIOS, CASSETTES, AND TAPE RECORDERS: If you want to get rock-bottom prices on these items, head to **Kardonski Hermanos**— actually a wholesaler—at Avenida Central, no. 10A-53, off the main street. Enter the side door and head upstairs to the showroom. A salesgirl will write up your selection by model number without a price. Head downstairs and Polish-born Señor Kardonski will establish your price. He's honest, but mild bargaining may help. If you don't find what you want here, try **Fotokina,** on Avenida Central at the Plaza 5 de Mayo.

PIÑATAS: For the child back home or with you, stop at **Piñatas Especiales,** Avenida Justo Arosemena and Calle 39, or at **Piñatas Flormarily,** on Calle 55 near Via Argentina. Piñatas make great party gifts, but don't forget to choose one in a size you can carry home easily.

NATIVE ART: Panamanian handcrafts, as well as those from all parts of Latin America, are on sale at **Artesanías Nacionales,** in Panamá Vieja, and at a small shop alongside the San José Church on Avenida A. Or check out the **Mercado Publico,** on Sal Si Puedes off Avenida Central; offer half the price and then go up a bit. But leave your purse at home, and exercise extreme caution as pickpocketing and muggings are very frequent.

You can order molas by mail from **Flory Saltzman's** shop in the Via Veneto building on Via España near El Panamá Hotel (mail address: Apartado 1719, Balboa). She has a wonderful selection in a variety of sizes.

Reproductions of huacas (decorative pre-Columbian artifacts found in Indian burial grounds) make unusual gifts. **Reprosa** is the firm that created the process by which these items are cast. While the originals were in gold, these modern versions are in sterling silver and some have a gold overlay. If you are really enthralled, you can buy an 18-karat gold one. Reprosa shops can be found in El Panamá Hotel and the Marriott, but the main store is on Avenida Samuel Lewis near the Sanctuario Nacional Church.

8. TRANSPORTATION NOTES AND ODDS 'N' ENDS

PANAMA CANAL CRUISE: You can visit Panama's islands and beaches, and go through the canal on an **Exploration Cruise Line** trip, which varies in length and goes several times a year. Travel agents can get the latest details for you.

TAXIS: Cabs here have no meters, so you must set the price in advance. Fares vary with the number of passengers and the distance to be traveled. For example, within a single zone a lone passenger would be charged $2.25 while four passengers would pay $6. A trip into a second zone would cost one passenger an additional $1.50 and four passengers an additional $3.75. The hourly rate is $5 for the first hour and $3 for each subsequent hour. You can bargain before you get into the cab. There are small and large cabs—small ones charging less.

AUTO RENTALS: You must be 23 years old and hold a valid license to rent a car. All the major international companies are here and there are local rental agencies too. Shop around for the best price.

ODDS AND ENDS: Here are a number of miscellaneous traveler aids:

The Press: The *International Herald-Tribune* is available at the larger hotels, and some newsstands. *Time* magazine is $1.95 (International Edition).

Banking: Panamá is an international banking center with over 120 banks. Banks do not have fixed hours, so make sure to check on hours at the branch you want to use.

U.S. Embassy: The U.S. Embassy is at Avenida Balboa and Calle 37 (tel. 27-1777). Hours are weekdays from 8 a.m. to noon and 1 to 4 p.m.; closed weekends.

Post Offices: All post offices, including the Balboa branch in the Canal Area, are open from 7 a.m. to 6 p.m. Monday through Saturday. Airmail to the U.S. is 30¢, and to Europe, 37¢.

Telephones: Local calls are 10¢. You can dial direct from many hotels here or the operator will make the call for you. Check on the charge added by the hotel before placing the call. You can also call from an INTEL office.

American Express: AMEX is represented by **Boyd Bros.,** on Avenida de los Martires.

Drugstore: The **Farmacía Arrocha,** near the Chase Manhattan Bank off Via España (tel. 23-4505), is open 24 hours a day.

Electricity: Panamá has the same 110-volt current as the U.S. No adapter necessary.

Airport Tax: Prepare to pay $15 per person when flying out of Panamá.

Gasoline: Quite expensive—over $2.35 a gallon.

Television: Channel 8 is English-language, with news at 6 and 10 p.m. nightly. You can catch U.S. films and TV shows, including "Sesame Street." No commercials. English-language newspapers carry listings daily. The station is part of the U.S. Southern Command Network.

Time: Panamá's time zone is the same as the U.S. Eastern Standard Time.

Rain: The Atlantic side of Panama (Colón) receives almost twice as much rain as the Pacific (Panamá) side.

Kosher: Panamá's sizable Jewish population buys its provisions at **Comisariato Kosher,** a supermarket in Albert Einstein Plaza off Calle 65 in El Cangrejo. Closed Saturday, it is open Sunday. Here they have salamis, gefilte fish, herring, and much more.

Tipping: Service is not included in your hotel or restaurant bill. A 10% to 15% tip is standard.

CAPSULE VOCABULARIES AND MENU TRANSLATIONS

□ □ □

1. PORTUGUESE
2. SPANISH

As you certainly know by now, Portuguese is the language of Brazil, while Spanish—or, more accurately, "Castellano"—is spoken almost everywhere else in South America. Although it helps tremendously to know either Spanish or Portuguese, you will find that English is the second language of the educated South American and that you will have no trouble being understood. Certainly, the hotels have at least one clerk apiece who speaks English, many restaurants have bilingual menus, and many shops have an English-speaking salesperson.

Nevertheless, the knowledge of a few phrases will help you considerably, as will translation of the menu terms you're most likely to encounter. That's what follows now—first for Portuguese, then for Spanish, with phonetic pronunciations set forth in parentheses following most words.

PORTUGUESE

NUMERALS

1 **Um** (oohn)
2 **Dois** (doys)
3 **Três** (trays)
4 **Quatro** (kwatro)
5 **Cinco** (seenko)
6 **Seis** (says)
7 **Sete** (*set*-tay)
8 **Oito** (*oy*-to)
9 **Nove** (*no*-vay)
10 **Dez** (dayss)
11 **Onze** (*un*-zay)
12 **Doze** (*do*-zay)
13 **Treze** (*tray*-say)
14 **Quatorze** (kwa-*tor*-zay)
15 **Quinze** (*keen*-zay)
16 **Dezesseis** (dayse-*says*)
17 **Dezessete** (dayse-*set*-tay)
18 **Dezioto** (dayss-*oy*-to)
19 **Dezenove** (dayse-*no*-vay)

20 **Vinte** (*veen*-tay)
30 **Trinta** (*treen*-tah)
40 **Quarenta** (kwa-*ren*-tah)
50 **Cinquenta** (seen-*kwen*-tah)

60 **Sessenta** (se-*sen*-tah)
70 **Setenta** (set-*ten*-tah)
80 **Oitenta** (oy-*ten*-tah)
90 **Noventa** (no-*ven*-tah)

100 **Cem** (sayn)
    Cento (*sen*-to)
200 **Duzentos** (do-*zen*-tos)
1,000 **Mil** (meel)

DAYS OF THE WEEK

Sunday	**Domingo**	do-*meen*-go
Monday	**Segunda-Feira**	say-*goon*-da *fay*-ra
Tuesday	**Terça-Feira**	*tayr*-sa *fay*-ra
Wednesday	**Quarta-Feira**	*kwar*-ta *fay*-ra
Thursday	**Quinta-Feira**	*keen*-ta *fay*-ra
Friday	**Sexta-Feira**	*says*-ta *fay*-ra
Saturday	**Sábado**	sa-ba-do

USEFUL EXPRESSIONS

Very good	**Muito bém**	Mo-eeto ben
Good night	**Boa noite**	Bo-ah noyte
Good afternoon	**Boa tarde**	Bo-ah tahrdge
Why, because	**Porque**	Por-*keh*
The day	**O dia**	O *dee*-ah
Where is . . .?	**Onde está . . .?**	Ohnde esta. . . .?
Hotel	**Hotel**	O-*tel*
Restaurant	**Restaurante**	Res-ta-oo-*rahn*-tay
Toilet	**Toucador**	To-ca-*dorh*
Airport	**Aeroporto**	Ah-airo-*por*-to
Post office	**Correio**	Kor-a-yoo
Beach	**Praia**	*Pray*-ya
Taxi	**Taxi**	*Tak*-see
I want . . .	**Quero . . .**	*Ke*-ro . . .
Mr.	**Senhor**	Seyn-*nor*
Mrs.	**Senhora**	Seyn-*nyor*-a
Miss	**Senhorita**	Seyn-nyor-*ee*-ta
Hello	**Olá**	Oh-*la*
When?	**Quando?**	*Kwan*-do
The check	**A conta**	A *kon*-ta
To eat	**Comer**	Coh-*mer*
A room with bath	**Quarto con banho**	*Kwar*-to kon *ban*-yo
Here	**Aqui**	A-*kee*
How much?	**Quanto custa?**	*Kwan*-toh *kus*-ta
Less expensive	**Mais barato**	Mays ba-*ra*-to
Good	**Bom**	Bon
Yesterday	**Ontem**	*Oyn*-ten
Today	**Hoje**	*O*-zjeh
Tomorrow	**Amanhã**	A-man-*yan*
What is . . .?	**Que é . . .?**	Keh *eh* . . .?
What time is it?	**Que horas são?**	Keh *oh*-rah sown?

It is cold	**Faz frio**	Fahs *free*-o
It is hot	**Faz calor**	Fahs ka-*lor*
It's sunny	**Faz sol**	Fahs *sol*
Left	**Esquerdo**	Ez-*ker*-do
Right	**Direita**	Dee-*ray*-ta
Yes, sir	**Sim, senhor**	Seen, sen-*yohr*
No	**Não**	Noun
Thank you	**Obrigado**	O-bree-*ga*-do
Please	**Por favor**	Por fa-*vor*
Money	**Dinheiro**	Deen-*yay*-ro
Until tomorrow	**Até amanhã**	Atay a-man-*yan*
Red	**Vermelho**	Ver-*mel*-yo
White	**Branco**	*Bran*-ko

RESTAURANT TERMS

Waiter	**O garção**	Oh gar-*sown*
Menu	**Cardápio**	Kar-*dap*-yo
Please bring me the check	**O favor de me trazer a conta**	Oh fa-*vor* day may tra-*zer* ah *kon*-ta
Breakfast	**Café**	Kah-*fay*
Lunch	**Almôço**	Al-*mo*-soo
Dinner	**Jantar**	Zhan-*tar*

SOUPS (SOPAS)

Caldo de carne	Meat bouillon	**Creme de espargos**	Cream of asparagus soup
Caldo de cebola	Onion soup	**Sopa de galinha**	Chicken soup
Caldo de verde	Vegetable soup	**Sopa de tomate**	Tomato soup

CONDIMENTS (CONDIMENTOS)

Açúcar	Sugar	**Pão**	Bread
Geléia	Marmalade	**Pimenta**	Pepper
Manteiga	Butter	**Sal**	Salt

SANDWICHES

Americana	Hot open combination sandwich, ham-cheese, egg salad	**Presunto**	Ham
		Queijo	Cheese
Misto	Ham and cheese	**Queijo presunto**	Ham and cheese

MEATS (CARNES)

Alcatra	Roast beef	**Filet mignon**	Filet mignon
Bife	Beef steak	**Frango**	Seasoned chicken and Spanish rice
Carne de porco	Pork		
Carne de vaca	Beef	**Galinha**	Chicken
Chorizo	Sausage	**Língua**	Tongue
Churrasco	Barbecue	**Pato**	Duck
Churrasco mixto	Mixed barbecued grill	**Perú**	Turkey
		Rosbife	Roast beef
Cordeiro	Lamb	**Salsichão**	Sausage
Costeletas de carneiro	Lamb chops		

FISH (PEIXES)

Bacalhau	Codfish	**Linguado**	Sole
Camarão	Shrimp	**Ostras**	Oysters
Lagosta	Lobster	**Sardinhas**	Sardines

EGGS (OVOS)

Ovos estrelados	Fried eggs	**Queijo frito**	Grilled cheese
com batatas fritas	with fried	**Omelete**	Omelet
	potatoes	**Ovos mexidos**	Scrambled eggs
Legumes	Vegetables	**Ovos quentes**	Soft boiled eggs
Presunto	Ham		

SALAD (SALADA)

Salada de alface	Lettuce salad	**Salada de maionaise de**	Chicken
Salada de batata	Potato salad	**galinha**	salad
Salada mixta	Mixed salad	**Salada tomate**	Tomato salad

VEGETABLES (LEGUMES)

Alface	Lettuce	**Cenouras**	Carrots
Arroz	Rice	**Couve-flor**	Cauliflower
Batatas	Potato	**Espinafre**	Spinach
Fritas	Fried	**Farofa**	Farfel
Puré	Mashed	**Feijão verde**	Stringbeans
Cebola	Onion	**Repôlho**	Cabbage

DESSERT (SÔBRE MESA)

Fruta	Fruit	**Queijo**	Cheese
Mamão	Papaya (Brazilian)	**Sorvete**	Ice cream
Pasteis	Cake	**Salada de frutas**	Fruit salad
Pêssego Melba	Peach Melba	**Torta**	Pie
Pudim	Custard	**Torta de maçã**	Apple pie

BEVERAGES (BEBIDAS)

Água	Water	**Cerveja**	Beer
Água mineral	Mineral water	**Chá**	Tea
Cacao	Cocoa	**Chocolate**	Chocolate
Café-puro	Black coffee	**Leite**	Milk
Café com leite	Coffee with milk	**Suco**	Juice

FRUIT (FRUTA)

Fruta	Fruit	**Maçã**	Apple
Abacate	Avocado	**Morango**	Strawberry
Abacaxi	Pineapple	**Pêra**	Pear
Banana	Banana	**Pêssego**	Peach
Laranja	Orange	**Uvas**	Grapes
Lamão	Lemon		

2. SPANISH

USEFUL EXPRESSIONS

Good day	**Buenos días**	Bway-nohss *dee*-ahss
How are you?	**Cómo está usted?**	Koh-moh es-*tah* oos-*ted*?
Very well	**Muy bien**	Mwee *byen*
Thank you	**Gracias**	*Grah*-see-ahss
Good-bye	**Adiós**	A-dee-*ohss*
Yes	**Sí**	See
No	**No**	Noh
Excuse me	**Perdóneme**	Pehr-*doh*-neh-may
When?	**Cuando?**	*Kwahn*-doh
Yesterday	**Ayer**	Ah-yayr
Today	**Hoy**	Oy
Tomorrow	**Manaña**	Man-*yah*-nah
Where are you going?	**A dónde va usted?**	Ah *dohn*-day vah oos-*ted*?
Where is . . . ?	**Dónde está . . .?**	Dohn-day ess-tah . . . ?
the station	**la estación**	La ess-tah-*syohn*
a hotel	**un hotel**	Oon oh-*tel*
a restaurant	**un restaurante**	Oon res-tow-*rahn*-tay
the toilet	**el retrete**	Ell ray-*tray*-tay
the shop	**la tienda**	Lah tee-*en*-dah
the market	**el mercado**	Ell mayr-*kah*-doh
post office	**el correo**	Ell koh-*rray*-oh
I want a single room	**Quiero un cuarto individual**	Kee-*ay*-roh oon *quahr*-toh in-de-ve-doo-*ahl*
a double room	**un cuarto para dos personas**	Oon *quahr*-toh pah-rah dohss payr-*sohn*-ahss
with bath	**con baño**	Kohn *bahn*-yoh
without bath	**sin baño**	Seen *bahn*-yoh
How much is it?	**Cuánto?**	*Kwahn*-toh?
Too much	**Es demasiado**	Ayss day-mah-see-*ah*-doh
Cheaper	**Mas barato**	Mahss bah-*rah*-toh
Better	**Mejor**	Mah-*hohr*
I don't like it	**No me gusta**	No may *goos*-tah
Money	**Dinero**	Din-*ay*-ro
My name is. . . .	**Mi nombre es. . . .**	Mee nohm-bray ayss. . . .
Black	**Negro**	*Nay*-groh
Red	**Rojo**	*Roh*-hoh
Blue	**Azul**	Ah-*zool*
White	**Blanco**	*Blahn*-koh
Green	**Verde**	*Vayr*-day
Yellow	**Amarillo**	Ah-ma-*ree*-yoh

NUMERALS

1	**Uno** (Oo-no)	**14**	**Catorce** (Kay-*tor*-say)	**50**	**Cincuenta** (Seen-*kwen*-tah)	
2	**Dos** (Dose)	**15**	**Quince** (*Keen*-say)	**60**	**Sesenta** (Say-*sen*-tah)	
3	**Tres** (Trayss)	**16**	**Dieciseis** (Dyes-ee-*sayss*)	**70**	**Setenta** (Say-*ten*-tah)	

1 **Uno** (Oo-no)
2 **Dos** (Dose)
3 **Tres** (Trayss)
4 **Cuatro** (*Kwah*-tro)
5 **Cinco** (*Seen*-ko)
6 **Seis** (Sayss)
7 **Siete** (*Syeh*-tay)
8 **Ocho** (*Oh*-choh)
9 **Nueve** (*Nway*-bay)
10 **Diez** (Dyes)
11 **Once** (*Ohn*-say)
12 **Doce** (*Doy*-say)
13 **Trece** (*Tray*-say)

14 **Catorce** (Kay-*tor*-say)
15 **Quince** (*Keen*-say)
16 **Dieciseis** (Dyes-ee-*sayss*)
17 **Diecisiete** (Dyes-ee-*sye*-tah)
18 **Dieciocho** (Dyes-ee-*oh*-choh)
19 **Diecinueve** (Dyes-ee-*nway*-bay)
20 **Veinte** (*Bayn*-tay)
30 **Treinta** (*Trayn*-tah)
40 **Cuarenta** (Kwah-*ren*-tah)

50 **Cincuenta** (Seen-*kwen*-tah)
60 **Sesenta** (Say-*sen*-tah)
70 **Setenta** (Say-*ten*-tah)
80 **Ochenta** (Oh-*chen*-tah)
90 **Noventa** (No-*ben*-tah)
100 **Cien** (Syen)
200 **Doscientos** (Dose-*syen*-tohs)
1,000 **Mil** (Meel)

DAYS OF THE WEEK

Sunday	**El Domingo**	Doh-*meen*-goh
Monday	**Lunes**	*Loo*-nayss
Tuesday	**Martes**	*Mahr*-tayss
Wednesday	**Miércoles**	Mee-*ayr*-koh-layss
Thursday	**Jueves**	Hoo-*ay*-vayss
Friday	**Viernes**	Vee-*ayr*-nayss
Saturday	**Sábado**	*Sah*-bah-doh

RESTAURANT TERMS

Breakfast	**El desayuno**	Day-sah-*yoo*-noh
Lunch	**El almuerzo**	Ahl-moo-*ayr*-so
Dinner	**La comida**	Koh-*mee*-dah
The check	**La cuenta**	*Quen*-tah
Water	**Agua**	*Ah*-gwah
The waiter	**Mozo**	*Moh*-so

SOUPS (SOPAS)

Arroz al caldo	Consommé with rice	**Crema de esparragos**	Asparagus soup
Caldo de gallina	Chicken soup	**Crema de tomates**	Tomato soup
Consommé a la reina	Consommé with egg	**Sopa de cebolla**	Onion soup
		Sopa de gallina	Chicken soup

MEAT (CARNE)

Aves	Poultry	**Jamón**	Ham
Bife	Baby beef	**Lengua**	Tongue
Carne asado	Prime ribs (also barbecued beef)	**Lomo**	Porterhouse
		Milanese	Veal
Chuleta	Chops	**Parrillada**	Barbecued beef
Chivito	Kid (goat)	**Pavo**	Turkey
Chorizos	Sausage	**Pollo**	Chicken
Churrasco	Tenderloin	**Riñónes**	Kidneys
Cordero	Lamb		

Gallina	Chicken	Salchicha	Sausage
Higado	Liver	Ternera	Veal
		Tocino	Bacon

FISH (PESCADO)

Albacora	Swordfish	Congrio	Eel
Almejas	Clams	Corvina	White bass
Anchoa	Anchovy	Erizos	Sea urchin
Atún	Tuna	Langostinos	Lobster
Calamares	Squid	Ostras	Oysters
Camarones	Shrimp	Ostiones	Scallops
Choritos	Mussels		

EGGS (HUEVOS)

Fritos	Fried	Revueltos	Scrambled
Pasados por agua	Boiled	Tortilla	Omelet

BEVERAGES (BEBIDAS)

Agua	Water	Jugo de naranja	Orange juice
Agua mineral	Bottled mineral water	Leche	Milk
Café	Coffee	Té	Tea
Cerveza	Beer	Vino	Wine

DESSERTS (POSTRES)

Postre	Dessert	Macedonia	Fruit salad
Dulce	Sweetmeat, cake	Panqueques	Pancakes
Flan	Custard	Torta	Cake
Helado	Ice cream		

CONDIMENTS AND OTHERS (CONDIMENTOS)

Aceite	Oil	Mermeladas	Jam
Ajo	Garlic	Pan	Bread
Azúcar	Sugar	Panecillo	Rolls
Hielo	Ice	Sal	Salt
Mantequilla	Butter	Tostada	Toast

Index

NOW!
ARTHUR FROMMER LAUNCHES HIS SECOND TRAVEL REVOLUTION
with

The New World of Travel

The hottest news and latest trends in travel today—heretofore the closely guarded secrets of the travel trade—are revealed in this new sourcebook by the dean of American travel. Here, collected in one book that is updated every year, are the most exciting, challenging, and money-saving ideas in travel today.

You'll find out about hundreds of alternative new modes of travel—and the many organizations that sponsor them—that will lead you to vacations that cater to your mind, your spirit, and your sense of thrift.

Learn how to fly for free as an air courier; travel for free as a tour escort; live for free on a hospitality exchange; add earnings as a part-time travel agent; pay less for air tickets, cruises, and hotels; enhance your life through cooperative camping, political tours, and adventure trips; change your life at utopian communities, low-cost spas, and yoga retreats; pursue low-cost studies and language training; travel comfortably while single or over 60; sail on passenger freighters; and vacation in the cheapest places on earth.

And in every yearly edition, Arthur Frommer spotlights the 10 GREATEST TRAVEL VALUES for the coming year. 400 pages, large-format with many, many illustrations. All for $14.95!

ORDER NOW
TURN TO THE LAST PAGE OF THIS BOOK FOR ORDER FORM.

NOW, SAVE MONEY ON ALL YOUR TRAVELS!
Join Frommer's™ Dollarwise® Travel Club

Saving money while traveling is never a simple matter, which is why, over 27 years ago, the **Dollarwise Travel Club** was formed. Actually, the idea came from readers of the Frommer publications who felt that such an organization could bring financial benefits, continuing travel information, and a sense of community to economy-minded travelers all over the world.

In keeping with the money-saving concept, the annual membership fee is low—$18 (U.S. residents) or $20 U.S. (Canadian, Mexican, and foreign residents)—and is immediately exceeded by the value of your benefits which include:

1. The latest edition of any TWO of the books listed on the following pages.

2. A copy of any Frommer City Guide.

3. An annual subscription to an 8-page quarterly newspaper *The Dollarwise Traveler* which keeps you up-to-date on fastbreaking developments in good-value travel in all parts of the world—bringing you the kind of information you'd have to pay over $35 a year to obtain elsewhere. This consumer-conscious publication also includes the following columns:

Hospitality Exchange—members all over the world who are willing to provide hospitality to other members as they pass through their home cities.

Share-a-Trip—requests from members for travel companions who can share costs and help avoid the burdensome single supplement.

Readers Ask . . . Readers Reply—travel questions from members to which other members reply with authentic firsthand information.

4. Your personal membership card which entitles you to purchase through the club all Frommer publications for a third to a half off their regular retail prices during the term of your membership.

So why not join this hardy band of international Dollarwise travelers now and participate in its exchange of information and hospitality? Simply send $18 (U.S. residents) or $20 U.S. (Canadian, Mexican, and other foreign residents) along with your name and address to: Frommer's Dollarwise Travel Club, Inc., Gulf + Western Building, One Gulf + Western Plaza, New York, NY 10023. Remember to specify which *two* of the books in section (1) and which *one* in section (2) above you wish to receive in your initial package of member's benefits. Or tear out the next page, check off your choices, and send the page to us with your membership fee.

FROMMER BOOKS
PRENTICE HALL PRESS
ONE GULF + WESTERN PLAZA
NEW YORK, NY 10023

Date_____

Friends:
Please send me the books checked below:

FROMMER™ GUIDES

(Guides to sightseeing and tourist accommodations and facilities from budget to deluxe, with emphasis on the medium-priced.)

☐ Alaska	$13.95	☐ Cruises (incl. Alask, Carib, Mex, Hawaii,	
☐ Australia	$14.95	Panama, Canada, & US)	$14.95
☐ Austria & Hungary	$14.95	☐ California & Las Vegas	$14.95
☐ Belgium, Holland, Luxembourg	$13.95	☐ Florida	$14.95
☐ Brazil	$14.95	☐ Mid-Atlantic States	$13.95
☐ Egypt	$13.95	☐ New England	$14.95
☐ France	$14.95	☐ New York State	$13.95
☐ England & Scotland	$14.95	☐ Northwest	$14.95
☐ Germany	$14.95	☐ Skiing in Europe	$14.95
☐ Italy	$14.95	☐ Skiing USA—East	$13.95
☐ Japan & Hong Kong	$13.95	☐ Skiing USA—West	$13.95
☐ Portugal, Madeira, & the Azores	$13.95	☐ Southeast & New Orleans	$14.95
☐ South Pacific	$13.95	☐ Southeast Asia	$14.95
☐ Switzerland & Liechtenstein	$13.95	☐ Southwest	$14.95
☐ Bermuda & The Bahamas	$14.95	☐ Texas	$13.95
☐ Canada	$14.95	☐ USA	$15.95
☐ Caribbean	$14.95		

FROMMER'S™ $-A-DAY® GUIDES

(In-depth guides to sightseeing and low-cost tourist accommodations and facilities.)

☐ Europe on $30 a Day	$14.95	☐ New Zealand on $40 a Day	$12.95
☐ Australia on $30 a Day	$12.95	☐ New York on $50 a Day	$13.95
☐ Eastern Europe on $25 a Day	$13.95	☐ Scandinavia on $60 a Day	$13.95
☐ England on $40 a Day	$13.95	☐ Scotland and Wales on $40 a Day	$12.95
☐ Greece on $30 a Day	$12.95	☐ South America on $30 a Day	$13.95
☐ Hawaii on $50 a Day	$13.95	☐ Spain and Morocco (plus the Canary Is.)	
☐ India on $25 a Day	$12.95	on $40 a Day	$13.95
☐ Ireland on $35 a Day	$13.95	☐ Turkey on $25 a Day	$12.95
☐ Israel on $30 & $35 a Day	$13.95	☐ Washington, D.C., & Historic Va. on	
☐ Mexico (plus Belize & Guatemala)		$40 a Day	$13.95
on $25 a Day	$13.95		

FROMMER'S™ TOURING GUIDES

(Color illustrated guides that include walking tours, cultural & historic sites, and other vital travel information.)

☐ Australia	$9.95	☐ Paris	$8.95
☐ Egypt	$8.95	☐ Scotland	$9.95
☐ Florence	$8.95	☐ Thailand	$9.95
☐ London	$8.95	☐ Venice	$8.95

TURN PAGE FOR ADDITONAL BOOKS AND ORDER FORM.